# THE
# ANATOMY
# OF
# ACCOUNTING

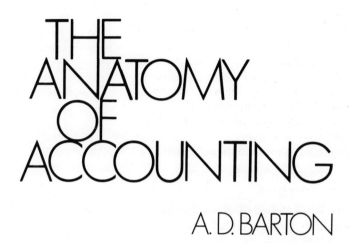

# THE ANATOMY OF ACCOUNTING

## A. D. BARTON

Second Edition

UNIVERSITY OF
QUEENSLAND PRESS

First edition 1975
Reprinted 1976
Second edition © University of Queensland Press,
St. Lucia, Queensland, 1977

Printed and bound by Silex Enterprise &
Printing Co., Hong Kong

Distributed in the United Kingdom, Europe,
the Middle East, Africa, and the Caribbean
by Prentice-Hall International,
International Book Distributors Ltd.,
66 Wood Lane End, Hemel Hempstead, Herts.,
England

National Library of Australia
Cataloguing-in-publication data
Barton, Allan D.
  The anatomy of accounting.

  Index.
  ISBN 0 7022 1482 5.
  ISBN 0 7022 1460 4  Paperback.


  1. Accounting.  I. Title.

657

# Contents

## Part 4: Analysis and Interpretation of Financial Reports 445

# Preface to Second Edition

In the three years since *The Anatomy of Accounting* was completed, two major developments have taken place and I have taken advantage of them in revising the text. The publication of the A.I.C.P.A. report, *The Objectives of Financial Statements*, in October 1973 has stimulated interest in the objectives of accounting, and I have revised chapter 3, Financial Information Requirements and Standards, in the light of recent discussion. The analysis has been simplified by combining the standards for accounting information with the guidelines for its communication , and several of the standards have been made more comprehensive. The development of normative accounting objectives has strengthened the need to use an analytical approach in the study of accounting.

Secondly, inflation has become a serious economic and social problem over the past few years and it has dramatized many deficiencies in conventional accounting. Official government enquiries in Australia and the United Kingdom which examined the problems caused by inflation on the measurement of business income and financial position both recommended the adoption of current value accounting based primarily on current costs of resources. The United States Securities and Exchange Commission has also recommended the publication of supplementary current value data for large corporations. The United Kingdom Institute of Chartered Accountants has recommended the adoption of price-level adjusted historic cost accounting as a solution to measuring the impact of inflation on the financial results and position of a business. There is no generally accepted solution as yet. Because of the urgency to develop acceptable methods of inflation accounting, the analysis in chapters 22, 23, and 24 has been expanded substantially. Chapter 21 concerning income theory has been simplified in order to serve as a better introduction to the inflation accounting analysis. However, inflation accounting is necessarily a complex matter, and in extending the treatment of it, the analysis has been taken beyond what one can cover in an introductory course. The detailed analysis and problem solving in these chapters and that in Chapter 25 on Present Value Accounting should be reserved for advanced courses in accounting. Only general matters covering the nature of and concepts used in each system, and the uses and limitations of each, should be covered in first year courses.

Because of these additions, this revised edition is suitable for use in advanced financial accounting courses wherein inflation accounting forms a major part of the course, as well as in introductory courses.

The appropriateness of *The Anatomy of Accounting* to introductory and advanced courses makes its use more flexible in the overall accounting sequence as students can take up the more difficult topics at a later stage of their programme.

In revising *The Anatomy of Accounting*, I have benefited from a detailed review of the book by Dr. B. Feller of the Australian Accounting Research Foundation in *The Australian Accountant*, October 1975. Many of his suggestions have been incorporated in the revision. Mrs. C. Eakin and my wife have been invaluable in providing secretarial assistance, and to them I offer my sincere thanks.

Allan D. Barton
Canberra
June 1976

# Preface to First Edition

For some time now the accounting profession has been under mounting pressure to solve the many problems being thrown up by the increasingly complex nature of business operations and a rapidly changing economic environment. This pressure for progress has reached back to the university classroom and there has been a growing realization that the traditional approach to teaching accounting, with its emphasis on techniques, provides inadequate preparation for the accountant of the 1970s and beyond. *The Anatomy of Accounting* represents a complete break with that tradition. A broadly based conceptual and analytical approach to financial accounting is developed which relates the requirements for accounting information to the information processing system. Accounting is taken to be a financial information system which should provide useful information to many groups of users. Their requirements set the objectives of the accounting system, and this study is based on how the requirements for general-purpose financial information can be met by the accounting system. The approach adopted is based on that formulated in the American Accounting Association's *A Statement of Basic Accounting Theory* and since 1968 it has been used for teaching first-year undergraduates (both accounting and non-accounting majors) and M.B.A. candidates at Macquarie University. It is largely in accord with the recommendations made in the report of the study group sponsored by the Price-Waterhouse Foundation, entitled *A New Introduction to Accounting* (July 1971).

*The Anatomy of Accounting* is designed as a new introduction to accounting. It contains an examination of the requirements of major user groups for information about a firm's income, financial position, and prospects, and a detailed analysis of the major problems associated with the measurement of periodic income and financial position in periods of changing prices, inflation, and uncertainty, together with their solution. Various theories of income and financial position determination are examined and evaluated in relation to users' needs for information. The text is based on a reasoning analysis throughout, rather than on descriptions and rationalizations of current accounting practice. While all essential techniques for recording and processing accounting data are covered, they are de-emphasized by demonstrating how they fit into a theoretical framework and are simply logical applications of principles.

The analysis begins with an examination of the information requirements of users of accounting reports. The nature of the modern corporation and its business operations are analyzed, and it is shown how all transactions can be recorded by using a very simple "flow" approach. The problem then arises of how to transform a mass of transaction data into useful financial information. The historic cost valuation system is first developed and the reports produced from it — the cash flow, funds, income and financial position statements — are explained and evaluated in relation to users' information requirements. While these reports serve some purposes adequately, they have serious deficiencies for other uses. Alternative theories of income and financial position determination which take account of inflation, of changing asset prices, and of both inflation and changing asset prices, are then developed and evaluated to see whether they provide more useful financial information. Next, the present value system relating to the future is explained and its role in decision-making is examined. Finally, the analysis of financial reports is covered. Some principles of financial management to assist in the analysis and interpretation of financial reports are explained in an appendix, and an account is given of some recent events in Australian business operations which relate to accounting. An appendix on the application of linear algebra in computerized accounting systems demonstrates how modern mathematical techniques can be used with great advantage in the accounting system. This is likely to become a major development in accounting in the near future.

A large number of questions and exercises are included at the end of each chapter. The problems are carefully graded and are designed to permit students to review the major ideas in each chapter, to test their understanding of the theory, and to enable them to develop adequate technical expertise in the mechanics of accounting. Solutions to some of the exercises are provided in Appendix 4.

Although the book contains an advanced level of theory for an introductory course, experience has shown that beginning students can handle the theory quite well. A theoretical emphasis has been made necessary by the adoption of a new approach and the confused state of contemporary theory. Good theory is really only commonsense when seen in its appropriate context and it provides the broad framework for all analysis and procedures. It is essential for an understanding of accounting reports and for the development of improvements in them. Much of the detail in the theoretical chapters can be skimmed over by the more pragmatic reader as it serves mainly to provide the reasons for the conclusions reached.

The book can be used in a flexible way. Readers not particularly concerned with techniques can easily pass quickly over the details of accounting data processing without missing anything of substance. The techniques are concentrated in chapters 7 to 11. Some users may prefer to cover chapter 26, on the analysis of financial reports, after completing their study of the historic cost measurement system, so as to emphasize more fully the uses and limitations of historic cost reports for the satisfaction of users' information requirements; and to allow students more time to develop expertise in analyzing and interpreting financial reports.

In addition to aiding both undergraduate and postgraduate students who either intend to become accountants or merely require some understanding of accounting reports and processes, *The Anatomy of Accounting* should be of use to members of the accounting profession and to the principal users of accounting reports, particularly business executives and investors. Many of the major issues facing business, investors, and accountants are analyzed and solutions provided. For example, problems of accounting in times of inflation, accounting for various types of decision-making, company takeovers, deferred tax accounting, inventory valuation, and depreciation are examined in the context of the various asset valuation and income measurement systems.

Over the years that this course has been taught at Macquarie University, I have had the benefit of comments from many students and from members of staff who have assisted in teaching it, including Messrs. R. Bird, B. Branford, G. Harris, K. Lemke, H. Lindstrom, D. Round, D. Street, and Dr. A. McHugh, and I wish to record my gratitude for their assistance.

Mr. Deryl H. Street, Senior Lecturer in Accounting at Macquarie University, wrote Appendix 3 dealing with the use of linear algebra for computerized accounting; without his authorship this important topic could not have been included.

I should also like to acknowledge my indebtedness to colleagues in other Australian universities who over the years have influenced my ideas in accounting, particularly Professors R. J. Chambers of Sydney University, L. Goldberg of Melbourne University, R. L. Mathews of the Australian National University, and W. J. Stewart of the University of New South Wales. Professor W. J. Vatter, recently retired from the University of California at Berkeley, has been the source of many ideas and philosophies incorporated in the book. Professor W. B. Reddaway, Chairman of the Faculty of Economics and Politics at the University of Cambridge, and Professor A. B. Pippard, F.R.S., President of Clare Hall, Cambridge, have provided congenial facilities at Cambridge which have allowed me to complete the manuscript whilst on sabbatical leave from Macquarie University. Miss Lin Sadgrove kindly typed Appendix 3. Finally, my wife Val has been of tremendous assistance to me in many ways.

Allan D. Barton
Cambridge
May 1973

# Part 1
# Accounting and the Economic Activity of the Firm

# Chapter 1
# Nature and Scope of Accounting

## THE FIELD OF ACCOUNTING

Accounting is not a precisely defined discipline or area of professional practice; in both instances it overlaps other areas to a substantial degree, and it is a matter of dispute as to just where accounting begins and where it ends. However, the same can be said about most fields of study, particularly where the field in question is closely allied to a particular profession (as accounting is), since what the profession does frequently exceeds the boundaries of the discipline as normally defined. A distinction should be made between the area of study, i.e., the discipline of accounting, and the vocation of accountancy, i.e., what accountants do in practice. Accountants in practice generally take an active part in areas beyond the discipline of accounting; in particular, many play an active role in management.

Various definitions of the discipline of accounting have been proposed, but there is not much difference between them. The one to be used here was framed by a committee of the American Accounting Association (the A.A.A., which is the body of academic accountants in the U.S.). They defined accounting as "the process of identifying, measuring and communicating economic information to permit informed judgments and decisions by users of the information".[1] This is a somewhat broader definition of accounting than most previous ones, and it places more emphasis on the use of accounting information for evaluating the results of past activities and for making decisions concerning future action.

An examination of the parts of the definition shows what is involved in accounting work, though many of its implications will not become clear until the course progresses. First, accounting involves the identification of that information which is required for the end-uses of the data, i.e., the making of informed judgments and decisions by users. Accounting data must be relevant to the uses for which they are required. Accounting data must be capable of measurement in common measuring units so that they can be aggregated. Moreover, the common measuring unit must be the unit of currency, i.e. the dollar, because the information relates to economic events. The information must be communicated to the user in an effective way to enable him to evaluate past performance and to make decisions about future actions. Effective communication requires that the information be classified appropriately and summarized so that magnitudes which are significant for the end-use are highlighted. A mass of unclassified and unsummarized data is meaningless as a source of information for decision-making. The data are communicated in reports, and hence accounting includes the preparation and presentation of these. Economic information comprises all data that relate to the use of scarce economic resources — cash, inventories, plant, labour, management, and so on — in achieving the objectives of the accounting entity, for example, a business firm. It can always be measured in money terms. Such information is required in order that the user can make informed judgments, i.e., those based on reliable and relevant data as against guesses, about results of past economic activity, and evaluate those results against the environmental conditions in which the entity operated. Finally, he uses the information to make decisions about future economic action, i.e., how to use his scarce economic resources. In the case of business, this involves questions of how to operate in the future, i.e., what prices to charge, products to make, methods of production to use, and so on. Decisions are based upon expected future events, and the best single means of forecasting the future is to have a reliable knowledge of what happened in the past and what factors caused the results of past activities to be achieved. Historical accounting is required for forecasting purposes as well as for the measurement of achieved results. Forecasts are integrated into a set of accounting reports called budgets. Budgeting forms a major part of accounting for decision-making and control purposes.

In summary, then, accounting is an information-gathering and communication system maintained for the purposes of making decisions about the use of economic resources, for enabling effective control over the utilization of those resources, and for evaluating the results of economic activity. It may be briefly described as a financial information system.

Earlier definitions of accounting tended to place more emphasis on the procedural aspects of accounting and restricted it to a history-recording process. Thus the American Institute of Certified Public Accountants (the A.I.C.P.A. — the body of practising accountants) in 1941 defined accounting as the "art of recording, classifying and summarizing in a significant manner and in terms of money, transactions and events which are, in part at least, of a financial character, and interpreting the results thereof".[2] This definition points out some of the main components of accounting work. Thus, accounting encompasses the recording of financial transactions by the entity, for example, sales of goods. This is often called "bookkeeping". Financial transactions are all those which involve money or money's worth, and occur between the entity and someone outside it. Events which are at least partly of a financial character can be interpreted as covering the transfer of resources within the entity from one segment to another. Moreover, the recording processes must be systematic and not spasmodic ones. Secondly, it covers the classification of financial data. Recorded data are fairly useless unless they can be classified so that all similar items can be grouped together to distinguish them from dissimilar ones, and then aggregated. Classification enables a mass of data to be summarized and reported. Thirdly, the data must be communicated to users in accounting reports which summarize and highlight significant magnitudes (for example, sales, profit, total assets) and relationships (for example, net profit percentage to sales and to investment). Finally, the definition covers the analysis and interpretation of accounting reports, i.e., what the reports mean.

However, this definition of accounting is too narrow for our purposes. As well as placing insufficient emphasis on the evaluation and decision-making functions of accounting data, it omits the use of accounting data for forecasting purposes. The planning of future activities and their effective execution requires that estimates be made of major magnitudes (for example, future sales, expenses, cash, inventories, and loans) and that these estimates be integrated into a set of budgeted accounting reports. By confining the accounting record to "transactions and events", it appears to omit consideration of changes in the prices of existing assets and changes in the value of the dollar.

In addition, both definitions omit another major part of accounting work, viz., auditing. Auditing involves an examination and a review of the accounting procedures, records, and reports to ensure that the reports have been fairly prepared in accordance with the entity's policies, good accounting practice, and the law.

We shall use "accounting" in its broad sense of an information-gathering and reporting system for use in making economic decisions and overall plans for the future, for evaluating past activities, and for controlling activities. Because of the emphasis on accounting for these purposes by users, we must study their information needs as they govern the data to be collected. In this higher realm of accounting, the work of the accountant frequently becomes inextricably linked with that of the user, particularly in business management.

In common parlance, several fields of accounting work are distinguished, and a brief mention of them may be useful. *Bookkeeping*, mentioned above, covers the procedural aspects of accounting work, and embraces the recording function. Bookkeeping procedures are governed by the end products — the accounting reports — which in turn are determined by the informational needs of users. Such procedures must be understood in order that the accounting reports can be interpreted correctly. *Management accounting* is directed towards the provision of accounting data, particularly on activities within the entity and for segments of the entity's activities, for use by management. It embraces cost accounting, budgeting, and the use of accounting data for decision-making, control, and evaluation purposes. *Financial accounting,* on the other hand, is directed towards the overall measurement of the financial results of operations — for example, cash surplus, income, and financial position; to reporting such data to outside users; and to internal administration, such as ensuring that debts are paid or collected on time. At the higher levels, management and financial accounting necessarily overlap to a substantial degree, and financial accounting includes budgeting and the use of accounting data for decision-making, control, and evaluation purposes for the entity as a whole. Both management and financial accounting include the accountant in industry, or in the public service, who works within the entity. *Professional accounting* embraces the work of accountants outside the entities who audit the accounting records and financial accounting reports for publication, provide secretarial assistance, and frequently prepare the taxation returns for the entity. Such accountants are employed by firms of public accountants. However it should be noted that the accounting profession embraces all fields of accounting practice and that it is not confined to the "professional accountant".

### ACCOUNTING AND RELATED DISCIPLINES

Accounting is closely related to several other disciplines, and the good accountant should be conversant with the parts of these disciplines relevant to his own. They overlap accounting and the accountant should have some knowledge of them in order that he can either apply them in his own work (where he is competent to do so), or recognize that a legal problem, for example, exists and communicate intelligently about the problem with a lawyer (where his own expertise is inadequate).

### 1. Economics

Economics can be called the science of rational decision-making about the use of scarce resources. It is concerned with the analysis of how to use scarce resources to maximize the benefit from their use. Thus it covers the principles governing efficiency in the use of resources (cash, labour, inventories, plant, etc.), the maximization of revenue from output, the optimum rate at which to expand, the best methods of finance to use, and so on. These principles must be applied in the accounting entity in order for it to achieve its objectives as far as the supply of limited resources permits. The accounting system supplies much of the information on which economic decisions are based, and normally the accountant has to decide which information is relevant to the problem. He should, therefore, understand economics so as to be proficient in this task, particularly in management accounting.

## 2. Statistics

Accounting is one form of statistics. A business or government collects a wide variety of statistics in addition to those provided in accounting reports. Many of these statistics are used to supplement accounting reports, for example, physical data on inventories, production, and sales, while others may not be related at all to the accounting system, for instance, statistics on industry performance. Accounting is a form of statistics possessing certain distinguishing characteristics — accounting data relate to transactions or to the transfer of resources within the entity, either historic or projected; they are always recorded in money terms; the twofold aspect of the item is always recorded; and the end result of the accounting process is summarized in *financial* reports. Statistical methods are useful in developing accounting data and in their interpretation. For example, regression analysis is most useful in budgeting and cost control; significance tests can be used in the analysis of budget and standard cost variances; while sampling techniques and significance tests are valuable aids in auditing.

## 3. Mathematics

Double-entry bookkeeping can be taught as a form of algebra, and indeed the first known book on the subject was part of a treatise on algebra. In 1494 Father Luca Pachioli, a Franciscan monk living in Renaissance Northern Italy, published his *Summa,*[3] which in fact was, as well, the first printed text on algebra. Pachioli included in his *Summa* an extensive and rigorous analysis of bookkeeping, "De computis et scripturis". The recording of economic transactions lends itself to algebraic analysis because each transaction necessarily involves a twofold effect which forms the basis of any algebraic equation.

With the recent advent of the computer, mathematics is again becoming vital to accounting. Instead of transactions being recorded in traditional accounts, they may all be recorded in a matrix, and the rules of matrix algebra can be applied in processing and summarizing data.[4] Some knowledge of mathematics is required to gain proficiency in the use of computers in accounting.

Other parts of mathematics are in constant use by accountants. For example, the compound interest formula and its variants must frequently be used wherever cash receipts or payments over time are involved in a transaction or in a valuation problem.

## 4. Organization Theory

The way in which a business is organized on hierarchical and functional lines always forms one of the bases for classifying accounting information. A knowledge of the organization of a business is necessary for the proper preparation and interpretation of all accounting reports relating to a particular segment of the business. Such reports form the basis of "responsibility accounting", wherein the performance achieved by individual managers or departments of a business is assessed and which is an integral part of the planning and control functions of management accounting.

### 5. Law

All businesses operate within a legal environment. All transactions with suppliers or customers are governed by the laws of contract, sale of goods, and so on. Companies are bodies incorporated under law and have a legal personality of their own. Taxation laws are all-pervasive in business. It goes without saying that the accounting system must conform to the requirements of the law.

Much of the work in financial and professional accounting is governed directly by law. The legal system regulates fairly closely the fiduciary areas of accounting — partnership and agency agreements, responsibilities of directors in managing the funds of shareholders and in reporting to them on the stewardship of such funds, auditing, bankruptcy accounting, and trustee and executor accounting. This form of accounting can be contrasted with accounting for economic decision-making and control, such as in management accounting, wherein economic analysis dominates.

### ACCOUNTING AND MANAGEMENT

Management is a broad occupational field which comprises many functions and involves the application of many disciplines, including those mentioned above. The accountant is frequently well placed to play an integral role in management, and in most business organizations of any size the accountant is a member of the top managerial team. The boundaries between accounting and management overlap extensively. A large proportion of the accounting information is prepared for the use of management, and the accountant is often in a better position to make decisions on the basis of such information. In addition, he may have greater expertise than other executives in some areas of management, for example in financial planning, because of his education in these areas. In the reverse direction, an active role in management can facilitate his work as an accountant, first in that he can more readily see any limitations of the accounting system in providing information for managerial purposes, and secondly in designing accounting reports which contain the information relevant to particular uses.

## MAJOR INFLUENCES ON ACCOUNTING

Historically, accounting has not developed as a separate discipline subject to rigorous, logical analysis. Rather, like Topsy, it has just "growed" as a service function according to the practical needs of the times. As a consequence accounting suffers from a wide diversity of inconsistent theories and practices. It is not long since public accountants worked as clerks of lowly status in solicitors' offices where they were employed to do all the bookkeeping required to satisfy the requirements of the law − in particular, trustee, company, bankruptcy, and taxation laws. Financial and professional accounting are especially dominated by company and taxation law, and by the interests of owners and managers. For instance, when owners or managers are pessimistic or optimistic about the *future*, their psychology can be transplanted into valuations included in accounting reports of *past* operations. The desire to minimize taxes is used as the sole reason for many accounting practices in inventory valuation, etc. Legal requirements often cause excessive emphasis on the use of past valuations because they are more readily verifiable for audit purposes even though they are not relevant to the use made of them. These influences all serve to distort accounting measurements of income and financial position and the effects of some of them are considered later. The lack of independence of accountants to formulate their own principles, combined with the absence of agreement in the profession about the fundamental objectives of accounting and of the method of developing accounting principles, comprise the major obstacles to the development of a coherent body of 'good ' *scientific* accounting practices.

### FURTHER READING

A.A.A., Committee to Prepare a Statement of Basic Accounting Theory. *A Statement of Basic Accounting Theory.* Evanston, Ill.: A.A.A., 1966. Chap. 1.

Hatfield, H. R. "An Historical Defense of Bookkeeping." In *Studies in Accounting Theory,* edited by W. T. Baxter and S. Davidson. London: Sweet & Maxwell, 1962.

### NOTES

1. A.A.A., *A Statement of Basic Accounting Theory,* p. 1.
2. Committee on Accounting Procedure and Terminology, *Accounting Research and Terminology Bulletins,* final ed. (New York: A.I.C.P.A., 1961), p. 9.
3. Hatfield, "An Historical Defense of Bookkeeping".
4. See Appendix 3.
5. See chapter 2.

# Chapter 2
# The Methodology of Accounting

Before we begin the study of accounting reports and techniques, a study of the methodology of accounting and the role of theory in accounting is desirable in order to understand the development of the course, and to gain additional insight into accounting practice and solutions to problems facing the profession.

## TYPES OF THEORY

Several approaches can be used to develop a course in accounting, the two most important being the pragmatic one of teaching practices currently used by accountants and a theoretical one based on deductive reasoning. The *pragmatic approach* involves teaching the rules and procedures used in everyday practice; it is essentially a descriptive method detailing what is done in current practice and it emphasizes techniques. It is a good approach for teaching those aspiring practitioners who are satisfied with doing the routine work in accounting. Accounting is just a practical art to most practitioners.

This approach, however, has serious defects for those who aspire to the more creative levels in accounting. There are many thousands of procedures and practices to be learned and so the method is time-consuming and repetitious; many of the practices are inconsistent and there is no guide for choosing between them; they cannot handle new situations facing business; there is no structure to the study of accounting other than what accountants do; justifications for the use of practices are frequently lacking and what is done is confused with what ought to be done; and so forth.

A *theoretical approach* using deductive reasoning is adopted here. This methodology is a fairly standard type of scientific method of analysis which is successfully used throughout the physical sciences and the more advanced social sciences. It is often referred to as a "model-building" approach. Theory concerns the study of the fundamental nature of a field rather than a study of its minutiae. A theory (or a model) is a coherent and mutually consistent set of concepts, assumptions, and propositions combined through logical reasoning which states how specified objectives can be reached in given circumstances. Since accounting is defined in terms of its being a financial information system, accounting theory is concerned with the process by which the financial information needs of users are satisfied. It provides the framework of analysis linking the need for information with the practical task of supplying that information. Deductive theory models are developed within a general "ends-means-constraints" framework of analysis. It tells one how to get from present position A to objective position B, subject to certain restrictions.

Deductive theory is normative and prescriptive rather than descriptive of the current state of the art — it is concerned with what ought to be done rather than with what is done.

The *components of a theoretical model* comprise:

1. A statement of objectives to guide the development of the theory.

2. Definitions of concepts or key items in the theory.

3. Assumptions which describe the environment in which the firm and the accounting system function. They are generally observations of a set of real world conditions simplified so that the task of developing logical relationships is made easier and so that these relationships can be highlighted. They describe the starting point. They need not be exact representations of reality, but they should at least be reasonable abstractions of the most relevant aspects of reality. They help in the task of sorting out "the wood from the trees" in the theory. All assumptions necessary for the conclusions of the model must be specified. The complete set of necessary assumptions is called the necessary and sufficient conditions for the model.

4. Constraints, i.e., restrictions on the means to achieving the desired ends. They are those assumptions about the environment which state what cannot be done.

5. Propositions or hypotheses which are logical deductions stating how objectives can be achieved within the given environment. They generally take the form: "if . . . , then . . . "

6. Principles. These are propositions which have been confirmed as correct by empirical application, i.e., they work in practice. Principles are therefore broad generalizations as to how specified objectives can be reached within a given environment, while a theory can be redefined as a coherent and mutually consistent set of principles.

7. Rules, i.e., detailed applications of principles. They are mechanical methods of applying principles to the accounting process. The rules of accounting measurement, recording, summarizing, and reporting are derived from accounting principles. There is a continuous chain of reasoning from principles to rules with the result that in the middle of the chain it is not possible to distinguish between minor principles and major rules.

In the deductive process, a number of languages can be used, such as normal prose, mathematics, geometry, flow charts, and computer programming languages.

A map is an everyday example of a theoretical model expressed in a pictorial flow chart. For example, if I am in Sydney and want to drive to an address in Melbourne, a general-purpose road map shows various alternative routes to Melbourne. Some routes can be ruled out by the constraints, e.g., via Broken Hill, if the constraints stipulate that the shortest route is to be taken. To ensure that I do not become lost, a series of general reference points may be given to the world between Sydney and Melbourne. These comprise major road names, and towns and mileages en route. The map is a very general one which describes only the most important features of reality along the route — it does not need to give precise details of every tree, house, and crossroad to be passed. However, once I reach Melbourne I need a much more detailed road map — a street directory — showing the myriad of streets to take me to a precise point. One cannot say that one map is more realistic or more useful than another, *only* that one is more general than another. Realism and usefulness can only relate to the objectives served by each — do they enable the objectives to be reached? Both maps are abstractions of reality, and both are useful within their stated objectives if they enable me to reach my destination.

And so it is with theoretical accounting models. Some are general-purpose models designed to answer questions of a general nature, while others are specifically related to precise questions about a particular thing. The concern of this course is with general-purpose models.

As an example of this methodology in accounting, users of accounting information want to know the firm's income earned from its operations and its financial position from time to time. This information should be of sufficient quality to satisfy the standards for accounting information. However there are several concepts of income and of financial position; for example, historic cost income and financial position, and current value income and financial position. The choice of the concept depends on the use to be made of the information, and here again the standards of an accounting information system are relevant. Some assumptions may be necessary to simplify the task of measuring income and financial position. For example, although it is accepted that all business effort contributes towards the making of profits, revenue and hence profit may be recognized at one particular point in the operating cycle, and an assumption must be made as to the most appropriate point. Some measures depend upon assumptions made about the future course of events — for example, whether the firm is to continue operations into the future. Next, any restrictions on the ability to provide the data have to be considered. For example, current market prices may not be available; future data are relevant for decision-making purposes but they cannot be obtained; the cost of acquiring the data may be a deterrent. Given the objectives and the environment, propositions are then made about the appropriate valuation bases for assets and liabilities, the methods of analyzing and recording transactions, items to be charged as expenses, etc.; and, if they are found to be empirically valid, they are elevated to the status of principles. Since the measurements of income and financial position are interdependent, the one set of valuation principles must be applied to the concepts being measured. For example, if historic cost income and financial position are to be measured, then all items should be valued at historic transaction prices; if current value income and financial position are to be measured, then all items are valued at current market prices. This combination of a set of mutually consistent and interdependent principles forms a theory of income determination. The next step is to derive the rules from the principles for recording transactions and measuring the items involved (for example, rules for double-entry recording and for measuring depreciation), and for summarizing the data (for example, classification rules). Finally, the information so derived is provided to users in accounting reports, and these reports should comply with the standards for accounting data.

The phases in the methodology of accounting can be summarized in the form of a continuous loop diagram to emphasize the logical nature of the accounting process and the interdependence of all stages (Fig. 2–1).

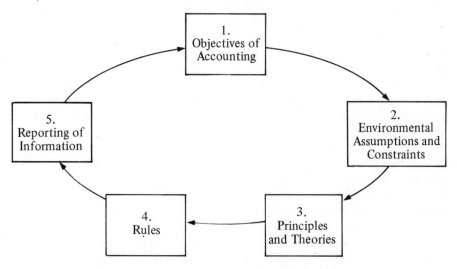

**Figure 2–1.** Phases in the methodology of accounting

Thus, the objectives of accounting are to satisfy the information requirements of users. The information prepared for them is governed by a particular set of environmental factors. Propositions are made as to how the information can be obtained, and the rules for processing the data are then deduced. The information reported at the end of the chain should satisfy users' requirements. The quality of the information provided should be judged with reference to the standards for accounting information.

### TESTING OF THEORIES

A vital stage in the theoretical approach is that of testing the theory. Before they can be accepted, all theories must be tested against reality in order to show whether they work. Does the theory answer the questions or solve the problems in real life that it was designed for? All theories must be tested empirically to see if they work. Testing occurs in the end phase where the information reported is compared with what was wanted. In the case of accounting, the test is whether the accounting system has produced the information required by users. If it does, the theory is accepted, however the theory must be rejected if it produces irrelevant or inadequate information. In this case the theory should be modified and tried again, or alternatively another theory should be applied and tested. An untested theory is no more than a series of unconfirmed propositions about what ought to be done, and it cannot be accepted while it remains untested.

Where the information does not satisfy the user's needs, the theory could be at fault at various points. First, the objectives, assumptions, or constraints may not be sufficient approximations to reality. This can occur where they are too general for the purpose in hand, they may be irrelevant, or a crucial assumption may be omitted. Secondly, the deductive logic joining the conclusions to the assumptions may be faulty. Finally, the results may not have been effectively communicated to users.

A theory ought to be tested and confirmed at every point possible — the assumptions, intermediate implications, and final conclusions — before it is accepted as a valid theory. There is a risk that if only the conclusions of a theory are confirmed, then its predictive ability has resulted from chance. The theory cannot be relied upon in such circumstances, and it cannot explain why the sequence of events happened. The testing of theories in most physical sciences is assisted by the ability to set up controlled laboratory experiments. Unfortunately this is not feasible in most social sciences and it is often difficult to acquire sufficient evidence to confirm or reject theories. As a consequence, the social sciences abound with untested theories.

### THE NEED FOR ACCOUNTING THEORY

There is a pressing need for an improvement in the state of current accounting theory. For centuries accounting has developed as a pragmatic art and countless "principles" have been developed to solve specific practical problems.[1] These "principles" are generally no more than rationalizations of current practices. One result of this piecemeal development is that current accounting practice is plagued by a proliferation of contradictory methods and accounting reports frequently fail to satisfy the information needs of users.[2]

Accounting theory, as with all theory, has various uses. First, it helps in "explaining and guiding the accountant's action in identifying, measuring and communicating economic information".[3] Theory is needed to *explain* why the accountant adopts this valuation principle for assets and not that one; or why he adopts this rule for measuring periodic depreciation and not that one. Likewise, it is needed to *guide* the accountant in the selection of principles and rules to apply in a particular circumstance. Theory provides a broad framework for the accountant's selection of practices. For example, does historic cost income or current value income provide a better basis for control, evaluation, and prediction? Third, theory is useful for *analyzing* the logical relationships in an accounting system and hence to establish the cause and effect relationships in the system. Next, theory has an important normative role in the *evaluation* of accounting practices. "The purpose in developing a theory of accounting is to establish standards for judging the acceptability of accounting methods. Procedures that meet the standards should be employed in the practice of accounting; those failing to meet the standards should be rejected."[4] It helps the accountant to answer questions of the type — Have the most appropriate practices been adopted, or is there scope for the use of better ones? Are all the practices mutually consistent? A good theory provides criteria by which one can accept or reject existing accounting methods. Fifth, theory can assist in making *predictions* of the likely outcome of actions in a given set of circumstances or the effects of changes in these circumstances; for example, what would be the effects of a change in inventory pricing methods on reported profits and balance sheet inventories. Sixth, theory is required to *synthesize* the existing body of accounting principles into a consistent whole and to eliminate the superfluous, inconsistent, and unsound ones. This synthesization would substantially reduce the number of generally acceptable accounting practices, simplify accounting and make for more uniformity in accounting. Finally, theory is a valuable aid in *research* to improve upon existing practices and to develop new practices to solve new problems thrown up by an ever changing business environment, for example, the problems created by inflation for profit measurement.

## DEVELOPMENT OF THE COURSE

The methodology outlined above is applied in the development of this course in financial accounting. We begin by examining the objectives of financial accounting, viz., to provide information about the financial activities of a firm to interested parties, and the standards which such information ought to achieve for it to satisfy users' needs. The economic activities of firms are then considered, and various rules are devised for recording and summarizing transaction data.

The major problem studied in the course is how to convert this mass of transaction data into useful information for users, and for this we must study several theories of income and financial position determination. The first of these theories is the historic cost theory. A series of financial reports based on historic cost showing the income earned, the distribution of that income, the resources and debts of the firm, and cash and finance flows, are prepared. Many adjustments must be made to the transaction data to obtain some of this information, and rules are derived for this purpose. Concepts are defined and assumptions are made explicit at appropriate points. The quality of these financial reports is judged with respect to the users' needs, and their limitations are noted. Modifications made to them in practice to overcome their inadequacies or to accommodate external influences on accounting are then examined and assessed.

Next, a series of alternative valuation theories based on a constant value of the dollar, on current market prices, on combinations of the two, and on present values, are studied to see how they overcome limitations of historic cost reports in providing useful financial information. Finally, techniques for the analysis of financial reports are studied, and an appraisal is made of the merits of each valuation system. Some empirical evidence about information requirements, inadequacies of information currently provided and its consequences is included in Appendix 2.

### FURTHER READING

A.A.A., Committee to Prepare a Statement of Basic Accounting Theory. *A Statement of Basic Accounting Theory.* Evanston, Ill.: A.A.A., 1966. Chap. 1.

### NOTES

1. See, for instance, the list of "principles" in P. Grady, *Inventory of Generally Accepted Accounting Principles for Business Enterprises,* Accounting Research Study No. 7 (New York: A.I.C.P.A., 1965); and W. J. Kenley, *A Statement of Australian Accounting Principles* (Melbourne: Accountancy Research Foundation, 1970).
2. See, for instance, "What's Wrong with Financial Statements", *Australian Accountant* (July 1968).
3. A.A.A., *A Statement of Basic Accounting Theory,* p. 2.
4. Ibid., p. 6.

### QUESTIONS

Prepare brief written answers to each of the following questions.

1. Why bother with theory in accounting? Why not just look at the "facts" in the real world?

2. Distinguish between two major approaches to the development of theory. What are the advantages and disadvantages of each approach?

3. Explain the phases in the methodology of an accounting system.

4. Explain the role of assumptions in theory construction. Do they have to be relevant to the real world?

5. "It's all right in theory but it doesn't work in practice". Comment critically.

6. Distinguish between accounting principles, theories and rules. Give examples of each.

7. What are the major components of a deductive theory?

8. Distinguish between necessary conditions, and the necessary and sufficient conditions, of a theory. Give examples.

9. What test is used to evaluate the validity of a theory?

# Chapter 3
# Financial Information Requirements and Standards

Because the approach to accounting in this course is a theoretical one, we must first study the information requirements of users as the end-purpose of the accounting system and the quality which such information ought to attain in order to be of most use. To do this involves an examination of who are the major users of accounting information and for what purposes they require such information, and secondly a set of standards for accounting information and guidelines for its communication.

## THE MAJOR USERS AND THEIR REQUIREMENTS

### 1. Short-Term Creditors

Short-term creditors comprise those creditors whose claims are due for payment within the coming year. Their claims arise in various ways. Suppliers of materials, merchandise, and services frequently grant trade credit, i.e., delayed payment terms, to their customers who are other businesses. Trading banks provide overdraft facilities and other financial institutions frequently advance short-term loans to businesses. The public may lend money to companies in the form of short-term deposits; and so on. Short-term creditors are concerned with the ability of the business to repay the loans in the near future, and to pay interest where it is charged; i.e., they want information about its immediate liquidity in order to assess the creditworthiness of the business, which in turn determines whether they will lend to it. The accountant can provide data on short-term liquidity, though in most cases external users other than banks do not have access to it except when the annual accounting reports are published by companies.

### 2. Long-Term Creditors

Businesses often borrow money for long periods of time (i.e., for greater than one year), and they must pay interest for this finance and repay the sum borrowed at the due date. Common forms of long-term loans comprise debentures, mortgages, notes, and straight loans. In many cases, the loans are secured to some asset, such as land and buildings, and the business cannot dispose of the stipulated asset (i.e., the collateral) before repayment of the loan. In the event of arrears in interest payments or loan repayment, the secured creditor normally has the right to take over the asset and sell it.

Long-term creditors require information about the long-term credit-worthiness of the business, i.e., its ability to pay interest and repay the loan. This ability is indicated by the expected future financial position of the business, i.e., its financial structure, liquidity, and market values of assets, and its long-term profit prospects. Budgeted accounting reports for future periods would be most relevant for this assessment, but normally these are not available to external users. Large financial institutions, however, often insist on them, and they have the power to do so in a capital market in which finance is scarce. In place of budgeted reports, long-term creditors normally must rely on historic accounting reports and evidence that the business has always met its interest and repayment commitments on time. Financial structures do not change substantially over time in well-run businesses, so that the current situation can be a good basis for predicting future financial structure and financial security.

### 3. Owners, Proprietors, or Shareholders

Owners provide the risk capital for businesses, and consequently they own the resources remaining after payment of all debts. All profits remaining after taxes and interest accrue to them. The form of ownership determines the legal characteristics of the business. Both "sole traders" (where there is only the one owner) and partnerships (where there are several joint owners) are unincorporated bodies in law, i.e., "firms", and their liability for business debts incurred is not limited to the assets of the business. The owner's personal property is liable to be used for the payment of business debts. The ability of such firms to borrow money to finance expansion is very restricted and they are always of small size.

In Australia, the business sector is dominated by companies. These are bodies incorporated under the Companies Acts of the various states, or under special acts of parliament (particularly for government business undertakings), or in rare cases by Royal Charter. The owners purchase shares in the company, and their liability for the debts of the company is limited to any amount unpaid on their shares up to the full nominal (or legal) value of the share. Companies may be "proprietary limited" or, in the case of public companies, simply "limited". The first group comprises companies which are owned by other companies, i.e., subsidiary companies, and generally small, privately owned companies.

The maximum number of owners of "pty. ltd." companies is restricted to fifty, and their shares cannot be sold on stock exchanges. This restricts the potential size of the privately owned company because it does not have access to the general market for share capital. Subsidiary companies, on the other hand, may be giants. Most overseas companies operating in Australia are subsidiaries of an overseas public· company (for example, General Motors-Holden's Pty. Ltd. is a subsidiary of General Motors Corporation of the U.S.); while the subsidiaries of some Australian companies are also very large (for example, Australian Iron & Steel Pty. Ltd. is a subsidiary of the Broken Hill Proprietary Co. Ltd.). Public companies can grow to a very large size because there is no natural limit to their life, there is no legal limit to the number of shareholders, and because of their access to the general capital market for funds. For example, in 1975 the B.H.P. Co. Ltd. had a share capital of $392m., total shareholders' funds of $1,587m., and 191,000 shareholders; and it ranks in the world's hundred largest companies outside the U.S.[1] Shareholders can sell their shares at any time, and any person can buy shares in a public company in virtually any volume. Public companies must publish their annual financial reports, duly audited by licensed company auditors, for the use of shareholders and investors generally.

A feature of the modern public company is the separation of ownership from control of the company's operations. Shareholders take no part in the management of the company; rather, they delegate their responsibilities through a board of directors, who hire a professional management to operate the company. Shareholders who are dissatisfied with the company's management may in law endeavour to have it changed through electing directors of their choice, but this is normally impracticable and the shareholder's solution is to sell his shares in the company. In law, directors have a fiduciary relationship with shareholders, i.e., one of the utmost good faith, and they are required to account each year to shareholders on the stewardship of the funds entrusted to them by shareholders. In particular, they are required to show that no funds have been misappropriated, that the company has operated within its legal charter, and that all assets and liabilities have been accounted for. This accounting to shareholders is done through the published annual accounting and directors' reports of the company.

Owners require a wide range of accounting information in order to help them decide on whether to leave their funds invested in the business or to increase their investment. Because they bear the ultimate risks of the business, they require information which helps them to assess whether the risk is worth undertaking. Hence information about the risks involved in the business, risks involved in alternative investment opportunities (for example, in other companies' shares), and the rewards for their sacrifice of funds, is required. Owners of "firms" can easily obtain such data as are available because they are also the managers and have access to all the data available. However share-holders of public companies are provided with only a limited amount of information, notwithstanding that the purchase of shares on a rational basis is a very complex task. These complexities become apparent when it is considered what the purchase of a share means in terms of economics.

When an investor buys a share in a public company, he purchases in effect ownership rights to a part of the company's net assets and profits generated by those assets, plus some other rights such as the power to vote for directors and to participate in new share issues. However both the profit stream and net assets are risky because the company cannot guarantee that it will always earn profits and that its assets will always maintain their values, and secondly because all creditors of the company rank ahead of shareholders in their claims for interest payments and repayment of debts. Shareholders' claims rank last — they are entitled only to what is left after all creditors' claims have been met.

Shareholders are concerned with the risk involved in the investment and the returns expected from it. The returns must outweigh the risks for the investment to be profitable. Moreover, the investor can purchase the shares of any public company and, if he is rational, he will seek to maximize the returns from his investment outlays. To do this, he must compare the returns and risks associated with the shares of each company and select those offering the highest returns in relation to risks. Risk arises from two sources — from trading operations and financial structure. Operating risks are those inherent in the company's trading activities — the various market risks arising from its own and its competitors' business policies and from the state of the economy. They can be judged from the size, stability, and trend of profits and sales, reliability of investment in assets (i.e., the liquidity of assets and their current market values compared with their historical costs), and net assets per share. Financial risks are additional ones arising from the use of debt finance. They are reflected in the company's financial structure — the proportion of finance provided by creditors judged in relation to the security of investment in its assets, and the proportion of profits absorbed by fixed financial charges. A company can be operating profitably, yet become bankrupt because of an inappropriate financial structure which prevents it from repaying loans or paying interest charges.

The investor's problem is further complicated by the fact that returns to shareholders may come in various forms — dividends, appreciation in share prices (due to reinvestment of profits, improved profit prospects, appreciation in asset values, speculation, and so on), rights to new share issues, bonus issues, etc. The investor must predict the returns from each source over the future. Technically, a share price is the present (or discounted) value of these expected future returns, with the discount rate depending on interest rates in the capital market and the degree of risk incurred in purchasing the company's shares. When an investor buys a share, he is really paying for these expected future returns.[2]

The performance of companies and their financial positions thus determine in large measure the rewards for and the risks undertaken by shareholders, and consequently they require reliable information on these matters. In order to assess achieved performance, shareholders ought to have data on profits earned in terms of current dollar values, profit rates on investment, and profits per share, again in terms of current dollar values; dividends per share; sales and market shares; growth rates achieved compared with those of competitors or the industry; and so forth. Financial position and financial structure can be reliably measured only if all the firm's assets and liabilities are shown at current market values. The prospects for future success of a company can be gauged from its past achievements, its current financial position, the management's overall policies for future action, and the economic trends in the industry. A judgment of the risks involved should likewise be based upon the above data. For various reasons which will be considered later, the information contained in the published reports of companies falls far short of these ideals in Australia. Most companies publish only what is required by law. This legal minimum is determined basically by the stewardship function of directors rather than by the needs of shareholders for information on which to assess accurately the company's achieved performance, its financial position, its prospects for future success, and the risks involved.

### 4. Potential Shareholders

Potential shareholders have the same interests in the financial affairs of a public company as existing shareholders. Essentially they make the same decisions – to buy shares, to retain them, or to sell them. Large companies depend upon the ready marketability of their shares as a factor in maintaining share prices, and therefore in maintaining investor confidence. Typically in the large company, membership of the body of shareholders changes every day on which the stock exchanges operate. A company may wish to tap the resources of potential investors in order to help finance expansion beyond the resources provided by its own funds and those of its existing shareholders.

### 5. Taxation Authorities

The government raises most of its revenue from taxation, the forms of which and the rates to be applied being specified in its annual budget. Accounting information forms the basis of any taxation assessment for personal income, company, payroll, sales taxes, and so on. The informational needs of taxation authorities, particularly the items which must be included in the assessment and their method of valuation, are always specified by the government. The tax department has direct access to the data it wants and it does not have to rely on published company reports.

## 6. Employees and Trade Unions

Employees and labour unions are vitally concerned with the operating results of a business and its financial position. Many employees work for the one business for the greater part of their lives and they have a long-term interest in the prosperity of the business. The success of any business depends substantially on the calibre of its employees. Employees are concerned with the financial success and stability of the business because it indicates the scope for possible wage and fringe benefit increases, the security of employment and retirement benefits, and the scope for promotion. These are obviously greater in stable, profitable expanding businesses than in other ones.

## 7. Competitors

Competitors of public companies are always interested in the operating results and financial positions of their rivals. They wish to compare such results with their own. The achievement of better results by competitors signifies that they are adopting more effective business policies, in which case there may be scope for the business to copy some of them. Imitation of policies which have achieved success is one of the best and simplest maxims for a business to follow. Such a business will not be the market leader, but it is likely to survive and prosper. Competitors should watch their rivals' cash and inventory positions. Excessive inventories are likely to lead to price cuts, as will an acute state of illiquidity. High liquidity provides a company with the means to significant future action, particularly internal expansion or the taking-over of another company whose share prices are depressed in relation to the current values of its net assets or its profit potential. A study of competitors' accounting reports can, therefore, forewarn the firm of possible future action.

## 8. Customers

Where large contracts are involved in transactions between companies (for example, construction projects or the supply of a big volume of materials and merchandise), the customer often insists on having a copy of the contractor's statement of financial position. Because it is difficult for other contractors to take over the job in the event of bankruptcy, the customer is concerned with the contractor's ability to complete the project on time. A statement of financial position can indicate the contractor's financial ability to undertake the project.

### 9.  Government Regulatory Bodies

Governments, both Commonwealth and state, are playing increasing roles in the direct guidance and regulation of business, as well as indirectly through their general economic and legal policies. Some state governments exercise price control over commodities such as bread and petrol, and accounting data on costs of production are used as the basis for the prices determination. Similar considerations apply as well to many primary products (for example, wheat, sugar, and dairy products) whose marketing is governed by marketing boards. All large companies are required to justify, on a cost basis, their case for price increases on products to the Prices Justification Tribunal. The Australian Industries Assistance Commission grants tariff protection to the greater part of Australian manufacturing industry to protect it from excessive overseas competition, and its assessment of the tariff level required is based partly upon cost of production data. The (restrictive) Trade Practices Tribunal makes extensive use of accounting data on costs and profits in its examination of charges relating to price discrimination, monopolization, collusive tendering, and so on.

### 10.  Management

The informational requirements of management are far more pervasive than those of other users, and this is particularly true for the large company with diversified activities covering many products and territories. The functions of management may be described as planning, controlling, evaluating, and reporting, and accounting information must be provided to facilitate these functions. Unlike most other users, management has access to all the internal data available, and it can always direct that additional information be obtained where the existing data are inadequate.

The planning or decision-making function of management revolves around the choice of objectives for the business and the decisions about how to use scarce resources to satisfy those objectives. All businesses have objectives such as a profit target, growth, sales value, a share of the market, efficiency, and so on, and management must formulate its plans according to these objectives. However, there are restrictions on their achievement caused by the stock of existing resources and the projected increase in resources of the business, together with the actions of competitive firms. Management must plan all the activities of the business in the fields of products to be made, methods of production to be used, sources of finance to be used, prices to be charged and selling methods to be adopted, and so on. These plans must then all be coordinated in a set of integrated budgets; otherwise, chaos may result when excessive inventories accumulate because production far outstrips sales, cash is not available to pay debts, and so forth.

The control function concerns the effective implementation of the plans. On the operating side, factors of production must be acquired at the time they are needed for production, the correct production must be made, the planned levels of efficiency, output and sales must be achieved, etc. On the financial side, cash must be carefully controlled so that all debts maturing to the business are collected on time, while it pays its own debts on time. Arrangements must be made in advance to bridge any temporary cash deficit.

Evaluation involves an assessment of how well the firm, a manager, or a department has performed over the period, and of where the firm currently stands with respect to its financial position, trading position, and so forth. The assessment should be made against norms such as the firm's own objectives and the performance of its competitors. It should answer questions such as − to what extent have the firm's objectives been achieved; what particular problems were encountered in operations; has the firm performed better than its competitors, and if not, why not? Various yardsticks may be used to assess performance, the most important being total profits and rates of profit on investment. Financial position is assessed mainly in terms of short-term and long-term liquidity and financial structure.

The reporting function of management applies only to companies, as here the management must report to shareholders on their stewardship of the shareholders' funds. The informational requirements of shareholders have been considered above. The reporting function is largely dictated to management by the law and stock exchange regulations, though management has the right to publish information beyond the prescribed minimum.

A great variety of information is required for planning purposes, and only some of it can come from the accounting system. Planning is the prerogative of top management, and much of the "data" used consist of nothing more than hunches or "guesstimates". Decisions must be made and plans prepared in the face of uncertain knowledge of what is likely to happen in the future. Management does not know what sales volume will be achieved, how a new product will sell, how efficient a new method of production will be, what competitors may do, and so on. Yet a watertight set of plans presupposes perfect knowledge of all these, as well as other items. Nevertheless, the accountant can provide much useful information to reduce the extent of uncertainty of future events, particularly where rapid changes are not occurring in the business or industry, and it is normally his function to coordinate and integrate the plans in quantitative economic terms.

Although the objectives of the business are determined by top management, the accountant can indicate their feasibility by providing a reliable measure of past achievements. Top management will consider a host of alternative ways of achieving the targets. For example, it will consider different marketing policies − different price, advertising, product-mix, and sales volume combinations; different production methods — which materials, plant, and type of labour to use; different methods of product styling or the introduction of new products; different methods of financing — short-term or long-term loans, trade credit, leasing, or retained profits; and so forth. Personnel engaged in marketing, production and finance will provide much of this advice. The accountant should help in the task of quantifying, in money terms, the series of alternatives and making explicit the implications of each (for instance, the effects of the plan on profits and liquidity) so that management can then choose between the alternative plans on a rational, informed basis. Finally, the plans tentatively selected must be integrated into a set of budgeted accounting reports which give a complete picture of the effects of the plans on production, sales, costs, profits, and financial position. Revisions of the plans will be made if any avoidable, undesirable features are made evident by the set of budgets.

Because the control function concerns the conformance of actions to plans, it is necessary that there be constant comparisons between plans and achievements to date. A feedback mechanism in the information system is required to check on both the feasibility of the plans and the effectiveness of their implementation. Effective control of operations cannot be made merely through recording what has happened. Events occur both by design and by accident or default. Likewise, business conditions change from those expected, and consequently the plans may require some amendment. Variations between budgeted and achieved results should be spotlighted and the reasons for them investigated immediately by management so that corrective action may be taken before it is too late. Typical of the problems that arise are: why have sales fallen below the target, why are expenses greater than expected, why is there a cash shortage?

The information requirements of management can be summarized in chart form as in Figure 3–1.[3] Note that the interrelationships between the phases form an endless loop in the information chain. The external reporting function can as well be joined onto the loop to complete the pattern.

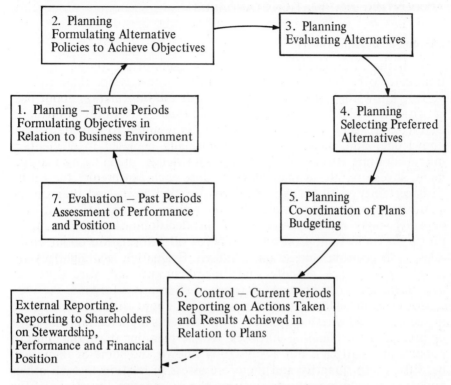

**Figure 3—1.** Cycle of management functions

## SUMMARY OF MAIN FUNCTIONS OF ACCOUNTING DATA

From the above it can be seen that the purpose of an accounting system is to provide financial information which satisfies the following functions:

1. Measurement: measurement of past performance and current financial position for all types of accounting entities

2. Forecasting: to provide historical data as the basis for forecasting future events by all types of users

3. Decision-making: to provide data for planning future activities, particularly by management and investors

4. Control: to report on actions taken and results achieved in relation to the plans formulated, particularly in business and government administration

5. Evaluation: assessment of achieved performance and current position in relation to the firm's objectives and the performance of competitors.

6. Stewardship: accounting for the use of owners' funds by a professional management in public companies, or by a government to its citizens, and so forth

7. Government regulation and taxation: to facilitate achieving the government's economic and social objectives and to provide revenue for the government.

## ACCOUNTING INFORMATION STANDARDS

### Information Systems Theory

If all the information requirements of users of accounting information were to be fully satisfied, it would be necessary for them to have perfect knowledge of all relevant data. All the information about past activities and about the future should be freely and readily available to all users. A "total information system" is required to provide perfect knowledge, and such a system is normally assumed in elementary microeconomic theory. With perfect knowledge, planning by management, investors, etc. is made easy because each can predict the future with certainty — the range of alternatives is known, and they can be quantified so that the choice between them is straightforward and depends solely on the objective of the decision-maker, for example, profit maximization. Control is easy, as all information about costs, sales, cash position, and so on is known. Evaluation is straightforward as the results are definite and unambiguous, and yardsticks for assessment are easily obtained in terms of alternatives forgone.

However, in reality, users of information about firms are not placed in such a knowledgeable position. Future events are uncertain and must be predicted for planning purposes. At the planning stage, the range of possible alternatives is not always fully known and some of them may be difficult to quantify and therefore assess in relation to each other; budgeted accounting reports covering the prospective operations of the future may be based on some wild guesses; and wrong courses of action may be adopted. The control function is hampered by both budgets of doubtful validity and incomplete data on current operations. Evaluation is made difficult because the measures of performance and position can be ambiguous in an uncertain world complicated by changing market prices and inflation.

Accounting information must be useful to users, otherwise it is pointless to collect it. The utility of information lies in its ability to inform users of relevant facts, estimates, and possibilities that were not already known, i.e., to reduce the existing state of ignorance. The accounting system is the firm's financial information system which is maintained for the purpose of informing interested parties about the economic activities of the firm and to satisfy the requirements of regulatory authorities. It forms the major single part of a firm's information system. However, information is not a free commodity and the firm must spend some money on maintaining its accounting system. The decision regarding expenditure on it should be judged according to the general economic principles of resource allocation and in a way similar to expenditures on any other item; namely, does the benefit to be derived from having the additional information outweigh the cost of obtaining it? A good accounting system must be economic, i.e., the benefits must exceed the cost. This does not mean that it provides complete information about everything such that all users have perfect knowledge. The state of perfect knowledge is normally both impracticable and uneconomic to attain in realistic conditions, and firms' accounting systems fall far short of this state. In general, the cost of information varies with how feasible it is to obtain it — some data can be easily collected and processed (e.g., historical transaction data), while other data cannot be (e.g., some data relating to future events — the efficiency of a new production process, the popularity of a new product, the effect of a change in price of the firm's product, and so on). Some business decisions must be made in a state of almost complete ignorance of relevant data — these are pure gambling decisions, for which a high potential return is required to compensate for the high degree of risk involved.

Because the value of information is frequently difficult to assess, the optimum expenditure on an accounting information system, i.e., that amount of expenditure at which the marginal benefits from the additional data are exactly offset by the cost of obtaining it, cannot be determined with any precision. Instead, the only practical approach appears to be to assess the cost of obtaining the extra information against several standards concerning its usefulness. These standards must be satisfied by an economic information system. If any of these standards is not adequately satisfied, then the benefits may not be sufficient to justify the cost of providing the information. It is up to the management to judge whether the benefits exceed the cost involved.

The standards for accounting information ought to be attained by an accounting system in providing the information needed by users. The standards determine the quality of information and hence the usefulness of accounting data. In addition, they constitute a basis for the inclusion or exclusion of data; they form the yardstick against which to judge the adequacy of various accounting systems and hence to indicate where improvements should be made, and they provide a checklist against which to judge the quality of information. With the introduction of computers having an enormous capacity for processing accounting data, it is becoming increasingly important to test accounting information against these standards and justify the cost of obtaining it.

The standards are not absolute in the sense that each and every standard must be fully satisfied before the information is useful — such a position is normally impossible of achievement in an uncertain world; rather, they must be used with judgment in assessing the adequacy of particular information.

While standards are closely related to accounting theory, there is a difference between the two in that accounting theory is concerned with the attributes of the accounting system itself, whereas accounting standards are concerned with the quality of the information generated by that system. But the distinction cannot be a sharp one as the information standards help determine the theory and consequently accounting practices, which in turn affect the quality of the information provided.

### The Standards

The standards of a good accounting information system comprise relevance of the data, verifiability, freedom from bias, timeliness, comparability, reliability, and understandability. Other standards are sometimes used; however they are mainly coextensive with the above. The standards are closely interrelated and overlap to some extent.

## 1. Relevance

"Relevance is the primary standard and requires that the information must bear upon or be usefully associated with actions it is designed to facilitate or results desired to be produced."[4] The concept of relevance only has meaning when it is related to a particular use — for what purpose is the information required? — and to particular users or classes of users — for whom is it required? To be relevant, the information must at least potentially influence the user's decisions or control actions. Likewise, such information should be significant for the end-use. If the information has no potential effect upon the user's decisions and actions, it is not relevant or significant; neither is it relevant or significant if a change in the information does not cause a change in the decision made. A different set of information should lead to different decisions.

The same data are not relevant for all users and uses, though most users must content themselves with the general-purpose published annual reports of companies. General-purpose and specific-purpose reports should be distinguished. Management and taxation authorities make most use of special-purpose reports, and these must be tailored to suit the needs of the specific users. As examples, reports for creditors and government regulatory bodies, and reports for shareholders and for management, should frequently differ because the informational requirements of each differ. Likewise, different valuation rules may be relevant for different purposes. For example, historic costs are relevant for some purposes (e.g., in stewardship reports to shareholders), but not for others (e.g., in evaluating a company's economic performance).

All accounting information that materially bears upon the end use should be provided to the user, i.e., the information should be complete and be material. The omission of some relevant information can lead to incorrect decisions and is a source of bias. Likewise the information should be material to the end use — the inclusion of insignificant details can confuse the user. The information should be presented in a form which enables significant causal and structural relationships in the data to be determined. This permits effective summarization of the data and highlights the major information in it. Determination of the relevance of data is assisted by specifying the area covered by the data (e.g., the accounting entity and period), the valuation principles employed (e.g., historical cost, current values, inventory valuation methods), and the assumptions underlying forecasts of future events, (e.g., the expected state of the economy, the business is to continue operations in the future).

Relevance is the primary requirement of a good information system and it takes precedence over the other requirements, particularly for decision-making. It is the main determinant of the benefits to be derived from the information. At best, irrelevant information is useless if it is disregarded — i.e., it has zero benefits. But, where irrelevance is not detected, use of the data can lead to costly wrong decisions — here, its benefits are negative.

## 2. *Verifiability*

"Verifiability requires that essentially similar measures or conclusions would be reached if two or more qualified persons examined the same data."[5] The events must be independently observable and testable. However, this standard does not always require identical results.

Verifiability is necessary to ensure that the data are dependable. Many users of accounting information have no direct access to the data and they have no alternative but to rely on that which is provided. Frequently accounting data are used by parties who have opposing interests and it is likely to be prepared by one party for use by the other who has no access to the accounting records. The assumptions underlying the choice of methods used in accounting (e.g., inventory and depreciation methods) and estimates (e.g., asset lives) which influence the final information should be explicit so that the user can test them. Auditing is feasible only where the data can be verified. Verifiability of data is particularly important for the stewardship function of directors and for all legal and taxation purposes.

However, for most decision-making purposes, data which cannot be verified may have to be used. This applies to all forecast data, which are necessarily no more than subjective estimates of future events, required for planning purposes. Here, verifiability must play a very secondary role to relevance. In any conflict between relevance and verifiability, the first requirement is for relevance in so far as decision-making is concerned.

The conflict between verifiability and relevance poses one of the greatest dilemmas in external reporting by companies. The greater the relevance of data for decision-making by investors, the less verifiable it becomes; and vice versa. Existing accounting practice in, and legal requirements for, external reporting emphasize verifiability; hence published company reports are not always satisfactory for the decision-making functions of investors.

### 3.  Freedom from Bias

"Freedom from bias means that the facts have been impartially determined and reported. It also means that techniques used in developing data should be free of built-in bias."[6] Accounting information has to satisfy the requirements of various users, some of whom have conflicting interests – information is provided to both buyers and sellers, to taxpayer and tax collector, to debtor and creditor. The information must be free from bias for it to serve the interests of various users, i.e., it must be neutral as between them and not favour one party against the other. The bias may be of a personal nature (e.g., use of the lowest recorded market values of assets in the balance sheet) or it may result from the use of inappropriate accounting techniques (e.g., in allocating fixed overhead costs to departments or products), from reporting incomplete data, or from excessive caution in the making of estimates.

The standards of verifiability and freedom from bias are generally treated as one in accounting literature, under the heading of "objectivity". This term has, however, been the subject of much dispute and is better avoided through the use of the two separate standards.

### 4.   Timeliness

Accounting information must be processed and reported within appropriate time periods for it to be economic. Both benefits and costs depend to a large extent on how quickly the information is processed and reported. The timeliness standard can be analyzed in terms of two related aspects of the frequency of reporting and the time lag in reporting. The optimum reporting interval (i.e., the time between the event and its reporting) varies according to the type of information. Customers booking an airline flight may want to know immediately whether they can get a seat on a particular flight. Control information on some aspects of costs or cash flow, for example, is required on a daily basis so that inefficiencies or illiquidity can be reported and rectified immediately. Data on other aspects of costs, performance, and overall financial position are best provided in summary form for longer periods – for example, a month, quarter, or year – so that distortions caused by irregular or random factors and by arbitary allocations of data are minimized. More accurate assessments of operations are then possible. Data processing systems can be installed to suit the required reporting interval. On-line computer systems are required for the provision of immediate answers, whereas the cheaper batch systems suffice for situations where reporting intervals cover a period.

The time lag aspect concerns the lag between the end of the reporting period and the time at which the information is given to the user. Stale information is of little use. Market opportunities will not wait on the accountant to acquire the necessary decision-making information. Control data are useless unless they can be obtained in time to permit the rectification of the inefficiencies occurring. But on the other hand, the constant reporting of data can be expensive and it is generally more economical and in some cases more useful to store the data for some time and report them in summary form at a later date, i.e., the optimum reporting interval must be considered.

## 5. Comparability

Accounting information is more useful if it facilitates comparisons as all decision-making, control, and evaluations involve comparisons. Comparability means that like things are measured and reported similarly, and that these are distinguished from unlike things. Comparability is required between businesses, between segments of operations within a business, between forecast results and actual results, and over time. Comparability requires that a consistent set of accounting principles, definitions, assumptions, data processing and measurement techniques, classifications of data and reporting intervals are applied throughout the accounting system. For example, the income measurement system (e.g., historical cost, current value) must be consistently applied to all items; the points at which sales transactions are assumed to give rise to revenue and assets must be consistently applied; information processing methods must be consistently applied so that the data can be meaningfully aggregated and interpreted, and the classification of items in accounting reports must be consistent. Comparisons are facilitated if the accounting system incorporates an automatic feedback mechanism. This mechanism is required in particular for effective control purposes. Hence budgeted and achieved performance should be compared as time unfurls immediately after the activity has taken place. Any avoidable inefficiencies are then highlighted by the comparison, and remedial action can be taken almost immediately.

In addition to ensuring comparability, consistency also acts as a safeguard against bias.

## 6. Reliability

The data provided by the accounting system must be reliable for it to be useful. Unreliable information can lead to incorrect decisions and judgments. Reliability is that quality which permits users of the information to depend upon it with confidence. To a large extent, this standard follows from the five above — data should be reliable if they comply with the above requirements. However it is not coextensive with them as for example a historical fact may be a reliable piece of information but not a relevant one for a particular purpose.

Users should be able to assess the reliability of information. This assessment is helped by the separation of estimated data from factual data (e.g., accumulated depreciation and plant cost). The assumptions underlying forecasts, estimates, measurement techniques and interpretations should be made explicit, and users should be informed of the limitations of the data where it is not factual. Users should be able to compare the information against the environment whose aspects are measured to test its reliability (e.g., sales data with trading conditions, and higher asset values with inflation in the economy). There should be a close correspondence between the information reported and reality.

## 7.  Understandability

The accounting information should be reported in a form that is understandable by a reasonably competent user. He must be able to interpret it correctly so as not to be misled by it. Information that is not understandable is not useful. Understandability requires that information be expressed as simply and as clearly as possible. The forms of presentation of information, classification of items and titles used in accounting reports are important in making the reports easy to read and understand. Various forms of presentation are available and the ones which most clearly communicate information should be employed. Logical and relevant bases of classification of data which highlight important relationships within the reports should be adopted. The titles of accounting reports, classification groups and accounts should describe their contents fairly accurately; otherwise the user can be misled or not understand what they relate to. Published accounting reports abound with meaningless (e.g., reserve for contingencies) or misleading (e.g., goodwill on consolidation) account titles, and classification groups (e.g., reserves and provisions). The assumptions embodied in the reports and concepts measured should be explicit for the reports to be reliably understood.

### FURTHER READING

A.A.A., Committee to Prepare a Statement of Basic Accounting Theory. *A Statement of Basic Accounting Theory.* Chapter 2, for information standards; chap. 3, pp. 19–30, and chap. 4, pp. 37–56, for information requirements.

A.I.C.P.A. Report of the Study Group on the Objectives of Financial Statements, *Objectives of Financial Statements,* New York: 1973.

Andersen, A. *Objectives of Financial Statements.* Chicago. A. Andersen and Co. 1972. Chaps. 1 and 2.

Kenley, W. J. and Staubus, G. J. *Objectives and Concepts of Financial Statements.* Melbourne: Accountancy Research Foundation, 1972. Chaps. 2, 8–10.

## NOTES

1. The 1975 annual report of the B.H.P. Co. Ltd;
2.
$$P_0 = \frac{R_1}{(1+r)^1} + \frac{R_2}{(1+r)^2} + \dots \quad \frac{R_n}{(1+r)^n} = \sum_{t=1}^{n} \frac{R_t}{(1+r)^t}$$

   where $P_0$ = the current share price
   $R$ = the expected stream of returns each year
   $r$ = the appropriate discount rate
   $t = 0 \dots n$ are years.
3. Adapted from A.A.A., *A Statement of Basic Accounting Theory*, p. 50.
4. Ibid, p. 7.
5. Ibid.
6. Ibid.

## QUESTIONS

Prepare brief written answers to each of the following questions:

1. Before a firm sells merchandise to another on credit, what information should it obtain about the buying firm?

2. When a company applies for a bank overdraft, what information will the bank probably require?

3. What are debentures? What information about a company does a potential investor in debentures require before he buys them?

4. What major economic functions are served by shareholders?

5. What in fact does an investor pay for when he buys shares in a public company?

6. You have $100 with which to buy shares in a public company. What information would you desire before purchasing the shares of any company?

7. You own 100 shares in the Broken Hill Proprietary Company Ltd. What information would you like to have to help you decide on keeping or selling the shares in order to purchase other shares?

8. Explain the main economic functions of management in the modern public company. Give examples of each function. What types of information are required for each function to be performed satisfactorily?

9. Explain the main functions of accounting data.

10. What should be the major objectives of the financial reports published by companies?

11. What principle should be applied in deciding whether to obtain additional information about a matter under consideration?

12. Explain the nature of the standards of a good information system. Why are they needed? What are the major standards?

13. What are the major standards for accounting information? Briefly explain each one.

14. Why is relevance regarded as the most important single standard for accounting information?

15. Why does a clash sometimes occur between the relevance and objectivity standards?

16. Criticism is frequently made of the "red tape" collected by businesses and governments. How would you define "red tape"?

# Chapter 4
# Some Basic Accounting Concepts

Several concepts which are used throughout all types of accounting are now examined. They are the accounting entity, monetary valuation, continuity of activity, and period concepts. Additional concepts will be added later. These concepts are frequently called "accounting conventions" in the literature.

## 1. THE ACCOUNTING ENTITY

All accounting records and reports are prepared for an accounting entity. The A.A.A. defines an accounting entity as "an area of economic interest to a particular individual or group".[1] In other words, it is the area of activity covered by the accounting records. The boundaries of an accounting entity are identifiable by determining (i) the interested individual or group, and (ii) the nature of the interest.[2] Hence the boundaries of the entity are determined by the user's interest. Note that the entity relates to an area of economic interest, i.e., an area in which economic activity occurs. Accounting is concerned with recording and reporting on such economic activity.

The accounting entity may be coextensive with the business unit (e.g., sole proprietor firm, partnership firm, or company, or a government business undertaking), or some defined part of a business (e.g., a department), or an amalgamation of related businesses (e.g., a holding company group), depending on the user's needs. It can also be any non-business group (e.g., person, club, church, or government), which engages in economic activities.

The accounting entity can be fairly complex in the case of holding company groups. A holding company group comprises an association of companies in which one company (the parent) owns a majority of the shares in another (the subsidiary). Virtually all large and medium-sized companies in Australia belong to a holding company group. For example, the B.H.P. Co. Ltd. is a holding company which had sixty-seven subsidiaries in 1975, including Australian Iron & Steel Pty. Ltd.[3] The arrangements within a holding company group can become very complicated where there are several tiers of subsidiary companies (i.e., one subsidiary has other subsidiaries), where subsidiaries own shares in other subsidiaries elsewhere in the group, and where outside investors also own shares in subsidiaries. For published reports, holding company groups follow the legal definition of a parent-subsidiary company relationship, and accounting reports are published for the parent company and the group as a whole, or alternatively for the parent company and each subsidiary company. The first alternative is the one normally chosen. The separate reports of each company are consolidated to form the group report through the elimination of all intercompany transactions, and in this way the group is treated as if it were one large company. However it is important to realize that a holding company group, while it is an accounting entity (for annual reports only) and an economic entity, is not a legal entity. Legal claims against one member of the group cannot normally be pressed against other members of the group, and the liability of each company is limited to its own resources plus any unpaid amounts on its shares. While shareholders and investors are interested in the results of the group, creditors are interested in the reports of the particular company with whom they traded. Unfortunately the reports of each company are not normally published and so they receive no data on the financial position of the relevant company. This is a serious deficiency in company law. The position of creditors of subsidiary companies is further aggravated by the fact that the registered capital of many subsidiary companies amounts to a few dollars only.

In addition to its subsidiary companies, a holding company may have a substantial share investment in other companies which constitutes only a minority holding in those other companies. For example, in 1975 the B.H.P. Co. Ltd. had a shareholding varying from 20 per cent to 50 per cent in twelve other companies. These are called associated companies.[4] One company does not normally need majority ownership of another for it to control effectively the business policies of the other company — frequently ownership of 10 per cent or less is sufficient to give it such control. While the group of subsidiary and associated companies would constitute an economic entity where the associated companies are controlled by the parent company, they do not constitute a legal entity or normally an accounting entity.

The entity concept has three major implications for accounting. First it delimits the area to be covered by accounting records and reports. This is needed to help identify that information which is relevant, and to leave out that which is irrelevant. For example, in the accounting records of subsidiary company A, no transactions between subsidiary company B and its customers are relevant. But of course they are relevant for the accounting records of subsidiary company B and for the holding company group. The management of company A is not concerned with company B's transactions, but the parent company management is. Similar considerations apply to accounting for the departments within a business. Second, all transactions are recorded from the viewpoint of the entity itself and not from the viewpoint of other parties, such as owners, managers, or customers. For example, when a firm sells goods to customers, this is recorded as sales by the firm, and not as purchases by customers. Similarly, all assets or resources are those owned by the firm, not the owners; and all liabilities are debts of the firm and not of the owners. Third, the entity concept underlies the accounting concept of profits, in which a sharp distinction is made between the expenses of operating the business and payments to owners. All payments to owners take the form of repayments of capital or loans, or a distribution of profits. Such a distribution may take various names depending on the legal form of the business – drawings, salary, or interest payments to a sole proprietor or partner, or dividends to shareholders in companies. They are not treated as business expenses. In unincorporated firms, owners can then judge whether the total returns they derive are adequate to compensate them for the funds and work they put into the business, i.e., whether they are at least equal to their opportunity costs. Divisions of profit between interest on capital, wages, and profits is arbitrary in such firms. Conversely, living expenses incurred by owners are personal expenses and not business expenses – they are not related to the operating activity of the business.

For the sake of brevity in subsequent discussions, the economic concept of the firm will be used to denote any form of business enterprise, and the particular legal form, that is, company, partnership, or sole proprietor, will be used only where it is relevant for the analysis.

### 2. MONETARY VALUATION

All accounting records of the firm are kept in monetary terms. The dollar is the common unit of measurement for economic events and plans in Australia – it is the legal tender used as the medium of exchange in market transactions. Accounting data must be quantified so that data can be aggregated and hence summarized. Purely qualitative information lacks precision and makes summarization difficult. Nevertheless qualitative information is useful for the interpretation of figures; for example, information on market conditions helps to explain why sales volume declined. Secondly, to quantify a diverse range of data, a common measuring unit must be used so that quantities involved in the diverse range of transactions and resources can be aggregated in comparable units, and profits and financial position determined. For example, the typical retailer sells thousands of lines of merchandise, incurs a wide range of expenses on purchasing merchandise, hiring labour services, buying premises and so on. The use of the dollar as the common measuring unit enables all this activity to be summarized into a few figures of total sales value and total expenses, and profit can then be determined. Again, the use of quantitative data in other units, for example production and sales volumes, can provide useful supplementary information to the financial data. A further reason for the use of monetary measurement is that managerial planning and control must take place in monetary terms, as must that for owners. The central objective of a firm is to make profits, and all planning is directed towards this end. Optimum sales policies and efficiency in the use of resources can be determined only in terms of market prices. For instance, a rise in wage rates will not of itself affect the productivity of workers and hence the physical efficiency of operations, but unless the firm can economize on the use of the now dearer labour, it is not as economically efficient after the wage increase as before.

While there is universal agreement amongst accountants on the necessity for monetary measurement, there is considerable controversy about which properties of the dollar should be used in accounting. The dollar has various properties which can form the basis for accounting measurements, in much the same way as most objects or events have various properties. Fruit, for example, has properties of type, size, weight, and so on. For some purposes, it is meaningful to add apples and oranges together and measure fruit in terms of weight; for other purposes they cannot be measured together. With the dollar its properties can be its general convertibility as legal tender into goods and services (i.e., its medium of exchange or its exchange price property); and its ability to buy goods and services in general (i.e., its general purchasing power property). The dollar can have other properties as well, e.g., its convertibility into other currencies, but they are of no concern here. At the time of an initial transaction, both these properties of the dollar coincide. However, over time they can diverge because of changes in market prices of goods and services in general. Hence the general purchasing power of the dollar, i.e., its general exchange value, no longer coincides with its initial exchange value.

Difficult problems in accounting are caused by these changing properties of the dollar over time and they have been the source of substantial confusion in accounting and in the business world generally. Each property may be used as the basis of monetary measurement. Where the *medium of exchange property* is used, all transactions are recorded in terms of the numbers of dollars received or expended in the transactions and all subsequent measures of income and financial position are made in these dollars. This is the appropriate measurement property where one is concerned with accounting for the *numbers* of dollars in transactions. It is used, for example, in the historic cost system of accounting. Where the *general purchasing power property* of the dollar is used, all transactions are recorded in terms of the numbers of dollars involved in the transactions as measures of the general purchasing power of the dollars then applying. If the general level of prices in the economy changes over time, the recorded dollar values are amended by the extent of the price change over the period (as shown by a price-level index) and all measures of income and financial position are based on the price-level adjusted dollar values. This property should be used where one is accounting for dollars as general purchasing power units. This property is used in the constant dollar value and real value accounting systems.

Each of these dollar measurement systems is logically sound and all the rules of mathematics can be applied to each. The dollar is a homogeneous unit of measurement in each according to the property specified. Thus it is valid to add 1960 dollars to 1975 dollars in the historic cost system because the system is only concerned with the number of dollars being used in market exchanges at the two dates. But it is not valid to add 1960 and 1975 dollars together if inflation has occurred and the general purchasing power property of the dollar is the unit of measurement. The dollars of each period must first be converted into units of general purchasing power as of a common date before they can be compared or added. For example, the 1960 dollars can be converted into equivalent 1975 purchasing power units by multiplying them by the ratio of the 1975 to the 1960 general price level index. The particular property of the dollar which is used as the unit of measurement in the accounting system must be specified so that the units of measurement are not mixed. Mixing of dollar properties must not occur — it is the cardinal sin of measurement theory and the end result lacks meaning.

### 3.  CONTINUITY OF ACTIVITY AND THE ACCOUNTING PERIOD

For normal accounting purposes, it is assumed that the life of the firm stretches indefinitely into the future. Cessation of business activities is not normally contemplated. This assumption is realistic for most firms because they have a basic urge to survive. A long, indefinite life is particularly appropriate for large public companies financed from the general capital market and operated by professional managements. Here, the life of the company is completely independent of the lives of its managers and shareholders, and some companies in the United Kingdom have been in existence for several hundred years. Australia's oldest public company is the Bank of New South Wales Ltd., established in 1817. It is true that the mortality rate amongst owner-operated firms is high, but even here the life of those firms that survive the initial establishment period can be quite long.[5]

However the users of accounting reports cannot wait until the end of the firm's life for information. Rather, they require information on the firm's liquidity, financial position, sales, expenses, profits, and so on at regular intervals. The optimum reporting interval varies according to the type of information required and the user's needs. Management may require information on sales, inventories, and liquidity daily, and information on profits and financial position on a monthly basis. Annual information may suit investors and long-term creditors, etc. Taxation returns on profits earned must be submitted annually. Companies are required to publish their main accounting reports annually, and to indicate their progress to shareholders each half year. Shareholders expect dividends to be paid at least once a year. Budgets are prepared on an annual basis, together with ones for shorter and longer periods.

It is necessary, therefore, to divide the indefinite life of the firm into regular accounting periods. Such periods may be days, weeks, months, quarters, half-years, and years, according to the needs of the users and legal requirements. Even though operating activity is continuous from the end of one accounting period to the beginning of the next — production and selling do not stop at the period's end — the accounting reports are prepared on the assumption of such an interruption in the continuity of activity.

At the end of the accounting period, a snapshot of the firm's position is taken to ascertain what resources and obligations it has at that point of time, and to enable measurement of flows of cash, funds, revenue, and expenses through the firm over the intervening period. In other words, the life of the firm is cut up into time-segments so as to measure financial position at the end of the period and results of operations over the period. However to do this requires making assumptions about the future course of events, as many transactions are only partially completed, many resources only partially used up, and so on, at the end of the period. For example, goods sold have not been paid for, and so the amount expected to be collected must be estimated; labour services have been used by the firm but not yet paid for, and the amount owing must be taken into account; the cost of using the firm's own plant and equipment during the period must be determined and this calculation depends upon the expected life of the plant and its future resale value. A completely factual set of accounting reports containing no estimates based on future events can be prepared only after the firm's life has ·come to an end. Only then have all transactions been completed, all resources converted into cash, all debts to creditors paid, and the balance remaining paid to owners as repayments of capital investment plus profits. Until this stage is reached, most accounting reports must be partly tentative.

### FURTHER READING

A.A.A. "The Entity Concept." *Accounting Review* (April 1965).
Gordon, M. J., and Shillinglaw, G. *Accounting: A Management Approach.* 4th ed. Homewood, Illinois: Richard D. Irwin, 1969. Chap. 1.

## NOTES

1. A.A.A., "The Entity Concept", p. 358.
2. Ibid.
3. *Annual Report of the Broken Hill Proprietary Co. Ltd.*, 1975.
4. Ibid.
5. Some data on company mortalities in New South Wales are given in the 1972 *Annual Report of the Corporate Affairs Commission* (Sydney: N.S.W. Government Printer, 1972). Over the period 1 July 1962—30 June 1971, 1,567 companies were wound up by court order. Some interesting aspects about these companies were:
   i. Paid-up capital: 589 had a paid-up capital of $20 or less, and it could not be ascertained for another 141 companies.
   ii. Life: 63 per cent of the failed companies did so within six years of incorporation, and 75 per cent failed within eight years.
   iii. Industries: the industries in which most failed companies operated were — building and construction, 408; wholesale and retail distribution, 166; light manufacturing, 143; leasing and hire-purchase, 121; real estate development, 103; electrical sales and manufacturing, 84.
   Another 578 companies were wound up under creditors' liquidations during period 1 July 1966—30 June 1972.
   In addition, about 6,000 other companies were subject to action for removal from the Register of Companies.
   There were over 118,000 companies registered in New South Wales on 31 December 1972, and 11,424 new companies were registered during 1972.

## QUESTIONS

Prepare brief written answers to each of the following questions.

1. Distinguish between:
   i.   an unincorporated firm
   ii.  a public company
   iii. a proprietary limited company
   with respect to both legal and economic characteristics.

2. What is:
   i.   A holding company?
   ii.  A subsidiary company?
   iii. A holding company group?
   iv.  An associated company?

3. What is an accounting entity? Give examples. Is each of the companies in Question 2 an accounting entity? Are accounting entities necessarily legal entities?

4. Why is it important to define the accounting entity?

5. Why must accounting records be kept in money terms?

6. Conceptually, the accountant has some choice in the selection of the properties of a monetary unit. What two properties could he use? Why not use both at once?

7. Why are accounting periods necessary?

# Chapter 5
# Recording the Economic Activity of the Firm

## NATURE OF A FIRM'S ACTIVITY

The economic function of any business firm in the economy is to acquire productive resources from the factor markets (i.e., factors of production), combine them into products for which there is a demand, and sell them to users in the product markets. A firm is always an intermediary in the economic process. Resources are available in the factor markets — labour services, land, natural resources, finance for investment — but consumers want finished goods and services — groceries, cars, electricity, etc. It is the function of the firm to acquire those resources and convert them into a demanded finished product. To the firm, a resource is anything which can contribute to the process of production.

All transactions of the firm incurred in performing its economic function can be considered in terms of flows of physical and financial resources between the firm and its markets. On the factor market side, the resources acquired by the firm, i.e., its inputs, comprise investment funds provided by the owners, and loans from outside investors (both generally in the form of cash which represents command over goods and services in general); plus all purchases by the firm of raw materials (e.g., coal, steel, wheat), manufactured merchandise (e.g., groceries, clothing, cars), labour services (e.g., managerial, operative, and sales), tertiary services (e.g., insurance), facilities for use by the firm (e.g., plant, buildings, and land), and, in some cases, knowhow (e.g., patents). The firm then converts these resources into a saleable form for customers. In the conversion process, some resources are used up almost immediately (e.g., raw materials and labour services), while others may last many years (e.g., plant and buildings) or indefinitely (e.g., land). The nature of the conversion process in the firm differs according to whether the firm is a manufacturer or distributor. The manufacturer changes the form of the resources acquired, while the distributor makes the manufactured product available to customers in the location and quantities desired.

However the firm must pay for its purchases and it is liable to return borrowed resources, and also pay a hiring charge for their use. All acquisition of resources by the firm must simultaneously involve an outflow of financial claims on it. The claim may be for immediate cash payment, i.e., a cash transaction, or for payment at a later date, i.e., a credit transaction. Both cash and credit constitute the forms of finance for the firm's transactions. The payments to the factors of production represent their rewards.

Hence, on the factor market side of the firm's operations, there is a cycle of transactions involving the acquisition of resources and their financing; or a flow of resources (physical and financial) into the firm offset by an outflow of cash and financial claims to the factor markets.

A similar cycle occurs on the product market side. Having converted the resources into saleable form, the firm sells the final goods and services. Customers may be other firms engaged in manufacturing (e.g., B.H.P. Co. Ltd. sells steel to Chrysler Australia Ltd. for the manufacture of cars) or in retailing (e.g., Kelvinator Australia Ltd. sells refrigerators to Grace Bros. Ltd.), or final consumers. Customers constitute the product market for the firm. On the sale, goods flow out of the firm, but in return customers must pay for them and hence there is a simultaneous inflow of financial claims to the firm. The financial claims may be extinguished immediately, as in a cash sale, or at a later date, as in a credit sale. Again, there is a complete cycle of outward and inward resource flows.

The simultaneous inflows and outflows of resources between the firm and its factor markets and between the firm and its product markets are illustrated in the transactions flow diagram (Fig. 5-1).

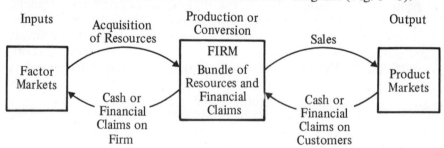

Figure 5-1. Transactions cycle of the firm

Accounting is concerned with recording, measuring, and reporting the transactions giving rise to these flows. In manufacturing firms, the details of the conversion process within the firm from raw materials to finished products are recorded as well. This is the subject matter of cost accounting.

The firm at any point of time can be viewed as a bundle of resources (i.e., assets) and financial claims on them (i.e., by creditors and owners). It engages in economic activity so long as the long-run prospects of cash inflow from the sales exceeds the cash outflow on the purchases of resources used to generate sales. This surplus, which is measured by the increase in the net stock of resources on hand, is profit and it belongs to the owners. It is the reward for owners sacrificing their investment funds over time at some risk of loss. Conversely, a loss reduces the net stock of resources of the firm, and it is borne by owners.

It should be noted that every transaction of the firm involves a two-fold flow aspect. First, on the factor market side, there is a flow of resources *into* the firm and a flow of cash or financial claims *out of* the firm to the factors of production. On the subsequent payment of a financial claim, there is a flow of cash *out of* the firm and the claim flows back into the firm. Secondly, on the product market side, there is a flow of resources *from* the firm to customers and a flow of cash or financial claims back *into* the firm. On the subsequent payment of the claims, there is a flow of cash *into* the firm from customers and the financial claim flows *out*. Hence all transactions involve a flow of resources or financial claims into the firm (from factors or customers) and a simultaneous flow of resources or financial claims *out of* the firm (to factors or customers). It is axiomatic that the inflows and their corresponding outflows must come from or go to the same source.

It is essential that each aspect of a transaction is recorded. The whole accounting system is based on this fundamental notion of the twofold aspect of each transaction, and it gives rise to the principle of *double entry*. It is for this reason that recording can be done in algebraic form, for example, in a matrix.

Furthermore, it may be noted that all purchase and sales transactions (as distinct from borrowing and lending ones) always involve a physical aspect and a simultaneous financing aspect. The physical aspect concerns the movement of goods and services into or out of the firm; the financing aspect concerns the reverse flow of finance (i.e., cash or financial claims). For example, when a retailer buys merchandise, there is an inward flow of merchandise to the retailer, and an outward flow of cash or a financial claim from the retailer. When the retailer sells merchandise, there is an outward flow of merchandise offset by an inward flow of cash or financial claims on customers.

Several bases of accounting record can be derived from the operating cycle of economic activity engaged in by the firm. *The cash basis of accounting* is used where the accounting record is restricted to those transactions where a cash transfer occurs. No accounting records are made when goods and services are bought or sold on credit; rather, the recording of the transaction is delayed until the cash payment actually takes place. The only signal used to record the transaction is that of cash changing hands. In other words, the purchase or sale is not recognized in accounting until it is paid for.

*The accrual basis of accounting* is used where *all* transactions between the firm and its markets are recorded, whether they be for cash or credit. The record is made at the time of the transaction. In the case of credit transactions, the subsequent payment of cash cancels the financial claim and this is treated as a second transaction. The accrual basis is subdivided into partial and full accrual bases. The partial accrual basis encompasses the recording of all external transactions, whereas in the full accrual basis various internal adjustments to the transaction data are made in order to measure periodic income from operations and financial position at the end of the period.

Selection of the accounting basis depends upon the information required. Where only knowledge of cash position and cash flows is wanted, the cash basis of accounting is sufficient. If, in addition, information on all types of financing and on debtors and creditors is required, the partial accrual basis is appropriate. However, where information on income earned and financial position is needed, the full accrual basis of accounting must be used.

### RECORDING CASH TRANSACTIONS

The simplest form of accounting system is that in which only cash transactions are recorded. Only those transactions in which cash flows from or into the firm are recorded, and all transactions involving credit are disregarded for accounting purposes. The receipt or payment of cash is the sole signal permitted for the recording of a transaction. The only accounting report which can be prepared is a cash flow statement showing sources and uses of cash over the period and cash on hand at the end of the period.[1] The operating cycle of the firm is as shown in Figure 5–2.

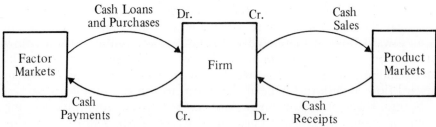

Figure 5–2. Cash transactions cycle of the firm

#### Accounts and the Ledger

The details of transactions are recorded in accounts. *Accounts* are merely chronological lists of transactions relating to the same item and which are prepared on a double-entry basis. A separate account is kept for each main item involved in transactions for which separate information is useful. For example, all cash transactions are recorded in the cash account, all wage payments in a wages account, all merchandise purchases in a merchandise account, and so on. Similar items may be recorded in one account if the information about separate items is not required; for example, a separate merchandise account may be kept for each type of merchandise, or all types of merchandise may be recorded in the one account. The name of the account should be descriptive of its contents though in practice there is a fairly conventional list of account titles. The complete collection of accounts is called the *ledger*.

The form of the ledger account varies according to whether the records are handwritten, recorded by an accounting machine, or by a computer. We shall use the tabular form suitable for use in machine accounting. This is the most common form in use in industry and is used by most firms, excluding perhaps the smallest which still use hand-written methods, and the largest which use computers or punch-card machines. In computerized accounting, transactions are recorded in a matrix, or an input-output table, and each transaction is entered into a cell of the matrix. But, even in this case, the final accounts may be printed out in tabular form. In a high labor-cost economy, clerical labor is too expensive to employ on record-keeping, and the job can be done more efficiently and quickly on machines or computers.

The twofold aspect of every transaction is recorded in each account as a *debit* aspect and a *credit* aspect, and a column is provided for each. A third column is provided for the balance of the account. The terms "debit" and "credit" originate from debitor (i.e., debtor) and creditor, both used by Pachioli.

The tabular form of account is as shown in Example A.

| | Name of Account (e.g., Cash) | | | |
|---|---|---|---|---|
| Date | Transaction (or Name of Related Account) | Dr. $ | Cr. $ | Balance $ |
| | | | | |

**Example A.** Tabular form of account

The traditional form of account, as used in virtually all textbooks and in handwritten records since the time of Pachioli, is called the "T-form". It differs from the tabular form in that the debit entries and credit entries stand on each side of the account, as in Example B.

*Name of Account*

Debit                                                      Credit

| Date | Name of Related Account | $ | Date | Name of Related Account | $ |
|------|------------------------|---|------|------------------------|---|
|      |                        |   |      |                        |   |
|      |                        |   |      |                        |   |

**Example B.** Traditional form of account

At the end of the accounting period, a list of the balances remaining in each account is made, and, if for every debit entry there is a credit entry, the sum of the debit and credit balances must be equal. This list is called a *trial balance.* Although the trial balance provides a valuable check on the ledger, it is not a conclusive test of accuracy since it will not indicate that some transactions have been omitted altogether, that some transactions have been recorded in the wrong accounts, or that incorrect amounts have been recorded. It provides nothing more than a check on the equality of debit and credit entries.

### Recording the Twofold Aspect of Transactions

In the analysis of transactions, it is necessary that they be recorded from the viewpoint of the firm itself, i.e., the entity concept must be applied. As can be seen from the operating cycle of activity, all transactions involve a flow of resources or cash into the firm and a reverse flow of cash or resources out of the firm to the particular source concerned. Thus, when resources are purchased from the factor markets, resources flow in and cash is paid out; when the firm sells goods and services, resources flow out and cash flows in. *On the input side, all inward flows* of purchased resources are *debited* in the relevant resource accounts, and the *related cash outflow* to the factors *is credited* in the cash account. *On the output side, all outward flows* of goods and services *are credited* in the sales account, and *the cash received* in return *is debited* to the cash account. For example, merchandise purchased for cash is debited to a merchandise purchases account and credited to the cash account; labour services purchased are debited to a wages account and credited to the cash account; merchandise sold is credited to a merchandise sales account and debited to the cash account. It can be seen that only *two rules* are needed for determining which aspect of a transaction to debit and which to credit – *all inward flows are debited* in the appropriate account, and *all outward flows are credited* in the related account. Since each inward flow comes from a particular source and the related outflow necessarily goes to that source, or conversely each outflow from the firm goes to a particular person and the related inflow comes from that source, the rules for debit and credit may be restated simply as: *debit the account into which the item flows (where to?), and credit the account from which it flows (where from?).* The *credit account* can be referred to in general terms as the *source account,* and the *debit account* as the *inflow account.* These two rules for debit and credit are completely general and they cover all credit transactions plus all internal transfers of values (for example, "balance day adjustments") or of resources (for example, inventory issues) within the firm where no transactions are involved.

It should be noted that each transaction must affect two accounts. Every transaction must have a debit in one account and an equal credit entry in another if the two-way flow aspects are both recorded. Where purchase and sales transactions are concerned, the two-way flow encompasses the physical flow in one direction and the financing flow in the other. Thus, for all transactions involving cash payments, the cash account is credited as the source of finance for the transaction and the recipient account is debited with the payment; while for all transactions involving cash receipts, the owner's capital account, sales account, and so on are credited as the source of finance and the cash account is debited. The accounting system is maintained in balance only through recording the two aspects of each transaction in separate accounts and as both a debit and a credit.

## An Example

Joe Spartacus decides to start up The Deep Blue Sea fish and chip shop. His transactions during the first week were:

Feb. 1.  Opens a business bank account with a deposit of $2,000. All payments are to be made by cheque, and all receipts banked daily, except for $10 till-money. Obtains use of a shop for $100 rent, payable monthly in advance. Pays rent with cheque 1.

2.  Buys cooking range $500 (cheque 2), refrigerator $400 (cheque 3), and cooking utensils $100 (cheque 4).

3.  Employs assistant at $30 per week. Buys supplies of fish, potatoes, and sundry cooking items $60 (cheque 5). Withdraws $10 for till-money (cheque 6).

4.  Commences trading. Cash sales for day $20.

5.  Cash sales $30.

6.  Buys additional supplies $60 (cheque 7). Cash sales $80.

7.  Cash sales $30. Pays assistant's wages due $30 (cheque 8). Withdraws $100 as personal wages (cheque 9).

*Required:*
Record all transactions in ledger accounts, and prepare a trial balance.

The Deep Blue Sea Ledger

## Bank Account

| Date | Transaction | Chq. No. | Dr. $ | Cr. $ | Balance | $ |
|---|---|---|---|---|---|---|
| Feb. 1 | J. Spartacus capital | | 2,000 | | 2,000 | Dr. |
| | Shop rent | 1 | | 100 | 1,900 | Dr. |
| 2 | Shop equipment – Cooking range | 2 | | 500 | 1,400 | Dr. |
| | Shop equipment – Refrigerator | 3 | | 400 | 1,000 | Dr. |
| | Shop equipment – Utensils | 4 | | 100 | 900 | Dr. |
| 3 | Supplies | 5 | | 60 | 840 | Dr. |
| | Cash on hand | 6 | | 10 | 830 | Dr. |
| 4 | Sales | | 20 | | 850 | Dr. |
| 5 | Sales | | 30 | | 880 | Dr. |
| 6 | Supplies | 7 | | 60 | 820 | Dr. |
| | Sales | | 80 | | 900 | Dr. |
| 7 | Sales | | 30 | | 930 | Dr. |
| | Wages | | | 30 | 900 | Dr. |
| | Drawings | | | 100 | 800 | Dr. |

## J. Spartacus Capital Account

| Feb. 1 | Bank | | | 2,000 | 2,000 | Cr. |
|---|---|---|---|---|---|---|

## Shop Rent Account

| Feb. 1 | Bank | | 100 | | 100 | Dr. |
|---|---|---|---|---|---|---|

## Shop Equipment Account

| Feb. 2 | Bank – Cooking range | | 500 | | 500 | Dr. |
|---|---|---|---|---|---|---|
| | Refrigerator | | 400 | | 900 | Dr. |
| | Utensils | | 100 | | 1,000 | Dr. |

## Supplies Account or Purchases Account

| Feb. 3 | Bank | | 60 | | 60 | Dr. |
|---|---|---|---|---|---|---|
| 6 | Bank | | 60 | | 120 | Dr. |

## Cash On Hand Account

| Feb. 3 | Bank | | 10 | | 10 | Dr. |
|---|---|---|---|---|---|---|

## Sales Account

| Feb. 4 | Bank | | | 20 | 20 | Cr. |
|---|---|---|---|---|---|---|
| 5 | Bank | | | 30 | 50 | Cr. |
| 6 | Bank | | | 80 | 130 | Cr. |
| 7 | Bank | | | 30 | 160 | Cr. |

Wages Account

| Feb. 7 | Bank | | 30 | | 30 | Dr. |
|--------|------|--|-----|--|-----|-----|

Drawings Account

| Feb. 7 | Bank | | 100 | | 100 | Dr. |
|--------|------|--|-----|--|-----|-----|

*Trial Balance as at 7 February*

|  | Dr. $ | Cr. $ |
|--|-------|-------|
| Bank | 800 | |
| J. Spartacus Capital | | 2,000 |
| Shop Rent | 100 | |
| Shop Equipment | 1,000 | |
| Supplies | 120 | |
| Cash on Hand | 10 | |
| Sales | | 160 |
| Wages | 30 | |
| Drawings | 100 | |
|  | $2,160 | $2,160 |

*Points to Note:*

1. Twofold aspect recorded for each transaction. For example, cash comes into the firm when Spartacus deposits $2,000 in its bank account; hence debit Cash at Bank account and credit where it came from, viz., Spartacus Capital. Purchase of shop equipment – a resource comes into the firm; hence debit Shop Equipment account, and credit Cash at Bank account since it was the financial source of the purchase. Sales of merchandise are an outflow and hence credited, and the cash which comes in is debited to Cash at Bank account.

2. Employment of assistant – not recorded as a transaction until wages paid. All payments for services rendered are best interpreted as purchase of services for cash.

3. All items bought for resale are debited to a Purchases, Merchandise, or Supplies account. These are kept separate from resources bought for use within the business, which are debited to their own appropriate accounts.

4. All merchandise or trading items sold are credited to a sales account rather than a purchases or merchandise account because the former is kept at retail prices whereas the latter account is kept at cost price. The two accounts are brought together at a subsequent stage to determine profit.

5. Wages paid to owner are treated as a withdrawal of capital or profit, and called Drawings. Note entity concept.

6. Trial balance totals are equal, and this confirms that a debit entry has been made for each credit one.

**Use of Cash Basis Accounting**

Cash basis accounting is used in some sectors of the economy, though not to any extent in business operations as the only accounting report which can be prepared from it is a cash flow report. Cash basis accounting can be adequate as a financial information system where mainly stewardship reports are required. Frequently a record of cash receipts and payments makes a sufficient accounting record for people engaged in professional practice — doctors, public accountants, and so on — and in small firms with few resources and dealing in cash transactions. The cash surplus on operations is treated as income. Likewise, clubs and societies often find it adequate for their needs. The accounts of trustees and executors of deceased estates are normally related to cash transactions only. Secondly, cash basis accounting is used extensively by the government where special considerations make it appropriate.[2]

However, while cash flow reports are vital for cash planning and control by business, cash basis accounting by itself is inadequate because it cannot provide much of the information required by management, shareholders, and so on. All transactions not immediately involving cash, all movements of resources within the firm and the using up of long-term resources in production, are disregarded. Hence no information is provided on total sales of the period; total expenses of production, profit earned, total resources owned by the firm, total debts due to or owing by the firm, and its current financial position; that is, an income statement and balance sheet cannot be prepared.

Management, owners, etc. must have this information for effective decision-making and control in a profit-making entity. For instance, management must have information about the firm's customers who have not paid for their purchases, in order to collect the money from them; likewise it must have data on debts to suppliers so that they can be paid on time. A firm must have a full accrual system of accounting to provide all such information; however, the cash flow reports which can be extracted are an integral part of the financial information system.

### A Note on Use of the Flow Approach

The flow approach for analyzing transactions into their debit and credit components is not normally used in accounting.[3] Rather, other approaches such as the balance sheet one are used. The flow approach is adopted here for several reasons. It is a more basic one, being related to the economic nature of transactions themselves which are the subject of the recording procedure, rather than to an accounting report, i.e., the balance sheet, which is derived from the record of transactions. Being more basic, it is simpler to apply and results in only two rules for debit and credit — debit the account to which the item flows, and credit the account from which it flows. The balance sheet approach on the other hand has eight rules for debit and credit. Since all debit components of transactions must have something in common, and likewise all credit components, there should be one basic rule for debit entries and the reverse rule for credit entries. The flow approach can be easily generalized to cover non-transaction entries such as the many internal transfer items recorded in product costing. It has to be used in designing computer programmes for accounting systems and it is capable of mathematical application.[4] Finally, under the name of network analysis, the approach is used in operations research, and its adoption in accounting should enable the closer integration of these related fields.

### RECORDING CREDIT TRANSACTIONS

The recording of transactions is now extended to cover transactions made on a credit basis. Not all transactions entered into by the firm involve immediate cash receipts or payments. Many purchases and sales are made on credit terms and the transfer of cash to extinguish the debt takes place at a later time. The later payment may be made in full shortly afterwards, or be spread in instalments over a long period, as in the case of hire purchase sales. Hence credit transactions give rise to two sets of transactions — the initial one involving the sale or purchase of resources, and the subsequent cash transaction(s) to settle the account. Each is recorded separately at the time it occurs.

However, as a matter of convenience, the record of a credit purchase of those resources acquired continuously may not be made until a bill is sent or the payment is made. Many services (e.g., labour, electricity, telephone) are acquired continuously and on credit, and they are paid for at regular intervals. In the case of wages and salaries, the purchase of labour services is recorded at the time of the wage payment; where bills are sent by the supplier, for example, for electricity used, the purchase is recorded on receipt of the bill.

The accounting system under which all transactions of the firm with its markets are recorded is the partial accrual basis of accounting. Under this basis, all cash and credit transactions are recorded as they occur. The occurrence of a transaction between the firm and its markets is the signal for recording, and not the transfer of cash alone. All purchases of resources on credit give rise to *creditors* or accounts payable. These are *liabilities* of the firm — it is liable to pay its creditors by some specified date. Conversely, all sales of resources on credit give rise to *debtors* or accounts receivable. These are resources or *assets* of the firm — they represent a financial claim on customers for the value of the sale. The operating cycle of activity shown in Figure 5−1 applies to accrual accounting.

The firm needs to maintain a record of all transactions to enable managerial control over debtors and creditors, that is, to ensure that debts are collected on time, and creditors are paid on time. Under the accrual basis, debts due to the firm and its liabilities are recognized immediately they are incurred. In addition, the time at which transactions occur is normally the best time to recognize them for purposes of measuring the sales of the period and the expenditures incurred during the period, even though cash has not changed hands. Cash receipts are typically incidental to the recognition of sales and cash disbursements are merely the settlement of liabilities.

The accounting report prepared at the end of the period summarizing the firm's external transactions is known as the funds statement.[5] This statement summarizes the sources of finance or funds obtained over the period (from sales, creditors, and investors) and the uses made of those finances in its operations. All credit accounts represent sources of finance, and all debit accounts show uses of finance. Additionally, a cash flow report may be extracted from the cash account.

The circumstances in which use of the partial accrual basis of accounting is appropriate are similar to those governing the use of cash basis accounting, except that credit transactions are important and a record needs to be kept of debtors and creditors. As with cash basis accounting, the partial accrual basis is inadequate for most business operations.

The recording of transactions involving purchases and sales on credit is very similar to that for cash transactions. The twofold aspect of each transaction must be recorded in separate accounts as a debit and a credit. However there are two sets of transactions involved — the initial credit transaction and the subsequent cash transaction — and each set is recorded separately. On the input side, all purchases of resources on credit involve an inward flow of resources and hence a debit to the relevant merchandise, electricity, rent, etc. account, while the supplier who provided the resources and therefore financed them is credited with his financial claim. On payment of the liability by the firm, the cash account is credited because cash flows out, while the financial claim flows back to the firm and the supplier's account is debited. Or more simply, credit the source account and debit the account to which the item flows. This entry extinguishes the claim, assuming full payment.

Conversely on the output side, all credit sales involve an outflow and are therefore credited to the sales account, while the firm receives financial claims on customers, whose accounts are debited. When the debt is collected, the financial claim flows out (hence credit customers accounts), while cash flows in (and hence debit the cash account). Or more simply, credit the source account (the customer) and debit the inflow account (cash). Note the physical and financing characteristics of each initial transaction, and how the account to which the item flows is debited and the account from which the item comes is credited.

**Example of Credit Transactions Recording**

Westside Retailers Limited was formed on 1 February to establish a shopping emporium. Fifty thousand shares of $1.00 each were offered for public subscription, and the issue was fully subscribed by 10 February, and the cash banked. Transactions for the remainder of the month were:

Feb. 12. Employed five sales staff at $60 each weekly.
15. Purchased premises for $30,000, of which $20,000 was paid in cash and the remainder borrowed on mortgage.
18. Purchased merchandise $12,000 on credit.
20. Paid salaries $300; advertising $1,000.
23. Sales: cash $2,000; credit $3,000.
24. Sales: cash $2,500; credit $4,000. Purchased merchandise for cash $3,000.
27. Sales: cash $2,000; credit $3,500. Paid Salaries $300. Paid creditors $10,000.
28. Sales: cash $3,000; credit $4,500. Purchased merchandise on credit $2,500. Received from debtors $7,000.

*Required:*
Record all transactions in ledger accounts and prepare a trial balance as at 28 February.

Westside Retailers' Ledger

Bank Account

| Date | Transaction | Dr. $ | Cr. $ | Balance $ |
|---|---|---|---|---|
| Feb. 10 | Capital | 50,000 | | 50,000 Dr. |
| 15 | Premises | | 20,000 | 30,000 Dr. |
| 20 | Salaries | | 300 | 29,700 Dr. |
| | Advertising | | 1,000 | 28,700 Dr. |
| 23 | Sales | 2,000 | | 30,700 Dr. |
| 24 | Sales | 2,500 | | 33,200 Dr. |
| | Merchandise | | 3,000 | 30,200 Dr. |
| 27 | Sales | 2,000 | | 32,200 Dr. |
| | Salaries | | 300 | 31,900 Dr. |
| | Creditors | | 10,000 | 21,900 Dr. |
| 28 | Sales | 3,000 | | 24,900 Dr. |
| | Debtors | 7,000 | | 31,900 Dr. |

Capital Account

| | | | | |
|---|---|---|---|---|
| Feb. 10 | Bank | | 50,000 | 50,000 Cr. |

Premises Account

| | | | | |
|---|---|---|---|---|
| Feb. 15 | Bank | 20,000 | | 20,000 Dr. |
| | Mortgage | 10,000 | | 30,000 Dr. |

### Mortgage Account

| | | | | | |
|---|---|---|---|---|---|
| Feb. 15 | Premises | | | 10,000 | 10,000 Cr. |

### Merchandise Account (or Purchases Account)

| | | | | | |
|---|---|---|---|---|---|
| Feb. 18 | Creditors | 12,000 | | | 12,000 Dr. |
| 24 | Bank | 3,000 | | | 15,000 Dr. |
| 28 | Creditors | 2,500 | | | 17,500 Dr. |

### Creditors Account (or Accounts Payable Account)

| | | | | | |
|---|---|---|---|---|---|
| Feb. 18 | Merchandise | | | 12,000 | 12,000 Cr. |
| 27 | Bank | 10,000 | | | 2,000 Cr. |
| 28 | Merchandise | | | 2,500 | 4,500 Cr. |

### Salaries Account

| | | | | | |
|---|---|---|---|---|---|
| Feb. 20 | Bank | 300 | | | 300 Dr. |
| 27 | Bank | 300 | | | 600 Dr. |

### Advertising Account

| | | | | | |
|---|---|---|---|---|---|
| Feb. 20 | Bank | 1,000 | | | 1,000 Dr. |

### Sales Account

| | | | | | |
|---|---|---|---|---|---|
| Feb. 23 | Cash | | | 2,000 | 2,000 Cr. |
| | Debtors | | | 3,000 | 5,000 Cr. |
| 24 | Cash | | | 2,500 | 7,500 Cr. |
| | Debtors | | | 4,000 | 11,500 Cr. |
| 27 | Cash | | | 2,000 | 13,500 Cr. |
| | Debtors | | | 3,500 | 17,000 Cr. |
| 28 | Cash | | | 3,000 | 20,000 Cr. |
| | Debtors | | | 4,500 | 24,500 Cr. |

### Debtors Account (or Accounts Receivable Account)

| | | | | | |
|---|---|---|---|---|---|
| Feb. 23 | Sales | 3,000 | | | 3,000 Dr. |
| 24 | Sales | 4,000 | | | 7,000 Dr. |
| 27 | Sales | 3,500 | | | 10,500 Dr. |
| 28 | Sales | 4,500 | | | 15,000 Dr. |
| | Bank | | | 7,000 | 8,000 Dr. |

Trial Balance as at 28 February

|  | Dr. $ | Cr. $ |
|---|---|---|
| Bank | 31,900 |  |
| Capital |  | 50,000 |
| Premises | 30,000 |  |
| Mortgage |  | 10,000 |
| Merchandise | 17,500 |  |
| Creditors |  | 4,500 |
| Salaries | 600 |  |
| Advertising | 1,000 |  |
| Sales |  | 24,500 |
| Debtors | 8,000 |  |
|  | $89,000 | $89,000 |

*Points to Note:*
1. At this stage where no customers' or suppliers' names are given, the one total debtors' account and the one creditors' account should be used. Where names are given, individual accounts should be opened for each debtor or creditor. The use of control accounts which combine both the total account and the individual personal accounts for debtors and for creditors is covered in chapter 11.

### NOTES
1. Cash flow reports are considered in chap. 17.
2. See chap. 17.
3. The flow approach was originated by Professor W. J. Vatter, of the University of California at Berkeley (see his *Managerial Accounting* (Englewood Cliffs, N.J.: Prentice-Hall, 1950).
4. See Appendix 3.
5. See chap. 18.

### QUESTIONS AND EXERCISES
[Solutions to problems marked * are given in Appendix 4.]

Prepare brief written answers to each of the following questions:
1. Explain the transactions cycle of firms.
2. Must there always be a twofold aspect to each transaction? Explain with reference to the following transactions:
   i.   Purchase of merchandise for cash by the firm
   ii.  Purchase of merchandise on credit by the firm
   iii. Payment of the supplier for the above merchandise
   iv.  Payment for the labour services of an employee
   v.   Sale of goods to customers for cash
   vi.  Sale of goods to customers on credit
   vii. Receipt of cash from customers for above sales
   viii. Investment in the firm by the owners.
3. Explain the physical and financing aspects of purchase and sale transactions.
4. What is:   i.   An account?   ii.   The ledger?   iii.   A trial balance?
5. Which aspect of a transaction should be debited, and which credited?

Record the following transactions in ledger accounts and prepare a trial balance at the end of each problem. Assume all transactions are for cash.
6. R. Martin decides to establish a milk bar. On 1 July he opens a business bank account with a deposit of $8,000. He leases suitable premises, paying $2,000 in advance for a year's lease. He purchases equipment (refrigerators, mixing machines, tables, and chairs) for $3,000, and merchandise for $500. During the first month, his sales amounted to $700, and he withdrew $100 as a personal salary.

7. Mick Slob opens a pie and soup kitchen outside the Opera House. He opens a business bank account with $5,000. He buys an old motor van for $300, has it converted and decorated for a further $1,500, and installs kitchen equipment in it for another $900. He pays a year's fee to the Council ($600) for permission to conduct operations on the site. During the first month of operations, he purchased cooking ingredients $150; gas $30; petrol $60; sauce $20. His takings for the month amounted to $350, and he paid himself a salary of $120.

8. To exploit the scenic underwater wonders of Sydney Harbour, Bob Marlin invests $20,000 in Submarine Cruises and buys a disused atomic submarine for $600 in March. He fits extensive panoramic windows along the sides at a cost of $8,000 in April and has the ship painted a luminous orange for $3,500 in June. He then commences operations. His transactions for the next three months are as follows:

July  Hires three ex-submariners on 1 July at a salary of $200 per month each and pays them on 31 July; advertising $400; fuel $3,000 (to last several years); anchorage and wharfage facilities $100; takings $900.
Aug.  Salaries $600; advertising $500; anchorage $100; takings $1,700.
Sept. Salaries $600; advertising $500; anchorage $100; takings $2,800.

9.  Dec.  1.   G. Allsopp invested $10,000 in Hotrod Car Sales.
          2.   Leased a suitable allotment for $2,000 p.a.
          2.   Purchased three cars at $800 each.
          3.   Sold two of these for $1,400 each.
          5.   Bought four more at $1,200 each.
          5.   Paid repair costs $170.
          6.   Sold three cars for $1,500 each.
          8.   Sold one car for $600.
          10.  Bought three more at $900 each.
          12.  Withdrew for private use $240.
          13.  Sold two cars at $1,300 each.
          14.  Paid employees wages and commission $200.

10.  Apr.  1.   J. Burns invested $4,000 in Boutique.
           1.   Rented a shop for $100 monthly, payable in advance.
           2.   Paid $700 for fittings to shop.
           2.   Bought merchandise for $1,300.
           4.   Sold merchandise for $280.
           6.   Purchased merchandise for $640.
           6.   Paid for advertising $150.
           8.   Sold merchandise $410.
           10.  Withdrew for private expenses $180.
           12.  Sold merchandise for $240.
           12.  Paid assistant's salary $80.

11. On 1 March, B. Abel paid $3,000 into the bank as capital of Abel Trading Store.
    Mar.  1.   Paid month's rent $80.
          2.   Paid for purchases $220.
          4.   Banked sales takings $180.
          7.   Paid for purchases $160.
          9.   Paid salaries $60.
          10.  Banked sales takings $270.
          12.  Paid for purchases $180.
          12.  Paid advertising $40.

14. Sales takings banked $190.
16. Paid salaries $60.
17. Sales takings banked $200.
18. Personal drawings $120.

For each of the following problems, record the transactions in appropriate ledger accounts and prepare a trial balance. Note that both cash and credit transactions are involved.

12. i.  R. Davis paid $100,000 into bank account to establish his new sports goods store.
    ii.  Bought 5-year lease of shop for $20,000 cash; shop fittings for $5,000 cash; delivery van for $3,000, payable $1,000 in cash and balance in 30 days.
    iii.  Bought merchandise $25,000 on credit.
    iv.  Paid salaries $1,000; advertising $5,000.
    v.  Sold goods for cash $8,000; on credit $5,000.
    vi.  Proprietor withdrew $500 as personal salary.
    vii.  Sales for cash $9,000; for credit $7,000.
    viii.  Bought merchandise $36,000 on credit.
    xi.  Sales for cash $13,000; for credit $12,000.
    x.  Paid creditors for merchandise previously bought $18,000; creditors for delivery van $2,000.
    xi.  Collected from customers $9,000.
    xii.  Sales for cash $7,000; for credit $11,000.

13. Jan. 1.  F. James deposited $6,000 in a business ban  account to establish his business for servicing and selling precision instruments.
    2.  Purchased tools and equipment from T. Murphy for $1,400 on credit.
    3.  Paid T. Murphy $400 cash.
    5.  Paid $80 to Black & Co. for two weeks' rent.
    9.  Charged Zipp Manufacturing Co. $700 for servicing their equipment.
    11.  James withdrew $300 to meet personal expenses.
    12.  Paid $90 for advertising, and $200 for materials.
    12.  Received commission, $260, from The Excelsior Co. for selling twelve of their instruments.
    13.  Charged Jet Airline Co. $460 and Medical Instruments Co. $600 for servicing their equipment.
    14.  Received a cheque for $500 from Zipp Manufacturing Co. Paid wages $300.

14. Feb. 1.  V. Abbott opened Priory Store with $2,600 capital.
    2.  Paid month's rent in advance $160.
    3.  Cash purchases $400.
    3.  Sales to T. Drucker on credit $160.
    4.  Credit purchase from B. Mustard $70.
    5.  Received from T. Drucker $160.
    5.  Credit sale to A. Allen $220.
    5.  Credit purchase from T. Reid $130.
    5.  Freight inwards paid $30.
    5.  Paid B. Mustard $70.
    6.  Paid salesmen's salaries $90.
    6.  Cash sales $140.

15. July   1.   B. Quick opened a business account with $2,000.
             2.   Cash purchases $260.
             3.   Purchased goods from M. Last on credit $420.
             4.   Sold goods on credit to J. Docker $110.
             5.   Credit purchase from J. Edwards $70.
             6.   Paid M. Last $420.
             8.   Paid rent $60.
             9.   Sold goods on credit to B. James $90.
          11.   J. Docker paid on account $50.
          13.   Cash sales $170.
          14.   Paid wages $80.
          15.   Paid rent $60.
          17.   Purchased on credit from M. Last goods for $120.
          19.   Received cheque from B. James $70.
          22.   Paid J. Edwards in full $70.
          24.   Made a credit sale to B. James $140.
          27.   Cash sales $230.
          28.   Paid wages $80.

16. July   1.   R. Tyler opened business account $4,500.
             1.   Cash purchases $1,000.
             2.   Paid month's rent $120.
             3.   Sold to K. Grace on credit $400.
             6.   Sold to P. Shaw on credit $340.
             6.   Advertising paid $70.
             6.   Personal drawings by Tyler $100.
             6.   Paid wages of assistant $50.
             8.   Received from K. Grace $100.
          10.   Cash purchases $410.
          12.   Cash sales $540.
          14.   Personal drawings $100.
          14.   Paid wages $50.

17. J. Tickle commenced a business, paying $5,000 into a business bank account on 1 March.
The following transactions occurred during his first two weeks of business:

Mar.   2.   He paid $80, being one month's rent in advance. He bought stock from D. Davis on credit — $275. He paid telephone rent in advance to 1 September — $25. He bought trading stock for cash $225.
          3.   Cash sales $75.
          4.   Bought stock from E. Evans on credit $425. Paid D. Davis $275. Cash sales $225.
          5.   Paid wages $62. Cash sales $120. Bought trading stock from R. Roberts on credit $325.
          8.   Cash sales $100. Paid E. Evans $425. Sold goods to S. Small on credit $170.
          9.   Cash purchases $190. Sold goods to H. Hope on credit $200.
         10.   Sold goods to W. Wall on credit $80. Bought a cash register from Cash Registers Ltd., for $500. He paid $200 cash and agreed to pay the balance in one month.
         11.   Cash purchases $25. S. Small settled his account $170.
         12.   Paid wages $80. H. Hope settled his account $200.
         13.   Cash sales $135.

18. On 1 August, the A.B.C. Co. Ltd. was formed to establish a retail hardware store. It offered 100,000 shares to the public at their registered value of $1.00 each. By 10 August, the issue was fully subscribed, the cash collected and banked. A manager was appointed to control the company. Transactions for the remainder of the month were:

Aug. 15. The company purchased suitable premises for $60,000. It paid $40,000 in cash and arranged for a mortgage to finance the remainder.

20. Purchased initial inventory of merchandise from Super Timber Co. Ltd. $4,000, payable in 30 days; Stone Pipe Co. Ltd. $1,500, payable in seven days; Mortland Cement Co. Ltd. $2,000, payable in seven days; and Bright Paint Co. Ltd. $5,000, payable in thirty days.

21. Hired two salesmen, salaries $60 per week each.

22. Paid for advertising $200.

23. Had shop fittings installed $2,500, payable in seven days to Shop Fitters Limited.

24. Opened for business. Sales for day: cash $90; credit (payable in seven days) — R. Jones $150, M. Smith $200, Model Building Co. $400.

25. Sales: cash $270; credit (seven days) — Jerry Home Builders $700, M. Smith $420.

26. Purchases from Mortland Cement Co. Ltd. $1,500 (seven days). Paid Stone Pipe Co. Ltd. $1,500; Mortland Cement Co. Ltd. $2,000.
Sales: cash $350; credit: R. Jones $120, Model Building Co. $600.

28. Paid salesmen's salaries $120; manager's salary $200. Purchased delivery truck for $3,000 for cash.

30. Paid Shop Fitters Ltd. $2,500.

31. Received cash from Jones $150, Smith $200, and Model Building Co. $400.

19. Record the following transactions in ledger accounts after including the opening balances from the trial balance below, and prepare a trial balance at the end of the period, for Smith and Co. Ltd.

|  | Dr. $ | Cr. $ |
|---|---|---|
| Cash at Bank | | 10,000 |
| Accounts Payable | | 14,000 |
| Mortgage | | 25,000 |
| Paid-up Capital | | 50,000 |
| Accounts Receivable | 24,000 | |
| Merchandise Inventory | 33,000 | |
| Delivery Vehicles | 6,000 | |
| Premises | 36,000 | |
| | $99,000 | $99,000 |

i.     Purchased merchandise on credit $7,000
ii.    Sales of merchandise: cash $4,000; credit $2,000.
iii.   Sold additional shares to owners $20,000.
iv.   Paid wages $2,000.
v.     Received bill for rates and taxes $5,000.
vi.   Sales of merchandise: cash $6,000; credit $8,000.
vii.  Collected cash from customers $10,000.
viii. Paid creditors $7,000.
ix.   Purchased a new delivery van for cash $4,000.
x.     Purchased additional premises $15,000, financed by mortgage.
xi.   Purchased merchandise $11,000 on credit.
xii.  Paid dividends $5,000.

# Part 2
# The Historic Cost Measurement System

# Chapter 6
# The Income Statement and Balance Sheet

After all the firm's economic activities for a period, as evidenced by its transactions, have been recorded and summarized in the trial balance, it is necessary to take some *measurements of its activities over the period and its position at the end of the period* for the information of various people. One of the major functions of the accounting system is to convert the mass of transaction data into useful information — the summary of the data shown in the trial balance is of very little use in itself. Rather, various measurements must be taken from this data and the results reported to users in accounting reports. Several sets of measurements may be taken:

1. The income earned from trading activities over the period. This calculation is made in the profit and loss (or income) statement.

2. The financial position of the firm at the end of the period — made in the balance sheet

3. The cash received from various sources over the period, and the manner in which this cash has been used — made in the cash flow statement

4. The finance (cash and credit) received from various sources over the period and the ways in which this finance has been used — made in the funds statement.

After these measurements have been made, management can determine policy relating to the distribution of income, and this is summarized in the appropriation statement.

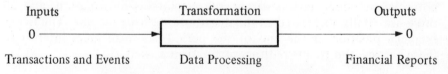

**Figure 6—1.** Outline of an information system

In terms of the operation of an information system, the transaction input data must be transformed into useful financial information, as illustrated in Figure 6—1. The input data comprise the raw transaction data; internal events relevant to specified concepts (e.g., consumption of the firm's own resources); and, in some systems, changes in the market prices of assets and the general purchasing power of the dollar. The transformation process covers the entire data processing system and it involves a study of the concepts to be measured (e.g., income and financial position) and the accounting techniques applied to the input data so as to measure these concepts. A host of adjustments must be made ·to revenue and expense, and asset and liability accounts, to measure income and financial position. The outputs of the information system comprise the accounting reports which contain the appropriate financial information.

To begin with, we shall confine our attention to the measurement of income and financial position and to profit distribution decisions. The three reports in which these measurements are made are often referred to collectively as the *final accounting reports.* Although cash flow and funds statements are easier to prepare than the final accounting reports because they are more factual, we shall postpone their consideration until after the final accounting reports have been prepared. The classification in the cash flow and funds statements, and some of the concepts measured, are derived from the income statement and balance sheet.

The preparation of the final accounting reports requires an understanding of what is being measured, and so first of all the concepts of income and financial position must be examined. Next, the content and form of presentation of the final reports are considered. Finally, the detailed adjustments to the transaction data which are necessary for the preparation of the reports are examined. The inclusion of these adjustments upgrades the accounting system to the *full accrual basis of accounting.*

The need for periodic accounting reports by various users was examined in chapter 3. Three of the most important items of information about a firm concern its income for the period, the distribution of that income, and its financial position. In general, the pursuit of income is the basic reason for the existence of the firm, and the amount of income earned is the primary measure of the firm's performance as an economic entity. Management, shareholders, and potential investors have a strong interest in this information; and all three are vitally interested in the distribution of the income. The firm's financial position at the end of the period is also of great interest to these parties, and to all creditors of the firm as well.

## KEY CONCEPTS

The meaning of the concepts of income and financial position must first be clearly understood before they can be measured. Both are part of a family of interrelated concepts of wealth, assets, capital, liabilities, and maintaining capital intact. There is much confusion about all these concepts. One of the greatest defects in current accounting theory is that they are frequently not defined precisely and as a result there are many glaring inconsistencies in current accounting practices. The confusion has been aggravated by the existence of two sets of terminology – one deriving from classical economics and the other from accounting – and both are commonly used in business. The following discussion adopts the language of economics but uses the standard accounting balance sheet symbols.

### Wealth

Wealth is the value of the stock of resources owned by the firm at any point of time (or in accounting terminology, the assets). Resources may be provided by creditors (as a result of credit purchases or loans) and by owners, and they may be generated from the firm's own operations. The net wealth of owners – which is their capital investment in the firm – can be determined by deducting the financial claims of creditors from total wealth. Symbolically:

$$A_t = L_t + P_t$$
$$\text{and} \quad P_t = A_t - L_t = NA_t$$

where
$$A = \text{total wealth or assets}$$
$$NA = \text{net wealth or net assets}$$
$$P = \text{owners' capital or proprietorship}$$
$$L = \text{liabilities or financial claims of creditors}$$
$$t = \text{a specified date.}$$

Because all transactions involve a flow of resources into or out of the firm, they must affect the stock of resources. If the resource inflow generated by transactions exceeds the outflow, the net stock of resources must be increased. The wealth of the firm can be measured again after a period of activity and the net wealth determined.

i.e., $NA_1 = P_1 = A_1 - L_1$
where $t = 1$ is the end of a period.

### Income

The net wealth at time 1 can be divided into two subsets of capital and income. After removing the effects of any additional capital contributions or withdrawals by owners from the initial capital investment $P_0$, the increase in net wealth is the income of the period. Assuming no such direct capital contributions or withdrawals by owners, income is measured as:

$$\begin{array}{ll}
& P_1 = \; A_1 - L_1 \\
\text{less} & P_0 = \; A_0 - L_0 \\
\hline
& \Delta P = \Delta(A-L) = Y = \Delta NA
\end{array}$$

where   $t$ = 0 refers to the start of the period
        $Y$ = income or profit for the period.

### Maintaining Capital Intact

An alternative method of defining income is to define it as the increment in net wealth over a period after maintaining intact the firm's capital, i.e., the level of capital at the beginning of the period. "Capital" when used in this phrase may refer to the economist's or the accountant's concept. "Capital" in economics refers to the resources of the firm, and "maintaining capital intact" means that any resources used up in the operating cycle are replaced before any income is reckoned to be earned. "Capital" in accounting refers to owner's investment in the firm, and "maintaining capital intact" means that this investment is kept at a constant level without having to resort to additional contributions by owners. Since proprietors own the net resources of the firm, both sets of terminology amount to the same thing.

The two alternative methods of defining income are identical. Income is an increment in wealth and as such it must be related to a base level of wealth or owners' capital. It can be measured only after the value of any resources or of owners' investment used up in operating activity has been replaced. The concept of maintaining capital intact is important because it is used as the benchmark for the definition and measurement of income. Both concepts are inseparable, and income cannot be defined without reference to a base level of capital or wealth.

The relationship between wealth, capital, and income is illustrated in Figure 6–2.

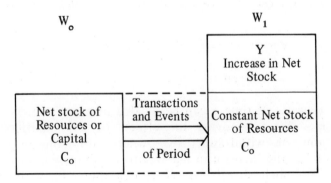

**Figure 6–2.** Relationship between Capital and Income

Unfortunately the concepts of wealth, income, and maintaining capital intact are not as simple as appears at first sight, and a host of problems occurs in both their definition and measurement. They depend not only upon the physical fact of the firm having a stock of resources on hand, but also upon the method used to value the resources and, in some cases, upon other criteria which may be used to distinguish the base from the increment. In normal conditions, a resource can possess several values simultaneously. The major concepts of value comprise the historic transaction price of the resource (i.e., the historical cost value), the current market buying price of the resource (i.e., the current replacement cost value), the current market selling price, the current market (buying or selling) value adjusted for inflation (the real value system), and the expected future selling prices of the resources adjusted for the cost of money over time (the present value system). Under each of these systems, income is the increment in net wealth. Furthermore, criteria in addition to the increase in value may be used in the concept of income. It may be necessary for the increment to be physically separated from the base stock, or for it to be realized through sale and hence held in the form of cash or financial claims. Where these criteria are applied and not met, the increment in wealth is treated as capital growth rather than income. The different concepts of income will be examined in some detail later in the course. For the moment, the analysis is confined to the simplest concepts of wealth, capital and income — the historic cost valuation system. The (recorded) medium of exchange measurement property of the dollar is used throughout the historic cost system.

It is essential that a consistent basis of valuation is applied to the measures of income and maintaining capital intact. Both are parts of wealth and the same method of valuation must be applied to all components of it. The measure of income is in fact part of the problem of asset valuation, and income cannot be defined without reference to the method of asset valuation. The bases of valuation are referred to as valuation principles, and use of a mutually consistent set of valuation principles provides a theory of income and asset measurement. The choice of the valuation principles to be employed depends upon the use to be made of the income and asset measures — one concept of income is appropriate for some purpose, another concept may be appropriate for a different use. Given the concept to be measured, rules can be derived from the principles to facilitate its measurement.

Although the firm's income can be determined from a comparison of its balance sheets at the beginning and end of the accounting period, it is preferable to calculate it from the profit and loss statement for the period. This statement summarizes the flows of resources through the firm on account of operations and thereby shows the details of how the income was earned.

### Financial Position

The concept of financial position in general terms is synonymous with wealth as it refers to how well off the firm is at a particular date. But more specifically it embraces consideration of the value and liquidity of the firm's assets, in relation to the value and maturity dates of its liabilities. The measure of financial position is needed to help assess the firm's ability to meet its liabilities as they fall due for repayment, i.e., to assess its short-run and long-run creditworthiness; to help determine its future borrowing capacity; and to provide a measure of the resources currently owned by the firm and which are available for use in its future operations. This information is required by management, short and long-term creditors, owners, and all potential investors and creditors.

The balance sheet is used as the major accounting report to indicate current financial position (though for evaluating the long-term position it ought to be supplemented by cash or funds flow budgets). As with the measure of income, the measure of financial position depends upon the fact of the existence of the firm's assets and liabilities, and upon their valuation. The same valuation systems used to measure income may be used to measure financial position, though we shall see later on that some of these systems are inappropriate for this purpose. For the time being, financial position is measured according to the historic cost valuation system.

## AN ILLUSTRATIVE SET OF FINAL ACCOUNTING REPORTS

An illustrative set of final accounting reports is presented below. The reports are prepared from a trial balance extracted from the ledger after the recording of all external transactions of the period and all subsequent internal adjustments necessary for the determination of income and financial position.[1]

Northside Trading Co. Ltd.

*Income Statement for the Year Ended 31 December 197X*

|  | $ | $ | $ |
|---|---|---|---|
| Sales Revenue |  |  | 140,000 |
| Less Estimated Credit Losses |  |  | 6,000 |
| *Net Sales* |  |  | 134,000 |
| Less Cost of Goods Sold |  |  | 100,000 |
| *Gross Profit* |  |  | 34,000 |
| Less  *Selling Expenses* |  |  |  |
| Advertising | 3,000 |  |  |
| Salesmen's Salaries | 6,000 |  |  |
| Depreciation of Shop Fittings | 1,000 | 10,000 |  |

| | | | |
|---|---|---:|---:|
| Less | *Administration Expenses* | | |
| | Directors' Fees | 1,000 | |
| | Office Salaries | 2,000 | |
| | Depreciation of Buildings | 3,000 | 6,000 |
| Less | *Finance Expenses* | | |
| | Interest | | 1,000 | 17,000 |

| | | | |
|---|---|---:|---:|
| *Net Operating Profit* | | 17,000 |
| Less *Non-Operating Expenses* | | |
| Loss Due to Fire | | 6,000 |
| *Net Profit* | | $11,000 |

### Profit Appropriation Statement for the Year Ended 31 December 197X

| | | |
|---|---:|---:|
| Balance of Retained Profits 1 Jan. | 5,000 | |
| Add Net Profit for Year | 11,000 | 16,000 |
| Less Dividends | 4,000 | |
| Taxation | 5,000 | |
| Goodwill Written Off | 2,000 | |
| Transfer to Reserve | 3,000 | 14,000 |
| Balance of Retained Profits 31 Dec. | | $ 2,000 |

### Balance Sheet as at 31 December 197X

*Assets*
*Current Assets*

| | | | |
|---|---:|---:|---:|
| Accounts Receivable | 30,000 | | |
| Less Estimated Bad Debts | 3,000 | 27,000 | |
| Merchandise Inventory | | 32,000 | |
| Prepayments | | 1,000 | 60,000 |

*Long-Term Assets*

| | | | |
|---|---:|---:|---:|
| Shop Fittings | 12,000 | | |
| Less Accumulated Depreciation | 3,000 | 9,000 | |
| Land and Building | 48,000 | | |
| Less Accumulated Depreciation | 18,000 | 30,000 | |
| Goodwill | | 6,000 | 45,000 |
| *Total Assets* | | | $105,000 |

*Liabilities*
*Current Liabilities*

| | | |
|---|---:|---:|
| Bank Overdraft | 3,000 | |
| Accounts Payable | 12,000 | |
| Dividend Payable | 2,000 | |
| Taxation Payable | 5,000 | |
| Accrued Expenses | 1,000 | 23,000 |

| *Long-Term Liability* | | |
|---|---|---|
| Mortgage | | 20,000 |
| *Total Liabilities* | | 43,000 |
| *Owners' Equity* | | |
| Paid-up Capital (50,000 shares of $1.00 each) | 50,000 | |
| Reserves | 10,000 | |
| Retained Profits | 2,000 | 62,000 |
| *Total Liabilities and Owners' Equity* | | $105,000 |

## THE PROFIT AND LOSS, OR INCOME, STATEMENT

The profit and loss statement is prepared in order to measure the firm's net income from its operations over the accounting period. It summarizes the revenue earned by the firm and the expenses and losses incurred over the period, and the difference between them is the net profit or loss. The profit and loss statement is presented in two parts. The first summarizes the results of its normal trading operations, and shows the net operating profit earned. Non-operating items are then included to determine net profit or income.

### 1. Definition of Terms

i. *Operating revenue and expenses.* All items relating to the normal trading operations of the firm, or to its major activities as distinct from incidental ones, are classified as operating revenue and expenses. Unless otherwise specified, it is assumed that all revenue and expenses are operating items.

ii. *Operating revenue* is the value of the cash and financial claims recognized as having been earned during the period from selling transactions related to the firm's major activities.

iii. *Operating expenses* represent the value of the resources necessarily used up in earning the current period's revenue. No revenue can be earned without expenses being incurred. For example, revenue from sales cannot be earned without incurring the expense of buying the merchandise sold, and of the salaries of salesmen.

iv. *Losses* are the costs of those resources which yield no benefit to the firm's operations. The resources may have been accidentally damaged or destroyed by fire, etc.; they may have deteriorated as the result of natural causes; or they may have been wasted because of wrong decisions by management or through ineffective control of operations. They should be segregated into operating and non-operating categories.

v. *Net operating profit* is the excess of the operating revenue earned during the period over the expenses incurred in earning that revenue. Since revenue represents the resources (cash and financial claims) acquired from sales, and expenses constitute the resources used up or consumed in the process of selling the period's revenue, net operating profit is the net increase in resources from normal operations. This net increase must appear in the firm's balance sheet as an increase in net assets over the period and hence in owners' investment.

vi. *Non-operating items* relate to incidental activities of the firm or to abnormal items which are not expected to recur. They are shown in a separate section of the profit and loss statement so as not to distort the data relating to the firm's normal and major operations. Examples of non-operating revenue for a retailer are interest and dividends received on financial investments and rent from premises leased out to other users. Non-operating expenses comprise resources consumed in earning non-operating revenue – for example, depreciation of rented-out premises, and losses incurred by the firm on the destruction of its resources by theft, fire, flood, and so on, to the extent not covered by insurance. Losses should always be recognized immediately they occur – they should never be "capitalized" in the balance sheet. Profits and losses on the disposal of long-term assets may also be shown as non-operating items where the amount is sufficiently significant; otherwise they are taken as an adjustment to depreciation expense.

vii. *Net profit.* The firm's net profit, obtained by adjusting net operating profit for non-operating items, is defined analogously to net operating profit. It is total revenue less total expenses and losses, or the increase in the firm's net resources over the period after eliminating payments to or by proprietors and income tax payments. Net profit represents that amount of resources which the firm could distribute in tax payments and to proprietors without impairing the net capital investment of the start of the period. It is the distributable surplus of resources resulting from the period's operations and events after maintaining capital intact. Net profit could be determined from comparative balance sheets, that is, the balance sheet on 1 January and that on the following 31 December. It represents the increase in net assets over the year after eliminating any payments by or to proprietors, and taxation. However such a method of determination hides valuable information on *how* the profit was earned, and it is preferable to show these details in the profit and loss statement as part of the accounting information system.

## 2. Classification in the Profit and Loss Statement

Classification of data in the profit and loss statement should be governed by the standards for accounting information, and in particular, be appropriate to its expected use and disclose significant relationships. The needs of management for information about various aspects of performance (for example, sales, gross profit, net operating profit, and net profit), and about expenses for expense control (for example, the proportion of sales revenue absorbed by the cost of goods sold, etc.) dominate the classification of data in the profit and loss statement. Consequently, it is important to distinguish between operating and non-operating items; and, in the operating section, between cost of goods sold and other groups of functionally related expenses. The surplus of operating revenue over cost of goods sold is called *gross profit,* and this amount is significant for various managerial planning and control purposes. Gross profit represents the amount from which must be recouped all the expenses of selling and administration and the expenses of borrowed finance, and a net operating profit obtained. These expenses may be classified into the functional areas of selling expenses, administration expenses, and finance expenses, as in the

Northside Trading Co. Ltd. illustration, or merely listed under the heading "Operating Expenses", according to the user's needs.

*Selling expenses* comprise all those expenses related to the selling or marketing function in the business. Hence all expenses incurred in the sales department (for example, salesmen's salaries, depreciation of shop fittings), sales promotion expenses (that is, advertising), and delivery expenses are included under this heading.

*Administration expenses* comprise all items related to the general administration, supervision, and control of the firm and its general facilities, such as office salaries and expenses, depreciation of office equipment, directors' fees and audit fees, plus rents, rates, and taxes and depreciation of buildings (except where they relate to the sales facilities).

*Finance expenses* comprise all expenses related to the use of borrowed finance, that is, interest. It does *not* include payments to proprietors for the use of their finance — these must all be shown as payments from profits.

Further information can be communicated to management through the use of additional bases of classification. Thus the classification of operating expenses into variable and fixed components, and the classi-fication of revenue and directly traceable expenses to selling depart-ments, provides very valuable information to management.

### 3. The Matching Principle

The method of calculating net operating profit by charging expenses against revenue is called the matching principle. It is one of the most important principles in accounting and many of the difficult problems in accounting are encountered in applying it. The matching principle states that the value of all resources consumed in the process of earning the current period's revenue must be charged against that revenue before any net operating profit is earned. This charging of expenses against revenue has the effect of recovering the value of resources consumed from revenue before any profit is allowed to be made and net assets are increased. It thereby ensures that the firm's initial capital (or net assets) is maintained intact before any profit is made.

The matching principle can be applied to all historically based valuation systems used to determine net income. In the measurement of historic cost income, all non-monetary assets are valued at their actual transaction prices, i.e., at historical acquisition cost. Expenses are measured in terms of the prices at which the resources consumed were bought, and the increase in net assets is measured in terms of the purchase prices of those assets.

The whole matching process pivots on the current period's revenue, and it must be defined before expenses can be identified. There are two major problems concerning the definition of current revenue, viz., the point at which to recognize a sale as current revenue, and secondly, how much revenue to recognize. These problems are considered later. If resources are used up in the process of earning the current period's revenue, then the value of the resources so consumed are expenses of the period. If resources used up in the period do not benefit the current period's revenue, but should benefit the revenue of a future period, then those resources remain on hand at the end of the period and are an asset of the firm. In this case, the initial resources will have been transformed into another asset (for example, raw materials and labour services will have been transformed into a finished product awaiting sale next year and hence become part of the asset, merchandise inventory). They remain an asset until the product in which they are embodied is sold.

In fact, most assets other than monetary ones are simply resources waiting to be used up in the process of earning revenue, and whose costs will be matched as expenses against the revenue of the periods which they benefit. They are stores of future expense, and the cost of the asset is "expensed" as the asset benefits revenue. For example, the costs of plant and buildings are matched in the form of depreciation expense against the revenue of each period in which the products of the plant and buildings are sold; the cost of merchandise purchased is charged to revenue as the expense, "cost of goods sold", when the merchandise is sold. The only economic difference between an outlay on resources such as merchandise or labour services, and plant or buildings, is that of time. The first items are likely to be embodied in sales of the near future, whereas the second group should benefit the sales of many future periods. However, as a matter of convenience, the purchase of resources likely to be used up in the near future is treated immediately as an expense (with an adjustment for any amount unused at the end of the period as an asset — for example, a prepaid expense, stock of stationery on hand), while the purchase of resources whose expected use extends over a long period is treated as an asset (with an adjustment to record the amount used up in each period as the expense — for example, depreciation).

Application of the matching principle automatically affects the firm's balance sheet as well as the profit and loss statement. Any item which affects income automatically affects assets or liabilities as part of the twofold effect of each transaction, and of course it must affect proprietorship to the extent of the profit or loss made. For example, all sales transactions increase revenue and either cash or debtors; all expenses involving transactions increase expenses and either reduce cash or inventories or increase liabilities, all expenses not involving transactions increase expenses and reduce a long-term asset.

The full accrual basis of accounting must be used in the matching process so that the recognition of revenues and expenses is made invariant to the actual time of cash transfer, and to enable the recognition of those expenses which do not require the use of cash.

Because the matching process concerns revenue and expense recognition, and it pivots on the sales to be recognized as the revenue of the period, it is necessary to consider in turn:

1. When to recognize a sale as current revenue
2. How much revenue to recognize
3. How much expense to charge against the revenue.

### 4.  The Point of Revenue Recognition

Here, the problem is to determine the critical event in the selling cycle at which the sale can be recognized as having been accomplished. Frequently there are four events in a sales transaction — the points of production, order, delivery, and cash collection — and each event can be used as the signal for recognizing the sale in appropriate circumstances. In the simple case of the cash and carry sale, the last three events occur simultaneously, and there is no problem concerning the choice of the critical event in the transaction.

The use of a particular point of revenue recognition is normally not mentioned in a profit and loss statement, but the standards for accounting information would require that it be disclosed to facilitate more accurate interpretation of the sales figure. For example, in the case of hire-purchase sales, where the cash collection basis for sales recognition is used, an increase in goods ordered and delivered this year may not raise the sales figure till later years when the customers pay their accounts. In terms of the volume of economic activity in the firm, the current year's revenue may understate the activity, while the future years' revenues overstate it.

### 5.  The Amount of Revenue to Recognize

The quoted sales price may not be the ultimate value of the sale to the firm, that is, the amount of cash it finally collects from the sale. We shall define revenue as this amount, that is, as the net sales value. The net sales value is likely to be less than the gross sales value because of cash discounts granted to customers for prompt payment, goods returned by customers or allowances made for inferior quality, breakages, and so on, and credit losses (i.e., bad debts). Such items should be deducted from gross sales to determine the amount of cash which the firm should ultimately collect from its sales transactions. However many estimates are involved in determining the deductions from the current year's gross sales, as for example it may be two or more years before the firm discovers that a customer will not pay the amount he still owes it.

In Australia, allowances for credit losses and discounts are normally shown as expenses of earning revenue. However, these items do not comply with our definition of expense as the cost of resources used up in earning revenue. Rather, they are sales revenue cancellations, and they should be deducted directly from sales in the profit and loss statement to determine net sales, as illustrated in Northside Trading Co. Ltd.

### 6. Expense Recognition

The problem in expense recognition is to associate the consumption of resources with the relevant revenue, that is, the revenue of that period to which the resources have contributed. The actual time of cash expenditure is irrelevant for this purpose, as is also the question of whether the resources consumed have involved the use of funds in the current period. Outlays on the purchase of short-term resources during the period do not comprise the expenses of the period. The problem would be easy if each resource acquired was physically embodied and identifiable in the product sold (the path of all resources purchased could then be traced through the firm and unambiguously identified in the products sold), if there were no difficulties in forecasting future events, and if there were no changes in market values away from historical purchase prices. Consider the following examples which illustrate these points. Merchandise purchased for resale can in many instances be identified as it is sold, and the expense, "cost of goods sold", easily ascertained. But if many units of the same product are acquired at different prices, and the products are all stored together so that they lose their purchase price identities, which purchase price should be applied to the item sold? In a manufacturing firm, the services of factory labour engaged in making the products are traceable to each product, but the services of managerial labour may not be. Similarly, in retailing, salesmen's salaries can be traced to selling trans-actions, but office salaries cannot be. Depreciation charges for the use of long-term assets in each period depend upon estimates of asset lives and resale values.

To aid in the matching process, a broad distinction is made between fixed and variable expenses. *Fixed expenses* refer to the costs of those resources which provide the firm's capacity to operate for the period. They are the costs of those resources which expire with the passing of time and which do not fluctuate with changes in the volume of sales. Fixed expenses are often called time costs or period costs. They comprise items such as all contractual costs of the firm (for example, staff salaries, rent, interest on fixed term loans), municipal rates and taxes, electric lighting, depreciation and amortization (where the allocations are based on time and not on use). In retailing it is assumed that the entire benefit from the use of these resources accrues to the current period's sales, and that nothing can be carried forward in assets as a charge against the sales of the next period. Rather, the next period has to bear its own charges for these items. If the resources are not fully utilized in the current period — for example, staff are underworked, the building has idle space — then the firm has excess capacity, but its expenses are not reduced. Likewise, the firm can increase its sales up to some limit without having to acquire additional fixed resources.

*Variable expenses* on the other hand comprise the costs of all those resources which must be acquired to increase the sales of the period. They vary with changes in the volume of sales — if sales are to be increased, total variable expenses must increase, while, if sales decline, total variable expenses can be reduced. Variable expenses are often called volume costs. Typical variable expenses are the cost of merchandise sold, salesmen's commissions, part of advertising expense, and depreciation (where it is based on asset use and not on time). If variable resources acquired are not used this year — for example, merchandise — they are assets of the firm at the end of the year, that is, merchandise inventory, and consequently are not part of the current year's expenses. In the Northside Trading Co. Ltd. report, the cost of goods sold is a variable expense, and part of advertising expense and salesmen's salaries would be a variable expense if they fluctuated with changes in sales. Otherwise, they would be fixed expenses along with all the other operating expenses.

Within the general context of the distinction between fixed and variable expenses, particular accounting problems in expense recognition concern the determination of the cost of goods sold during the period, depreciation and amortization, adjustments for services paid for in advance of their use (that is, prepayments) or after their use (that is, accrued expenses), and adjustments for stocks of sundry non-merchandise items on hand at the end of the period (for example, stocks of stationery).

### 7. Tentativeness of Periodic Income Measurement

· It should always be remembered that the calculation of periodic income is necessarily tentative to some extent. This tentativeness occurs because all the transactions of a particular stretch of time are arbitrarily hived off from a continuing sequence of transactions in the indefinite life of the firm, notwithstanding the fact that many of the transactions are only partly completed and many resources acquired in earlier periods are used in the operations of the current period. Forecasts of future events must be made for many items of revenue and expense, and hence estimates as well as accomplished facts are incorporated in the profit and loss statement. The amount of cash to be received from customers for credit sales must be estimated, long-term asset lives must be estimated for the calculation of depreciation expense, and so on.

Where estimates are involved, the criteria of a good information system should be satisfied. The assumptions on which the estimates are made should be explicit, the evidence on which they are based should be as verifiable as circumstances permit, and the estimates should be free from bias. Income measurement can be factual only where there is perfect knowledge of the future or where the firm's life has come to an end.

In the case of the Northside Trading Company Ltd., the net profit, calculated as revenue minus expenses and losses, is estimated at $11,000 and this sum is embodied in an increase in the firm's net assets (that is, total assets less liabilities) over the year. The increase need not be represented in any particular assets and the specific assets in which it is invested do not matter for income determination purposes. That is a matter for financial policy. The figure of $11,000 for net profit for the year is only an estimate, although it should of course be the best estimate possible in the existing state of knowledge about future events. Assumptions have been made concerning estimated credit losses, the cost of merchandise sold, and depreciation. The $11,000 increase in net assets refers to the extra finance invested in them during the year, and it may well be that the current market values of some of the assets acquired are no longer the same as those when they were bought by the company.

## THE PROFIT APPROPRIATION STATEMENT

The profit appropriation statement shows the various forms of profit distribution. Net profit is added to the amount of undistributed profits (or retained earnings) from the end of the previous period to show the total profits available for appropriation. Profits may be appropriated as follows:

1. For payment of company profits taxes (but not other forms of taxation such as sales, payroll, or personal income taxes)
2. For payment of dividends to shareholders; or salaries, drawings, and interest to proprietors of unincorporated businesses
3. For transfers to revenue reserves
4. For amortizing some intangible assets such as goodwill and preliminary expenses
5. For adjustments to the recorded profits of previous years.

The balance in the statement represents the retained earnings of the firm which have not been earmarked for any specific undistributed profits account. However, from a financial viewpoint, all revenue reserve accounts contain undistributed profits, and there is no transfer of resources involved in the "distribution" of profits to revenue reserve accounts.

The profit appropriation statement is not used in the United States. Rather, the "all-inclusive" income statement is used, in which non-operating items and profit distribution items are shown in the income statement immediately below the net operating profit. An important advantage of this method is that it shows company tax as the first charge on profits, and the profits after tax which are available for allocation by management. After-tax profits is the concept which is of prime interest to shareholders and to management for income distribution decisions, and they are not shown where a separate appropriation statement is used. The relevant part of the income statement appears as:

|  | $ |
|---|---|
| Net Income | 11,000 |
| Less Company Income Tax | 5,000 |
| Net Income after Tax | 6,000 |
| Add Retained Income, 1 Jan. | 5,000 |
| Income Available for Distribution | 11,000 |
| Less Allocations (detailed) | 9,000 |
| Balance of Retained Income, 31 Dec. | $2,000 |

## THE BALANCE SHEET

### 1. Nature of the Modern Balance Sheet

The balance sheet is a statement of the firm's assets, liabilities, and ownership equity as at the end of the accounting period. Assets are all those resources owned by the firm and available for its future use. Liabilities are financial obligations of the firm which must be paid at a future date. Proprietorship forms the residual claim on the firm's assets after its liabilities have been repaid.

Because the balance sheet shows assets, liabilities, and proprietorship, it is used as a statement of financial position. However, its use for this purpose is not always reliable because the measure of financial position depends upon the valuation of assets and liabilities as well as upon their mere existence. Where current market values of assets diverge from their historical purchase prices, the balance sheet does not provide a reliable measure of the firm's current financial position.

The balance sheet must be based upon a valuation system for assets and liabilities, and specifically it must use the valuation system embodied in the concepts of maintaining capital intact and net income employed in the profit and loss statement. At this stage of our analysis, all asset values are based on historical acquisition cost, and the capital to be maintained intact is the proprietary investment in assets at the start of the period, valued at their historical cost (less depreciation where relevant). Subsequent changes in the market prices of assets are disregarded for balance sheet purposes and the measure of financial position is in terms of historical market prices.

The results of all trading and financial activities for the past period are incorporated in the assets, liabilities, and ownership equity at the end of the period, and hence, unlike the income statement, the balance sheet includes the effects of *all* transactions. The net effects of trading transactions and events are summarized in the increases in proprietorship and assets.

In the balance sheet, total assets must always equal liabilities plus proprietorship. This results from the twofold nature of all transactions – the assets of the firm must come from somewhere, and they must ultimately be owned by someone outside the firm itself. Ownership of net assets (that is, total assets less liabilities) is always vested in proprietorship as owners have the residual claim to the assets of the firm, and profits accrue to them after taxes have been met. These relationships are symbolized in the balance sheet equation:

Assets = Liabilities + Proprietorship.

The nature of the balance sheet has changed over time with the increasing complexity of modern business. In early times, when business firms were operated by a sole trader in a simple business environment, all liabilities arose from goods and services supplied to the firm and all assets were resources owned by it, and the balance sheet was a statement of sources of finance on a particular date and the investment of those funds in particular assets; that is, it was a funds statement as for a particular date.

However, since the advent of the modern corporation, the nature of liabilities, and of assets, has undergone change. Not all liabilities result from loans to the company and purchases on credit by it; they also arise from management's intentions or obligations arising from past activities to meet warranty costs on goods sold, income tax and dividend payments, long service leave gratuities to employees, and so on. But even the concept of present obligations may not be broad enough to cover all liabilities and proprietorship items, and the broad concept of "future restrictions on assets" has been advocated. All liabilities involve a restriction on the future use of assets – the liabilities must be repaid from them, and this thereby prevents some assets being used for other purposes. Likewise, decisions by management to transfer retained profits to reserves represent an expression of intention to invest those profits in the company's operating assets rather than leave them available for possible dividend distribution, even though there is no actual movement of funds involved. An analogous situation occurs with the issue of bonus shares from share premium reserves. Similarly, there are various concepts of assets which may be employed in the balance sheet. Rather than assets being thought of as financial and productive resources of the company, they may be described in terms of service potential or their future usefulness. Resources which have no service potential are not assets under this concept. Alternatively, assets may be described as financial claims and deferred charges to future revenues. Non-monetary assets such as inventories, plant, buildings, and so on are included in the balance sheet so that their costs can be charged against the revenues of future periods as they are used up, i.e., as expenses. These assets differ from current expenses only with respect to the time period involved. According to this point of view, the balance sheet is no more than a connecting link between successive income statements and it is not meant to be a statement of financial position. The balance sheets prepared to represent each of these viewpoints can differ somewhat in the items that are included as assets and liabilities.

Some of the current controversies in accounting practice revolve around the concepts of assets and liabilities to be used in the balance sheet — for example, whether leases should be shown as assets and liabilities, whether goodwill should be shown as an asset, and whether deferred income taxes should be shown as liabilities. Whichever concepts are adopted, they must be mutually consistent throughout their applications to revenue, expenses, assets, and liabilities; otherwise the accounting reports are not valid.

Whatever viewpoint about the modern balance sheet is adopted, it may always be viewed as a snapshot of a firm's position (however defined) at the end of an artificial accounting period which shows all those items which run on from the past period to the future. It represents the bridge between succeeding accounting periods, and the balance sheet items become the opening balances in the ledger accounts of the new period.

### 2.  Classification in the Balance Sheet

The classification of assets, liabilities, and proprietorship into significant groups in the balance sheet is governed by the end uses of the statement, and the standards for accounting information should be applied. Because the balance sheet is used as a statement of financial position, assets are classified primarily according to their degree of liquidity or time of conversion into cash, while liabilities are shown in order of maturing or repayment dates. By ranking assets and liabilities in this order, it is easy to check across from the short-term assets to the short-term liabilities to see that the firm has sufficient reasonably liquid resources to cover its immediate debts. In establishing the liquidity of assets, both the elements of time and intended use are considered. Although some assets could readily be sold for cash, for example securities and premises, the firm may intend to keep them for a long time and therefore they are not classified as short-term assets.

Assets are classified into current (or short-term) and long-term (or fixed or non-current) categories. *Current assets* comprise all those assets which are in cash form (cash on hand or at bank) or are likely to be converted into cash or used up within the firm, within the coming year. However, by convention, this rule is not applied rigorously to particular components of an asset group; hence, for example, all debtors may be shown as current assets even though some parts of debtors' accounts are not liable for payment before the end of the following year, and all merchandise inventories are shown as current assets although some items may not be sold in the next year. Typical current assets are shown in the balance sheet of the Northside Trading Co. Ltd.; other typical ones are cash and investments in securities held for resale. Within the current asset group, the assets are shown in rough order of liquidity.

*Long-term assets* are those which are not expected to be converted into cash, or to be substantially used up in the firm's operations, within the year. Normally such assets are held for use within the firm and are not held for purposes of resale. Typical long-term assets include those in the balance sheet of the Northside Trading Co. Ltd., plus plant, long-term investments in securities, leases, goodwill, and patents. Long-term assets are normally called "fixed" assets in practice, and indeed company law in Australia requires the use of this title. However the term is not altogether appropriate since many assets are not fixed in the physical sense (for example, motor vehicles) and their fixity with respect to time is a matter of degree. "Long-term" denotes a more accurate description of the nature of these assets. The term came into accounting from classical economics, where "fixed capital", as distinguished from "working capital", denoted investment in the long-term resources of the firm.

A further sub-classification of long-term assets into *tangible* and *intangible assets* is sometimes made. Although tangible assets are defined as those long-term assets having a physical embodiment (for example, plant and buildings), legal rights such as leases and securities are normally included in the group. Intangible assets generally comprise items such as the purchased goodwill of another firm taken over, pre-liminary expenses incurred on the formation of the company or on a new share issue, debenture discount where debentures are sold at a price below their par value, patents and trade marks, and capitalized expenditures on research and development. The main reason for separating the "tangible" from "intangible" assets is not their tangibility but the arbitrary methods used for the valuation of intangible assets. For example, although the price paid for goodwill, and the amounts spent on preliminary expenses, research, development, and patents, may be objective, the amortization of these items as charges against revenue or profit is often very arbitrary. Frequently the amortization depends upon "what the profits will bear". The classification of long-term assets according to their "tangibility" serves no useful purpose unless the valuation of the "intangible assets" is arbitrary (in which case it is a valuation problem and not a question of physical embodiment). Investment analysts normally omit "intangible assets" in their measures of the net worth of a company; hence they calculate the value of "net tangible assets per share" as the sum of total assets less "intangible" assets, and less liabilities, divided by the number of shares. (This asset backing per share is then compared with the current share price to serve as one measure of the riskiness of shareholders' investment in the company and as an indicator of the company as a takeover prospect.) Another distinguishing characteristic of intangible assets is that they are normally non-severable from the firm – they cannot be sold as separate assets – and hence do not have separate market values.

It is important to disclose separately the historic cost value of assets and any subsequent deductions from them, as the first is a factual amount and the second an estimate. Moreover, the separate disclosure helps the user to assess the adequacy of the allowance. Thus estimated bad debts should be openly deducted from debtors in the balance sheet to ascertain the net value of debtors – that is, the amount expected to be collected in cash from them. The accumulated depreciation of long-term assets should likewise be openly deducted from the cost of the assets to derive their net values, and company law now requires this. Furthermore, these deduction items must be offset against the assets to which they relate, and not shown as liabilities merely because they have credit balances. They are asset deductions, not liabilities.

*Liabilities and proprietorship* are frequently called *equities*. However, the term "equity" has a strict legal meaning (that is, rights under a law of equity) and is not altogether appropriate in the balance sheet. Liabilities arising from the purchase of resources or the loan of cash confer rights under common law and the purchase of shares conveys rights under statute law, while some "liabilities" do not confer legal rights at all but are an expression of managerial intention.

*Current liabilities* are those obligations payable within the coming year, or alternatively those restrictions on the use of assets which should be removed within the year. The liabilities are arranged in approximate order of payment so that they can be more readily compared with the more liquid of the current assets.

*Long-term (or deferred) liabilities* are those payable beyond the coming year. Alternatively they represent those restrictions on the use of assets which will not be removed in the coming year. In the case of some long-term liabilities, particularly debentures and mortgages, the restrictions are specified in the contract and they are much more than a general financial restriction on the firm's asset – for example, they may restrict the firm's borrowing powers.

*Proprietorship, owners' equity, or shareholders' funds* comprise three groups of items which are listed in the order below, though without the subgroup titles.

i.  *Contributed capital of owners* – paid-up capital, or in the United States, common stock. This represents the paid value of the shares issued by the company. It may comprise not only those shares paid for by shareholders; it includes as well all bonus shares issued to shareholders. The paid-up capital may comprise ordinary and preference shares. Preference shares carry different legal rights, which are specified in the company's registered articles of association, from those of ordinary shares. Normally, preference shares have fixed dividend rights which rank ahead of ordinary dividend rights, prior rights to the return of capital in the event of liquidation of the company, and restricted voting rights on the policies of the company. Ordinary shares normally carry the ultimate risk with respect to return of capital and dividends, and are given the main voting rights. The profits and assets remaining after satisfaction of preference shareholders' rights normally belong to them.

Full details of the company's capital structure should be shown in the balance sheet. Registered capital shows the legal, registered capital of the company, and it represents the maximum number and value of the shares that can be issued by the company. Issued capital comprises the value of the shares issued by the company. Called-up capital represents the amount that shareholders have been asked to pay on the issued shares towards their nominal value. Uncalled capital represents the shareholder's future liability for the debts of the company, and it is to this amount that his liability is limited (assuming he has no calls in arrears). If shares are issued fully paid, the shareholder has no further liability for the debts of the company. In the United States, all corporation shares are sold fully paid; in Australia, most shares are fully paid. The paid-up capital is the significant figure in the balance sheet for accounting and economic purposes. The current market price of the share can exceed or be less than this value.

The different concepts of capital are illustrated below:

|  | $ |
|---|---|
| Registered Capital (100,000 shares of $1.00 each) | 100,000 |
| Less Unissued Capital (40,000 shares of $1.00 each) | 40,000 |
| Issued Capital (60,000 shares of $1.00 each) | 60,000 |
| Less Uncalled Capital (60,000 shares at 20 cents each) | 12,000 |
| Called-up and Paid-up Capital (60,000 shares at 80 cents) | $48,000 |

ii. *Capital reserves* arise from the sale of shares at a price greater than their nominal (or par) value, that is, share premium reserves, and from the upward revaluations of assets, that is, asset revaluation reserves. The share prices of successful companies exceed their par values, and such companies often make new share issues at a price greater than par. For example, the current market price for a $1.00 share may be $2.50; if the company makes a share issue, it may charge $1.80 for the share. Hence the share premium is 80 cents. (The additional 70 cents above the issue price is a valuable benefit to the shareholder: it represents the "rights" value of the share, which the shareholder can sell if he decides not to purchase the new share.) Capital reserves are normally (although not necessarily) the source from which bonus share issues are made. Such an issue incorporates the capital reserves into the company's permanent share structure. Bonus shares are normally indistinguishable from ordinary shares, and carry the same rights. The company in fact does not distribute anything to the shareholder in a bonus issue; it merely increases the number of paper titles to the shareholder's existing property. However share prices frequently respond favourably to bonus issues.

iii. *Revenue reserves* are retained earnings of the firm. They may be listed under various titles — general, asset replacement, dividend equalization, and special reserves — as well as the appropriation account balance.

### 3. Form of Presentation of Balance Sheet

There is no fixed form of balance sheet presentation, and several forms may be used. The balance sheet of the Northside Trading Co. Ltd. is shown in a narrative form. Another narrative form which emphasizes shareholders' funds and their investment in working capital and net assets is as depicted below:

|  | $ |
|---|---|
| Owners' Equity | $62,000 |
| This is invested as follows in: |  |
| Current Assets | 60,000 |
| Less Current Liabilities | 23,000 |
| Working Capital | 37,000 |
| Plus Long-Term Assets | 45,000 |
|  | 82,000 |
| Less Long-Term Liabilities | 20,000 |
| Net Assets | $62,000 |

Working capital represents the investment of long-term funds in the net short-term assets of the firm and thus provides an indication of short-term financial solvency. It is the surplus of reasonably liquid assets over liabilities due for payment in the coming year.

Frequently, balance sheets are shown in "T" form, with assets on the left-hand side in the United States, but on the right-hand side in Australia. The Australian "T" form can be traced back to the origins of accounting wherein the balance sheet was a "balance account" in the ledger. In the fifteenth century, Pachioli recorded the balances of all asset, liability, and proprietorship accounts on the opposite side in a "balance account" at the end of a business venture or an accounting period. Hence for asset accounts with left-hand-side debit balances, the entry was made in the balance account on the credit right-hand side; and vice versa for liabilities and proprietorship. This balance account later became the balance sheet. But the balance sheet is not a ledger account, and it is confusing for assets with debit balances and entries on the left-hand side of a "T" account to appear on the right-hand side of a balance sheet; and vice versa for liability and proprietorship accounts.

## USE OF THE INCOME AND APPROPRIATION STATEMENTS AND BALANCE SHEET

These three statements are the most widely used of all accounting reports and they must be published annually by public companies. Some companies publish funds statements as well. The amount of detail which must be published in the profit and loss statement is very minimal, and most companies do not go beyond the legal minimum. Published reports are generally inadequate as an information system for the needs of outside users — creditors, shareholders, and so on — and they concentrate on fulfilling the stewardship function rather than serving as a good basis for decision-making.

Nevertheless, outside parties must use them and they do contain some very useful information. Management of course has access to all the information contained in the reports. The profit and loss statement reports on the performance achieved by the firm. The making of profits is the major objective of the firm, and the major determinant of whether it can survive, so that the profit and loss statement plays a crucial role in reporting on its achieved success. Related measures of performance are the rates of profit on total assets and on shareholders' funds. Management, long-term creditors, shareholders, and potential investors all require this information. The last three groups also require the information contained in the appropriation statement showing the management's profit distribution policies and the extent to which the company finances its growth from retained earnings.

All users need the information contained in the balance sheet. It reports on the firm's financial position on the date of the balance sheet, and it is a necessary basis for assessing the firm's short-term and long-term creditworthiness and the riskiness of investment in its securities.

The limitations of the final reports as part of an information system arise from the reliability of the estimates necessarily contained in them, from changes in market values of assets subsequent to their purchase, and from changes in the value of the dollar. Like all historical reports, they suffer from the unavoidable fact that they must relate to past operations, whereas all users would desire information about the future for decision-making purposes.

Management should prepare a series of budgeted final reports for some years ahead so as to coordinate satisfactorily its present decisions which have long-term effects, that is, decisions concerning long-term financing, investment in long-term assets, growth plans, and so on. The budgeted income and appropriation statements and balance sheets summarize the estimated effects of all decisions and plans of the firm, and will highlight any unsound long-term effects. If they are not prepared, the firm may find itself in an unsound position in, say, ten years' time as a consequence of decisions taken now. Such reports also fulfill a valuable control function as time passes and the plans are being put into operation.

A more detailed examination of the uses and limitations of historic final reports is made later on.

### CLASSIFICATION IN ACCOUNTING

It has been shown how the data in accounting reports can be classified into various groups so as to make the reports more meaningful to users. Classification is one of the most important functions in accounting, as only through the process of classification can the mass of transaction data be summarized, significant groups of items be compiled (e.g., expenses), significant relationships between groups be determined (e.g., current assets and current liabilities), and the results reported to users. Thus the whole process of separating the current period's transactions from those of other periods, and the separation of items between the three accounting reports, is one of classification. It is evident that an income statement without any classification of expenses, or a balance sheet without any classification of assets or of liabilities and proprietorship, would have very restricted usefulness.

Classification is the logical arrangement of data into groups where each group has some common significant characteristic which distinguishes it from other groups. In classifying data, it is essential that the groups are mutually exclusive and that, taken together, they are exhaustive of the whole class of items. Three rules of classification should be noted:

1. The basis of division should be some common and significant (to the end-use) quality possessed by the whole class of items.

2. Each act of division must have one basis only so as to avoid cross division.

3. All groups taken together must cover the classification of all items.

A variety of bases of classification are used in accounting, of which the more important ones are as follows:

1. Inherent properties or natural classification of items (e.g. cash, wages, sales), which forms the basis for the initial classification of the aspects of each transaction into accounts.

2. Time periods. Time underlies the division of items between accounting periods, and the classification of assets according to liquidity and of liabilities according to dates of payment, and to a large extent the division of expenses between fixed and variable.

3. Functions. The three final accounting reports are functionally divided between items relating to the earning of income, the allocation of income, and the financial position of the firm. Expenses in the income statement are divided according to the selling, administrative, and financing functions of operations.

4. Administrative responsibility to reflect staff responsibilities where delegation of authority is an essential feature of the organization. Staff may be assigned according to functions, departments, territories, and so on.

5. Relationship to major activities. This is used to distinguish between operating and non-operating items in the income statement.

6. Normality of occurrence. This may displace or supplement major activity as the basis for distinguishing between operating and non-operating items.

7. Relationship to changes in volume of activity enables the distinction between fixed and variable expenses to be made.

8. Sources of funds. The distinctions between liabilities and proprietorship, and the distinctions within each group, are made according to this criterion.

9. Tangibility is applied as a basis of classification for some assets.

10. Intended use is used to supplement the time basis in the classification of assets according to liquidity.

The standards for accounting information must be borne in mind when selecting the bases of classification for use in accounting reports. The bases must enable information to be provided which is appropriate to the user's needs and to disclose all significant relationships in the reports. The bases used must be applied consistently to enable valid comparisons of items or groups within the reports and over time. It may be necessary to present the same reports classified in alternative ways so as to convey all the significant relationships required. For example, one version of the income statement may emphasize results by territories or departments, and another one the variability of items according to changes in the volume of activity.

There is significant scope for classification improvements in the reports of many Australian companies. A commonly used classification of assets is that into current, investments, fixed and intangible assets; while liabilities and proprietorship are often classified as current and deferred liabilities (separately), reserves and provisions, and proprietorship. Revenue contra items are frequently classified as expenses even though the closest basis of association is with revenue and not the using up of resources. Company profit tax is normally shown as an expense, notwithstanding that its basis of association is taxable income and not revenue or the using up of resources to generate revenue.

### FURTHER READING

A.A.A. "The Matching Concept." *Accounting Review* (April 1965).
Fitzgerald, A. A., and Schumer, L. A. *Classification in Accounting.* Sydney: Butterworths, 1952. Chaps. 1 and 4.
Gordon, M. J., and Shillinglaw, G. *Accounting: A Management Approach.* 4th ed. Homewood, Illinois: Richard D. Irwin, 1969.
Mathews, R. L. *The Accounting Framework.* 3rd ed. Melbourne: Cheshire, 1971. Chaps. 2 and 3.

### NOTE

1. The trial balance and adjustments are examined in chap. 10.

### QUESTIONS AND EXERCISES

[Solution to problem marked * is given in Appendix 4.]

Prepare brief written answers to each of the following questions:

1.  a.   Explain in general terms the concepts of income, maintaining capital intact, and financial position.
    b.   Explain the above concepts in terms of the historical cost valuation system.

2.  Briefly distinguish between the functions served by, and the contents of, the income and appropriation statements and the balance sheet.

3.  What general objectives govern the classification of accounting reports?

4.  What are the main rules of classification?
    Is the following classification of the Australian population logical? How should it be classified?

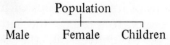

5.  In the income statement, what is the distinction between:
    i.    Operating and non-operating items?
    ii.   Expenses and losses?
    iii.  Fixed and variable expenses?
    iv.   Selling, administration, and finance expenses?
    Illustrate your answer in each case, and indicate the basis of classification used.

6.  Explain the concepts of gross profit, net operating profit, and net profit.

7. Explain the matching principle. What major problem areas are involved in its application?

8. Explain and illustrate the statement that "most assets other than monetary ones are simply resources waiting to be used up in the process of earning revenue".

9. Are periodic income statements completely factual? Discuss.

10. In the balance sheet, distinguish between:
    i.   Current and long-term assets
    ii.  Current and long-term liabilities
    iii. Liabilities and proprietorship
    iv.  Contributed capital, capital reserves, and revenue reserves.
    Illustrate your answer in each case and indicate the basis of classification used.

11. Frequently, in the published reports of Australian companies, assets are classified into: current, fixed, investments, and intangible assets. What bases underlie this classification? Is it a logical one?

12. What is the balance sheet equation? How would you relate it to the twofold flow aspects of transactions involving balance sheet items?

13. The assets, liabilities and proprietorship of Carter's Corner Store are listed below. Arrange them in the form of a balance sheet.

|  | $ |
|---|---|
| Cash on Hand | 80 |
| Bank Overdraft | 700 |
| Accounts Receivable | 290 |
| Accounts Payable | 200 |
| Salaries Payable | 100 |
| Premises | 15,000 |
| Merchandise Inventory | 1,630 |
| G. Carter Capital | 10,000 |
| Mortgage | 8,000 |
| Shop Fixtures | 2,000 |

For each of the following firms, trial balances have been extracted from the ledgers after all appropriate internal adjustments have been made to the transaction data to permit the preparation of final accounting reports. Determine the income earned for the year and the financial position of the firm at the end of the year, in appropriately classified accounting reports. Briefly explain the significance of the income figures calculated and the measures of financial position.

*14. T. Bee – Pharmacist

*Trial Balance as at 31 December 197X*

|  | Dr. $ | Cr. $ |
|---|---|---|
| Accounts Receivable | 760 | |
| Accounts Payable | | 900 |
| Advertising | 200 | |
| Bank | 2,970 | |
| Cost of Merchandise Sold | 10,300 | |

| | | |
|---|---:|---:|
| Interest | 150 | |
| Merchandise Inventory | 1,260 | |
| Mortgage | | 4,000 |
| Salary (of employee) | 2,400 | |
| Salary Owing | | 100 |
| Shop Fittings | 1,600 | |
| Shop Premises | 10,000 | |
| Sales | | 18,000 |
| Sundry Expenses | 360 | |
| T. Bee Capital | | 7,000 |
| | $30,000 | $30,000 |

15.   T. Ford's Service Station

*Trial Balance as at 31 December 197X*

| | Dr. $ | Cr. $ |
|---|---:|---:|
| Accounts Receivable | 640 | |
| Accounts Payable | | 1,500 |
| Advertising | 470 | |
| Accumulated Depreciation of Building | | 3,000 |
| Building (at cost) | 10,000 | |
| Cash at Bank | 820 | |
| Cost of Petrol Sold | 26,000 | |
| Council Rates | 330 | |
| Depreciation of Buildings | 500 | |
| Electricity | 640 | |
| Interest | 500 | |
| Inventory | 2,000 | |
| Land | 15,000 | |
| Mortgage | | 7,000 |
| Sales | | 39,000 |
| T. Ford – Capital | | 15,000 |
| T. Ford – Drawings | 3,000 | |
| Wages (of employees) | 5,600 | |
| | $65,500 | $65,500 |

16.   Avant Garde Boutique Pty. Ltd.

*Trial Balance as at 30 June 197X*

| | Dr. $ | Cr. $ |
|---|---:|---:|
| Accounts Receivable | 7,400 | |
| Accounts Payable | | 2,500 |
| Advertising | 2,400 | |
| Bank Overdraft | | 1,800 |
| Cost of Merchandise Sold | 27,000 | |
| Dividends Paid | 3,000 | |
| Income Tax | 2,700 | |

| | | |
|---|---:|---:|
| Income Tax Payable | | 2,700 |
| Insurance | 700 | |
| Lighting | 500 | |
| Merchandise Inventory | 10,600 | |
| Paid-up Capital | | 12,000 |
| Rent | 1,800 | |
| Rent Paid in Advance | 400 | |
| Reserves | | 3,000 |
| Salaries | 7,600 | |
| Sales | | 45,000 |
| Shop Fittings | 4,600 | |
| Unappropriated Profits, 1 July | | 1,700 |
| | $68,700 | $68,700 |

17.   Trading Enterprises Pty. Ltd.

*Trial Balance as at 30 June 1970*

| | Dr. $ | Cr. $ |
|---|---:|---:|
| Paid-up Capital | | 25,000 |
| Trade Creditors | | 12,250 |
| Mortgage | | 25,000 |
| Trade Debtors | 26,250 | |
| Bank | | 5,400 |
| Commonwealth Bonds | 5,000 | |
| Land and Buildings | 51,000 | |
| Advertising | 5,000 | |
| Sales | | 140,000 |
| Cost of Goods Sold | 80,000 | |
| Merchandise Inventory (30.6.70) | 18,000 | |
| Goodwill | 11,850 | |
| Interest on Bonds | | 200 |
| Interest on Mortgage | 425 | |
| Rates          ) Paid 1.7.69 | 700 | |
| Insurance ) | 300 | |
| Office Salaries | 5,200 | |
| Salesmen's Salaries | 10,000 | |
| Delivery Expenses | 4,250 | |
| Sundry Office Expenses | 2,725 | |
| Audit Fees | 475 | |
| Directors' Fees | 2,700 | |
| Dividends Paid | 12,000 | |
| Company Tax Paid | 7,200 | |
| Appropriation Account (1.7.69) | | 17,150 |
| General Reserves | | 21,000 |
| Salesmen's Commissions | 3,925 | |
| Accum. Depreciation of Buildings | | 6,000 |
| Estimated Bad Debts | | 1,250 |
| Depreciation of Buildings | 3,000 | |
| Estimated Credit Losses | 3,250 | |
| | $253,250 | $253,250 |

18. Explain why all transactions affecting the income statement automatically affect the balance sheet, and why the reverse situation does not hold. Illustrate your answer using the following transactions:

|      |                              | $      |
|------|------------------------------|--------|
| i.   | Cash sales                   | 1,000  |
| ii.  | Credit sales                 | 3,000  |
| iii. | Purchases on credit          | 2,500  |
| iv.  | Wages paid                   | 800    |
| v.   | Purchase of plant on credit  | 10,000 |
| vi.  | Payment of creditors         | 6,000  |
| vii. | Cash collected from debtors  | 5,000  |

19. Demonstrate that income is the increase in net assets over a period using both the income statement approach and the comparative balance sheet approach. Use the following data for the demonstration:

|      |                                     | $       |
|------|-------------------------------------|---------|
| 1.   | Sales of merchandise for cash       | 120,000 |
| ii.  | Cost of merchandise sold            | 76,000  |
| iii. | Wages paid                          | 21,000  |
| iv.  | Advertising paid                    | 3,000   |
| v.   | Depreciation of buildings           | 5,000   |
| vi.  | Purchases of merchandise on credit  | 83,000  |
| vii. | Cash paid to creditors              | 74,000  |

There were no other operating items during the period. The balance sheet at the beginning of the period was:

|                      | $       | $        |           | $        |
|----------------------|---------|----------|-----------|----------|
| Cash                 |         | 31,000   | Creditors | 25,000   |
| Inventories          |         | 34,000   | Capital   | 115,000  |
| Buildings            | 100,000 |          |           |          |
| Less Assumulated     |         |          |           |          |
| Depreciation         | 25,000  |          |           |          |
|                      |         | 75,000   |           |          |
| Total Assets         |         | $140,000 | Total Funds | $140,000 |

What is the income of the period and the capital maintenance amount? Prepare an income statement and an end-of-period balance sheet as part of your answer.

# Chapter 7
# Accounting for Revenue Adjustments

The measurement of periodic income must begin with the determination of revenue for the period. In accounting for revenue, two major problems must frequently be resolved — when to record a selling transaction as giving rise to revenue, and how much revenue to recognize in the transaction. These problems may not occur in the simplest situation of the cash and carry sale, but they can be important issues in other situations. Since the first problem raises complicated issues, its analysis is postponed until the more procedural work is completed, and, until then, it is assumed that the sale is recorded on the point of delivery of the goods.

The second set of problems in accounting for revenue is considered here. These problems arise because the quoted sale price need not be the ultimate amount collected in cash from the sale. Rather, adjustments to gross revenue for discounts, sales returns, and allowances, and, in the case of credit sales, for expected credit losses, may need to be made to determine the net revenue earned in the period.

Net revenue is the eventual amount of cash likely to be collected from the sales (as recognized) of the period. Selling transactions which do not ultimately materialize in cash are not sales, and the effect of the original sale entry should be nullified. However the method used in accounting to accomplish this does not directly cancel the initial entry; rather, a *contra entry* is used. A contra entry is one made in a special contra ledger account to offset an earlier entry in a related account. The contra account must always be shown as a deduction from the related account — it should never appear as an independent account. Thus, debit items are accumulated in a contra account to offset credit entries in the main account in order to obtain aggregate debits and aggregate credits relating to the item, rather than just the net balance, because the gross figures are useful; and vice versa for credit contra accounts to offset main debit accounts.

## SALES OR CASH DISCOUNTS

Sales or cash discounts are those allowed for prompt payments of accounts. Frequently firms grant trade credit to customers, and discounts are given as an incentive for prompt payment of amounts owing on credit sales. Generally the discount rate represents a very high effective annual interest rate; for example 2/10, n/30 (2 per cent discount for payment within ten days; otherwise full price is payable within the maximum credit period of thirty days) is approximately 37 per cent per annum simple rate of interest – the 2 per cent discount represents a 2 per cent interest charge on a loan for twenty days. These interest rates are much higher than the rates normally payable on borrowed finance, and they represent a strong inducement to pay within the discount period.

Sales discounts must be distinguished from trade discounts, which are reductions off the retail price for various classes of buyers or sizes of orders. Trade discounts are merely devices for quoting different prices to different buyers, and no record is made of them. The sale is recorded at the relevant price charged to the customer.

Two methods of recording sales discounts may be used. Under the *gross price method,* sales are recorded at the full price charged and no record is made of the discount at the time of sale. The discount is recorded at the time of cash receipt if the customer takes advantage of the discount terms and pays within the stipulated period; otherwise no record of the discount is made. The entry on sale is:

|  |  | $ |  |
|---|---|---|---|
| Accounts Receivable | Dr. | 100 | (gross price) |
| Sales | Cr. | 100 | |

On cash receipt within the discount period, the entry is:

| Cash | Dr. | 98 |
|---|---|---|
| Sales Discount Allowed | Dr. | 2 |
| Accounts Receivable | Cr. | 100 |

If the customer pays beyond the discount period, and forfeits the discount, the entry is:

| Cash | Dr. | 100 |
|---|---|---|
| Accounts Receivable | Cr. | 100 |

Hence only the discounts taken are recorded, and the discounts not taken are hidden in sales revenue. The Sales Discount account is a *contra account,* and it must be deducted from sales in the profit and loss statement. The method has the advantage of simplicity, but it is criticized because it hides the discounts lost in sales revenue.

At the end of the accounting period, the discounts liable to be taken by customers on account of recent sales should be estimated and be deducted from both sales and accounts receivable, if the amount is significant. This entry reduces both accounts to their expected realizable values. The entry is:

| Sales Discounts Allowed | Dr. |
|---|---|
| Estimated Discount Allowable | Cr. |

as mentioned above. Sales Discount Allowed is a sales contra account, while the Estimated Discount Allowable is a contra account deducted from accounts receivable in the balance sheet.

Under the *net price method* of recording discounts, discounts allowable are recorded at the time of the sale, and sales are recorded at the net price as the firm expects to receive this amount only. However the customer is still debited with the full amount. The entry to record the sale is:

|  |  | $ |
|---|---|---|
| Accounts Receivable | Dr. | 100 |
| Sales | Cr. | 98 |
| Sales Discount Allowable | Cr. | 2 |

On receipt of cash within the discount period, the entry is:

|  |  | $ |
|---|---|---|
| Cash | Dr. | 98 |
| Sales Discount Allowable | Dr. | 2 |
| Accounts Receivable | Cr. | 100 |

On receipt of cash beyond the discount period, the entry is:

|  |  |  | $ |
|---|---|---|---|
| (a) | Bank | Dr. | 100 |
|  | Accounts Receivable | Cr. | 100 |
| (b) | Sales Discount Allowable | Dr. | 2 |
|  | Cash Discount Gained | Cr. | 2 |

Where the customer pays his bill too late to take advantage of the discount, that discount is gained by the firm. This is regarded as a profit made on financing customers rather than on selling and is shown as an item of non-operating revenue in the profit and loss statement.

Thus under this method, the Sales Discount Allowable account is credited each time a credit sale is made with the customer's discount entitlement and debited each time cash is received within the discount period or the credit period expires. The balance in the account at any time represents the discount that customers are entitled to if they pay their debts on time. Thus there is no need for any entry to recognize unclaimed discounts at the end of the financial year as in the gross price method. The Sales Discounts Allowable account is a contra account to debtors in the balance sheet. Discounts not claimed are shown as a gain to the firm, and sales are shown at the net realizable amount throughout.

## SALES RETURNS AND ALLOWANCES

Customers may return goods because they differ from those ordered, they are defective or damaged, and so on. Similarly, allowances for these reasons or for overcharging may be made to the customer where he retains the goods. Returns and allowances are recorded as:

|                               |     | $  |
| ----------------------------- | --- | -- |
| Sales Returns and Allowances  | Dr. | 20 |
| Accounts Receivable           | Cr. | 20 |

The Sales Returns account (or returns inwards) is a contra account which is deducted from sales in the profit and loss statement. Management should be informed of the total sales returns, as they indicate the selling of defective products, careless packing, and so on, and these factors can jeopardize the firm's trading reputation. Debiting them directly to the sales account hides this information from management.

### BAD DEBTS OR CREDIT LOSSES

Where the firm sells goods on credit, bad debts or credit losses are incurred if a customer does not pay for the merchandise purchased. Bad debts have been a primary factor in most of the recent spectacular crashes of large retailing companies, and many millions of dollars were lost. In all these cases, the credit control procedures were excessively lax, and hopelessly inadequate allowances were made for bad debts.

The accounting for bad debts involves a classification of customers accounts into three categories — good, doubtful, and bad. Good debts are those which the firm confidently expects to be paid in full; doubtful debts are those which the firm expects *may* not be paid; while bad debts are those that the firm has given up all hope of collecting and are recognized as worthless. The major problem being analyzed here concerns the middle class of doubtful debts, as they must be estimated and recorded appropriately. The potential bad debts associated with the current year's credit sales must be estimated because it may be several years before the debt is finally declared to be bad. This occurs when the debtor is declared bankrupt, or has been missing for some time, and so on, and the firm has given up hope of recovering the money. The doubtful debts included in the current year's credit sales must be estimated and deducted from sales in a contra account (Estimated Credit Losses); and the doubtful debts included in accounts receivable must be estimated and deducted therefrom in a contra account (Estimated Bad Debts). Use of the word "estimated" in each account title signifies that the debts are in the doubtful stage. Revenue, profits, and accounts receivable are overstated if the doubtful debts are not estimated and deducted from revenue and accounts receivable. Both these accounts should show the cash expected to be ultimately received.

A combination of several methods should be used to estimate doubtful debts. Past experience should be analyzed to determine the proportion of bad debts in credit sales, and the factors with which bad debts seem to be associated, such as particular classes of customers, geographical areas, branches or departments of the firm, high-pressure salesmanship, and state of the economy (and in particular, the extent or absence of overtime work and full employment). No fixed proportion of credit sales should be used because the determinants of bad debts are not constant. As a complementary method, the accounts receivable should be "aged", i.e., ranked in groups according to their age, and past experience, plus information about particular debtors who show signs of defaulting in their payments, used to determine the proportion of bad debts likely to exist in each age group. In general, the older the age group, the higher the proportion of bad debts included in it. Overdue customers' accounts should be carefully scrutinized and assessed. The operation of the credit system and the debt-collection processes should be reviewed to ensure that proper assessments of customer credit-worthiness are made and that credit sales are not necessarily made to everyone who wants them, that customers are notified of instalments due, and that the firm takes prompt action to recover overdue instalments. Laxity in the credit department of the firm is likely to result in the proportion of overdue debts, and ultimately bad debts, increasing significantly. These reviews and estimates ought to be made at least monthly for the effective control of credit policy and for the preparation of interim accounting reports. They ought to be recorded in the ledger at the time each review is made, rather than only at the end of the year.

The recording procedure in accounting for doubtful debts is as follows. Where the estimate for bad debts is first made, the entry is:

| | | |
|---|---|---|
| Estimated Credit Losses | Dr. | (or Doubtful debts account) |
| Estimated Bad Debts | Cr. | (or Provision for doubtful debts account) |

The Estimated Credit Losses account is a sales contra account and must be deducted from it in the profit and loss statement. Estimated credit losses should never be debited to the sales account because the amount involved is only an estimate of what sales will eventually be nullified, and management should be informed of their amount. At this stage of the proceedings, the credit sales are not bad ones, but there is the expectation of them being so, and the account title should indicate this. The loss results from selling on credit during the period and, as it has to be anticipated, the name "Estimated Credit Losses" appropriately describes the content of the account. Likewise, the Estimated Bad Debts account is a contra one attaching to the Accounts Receivable account in the balance sheet. The account is as its name implies – an estimate of future bad debts included in debtors' balances, i.e., of doubtful debts. Expected bad debts should never be credited to Accounts Receivable, since this would eliminate the debts due in the same way as cash payments by debtors. The debts remain due in the firm's accounts until they are written off as bad. Of course, this does not affect the firm's legal rights to pursue recovery of the debt still further; it merely records the firm's belief about the chances of recovering the money so as to provide a more accurate measure of income and financial position.

By accounting for doubtful debts in this way, credit losses are anticipated and recognized in the income statement for the period in which the sale takes place rather than that in which the cash is finally considered to be uncollectable, and the value of debtors in the balance sheet is reckoned at the amount expected to be collected from them.

It should be understood that, in both cases, the deductions are of *estimated* amounts for credit losses and bad debts because of the time lag between the point of sale and ultimate recognition that the cash will not be collected. The estimated credit losses included in the gross credit sales of the period are deducted from sales in the income statement under the name of credit losses in order to determine the amount of cash expected to be ultimately collected from the period's credit sales; and the estimated bad debts included in gross accounts receivable are deducted therefrom in the balance sheet to show the cash expected to be ultimately collected from the customers owing money at the end of the period.

Secondly, when at a later date the firm decides to write off a doubtful debt as a bad debt, the amount is charged to the Estimated Bad Debts accounts. This has the effect of matching the subsequent fact of the bad debt against the previously made estimate. Given perfect foresight, the two would cancel out. The estimate was inadequate if bad debts exceed it; while, if there is a credit balance in the Estimate account, either the estimate was excessive or some doubtful debts have still to be written off if all cash from the relevant period's sales has not yet been collected. In any case, the balance is carried forward and is brought up to date again at the end of the next accounting period. Bad debts should not be charged against the Estimated Credit Losses Account unless the bad debts relate to the *current* period's sales. However, because of the time lag involved, along with the regular updating of the bad debts estimate, this would be an unusual circumstance. The entry to record a bad debt is:

Estimated Bad Debts              Dr.
Accounts Receivable              Cr.

The credit entry to Accounts Receivable eliminates the debt from the balance of that account. It should be noted that there is no separate account for bad debts written off under this method.

If it should happen that a bad debt is subsequently recovered, the entry is:

Accounts Receivable              Dr.
Bad Debts Recovered              Cr.

The debit to Accounts Receivable reinstates the debt, and the cash received from the debtor is recorded in the usual way. The Bad Debts Recovered may be shown as an item of non-operating revenue in the income statement.

A Bad Debts Recovered account is credited rather than the entry to write off the bad debt being reversed, so as not to distort the balance in the Estimated Bad Debts account (which is the amount of doubtful debts included in current debtors balances).

### Examples

1.  The following information is extracted from a firm's trial balance as at 30 June.

|  |  | $ |
| --- | --- | --- |
| Accounts Receivable | Dr. | 30,000 |
| Estimated Credit Losses | Dr. | 2,000 |
| Estimated Bad Debts | Cr. | 1,500 |
| Sales | Cr. | 75,000 |

After an analysis of debtors' accounts at the end of the year, it is proposed that (1) additional bad debts of $1,200 be recognized and written off, and (2) that the estimate for bad debts on remaining debtors' balances be raised to $1,900.

Record this information in ledger accounts, and show the relevant sections of the final reports.

Accounts Receivable Account

|  |  | Dr. $ | Cr. $ | Balance $ |
| --- | --- | --- | --- | --- |
| June 30 | Balance |  |  | 30,000 Dr. |
|  | Estimated Bad Debts (1) |  | 1,200 | 28,800 Dr. |

Estimated Bad Debts (Contra Accounts Receivable)

|  |  |  |  |  |
| --- | --- | --- | --- | --- |
| June 30 | Balance |  |  | 1,500 Cr. |
|  | Accounts Receivable (1) | 1,200 |  | 300 Cr. |
|  | Estimated Credit Losses (2) |  | 1,600 | 1,900 Cr. |

Sales Account

|  |  |  |  |  |
| --- | --- | --- | --- | --- |
| June 30 | Balance |  |  | 75,000 Cr. |

Estimated Credit Losses (Contra Sales)

|  |  |  |  |  |
| --- | --- | --- | --- | --- |
| June 30 | Balance |  |  | 2,000 Dr. |
|  | Estimated Bad Debts (2) | 1,600 |  | 3,600 Dr. |

*Profit and Loss Statement*

|  | $ |
|---|---|
| Sales | 75,000 |
| Less Estimated Credit Losses | 3,600 |
| Net Sales | $71,400 |

*Balance Sheet*

|  | $ |
|---|---|
| Accounts Receivable | 28,800 |
| Less Estimated Bad Debts | 1,900 |
| Net Accounts Receivable | $26,900 |

NOTE:

i.   The Estimated Credit Losses account is already open from the regular review of debtors' accounts made during the year and/or from charging a given percentage of credit sales to it.

ii.  Bad debts recognized during the year have already been written off, and the balances of Accounts Receivable and the Estimated Bad Debts accounts are derived after this event.

iii. New bad debts are written off against the Estimated Bad Debts account, and not in the Estimated Credit Losses account.

2.   Superfi Electronics is a specialized retailer of high-quality sound reproduction equipment. All sales are made on credit. Company policy is to provide initially for estimated credit losses at the rate of 1 per cent of credit sales, and subsequently to review customers' accounts regularly for the possibility of bad debts. An ageing schedule of debtors' balances is prepared as part of this review.

The trial balance for 30 November includes the following account balances:

|  |  | $ |
|---|---|---|
| Accounts Receivable | Dr. | 800,000 |
| Estimated Bad Debts | Cr. | 30,000 |
| Sales | Cr. | 9,000,000 |
| Estimated Credit Losses | Dr. | 90,000 |

Transactions for December were:

i.   Sales (all credit) $1,200,000
ii.  Cash collected from current customers $500,000
iii. $3,000 was recovered from one former customer whose debt had been written off as bad a year previously.

The ageing schedule of debtors' balances revealed the following situation:

| Age of Accounts | Amounts Receivable | Uncollectable Estimate |
|---|---|---|
|  | $ | % |
| 0 – < 1 month | 1,200,000 | 1 |
| 1 – < 4 months | 200,000 | 6 |
| 4 – <12 months | 90,000 | 10 |
| 1 year and over | 10,000 | 100 |
|  | $1,500,000 |  |

It was decided to write off the debts more than one year overdue as bad, and to revise the estimate of bad debts on remaining debtors balances in accordance with the ageing schedule.

Record the above information in ledger accounts and show the relevant parts of the final reports.

Accounts Receivable Account

|  |  | Dr. $ | Cr. $ | Balance $ |
|---|---|---|---|---|
| Nov. 30 | Balance |  |  | 800,000 Dr. |
| Dec. 31 | Sales | 1,200,000 |  | 2,000,000 Dr. |
|  | Bank |  | 500,000 | 1,500,000 Dr. |
|  | Bad Debts Recovered | 3,000 |  | 1,503,000 Dr. |
|  | Bank |  | 3,000 | 1,500,000 Dr. |
|  | Estimated Bad Debts |  | 10,000 | 1,490,000 Dr. |

Estimated Bad Debts Account

| Nov. 30 | Balance |  |  | 30,000 Cr. |
|---|---|---|---|---|
| Dec. 31 | Estimated Credit Losses |  | 12,000 | 42,000 Cr. |
|  | Accounts Receivable | 10,000 |  | 32,000 Cr. |
|  | Estimated Credit Losses |  | 1,000 | 33,000 Cr. |

Sales Account

| Nov. 30 | Balance |  |  | 9,000,000 Cr. |
|---|---|---|---|---|
| Dec. 31 | Accounts Receivable |  | 1,200,000 | 10,200,000 Cr. |

Estimated Credit Losses Account

| Nov. 30 | Balance |  |  | 90,000 Dr. |
|---|---|---|---|---|
| Dec. 31 | Estimated Bad Debts | 12,000 |  | 102,000 Dr. |
|  | Estimated Bad Debts | 1,000 |  | 103,000 Dr. |

Bank Account

| Dec. 31 | Accounts Receivable | 500,000 |  | 500,000 Dr. |
|---|---|---|---|---|
| Dec. 31 | Accounts Receivable | 3,000 |  | 503,000 Dr. |

Bad Debts Recovered Account

| Dec. 31 | Accounts Receivable |  | 3,000 | 3,000 Cr. |
|---|---|---|---|---|

*Profit and Loss Statement*

|  | $ |
|---|---|
| Sales | 10,200,000 |
| Less Estimated Credit Losses | 103,000 |
|  | $10,097,000 |
|  |  |
| Non-operating Income |  |
| Bad Debts Recovered | $3,000 |

*Balance Sheet*

|  | $ | $ |
|---|---|---|
| Bank |  | 503,000 |
| Accounts Receivable | 1,490,000 |  |
| Less Estimated Bad Debts | 33,000 | 1,457,000 |
|  |  | $1,960,000 |

## ACCRUED INCOME

In some cases a firm receives income from sundry sources. It may receive interest or dividend income on investments, commission on selling the products of other firms, rent from part of its premises leased out, and so on. Where any such income is owing to it at balance date, the amount should be estimated and recorded as income accrued. For example, if $5,000 interest on government bonds is accrued on 30 June, the entry is:

|  |  | $ |
|---|---|---|
| Interest Receivable Accrued | Dr. | 5,000 |
| Interest on Bonds | Cr. | 5,000 |

The first account is shown as a current asset in the balance sheet, while the second appears as non-operating income in the profit and loss statement.

## FURTHER READING

A.S.A. Pronouncement. "The Valuation of Book Debts, Bad Debts and the Provision for Doubtful Debts." *Australian Accountant* (December 1967).

Carrington, A. S., Battersby, G. B., and Howitt, G. *Accounting. An Information System.* Christchurch. Whitcombe and Tombs, 1975. Chaps. 7 and 9.

Gordon, M. J., and Shillinglaw, G. *Accounting: A Management Approach.* 4th ed. Homewood, Illinois: Richard D. Irwin, 1969. Chap. 5, pp. 134–40.

Mathews, R. L. *The Accounting Framework.* 3rd ed. Melbourne: Cheshire, 1971. Chap. 3.

## QUESTIONS AND EXERCISES

[Solutions to problems marked * are given in Appendix 4.]

Prepare brief written answers to each of the following five questions:

1.  What is the distinction between gross revenue and net revenue? What items can account for the difference?

2.  Explain the nature of, and reasons for the use of, contra accounts. Give illustrations.

3.  Distinguish between bad debts and doubtful debts.

4.  What purpose is served by "ageing" customers' accounts?

5. Explain the rationale underlying the method of accounting for bad and doubtful debts.

6. i. Record the following transactions in the ledger accounts of Jason and Sons, using:
   a. the gross price method
   b. the net price method
   for recording sales discounts.
   ii. Show the revenue section of the income statement.
   iii. Consider the merits of each approach.
   Aug. 1. Sold goods to A. Green $500, terms 2/10, n/30.
   Sold goods to J. Brown $100, terms 2/10, n/30.
   Sold goods to C. Black $200, terms 2/10, n/30.
   Aug. 9. Green settled his account.
   Aug. 28. Brown settled his account.

*7. Record the following transactions in ledger accounts and show the revenue section of the income statement.

   Apr. 1. Sold goods to B. Jay on credit $670.
   Apr. 1. Sold goods to R. Dunn for cash $480.
   Apr. 3. Jay returned defective goods and was allowed $120 for same.
   Apr. 3. Dunn claimed he was overcharged by $40, and after investigation the claim was allowed and the money refunded.

8. Record the following transactions in the ledger accounts of Jolly Enterprises, using:
   i. the gross price method
   ii. the net price method
   of recording sales discounts, and show the revenue section of the income statement.
   Mar. 1. Sold goods to A. Allan $400, terms 2/10, n/30.
   Sold goods to B. Black $300, terms 2/10, n/30.
   Sold goods to C. Cliff $200, terms 2/10, n/30.
   Mar. 9. Allan settled his account.
   Mar. 28. Black settled his account.

9. Record the following transactions in the ledger accounts and show the revenue section of the income statement for PBX Ltd.

   Mar. 1. Sold goods to A.B. on credit $540.
   Sold goods to C.D. for cash $460.
   Mar. 7. A.B. returned defective goods and was allowed $140 for same.
   Mar. 9. C.D. claimed he had been overcharged by $60. After investigation the claim was allowed and the money refunded.

Record the following items in ledger accounts and show the relevant sections of the income statement and balance sheet.

10. Year 1 Sold goods to A. Hanson $2,000, B. Allan $3,000 and D. Munro $1,500. By the end of the year, had collected from Hanson $1,600, Allan $2,400 and Munro $1,100. Hanson's balance was long overdue, and, as constant efforts had failed to make him pay the amount owing, it was decided to provide for it as a possible bad debt.
    Year 2 Collected amounts owing from all debtors except Hanson, who was declared bankrupt and was able to pay only 20 cents in the dollar.

*11. The Ajax Textile Co. adopts the practice of providing for expected credit losses at the rate of 3 per cent of its credit sales. During 197X, its credit sales amounted to $650,000 and it recognized customers' debts of $14,000 as uncollectable. Record these items in ledger accounts.

12. The Pie Squared Co. has found from experience that 2 per cent of its credit sales eventually prove to be uncollectable and it records anticipated bad debts monthly on this basis. During May, credit sales were $100,000; one customer who owed $1,400 was declared bankrupt but able to pay 50 cents in the dollar, and this was duly paid; a former customer whose debt for $600 was written off as bad a year previously has now paid the amount owing by him. Record these items in ledger accounts.

13. Mammoth Trading Enterprises Ltd. began trading operations on 1 January 1969. The following information has been extracted from the firm's trial balance of 31 December 1969:

|  |  | $ |
|---|---|---|
| Accounts Receivable (Debtors) | Dr. | 30,000 |
| Cash — Sales | Cr. | 150,000 |
| Credit | Cr. | 150,000 |

Management estimates that 2 per cent of the outstanding debtors' balances will not be recovered.

*Required:*
1. Record the estimate of credit losses in the ledger accounts.
2. Show the relevant sections of the final reports.

14. The following information is extracted from Dalton's Ltd. trial balance as at 30 June.

|  |  | $ |
|---|---|---|
| Accounts Receivable | Dr. | 45,000 |
| Estimated Credit Losses | Dr. | 2,500 |
| Estimated Bad Debts | Cr. | 2,250 |
| Sales — Cash | Cr. | 30,000 |
| — Credit | Cr. | 160,000 |

An analysis of debtors' accounts indicates that additional bad debts of $1,500 should be recognized and written off and that the estimate for bad debts on remaining debtors' balances should be raised to $3,000.
*Required:*
i. Record this information in the relevant ledger accounts.
ii. Show the relevant sections of the final reports.

15. Sellers Ltd. has found from experience that 2 per cent of its credit sales eventually prove to be uncollectable and it records anticipated bad debts monthly on this basis. The following information relates to March:

i. Credit sales for month $150,000.
ii. A customer who owed $800 was declared bankrupt but was able to pay 40 cents in the dollar. This was duly paid.
iii. A former customer whose debt of $500 had been written off as bad a year previously paid the amount owing by him.

*Required:*
a. Record these transactions in the ledger accounts.
b. Show the relevant sections of the final reports.

16. The Hasty Mail Order Co. determines its estimate of bad debts from an analysis of its debtors' accounts, and on 30 June an "ageing" schedule revealed the following data:

| Age of Accounts | Amounts Receivable | Uncollectable |
|---|---|---|
| | $ | % |
| 0 – 60 days | 120,000 | 1 |
| 61 – 120 days | 100,000 | 2 |
| 121 – 180 days | 70,000 | 10 |
| Over 180 days | 40,000 | 20 |

At 30 June, the existing credit balance in the Estimated Bad Debts account was $3,000 and balance in the Estimated Credit Losses account was $46,400 debit.

Record in ledger accounts the adjustment necessary to provide for the revised estimate of bad debts.

17. The practice of the management of the Dazzle Corporation has been to provide for credit losses on a monthly basis at the rate of 1 per cent on credit sales, and at the year's end to make a detailed analysis of accounts receivable to determine more accurately the allowance for uncollectable accounts. Credit sales for the year amounted to $300,000; the bad debts written off were $1,400; and the cash collected was $250,600. The balances in the Accounts Receivable and Estimated Bad Debts accounts on 1 January last were $50,000 debit and $1,500 credit, respectively.

On 31 December, an age analysis of accounts receivable showed the following:

| Age of Accounts | Amounts Receivable | Uncollectable |
|---|---|---|
| | $ | % |
| 0 – 30 days | 60,000 | ¼ |
| 31 – 60 days | 20,000 | 2 |
| 61 – 90 days | 10,000 | 5 |
| 91 – 120 days | 5,000 | 20 |
| Over 120 days | 3,000 | 50 |

On the basis of past experience and evidence about individual overdue customers accounts, management estimated the uncollectable proportions as given above, and the estimate of bad debts is to be revised accordingly. Record the above information in ledger accounts and show the relevant parts of the final reports. How should you interpret the net revenue and net accounts receivable figures?

18. The following information is extracted from a firm's trial balance on 31 December:

| | | $ |
|---|---|---|
| Accounts Receivable | Dr. | 200,000 |
| Estimated Bad Debts | Cr. | 4,000 |
| Estimated Credit Losses | Dr. | 8,000 |
| Sales | Cr. | 690,000 |

After an analysis of overdue customers' accounts, it is recommended that bad debts of $5,000 be recognized and written off, and that the estimate for bad debts on remaining debtors' balances be $6,000.

Record the above items in ledger accounts and show the relevant sections of the final reports.

19. Balances on 31 May in the following accounts were:

|  |  | $ |
|---|---|---|
| Accounts Receivable | Dr. | 420,000 |
| Estimated Bad Debts | Cr. | 13,000 |
| Sales | Cr. | 1,600,000 |
| Estimated Credit Losses | Dr. | 16,000 |

During June, sales (all credit) were $150,000, and credit losses were expected to be 1 per cent of sales; Accounts Receivable of $4,500 were recognized as bad and written off as uncollectable; $1,000 was received from a customer whose account had previously been written off as uncollectable; and $120,000 was collected from current customers.

After a review of customers' accounts at the end of June, it was estimated that $11,000 could prove to be uncollectable and that the Estimated Bad Debts account should be adjusted accordingly. Record the above items in ledger accounts and show the relevant sections of the final reports.

*20. Balances in the following accounts of Shindig Company on 30 November were:

|  |  | $ |
|---|---|---|
| Accounts Receivable | Dr. | 800,000 |
| Estimated Bad Debts | Cr. | 30,000 |
| Sales | Cr. | 9,000,000 |
| Estimated Credit Losses | Dr. | 90,000 |

Transactions for December were:

i.   Sales (all credit) $1,000,000.
ii.  Cash collected from customers $500,000.
iii. $2,000 was recovered from one former customer whose debt had been written off as bad a year before.

Company policy was to provide for estimated credit losses at the rate of 1 per cent of credit sales, and to review customers' accounts regularly for the possibility of bad debts. The review on 31 December revealed the following situation:

| Age of Accounts | Amounts Receivable $ | Uncollectable Estimate % |
|---|---|---|
| 0 – 1 month | 1,000,000 | 1 |
| 1 – 4 months | 200,000 | 5 |
| 4 – 12 months | 88,000 | 10 |
| Over 1 year | 12,000 ✓ | 100 |
|  | $1,300,000 |  |

It was decided to write off the debts more than one year overdue as bad, and to revise the estimate of bad debts on remaining debtors' balances in accordance with the ageing schedule.

Record the above information in ledger accounts and show the relevant parts of the final reports. What do the figures for net revenue and net accounts receivable mean?

21. The Bunyeroo Department Store provides for estimated credit losses at the rate of 2 per cent on credit sales, and periodically checks on the adequacy of this estimate by ageing its debtors' accounts. Its trial balance for 31 May includes the following account balances:

|  |  | $ |
|---|---|---|
| Credit Sales | Cr. | 480,000 |
| Estimated Credit Losses | Dr. | 9,600 |
| Accounts Receivable | Dr. | 88,000 |
| Estimated Bad Debts | Cr. | 4,700 |

During June, its credit sales were $42,000, it collected $46,000 from customers, and it wrote off bad debts of $3,000. The final estimate of bad debts is to be revised according to the following ageing schedule of debtors' balances.

| Age of Accounts | Amounts Receivable | Uncollectable Estimate |
|---|---|---|
| | $ | % |
| 0 – 30 days | 42,000 | 1 |
| 31 – 60 days | 28,000 | 5 |
| 61 – 90 days | 7,000 | 10 |
| Over 90 days | 4,000 | 20 |
| | $81,000 | |

Record the above information in ledger accounts.

22. The following accounts are extracted from the trial balance of Hopeful Traders as at 30 November:

| | Dr. $ | Cr. $ |
|---|---|---|
| Accounts Receivable | 290,000 | |
| Estimated Bad Debts | | 12,000 |
| Sales | | 1,400,000 |
| Estimated Credit Losses | 28,000 | |
| Sales Returns | 46,000 | |

During December its sales (all credit) were $100,000; sales returns were $4,000; credit losses at the rate of 2 per cent are to be allowed for; several customers with long overdue accounts to the value of $4,000 were declared bankrupt and they paid 25 cents in the dollar, with the remainder of their accounts being written off as bad debts; $2,000 was recovered from a customer whose account had been written off as a bad debt in the previous year; and $110,000 was collected from current customers. After a review of debtors' accounts at the end of December, it was estimated that $10,000 could prove to be uncollectable, and the Estimated Bad Debts account is to be revised accordingly.

Record the above data in ledger accounts. Show the relevant parts of the final reports, and explain the effect of the final adjustment to the Estimated Credit Losses and Estimated Bad Debts Accounts.

23. Crooks Limited operate a chain of retail stores selling household appliances. All sales are made on credit, and estimated credit losses are initially provided for at the rate of 3 per cent on sales. In addition, an age analysis of customers' accounts is regularly made and the estimate of bad debts is revised in the light of this age analysis and other relevant information.

The trial balance for 30 November includes the following account balances:

|  |  | $ |
|---|---|---|
| Sales | Cr. | 860,000 |
| Estimated Credit Losses | Dr. | 25,800 |
| Accounts Receivable | Dr. | 240,000 |
| Estimated Bad Debts | Cr. | 8,600 |

During December, sales were $140,000, collections from customers were $106,600, and bad debts of $3,400 were recognized and written off. The final estimate of bad debts is to be revised according to the following ageing schedule of customers' accounts:

| Age of Account | Accounts Receivable | Uncollectable Estimate |
|---|---|---|
|  | $ | % |
| 0 – 60 days | 140,000 | 1 |
| 61 – 120 days | 70,000 | 5 |
| 121 – 240 days | 45,000 | 10 |
| Over – 240 days | 15,000 | 20 |
|  | $270,000 |  |

*Required:*

i. Record the above information in ledger accounts.
ii. Show the relevant parts of the income statement and balance sheet as at 31 December.
iii. Briefly explain the meaning of the two sets of items in each final report.

# Chapter 8
# Accounting for Expenses

Having determined the revenue for the period, the next step in the measurement of periodic income and financial position at the end of the period is to measure the resources used up in earning revenue. As with accounting for revenue, several types of problems are involved in measuring the expenses of the period, and the more complicated issues involving valuation problems are postponed until after the technical aspects of preparing the final accounting reports have been completed. The problems in expense recognition to be considered here comprise the determination of the cost of the goods sold during the period, depreciation and amortization, adjustments for services paid for in advance of their use (i.e., prepayments) or after their use (i.e., accrued expenses), and adjustments for stocks of sundry non-merchandise items on hand at the end of the period (e.g., stocks of stationery). These problems are all part of the process of determining periodic income by applying the matching principle and involve the apportionment of items between this accounting period and the future. Some of the items to be recorded do not involve external transactions (for example, depreciation) and these are referred to in accounting as events. However the rules for debit and credit developed for external transactions still apply, viz., debit the account to which the item flows, and credit the account from which it comes.

## INVENTORIES AND THE COST OF MERCHANDISE SOLD

### 1. Time of Recognition of Purchase

The problem here is somewhat analogous, though much simpler, to that of sales recognition. In general, three points of purchase recognition may be considered — the times of order, receipt of the goods, and payment. Time of delivery is normally used — the seller has completed his part of the contract, the price is known, the goods received can be checked against the order to ascertain that the order has been accurately fulfilled, and that there are no defects. If the delivery basis is used, goods on order but not received are not included in purchases, in inventory balance, or in accounts payable.

### 2. The Value of Purchases and Purchase Discounts

Again, analogous to the sales problem. Purchases may be recorded at the gross or net price after allowance for cash discounts for prompt payment. Trade discounts are always disregarded.

### i. Gross Price Method

No record is made at the time of purchase of the discount which the firm can claim if it pays the supplier within the discount period, and the purchase is recorded at the gross price. The discount is recorded when and if payment is made in the discount period; but no record is made of the discount lost by late payment.

The entries are:

| | | | $ | |
|---|---|---|---|---|
| a. On purchase: | | | | |
| Merchandise Inventory | Dr. | | 100 | N.B |
| Accounts Payable | Cr. | | 100 | |
| b. On payment within the discount period: | | | | |
| Accounts Payable | Dr. | | 100 | |
| Bank | Cr. | | 97 | |
| Purchase Discounts Received | Cr. | | 3 | |
| c. On late payment: | | | | |
| Accounts Payable | Dr. | | 100 | |
| Bank | Cr. | | 100 | |

Purchase Discounts Received is a contra account which is credited to Merchandise Inventory account. It is not an item of revenue — no goods have been sold — but there is a reduction in cost.

The amount of discounts receivable on the non-overdue creditors at the end of the year should be calculated and recorded as a balance-day adjustment so as to determine the net cost of purchases for the period and the cash value of creditors. However, this adjustment is generally not made unless the amount involved is significant.

### ii. Net Price Method

The discount to which the firm is entitled for prompt payment is recorded at the date of purchase and purchases are recorded at the net price only. The discount received is matched against the entitlement upon payment of the supplier within the discount period, so that there is a continuing tendency for the account to be balanced out. But if the payment is made late, an entry is made to record the discounts lost. Any balance in the account at the end of the year represents the discounts which the firm can get on its creditors, and it should be deducted from them in the balance sheet so as to show their net cash value.

The entries are:

NB

|  |  | $ |
|---|---|---|
| a. On purchase: | | |
| Merchandise Inventory | Dr. | 97 |
| Purchase Discounts Receivable | Dr. | 3 |
| Accounts Payable | Cr. | 100 |
| | | |
| b. On payment within the discount period: | | |
| Accounts Payable | Dr. | 100 |
| Bank | Cr. | 97 |
| Purchase Discounts Receivable | Cr. | 3 |
| | | |
| c. On late payment: | | |
| Accounts Payable | Dr. | 100 |
| Bank | Cr. | 100 |
| Purchase Discounts Lost | Dr. | 3 |
| Purchase Discounts Receivable | Cr. | 3 |

Purchase Discounts Lost is shown as a finance expense as it represents payment for extended credit terms.

The net price method has two main advantages. It highlights the discounts lost because of illiquidity or laxity in payment. Management should know this figure so that corrective action can be taken to eliminate the cost of the discounts lost. It represents a most expensive form of finance and a financially efficient firm would avoid it. Secondly, it treats the cost of merchandise as the net amount, as this is all that the firm is required to pay if it is efficiently managed. The costs of its main operations are therefore not distorted by laxity in financial management.

### 3. Purchase Returns and Allowances

Again, treated analogously to sales returns:

|  |  | $ |
|---|---|---|
| Accounts Payable | Dr. | 50 |
| Purchases Returns | Cr. | 50 |

Purchases Returns account is a contra account transferred to Merchandise Inventory account at end of period. It indicates the efficiency of suppliers in meeting the firm's purchase orders.

### 4. Recording the Cost of Sales

Two methods of recording the cost of merchandise sold are available.

Under the *perpetual inventory system,* detailed stock records of all movements of inventory are kept. Each line of merchandise has an additional and separate (subsidiary) ledger account recording inward and outward movements, and balance on hand.[1] When a sale is made, the transaction is recorded simultaneously at selling price and at cost price. For example in a department store, the cost price is frequently recorded in code on the price tag, and, when a sale is made, both cost and selling prices are recorded. Most large retailing and manufacturing firms use the perpetual inventory system for all those items having sufficient value to justify the cost of maintaining it.

As an example, if goods costing $400 are sold for $600 cash, the entries to record the transaction are:

| | | $ |
|---|---|---|
| i. Entry at selling price: | | |
| Cash | Dr. | 600 |
| Sales | Cr. | 600 |
| | | |
| ii. Entry at cost price: | | |
| Cost of Goods Sold | Dr. | 400 |
| Merchandise Inventory | Cr. | 400 |

The second entry recognizes the expense incurred on the sale, and transfers an asset to an expense account. The credit to Merchandise Inventory reduces the asset balance. Essentially, the Merchandise Inventory account is treated like most asset accounts – all movements into it are debited, and all movements out are credited; the balance in the account is the inventory on hand. The account is always kept at *cost.* It is for this reason that sales at retail are not credited to the merchandise account.

Shown below are the entries to record the following items:

| | | $ |
|---|---|---|
| Jan. 1. | Merchandise on hand at cost price | 300 |
| 30. | Credit purchases for month | 500 |
| 30. | Cash sales | 600 |
| 30. | Cost of merchandise sold | 400 |

Merchandise Inventory Account

| | | Dr. $ | Cr. $ | Balance $ |
|---|---|---|---|---|
| Jan. 1 | Balance | | | 300 Dr. |
| 30 | Accounts Payable (for purchases) | 500 | | 800 Dr. |
| 30 | Cost of Merchandise Sold | | 400 | 400 Dr. |

Accounts Payable Account

| | | | Cr. $ | Balance $ |
|---|---|---|---|---|
| Jan. 30 | Merchandise Inventory | | 500 | 500 Cr. |

Sales Account

| Jan. 30 | Cash | | | 600 | | 600 Cr. |
|---------|------|---|---|-----|---|---------|

Cash Account

| Jan. 30 | Sales | | 600 | | | 600 Dr. |
|---------|-------|---|-----|---|---|---------|

Cost of Merchandise Sold Account

| Jan. 30 | Merchandise Inventory | | 400 | | | 400 Dr. |
|---------|----------------------|---|-----|---|---|---------|

NOTE: The balance in the Merchandise Inventory account indicates the stocks that *should* be on hand at 30 January.

A second method for recording the cost of merchandise sold is the *retail inventory system*. Instead of detailed outward movements of merchandise at cost price being kept, the gross profit margin is deducted from sales at the retail price. For example, merchandise is sold for $600 cash, on which the gross profit margin is 33 1/3 per cent on the retail price. Hence the cost of the merchandise sold is: 600 x 2/3 = $400, i.e., the cost proportion of the retail price. This method is frequently used in variety stores and supermarkets where the selling price of goods is low and it is both inconvenient and uneconomical to keep individual cost records. Sales for the period are determined from cash register tapes and sales invoices.

Regular information on the cost of goods sold and inventory levels is essential in firms of any size. In addition to their use for measuring gross and net profits earned and assets on hand, these inventory data are required by the firm's buyers to help them determine replacement orders for new merchandise and to help maintain desired quantities of merchandise on hand. The buying department needs regular information on how much and what types of merchandise should be purchased to meet expected sales. The firm may lose sales if its stocks of particular lines of merchandise are inadequate, while excessive stocks of merchandise tie up investment funds and storage space and frequently have to be disposed of at cut prices. In addition, the data for inventories which should be on hand are necessary for effective stock control. The balance in the inventory account ought to be compared with the balance actually on hand (determined from a stocktake), and the reasons for any discrepancy (theft, inaccurate records, and so on) investigated and rectified.

Under a third system, *the periodic inventory system,* the cost of merchandise sold is not recorded directly, but is calculated by working back from the data for opening inventory, purchases, and the end-of-period inventory, determined by counting the stock on hand, i.e., a physical stocktake. Under this system, the cost of merchandise sold is determined as: opening inventory + purchases for period - purchase returns, etc. - closing inventory.

The periodic inventory system has serious defects for large firms. The cost of goods sold, income, and inventories on hand cannot be determined until a stocktake is made, and this cannot be done frequently. Secondly, the cost of merchandise sold includes all merchandise lost for other reasons such as theft and deterioration, and hence there is no check on the amount of inventory that should be on hand. Thirdly, no information can be provided to the buying department about stock replacement needs. However the system can be appropriate for small firms — it is cheap to operate, and the owner can tell from observation of his shelves what goods are still on hand and which ones need replacing.

The balance of stock on hand determined from the stocktake can be recorded as the balance in the Merchandise Inventory account (there is no double entry for this), and then the Cost of Goods Sold is recorded in the usual way; or alternatively a special "balance day adjustment account", the Stock on Hand account, may be opened. In this case, purchases are debited to a Purchases account and not a Merchandise Inventory account. The Purchases account is classified as an expense account (as, for example, wages are), and not an asset account, and is transferred to a Cost of Goods Sold account at the end of the year.[2] If, for example, a physical stocktake establishes the closing stock in the above illustration at $350, the entry for it in this system is:

|  |  | $ |
|---|---|---|
| Stock on Hand | Dr. | 350 |
| Cost of Goods Sold | Cr. | 350 |

The Cost of Goods Sold is then calculated at $450. It should be noted that the $50 discrepancy in both figures will not be known unless the perpetual inventory system is supported by an occasional physical stocktake. The discrepancy could be explained by clerical errors, theft, and so on, and it is included in the Cost of Goods Sold.

The entries and accounts required for the periodic inventory system are illustrated below:

|  |  |  | $ |
|---|---|---|---|
| Data: | 1. | Stocks on hand 1 Jan. (at cost) | 6,600 |
|  | 2. | Purchases (all credit) for year | 32,000 |
|  | 3. | Sales (all credit) for year | 45,000 |
|  | 4. | Purchases returns for year | 800 |
|  | 5. | Stocks on hand, 31 Dec. (at cost per physical stocktake) | 4,600 |

Stock on Hand Account (Asset)

|  |  | Dr. $ | Cr. $ | Balance $ |
|---|---|---|---|---|
| Jan. 1 | Balance |  |  | 6,600  Dr. |
| Jan. 1 | Cost of Goods Sold (1) |  | 6,600 | — |
| Dec. 31 | Cost of Goods sold | 4,600 |  | 4,600  Dr. |

Purchases Account (Expense)

| Dec. 31 | Accounts Payable (2) | 32,000 | | 32,000 | Dr. |

Purchases Returns Account

| Dec. 31 | Accounts Payable (4) | | 800 | 800 | Cr. |

Sales Account

| Dec. 31 | Accounts Receivable (3) | | 45,000 | 45,000 | Cr. |

Cost of Goods Sold Account

| Jan. 1 | Stock (1) | 6,600 | | 6,600 | Dr. |
| Dec. 31 | Stock (5) | | 4,600 | 2,000 | Dr. |

Accounts Payable Account

| Dec. 31 | Purchases (2) | | 32,000 | 32,000 | Cr. |
| | Purchases Returns (4) | 800 | | 31 8 )) | Cr. |

Accounts Receivable Account

| Dec. 31 | Sales (3) | 45,000 | | 45,000 | Dr. |

The income statement would appear as:

|  | $ | $ | $ |
|---|---|---|---|
| Sales | | | 45,000 |
| Less Cost of Goods Sold: | | | |
| Stock on hand, 1 Jan. | | 6,600 | |
| Add purchases | 32,000 | | |
| Less purchases returns | 800 | 31,200 | |
| | | 37,800 | |
| Less stock on hand, 21 Dec. | | 4,600 | 33,200 |
| Gross Profit | | | $11,800 |

The first entry (1) in the Stock and Cost of Goods Sold accounts is a reversing entry (for the balance day adjustment made on the preceding day) which has the effect of closing off the Stock account for the year.[3]

## DEPRECIATION AND AMORTIZATION

In accounting, the concepts of depreciation and amortization refer to the systematic allocation of the net cost of a long-term asset over its revenue-producing life. The term "depreciation" is applied to physical assets, and "amortization" to intangible assets. The process of charging depreciation is one whereby the costs of long-term assets are charged as periodic expenses against the revenue of each period which benefits from the use of the asset; it is the process of expensing long-term costs.

This is done in order to recover systematically the expenditures on long-term assets from revenues generated over the lives of the assets before a profit is reckoned to be made, as part of the principle of maintaining capital intact. It would be inappropriate to recover the total expenditure from revenue in the year of purchase as such a procedure would seriously distort the measures of capital maintenance and periodic profit. Only the net cost is allocated as depreciation, i.e., purchase cost less salvage or retirement value.

Various methods of allocating long-term asset cost as depreciation charges are available, and the three most widely used methods are:

1. The straight line method
2. The reducing balance method
3. The production units method

### 1.  Straight line method

The net cost is allocated equally to each year of the asset's life.

$$D = \frac{C-S}{n}$$

where    D is the annual depreciation
C is the cost price
S is the scrap value
n is the life in years.

*Example*

Cost of plant:  $1,000
Estimated scrap value:  $100
Estimated life:  3 years

$$D = \frac{1,000 - 100}{3}$$

$$= \$300 \text{ p.a. for 3 years.}$$

Under this method, the periodic charge for depreciation is constant. In addition, it is a fixed expense which does not vary with changes in the intensity of use of the asset or with changes in revenue.

### 2.  Reducing balance method

A constant proportion of the net balance sheet value (i.e., cost less accumulated depreciation) is allocated to each year of the asset's life. This formula results in a steadily decreasing annual depreciation charge.

The aim is to allocate the net cost of using the asset so as to reduce the net book value (NBV) to S' at the end of n periods by applying a constant percentage rate to the NBV of the asset at the beginning of the period.

| | 0 | 1 | 2 | 3 | ... | n |
|---|---|---|---|---|---|---|
| Original Cost | C | C | C | C | ... | C |
| Depreciation Charge | | DC | DC (1-D) | DC (1-D)$^2$ | ... | |
| NBV | C | C (1-D) | C (1-D)$^2$ | C (1-D)$^3$ | ... | C (1-D)$^n$ |

$$\therefore \quad C(1-D)^n = S \quad \text{and} \quad D = 1 - \sqrt[n]{\frac{S}{C}}$$

*Example*

$$C = \$1{,}000, \quad s = \$100, \quad n = 3$$

$$D = 1 - \sqrt[3]{\frac{100}{1{,}000}} = 1 - 0.46 = 54\%$$

Depreciation in year 1: 54% of 1,000 = 540. Net balance sheet value $460.
Depreciation in year 2: 54% of 460 = 248. Net balance sheet value $212.
Depreciation in year 3: balance of 112.

Depreciation is a fixed expense as well under this method.

### 3. Production units method

The life of the asset is estimated in terms of its output potential, and net cost is averaged over this output. The year's depreciation charge is: output times depreciation per unit.

$$D = \frac{C - S}{q}$$

where q = a measure of total output.

*Example*

The life of a car is estimated to be 90,000 miles; its cost is $1,000 and its estimated trade-in value is $100.

$$D = \frac{1000 - 100}{90{,}000 \text{ miles}}$$

$$= 1 \text{ cent per mile.}$$

If car travels 40,000 miles in the first year, the depreciation charge for the year is (40,000 x 0·01) = $400. Under this method, depreciation is a variable expense which changes with the intensity of use of the asset.

### Recording Depreciation

The periodic depreciation expense is debited to a Depreciation account and credited to an Accumulated Depreciation account (or Provision for Depreciation account), which is a contra asset account. The debit entry is made in the Depreciation account as the charge flows to it, while it is credited in the Accumulated Depreciation account as the charge flows from it (in lieu of the asset itself). It must not be credited to the asset account because its historical cost should be shown separately from the portion of that cost charged as an expense. On disposal of the asset, the Accumulated Depreciation account is transferred to the asset account, and the sale or scrapping of the asset is then recorded. A profit or loss on sale may be made at this stage. For example, in the above illustration using straight line depreciation, if the plant is sold for $60 at end year 3, a loss of $40 is incurred on its sale. The entries in the relevant accounts are:

Plant Account (Asset)

|  |  | Dr. $ | Cr. $ | Balance $ |
|---|---|---|---|---|
| Year 1 Jan. 1 | Bank | 1,000 |  | 1,000 Dr. |
| Year 3 Dec. 31 | Accumulated Depreciation |  | 900 | 100 Dr. |
|  | Bank |  | 60 | 40 Dr. |
|  | Loss on sale |  | 40 | — |

Accumulated Depreciation of Plant Account (Contra Asset)

| Year 1 Dec. 31 | Depreciation |  | 300 | 300 Cr. |
|---|---|---|---|---|
| Year 2 Dec. 31 | Depreciation |  | 300 | 600 Cr. |
| Year 3 Dec. 31 | Depreciation |  | 300 | 900 Cr. |
|  | Plant | 900 |  | — |

Depreciation of Plant Account (Expense)

| Year 1 Dec. 31 | Accumulated Depreciation | 300 |  | 300 Dr. |
|---|---|---|---|---|
| Year 2 Dec. 31 | Accumulated Depreciation | 300 |  | 300 Dr. |
| Year 3 Dec. 31 | Accumulated Depreciation | 300 |  | 300 Dr. |

Loss on Sale of Plant Account

| Year 3 Dec. 31 | Plant | 40 |  | 40 Dr. |
|---|---|---|---|---|

Bank Account

| Year 1 Jan. 1 | Plant |  | 1,000 | 1,000 Cr. |
|---|---|---|---|---|
| Year 3 Dec. 31 | Plant | 60 |  | 940 Cr. |

*Balance Sheet Data, 31 December*

|  |  | $ | $ |
|---|---|---|---|
| Year 1 | Plant | 1,000 | |
|  | Less Accumulated Depreciation | 300 | 700 |
| Year 2 | Plant | 1,000 | |
|  | Less Accumulated Depreciation | 600 | 400 |
| Year 3 | — | | |

*Profit and Loss Statement Data, 31 December*

|  |  | $ | |
|---|---|---|---|
| Year 1 | Depreciation Expense | 300 | |
| Year 2 | Depreciation Expense | 300 | |
| Year 3 | Depreciation Expense | 300 | |
|  | Loss on Sale of Plant | 40 | (Non-Operating Expense) |

Conversely, a profit on sale (when the cash received exceeds net balance-sheet value) is debited to Plant account and credited to a Profit on Sale of Plant account. This is classified as Non-Operating Revenue in the income statement.

### PREPAID EXPENSES

Prepaid expenses occur when payments for short-term resources do not coincide with the using up of those resources within the accounting period and there are some remaining at its end. For example, where $600 rent is paid six months in advance on 1 November 19X2, the expense portion of it by 31 December 19X2 comprises only two months of the six. Hence rent expense for November–December is $200, and the $400 is an asset, Prepaid Rent, or Prepaid Expenses. The prepayment is transferred *from* the expense account (thereby reducing it) *to* an asset account (thereby increasing it). Assuming that $1,000 had been paid earlier in the year, the entries in the relevant accounts are:

Rent Account (Expense)

|  |  | Dr. $ | Cr. $ | Balance $ | |
|---|---|---|---|---|---|
| *19X2* | | | | | |
| Nov. 1 | Balance | | | 1,000 | Dr. |
| Nov. 1 | Bank | 600 | | 1,600 | Dr. |
| Dec. 31 | Prepaid Rent | | 400 | 1,200 | Dr. |

Prepaid Expenses Account (Asset)

|  |  | Dr. $ | Cr. $ | Balance $ | |
|---|---|---|---|---|---|
| *19X2* | | | | | |
| Dec. 31 | Rent | 400 | | 400 | Dr. |

·The balance in the Rent account ($1,200) represents the expense of the year charged against revenue in the profit and loss statement. This is the cost of the rental services used during the year, and it needs to be recovered from the year's revenue in order to maintain capital intact. The Prepaid Expense account shows the payment for part of next year's rental services; consequently it is shown as a current asset in the balance sheet. It is due to be recovered from next year's revenue. Normally one account is adequate for the record of all expenses paid for in advance.

### ACCRUED EXPENSES

Conversely, the opposite might occur and short-term resources are used up without their having been recognized or paid for. It is more convenient to recognize and hence record many items of expense at the date of payment or upon receipt of a bill rather than as the expense is actually incurred. For example, the wages expense is formally recognized and recorded only at pay day, even though the expense is being incurred on each working day; electricity and telephone expenses are formally recognized only upon the receipt of a bill. The expense incurred on such resources used before the time of payment is called an accrued expense. A liability for the expense is recognized and trans-ferred *from* a liability account *to* the expense account, thereby increasing the amounts in each account. In effect, an inflow of services from factors of production on credit is being recognized at balance date. For example, if the weekly wages of $200 are paid each Friday, and the accounting period ends on Wednesday 31 December, then on Wednesday an additional three days' wages expense of $120 has been incurred though the wages are not yet liable for payment. If $10,000 has been paid earlier in the year for wages, the entries in the relevant accounts are:

Wages Account (Expense)

|  |  | Dr. $ | Cr. $ | Balance $ |
|---|---|---|---|---|
| *19X2* | | | | |
| Dec. 26 | Balance | | | 10,000　Dr. |
| Dec. 31 | Accrued Wages | 120 | | 10,120　Dr. |

Accrued Expenses Account (Liability)

|  |  |  |  |  |
|---|---|---|---|---|
| *19X2* | | | | |
| Dec. 31 | Wages | | 120 | 120　Cr. |

Hence the period's wages expense is $10,120, and $120 is shown as a current liability in the balance sheet. The cost of the labour services used during the year is $10,120, and this is charged against the year's revenue to recover the funds expended so as to maintain capital intact. The additional $120 of labour services have been used this year but as they have been provided on credit by employees · it is necessary to recognize the liability for them.

## STOCKS OF SUNDRY ITEMS ON HAND

At the end of the accounting period, the firm may have unused stocks of sundry items on hand, such as advertising matter, packaging materials, stationery, and so on. If the amounts involved are significant, these stocks should be valued, and recorded in an appropriate stock account. The amount is transferred *from* the expense account (thereby reducing its balance from the amount purchased to the amount used) *to* a stock account (thereby recognizing an asset on hand).

For example, if purchases of stationery for the year were $2,500 and the stationery on hand at end of year is $300, the entries in the relevant accounts are:

Office Stationery Account (Expense)

|  |  | Dr. $ | Cr. $ | Balance $ |
|---|---|---|---|---|
| *19X2* |  |  |  |  |
| Dec. 31 | Balance |  |  | 2,500 Dr. |
| Dec. 31 | Stock of Stationery |  | 300 | 2,200 Dr. |

Stock of Stationery Account (Asset)

|  |  |  |  |  |
|---|---|---|---|---|
| *19X2* |  |  |  |  |
| Dec. 31 | Office Stationery | 300 |  | 300 Dr. |

This method of accounting for items of sundry stock on hand is the same as that for merchandise stocks where the periodic inventory system is used.

## ALTERNATIVE METHODS OF EXPENSE RECORDING

It should be noted that there are two alternative methods of accounting for the purchase of resources. (1) Where resources are either substantial items or are expected to be used over a long period, their purchase is recorded as an asset (hence Merchandise account is debited with purchases, Plant account with equipment bought, etc.), and any amounts used to earn the period's revenue are charged out as expenses (hence the asset accounts are credited with cost of goods sold and depreciation, and the relevant expense accounts are debited). (2) Where the resources acquired are used up quickly, (e.g., labour services) or are minor items (e.g., stationery), the purchase is debited directly to the relevant expense account. Any amounts unused at the end of the period are transferred from the expense account to an asset account (hence inventories are transferred from the cost of goods sold account to a stock account under the periodic inventory system, or rent is transferred to a prepaid expense account). Conversely, the liability for amounts used but not paid for are recognized and transferred from an accrued expenses account to the relevant expense accounts. There are no conceptual differences between the items recorded under each method — it is mainly a matter of convenience and internal control.

## FURTHER READING

Carrington, A. S.; Battersby, G. B., and Howitt, G. *Accounting: An Information System.* Christchurch: Whitcombe and Tombs, 1975. Chap. 7.

Gordon, M. J., and Shillinglaw, G. *Accounting: A Management Approach.* 4th ed. Homewood, Illinois: Richard D. Irwin, 1969. Chaps. 2, 3, and 5.

Mathews, R. L. *The Accounting Framework.* 3rd ed. Melbourne: Cheshire, 1971. Chap. 3.

## NOTES

1. Subsidiary ledger accounts are considered in chap. 11.
2. Closing entries for revenue and expense accounts are considered in chap. 10.
3. Reversing entries for "balance day adjustment" asset and liability accounts are also considered in chap. 10.

## QUESTIONS AND EXERCISES

[Solutions to problems marked * are given in Appendix 4.]

Prepare brief written answers to each of the following questions:

1. What are the main problems encountered in accounting for inventories?

2. Distinguish between the perpetual, retail and periodic inventory systems for accounting for the cost of goods sold and inventories on hand. What are the advantages of each method?

3. Explain the accounting concept of depreciation.

4. Explain three methods of measuring periodic depreciation charges.

### Purchase Discounts

5. Record the following transactions in ledger accounts using
   i. the gross price method
   ii. the net price method
   of accounting for purchase discounts.

   Mar. 1. Bought goods from S. Swan $500, terms 2/10, n/30.
   Bought goods from T. Turtle $400, terms 2/10, n/30.
   3. Bought goods from D. Duck $300, terms 5/10, n/20.
   8. Settled account with S. Swan.
   10. Settled account with T. Turtle.
   23. Settled account with D. Duck.

### Inventories

6. Record the following transaction at both cost and retail prices:
   Merchandise which cost $800 was sold for $1,100 cash.

7. The Swan Co. uses a perpetual inventory system. On 1 July, its inventory of merchandise was $22,500. During July, its purchases (all credit) were $34,000; merchandise returned to suppliers amounted to $1,500; sales (all credit) were $45,000; and the cost of merchandise sold was $37,000.
   Record this information in ledger accounts and determine the value of inventory which should have been on hand on 31 July.

8. Dime Retailers use the retail inventory system of accounting for inventories. The inventory on 1 September was $400 at cost; purchases for September were $900; and sales were $1,500. The profit margin on sales is 30 per cent.

   Record this information in ledger accounts and determine cost of goods sold and closing inventory.

9. A retail variety store marks selling prices of its goods at 25 per cent above cost (i.e., gross profit is 20 per cent of selling price).

   The following information has been extracted from the accounting records:
   Inventory at beginning of month $2,500
   Purchases during month $15,000
   Sales during month $19,000

   *Required*:
   i. Record information in ledger accounts.
   ii. Determine cost of goods sold and closing inventory.

10. From the following information relating to a firm using the periodic inventory system, show the calculation of gross profit in the income statement:

    Mar. 1   Stock on hand $4,500
    Mar. 31  Sales for month $16,000
    Purchases for month $9,500
    Returns to suppliers $500
    Stock on hand, as per stocktake $3,500

11. Department 6 of Ryde Retailers handles electric fans. A stocktake is made at the end of each quarter, and on 1 April its inventory comprised 70 fans costing $20 each, while on 30 June it was 48 fans. The purchases (all at $20 each) and sales (all at $30 each) for the quarter were:

    |       | *Purchases* | *Sales* |
    |-------|-------------|---------|
    | Apr.  | 50 fans     | 70 fans |
    | May   | 40 fans     | 40 fans |
    | June  | 20 fans     | 20 fans |

    Using aggregate figures for the quarter, record this information in ledger accounts using:

    i. The periodic inventory system (with Stock, Purchases, and COGS accounts)
    ii. The perpetual inventory system.

    How would you explain the discrepancy in the closing stock of fans on hand, and account for it under the second system?

*12. The hardware department of a retail store sells home tool kits. A physical stocktake is made at the end of each quarter. On 2 January, 100 tool kits costing $40 each were on hand. A physical stocktake on 31 March revealed that 74 tool kits were on hand.

    The purchases for the quarter (all at $40 and on credit) and sales for the quarter (all at $75 and on credit) were:

    |       | *Purchases* | *Sales* |
    |-------|-------------|---------|
    | Jan.  | 120         | 100     |
    | Feb.  | 80          | 140     |
    | Mar.  | 70          | 50      |

    Four tool kits (sold in March) were returned and the buyers were given a refund.

*Required*:

Record this information in ledger accounts using:

i.   the periodic inventory system
ii.  the perpetual inventory system

of recording purchases and cost of sales.

13.   Hifi Pty. Ltd. retails stereograms. On 1 January it had 60 stereos on hand which cost $120 each. During the year it purchased 300 stereos for $120 each, sold 320 units for $200 each, and returned 2 to the suppliers. The stocktake conducted on 31 December revealed that it had 35 units on hand.

Record this information in ledger accounts using:

i.   The periodic inventory system
ii.  The perpetual inventory system.

14.   Foresight Enterprises trades in crystal balls. A stocktake on 31 December last showed that it had 30 balls on hand. Its purchases and sales for the following three months were:

|      | *Purchases* | *Sales* |
|------|-------------|---------|
| Jan. | 40 balls    | 25 balls |
| Feb. | 20          | 30      |
| Mar. | 50          | 40      |

These balls cost $20 each, and are sold for $60 each. A stocktake on 31 March revealed that there were 44 balls on hand. Assume all transactions were for cash.

Record these data in ledger accounts using:
i.   The periodic inventory system (with closing entries to COGS account)
ii.  The perpetual inventory system.

How would you explain the discrepancy in the closing stock of balls, and account for it under the perpetual inventory system?

15.   Skyhigh Ltd. operates a franchise for light aircraft. A stocktake on 31 December last showed that it had 60 aircraft on hand. Its purchases and sales for the following three months were:

|      | *Purchases* | *Sales* |
|------|-------------|---------|
| Jan. | 70 planes   | 65 planes |
| Feb. | 40          | 55      |
| Mar. | 50          | 40      |

The planes cost $20,000 each, and are sold for $60,000 each. A stocktake on 31 March revealed that there were 54 planes on hand. Assume all transactions were for cash.

Record these data in ledger accounts using:

i.   The periodic inventory system (with closing entries to COGS account)
ii.  The perpetual inventory system.

How would you explain the discrepancy in the closing stock of aircraft, and account for it under the perpetual inventory system?

**Depreciation**

*16.   The Juggernaut Bus Company bought a bus on 1 January 1970 for $9,000 cash. In accordance with company policy, the bus would be run for three years, after which it would be traded in on a new vehicle. The resale value at that date was expected to be $3,000. The company uses straight line method of depreciation. At the end of 1972, the bus was traded in for $2,500.

Record the above information in ledger accounts for each of the three years and show the items in the balance sheet as at the end of the year. Assume that the company's financial year ends on 31 December.

17. The Hasty Taxi Truck Company bought a new truck on 1 January 1971 for $5,000. The company intended to use the truck for two years, after which it would be sold for an expected price of $1,000; and to depreciate it on the reducing balance basis. At the end of 1972, the truck was sold for $1,500 cash.

Calculate the depreciation rate to the nearest 5 per cent, and record the above information in ledger accounts and show the items in the balance sheet.

18. i. Coal Carters Limited purchased a truck for $20,000 and spent a further $16,000 on modifications on 1 July 1968. The estimated life of the truck was three years in which time it was expected to complete 500,000 ton miles of work. The estimated resale value at 30 June 1971 was $6,000. The truck performed the following work:

| Year | Ton Miles |
|---|---|
| 1 | 120,000 |
| 2 | 230,000 |
| 3 | 150,000 |

Required:

A. Calculate the charge for depreciation expense in each year using:

    a. Straight line method
    b. Reducing balance method
    c. Production units method.

B. Using the production units method, record purchase of the truck and:

    a. The periodic depreciation expense each year in the ledger
    b. The item "motor truck" in the balance sheet at the end of each year.

ii. Assume that the truck is sold for $8,500 on 30 June 1971 (end of year 3).

Required:

A. Record this transaction in the ledger.
B. Show the effect of the transaction on the presentation of the income statement at the end of year 3.

*19. On 1 February 1970, Property Developments Limited acquired a ten-year lease on a block of flats for $120,000 cash. The firm closes its books on 30 June each year.

Required:

i. Record the leasehold transaction in the relevant ledger accounts.

ii. Determine the amortization of leasehold for the current period (straight line method) and record in the ledger accounts.

iii. Show how the asset leasehold would appear in the firm's balance sheet as at 30 June 1970.

20. Chancit Airlines Ltd. bought a new jumbo jet aircraft on 1 January 1970 for $4,000,000 cash. Company policy was to fly the aircraft for 60,000 hours and then trade it in on a new model. The trade-in value at that stage was expected to be $1,000,000. During 1970, the aircraft logged 24,000 hours, 20,000 hours during 1971, and 12,000 hours during 1972 before it had a serious accident. The aircraft was written off as a total loss. The company depreciated its aircraft on the production units basis.

    Record the above information in ledger accounts. Show the asset in the balance sheet at the end of each year.

21. The Blue Line Bus Co. purchased a new bus on 1 January 1970 for $20,000 cash. The bus will be used for 4 years, at the end of which it will be traded in on a replacement. The estimated trade-in value is $3,000. The company charges depreciation on its buses at the rate of 40 per cent p.a. reducing balance. At the end of 1973 the trade-in value was $2,000.

    Record the above information in ledger accounts for each year and show the items in the balance sheet as at the end of each year, and in the income statement for the final year. The company's financial year ends on 31 December.

22. Harbour Hovercrafts Ltd. purchased a new hovercraft on 1 January 1970 for $1,000,000 for its ferry services. Company policy was to keep the craft for four years, after which it would be sold for an expected price of $250,000; and to depreciate it at 30 per cent per annum on the reducing balance basis.

    At the end of 1973, the craft was sold for $180,000 cash.

    i.   Record this information in the appropriate ledger accounts, including closing entries where relevant.

    ii.  Show the relevant parts of the income statement and balance sheet for each year.

    iii. Explain the meaning of the entries concerning the hovercraft in the income statement and balance sheet for year 2.

### Balance-Day Adjustments

23. The following account balances are extracted from a firm's trial balance as at 31 December, prepared after all transactions for the year have been recorded.

| | Dr. $ | Cr. $ |
|---|---|---|
| Buildings | 400,000 | |
| Accumulated Depreciation of Buildings | | 160,000 |
| Plant | 100,000 | |
| Accumulated Depreciation of Plant | | 40,000 |
| Rent | 8,000 | |
| Salaries | 22,000 | |
| Electricity | 3,000 | |
| Stationery | 2,000 | |

The above data require adjustment by the following items before the period's income can be measured and financial position determined:

    i.   Depreciation is to be charged on buildings at the rate of 5 per cent on net book value, and on plant at 10 per cent p.a. on cost.

ii. The rent is paid until 28 February next, and $2,000 relates to next year.

iii. Salaries accrued $1,000; electricity accrued $500.

iv. Stock of stationery on hand $400.

Record the above adjustments in ledger accounts, and briefly explain their effects on the measures of income and financial position.

24. The following accounts are taken from a firm's trial balance, prepared as for 30 June 1968:

| | Dr. $ | Cr. $ |
|---|---|---|
| Accounts Receivable | 96,000 | |
| Estimated Bad Debts | | 4,000 |
| Plant | 130,000 | |
| Accumulated Depreciation of Plant | | 55,000 |
| Retained Earnings | | 45,000 |
| Estimated Credit Losses | 6,000 | |
| Wages | 152,000 | |
| Municipal Rates | 16,000 | |

i. Open ledger accounts for each of the above items, and record the following adjustments in them:

a. After an examination of overdue Accounts Receivable, the credit manager has decided that $3,000 should be written off as bad debts and that the estimated bad debts allowance should be increased to $5,000.

b. Annual depreciation at the rate of 20 per cent on the net book value of plant is to be charged.

c. Wages owing at balance date $6,000.

d. The Council rates are paid in advance up to 30 September 1968, and $4,000 relates to the next financial year.

ii. Illustrate how Accounts Receivable, and Plant, should be shown in the balance sheet.

25. Record the following adjustments in ledger accounts of Black & Co. Ltd.

The accounting period ends on 30 June, and at that date the position includes the following:

i. Municipal rates of $4,800 relating to the year ending 30 September were paid on 3 January.

ii. Interest accrued on bank overdraft $850.

iii. The firm owns $100,000 6 per cent government bonds. Half-yearly interest is due on 1 August.

iv. An annual insurance premium of $480 for the year ending 31 March was paid on 5 April.

v. Rent is payable monthly in advance. The monthly rental of $280 was due and paid on 15 June.

vi.      The firm had sundry stocks of office stationery ($230) and advertising literature ($170) on hand. The advertising literature related to a sales promotion campaign conducted in January last.

vii.      The firm receives selling commissions of 3 per cent on some sales. Commissions earned are paid in the following month. Sales of the product on which commission is payable in June were $12,000.

viii.      Telephone rental of $156 for the year ended 30 May next had been paid on 10 June.

ix.      Interest on debentures of $2,100 was paid on 1 March for half year. A half-yearly interest payment is due on 1 September.

x.      The weekly pay day falls on 3 July, and $1,600 in unpaid wages have been earned by 30 June.

# Chapter 9
# Accounting for the Appropriation of Profits

All forms of profit distribution are summarized in the Profit Appropriation statement, and recorded in the Appropriation account in the ledger. Profits may be appropriated as follows:

1. For payment of company income or profits taxes

2. For payment of dividends to shareholders; or salaries, drawings, and interest to proprietors of unincorporated businesses

3. For transfers to revenue reserves

4. For amortizing some intangible assets such as goodwill and preliminary expenses.

In addition "capital losses" may be charged against profits in the Appropriation statement rather than charged as non-operating losses where the amount involved is large, and mistakes in the determination of previous year's profits may be corrected in the Appropriation statement.

The amount remaining in the Appropriation statement represents the retained profits of the firm which have not been earmarked for any specific accounting purpose. However, the total retained profits of the firm comprise this balance plus all the revenue reserves of the firm. Revenue reserves are merely retained profits under other names, and "transfers" to such reserves do not involve any external transaction or movement of funds. All retained profits form part of the owners' equity in the firm.

## 1. COMPANY PROFITS TAXATION

The Australian government raises a significant amount of its revenue from taxes on company profits. The tax rates on public companies in recent years have varied around 45 cents in the dollar on taxable profits. Taxable profit may not coincide with accounting profit in all firms, as the measure of taxable profit reflects to some extent the government's current fiscal policies, which may change from year to year, and certain administrative simplifications.[1] The calculation of taxable profit is governed by the Income Tax Assessment Act.

Profits taxes are not an expense of earning the firm's revenue of the period, and hence they are not a charge against revenue. They do not represent the cost of resources consumed in the revenue-earning process. Rather, they are a charge on profits — if there are no taxable profits, there is no tax; while, if taxable profits are made, the charge varies with the size of those profits. But, being a compulsory charge on profits, they are more accurately described as *expropriations* than as appropriations of profits.

Companies must estimate their liabilities for taxation for inclusion in the appropriation statement, in advance of receiving their taxation assessment from the government. Normally this estimate is made shortly after the end of the company's financial year, but the assessment is not received for six months or more, and generally the tax is not paid until after nine months have elapsed.

To record the estimated tax liability, the entry is:

|  |  | $ |  |
|---|---|---|---|
| Appropriation | Dr. | 1,000 | |
| Estimated Tax Payable | Cr. | 1,000 | (or Provision for Taxation) |

Upon subsequent payment of the tax, the entry is:

|  |  | $ |
|---|---|---|
| Estimated Tax Payable | Dr. | 1,000 |
| Bank | Cr. | 1,000 |

If the estimate is not accurate, the account would carry forward a balance (either debit if the estimate were too small, or credit if it were excessive) which would affect the allocation out of subsequent year's profits for future taxes.

It should be noted that the payment of personal income taxes by the owners of unincorporated firms is not recorded in the accounts of the firm. Such firms are not separate business entities for tax purposes, and the charge for tax is on the taxable personal incomes of owners. This is a private matter for owners. Similarly, the personal income taxes on shareholders of a company for dividends received are personal items only.

## 2. DIVIDENDS AND DRAWINGS

The directors of a company determine the amount of dividends to be paid by the company to its shareholders. However the dividends payment must be approved by shareholders before it can be made. This though is normally only a formality. Shareholders have the power to approve the recommended rate, or a lower rate, but they cannot vote themselves a higher rate than that recommended by directors. Dividends are normally paid twice a year — an interim dividend may be paid from the profits of the first half-year, while the final dividend is paid after the end of the year.

The entries to record the dividend declaration and payment are respectively:

|  |  | $ |  |
|---|---|---|---|
| 1. Appropriation | Dr. | 1,500 |  |
| Dividend Payable | Cr. | 1,500 | (or Provision for Dividend) |
|  |  |  |  |
| 2. Dividend Payable | Dr. | 1,500 | (or Provision for Dividend) |
| Bank | Cr. | 1,500 |  |

Alternatively, separate Dividend accounts may be kept for each class of share (ordinary, preference), is which case the Dividend accounts are debited first and are subsequently transferred to the Appropriation account.[2] The Dividend Payable account is shown as a current liability in the balance sheet until the dividend is paid. The choice between debiting a Dividend account or the Appropriation account depends on convenience. Separate Dividend accounts are useful to accumulate the total dividend charge where several dividends are paid; in simple circumstances a direct debit to the Appropriation account is sufficient.

In unincorporated firms, all payments to owners by whatever name — drawings, partners' salaries, interest on capital, share of profits, and so on — other than repayments of capital or loans, are distributions of profits and are recorded as such in the Appropriation statement. They are not shown as expenses of earning revenue. This is an application of the entity concept.

In the sole proprietor firm, the entry to record any payments from profit to the owner is:

|  |  | $ |
|---|---|---|
|  |  | |
| Drawings (etc.) | Dr. | 200 |
| Bank | Cr. | 200 |

No provision for future payments is required in these cases. The Drawings account is transferred at the end of the year to the Appropriation account[3] and is shown in the Appropriation statement as a distribution of profits.

The accounting for profit appropriations of a partnership firm follow the same principle, though the mechanics are more complicated. A separate Capital account is maintained for each partner and a Current account is required for each. All non-capital transactions between the firm and the partners are recorded in the Current accounts. The profit share, interest on capital and loans, salary entitlement, and so on, of each partner are credited to his Current account and debited to the Appropriation account, while all drawings or salary paid are debited to it and credited in the Bank account. A credit balance in the Current account represents undrawn profits, while a debit balance signifies overdrawn profits. The balance in the Current account is shown as part of proprietorship in the balance sheet; there should be no balance remaining in the Appropriation account. The distribution of net profits between partners is normally governed by the partnership agreement between them. However, in the unlikely event of no such agreement being made, the provisions of the relevant State Partnership Act are applied.

As an example, Ada and Elsie are in partnership. The partnership agreement provides that Ada's salary is $8,000 and Elsie's is $2,000 p.a.; 8 per cent interest on capital is payable to each; and residual profits are to be shared equally. Ada contributed $10,000 capital and Elsie contributed $50,000. The net profit for the year was $20,000; Ada has withdrawn $10,000 over the year, and Elsie $6,000. The Appropriation and Current accounts are shown below.

Appropriation Account

|  | Dr. $ | Cr. $ | Balance $ |
|---|---|---|---|
| Net Profit |  | 20,000 | 20,000 Cr. |
| Ada Current — salary | 8,000 |  | 12,000 Cr. |
|     — interest on capital | 800 |  | 11,200 Cr. |
| Elsie Current — salary | 2,000 |  | 9,200 Cr. |
|     interest on capital | 4,000 |  | 5,200 Cr. |
| Ada Current — profits share | 2,600 |  | 2,600 Cr. |
| Elsie Current — profits share | 2,600 |  |  |

Ada Current Account

|  | Dr. $ | Cr. $ | Balance $ |
|---|---|---|---|
| Bank — drawings | 10,000 |  | 10,000 Dr. |
| Appropriation — salary |  | 8,000 | 2,000 Dr. |
| Appropriation — interest on capital |  | 800 | 1,200 Dr. |
| Appropriation — profits share |  | 2,600 | 1,400 Cr. |

Elsie Current Account

|  | Dr. $ | Cr. $ | Balance $ |
|---|---|---|---|
| Bank — drawings | 6,000 |  | 6,000 Dr. |
| Appropriation — salary |  | 2,000 | 4,000 Dr. |
| Appropriation — interest on capital |  | 4,000 | — |
| Appropriation — profits share |  | 2,600 | 2,600 Cr. |

## 3. TRANSFERS TO REVENUE RESERVES

In companies, directors may decide to "transfer" part of the profits to revenue reserves. Reserves are created for many types of specific or vague purposes — asset replacement, dividend equalization, expansion, special, general, contingency, and so on. Under whatever name, they are all undistributed profits of the company, and sometimes the only purpose in creating them is to reduce the amount shown specifically as undistributed profits. Normally, no external transaction or cash is involved in the "transfer" of profits to reserves — the transfer is a "book entry" only. The entry to record the transfer is:

|  |  | $ |
|---|---|---|
| Appropriation | Dr. | 2,000 |
| General Reserve, etc. | Cr. | 2,000 |

All reserve accounts are included in the owners' equity section of the balance sheet.

In the unusual circumstance of the transfer to a reserve account being accompanied by the investment of cash in some asset such as securities, a separate transaction is involved and recorded as such. The entry to record this is the normal type for the purchase of any resource, for example:

|  |  | $ |
|---|---|---|
| Commonwealth Bonds | Dr. | 2,000 |
| Bank | Cr. | 2,000 |

The amount of the bonds purchased may or may not equal the "transfer" to the Reserve account. Government enterprises often set up such "sinking funds" to provide cash for some specific future purpose, but the method is rarely used by private enterprise.

## 4. AMORTIZATION OF INTANGIBLE ASSETS

Expenditures by companies on items known as "fixed intangible assets", such as preliminary expenses and goodwill, are amortized out of profits rather than out of revenue. Preliminary expenses are incurred by companies on their formation or at times of subsequent share issues. They comprise legal costs incurred in registering the company and the costs associated with the issue of shares — the issue of a prospectus inviting investors to subscribe to its shares, promotion costs, share-broking and underwriting costs, and so on. They are not expenses incurred to earn revenue and so are not amortized in the profit and loss account; rather they are fixed costs benefiting the entire life of the company. Goodwill arises from the payment of a price for purchase of another firm where that price exceeds the sum of the values of the net assets acquired. It represents a payment for the established organization and reputation of the firm purchased, and is made in the expectation of earning future profits from the firm. For example, if the sum of the values of the accounts receivable, inventories, premises, and so on taken over is $100,000, and the purchase price for the firm is $120,000, the value of goodwill is $20,000. The cost of such goodwill is amortized out of profits on some arbitrary basis, such as the ability of profits to bear the charge, i.e., the higher the profits, the higher the amortization charge until the goodwill is completely written off.

The entry to record purchase of goodwill is:

|  |  | $ |
|---|---|---|
| Goodwill | Dr. | 20,000 |
| Bank | Cr. | 20,000 |

If it is decided to write off $5,000 from goodwill, the entry is:

| | | |
|---|---|---|
| Appropriation | Dr. | 5,000 |
| Goodwill | Cr. | 5,000 |

This reduces the balance-sheet value of goodwill to $15,000 and the disclosed retained earnings of the business. Again, the entry is a purely internal transfer item, and no funds are involved in the transfer.

The recording of intangible assets' amortization differs from that of tangible assets in that the amortization is credited directly to the asset account and not to a contra account such as accumulated amortization of goodwill.

The logic underlying accounting for intangible assets is not always particularly sound, and current practice is often based more on reasons of accounting conservatism than logic. Because the values of intangible assets are often arbitrary, there is a tendency to write them off, i.e., amortize them, as quickly as profits permit. In some cases, goodwill should not be written off — for example, where it attaches to the site; while in other cases, where the goodwill is attached to the "personality" of the firm taken over, it should be amortized, but the period over which amortization should be made is difficult to determine.

### 5. WRITING OFF CAPITALIZED LOSSES

Sometimes substantial losses incurred by fire, flood, and so on are charged to the Appropriation account rather than to the Profit and Loss account as a non-operating loss, probably because the firm does not want to depress its net profit figure, as this can have a substantial effect on its share price. Likewise substantial holding losses on fixed assets are sometimes charged to the Appropriation account to avoid the depressing effect on net profit. However, these practices are rather suspect.

### 6. ADJUSTMENTS TO PREVIOUS YEARS' PROFITS

Where estimated data included in the income determination of a previous year turn out to be substantially incorrect, or items have been wrongly omitted from a previous year's reports, the adjustment may be made through the Appropriation account to retained earnings. This overcomes the need to go back and revise the reports of earlier years, and has the same effect on the end-of-period retained earnings. For example, substantial bad debts related to 1970 sales not foreseen till 1972 would be charged against retained earnings in 1972, in place of revising the 1970 and 1971 accounting reports. But minor errors due to imperfect foresight are simply carried forward in the estimate accounts for bad debts, accumulated depreciation, estimated taxation, and so forth, as part of their balances.

## FURTHER READING

Mathews, R. L. *The Accounting Framework.* 3rd ed. Melbourne: Cheshire, 1971. Chap. 10, pp. 251—56 (on partnerships) and pp. 258—77 (on companies).

## NOTES

1. The major differences between accounting and taxable incomes are discussed in chap. 15.
2. Closing and transfer entries are considered in chap. 10.
3. See note 2, above.

## QUESTIONS AND EXERCISES

[Solution to problem marked * is given in Appendix 4.]

1. What is the basis of the distinction between expenses and profit appropriations? Illustrate your answer.

2. Is company income tax an expense or a charge on profits? Justify your answer.

3. How should the personal income tax levied on the profits of an unincorporated firm accruing to the owner be classified? Justify your answer.

4. Explain why directors' salaries may justifiably be treated as a company expense, whereas the salaries of owners of unincorporated firms are treated as profit distributions.

5. Why do companies transfer undistributed profits to reserves? Is there any movement of cash or other assets involved in the transfer?

6. Why are some intangible assets amortized out of profits and not treated as an expense?

7. Why are "capital losses" frequently written off against profits or assets rather than treated as an abnormal expense? Is this practice justified?

8. i. The following information, for the year ended 30 June 1970, has been extracted from the records of Western Limited, a public company in its second year of operation.

|  | $ |
|---|---|
| Net Income for year | 72,000 |
| Appropriation Account (balance 1 July 1969) | Nil |
| Issued Capital | |
|     100,000 fully paid $1 ordinary shares | |
|     Preliminary (Floatation and Formation) Expenses | 4,250 |
| Directors have recommended an initial dividend rate | |
|     of 20 per cent on issued capital. | |

The company is liable for the payment of company income

tax. The company tax rate is currently 47.5 cents in the dollar.

The directors, concerned about the effects of inflation on the company's financial position, desire to make appropriate transfers from Appropriation Account to an Asset Replacement Reserve. They deem it prudent to set aside $10,000 of current profits for this purpose.

Preliminary Expenses are to be written down by $2,500.

*Required:*

a.   Record the above information in the relevant ledger accounts.
b.   Prepare an Appropriation statement.
c.   Show the relevant sections of the balance sheet.

ii.   The company sent dividend cheques to shareholders during August 1970. The income tax assessment for $31,750 was received and paid in April 1971.

*Required:*

Show the effect of these transactions in the relevant ledger accounts.

9.   The T.U.C. Company estimated its income tax liability for the year ended 31 December 1969 to be $19,500 and made the appropriate record in its accounts. During 1970 it received and paid a tax assessment for $17,750, and by the end of 1970 it had earned profits of $100,000. Record the tax liability for 1970. The company tax rate was 47.5 cents in the dollar.

*Required:*

Show the effect of these transactions in the relevant accounts.

*10.   Record the following adjustments in ledger accounts and prepare an Appropriation statement for Aphis Ltd. The following information relating to the year ending 30 June 1969 has been obtained from the company's records.

|  | $ |
|---|---|
| Net Income for Year | 100,000 |
| Appropriation Balance (1 July 1968) | 16,450 Cr. |
| General Reserve Account | 9,000 Cr. |
| Asset Replacement Reserve Account | 7,000 Cr. |
| Interim Dividends Paid | 16,700 Dr. |
| Taxation Paid | 29,000 Dr. |
| Taxation Payable Account | 27,500 Cr. |
| Goodwill Account | 7,000 Dr. |
| Formation Expenses Account | 2,750 Dr. |

On 30 June 1969, the directors decided to:

i.     Recommend a final dividend payment of $21,000.
ii.    Write off formation expenses.
iii.   Write down goodwill *by* $3,000.
iv.    Increase general reserves *by* $3,000 and asset replacement reserve *to* $20,000.
v.     Provide for an estimated tax liability of $37,500.

11. Darky and Joan are in partnership. The partnership agreement provides that:

 i. Partners' salaries are to be:
 Darky $5,000
 Joan $1,000

 ii. Each is to receive 10 per cent interest on capital before distribution of profits

 iii. Residual profits are to be distributed in the proportions of their contributed capital:
 Darky $20,000
 Joan $10,000

 Net profit for the year was $30,000. During the year the partners had withdrawn:
 Darky $ 5,000
 Joan $10,000

 *Required*:

 a. Record this information in the relevant ledger accounts.

 b. Prepare an Appropriation statement and show the Owners' Equity part of the balance sheet.

12. Big Pretzel and Slim Jane are partners in the Captivating Lonjeray Boutique. The balances in their capital and current accounts on 1 January were:

| | $ | |
|---|---|---|
| Big Pretzel Capital | 40,000 | Cr. |
| Slim Jane Capital | 10,000 | Cr. |
| Big Pretzel Current | 5,000 | Cr. |
| Slim Jane Current | 2,500 | Dr. |

 The partnership agreement provides that Big Pretzel be paid a salary $8,000 per annum and Slim Jane $15,000. Interest on capital at 10 per cent per annum is payable to each, and interest on overdrawn current accounts is payable at 20 per cent per annum on the opening balance where the amount is not extinguished before the end of the year. The residual profits are to be shared in proportion to capital contributions.

 Over the year, both partners had withdrawn $25,000 each, and profits earned were $48,000.

 *Required:*

 i. Record this information in relevant ledger accounts.
 ii. Prepare an Appropriation statement and show the Owners' Equity part of the balance sheet.

# Chapter 10
# Preparation of Final Accounting Reports

All transactions and adjustments thereto for the measurement of periodic income and financial position have now been completed, and the only matters remaining concern the mechanics of final report preparation and processing accounting data. In the preparation of the final reports, three matters are pertinent — the use of a trial balance worksheet, entries for closing the period's operating accounts, and reversing entries for some balance-day adjustments to be made on the first day of the new accounting period.

## TRIAL BALANCE WORKSHEET

Normally, a trial balance (the initial trial balance) is extracted from the ledger after all transactions for the period have been recorded, but before the adjustments necessary to bring the accounts completely up to date have been recorded. This is done as a partial check on the accuracy of the double-entry record of transactions, and any errors that become apparent should then be corrected before the final adjustments are made. The adjusted trial balance is prepared after the balance-day adjustments (made to enable a more complete estimate of the income earned over the period and the assets, liabilities, and proprietorship at the end of the period) have been recorded in the accounts. Any errors in the adjusted trial balance should then be confined to those adjustments.

One method which is often used to facilitate the practical task of preparing final accounting reports is the use of a worksheet. The worksheet is known as a ten-column (or twelve-column) trial balance. It shows the initial trial balance, adjustments thereto, a revised trial balance if deemed useful, and then the classification of the items into the three final accounting reports. The reports are then written up, with suitable classification of items, from these worksheet columns. Adjustments are recorded on the worksheet in addition to their being recorded in the accounts.

### Illustration — Northside Trading Co. Ltd.

The twelve-column trial balance worksheet is illustrated for the Northside Trading Co. Ltd., whose final accounting reports are shown in chapter 6. The initial trial balance, prepared after recording in the accounts all transactions for the year ended 31 December 197X, is to be amended by the following adjustments:

1. Bad debts of $2,000 are to be recognized and written off debtors' balances.
2. Expected bad debts included in debtors' balances are estimated to be $3,000.
3. $3,000 depreciation of buildings is to be charged.
4. $1,000 depreciation of shop fittings is to be charged.
5. $1,000 of advertising expenditure relates to advertising for the following year.
6. Expenses incurred but unpaid at balance day comprise: Interest $500, Salesmen's Salaries $300, and Office Salaries $200.
7. Company tax is estimated to be $5,000 and is to be provided for.
8. A final dividend of $2,000 is to be provided for.
9. $3,000 is to be transferred to Reserves.
10. The value of goodwill is to be reduced by $2,000.

These adjustments are recorded in the Adjustments columns opposite the relevant accounts where possible, and any new accounts are recorded below the set included in the initial trial balance. Although accounts should not be opened for profit appropriation items such as goodwill written off (for the reason that such accounts serve no purpose), it is useful to show these items separately on the worksheet so that they can be shown on the final reports. Similarly, Retained Profits at the beginning and at the end of the period, and Net Profits, are shown separately.

There is no classification of items within each pair of final report columns, and all contra accounts are shown in their correct debit or credit columns.

Although the worksheet is a useful aid in the preparation of final accounting reports for large or complicated problems, and for teaching students a systematic procedure for the preparation of final reports, it is a time-consuming procedure. For student purposes, a similar but time-saving method is to record all adjustments directly onto the initial trial balance given (by altering existing amounts when appropriate and writing in new accounts below the trial balance), classify the items into their three reports by means of putting a mark in a column for each report, and prepare the final reports directly from the adjusted trial balance.

Before commencing answers to a problem, the following three points should be noted in particular:

1. The period covered by the reports: for depreciation, accrued expense, and prepayment calculations.
2. The type of inventory system in use: where the periodic inventory system is used, the trial balance includes a Stock account balance for the beginning of the period, and a Purchases account; and the Cost of Goods Sold is calculated in the Profit and Loss statement. The end-of-period stock is shown as an adjustment item. Where the perpetual or retail inventory system is used, the Merchandise Inventory account shows the end-of-period inventory and the Cost of Goods Sold account is shown in the trial balance.

Northside Trading Co. Ltd.

*Twelve-Column Trial Balance Worksheet*

| | Initial Trial Balance | | Adjustments | | Adjusted Trial Balance | | Profit and Loss | | Appropriation | | Balance Sheet | |
|---|---|---|---|---|---|---|---|---|---|---|---|---|
| | Dr. $ | Cr. $ | Dr. $ | Cr. $ | Dr. $ | Cr. $ | Dr. $ | Cr. $ | Dr. $ | Cr. $ | Dr. $ | Cr. $ |
| Accounts Receivable | 32,000 | | | (1)2,000 | 30,000 | | | | | | 30,000 | |
| Accounts Payable | | 12,000 | | | | 12,000 | | | | | | 12,000 |
| Accumulated Depreciation of Shop Fittings | | 2,000 | | (4)1,000 | | 3,000 | | | | | | 3,000 |
| Accumulated Depreciation of Buildings | | 15,000 | | (3)3,000 | | 18,000 | | | | | | 18,000 |
| Advertising | 4,000 | | | (5)1,000 | 3,000 | | 3,000 | | | | | |
| Bank Overdraft | | 3,000 | | | | 3,000 | | | | | | 3,000 |
| Estimated Credit Losses | 3,400 | | (2)2,600 | | 6,000 | | 6,000 | | | | | |
| Cost of Goods Sold | 100,000 | | | | 100,000 | | 100,000 | | | | | |
| Dividends | 2,000 | | (8)2,000 | | 4,000 | | | | 4,000 | | | |
| Directors' Fees | 1,000 | | | | 1,000 | | 1,000 | | | | | |
| Estimated Bad Debts | | 2,400 | (1)2,000 | (2)2,600 | | 3,000 | | | | | | 3,000 |
| Fire Losses | 6,000 | | | | 6,000 | | 6,000 | | | | | |
| Goodwill | 8,000 | | | (10)2,000 | 6,000 | | | | | | 6,000 | |
| Interest | 500 | | (6) 500 | | 1,000 | | 1,000 | | | | | |
| Land and Buildings | 48,000 | | | | 48,000 | | | | | | 48,000 | |
| Mortgage | | 20,000 | | | | 20,000 | | | | | | 20,000 |
| Merchandise Inventory | 32,000 | | | | 32,000 | | | | | | 32,000 | |
| Office Salaries | 1,800 | | (6) 200 | | 2,000 | | 2,000 | | | | | |
| Paid-up Capital | | 50,000 | | | | 50,000 | | | | | | 50,000 |
| Reserve | | 7,000 | | (9)3,000 | | 10,000 | | | | | | 10,000 |
| Retained Profits 1 Jan. | | 5,000 | | | | 5,000 | | | | 5,000 | | |
| Sales | | 140,000 | | | | 140,000 | | 140,000 | | | | |
| Salesmen's Salaries | 5,700 | | (6) 300 | | 6,000 | | 6,000 | | | | | |
| Shop Fittings | 12,000 | | | | 12,000 | | | | | | 12,000 | |
| Depreciation of Buildings | | | (3)3,000 | | 3,000 | | 3,000 | | | | | |
| Depreciation of Shop Fittings | | | (4)1,000 | | 1,000 | | 1,000 | | | | | |
| Prepaid Expenses | | | (5)1,000 | | 1,000 | | | | | | 1,000 | |
| Accrued Expenses | | | | (6)1,000 | | 1,000 | | | | | | 1,000 |
| Taxation | | | (7)5,000 | | 5,000 | | | | 5,000 | | | |
| Estimated Taxation Payable | | | | (7)5,000 | | 5,000 | | | | | | 5,000 |
| Dividend Payable | | | | (8)2,000 | | 2,000 | | | | | | 2,000 |
| Transfer to Reserve | | | (9)3,000 | | 3,000 | | | | 3,000 | | | |
| Goodwill Written Off | | | (10)2,000 | | 2,000 | | | | 2,000 | | | |
| Net Profit | | | | | | | 11,000 | | | 11,000 | | |
| Retained Profits 31 Dec. | | | | | | | | | 2,000 | | | 2,000 |
| | $256,400 | $256,400 | $22,600 | $22,600 | $272,000 | $272,000 | $140,000 | $140,000 | $16,000 | $16,000 | $129,000 | $129,000 |

3. Finally it should be noted that the final accounting reports shown in chapter 6 are prepared last in order of time, i.e., after all adjustments to the transaction data recorded in the ledger accounts and the worksheet have been prepared, and decisions of profit appropriations made. The final reports were shown first of all to give an overview of the end result and to give direction to the adjustments necessary for the measurement of revenue and expenses, and assets and liabilities.

## CLOSING ENTRIES

At the end of each year when the final accounting reports are prepared, all non-balance-sheet accounts are closed off so that the new accounting period begins afresh with only the firm's Assets, Liabilities, and Proprietorship accounts in its ledger. A Profit and Loss account is opened up in the ledger in order that all Revenue, Expense, and Loss account balances can be transferred to it. In addition, a Cost of Goods Sold account may be opened where the periodic inventory system is used, and inventory balances, purchases, returns to suppliers, and so on are transferred to it to determine the cost of goods sold, which amount is then transferred to the Profit and Loss account. Likewise, all profit distributions debited to separate accounts (for example, Taxation and Dividends) are transferred to the Appropriation account to close them off, along with the net profit which is transferred from the Profit and Loss account. (It will be recalled that some charges on profits are debited direct to the Appropriation account — for example, transfer to reserves.) In unincorporated firms, the Appropriation account balance is transferred to the owner's Capital account or to the partners' Current accounts. After this procedure is completed, the only accounts remaining open are those shown in the balance sheet, and they represent the firm's assets, liabilities, and proprietorship as at the end of the accounting period and which are carried forward for the beginning of the next accounting period. New accounts are opened in the next period for all revenue, expense, loss, and profit distribution items. Hence this procedure enables the whole of the period's trading transactions and losses to be summarized in the ledger in accounts which relate to the current year only. But note that these closing accounts should not be confused with the accounting reports having similar names — they are prepared in addition to the accounting reports; and secondly that ledger accounts are not closed off for the preparation of interim accounting reports. The Profit and Loss account in the ledger was the forerunner of the modern form of published Profit and Loss statement.

The procedure for closing off operating activity accounts is a purely mechanical one, and the rules for double-entry recording of transactions and events do not apply. The transfers are made after all balance-day adjustments have been recorded in the accounts. The Profit and Loss account is not classified in any way, and is merely a list of debit and credit account balances.

The closing entries for the Northside Trading Company Limited, together with the final appropriations of profit, are illustrated below.

Northside Trading Company Limited

### Sales Account

| | | Dr. $ | Cr. $ | Balance $ |
|---|---|---|---|---|
| Dec. 31 | Balance | | | 140,000 Cr. |
| | Profit and Loss | 140,000 | | ——— |

### Estimated Credit Losses Account

| | | | | |
|---|---|---|---|---|
| Dec. 31 | Balance | | | 6,000 Dr. |
| | Profit and Loss | | 6,000 | ——— |

### Cost of Goods Sold Account

| | | | | |
|---|---|---|---|---|
| Dec. 31 | Balance | | | 100,000 Dr. |
| | Profit and Loss | | 100,000 | ——— |

### Fire Loss Account

| | | | | |
|---|---|---|---|---|
| Dec. 31 | Balance | | | 6,000 Dr. |
| | Profit and Loss | | 6,000 | ——— |

### Dividends Account

| | | | | |
|---|---|---|---|---|
| Dec. 31 | Balance | | | 4,000 Dr. |
| | Appropriation | | 4,000 | ——— |

### Taxation Account

| | | | | |
|---|---|---|---|---|
| Dec. 31 | Balance | | | 5,000 Dr. |
| | Appropriation | | 5,000 | ——— |

### Goodwill Account

| | | | | |
|---|---|---|---|---|
| Dec. 31 | Balance | | | 8,000 Dr. |
| | Appropriation | | 2,000 | 6,000 Dr. |

### Reserve Account

| | | | | |
|---|---|---|---|---|
| Dec. 31 | Balance | | | 7,000 Cr. |
| | Appropriation | | 3,000 | 10,000 Cr. |

### Profit and Loss Account

| | | | | |
|---|---|---|---|---|
| Dec. 31 | Sales | | 140,000 | 140,000 Cr. |
| | Estimated Credit Losses | 6,000 | | 134,000 Cr. |
| | Cost of Goods Sold | 100,000 | | 34,000 Cr. |
| | Advertising | 3,000 | | 31,000 Cr. |
| | Salesmen's Salaries | 6,000 | | 25,000 Cr. |
| | Depreciation of Shop Fittings | 1,000 | | 24,000 Cr. |
| | Directors' Fees | 1,000 | | 23,000 Cr. |
| | Office Salaries | 2,000 | | 21,000 Cr. |
| | Depreciation of Buildings | 3,000 | | 18,000 Cr. |
| | Interest | 1,000 | | 17,000 Cr. |
| | Fire Loss | 6,000 | | 11,000 Cr. |
| | Appropriation (Net Profit) | 11,000 | | — |

Appropriation Account

| | | | | | |
|---|---|---|---|---|---|
| Jan. 1 | Balance | | | | 5,000 Cr. |
| Dec. 31 | Profit and Loss (Net Profit) | | 11,000 | | 16,000 Cr. |
| | Dividends | 4,000 | | | 12,000 Cr. |
| | Taxation | 5,000 | | | 7,000 Cr. |
| | Goodwill | 2,000 | | | 5,000 Cr. |
| | Reserve | 3,000 | | | 2,000 Cr. |

It should be noted that the Goodwill, Reserve, and Appropriation accounts are balance sheet accounts which are not closed off.

## REVERSING ENTRIES

At the beginning of a new accounting period, the entries made at the close of the preceding period for accruals and prepayments, and for stocks on hand where a periodic inventory system is used, are reversed. The same applies to any balance-day adjustment entries for discounts receivable or payable or income accrued. In the case of accrued and prepaid expenses, the reversal has the effect of adjusting the subsequent cash payment to the amount chargeable as an expense against the new period's revenue, and of closing-off the accrued and prepaid expense accounts. For example, if salaries of $500 are accrued at the end of the preceding accounting period, the cash payment for wages in the new period of, say, $8,000 includes $500 relating to the previous period. Assuming no accruals at the end of the new period, the wages expense for that period is $7,500. Conversely, for prepayments, if $400 of rates are prepaid at the end of the preceding period, and if total rates for the ensuing year are $2,000, then only $1,600 remains to be paid in that year. In the case of inventories, the reversing entry has the effect in the accounts of transferring the opening inventory to the Cost of Goods Sold account as an expense of operations for the new period; likewise with the reversing entry for sundry stocks on hand. The Stock account is thereby closed.

The position with respect to reversing entries for the Northside Trading Co. Ltd. is illustrated below.

Advertising Account

| | | | | | |
|---|---|---|---|---|---|
| Jan. 1 | Prepayments | | 1,000 | | 1,000 Dr. |

Prepayments Account

| | | | | | |
|---|---|---|---|---|---|
| Dec. 31 | Advertising | | 1,000 | | 1,000 Dr. |
| | Advertising | | | 1,000 | — |

Interest Account

| | | | | | |
|---|---|---|---|---|---|
| Jan. 1 | Accrued Expenses | | | 500 | 500 Cr. |

Salesmens' Salaries Account

| Jan. 1 | Accrued Expenses | | 300 | 300 Cr. |
|--------|------------------|--|-----|---------|

Office Salaries Account

| Jan. 1 | Accrued Expenses | | 200 | 200 Cr. |
|--------|------------------|--|-----|---------|

Accrued Expenses Account

| Dec. 31 | Sundry Expenses | | 1,000 | 1,000 Cr. |
|---------|-----------------|-------|-------|-----------|
| Jan. 1 | Sundry Expenses | 1,000 | | — |

The reversing entry for stocks on hand, where required, is:

| Jan. 1 | Cost of Goods Sold | Dr. |
|--------|--------------------|-----|
| | Stock on Hand | Cr. |

This entry closes off the Stock on Hand asset account by transferring it back to an expense account for the new year.

### FURTHER READING

Carrington, A. S., Battersby, G. B., and Howitt, G. *Accounting. An Information System*, Christchurch; Whitcombe and Tombs, 1975. Chaps. 7 and 9.

Gordon, M. J., and Shillinglaw, G. *Accounting, A Management Approach*. 4th ed. Homewood, Illinois: Richard D. Irwin, 1969. Chap. 6.

Mathews, R. L. *The Accounting Framework*. 3rd ed. Melbourne: Cheshire, 1971. Chap. 3.

### QUESTIONS AND EXERCISES

[Solutions to problems marked * are given in Appendix 4.]

Prepare final accounting reports for presentation to the owners or directors in each of the following:

1. The year's trading of Eastwood Store, owned by R. Green, produced the following trial balance at 30 June 19X0:

| | Dr. $ | Cr. $ |
|--|-------|-------|
| Sales | — | 26,780 |
| Sales Returns and Allowances | 520 | — |
| Cost of Goods Sold | 9,060 | — |
| Advertising | 1,720 | — |
| Salesmen's Salaries | 4,600 | — |
| Commission | 1,340 | — |
| Showroom Rent | 1,200 | — |
| Delivery Expenses | 1,260 | — |
| Office Salaries | 2,860 | — |
| Office Rent | 1,170 | — |
| Insurance | 680 | — |
| Sales Discounts | 894 | — |
| Interest Expense | 216 | — |
| Bank | — | 1,750 |

| | | |
|---|---|---|
| Accounts Receivable | 4,260 | – |
| Merchandise Inventory | 2,940 | – |
| Motor Van | 2,800 | – |
| Accumulated Depreciation of Motor Van | – | 360 |
| Office Equipment | 1,280 | – |
| Accumulated Depreciation of Office Equipment | – | 490 |
| Showroom Fittings and Fixtures | 2,400 | – |
| Accumulated Depreciation of Showroom Fittings | – | 600 |
| Accounts Payable | – | 1,580 |
| Long-Term Loan | – | 2,400 |
| R. Green – Capital | – | 8,000 |
| R. Green – Drawings | 2,760 | – |
| | $41,960 | $41,960 |

*Additional requirements:*

Office Rent paid in advance, $90. Interest owing, $56. Provide for depreciation of Motor Van at 10 per cent per annum, Office Equipment at 10 per cent per annum, and Showroom Fittings at 5 per cent per annum on cost.

2.  Reynolds' Retail Store

*Trial Balance at 31 December 19X6*

| | Dr. $ | Cr. $ |
|---|---|---|
| Debtors | 12,400 | – |
| Advertising | 870 | – |
| Delivery Truck Expenses | 1,250 | – |
| Shop Lighting | 476 | – |
| Wrapping Materials | 240 | – |
| Postage and Stationery | 148 | – |
| Furniture and Fittings | 2,240 | – |
| Fire Insurance | 196 | – |
| Delivery Truck | 3,400 | – |
| Cost of Goods Sold | 19,180 | – |
| Creditors | – | 7,690 |
| Rates and Taxes | 368 | – |
| Estimated Bad Debts | – | 500 |
| Estimated Credit Losses | 760 | – |
| Rent | 870 | – |
| Salaries – Office Staff | 2,630 | – |
| Salaries – Salesmen | 2,976 | – |
| Sales | – | 36,760 |
| General Expenses | 1,420 | – |
| Returns Inward | 960 | – |
| Merchandise Inventory | 13,840 | – |
| Accumulated Depreciation – Delivery Trucks | – | 960 |
| Accumulated Depreciation – Furniture and Fittings | – | 540 |
| Bank | – | 4,014 |
| J. Reynolds – Capital | – | 16,000 |
| J. Reynolds – Drawings | 2,240 | – |
| | $66,464 | $66,464 |

*Adjustments:*

a.  Stocks on hand 31 December 19X6: wrapping materials, $46, stationery, $66.

b.  Lighting, $48, and Advertising, $124, owing at 31 December 19X6.

c.  Insurance paid in advance, $82.

d.  Estimated Bad Debts to be increased to $700.

e.  Depreciation to be charged on Delivery Truck at 20 per cent per annum on cost and on Furniture and Fittings at 10 per cent per annum on net book value.

*3.  The following trial balance as at 30 June 19X8 has been extracted from the books of Fashion Retailers, owned and operated by T. Bowman:

|  | Dr. $ | Cr. $ |
|---|---|---|
| Accumulated Depreciation of Delivery Vans | — | 820 |
| Accumulated Depreciation of Store Fixtures | — | 260 |
| Advertising | 2,960 | — |
| Bank | — | 5,500 |
| Cost of Goods Sold | 19,200 | — |
| Creditors | — | 6,640 |
| Debtors | 12,600 | — |
| Delivery Van | 4,480 | — |
| Estimated Bad Debts | — | 480 |
| Estimated Credit Losses | 540 | — |
| Interest | 180 | — |
| T. Bowman – Capital | — | 12,000 |
| T. Bowman – Drawings | 2,240 | — |
| Office Salaries | 1,820 | — |
| Office Stationery and Expenses | 900 | — |
| Merchandise Inventory | 8,860 | — |
| Rent | 2,320 | — |
| Returns Inward | 520 | — |
| Sales | — | 37,300 |
| Store Fixtures | 1,760 | — |
| Travellers' Salaries | 3,300 | — |
| Travellers' Commission | 1,220 | — |
|  | $63,000 | $63,000 |

*Adjustments:*

i.  Depreciation to be charged: Delivery Vans 15 per cent per annum on cost; Store Fixtures 15 per cent per annum on net book value.

ii.  Estimated Bad Debts to be increased to $760.

iii.  Travellers' Commission $90, and Rent $120 for June unpaid.

iv.  Office Stationery on hand $120.

4.  The following trial balance has been extracted from the books of P. Glass & Co., hardware merchant, as at 30 June 19X8:

|  | Dr. $ | Cr. $ |
|---|---|---|
| Accumulated Depreciation of Store Fixtures | — | 500 |
| Accumulated Depreciation of Delivery Vans | — | 2,160 |
| Administration Expenses | 1,430 | — |
| Advertising | 1,610 | — |
| Bank | 1,550 | — |
| Creditors | — | 7,140 |
| Cost of Goods Sold | 10,800 | — |
| Debtors | 10,180 | — |
| Delivery Expenses | 1,270 | — |
| Delivery Vans | 4,600 | — |
| Estimated Bad Debts | — | 800 |
| Estimated Credit Losses | 600 | — |
| Fire Loss | 1,620 | — |
| Insurance | 1,280 | — |
| Office Stationery and Expenses | 260 | — |
| Mortgage | — | 7,000 |
| Merchandise Inventory | 3,400 | — |
| Premises | 10,000 | — |
| P. Glass — Capital | — | 20,000 |
| P. Glass — Drawings Account | 2,400 | — |
| Salaries and Wages — Office | 2,140 | — |
| Salaries and Wages — Salesmen | 4,000 | — |
| Salaries and Wages — Drivers | 3,600 | — |
| Sales | — | 29,000 |
| Sales Returns | 660 | — |
| Store Fixtures | 1,900 | — |
| Traveller's Salary | 2,800 | — |
| Traveller's Commission | 500 | — |
|  | $66,600 | $66,600 |

Prepare appropriate accounting reports for submission to P. Glass after making the following adjustments:

i.    Advertising account includes $110 paid in advance for next year.

ii.   Insurance account includes $220 premium paid on the life insurance policy of P. Glass.

iii.  Write off $400 additional Bad Debts, and increase Estimated Bad Debts to $1,020.

iv.   Depreciation to be charged on Delivery Vans at 15 per cent per annum on cost, and on Store Fixtures at 10 per cent per annum on cost.

v.    Traveller's Commission $40, and Traveller's Salary $200 are unpaid.

5.   Outback Trading Co.

### Trial Balance at 30 June 19X7

|  | Dr. $ | Cr. $ |
|---|---|---|
| Accumulated Depreciation of Office Equipment | — | 2,200 |
| Accumulated Depreciation of Shop Fittings | — | 3,000 |
| Advertising | 3,600 | — |

| | | |
|---|---:|---:|
| Bank | — | 3,510 |
| Long-Term Loan | — | 15,000 |
| Insurance — | | |
| Shop Fittings | 184 | — |
| Office Equipment | 66 | — |
| Interest | 930 | — |
| J. Palmer — Capital | — | 30,000 |
| J. Palmer — Drawings | 4,120 | — |
| Office Expenses and Stationery | 1,690 | — |
| Office Equipment | 4,400 | — |
| Office Salaries | 2,460 | — |
| Purchases | 104,450 | — |
| Repairs to Office Equipment | 240 | — |
| Rent | 2,800 | — |
| Returns Inward | 3,120 | — |
| Returns Outward | — | 1,690 |
| Sales | — | 139,800 |
| Salesmen's Salaries | 7,640 | — |
| Shop Fittings | 12,000 | — |
| Stock of Merchandise on Hand, 1 July 19X6 | 28,200 | — |
| Trade Creditors | — | 12,300 |
| Trade Debtors | 31,600 | |
| | $207,500 | $207,500 |

*Adjustments Required:*

a.   Stock of Merchandise on Hand, at 30 June 19X7, $32,740.

b.   Salaries, accrued to 30 June 19X7 — Office $150; Salesmen $320.

c.   Rent paid in advance $300. Rent to be apportioned four-fifths to shop, and one-fifth to office.

d.   Depreciation to be charged at the rate of 10 per cent per annum on cost of Office Equipment, and on Shop Fittings.

6.   Muggins and Co. Ltd.

*Trial Balance at 31 December 19X6*

| | Dr. $ | Cr. $ |
|---|---:|---:|
| Accounts Receivable | 27,380 | — |
| Accounts Payable | — | 9,240 |
| Advertising | 14,980 | — |
| Audit Fees | 1,800 | — |
| Bank | 14,470 | — |
| Bills Receivable | 1,260 | — |
| Cost of Goods Sold | 86,730 | — |
| Delivery Expenses | 7,030 | — |
| Directors' Fees | 3,000 | — |
| Dividend | 6,000 | — |
| Estimated Bad Debts | — | 2,730 |
| Estimated Credit Losses | 2,200 | — |
| Furniture and Equipment — Office | 5,000 | — |
| Furniture and Equipment — Showroom | 8,500 | — |
| Goodwill | 15,000 | — |

| | | |
|---|---|---|
| Inventory | 53,900 | — |
| Insurance | 1,200 | — |
| Interest | 2,000 | — |
| Lighting and Heating | 1,800 | — |
| Mortgage | — | 30,000 |
| Office Expenses | 4,720 | — |
| Office Salaries | 7,800 | — |
| Preliminary Expenses | 2,800 | — |
| Profit and Loss Appropriation Account, 1 Jan. 19X6 | — | 6,690 |
| Accumulated Depreciation — Office Furniture and Equipment | — | 1,600 |
| Accumulated Depreciation — Showroom Furniture and Equipment | — | 2,400 |
| Accumulated Depreciation — Travellers' Cars: | — | 3,600 |
| Accumulated Depreciation — Premises | — | 18,000 |
| Premises | 60,000 | — |
| Reserve | — | 8,000 |
| Sales | — | 198,600 |
| Sales Salaries | 15,240 | — |
| Travellers' Cars | 10,600 | — |
| Travellers' Salaries and Expenses | 7,450 | — |
| Paid-up Capital | — | 80,000 |
| | $360,860 | $360,860 |

*Adjustments Required:*

a.  Accrued Expenses at 31 December 19X6 — Lighting and Heating $420; Advertising $1,260; Office Salaries $490; Sales Salaries $780; Travellers' Salaries $260.

b.  Lighting to be apportioned 80 per cent as selling expense, 20 per cent general.

c.  Additional Bad Debts of $540 are to be written off, and Estimated Bad Debts of $3,200 are to be provided for on closing debtors' balances.

d.  Depreciation to be charged at 5 per cent per annum on cost of Furniture and Equipment, 20 per cent per annum on cost of Cars, and 5 per cent per annum on net book value of Premises.

e.  Provision to be made for Estimated Taxation on year's results $8,000, and Final Dividend $4,000.

f.  $5,000 be written off Goodwill, and $1,000 off Preliminary Expenses.

*7.  Nepean Co. Ltd.

*Trial Balance at 30 June 19X8*

| | Dr. $ | Cr. $ |
|---|---|---|
| Accounts Payable | — | $11,700 |
| Accounts Receivable | 27,600 | — |
| Accumulated Depreciation of Office Equipment. | — | 400 |
| Accumulated Depreciation of Shop and Store Fittings | — | 3,200 |
| Accumulated Depreciation of Building | — | 8,000 |

| | | |
|---|---:|---:|
| Advertising | 4,570 | — |
| Appropriation Account (balance at 1 July 19X7): | — | 7,300 |
| Audit Fees | 820 | — |
| Bank | — | 9,500 |
| Building | 40,000 | — |
| Cost of Goods Sold | 92,720 | — |
| Debentures | — | 8,000 |
| Directors' Fees | 2,000 | — |
| Estimated Bad Debts | — | 600 |
| Estimated Credit Losses | 2,400 | — |
| Goodwill | 14,000 | — |
| General Reserve | — | 6,500 |
| Insurance | 460 | — |
| Interest | 1,020 | — |
| Interim Dividend | 5,000 | — |
| Merchandise Inventory | 28,690 | — |
| Office Expenses and Stationery | 2,140 | — |
| Office Equipment | 4,400 | — |
| Office Salaries | 2,680 | — |
| Paid-up Capital | — | 40,000 |
| Repairs to Office Equipment | 270 | — |
| Sales Returns and Allowances | 3,790 | |
| Sales | — | 142,760 |
| Salesmen's Salaries | 6,400 | — |
| Shop and Store Fittings | 9,000 | — |
| Share Premium Reserve | — | 10,000 |
| | $247,960 | $247,960 |

*Adjustments Required:*

a. Salaries accrued to 30 June 19X8 — Office $150; Salesmen $186.

b. Insurance paid in advance, $120.

c. Straight-line depreciation to be charged at 10 per cent per annum on Office Equipment and Shop and Store Fittings, and 5 per cent reducing balance depreciation on Buildings.

d. Transfer $1,000 to General Reserve, and write $4,000 off Goodwill.

e. Write off Bad Debts $400, and revise the Estimate of Bad Debts to $1,000 on debtors' balances.

f. Provide for Company Taxation $5,000, and Dividends $7,000.

8. Macquarie Trading Company Limited

*Trial Balance at 30 June 19X2*

| | Dr. $ | Cr. $ |
|---|---:|---:|
| Accounts Receivable | 67,000 | — |
| Accounts Payable | — | 21,000 |
| Accumulated Depreciation of Delivery Vehicles | — | 1,600 |
| Accumulated Depreciation of Shop Fittings | — | 14,000 |
| Administrative Salaries | 5,200 | — |

| | | |
|---|---:|---:|
| Advertising | 10,200 | — |
| Bank | 16,600 | — |
| Cost of Goods Sold | 340,000 | — |
| Debentures | — | 20,000 |
| Delivery Expenses | 22,400 | — |
| Delivery Vehicles | 6,000 | — |
| Interim Dividend | 12,500 | — |
| Interest | 2,000 | — |
| Long-Term Investments | 13,000 | — |
| Merchandise Inventory | 92,000 | — |
| Paid-up Capital | — | 100,000 |
| Preliminary Expenses | 12,500 | — |
| Appropriation Account, 1 July 19X1 | — | 6,000 |
| Estimated Bad Debts | — | 3,400 |
| Long-Term Notes | — | 14,000 |
| Rent | 20,000 | — |
| Sales | — | 520,000 |
| Salesmen's Salaries | 40,600 | — |
| Shop Fittings | 36,000 | — |
| Estimated Credit Losses | 4,000 | — |
| | $700,000 | $700,000 |

*Additional Information Required to be Incorporated in the Final Report:*

i.  Depreciation is to be charged on Delivery Vehicles and Shop Fittings at 10 per cent per annum on cost.

ii.  Salesmen's Salaries owing $400.

iii.  After a review of the Accounts Receivable, management decided to write off Bad Debts $2,000, and to raise the Estimated Bad Debts to $5,400.

iv.  Provide for Company Income Tax payable $26,000.

v.  A Final Dividend of $12,500 is to be provided for.

vi.  $2,000 is to be written off Preliminary Expenses.

9.  Epping Retailers Limited

*Trial Balance at 30 June 19X9*

| | Dr. $ | Cr. $ |
|---|---:|---:|
| Accounts Receivable | 48,200 | — |
| Accounts Payable | — | 19,600 |
| Accumulated Depreciation of Shop Fittings | — | 2,000 |
| Advertising | 4,600 | — |
| Appropriation Account, 1 July 19X8 | — | 9,400 |
| Bank | — | 7,600 |
| Cost of Goods Sold | 168,700 | — |
| Directors' Fees | 2,000 | — |
| Estimated Bad Debts | — | 1,400 |
| Estimated Credit Losses | 2,600 | — |
| General Reserve | — | 16,000 |
| Interest | 2,800 | — |

| | | |
|---|---:|---:|
| Merchandise Inventory | 61,900 | – |
| Mortgage | – | 30,000 |
| Office Expenses | 2,900 | – |
| Office Salaries | 8,300 | – |
| Paid-up Capital | – | 100,000 |
| Premises | 94,000 | – |
| Sales | – | 234,000 |
| Sales Returns | 4,600 | – |
| Share Premium Reserve | – | 20,000 |
| Salesmen's Salaries | 19,400 | – |
| Shop Fittings | 20,000 | – |
| | $440,000 | $440,000 |

*Additional Information to Be Incorporated into the Reports:*

i.    Salesmen's Salaries unpaid $600.

ii.    Advertising paid in advance $400.

iii.    Depreciation is to be charged on Shop Fittings at 10 per cent of net book value.

iv.    Bad Debts of $500 are to be recognized and written off.

v.    The Estimate of Bad Debts is to be revised to $2,000.

vi.    Directors recommend payment of an 8 per cent Dividend on Paid-up Capital, and this amount is to be provided for.

vii.    Income Tax of $6,000 is to be provided for.

10.    Master Stores Limited

*Trial Balance at 30 June 19X8*

| | Dr. $ | Cr. $ |
|---|---:|---:|
| Accounts Receivable | 76,000 | – |
| Accounts Payable | – | 34,000 |
| Accumulated Depreciation of Vehicles | – | 8,000 |
| Advertising | 4,000 | – |
| Appropriation Account 1 July | – | 16,000 |
| Bank | 12,000 | – |
| Cost of Goods Sold | 183,000 | – |
| Debentures | – | 40,000 |
| Directors' Fees | 4,000 | – |
| Delivery Vehicles | 20,000 | – |
| Estimated Bad Debts | – | 3,000 |
| Estimated Credit Losses | 5,000 | – |
| Interest | 6,000 | – |
| Land and Buildings | 88,000 | – |
| Merchandise Inventory | 53,000 | – |
| Office Salaries | 14,000 | – |
| Paid-up Capital | – | 100,000 |
| Preliminary Expenses | 10,000 | – |
| Reserves | – | 15,000 |
| Sales | – | 274,000 |
| Salesmen's Salaries | 15,000 | – |
| | $490,000 | $490,000 |

*Additional Information to Be Incorporated in the Reports:*

i.   Salesmen's Salaries owing $1,000.

ii.  Depreciation is to be charged on Delivery Vehicles at 20 per cent per annum on cost.

iii. The Estimate of Bad Debts is to be increased by $1,000.

iv.  Dividends of $10,000 and Company Taxation of $17,000 are to be provided for.

v.   $6,000 is to be written off Preliminary Expenses.

*11. Balaclava Battlers Limited

*Trial Balance at 30 June 19X0*

|  | Dr. $ | Cr. $ |
|---|---|---|
| Accounts Receivable | 62,800 | – |
| Accounts Payable | – | 22,600 |
| Accumulated Depreciation of Shop Fittings | – | 4,000 |
| Advertising | 7,700 | – |
| Audit Fees | 1,000 | – |
| Appropriation Account, 1 July 19X9 | – | 11,300 |
| Bank | – | 9,400 |
| Cost of Goods Sold | 185,100 | – |
| Directors' Fees | 2,000 | – |
| Estimated Bad Debts | – | 1,700 |
| Estimated Credit Losses | 3,400 | – |
| General Reserve | – | 18,000 |
| Goodwill | 10,000 | – |
| Interest | 3,800 | – |
| Merchandise Inventory | 75,700 | – |
| Mortgage | – | 35,000 |
| Office Expenses | 3,300 | – |
| Office Salaries | 12,200 | – |
| Paid-up Capital | – | 120,000 |
| Premises | 100,000 | – |
| Rates | 4,400 | – |
| Sales | – | 278,000 |
| Sales Returns | 5,200 | – |
| Share Premium Reserve | – | 20,000 |
| Salesmen's Salaries | 23,400 | – |
| Shop Fittings | 20,000 | – |
|  | $520,000 | $520,000 |

*Additional Information to Be Incorporated into the Reports:*

i.   Salesmen's Salaries unpaid $800.

ii.  Rates paid in advance $1,400.

iii. Depreciation is to be charged on Shop Fittings at 10 per cent on cost.

iv.  Bad Debts of $1,200 are to be recognized and written off.

v.   The Estimate of Bad Debts is to be revised to $3,500.

vi.　Directors recommend payment of an 8 per cent Dividend on Paid-up Capital, and this amount is to be provided for.

vii.　Income Tax of $7,000 is to be provided for.

viii.　Goodwill is to be written down by $4,000.

*12.　Gold Coast Retailers Limited

*Trial Balance at 31 December 19X9*

|  | Dr. $ | Cr. $ |
|---|---|---|
| Advertising | 8,500 | — |
| Appropriation Account, 1 Jan. 19X9 | — | 12,200 |
| Audit Fees | 2,500 | — |
| Accounts Receivable | 64,800 | — |
| Accounts Payable | — | 15,090 |
| Accumulated Depreciation of Premises | — | 10,000 |
| Accumulated Depreciation of Office Equipment | — | 1,600 |
| Accumulated Depreciation of Travellers' Cars | — | 4,280 |
| Bank | 11,740 | — |
| Cost of Goods Sold | 156,000 | — |
| Debentures | — | 20,000 |
| Directors' Fees | 1,800 | — |
| Dividend | 5,000 | — |
| Estimated Credit Losses | 1,580 | — |
| Estimated Bad Debts | — | 1,700 |
| Goodwill | 30,000 | — |
| Interest | 2,800 | — |
| Merchandise Inventory | 46,730 | — |
| Office Equipment | 4,400 | — |
| Office Expenses | 5,760 | — |
| Office Salaries | 7,070 | — |
| Paid-up Capital | — | 80,000 |
| Premises | 50,000 | — |
| Rates on Premises | 2,080 | — |
| Reserve | — | 22,000 |
| Sales | — | 250,000 |
| Sales Returns | 6,000 | — |
| Share Premium Reserve | — | 12,000 |
| Salesmen's Salaries | 8,600 | — |
| Travellers' Cars | 7,200 | — |
| Travellers' Salaries | 6,310 | — |
|  | $428,870 | $428,870 |

*Additional Information to Be Incorporated in the Reports:*

i.　Expenses unpaid on 31 December 19X9: Travellers' Salaries $220; Interest $200.

ii.　Expenses paid in advance on 31 December 19X9: Rates $480.

iii.　Depreciation to be charged on Office Equipment and Travellers' Cars at 10 per cent per annum on cost, and on Premises at 5 per cent per annum on net book value.

iv.   Bad Debts of $1,600 to be recognized and written off.

v.   Estimated Bad Debts to be raised to $3,000.

vi.   Goodwill is to be written down by $4,000.

vii.   Provide for Income Tax at 40 cents in the $ of net profit.

viii.   Provide for Final Dividend of $7,000.

ix.   Transfer $6,000 to Reserve.

13.   The Glenrowan General Store

*Trial Balance at 31 December 19X0*

|  | Dr. $ | Cr. $ |
|---|---|---|
| Accounts Payable | — | 26,600 |
| Accounts Receivable | 45,800 | — |
| Accumulated Depreciation on Office Equipment | — | 1,000 |
| Accumulated Depreciation on Salesmen's Cars | — | 2,500 |
| Advertising | 6,200 | — |
| Audit Fees | 1,500 | — |
| Bank | 5,300 | — |
| Car Expenses | 3,200 | — |
| Capital — Edward Kelly | — | 50,000 |
| Capital — William Kelly | — | 40,000 |
| Current Account — Edward Kelly | 9,000 | — |
| Current Account — William Kelly | 7,800 | — |
| Insurance | 1,500 | — |
| Interest | 700 | — |
| Long-Term Loan | — | 18,500 |
| Office Equipment | 5,000 | — |
| Office Expenses | 7,200 | — |
| Office Salaries | 18,000 | — |
| Purchases | 150,000 | — |
| Purchases Returns | — | 2,000 |
| Rent | 8,600 | — |
| Sales | — | 243,000 |
| Salesmen's Cars | 12,500 | — |
| Salesmen's Salaries | 30,000 | — |
| Sales Returns | 2,700 | — |
| Shop Lighting | 600 | — |
| Stock on Hand, 1 Jan. 19X0 | 68,000 | |
|  | $383,600 | $383,600 |

*Additional Information to Be Incorporated into the Reports:*

i.   Stock of Merchandise on Hand, 31 December 19X0, $81,000.

ii.   Expenses unpaid on 31 December 19X0: Office Salaries $300.

iii.   Expenses paid in advance on 31 December 19X0: Rent $150.

iv.   Depreciation to be charged on Office Equipment at 20 per cent per annum on net book value, and Salesmen's Cars at 10 per cent on cost.

v   The partnership agreement provides that each owner is entitled to a salary of $8,000 per annum, and the residue of the profits is to be divided according to contributed capital.

14.   The Gordon Emporium Limited

*Trial Balance at 30 June 19X2*

|  | Dr. $ | Cr. $ |
|---|---|---|
| Accounts Receivable | 70,000 | — |
| Accounts Payable | — | 34,000 |
| Accumulated Depreciation on Vehicles | — | 6,000 |
| Advertising | 3,000 | — |
| Appropriation Account, 1 July 19X1 | — | 14,000 |
| Bank | 8,000 | — |
| Cost of Goods Sold | 124,000 | — |
| Debentures | — | 20,000 |
| Directors' Fees | 2,000 | — |
| Delivery Vehicles | 20,000 | — |
| Estimated Bad Debts | — | 4,000 |
| Estimated Credit Losses | 5,000 | — |
| Interest | 1,000 | — |
| Land and Buildings | 95,000 | — |
| Merchandise Inventory | 30,000 | — |
| Office Expenses | 4,000 | — |
| Office Salaries | 11,000 | — |
| Preliminary Expenses | 5,000 | — |
| Registered Capital | — | 200,000 |
| Reserves | — | 7,000 |
| Sales | — | 195,000 |
| Salesmen's Salaries | 22,000 | — |
| Unissued Capital | 80,000 | — |
| | $480,000 | $480,000 |

*Additional Information to Be Incorporated in the Reports*:

i.    Salesmen's Salaries owing $1,000.

ii.   Depreciation to be charged on Delivery Vehicles at the rate of 10 per cent per annum on cost.

iii.  Bad Debts to be written off — $1,000; and the Estimate of Bad Debts is to be increased to $5,000.

iv.   Dividend of $8,000 and Company Tax of $10,000 are to be provided for.

v.    $4,000 is to be transferred to Reserves.

Explain the reasons for making balance-day adjustments for items i, ii, and iii, above.

*15.  Pacific Retailers Limited

### Trial Balance at 31 December 19X0

|  | Dr. $ | Cr. $ |
|---|---|---|
| Accounts Receivable | 38,200 | – |
| Accounts Payable | – | 18,600 |
| Accumulated Depreciation of Office Equipment | – | 2,000 |
| Accumulated Depreciation of Delivery Vans | – | 6,000 |
| Accumulated Depreciation of Premises | – | 20,000 |
| Advertising | 8,800 | – |
| Appropriation, 1 Jan. 19X0 | – | 16,300 |
| Audit Fees | 2,000 | – |
| Bank | – | 14,300 |
| Bills Payable | – | 10,000 |
| Cost of Goods Sold | 216,000 | – |
| Directors' Fees | 3,000 | – |
| Delivery Expenses | 12,400 | – |
| Delivery Vans | 36,000 | – |
| General Reserve | – | 6,000 |
| Goodwill | 24,000 | – |
| Interest | 3,800 | – |
| Interim Dividend | 6,000 | – |
| Loss Due to Fire | 8,000 | – |
| Merchandise Inventory | 62,800 | – |
| Mortgage | – | 40,000 |
| Office Equipment | 12,000 | – |
| Office Expenses | 7,200 | – |
| Office Salaries | 24,400 | – |
| Premises | 90,000 | – |
| Registered Capital | – | 130,000 |
| Rates | 2,800 | – |
| Share Premium Reserve | – | 20,000 |
| Sales | – | 376,800 |
| Sales Returns | 6,200 | – |
| Salesmen's Salaries | 46,400 | – |
| Unissued Capital | 40,000 | – |
| Uncalled Capital | 10,000 | – |
|  | $660,000 | $660,000 |

*Additional Information to Be Incorporated in the Reports:*

i.   Expenses unpaid on 31 December 19X0 – Office Salaries $200; Salesmen's Salaries $400.

ii.   Expenses paid in advance on 31 December 19X0 – Rates $500.

iii.   Depreciation to be charged on Office Equipment: 10 per cent straight line; Delivery Vans 20 per cent straight line; Premises 5 per cent reducing balance.

iv.   The liability for Company Tax on the year's profits is estimated to be $11,000.

v.   The directors have recommended payment of a Final Dividend of $6,000.

vi.   $4,000 is to be written off Goodwill.

vii.   $6,000 is to be transferred to the General Reserve.

viii.   There is a contingent liability of $50,000 under a contract for the construction of additional premises.

# Chapter 11
# Processing Accounting Data

We have defined accounting as a financial information-gathering and communication system maintained by an entity for the purpose of enabling rational decisions to be made about the use of resources in its operations and for effective control over the use of these resources. The basic inputs for such an information system consist of facts about the firm's transactions with its factor and product markets and market prices of its resources. The system must convert or transform these facts into information (i.e., the output of the system) that is useful for prediction, decision-making, control, and evaluation purposes, and as well satisfy legal and taxation requirements. The operation of an information system takes the broad form shown in Figure 11−1.[1]

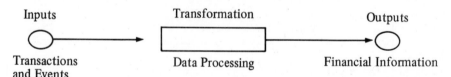

| Inputs | Transformation | Outputs |
|---|---|---|
| Transactions and Events | Data Processing | Financial Information |

**Figure 11−1.** Outline of information system

The data processing system encompasses the physical processes by which input data are transformed into the required financial information. It covers the sorting, classifying, recording, storing, aggregation, and summarization of data relating to transactions and events, and the preparation of accounting reports, i.e., the bookkeeping parts of accounting. The type of data processing system used by the firm depends upon its size and the nature of its business operations. It can range from manual systems with hand-written records appropriate for very small firms, through mechanical systems using accounting machines, to fully computerized systems in large firms. Moreover, substantial variations in format and procedures occur between firms in the same general systems category. Whatever the system used, it must be tailored to suit the informational requirements of the firm and be efficient. Only a very general format is outlined here, to show how several everyday accounting devices are used to facilitate data processing. These devices comprise the use of specialized journals, general and subsidiary ledgers and control accounts, and columnar accounts.

A typical procedure in a handwritten accounting system is for the documents relating to transactions — sales invoices, purchase invoices, receipts for cash paid and received, cash register duplicates, and so on — to be sorted; journals are written up from these documents; and the items are posted from the journals to the ledger accounts.

### JOURNALS

Journals are the normal books of originating entry in the handwritten accounting system. Journals are merely lists of transactions in chronological order, prepared in a specified format. The journal is a day-book in the nature of a memorandum record, used as the basis for the subsequent entries in the ledger accounts. In mechanized data processing systems, several stages can be handled simultaneously, and the journal is often a master carbon copy of all ledger account entries.

Two main types of journals are used — a general journal, and a series of specialized journals: Specialized journals are used where there are large numbers of transactions of the same type. All transactions and events not recorded in specialized journals are recorded in the general journal.

The form of the *general journal* is as follows:

| Date | Transactions | | Dr. $ | Cr. $ |
|------|--------------|---|-------|-------|
| 19X8 July 31 | Depreciation of Plant<br>Accumulated Depreciation of Plant<br>Depreciation charged on plant for the year at the rate of 10 per cent per annum on cost | Dr.<br>Cr. | 100 | 100 |

The transaction or event is analyzed according to the accounts affected and its twofold aspects, and a short description (the narration) of the transaction is given, together with any pertinent information concerning it.

*Specialized journals* are used to record the everyday transactions of the firm. Rather than each transaction being accorded a separate double entry in the general journal, all transactions of the same type are merely listed in the relevant specialized journal, and the totals are posted to the main ledger accounts. This system is more economical to operate; and, when the specialized journal includes a series of classification columns for analyses of the items, much more separate information can be provided. Typically, specialized journals are kept for cash receipts, cash payments, credit purchases, credit sales, payroll, and so on. The format and procedures required are illustrated in the problem below.

The general journal entries for closing the accounts of the Northside Trading Company Limited, and the reversing entries, are given below:

Northside Trading Company Limited

*General Journal*

| Date | Particulars | | Dr. $ | Cr. $ |
|---|---|---|---|---|
| Dec. 31 | Sales | Dr. | 140,000 | – |
| | Profit and Loss | Cr. | – | 140,000 |
| | Revenue account closed off to Profit and Loss account | | | |
| Dec. 31 | Profit and Loss | Dr. | 129,000 | – |
| | Estimated Credit Losses | Cr. | – | 6,000 |
| | Cost of Goods Sold | Cr. | – | 100,000 |
| | Advertising | Cr. | – | 3,000 |
| | Salesmen's Salaries | Cr. | – | 6,000 |
| | Depreciation of Shop Fittings | Cr. | – | 1,000 |
| | Directors' Fees | Cr. | – | 1,000 |
| | Office Salaries | Cr. | – | 2,000 |
| | Depreciation of Buildings | Cr. | – | 3,000 |
| | Interest | Cr. | – | 1,000 |
| | Fire Loss | Cr. | – | 6,000 |
| | Expense accounts closed off to Profit and Loss account | | | |
| Dec. 31 | Profit and Loss | Dr. | 11,000 | – |
| | Appropriation | Cr. | – | 11,000 |
| | Net profit transferred to Appropriation account | | | |
| Dec. 31 | Appropriation | Dr. | 14,000 | – |
| | Dividends | Cr. | – | 4,000 |
| | Taxation | Cr. | – | 5,000 |
| | Goodwill | Cr. | – | 2,000 |
| | Reserve | Cr. | – | 3,000 |
| | Profit appropriations charged to Appropriation account | | | |
| Jan. 1 | Advertising | Dr. | 1,000 | – |
| | Prepayments | Cr. | – | 1,000 |
| | Reversing entry for Prepaid Advertising | | | |
| Jan. 1 | Accrued Expenses | Dr. | 1,000 | – |
| | Interest | Cr. | – | 500 |
| | Salesmen's Salaries | Cr. | – | 300 |
| | Office Salaries | Cr. | – | 200 |
| | Reversing entry for Accrued Expenses | | | |

## LEDGERS

Along with the use of general and specialized journals, the ledger is divided into the main *general ledger* and specialized *subsidiary ledgers.* The *general ledger* comprises all the main accounts and a complete double-entry record must be maintained in it. The trial balances are prepared from the general ledger. *Subsidiary ledgers* comprise supplementary accounts which record, in detail, items included in the general ledger. The purpose of maintaining subsidiary ledgers is to permit the accumulation of extra detail on some aspects of the firm's operations without unduly expanding the main ledger and to enable the physical separation of work by the data processing staff. It is important to recognize that entries in subsidiary ledgers are *in addition to* the double entry maintained in the general ledger, and that there need not be double entry in the subsidiary ledgers. Rather, these ledgers are essentially just additional memoranda records. Accounts in the general ledger which are supported by additional data in specialized ledgers are known as *control accounts.* Normally, Accounts Receivable and Accounts Payable accounts are control accounts in the general ledger supported by the personal accounts for each debtor and creditor in the specialized debtors' ledger and creditors' ledger; Merchandise Inventory account is a control account supported by separate accounts for each line of merchandise in a specialized ledger; the Payroll (or Wages and Salaries) account is supported by the personal wages account of each employee; and so on. The entries in the control accounts should equal the sum of the amounts recorded in the relevant subsidiary ledger accounts, and the balances in the control accounts should equal the sum of the balances in the related subsidiary ledger accounts. Normally a schedule of subsidiary account balances is prepared at balance date to support the control account balance, and any discrepancy appearing should be resolved. The use of control accounts and subsidiary ledgers is a valuable aid in maintaining an accurate set of records.

Another method which enables the aggregation of additional detailed information is the use of *columnar accounts* in either ledger. Columnar accounts contain additional analysis columns showing a detailed classification of items, and they can be a substitute for control accounts where the amount of extra detail required is limited and can be handled with a few extra columns in the account. For example, in the illustration following, the Sales account shows the value of each product line sold in analysis columns. It is easier to do this than to have separate subsidiary ledger accounts for each product line sold where the number of product lines, or selling departments, is small.

The data flows and accounting records used are illustrated below.[2]

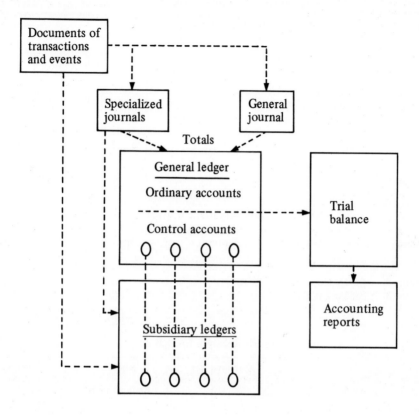

### An Illustrative Problem

T. Ray operates an electrical appliances store. His transactions for the first week in September were as follows:

Sept. 1.  Sold fan to M. Wiggins on credit $30. Sold radio to I. Joseph on credit $50. Cash sales — fans $60; radios $100.

2.  Purchased fans from Leroy Co. $160. Paid weekly rent $40.

3.  Sold radio to R. Grey on credit $50. Cash sales — radios $150. Purchased radios from Jackson & Co. $280. Paid council rates $80.

4.  Sold fan to J. Burke on credit $30. Cash sales — fans $90.

5.  Cash sales — radios $200. Paid salesmen's salaries $90. Paid office salaries $40. Paid Leroy in full $160. Received from M. Wiggins $20. Received from I. Joseph $50.

*Required:*

Record these transactions in specialized journals, post to general and subsidiary ledger accounts, reconcile balances in related general ledger control and subsidiary ledger accounts, and prepare a general ledger trial balance.

*Specialized Journals*

### Credit Sales Journal

| Date | Customer – Dr. Account | Amount $ | Radios $ | Fans $ |
|---|---|---|---|---|
| Sept. 1 | M. Wiggins | 30 | | 30 |
| | I. Joseph | 50 | 50 | |
| 3 | R. Grey | 50 | 50 | |
| 4 | J. Burke | 30 | | 30 |
| | | $160 | $100 | $60 |

### Credit Purchases Journal

| Date | Supplier – Cr. Account | Amount $ | Radios $ | Fans $ |
|---|---|---|---|---|
| Sept. 2 | Leroy Co. | 160 | | 160 |
| 3 | Jackson & Co. | 280 | 280 | |
| | | $440 | $280 | $160 |

### Cash Receipts Journal

| Date | Source – Cr. Account | Rec. No. | Amount Received $ | Account Receivable $ | Sales Radios $ | Sales Fans $ | Sundry | Bank Deposit $ |
|---|---|---|---|---|---|---|---|---|
| Sept. 1 | Sales | | 160 | | 100 | 60 | | 160 |
| 3 | Sales | | 150 | | 150 | | | 150 |
| 4 | Sales | | 90 | | | 90 | | 90 |
| 5 | Sales | | 200 | | 200 | | | |
| | M. Wiggins | | 20 | 20 | | | | |
| | I. Joseph | | 50 | 50 | | | | 270 |
| | | | $670 | $70 | $450 | $150 | | $670 |

### Cash Payments Journal

| Date | Payee – Dr. Account | Chq. No. | Amount Paid $ | Accounts Payable $ | Rent $ | Salesmen's Salaries $ | Office Salaries $ | Sundry $ |
|---|---|---|---|---|---|---|---|---|
| Sept. 2 | Rent | | 40 | | 40 | | | |
| 3 | Rates | | 80 | | | | | 80 |
| 5 | Salesmen's Salaries | | 90 | | | 90 | | |
| | Office Salaries | | 40 | | | | 40 | |
| | Leroy Co. | | 160 | 160 | | | | |
| | | | $410 | $160 | $40 | $90 | $40 | $80 |

*General Ledger*

Sales Account

| Date | | Dr. $ | Cr. $ | Balance $ | Radios $ | Fans $ |
|------|---|------|------|-----------|----------|--------|
| Sept. 5 | Accounts Receivable | | 160 | 160 Cr. | 100 | 60 |
| | Cash | | 600 | 760 Cr. | 450 | 150 |

Purchases Account

| Sept. 5 | Accounts Payable | 440 | | 440 Dr. | 280 | 160 |
|---------|------------------|-----|---|---------|-----|-----|

Accounts Receivable Control Account

| Date | | Dr. $ | Cr. $ | Balance $ |
|------|---|-------|-------|-----------|
| Sept. 5 | Credit Sales | 160 | | 160 Dr. |
| | Cash | | 70 | 90 Dr. |

Accounts Payable Control Account

| Sept. 5 | Credit Purchases | | 440 | 440 Cr. |
|---------|------------------|---|-----|---------|
| | Cash | 160 | | 280 Cr. |

Cash at Bank Account

| Sept. 5 | Accounts Receivable | 70 | | 70 Dr. |
|---------|---------------------|----|---|--------|
| | Sales — Radios | 450 | | 520 Dr. |
| | Fans | 150 | | 670 Dr. |
| | Accounts Payable | | 160 | 510 Dr. |
| | Rent | | 40 | 470 Dr. |
| | Salesmen's salaries | | 90 | 380 Dr. |
| | Office salaries | | 40 | 340 Dr. |
| | Rates | | 80 | 260 Dr. |

Rent Account

| Sept. 5 | Cash | 40 | | 40 Dr. |
|---------|------|----|---|--------|

Salesmen's Salaries Account

| Sept. 5 | Cash | 90 | | 90 Dr. |
|---------|------|----|---|--------|

Office Salaries Account

| Sept. 5 | Cash | 40 | | 40 Dr. |
|---------|------|----|---|--------|

Rates Account

| | | | | |
|---|---|---|---|---|
| Sept. 5 | Cash | 80 | | 80 Dr. |

*Subsidiary Ledgers*

*Debtors' Ledger*

M. Wiggins Account

| Date | | Dr. $ | Cr. $ | Balance $ |
|---|---|---|---|---|
| Sept. 1 | Sales — Fans | 30 | | 30 Dr. |
| 5 | Cash | | 20 | 10 Dr. |

I. Joseph Account

| | | | | |
|---|---|---|---|---|
| Sept. 1 | Sales — Radios | 50 | | 50 Dr. |
| 5 | Cash | | 50 | — |

R. Grey Account

| | | | | |
|---|---|---|---|---|
| Sept. 3 | Sales — Radios | 50 | | 50 Dr. |

J. Burke Account

| | | | | |
|---|---|---|---|---|
| Sept. 4 | Sales — Fans | 30 | | 30 Dr. |

*Creditors' Ledger*

Leroy Co. Account

| | | | | |
|---|---|---|---|---|
| Sept. 2 | Purchases — Fans | | 160 | 160 Cr. |
| 5 | Cash | 160 | | — |

*Schedule of Debtors' Balances*

| | $ |
|---|---|
| M. Wiggins | 10 |
| R. Grey | 50 |
| J. Burke | 30 |
| Total Accounts Receivable (per general ledger) | $90 |

*Schedule of Creditors' Balances*

| | |
|---|---|
| Jackson & Co. | 280 |
| Total Accounts Payable (per general ledger) | $280 |

*General Ledger Trial Balance*

|  | Dr. $ | Cr. $ |
|---|---|---|
| Sales |  | 760 |
| Purchases | 440 |  |
| Accounts Receivable | 90 |  |
| Accounts Payable |  | 280 |
| Cash at Bank | 260 |  |
| Rent | 40 |  |
| Salesmen's Salaries | 90 |  |
| Office Salaries | 40 |  |
| Rates | 80 |  |
|  | $1,040 | $1,040 |

*Points to Note:*

1.  The specialized journals have a total amounts column, followed by analyses columns according to the quantity of detail required.

2.  In the cash receipts journal, provision is made to record the amounts deposited at the bank, so as to facilitate comparison of the firm's cash receipts journal with its bank statement compiled by the bank. Normally, receipts are banked daily for control reasons. Provision can be made to record cash discounts by adding another column: in this case the gross amount is recorded in the Accounts Receivable column for credit to that account. Similar provision can be made in the cash payments journal for discounts allowed to customers.

3.  Payments should normally be made by cheque so as to facilitate cash control and reconciliation of the payments journal with the bank statement.

4.  In posting transactions to the general ledger, only the totals in the subsidiary journals are used. For example, the postings from:

|  |  |  | $ |
|---|---|---|---|
| i. | The credit sales journal are: |  |  |
|  | Accounts Receivable | Dr. | 160 |
|  | Sales | Cr. | 160 |
| ii. | The credit purchases journal are: |  |  |
|  | Purchases | Dr. | 440 |
|  | Accounts Payable | Cr. | 440 |
| iii. | The cash receipts journal are: |  |  |
|  | Cash at Bank | Dr. | 670 |
|  | Accounts Receivable | Cr. | 70 |
|  | Sales — Radios | Cr. | 450 |
|  | Fans | Cr. | 150 |
| iv. | The cash payments journal are: |  |  |
|  | Accounts Payable | Dr. | 160 |
|  | Rent | Dr. | 40 |
|  | Sales Salaries | Dr. | 90 |
|  | Office Salaries | Dr. | 40 |
|  | Rates | Dr. | 80 |
|  | Cash at Bank | Cr. | 410 |

An exception to this rule occurs for items in a Sundries column — these are posted individually to their separate accounts.

5. The Sales and Purchases accounts are supplemented by analysis columns for radios and fans.

6. The Accounts Receivable and Accounts Payable accounts are control accounts supplemented by personal accounts for individual debtors and creditors in subsidiary ledgers. Control accounts could be used for sales and purchases, but columnar accounts suffice in this simple illustration.

7. The entries to the subsidiary ledger accounts are posted from the body of the specialized journal. They comprise entries in addition to the double entry in the general ledger, and there need be no double entry in the subsidiary ledgers.

8. The schedule of balances in the subsidiary ledgers should agree with the balances in the related control accounts.

## CHART OF ACCOUNTS

A chart of accounts is a classified list of all accounts in the ledger. It is constructed according to the classification of accounts in the final accounting reports, and it thereby serves as an index to the ledger. Each ledger account is given a code number according to its position in the chart; and, if space is left in the numbering system, new accounts can be added as required. The structure and content of the chart depends upon the kinds of information required by users, as reflected in the accounting reports. A typical practice is to organize the accounts in the order illustrated below; other sequences may of course be used. An abbreviated chart of accounts showing only some of the accounts for the Northside Trading Co. Ltd. is as follows:

1. Assets

    11   Current Assets
       111  Cash at Bank
       112  Accounts Receivable
       112A Estimated Bad Debts

    12   Long-Term Assets
       121  Shop Fittings
       121A Accumulated Depreciation of Shop Fittings

2. Liabilities

    21   Current Liabilities
    22   Long-Term Liabilities

3. Shareholders' Funds

    31   Contributed Capital
       311  Paid-up Capital
    32   Retained Earnings
       321  Reserves
       322  Appropriation

4.  Operating Revenue
    41   Sales
    41A  Estimated Credit Losses

5.  Operating Expenses
    51   Cost of Goods Sold
    52   Selling Expenses
         521   Advertising
    53   Administrative Expenses
         531   Directors' Fees
    54   Finance Expenses
         541   Interest

6.  Non-Operating Revenue and Expenses

    61   Non-operating Revenue
    62   Non-operating Expenses
         621   Fire Loss

7.  Profit Disposition Accounts

    71   Dividends

8.  Closing Accounts

    81   Profit and Loss.

## MANUAL OF ACCOUNTS

A manual of accounts is a detailed set of instructions accompanying the chart, in which instructions are given as to what items should be recorded in each account, the amount of detail to be recorded, when accounts are to be closed off, and so on. It is prepared to guide the accounting staff in their work.

### FURTHER READING

Carrington, A. S., Battersby, G. B., and Howitt, G. *Accounting: An Information System*. Christchurch: Whitcombe and Tombs, 1975. Chaps. 2 and 4.
Gordon, M. J., and Shillinglaw, G. *Accounting, A Management Approach*. 4th ed. Homewood, Illinois: Richard D. Irwin, 1969. Chap. 7.
Mathews, R. L. *The Accounting Framework*. 3rd ed. Melbourne: Cheshire, 1971. Chaps. 2 and 5.

### NOTES

1. Mathews, *The Accounting Framework*, chap. 8.
2. Adapted from Gordon and Shillinglaw, *Accounting: A Management Approach*, p. 220.

### QUESTIONS AND EXERCISES

1.  A Brown's ledger is subdivided, inter alia, into a general ledger and a subsidiary debtors' ledger. Show how the following entries would be recorded in the two ledgers, and prepare a trial balance of general ledger balances at 31 December 19X0, supported by a schedule of debtors' balances:

Credit Sales Journal

| 19X0 | | Amount $ |
|---|---|---|
| Dec. 27 | B. Cooke | 117 |
| 28 | C. Drew | 71 |
| 29 | D. Egan | 64 |
| 30 | B. Cooke | 16 |
| 31 | E. Fisher | 162 |
| | | $430 |

Cash Receipts Journal

| 19X0 | | Amount Received $ | Debtors $ | Discount $ | Sales $ | Bank Deposit $ |
|---|---|---|---|---|---|---|
| Dec. 27 | Cash Sales | 18 | | | 18 | 18 |
| 28 | B. Cooke | 114 | 117 | 3 | | 114 |
| 29 | Cash Sales | 16 | | | 16 | 16 |
| 29 | C. Drew | 69 | 71 | 2 | | 69 |
| 30 | D. Egan | 64 | 64 | | | 64 |
| | | $281 | $252 | $5 | $34 | $281 |

2. C. Sturt is a merchant. His accounting records contain, inter alia, a general journal, cash receipts journal, and sales journal, as well as a general ledger and a debtors' ledger. During a given week in May 19X9, he entered into the following transactions with customers:

*19X9*
May   6.   Credit Sales to M. Flinders $44; J. Cook $33; W. Wentworth $28.

       7.   Cash Sales $47.

       8.   Credit Sales to W. Wentworth $22; J. Cook $29. Cash Sales $64.

       9.   Credit note sent to M. Flinders $12 − allowance on defective goods supplied on 6 May.

     10.   Cash Sales $69. M. Flinders paid $25 on account. W. Wentworth paid amount owing, less 2 per cent cash discount.

Assuming there are no other transactions, you are required to record the above transactions in the Sales and Cash Receipts journals and post to ledger accounts. After balancing the accounts as at 10 May, prepare a list of general ledger balances (in the form of a trial balance) supported by a schedule of debtors' balances.

3.    The following entries appear in the books of original entry of K. Williams:

*Purchases Journal*

| Date 19X5 | Particulars | Amount $ |
|---|---|---|
| Nov. 1 | B. Black | 75 |
| 2 | W. White | 52 |
| 3 | G. Green | 49 |
| 4 | T. Brown | 13 |
| 4 | B. Black | 30 |
| | | $219 |

*Cash Payments Journal*

| Date | Particulars | Amount Received $ | Creditors $ | Discount Received $ | Rent $ | Wages $ | Purchases $ |
|---|---|---|---|---|---|---|---|
| Nov. 1 | Cash Purchases | 14 | | | | | 14 |
| 2 | Rent | 20 | | | 20 | | |
| 3 | Cash Purchases | 17 | | | | | 17 |
| | Wages | 36 | | | | 36 | |
| 4 | B. Black | 73 | 75 | 2 | | | |
| | W. White | 50 | 52 | 2 | | | |
| | | $210 | $127 | $4 | $20 | $36 | $31 |

K. Williams's ledger is subdivided, inter alia, into a general ledger (containing a creditors' control account) and a creditors' ledger. Assuming there are no other transactions to be taken into account, you are required:

a.    To post the above entries to appropriate accounts in the two ledgers

b.    To prepare a schedule of general ledger balances as at 4th November, supported by a schedule of creditors' balances.

4.    Record the transactions of A.B.C. Co. Ltd. (see chapter 5) in appropriate specialized journals and the general journal, post to the general ledger and debtors' and creditors' ledgers, extract the general ledger trial balance and supporting schedules of debtors' and creditors' balances.

5.    What is the function of a chart of accounts? Prepare a specimen chart of accounts for Exercise 15, Pacific Retailers Ltd., chapter 10.

6.    Avionics Limited operates the franchise for Arrow and Super Arrow light aircraft, manufactured by the Arrow Aircraft Corporation Limited. The balance sheet of Avionics Limited as at 31 December 1973 is as follows:

|  | $ | $ |  | $ | $ |
|---|---|---|---|---|---|
| *Current Assets* | | | *Current Liabilities* | | |
| Bank | 26,000 | | *Accounts Payable | 110,000 | |
| *Accounts Receivable | 300,000 | | Tax Payable | 112,000 | |
| *Aircraft Inventory | 404,000 | | Dividends Payable | 100,000 | |
| Supplies Inventory | 6,000 | | Accrued Expenses | 2,000 | |
| Prepayments | 14,000 | 750,000 | | | 324,000 |

| *Long-Term Assets* | | | | *Long-Term Liabilities* | | |
|---|---|---|---|---|---|---|
| Equipment | 78,000 | | | Mortgage | | 100,000 |
| Less Accumulated | | | | | | |
| Depreciation | 14,000 | 64,000 | | *Shareholders' Equity* | | |
| Premises | 200,000 | | | Registered Capital | | |
| Less Accumulated | | | | ($1.00 shares) | 1,000,000 | |
| Depreciation | 24,000 | 176,000 | 240,000 | Less Unissued Capital | 500,000 | |
| | | | | Paid-up Capital | 500,000 | |
| | | | | General Reserve | 55,000 | |
| | | | $990,000 | Appropriation account | 11,000 | 566,000 |
| | | | | | | $990,000 |

The details of the control accounts (marked*) are summarized in the following schedules extracted from the subsidiary ledgers:

| | $ | | | $ |
|---|---|---|---|---|
| *Schedule of Accounts Receivable* | | | *Schedule of Accounts Payable* | |
| Cambridge Aero Club | 48,000 | | Arrow Aircraft Corporation | 100,000 |
| Sawston Soaring Society | 24,000 | | Bell Oil Co. | 10,000 |
| Alice Springs Pastoral Co. | 36,000 | | | |
| Kimberley Mining Co. | 96,000 | | | $110,000 |
| Chartair | 96,000 | | | |
| | | | | |
| | $300,000 | | *Schedule of Aircraft Inventory* | $ |
| | | | Arrows: Two at $42,000 each | 84,000 |
| *Schedule of Prepaid Expenses* | $ | | Super Arrows: Four at $80,000 each | 320,000 |
| Rates | 4,000 | | | |
| Insurance | 10,000 | | | $404,000 |
| | | | | |
| | $14,000 | | *Schedule of Accrued Expenses* | |
| | | | Salaries Payable | $2,000 |
| | | | | |
| | | | *Schedule of Supplies Inventory* | |
| | | | Fuel | $6,000 |

*General*

i.  All aircraft are purchased by Avionics from the Arrow Aircraft Corporation on the following terms:
Arrow Aircraft — purchase price $42,000
Super Arrow Aircraft — purchase price $80,000 (except where otherwise indicated)
Payment terms — 50 per cent deposit and balance in three months.

ii.  All aircraft sales are made by Avionics to their customers on the following terms:
Arrow aircraft — selling price $60,000.
Super Arrow aircraft — selling price $120,000.
Payment terms — 20 per cent deposit and balance to be paid in four equal instalments each three months.

iii.  Sales of aircraft are costed on a FIFO basis.

iv.  All fuel is bought from the Bell Oil Company on thirty days credit.

The following transactions were made during 1974:

Jan. 31. *Paid* salaries $12,000; sundry administrative expenses $1,300; aircraft maintenance charges $4,500; Bell Oil Co. $10,000; Arrow Aircraft Corporation $60,000. *Cash received* from Sawston Soaring Society $12,000; Kimberley Mining Co. $24,000. *Sales·* One Arrow aircraft to Cambridge Aero Club.

Feb. 28. *Paid* salaries $12,000; advertising $4,500; insurance on aircraft and premises for six months ending 31 August $38,000; aircraft registration fees $10,000; aircraft maintenance charges $4,800; sundry administrative expenses $1,300, dividends $100,000. *Cash received* from Cambridge Aero Club $12,000; Alice Springs Pastoral Co. $12,000. *Purchases*: Two Arrow aircraft; Fuel $3,500.

Mar. 31. *Paid* salaries $12,000; municipal rates on premises for year ended 31 March 1975 $16,000; sundry administrative expenses $1,400; aircraft maintenance charges $5,300; Arrow Aircraft Corporation $40,000; Bell Oil Co. $3,500. *Cash received* from Chartair $24,000. *Sales*: Two Super Arrows aircraft to Kimberley Mining Co.; one Arrow aircraft to Abington Aero Club.

Apr. 30. *Paid* salaries $12,000; power $800; advertising $11,000; sundry administrative expenses $1,300; aircraft registration fees $45,000; aircraft maintenance charges $8,700. *Cash received* from Sawston Soaring Society $12,000; Kimberley Mining Co. $24,000; Cambridge Aero Club $12,000. *Purchases*: Three Arrow aircraft, and six Super Arrow aircraft; fuel $3,000. *Sales*: Three Arrow aircraft to Hawkesbury Aeronautics.

May 31. *Paid* salaries $12,000; sundry administrative expenses $1,400; aircraft registration fees $10,000; aircraft maintenance charges $6,900; Arrow Aircraft Corporation $42,000; Bell Oil Co. $3,000. *Cash received* from Cambridge Aero Club $12,000; Alice Springs Pastoral Co. $12,000. *Sales*: Four Super Arrow aircraft to Nullarbor Airlines. *Purchases*: Two Arrows.

June 30. *Paid* salaries $12,000; advertising $7,200; sundry administration expenses $1,400; interest on mortgage $5,000; taxation $112,000; aircraft registration fees $15,000; aircraft maintenance charges $5,300. *Cash received* from Kimberley Mining Co. $48,000; Chartair $24,000; Abington Aero Club $12,000. *Sales*: Two Super Arrows to Skyways; two Arrows to Cambridge Aero Club. *Purchases*: Three Super Arrows; fuel $3,500. Raised a three-year loan of $250,000 from Bulli Finance Co. to improve the company's liquidity.

July 31. *Paid* salaries $14,200; sundry administration expenses $1,300; aircraft maintenance charges $6,700; Bell Oil Co. $3,500; interim. dividend 5 per cent on paid-up capital as of 30 June; Arrow Aircraft Corporation $303,000. *Cash received* from Kimberley Mining Co. $24,000; Hawkesbury Aeronautics $36,000; Cambridge Aero Club $12,000. *Sales*: One Super Arrow to Hawkesbury Aero-Nautics. Shares (200,000) issued to shareholders at par, payable in full on application — all money received by end July.

Aug. 31. *Paid* salaries $14,200; sundry administration expenses $1,300;

power $700; aircraft registration fees $10,000; aircraft maintenance charges $7,300; Arrow Aircraft Corporation $42,000. *Cash received* from Cambridge Aero Club $12,000; Nullarbor Airlines $96,000; Alice Springs Pastoral Co. $12,000. *Sales*: Two Arrows to Alice Springs Pastoral Co. *Purchases*: Two Super Arrows.

Sept. 30. *Paid* salaries $14,400; advertising $11,200; insurance for six months ended 28 February 1975 $42,000; sundry administration expenses $1,400; aircraft registration fees $15,000; aircraft maintenance charges $8,100; Arrow Aircraft Corporation $120,000. *Cash received* from Chartair $24,000; Abington Aero Club $12,000; Skyways $48,000; Kimberley Mining Co. $48,000; Cambridge Aero Club $24,000. *Sales*: Three Super Arrows to Chartair. *Purchases*: Three Arrows.

Oct. 31. *Paid* salaries $14,400; sundry administration expenses $1,600; aircraft registration fees $20,000; aircraft maintenance charges $8,800. *Cash received* from Kimberley Mining Co. $24,000; Hawkesbury Aeronautics $60,000; Cambridge Aero Club $12,000. *Sales*: Two Arrows to Abington Aero Club. *Purchases*: Four Super Arrows; fuel $4,000.

Nov. 30. *Paid* salaries $14,400; sundry administration expenses $1,700; aircraft registration fees $10,000; aircraft maintenance charges $9,200; Bell Oil Co. $4,000; Arrow Aircraft Corporation $80,000. *Cash received* from Cambridge Aero Club $12,000; Nullarbor Airlines $96,000; Alice Springs Pastoral Co. $24,000. *Sales*: Three Super Arrows to Nullarbor Airlines. *Purchases*: Two Arrows.

Dec. 31. *Paid* salaries $16,000; sundry administration expenses $1,800; advertising $6,000; interest $17,500; aircraft registration fees $10,000; aircraft maintenance charges $9,400; Arrow Aircraft Corporation $63,000. *Cash received* from Chartair $96,000; Abington Aero Club $12,000; Kimberley Mining Co. $48,000; Cambridge Aero Club $24,000; Skyways $48,000. *Sales*: One Arrow to Sawston Soaring Society. *Purchases*: Two Super Arrows at the new price of $90,000 each; fuel $5,000.

*Instructions:*

a. Record all transactions in journals, using cash receipts, cash payments, credit sales, credit purchases, and a general journal.

b. Post all entries to ledger accounts at end of each month, using control accounts and subsidiary ledger accounts where appropriate.

c. Record all reversing entries on 1 January in the general journal and ledger accounts.

d. Prepare interim accounting reports for the six months ended 30 June. Do not close off the operating accounts but prepare the reports from a worksheet. Additional information on 30 June (not to be incorporated in the accounts).

Fuel stocks on hand (as per measurement) $4,000
Rates and insurance prepaid
Salaries owing $3,000
Depreciation to be charged on equipment at the rate of 20 per cent per

annum on cost, and on premises at 5 per cent per annum on net book value.

Provide for 5 per cent interim dividend on paid-up capital and company tax at 40 per cent on net profits.

e.  Prepare final accounting reports for the year ended 31 December.
Record all balance-day adjustments in the journals and ledger accounts.
Additional information on 31 December.
Fuel stocks on hand (as per measurement) $5,000
Rates and insurance prepaid
Salaries owing $3,000
Depreciation to be charged on equipment at the rate of 20 per cent per annum on cost, and on premises at 5 per cent per annum on net book value.
Provide for a final dividend of 8 per cent on the enlarged paid-up capital, and company tax at 40 per cent on the year's profits. Transfer $10,000 to General Reserve.
Close off all operating accounts to a Profit and Loss account.

# Chapter 12
# Revenue Recognition

The techniques required for recording and summarizing transaction data and for measuring the results of the firm's economic activity over an accounting period have now been covered. However several fundamental conceptual problems concerned with the measurement of periodic results were assumed away so as to simplify preparation of the periodic accounting reports, and we must now examine these problems. Logically, answers to them must be given before any measure of income or financial position can be made within the historical cost valuation system. These problems are, first, when to recognize the revenue from a selling transaction; second, the inventory valuation method to be used in a period of changing prices; and third, the depreciation method to be adopted. There is no uniform opinion in the accounting profession about these issues, and they are all the subject of controversy.

## THE TIMING OF REVENUE RECOGNITION

Revenue recognition refers to the point in the operating cycle of transactions at which it is considered that the revenue from operating activity has been earned. The term "revenue realization" is alternatively used to describe this point. However this alternative term is not favoured here since it is frequently used as well to mean the point at which cash is collected or a financial claim is created by a sales transaction. The use of both terms has been the cause of some confusion in the analysis of the revenue recognition problem.[1]

The problem of revenue recognition does not arise in the simplest situation of the cash and carry sale, but it can be a crucial problem in more complicated cases. For instance, consider the following situations. When a person takes out a cash subscription to a magazine for the coming year, ought the revenue to be recognized at that point even though the magazines are yet to be published and the costs are yet to be incurred? Where goods are sold on hire-purchase, ought the revenue be recognized at the time of order, delivery, cash instalment, or final cash payment when the legal title passes to the buyer? Should the revenue be recorded on the award of the contract, on the completion of the job, or according to the stages of production, in the case of a large construction project to be carried out by a firm? In each case, there can be genuine differences of opinion as to when revenue ought to be recognized and therefore treated as sales of the period.

The timing of the revenue recognition has important effects on the measure of periodic income earned and financial position. Until an event is recorded as a sale, there can be no revenue recognized or expense charged, and hence profit earned, no increase in accounts receivable, and the merchandise remains in inventory. If a sale is recorded before the firm acquires or produces the goods, there can be no transfer from inventories to cost of goods sold to recognize the expense incurred on the sale, and so the whole sales revenue would appear immediately as profit, to be followed subsequently by expenses which have no current sales against which to be attached. Therefore, timing of revenue recognition is crucial to both the profit and loss statement and the balance sheet. However it should be understood that, in the long run covering many accounting periods, the effects of using different points of revenue recognition will cancel out. The impact of selecting the appropriate point is on the measurement of *periodic* results — according to which point is selected, revenue recognition will be brought forward to the current period or postponed till a later period.

The matching principle of profit determination requires that expenses associated with a given revenue must be charged against that revenue. Until the revenue is recognized, inventory costs must be carried in asset values and they are expensed as the cost of goods sold when the revenue is recognized. If revenue recognition is deferred, inventories are increased, while sales, accounts receivable, and profit are reduced.

Although it can be argued that in general profit is earned from the total operations of the firm, it cannot be recognized on each unit of activity within the firm because of insoluble profit allocation problems which arise particularly where all factors of production combine together in a joint effort. Consequently, profit has to be recognized at a moment of time, but at which moment? The accountant needs an appropriate signal from the chain of events in the normal operating cycle to justify the recognition of revenue and hence profit. There are five events in the normal cycle, though they need not occur in the order given below:

1. Acquisition of resources (for a manufacturer), or of merchandise (for a retailer)
2. Production of the goods (for a manufacturer)
3. Receipt of customer order
4. Delivery of the goods
5. Cash collection.

Which of these events should be used as the point of recognizing revenue? The most favoured solution is to select the critical event in the cycle, and this event could be any one of the five, according to the circumstances of the business. The critical event occurs when the most crucial decision is made or the most difficult task performed in the cycle of the complete transaction.[2] Revenue is then recognized once the critical event has been completed.

However, where the critical event is difficult to distinguish — and this may be a common situation — the following criteria may be used as guides to determine the most appropriate point for revenue recognition.[3]

1. The main revenue producing service has been performed
2. Any further costs that are necessary to create revenue are either negligible or can be accurately predicted
3. The amount ultimately collectable in cash can be estimated within an acceptable error range
4. Revenue and profit accord with the volume of economic activity in the firm during the period.

The first point is included to ensure that revenue is not anticipated before the products are available for delivery to the customer; the second and third criteria are included to avoid excessive reliance on those estimates which are difficult to make so as to satisfy the objectivity standards; and the fourth criterion is included to prevent undue distortion of periodic results. This could happen where a large share of the cycle occurred in previous periods and revenue recognition is unduly delayed so that the first three criteria are fully satisfied. The *first* point in the operating cycle that reasonably satisfies these criteria should be used as the point of revenue recognition. It should not be delayed until the whole cycle is completed and the cash collected unless cash collection is the critical event.

The application of the critical event and the above criteria to each stage of the operating cycle are now considered for various types of business situations.

### 1. Acquisition of Resources or Purchase of Merchandise

This is not used in practice because it normally does not satisfy any of the criteria. However its use could be justified where the market for the product is assured and the production costs are known in advance, but where the critical event is to acquire the resources which are in scarce supply — for example, precious metals or any rationed commodity. Its use is implicit in the static economic theory of the firm and in the current cash equivalent system of accounting valuation wherein all assets are revalued at current realization prices.

### 2. Production

Production by the firm creates value, so that revenue could be recognized on this basis. However the production basis has some serious limitations in many situations. Both production and marketing are required to create value — all the value-adding services have not been performed at the end of the production stage — and it is difficult to separate the contribution of each, unless one assumes that each dollar of expenditure makes the same contribution to profit. But this assumption can be easily shown to be false, since it implies that the greater the expenditure, the greater the profit, and hence that there is no limit to the size of the firm; and secondly that all expenditures are equally profitable and hence, that there is no optimum method of operation. In addition, the amount of cash ultimately collectable may be too uncertain to justify the use of the production basis.

Nevertheless, there are everyday situations in which production is the critical event in the cycle. Marketing costs may be small, and sales and cash collection assured. The analysis of production as the critical event may be separated into two categories — at the completion of production or according to the stages of the production process. Revenue may be recognized at the point of completion of production of precious metals in the case of mining companies, where goods are manufactured to order under a supply contract to another firm, or in agriculture where the output is sold through government marketing schemes. In these cases, completion of production is the critical event if market demand and price are assured, and if subsequent marketing costs are known and are relatively small.

In other situations, revenue may appropriately be recognized according to the stages of completion of production — for example, in contracts involving the supply of services or in long-term contracts involving large construction projects whose period of production extends over several years. In the former case, the service is usually performed under the terms of a prior agreement, and the performance gives rise to a claim for services rendered. This occurs with personal services, interest, rent, electricity, and so on. In the case of long-term contracts, revenue recognition at the time the contract is obtained, or at the time of completion and delivery of the project to the customer, would result in large isolated sales and profits occurring in occasional years, with large expenses and losses being incurred in the in-between years. Profits would be distorted away from the actual flow of economic activity in the firm and they would not reflect accurately the firm's performance for each period, nor would the balance sheet reflect its financial position at the end of each period.

In cases where production is the critical event, periodic revenue is recognized according to the production accomplished, or the proportion of completion of the project. For example, if a project is 25 per cent completed from the year's work, then 25 per cent of the contract price is recorded as the year's revenue, and profit calculated accordingly. The proportion of work completed is generally judged from the costs incurred to date in relation to the estimated total cost of the project.

### 3.   Receipt of Customer Order

The order is a significant event in the operating cycle as it signifies a customer's intention to buy. It can be a sound basis for revenue recognition if the goods are in stock when the order is received and the number of order cancellations is small. Delivery may be fairly automatic upon receipt of the order and with little delay. The order may constitute the critical event where sales are not assured, and the four criteria can be satisfied in the circumstances mentioned above. But in these situations, the time of delivery may nearly coincide with the order time, so that whichever basis is the more convenient would be used. Where there is some delay in fulfilling the order, then the delivery basis, or the production basis for a long-term contract, is more appropriate. Essentially, the order basis is used where it gives rise to a valid claim against the customer, the amount is objectively determined, and there is no substantial delay in final delivery.

But even where the order basis is not used for sales recognition, it can still be important in its own right. Firms often list orders for managerial use and they may report them to shareholders where the time-lag in delivery is long, as the size of the order list indicates the level of future activity in the firm. Likewise, production may not commence until a sufficient number of orders is received, as with new aircraft types.

### 4.   Delivery of Goods

The delivery point normally occurs where the goods leave the seller's hands. It often coincides with the order point and, in the case of a cash sale, with the point of cash collection. In the case of large construction projects, the time of delivery may be taken as the time at which the client can be billed for the job. This normally occurs as the stages of a job are completed and checked by the client, and the billing is authorized by him.

The delivery point should be used where delivery is the critical point in the cycle. Here, most costs will have been incurred, the sales price is known, and the firm can rely on collecting the cash.

The term "time of sale" in ordinary language may refer to either the times of order or of delivery.

### 5.   Cash Collection

Where the firm is uncertain about its customers paying for their merchandise, the collection of cash may be the critical event in the operating cycle. The cash basis is often used by small firms, professional people, and the government, and for hire-purchase sales by large firms (or at least a variant of it). Frequently, the checks on the creditworthiness of hire-purchase customers are inadequate, and there is much uncertainty of ultimate cash collection. Moreover, there may be substantial debt collection and product reclamation costs incurred after the point of delivery, so that the amount of net revenue to be recognized is difficult to estimate.

But it should be pointed out that, if cash collection on hire-purchase sales is excessively uncertain, then the sale should not be made in the first place. Otherwise, the firm is doomed to bankruptcy, as no firm can incur expenditures on merchandise purchased, labour services, advertising, and so on, and then give away the merchandise to customers who are unlikely to pay for it. In a well-managed firm, cash collection on hire-purchase sales should not be uncertain to any significant degree.

However the principal reason for the use of the cash collection basis for hire-purchase sales in Australia is a taxation one. If firms record as sales the value of hire-purchase goods delivered within the year, then the gross value of the sales is assessed as taxable income (though this is offset by expenses incurred) and the firm pays tax accordingly, even though it has not received the cash from its customers. Hence the firm may encounter financial problems — it must pay out cash to the government before it receives the cash from its customers — while, if the debt turns out to be a bad one, the firm has overstated its sales and profits, and hence paid excessive taxation. Although it can claim this excess back, it has been denied the use of the cash in the meantime.

Under the straight cash basis of recording sales, no accounting record is made of goods delivered, or debts created, by the initial selling transaction. Hence there are no debtors' accounts or bad debts recorded in the ledger. These items may, of course, be included in non-accounting records for administrative purposes. Sales are recorded as the cash is received in each period, and costs are allocated to the cost of goods sold on this basis.

In general, the cash collection method for hire-purchase sales is not recommended by the accounting profession. Alternative methods of recognizing revenue at the point of sale, together with an adequate estimate of bad debts, are recommended.[4] The methods of accounting for hire-purchase transactions in reality are fairly complex and are beyond the scope of this course. In addition to the straight cash collection method (the "income emerging" basis), there are at least three variants of the delivery basis in use — the annuity, rule of 78, and simple-interest methods. In these three methods, the selling price of a good is divided into two parts — cash price and the full hire-purchase price, which exceeds the cash price by a hiring or interest charge. Sales at the full price are debited to customers in the usual way, but only the cash price is credited to the sales account. Thus "trading profit" (cash price less cost of goods sold) is recognized at this point. The hiring charge is credited to an "unearned income" (or similar name) account. It is a contra debtors account. The "unearned income" is then amortized to current revenue as the instalments are received according to the annuity, rule of 78, or simple-interest methods. Hire-purchase debtors are shown in the balance sheet at their gross value less the "unearned income"; the net value represents what the debtors would have to pay the firm to extinguish their debts *now*.

### The Importance of Consistency

It is most important that the basis of revenue recognition adopted by the firm is applied consistently over time because of its impact on the reporting of profits and assets. If a change in the basis is warranted by a change in the operating conditions of the firm, then the effects of the change on profits and assets must be reported.[5]

Consistency does not necessarily mean however that all segments of a firm should adopt the same basis of revenue recognition. A diversified firm could justify the use of several bases simultaneously in different segments of its operations where the conditions relating to each segment differ considerably.

### An Example

The Waddy Construction Company has obtained a government contract for the building of a bridge and approach roads over the Blackyarra River. The contract price is $500,000, to be billed as follows:

1. Sixty per cent after all earthwork, and also foundations and piers for the bridge, have been completed to the satisfaction of a government inspector

2. An additional 25 per cent after the decking on the bridge has been completed and approved, and the concrete for the road poured and approved

3. A further 15 per cent on completion of the whole project.

Payments are to be made within a month of billing. The job is estimated to cost $400,000.

At the end of the first year, the job is appraised as 90 per cent complete and costs are coinciding with the original estimates. Expenses of $360,000 have been incurred so far. The government inspector has checked and approved the first two stages of the work, the government paid the first instalment on time, and it has just been billed for the amount due on the second stage.

*Required:*

Compute income for the year, and the values of Inventory (i.e., works in progress) and Accounts Receivable at the end of the year on the basis of recognizing revenue on the basis of:

1. Production
2. Billing the government for the work completed and inspected
3. Receipt of cash.

*Solution*

1. *Revenue recognition at point of production*

Cash

|  | Dr. $ | Cr. $ | Balance $ |
|---|---|---|---|
| Inventory |  | 360,000 | 360,000 Cr. |
| Accounts Receivable | 300,000 |  | 60,000 Cr. |

Inventory (or Job in Process)

|  | Dr. $ | Cr. $ | Balance $ |
|---|---|---|---|
| Cash | 360,000 |  | 360,000 Dr. |
| Cost of Goods Sold (90% of total cost) |  | 360,000 | — |

Cost of Goods Sold

|  | Dr. $ | Cr. $ | Balance $ |
|---|---|---|---|
| Inventory | 360,000 |  | 360,000 Dr. |

Accounts Receivable (or Government)

|  | Dr. $ | Cr. $ | Balance $ |
|---|---|---|---|
| Sales | 450,000 |  | 450,000 Dr. |
| Cash |  | 300,000 | 150,000 Dr. |

Sales

|  | Dr. $ | Cr. $ | Balance $ |
|---|---|---|---|
| Accounts Receivable (90% of total price) |  | 450,000 | 450,000 Cr. |

*Income Statement for Year 1*

|  | $ |
|---|---|
| Sales | 450,000 |
| Less Cost of Goods Sold | 360,000 |
| Profit | $90,000 |

*Balance Sheet Assets at End of Year 1*

|  | $ |
|---|---|
| Accounts Receivable | 150,000 |
| Inventory | — |

2. *Revenue recognition at time of billing*

Cash

|  | Dr. $ | Cr. $ | Balance $ |
|---|---|---|---|
| Inventory |  | 360,000 | 360,000 Cr. |
| Accounts Receivable | 300,000 |  | 60,000 Cr. |

Inventory

| | Dr. $ | Cr. $ | Balance $ |
|---|---|---|---|
| Cash | 360,000 | | 360,000 Dr. |
| Cost of Goods Sold (85% of total cost) | | 340,000 | 20,000 Dr. |

Cost of Goods Sold

| | | | |
|---|---|---|---|
| Inventory | 340,000 | | 340,000 Dr. |

Accounts Receivable

| | | | |
|---|---|---|---|
| Sales | 425,000 | | 425,000 Dr. |
| Cash | | 300,000 | 125,000 Dr. |

Sales

| | | | |
|---|---|---|---|
| Accounts Receivable (85% of total price) | | 425,000 | 425,000 Cr. |

### Income Statement for Year 1

| | $ |
|---|---|
| Sales | 425,000 |
| Less Cost of Goods Sold | 340,000 |
| Profit | $85,000 |

### Balance Sheet Assets at End of Year 1

| | $ |
|---|---|
| Accounts Receivable | 125,000 |
| Inventory | 20,000 |

### 3. Revenue recognition at time of cash receipt

Cash

| | Dr. $ | Cr. $ | Balance $ |
|---|---|---|---|
| Inventory | | 360,000 | 360,000 Cr. |
| Sales | 300,000 | | 60,000 Cr. |

Inventory

| | | | |
|---|---|---|---|
| Cash | 360,000 | | 360,000 Dr. |
| Cost of Goods Sold (60% of total cost) | | 240,000 | 120,000 Dr. |

Cost of Goods Sold

| | | | |
|---|---|---|---|
| Inventory | 240,000 | | 240,000 Dr. |

Sales

| | | | |
|---|---|---|---|
| Cash (60% of total price) | | 300,000 | 300,000 Cr. |

### Income Statement for Year 1

|  | $ |
|---|---|
| Sales | 300,000 |
| Less Cost of Goods Sold | 240,000 |
| Profit | $60,000 |

### Balance Sheet Assets at End of Year 1

|  | $ |
|---|---|
| Accounts Receivable | — |
| Inventories | 120,000 |

*Points to note:*

1. For simplicity, it is assumed that all costs incurred are cash costs.

2. The effects of the three alternative points of revenue recognition on Sales, Cost of Goods Sold, Profit, Accounts Receivable, and Inventories.

   i.   Where revenue is recognized at the point of production, there is an automatic transfer from the Production or Inventory account to the Cost of Goods Sold account (and hence no inventories remain on hand) in accordance with the matching principle; and simultaneously from Sales to the client's account. As compared with the other methods, the revenue and profits are maximized in year one but would be less in the subsequent year when the job is finished.

   ii.  Under the billing or delivery basis, the sale is recorded at the date of billing, and the transfer from Inventory to Cost of Goods Sold is made at that point. Revenue is less than under method (1) to the extent of the selling value of the inventory, and profit is less to the extent of the unrecognized profit margin on the inventory valued at cost.

   iii. Under the cash receipts basis, no sales are recognized until the cash is received (and hence there are no debtors accounts), and the transfer from inventory to cost of goods sold is made at the time of cash receipt. Revenue is less than under method 1 to the extent of the selling value of work completed but not yet paid for; while profit is less by the amount of the unrecognized profit on inventory valued at cost. Inventory is higher than under the previous methods because the point of sale recognition occurs at a later stage in the cycle.

3. The different bases of revenue recognition do not affect the total revenue or profits over two years (i.e., the life of the project); it is only the periodic measurements that are affected, i.e., the allocations of revenue, cost, and profits between year 1 and year 2. The different methods have the effect of either bringing forward or of postponing the recognition of profits. This effect would be even more pronounced if the two extreme bases of total profit recognition at the times of winning the contract or of job completion were used. In the former case, the entire profit of $100,000 would be recognized in year 1, and in the latter it would be recognized in year 2. Postponing profit recognition produces more conservative results.

### FURTHER READING

A.A.A. "The Realization Concept." *Accounting Review* (April 1965).

Gordon, M. J., and Shillinglaw, G. *Accounting: A Management Approach*. 4th Ed. Homewood, Illinois: Richard D. Irwin, 1969. Chap. 5, pp. 120–33.

Myers, J. M., "The Critical Event and the Recognition of Net Profit", in Zeff, S., and Keller, W. *Financial Accounting Theory*. New York: McGraw-Hill, 1964.

## NOTES

1. See, for example, the A.A.A. report, "The Realization Concept", where the term "realization" is inadvertently used in both senses.

2. Myers, "The Critical Event and the Recognition of Net Profit".

3. The first three criteria are taken from Gordon & Shillinglaw, *Accounting: A Management Approach*, chap. 5.

4. See, for example, A.S.A., *Accounting Principles and Practices Discussed in Reports of Company Failures, 1966*. The sections in this report on hire-purchase accounting answer some criticisms arising from the Reid Murray case.

5. Ibid.

## QUESTIONS AND EXERCISES

[Solution to problem marked * is given in Appendix 4.]

1. What does the term "revenue recognition" mean? Distinguish it from "revenue realization".

2. Why is determination of the point of revenue recognition crucial to the accounting process?

3. What are the five critical points in the normal operating cycle at which revenue may be recognized?

4. Explain the concept of the "critical event" used in determining the point of revenue recognition.

5. Under what conditions may the following practices in revenue recognition be justified? Recognition at time of:

    i. Purchase of a highly desired city allotment in the case of a land speculator

    ii. Production in the case of a gold miner

    iii. Stages of completion of a large building in the case of a construction company

    iv. Customer order for refrigerators in the case of a department store

    v. Cash receipt by a fashion retailer for sales on hire purchase

    vi. Receipt of subscriptions by a magazine publisher.

6. "Under the production basis of revenue recognition, there are no inventories on hand; while under the cash receipts basis, there are no debtors (and hence no bad debts can occur)." Explain.

7. In the case of a firm with a normal operating cycle, what are the main effects on assets and profits of recognizing revenue at the point of cash receipt rather than at the point of production?

8. "Profit is earned at the moment of making the most critical decision or of performing the most difficult task in the cycle of a complete transaction. Just what this event is may not be easy to distinguish in many cases." — J. M. Myers, "The Critical Event and the Recognition of Net Profit".

   Explain this statement. Illustrate your answer with reference to the economic cycle of a retailer.

9. On 1 January 1971, A purchased for $960.43 a $1,000 4 per cent bond which matured on 31 December 1980. The price paid means that A will receive a return of 4½ per cent per annum on his outlay.

   The purchase of the bond entitles A to receive:

   |  | $ |
   |---|---:|
   | On maturity (in ten years) | 1,000 |
   | Interest at the rate of $40 at the end of each year for ten years | 400 |
   |  | $1,400 |

   A intends to hold the bond until it matures. How much revenue should be recognized as being earned in each year?

10. The Gumeracha Building Co. Ltd. has just been awarded a $20m. contract to build a new concert hall for the Oodnadatta City Council. The project is expected to take three years to complete and to cost $15m. The terms of the contract stipulate that progress payments are to be made three months after the completion of each major phase of the project.

    As accounting consultant to the company, you are asked to prepare a report to the directors outlining the alternatives open to the company for the recognition of periodic revenue and profit, and to recommend one particular alternative. Your recommendation should be supported by the reasons for it.

11. The following is a summary of the motor cars sold on hire purchase and instalments collected by Never-Never Car Sales for the quarter ended 30 June 19X1:

    | Month | No. of Cars Sold | No. of instalments Collected |
    |---|---|---|
    | Apr. | 20 | 20 |
    | May | 16 | 36 |
    | June | 14 | 50 |

    *Other Data:*

    i.  Selling price per car, $2,000.
    ii. Cost price per car, $1,400.
    iii. Monthly instalments per car, $200. The first instalment is payable on purchase of the car.
    iv. Stock of cars on hand 1 April, 70 cars.
    v.  Operating expenses incurred and paid for the quarter: $10,000.

    *Required:*

    A. Record the above data in ledger account, using:

       a. The sales basis for recognizing revenue
       b. The cash collection basis for recognizing revenue.

B.    Prepare an income statement and balance sheet according to each basis of revenue recognition.

C.    Explain the reason for profit and assets being less under the cash collection basis than under the sales basis.

*12.  A contract for the construction of twenty miles of concrete freeway is awarded to the Ryde Construction Company by the New South Wales Government. The contract price is $100,000 per mile, payable as follows:

i.    Fifty per cent on a mileage basis after the concrete is poured and approved by a government inspector

ii.    Forty per cent additional on a mileage basis after the work has been completed, including grading and seeding of embankments and centre strip, and approved by the inspector

iii.    The balance of 10 per cent when the entire job has been completed and approved by the inspector.

The job is estimated to cost $80,000 per mile.

At the end of the first year, ten miles of road are entirely completed and approved; concrete has been poured and approved on an additional stretch of five miles; and preliminary grading has been done on the remainder. Estimates of cost incurred are:

A.    On the completed stretch, $80,000 per mile
B.    On the second stretch, $60,000 per mile
C.    On the third stretch, $15,000 per mile.

It is expected that the unfinished stretches will be completed according to original cost estimates. The council paid the amounts due from it on time.
Record the above data in ledger accounts, using (a) the production basis, and (b) the billing basis, of revenue recognition.

What income has the Ryde Construction Company earned on the contract for the year?

13.    The Colossus Construction Company has been awarded a contract for the construction of fifteen miles of concrete freeway. The contract price is $150,000 per mile, payable as follows:

i.    Forty per cent on a mileage basis after the concrete is poured and approved by a government inspector

ii.    Forty per cent additional on a mileage basis after the work has been completed, including grading and seeding of embankments and centre strip, and approved by the inspector

iii.    The balance of 20 per cent when the entire job has been completed and approved by the inspector.

The job is estimated to cost $100,000 per mile.

At the end of the first year:

A.    Eight miles of road are entirely completed and approved

B.    Concrete has been poured and approved on an additional stretch of four miles

C.    Preliminary grading has been done on the remainder.

Estimates of the costs incurred were:

a.    On the completed stretch, $100,000 per mile
b.    On the second stretch, $75,000 per mile
c.    On the third stretch, $25,000 per mile.

It is expected that the unfinished stretches will be completed according to the original estimates. The Roads Board paid the amounts due from it on time.

*Required:*

i.    Record the above data in ledger accounts, using:

    a.    the production basis
    b.    the billing basis
    of revenue recognition.

ii.    What income has Colossus Construction Company earned on the contract for the year?

14.    Girth Pty. Ltd., a single venture enterprise, was formed for the purpose of purchasing a plot of standing timber for $1,500,000, with the intention of letting it stand for a further five years before cutting and sale.

The company incurred the following costs in the development and care of the lot during the first three years of ownership:

|  | $ |
|---|---|
| Development costs (access roads, etc.) | 100,000 |
| Timber care (wages etc.) | 150,000 |
| Miscellaneous other costs: | 50,000 |

During the third year the company was offered $2,200,000 for the timber. The cost of cutting and dressing the timber for shipment was quoted as $75,000. The company refused this offer. The directors felt that the expected rate of growth of the timber would justify postponement of its sale. The directors relied on the following data prepared by the accountant:

|  | Year 4 | Year 5 |
|---|---|---|
|  | $ | $ |
| Expected sale value of timber | 2,500,000 | 2,700,000 |
| Expected total cost of timber care | 100,000 | 75,000 |
| Expected cutting and dressing costs | 75,000 | 75,000 |

The company let the timber stand until the sixth year, when it was cut and sold for $2,750,000.

The costs incurred in the last three years were:

| Cost | Year 4 | Year 5 | Year 6 |
|---|---|---|---|
|  | $ | $ | $ |
| Development | 30,000 |  |  |
| Maintenance of roads | 5,000 | 3,000 | 1,000 |
| Timber care and other costs | 60,000 | 50,000 | 65,000 |
| Cutting and dressing |  |  | 75,000 |

The company planted young tree seedlings as a conservation measure at the end of year 6. The land was sold back to the original owner for $60,000.

*Required:*

i.  Indicate, giving reasons, the accounting net income or loss you would recognise on this stand of timber —

  a.  For the first three years
  b.  For year 4
  c.  For year 5
  d.  For year 6.

ii. What assumptions did you make in determining net income or loss and why?

# Chapter 13
# Cost of Sales and Inventory Valuation

To date the only problems considered in the determination of periodic cost of goods sold and balance sheet inventories were those concerning the method of recording inventory issues (i.e., the use of periodic or perpetual inventory systems); and those connected with the point at which a selling transaction should be recognized, and hence the point at which the transfer is made from the Merchandise Inventory account to the Cost of Goods Sold account. However, these are not the only problems associated with accounting for inventories – some awkward valuation problems are caused by fluctuating inventory purchase prices, and, as we shall see later on, by fluctuating selling prices as well. The problem of fluctuating purchase prices being considered here arises where the same line of product is purchased at varying prices over time.

Consider the following situation with respect to one line of merchandise, for example, widgets:

|  | No. of Units | Cost $ | Value $ |
|---|---|---|---|
| Jan. 1 Inventory balance | 1,000 | 0.60 | 600 |
| Jan. 31. Purchases | 800 | 0.70 | 560 |
| Feb. 28. | 600 | 0.80 | 480 |
| Mar. 31. | 1,000 | 0.90 | 900 |
| Apr. 30. | 600 | 1.00 | 600 |
| Total inventory available | 4,000 | | $3,140 |
| Sold during period | 3,000 | | |
| Apr. 30 Inventory balance | 1,000 | | |

How should the cost of goods sold be determined, and closing inventory be valued? Are the lower-priced goods sold first, with the higher-priced ones remaining in inventory? Or conversely are the higher-priced ones sold first with the lower-priced ones remaining in inventory? Or is there no particular order in which the goods are sold?

The cost of goods sold and the value of inventory on 30 April will differ according to the method used, even though all methods are based on historic acquisition costs and all aim to measure historic cost income and value balance sheet inventories at historic cost.

## PERPETUAL INVENTORY SYSTEM VALUATION METHODS

Where *perpetual inventory procedures* are used, several methods are available. The price actually paid by the firm for the particular widget sold may be recorded as the cost of the good sold (that is, the identified cost method) or an assumption made as to the order in which purchase prices are to be applied to goods sold. Such assumptions relate to the pricing order of selling inventories only, and they do not bear any necessary relationship to the actual physical order in which goods are sold. The three most popular methods in this category are known as FIFO, LIFO, and weighted average cost.

### 1. Identified Cost

The use of this method requires that individual cost records are kept for each good purchased so that the cost of each good in inventory is known. Its use is confined to fairly expensive commodities where it is worthwhile to maintain cost records for individual units of a commodity (for example, major consumer durables). However, note that, where two or more identical widgets are in inventory, the widget actually picked up and sold by the salesman may be a matter of chance. Likewise the value of cost of goods sold and balance sheet inventory will be affected by this chance factor, so that results are difficult to evaluate and they may not be comparable with those of previous periods.

### 2. FIFO — First In, First Out

Under this method, the *prices* of the goods acquired *first* are applied to the goods sold first, until the inventory acquired at that first price is exhausted, and so on down the line. The cost of the 3,000 units sold and the balance sheet inventory are calculated under FIFO as follows:

|  |  | No. of Units | Cost $ | Value $ |
|---|---|---|---|---|
| Cost of goods sold | Initial inventory | 1,000 at | 0.60 | 600 |
|  | Jan. purchases | 800 | 0.70 | 560 |
|  | Feb. purchases | 600 | 0.80 | 480 |
|  | Mar. purchases | 600 | 0.90 | 540 |
|  | Sold | 3,000 |  | $2,180 |

| Balance Sheet inventory | | | | |
|---|---|---|---|---|
| | Mar. purchases | 400 | 0.90 | 360 |
| | April purchases | 600 | 1.00 | 600 |
| | On hand | 1,000 | | $960 |

Hence the earlier purchase prices are applied in the determination of cost of goods sold, and the later prices in the valuation of balance sheet inventories.

If monthly reports are required, the cost of goods sold and inventory balance are calculated by applying FIFO to each month. The result over the total period is not affected by a monthly calculation.

### 3.  LIFO — Last In, First Out

The opposite pricing assumption is applied under this method, and the *prices* of the goods acquired *last* are applied to the goods sold first until that segment of the inventory is exhausted, and so on.

LIFO is applied as follows:

| | | No. of Units | Cost $ | Value $ |
|---|---|---|---|---|
| Cost of goods sold | Apr. purchases | 600  at | 1.00 | 600 |
| | Mar. purchases | 1,000 | 0.90 | 900 |
| | Feb. purchases | 600 | 0.80 | 480 |
| | Jan. purchases | 800 | 0.70 | 560 |
| | Sold | 3,000 | | $2,540 |
| Balance sheet inventory | Jan. inventory | 1,000 | 0.60 | $600 |

Hence, where LIFO is used, the most recent purchase prices are applied in determining the cost of goods sold, while the more historic prices are applied to determine the value of inventories in the balance sheet. Normally LIFO is applied to the year as a whole, with seasonal variations in inventory levels being disregarded.

### 4.  Weighted Average Cost

Under this method, it is assumed that individual items of merchandise lose their separate identities once they are put into inventory, and that all items of merchandise come out of the common pool and are made at the average cost of the inventory on hand. Whether this particular widget sold cost $.60 or $1.00, and when it was bought, are irrelevant in this method. The average cost is weighted according to the volume of inventory purchased at each price, as a simple average of prices would be misleading where different quantities are acquired at each price.

A new weighted cost must be calculated after each purchase where the purchase price does not equal the weighted average cost, and this can be cumbersome where the firm does not have a mechanized accounting system designed to calculate weighted averages. Alternatively, the firm may make periodic averages and apply the average cost to the period covered. For example, if the firm averages its prices over four months, the following results emerge:

$$\text{Weighted average cost} = \frac{\text{Total purchase cost}}{\text{Total inventory available}}$$

$$= \frac{3,140}{4,000}$$

$$= \$.785 \text{ per unit.}$$

Cost of goods sold  3,000 x 0.785 = $2,355
Balance sheet inventory  1,000 x 0.785 =  $785

The same price is applied to the cost of goods sold and the inventory in in the balance sheet.

## A COMPARISON OF FIFO, LIFO, AND WAC

A comparison of the three methods reveals systematic differences between them. Assume that the widgets are sold for $1.50 each in order to highlight the effect of each method on profits.

|  | FIFO | WAC | LIFO |
|---|---|---|---|
|  | $ | $ | $ |
| Revenue | 4,500 | 4,500 | 4,500 |
| Cost of goods sold | 2,180 | 2,355 | 2,540 |
| Net profit | $2,320 | $2,145 | $1,960 |
| Balance sheet inventory | $960 | $785 | $600 |

In a period of inflation, the FIFO method consistently results in a lower cost of goods sold (and hence higher profits), and a higher balance sheet valuation of inventory, than those obtained under LIFO or WAC. Conversely, LIFO always yields a higher cost of goods sold (and hence lower profits), and a lower balance sheet valuation of inventory, than those obtained under the other methods. The WAC method always gives results between LIFO and FIFO because of the averaging process involved.

Assuming that the opening stock of inventories is not reduced, then during an inflationary period the use of FIFO results in the closing stock of inventories being valued at prices approximating current replacement costs for the balance sheet because the most recent acquisition prices are applied to the inventory on hand. But, on the other hand, the earlier lower prices are applied to the goods sold and hence the firm does not recover sufficient funds from revenue to replace the inventories sold. In the example above, if the 3,000 widgets sold were all replaced at the end of April, their replacement cost would be $3,000; instead the firm has recouped only $2,180 with which to replace them. Thus the use of FIFO results in the understatement of costs and the overstatement of profits in terms of "current income" (a measure of profit based on maintaining physical capital — here, the level of inventories — intact).

Conversely under LIFO, the cost of goods sold is reckoned at nearer the replacement cost of the inventories sold because the more recent higher prices are applied to them. It will not equal the replacement cost however where prices have not stopped rising and where goods acquired in an earlier period are sold. In the above example, the replacement cost of the goods sold is $3,000 while their LIFO cost is only $2,540. As a consequence of the higher LIFO cost of goods sold, LIFO profit is less than FIFO profit, and it lies nearer "current income". But, against this advantage for income determination, the LIFO value of the balance sheet inventory can become ludicrously low in terms of current replacement costs since it may well relate to the time when the firm was established or to when it adopted the LIFO basis of inventory valuation. The use of LIFO can seriously distort the balance sheet to a far greater extent than FIFO can distort the income statement. LIFO inventory values can date back twenty years or fifty years and so on; whereas FIFO values in the income statement are unlikely to extend back beyond a year, and normally would extend back only a few months where inventories are turned over at least several times a year.

During a period of declining prices the opposite results occur, and the cost of goods sold under LIFO may be less than that under FIFO, while LIFO balance sheet inventories may exceed the FIFO inventory. However, firms in the U.S. who employ LIFO during an inflationary period endeavour to drop the LIFO basis once price falls take place.

No generalizations about the effects of LIFO as compared with FIFO are possible when prices fluctuate up and down, nor when the initial stock of inventories (i.e., the base stock) is depleted. If inventory levels are depleted from time to time, the inventory prices of some considerable time back may be applied to determine the cost of goods sold in the current period. The use of LIFO in either of these circumstances would destroy the comparability of accounting reports over time.

The accounting reports of companies which use FIFO are obviously not comparable with the reports of those companies using LIFO during a period of unstable prices.

## JUSTIFICATION FOR THE USE OF LIFO

LIFO is not recommended by any authoritative accounting bodies. While its use has been advocated on several grounds, the overwhelming reason for its widespread use in the U.S. is that of minimizing profits taxes. U.S. tax laws, unlike those in Australia, allow the use of LIFO in the assessment of taxable income, and during a long period of inflation the effect on income, and consequently on tax payments, can be very substantial. LIFO is rarely used in Australia because it is not permitted for the calculation of taxable income, and it is expensive to maintain two stock valuation systems concurrently.

Other reasons advanced in support of its use can be shown to be defective. The argument that the firm must maintain a minimum investment in inventories, that is, the base stock argument, is irrelevant as a justification for the method. A going-concern firm must maintain a minimum level of investment in most assets — in cash, accounts receivable where it relies on credit sales, plant, buildings, and so on — but this fact does not justify valuation at very historic prices where the specific assets acquired on establishment of the firm have long since been disposed of. The basis of asset valuation is an issue distinct from the need to maintain minimum levels of assets in a going concern. Secondly, LIFO is justified as a method of replacement cost valuation accounting as distinct from historical cost valuation accounting. The claim that the use of LIFO enables the measurement of the cost of goods sold at a value nearer the replacement cost of the goods sold, and hence enables the measurement of historic profit to approximate current income, is normally true; however, it does this by excessively distorting the balance sheet valuation of inventories. It is difficult to justify improving one accounting report at the expense of the other through the use of inconsistent valuation methods. And in any case a superior method is available, that is, the consistent use of current replacement costs of inventories in both reports where the objective is to measure current income and current financial position. The related argument that the use of LIFO eliminates from inventories the "unrealized gains" due to price rises likewise is not a sound justification where the superior replacement cost basis itself can be applied. These "unrealized gains" are measured by the differences between the two closing inventory values or by the profit differences between the two methods — here, $360. It is claimed that this additional $360 profit is illusory since the firm cannot replace its inventories from the FIFO cost of goods sold. While this argument is partly true, replacement cost accounting is superior to LIFO accounting in handling this problem. LIFO is not a good substitute for replacement cost accounting.

## INVENTORY VALUATION UNDER THE PERIODIC INVENTORY SYSTEM

Here, no precise measure of the cost of inventories sold can be made since no internal cost records are kept. However, it is likely that the closing inventories will be valued at either current replacement cost or recent purchase prices, and in this event the cost of goods sold will approximate that obtaining under the FIFO method, together with the undisclosed stock leakages.

## FURTHER READING

A.A.A. "A Discussion of Various Approaches to Inventory Measurement". Supplementary Statement no. 2. *Accounting Review* (July 1964).

Carrington, A. S.; Battersby, G. B.; and Howitt, G. *Accounting: An Information System.* Christchurch. Whitcombe and Tombs, 1975. Chap. 8.

Gordon, M. J., and Shillinglaw, G. *Accounting: A Management Approach.* 4th ed. Homewood, Illinois: Richard D. Irwin, 1969. Chap. 12.

Johnson, C. E. "Inventory Valuation: The Accountant's Achilles Heel". In Zeff, S., and Keller, W. *Financial Accounting Theory.* New York: McGraw-Hill, 1964.

Mathews, R. L. *The Accounting Framework.* 3rd ed. Melbourne: Cheshire, 1971. Chap. 6, pp.73—80.

## QUESTIONS AND EXERCISES

[Solution to problem marked * is given in Appendix 4.]

1.   What is the inventory pricing problem and how does it arise?

2.   Explain four methods of pricing inventories sold under a perpetual inventory system.

3.   Critically examine the reasons advanced for the use of LIFO.

*4.   Explain and contrast the use of the FIFO and LIFO methods of inventory pricing on income determination and asset valuation in a period of inflation. Illustrate your answer with respect to the following data:

| | | |
|---|---|---|
| Jan.   1 | Inventory | 100 units at 30 cents each |
| Jan.  31 | Purchases | 120 units at 40 cents each |
| Feb.  28 | Purchases | 110 units at 50 cents each |
| Mar.  31 | Purchases | 140 units at 60 cents each |
| Sales for period | | 400 units at 80 cents each |

5.   Jane Slimline is a professional share trader. Her dealings in the shares of Jasminex N. L., a tin-mining company, for the past six months were as follows:

| | Bought | | Sold | |
|---|---|---|---|---|
| | No. | Price per Share $ | No. | Price per Share $ |
| Jan. | 10,000 | 1 | — | — |
| Feb. | 7,000 | 5 | 12,000 | 9 |
| Mar. | 6,000 | 20 | 8,000 | 40 |
| Apr. | 9,000 | 60 | 5,000 | 80 |
| May | 4,000 | 75 | 6,000 | 50 |
| June | — | — | 1,000 | 4 |

Jane wants to know how much profit she made over the six months, and the value of her portfolio at the end of June.

(Show all calculations in your answer for three possible methods of share valuation.)

6. Purchases of a certain product during July are set out below:

$

| July | 1. | 100 units @ 10.00 |
| | 12. | 100 units @ 9.80 |
| | 15. | 50 units @ 9.60 |
| | 20. | 100 units @ 9.40 |

Units sold during the month were as follows:

| July | 10. | 80 units |
| | 14. | 100 units |
| | 30. | 90 units |

No opening inventories.

*Required:*

i. Determine the cost of goods sold for July under three different valuation methods.

ii. Discuss the advantages and/or disadvantages of each of these methods.

iii. A physical stocktake revealed a shortage of five units. Show how you would bring this to account.

7. Fresh Fisheries Limited operate a chain of retail sea food shops. Their wholesale distribution centre has the following records of boxes of fish.

| Week Ending | | No. of Boxes | Unit Cost $ | Total Cost $ |
| --- | --- | --- | --- | --- |
| Jan. 6 | Purchases | 400 | 21 | 8,400 |
| | Deliveries | 380 | | |
| Jan. 13 | Purchases | 525 | 25 | 13,125 |
| | Deliveries | 530 | | |
| Jan. 20 | Purchases | 420 | 34 | 14,280 |
| | Deliveries | 440 | | |
| Jan. 27 | Purchases | 500 | 30 | 15,000 |
| | Deliveries | 470 | | |

The January 1 inventory comprised 60 boxes at a unit cost of $17 per box.

Calculate the cost of fish delivered to the retail shops during the 4-week period, and the cost of the fish in the warehouse on January 27, using the:

i. first-in, first-out basis
ii. weighted average cost basis
iii. last-in, first-out basis.

# Chapter 14
# Depreciation and Long-Term Assets

The next problem to be considered in the measurement of periodic income and financial position concerns the measurement of depreciation on long-term assets. Several problems are encountered in accounting for long-term assets in a historical cost accounting system. These problems are:

1. What costs to include in the acquisition cost of the asset
2. What length of time the asset is expected to contribute to revenue
3. The residual value of the asset at the end of that period
4. The purpose to be served by expensing the asset's net cost (that is, depreciation or amortization) over that period
5. The method of depreciation.

### THE ACQUISITION COST OF A LONG-TERM ASSET

Although in most cases the acquisition cost of an asset is an objective, verifiable amount, problems can arise in some circumstances. The general principle to be applied in these cases is that all expenditures necessary to make an asset suitable for its intended use are part of its cost. Hence, costs of transporting the plant to its site, installing it, and putting it into working condition are essential parts of its cost; discounts allowed on purchase are not part of its cost.

Difficult problems, however, can arise in some circumstances, and the general nature of these problems only is indicated here. Frequently a manufacturing firm builds part of its own plant, or makes its own tools for use in production (for example, B.H.P. Co. Ltd. supplies its own steel for the construction of a new steel mill; Ford Motor Co. Pty. Ltd. makes some of its own tools, and buys in others). Should such items be costed at variable cost of production, variable cost plus a share of fixed costs, or that plus a profit margin, or should they be costed at the price that would have to be paid if they were bought from another firm? Where the government grants investment allowances to stimulate the installation of new plant, should the asset cost include or exclude such allowances? With existing assets, it is often difficult to distinguish improvements to the asset ("betterments") from maintenance, and maintenance from replacements. For example, a new facade on shop premises needing renovation may be a betterment or maintenance; a new engine or tyre on a truck to replace worn-out items constitutes both replacement and maintenance; painting of premises constitutes maintenance whose benefits extend beyond the current accounting period. In general, the expenditure is treated as a betterment if it extends the productive capacity (either annual or lifelong) of the asset, and as maintenance expenditure if it enables the full utilization of the asset as envisaged at the time of purchase. However, the dividing line between the two is not always distinct, and in doubtful cases the expenditure would be shown as maintenance. If the expenditure is classified as a betterment or a replacement, it is capitalized as part of the asset's cost; if it is maintenance, it is shown as current expense.

The accounting treatment of such items of expenditure on betterments, maintenance and replacement partly depends on the unit of account — is the building or truck depreciated as a whole, or are individual parts of it depreciated? This decision should depend on how important each component is, in cost terms, although in practice taxation laws and the doctrine of conservatism encourage firms to treat as many expenditures as possible as current maintenance.

## THE ASSET'S EXPECTED LIFE

Here, the problem varies according to the type of asset. In the case of those assets whose life is fixed by contract (for example, leases), there are no problems involved in determining the lifespan of the asset. Conversely, the problem does not arise with assets such as land which have an infinite life. However, the majority of long-term assets lie between these extremes, and they have finite lives determined by physical deterioration and obsolescence, or in Hatfield's words, by that "irresistible march to the junkheap".[1] Such deterioration causes a decline in the quantity or quality of output, or a rise in its cost because of increasing maintenance. At some stage it becomes cheaper for the firm to replace the asset rather than continue repairing it.

While we are not concerned here with estimating economic lifespans of physical assets, a general review of the two main determinants of physical life and obsolescence is made here to illustrate some of the complexities involved.

### 1. Physical Life

Engineers generally build a physical life factor into their design of a piece of equipment, building, and so on, which is based on scientific data about the materials used, stresses imposed on them through use, the expected type and intensity of use, maintenance, etc. However, they also build in a margin of error allowance (a "safety factor") to ensure that the asset will at least reach this design life, particularly where human safety is involved. The accountant uses such engineering life estimates as one of the basic factors in determining the expected lifespan of assets for accounting purposes.

However, there is generally a liberal margin surrounding the engineer's designed life in which a machine may come to the end of its physical life. The "safety factor" may enable the machine to be worked for a much longer period than that initially specified. Actual physical life depends critically on the firm's maintenance policy, and inadequate maintenance can curtail a machine's life quite drastically, whereas good maintenance can prolong it almost indefinitely. The machine may be used more or less intensively than anticipated at the time of purchase. These considerations mean that any estimate of physical life can be subject to a substantial margin of error.

## 2.  Obsolescence

Physical life is generally difficult to estimate, but obsolescence is much more so. Obsolescence of productive equipment and buildings can occur from both the product market side and from the production side. Changes in consumers' tastes (for example, fashion changes), technological improvements in products which render existing equipment unsuitable (for example, equipment for making piston-engined aircraft is inadequate for the manufacture of jet aircraft), or changes in popularity of retailing locations (for example, the shift from downtown Sydney has depressed property values in that area), cause obsolescence on the product market side. Similarly, it can occur on the production side because of the technological improvements in the equipment used to perform a given service (for example, computers replacing accounting machines).

A host of problems is involved in estimating effective lives of "intangible assets" such as goodwill, patents, and expenditures on research and development and advertising of new products. It is difficult enough to identify future benefits from these assets, let alone the period over which such benefits accrue, and for this reason the amortization of expenditures on such assets is often treated as a charge against profits rather than as an expense of earning revenue.

## RESIDUAL VALUE OF THE ASSET

The residual value of the asset at its disposal date must be estimated at the time of purchase in order that only the net outlay incurred on the asset is allocated over the revenue-producing periods. Where the asset is to be used until it is physically worn out or obsolete, residual value will be negligible. Likewise, it will be zero for assets based on legal contracts. At the other extreme, the residual value of buildings may be expected to be similar to, or exceed, current purchase price because of the appreciation occurring in property values. Firms sometimes replace assets such as cars regularly each year or so, long before they are worn out or obsolete, and in this case residual values form a high proportion of the new price. They can be estimated with reasonable accuracy where the items have established market prices for various stages of their secondhand state. However there can be a problem in the valuation of assets traded in on new ones because trade-in values can be fictitiously high and in fact represent in part a reduction in the price of the new assets. In this situation, the best guide is to use the cash purchase price of the new asset as its cost and the cash selling value of the existing one as its residual value. In most cases, then, the estimation of residual values is not a serious problem.

## THE PURPOSE OF CHARGING DEPRECIATION

In accounting, the objective of charging depreciation on long-term assets is to allocate the net outlay on those resources as expenses of earning revenue in order to measure periodic income. All outlays on resources used up in the revenue-earning process must be recouped out of revenue before a profit is earned, and the process of charging depreciation is one of allocating outlays on long-term resources against the revenues to which those resources made a contribution in order to recoup them and thereby maintain capital intact. Outlays on inventories, salesmen's salaries, and so on are fairly easy to trace through the firm to the revenue-earning process in particular periods, and hence to be charged as expenses. But this is not always the case with outlays on long-term assets because of the problems discussed above.

Hence the primary purpose of depreciation accounting is to allocate the net cost of a long-term asset over the periods comprising its effective working life during which it contributes to the earning of revenue. This is done as a requirement of the accounting theory of historical cost income determination, and it is part of the matching principle. The A.I.C.P.A. states that depreciation accounting is "a system of accounting which aims to distribute the cost . . . of tangible capital assets, less salvage (if any), over the estimated useful life of the unit . . . in a systematic and rational manner. It is a process of allocation, not of valuation".[2]

Much confusion surrounds the concept of depreciation because it is used in different ways by different professions. Engineers define depreciation in terms of physical wear. Economists sometimes define it as the decline in the market value of an asset due to all types of causes – wear, obsolescence, changes in market prices, and so on; at other times they define it in terms of a fund which must be accumulated to replace the asset. Businessmen as well often think of depreciation in terms of a replacement fund. But accounting depreciation is none of these things. It is a necessary expense incurred in earning revenue, and it must be charged as such to revenue in order to recover the net cost of the asset and thereby maintain intact the historic money investment in the firm before any profit is realized.

## THE CHOICE OF DEPRECIATION METHOD

The selection of the method used to allocate the net cost of a long-term asset over its effective working life can have an important effect on the periodic depreciation charges and hence on income and net asset values. Consider the following illustration. A machine costs $105,000, it has an estimated working life of 250,000 hours over 5 years, and an estimated residual value of $5,000. The machine can be depreciated according to the straight line, reducing balance or production units methods. Annual charges under each method are calculated at the following rates.

a)  Straight line depreciation.     $D = (\frac{100}{n})\% = (\frac{100}{5})\% = 20\%$ p.a.

b)  Reducing balance depreciation.  $D = 1 - 5\sqrt{\frac{5,000}{105,000}} = 46\%$ p.a.

c)  Production units.               $D = \frac{100,000}{250,000} = 40$ cents per hour.

| Year | S.L. Dep'n. | R.B. Dep'n | P.U. Dep'n | |
|------|-------------|------------|------------|---|
| | | | Prod'n Hours | Amount |
| 1 | 20,000 | 48,300 | 55,000 | 22,000 |
| 2 | 20,000 | 26,080 | 55,000 | 22,000 |
| 3 | 20,000 | 14,080 | 50,000 | 20,000 |
| 4 | 20,000 | 7,610 | 45,000 | 18,000 |
| 5 | 20,000 | 3,930 | 45,000 | 18,000 |
| Totals $100,000 | $100,000 | | 250,000 hours | $100,000 |

The depreciation method should be selected on the principle that the periodic depreciation charges should reflect the expected pattern of benefits obtainable in each period from its use. "The depreciation of an asset during a period should reflect the share of the asset's service potential that has expired during that period. Similarly, the net balance in the asset account at any point in time should reflect the unexpired portion of the asset's service potential."[3]

The three most common methods adopted are the straight line, reducing balance, and production units methods. Under the straight line method, the depreciation charge is constant each year; it declines, but at a diminishing rate, each year under the reducing balance method; while it varies proportionately with output in the final method. Hence the straight line method implies using up an equal amount of service potential each year; the reducing balance method a declining pattern of service potential exhaustion, and the production units basis a constant using up of service potential with increases in output.

How well do the assumptions underlying these three methods accord with reality? Except for those assets comprising rights over a fixed period of time (for example, leases), for which the straight line method is appropriate because the asset's service potential expires equally each period, any one method of depreciation can only approximate the time flow of potential benefits. The depreciation method chosen initially must be consistently applied over the asset's life; it cannot be changed from year to year.

A further problem to be solved in applying the benefits or service potential principle is whether the data should relate to potential gross or net benefits from the use of the asset; that is, before, or after, allowing for repair and maintenance expenditures on the asset. This issue is not yet resolved.

Where *gross benefit flows* are considered, the two patterns illustrated in Figures 14–1 and 14–2 are typical of reality.

1. Constant output in each period of the asset's life – the "one-hoss shay" assumption.

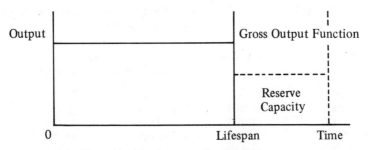

**Figure 14–1.** Constant Productivity case

Where machines form part of an integrated production line, they must be capable of maintaining their output rate so as to maintain the balance of capacities at each stage of production and the smooth flow of production. Imbalance in capacities, excessive breakdowns and so on cause bottlenecks in production which can seriously restrict the total output of the firm. The machines must be serviced to work effectively, and as soon as they cannot be economically serviced, they must be replaced by new machines.

Sometimes old plant is kept as 'reserve capacity' to meet peak demands or to act as a standby in the event of machine breakdowns. In such a case there is a downward step in the output function.

The constant periodic output potential applies also where benefits expire mainly or wholly with the expiration of time, for example, with leases and buildings.

2. Output declines at an increasing rate over time.

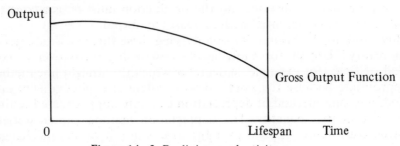

**Figure 14–2.** Declining productivity case

The periodic productivity of many assets declines progressively as physical depreciation, breakdowns, maintenance periods, and obsolescence increase over time. Generally the declining output function is concave to the origin — this reflects the increasing rate of decline in productivity as the asset ages. The asset is likely to be scrapped before its output declines to nothing, so that the output function has a vertical section at the lifespan of the asset.

If the decline in productivity over time is significant, assets with these characteristics should not form part of an integrated production line. Rather, they need to be operated as independent productive units so that their declining productivity does not restrict the output of other assets. The output functions of assets such as cars and trucks normally follow this pattern.

Where depreciation is mainly a function of use, the production units method enables an allocation of net asset cost in accordance with the matching principle if output fluctuates from period to period. Where output is fairly constant or is mainly a function of time, the straight line method is appropriate. If output declines substantially over the asset's life and the production units method cannot be applied, the reducing balance method is the appropriate method to use.

If the *net benefits* principle is used, allowance must be made for the time pattern of maintenance charges on the output function. Generally, these will increase over time until they become so large that it is more economical to replace the asset than to repair it. The pattern illustrated in Figure 14–3 is typical of the general trend, though there are likely to be significant steps in the function corresponding to major overhaul or renovation periods.

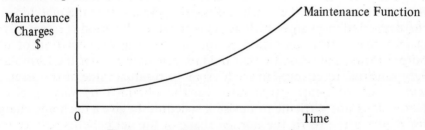

**Figure 14–3.** Rising maintenance charges

If maintenance charges are deducted from the value of output of the asset to derive its net output function, the function will in all cases decline. For example, the pattern illustrated in Figure 14–4 emerges where the gross output is constant each period.

The same general pattern applies if the gross output function is a declining one, but the negative slope of the net output function is greater.

The use of the net benefits principle justifies the use of a declining charge method of depreciation. The reducing balance method is the most widely used of the declining charge methods. Under this method,

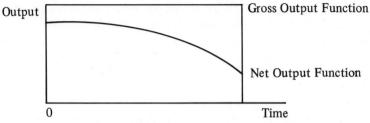

Figure 14–4. Declining net productivity case

the largest proportion of the net cost is charged in the first year when the asset's net productivity is greatest, and a declining charge is made each year as its productivity progressively declines. The pattern of depreciation charges follows the form of a curve convex to the origin and asymptotic to the time axis (Fig. 14–5).

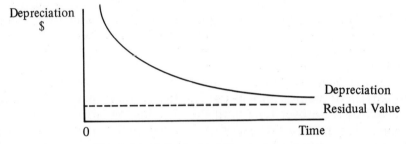

Figure 14–5. Reducing balance depreciation

The main defects in applying the reducing balance method to satisfy the requirements of the net benefits principle are that the matching of the depreciation charges with net benefits in each period is essentially a chance one — the allocation is not based on any calculation of net output flows; and secondly that the rate calculated under the formula is very sensitive to changes in the lifespan or residual value of the asset. A wide range of depreciation rates can be obtained by varying either factor. It is not difficult to devise a schedule to give a declining charge for depreciation to fit the normal shape of the net benefits pattern but this is not done in practice. Use of the reducing balance method of depreciation is generally justified on grounds other than the use of the net benefits approach.

The allocation of the net cost of an asset over its life according to gross or net output flows is a matter of contention. The gross basis is justified on the grounds that depreciation is a process of allocating a long-term cost over output which must be done irrespective of the size of maintenance expenses. Maintenance affects the asset's efficiency and length of life, but it is claimed that this should not affect the method of cost allocation. The net benefits basis is justified on the claim that the

cost of owning and using the asset, that is, depreciation plus maintenance, should be matched against output in each period, otherwise the
early years are charged with insufficient costs when maintenance costs
are low, while the later years bear excessive costs when maintenance
charges are high.

The gross benefits approach is used to support the straight line
method, while the net benefits one can be used to support the reducing
balance method. The effects of adding maintenance charges to straight
line and reducing balance depreciation are summarized in Figures 14–6
and 14–7.

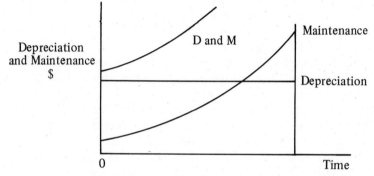

**Figure 14–6.** Straight line depreciation

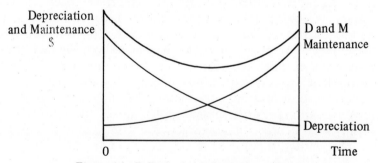

**Figure 14–7.** Reducing balance depreciation

However, in most cases other arguments are used to support the
application of the reducing balance method. Secondhand market values
of long-term assets often decline very rapidly in the early years,
followed by a less rapid rate of decline. Use of the reducing balance
method enables balance sheet values to follow this trend so that there is
less risk of the balance sheet value exceeding the secondhand value of
the asset. One can, however, question the relevance of this in a historic
cost system to assets whose continuing use in the firm is planned and
whose resale is not contemplated. The reducing balance method is
useful where the asset's life cannot be estimated with much confidence,

as the asset account always remains open until disposed under this method — the formula never allows the total net cost to be depreciated, and the charge in the later years becomes somewhat nominal. A final reason for its use, and by far the least justifiable, is that it is a most conservative method. It enables excessive depreciation charges to be made on new assets, and thereby profits and assets in those years to be understated. In effect part of the expenses of future periods is charged to the current period. As compared with the straight line method in its application to an asset whose life is short or residual value is low, the depreciation rate under the reducing balance method is several times that under the straight line method. The reducing balance rate is very sensitive to the lifespan and residual value of the asset — the shorter the lifespan, or the lower the residual value, the greater the difference between the two depreciation rates.

The reducing balance and straight line methods are widely used in Australia. However, the reducing balance method cannot be used in its pure form for tax purposes — rather, a variant of it is used in which a depreciation rate exceeding the straight line rate by 50 per cent is applied to the net book value of the asset. A similar position applies in the United States, except that double the straight line rate is applied to the net book value. The method is known as the "double declining balance" method.

Another method of depreciation which has acquired considerable popularity recently in the literature, though it has been known for many years, is the annuity method. Under this method, an implicit interest cost on the finance used to acquire the asset is recorded along with the depreciation charge in such a way as to hold the rate of return on investment constant each year. It is not recommended here because such an implicit interest cost is not relevant for the measurement of periodic historic cost income — the method belongs to the present value system of accounting. Furthermore, application of the annuity method results in rising depreciation charges over time, and this is hardly realistic. The method is not used to any extent in practice.

### FURTHER READING

A.A.A. "Accounting for Land, Buildings and Equipment". Supplementary Statement no. 1. *Accounting Review* (July 1964).

Carrington, A. S., Battersby, G. B., and Howitt, G. *Accounting. An Information System.* Christchurch. Whitcombe and Tombs, 1975. Chap. 8.

Gordon, M. J., and Shillinglaw, G. *Accounting: A Management Approach,* 4th ed. Homewood, Illinois: Richard D. Irwin, 1969. Chap. 10, pp. 295–301, and chap. 11.

Mathews, R. L. *The Accounting Framework.* 3rd ed. Melbourne: Cheshire, 1971. Chap. 6, pp. 180–84.

## NOTES

1. H. R. Hatfield, *Accounting* (N.Y.: Appleton, 1927), p. 130.
2. A.I.C.P.A., *Accounting Research Bulletin*, no. 43 (1953).
3. Gordon & Shillinglaw, *Accounting: A Management Approach*, p. 322.

## QUESTIONS AND EXERCISES

1.  What is the significance in the distinction between treating some expenditures on new assets as part of the asset's cost and others as expenses?

    What principles are applied in differentiating between the two?

    Why might a firm prefer to treat such expenditures as expenses in borderline cases?

2.  Comfort Motels purchases a block of land for $80,000, with the intention of building a motel on it. A dilapidated building, valued at $10,000, had stood on the land, and it cost $7,000 to demolish it and clear up the site. At what value should the land be shown in Comfort Motels' balance sheet?

3.  Diecasters Ltd. bought some new plant direct from the United States. The price quoted was $500,000 Aust. The company incurred the following expenditures in connection with the plant to get it into efficient working condition:

    i.    Cost of trip to the U.S. by a director to order the plant: $4,000
    ii.   Freight and insurance: $10,000
    iii.  Customs duty: $40,000
    iv.   Wages of own staff to instal the plant: $2,000
    v.    Running-in costs: $3,000

    At what cost should the new plant be shown in Diecasters' balance sheet?

4.  On what basis may betterment expenditures be distinguished from maintenance expenditures? What is the significance of the distinction for accounting purposes? How would you treat the following expenditures:

    i.    Extensive renovation of premises?
    ii.   Installation of a new engine in a taxi cab?
    iii.  A new set of tyres on a taxi cab?
    iv.   The regular 5,000 miles service on a cab?

5.  Distinguish between the concepts of depreciation as used in accounting, economics and engineering. What is the purpose of charging depreciation in accounting? Is the objective of accounting depreciation to provide funds for replacement of long-term assets?

6.  Why is it necessary to recognize depreciation as an expense of operations? In what way does depreciation expense differ from most other expenses?

7.  Why is depreciation of plant credited to Accumulated Depreciation of Plant account and not to Plant account?

8.  The annual report of X Company states: "It is not the policy of this company to charge depreciation on fixed assets. Our plant and equipment are always maintained in first-class condition, and the market value of our buildings appreciates each year." Discuss critically.

9.  What are the three main depreciation methods used in accounting? What factors are relevant in choosing between them? What is the relationship between maintenance activities and the choice of a depreciation method?

10. Company. A depreciates its equipment on a straight line basis and Company B on a reducing balance basis. Are the depreciation charges of the two companies necessarily non-comparable?

*11. Calculate the straight line and reducing balance depreciation rates and the annual charges under each for the following situations:

    i.   a    asset cost $1,000   resale value $400   estimated life 2 years
         b.   asset cost $1,000   resale value $400   estimated life 3 years

    ii.  a.   asset cost $1,000   resale value $100   estimated life 8 years
         b.   asset cost $1,000   resale value $  1   estimated life 8 years

Show your answer in the form of a table for the reducing balance method. Comment on a comparison of the results for each method, and on the effects of changing resale values and lifespans.

12. Calculate the straight line and reducing balance depreciation rates and the annual charges under each for the following situations:

    i.   a.   Asset cost $1,400   resale value $400   estimated life 2 years
         b.   Asset cost $1,400   resale value $400   estimated life 3 years

    ii.  a.   Asset cost $1,400   resale value $400   estimated life 10 years
         b.   Asset cost $1,400   resale value $100   estimated life 10 years

Present a comparison of the results for each method and comment upon the effects of changing resale values and lifespans.

13. In January 1959, Knitting Mills Pty. Ltd., placed in service a new machine costing $50,000. Its estimated useful like was twenty years and its salvage value zero.

In December 1962, certain improvements were added to this machine at a cost of $6,000. Eight years later, the machine was thoroughly overhauled and rebuilt at a cost of $12,000. It was estimated that the overhaul would extend the useful life of the machine by five years, or until the end of 1983. Depreciation charges in 1970 were unaffected by the overhaul.

*Required:*

    i.   Show the entries in the journal and ledger accounts to record the improvements added in December 1962, and the rebuilding in 1970.
    ii.  Compute depreciation for 1963 on a straight line basis.
    iii. Compute depreciation for 1971 on a straight line basis.
    iv.  Show the book value of the machine as at 31 December 1971.
    v.   Justify your treatment of the improvements and the overhaul.

14. On 1 January 1959, Paton Ltd. acquired a new machine for $40,000. The machine was installed at a cost of $5,000, of which $2,000 was wages paid to Woppa Ltd., a wholly owned subsidiary of Paton Ltd. The machine had an estimated useful life of twenty years with an estimated resale value of $3,000. The firm uses the straight line method of depreciation for machines of this nature.

In December 1964 certain improvements were added to this machine at a cost of $7,900. The estimated resale value of the machine was revised as being $3,200. In December 1971 the machine was thoroughly overhauled at a cost of $34,290. It was estimated that the overhaul would extend the life of the machine by ten years, after which its resale value would be $2,000.

Depreciation charges in 1964 and 1971 were unaffected by the work done on the machine.

*Required:*

i.    Record all transactions in ledger accounts

ii.    Compute the depreciation charges for 1963, 1965, and 1972, and record in the appropriate accounts.

iii.    Show the book value of the machine as at 31 December 1975.

iv.    Would your answer be any different if all the installation costs were paid to an unrelated company? Why?

# Chapter 15
# Accounting for Liabilities

A firm's liabilities are important from several points of view. In broad terms, they are the debts of the firm and hence are an integral part of the measure of its financial position. As a corollary, they are the link between the measures of the firm's gross and net wealth, and hence their measurement is linked with that of owners' equity and capital maintenance. Secondly, liabilities include all external sources of finance for the firm. They provide funds, i.e., cash or resources, for use in its operations. Hence the characteristics of liabilities — their maturity dates, preferential rights to repayment of principal and interest, and so on — must be included in the analysis of the financial structure of the firm. This in turn affects the degree of financial risk (as distinct from operating risk) borne by owners and the returns required by owners to reward them for providing the risk capital to the firm. A further consequence is that they affect the overall economic cost of financing the firm's operations, which in turn affects the profitability of all investment projects and the owners' investment in the firm. The financial structure decision of the firm is always a top management one because of its crucial nature and pervasive effects on all the firm's operations.

There can be no independent theory of liability recognition and measurement — rather, their recognition and measurement must be integrated with the decisions about assets and expenses and profit appropriations. For example, the decision to record merchandise purchases on credit affects the asset (inventory) and liabilities (accounts payable) simultaneously and for the same amount; likewise for recording accrued wages which affects the wages expense and the liability for accrued expenses. In other words, the accounting for liabilities is part of the process of measuring wealth, capital maintenance, income, and financial position. These concepts and their measurement are all part of an integrated theory. However, there are various aspects of accounting for liabilities which warrant examination here because they involve issues which tend to be implicit rather than explicit in their other contexts. These issues bear more explicitly on the liabilities themselves than upon the measurement of assets, expenses, and profit appropriations. They tend to concern the nature of liabilities and secondly the timing of their recognition — i.e., when to recognize them, rather than the valuation of liabilities, since the latter is explicitly analyzed in the context of asset or expense measurement.

## NATURE AND SCOPE OF LIABILITIES

The concept of a liability has been undergoing changes as the environment in which modern corporations operate becomes more complex.[1] While the common forms of items classified as liabilities (for example, trade creditors and loans) have always been and probably always will be classified as liabilities, there are differences of opinion with respect to some of the newer "liabilities" (for example, provisions for warranty costs, deferred income tax, pensions and long-service leave, and leases). In other words, there is the question of just how broadly liabilities should be defined.

Several concepts of liabilities have been proposed. Liabilities may be defined as sources of funds to the firm from sources other than the owners. In the modern situation, this definition is too restricting in that, for example, it would exclude dividend and tax liabilities, expected warranty costs on products sold, and so on. A second, broader definition is that they are the obligations of the firm. This concept would include the examples above in its ambit. However, the question then arises — do they have to be legal obligations? A firm is not legally required to pay any dividends, for example, though it may be foolish from other points of view not to do so. Likewise, it may carry out repairs on products sold beyond the terms of the warranty in order to protect its good trade name. It may provide pensions or long-service leave benefits to its employees above the legal minimum. Provisions for deferred company income taxes are not legal obligations; yet the accounting profession recommends that they be shown as liabilities. A third concept of liabilities is broader still, and it defines them in terms of restrictions that apply to the future use of assets by the firm. The termination of the liability will involve the use of assets in the future and hence restrict the firm's ability to use its assets for other purposes. Such restrictions may arise from legal or managerial considerations and they arise from obligations beyond legal ones. Thus if the company "stands behind its products", it may recognize a liability for warranty costs above the legal requirements; it recognizes the economic necessity to pay dividends to shareholders; and so on.

Although it might appear at first sight that all legal obligations should at least be included within the ambit of liabilities as such obligations are, in the normal course of events, unavoidable, in fact current accounting practice does not adhere rigidly to the legal concept. Legal liabilities arising out of executory contracts and those arising out of other arrangements where neither party has performed his part of the agreement are normally omitted from the accounts and balance sheet. These situations concern transactions involving an exchange of a promise for a promise. Thus leases, purchase commitments, and employment contracts are generally not recognized as accounting transactions until the services or goods specified in the contract are delivered or paid for. Such transactions affect both assets and liabilities simultaneously, and they are usually omitted from both groups on the grounds that until the goods or services are delivered or paid for, there is an unconditional right of set-off. Yet the buyer may not be able to cancel the contract without paying for the goods and services committed even though he has not received them. For example, a lessee cannot unilaterally cancel a lease; a company cannot cancel a contract for the construction of new buildings. Furthermore, these transactions normally meet the accounting standards of verifiability, freedom from bias, quantifiability, and relevance.

It should be obvious that not all balance sheet credit accounts are liabilities of the firm or part of owners' equity. A very prevalent practice in the past was to show all asset contra accounts as liabilities. Thus "reserves for bad debts" (i.e., estimated bad debts), "reserves for depreciation" (i.e., accumulated depreciation charged) were shown as liabilities, with the result that both the assets and liabilities of the company were overstated.

Selection of the concept of liabilities to be employed in the accounting system should depend on which concept enables the accounting reports to be more informative. Which concept satisfies best the user's needs for information about the financial position and the financial structure of the firm, about the stewardship of resources by management, and so on? Given this objective, then the same set of criteria should be applied consistently to all transactions and thereby to the recognition of assets, expenses, profit appropriations, and liabilities.

## BASIC CHARACTERISTICS OF LIABILITIES

Liabilities may be defined as currently existing obligations, which the firm intends to meet at some time in the future, to provide money, goods, or services to others outside the firm. Such obligations, whether arising from legal or managerial considerations, will impose restrictions on the use of assets. They should satisfy the following tests:

1. The liability must exist at the present time, i.e., it must have arisen out of a past transaction or event involving the firm with outside entities (and not owners). The non-liability aspect of the transaction must have been recognized, i.e., the asset purchase or the expense has been recognized and recorded. In general, obligations contingent upon the occurrence of future events are not existing obligations and should not be recorded as liabilities.

2. They must involve an expenditure of resources — cash, goods, or services — in the future.

3. The amount of the liability and the creditor's identity or group must be known

with reasonable accuracy. This requirement, of course, applies throughout all accounting. In some cases the value of the liability is a probabilistic figure only, and the creditor can be identified only as a member of a defined group.

4. The maturity date of the liability should be at least approximately known.

5. If there is no unconditional right of offset in executory contracts, the obligation should be shown as a liability.

## THE VALUATION OF LIABILITIES

The requirements for an accurate measure of financial position and financial structure should determine the basis of liability valuation. Their valuation should be consistent with the valuation of assets and expenses.

Liabilities may be valued at their face values or their net discounted values. For short-term liabilities, the two tend to coincide. The net discounted value is recommended because this is the amount for which the liability could be immediately discharged and as such it is more relevant for the measures of financial position and structure. Loans to the firm are shown at their net discounted value simply by not including future interest commitments as part of the liability. Hire-purchase creditors are shown at their gross value less unearned interest. Leasehold liabilities can be shown at their cash equivalent value; and so on.

## SOME PROBLEM AREAS IN ACCOUNTING FOR LIABILITIES

### 1. Contingent Liabilities

These are obligations which, although they refer to a past transaction or event, will arise in the future only if a specified event occurs. The obligations are contingent upon specified future events occurring. They are possible but not probable liabilities. However, the division between actual liabilities and contingent liabilities is not always easy to make. For example, the firm may be facing a claim for legal damages. If it is most probable that damages will be awarded against it, then the probable amount of the damages should be shown as a liability; but if the judgment is likely to be in its favour, then the damages should be shown as a contingent liability only. Contingent liabilities are recorded outside the double-entry process as memorandum footnotes to the balance sheet. Other generally recognized contingent liabilities are guarantees of a parent company to the creditors of the subsidiary, patent infringement claims, liability with respect to notes or accounts receivable discounted (where the company is responsible for carrying the burden of bad debts), and frequently the amounts committed under long-term construction contracts. In fact the liabilities under all executory contracts could be shown in this way.

## 2. Deferred Performance Liabilities

Deferred performance liabilities arise from sales to customers which are recorded in advance of the completion of the operating cycle — for example, the sales of subscriptions to a magazine ,or products under warranty, rent received in advance, etc. They are contractual obligations or intentions to perform services in the future, beyond the point of revenue recognition, and they should be recognized as liabilities. They are often called deferred credits or unearned income, but they are in fact liabilities. They are settled by delivering the magazines in the future, repairing the appliances sold, allowing the tenant to remain in the premises, and so on, rather than by the payment of cash. Here, a portion of the price applies to costs that have not yet been incurred. At the time of sale, the amount involved should be estimated and debited to estimated magazine costs to be incurred, or estimated warranty costs (an expense item), and credited to estimated liability to customers (a liability). Even though the identities of the customers who will require appliance-servicing may not be known, they are identifiable as a group; and the amount should be capable of reasonably accurate estimation in total.

## 3. Debentures and Bonds

A problem can arise where the issue price of the debenture or bond does not equal its maturity value. For example, a $100 7 per cent six-year bond may be sold for $98. The company must pay $7 interest each year, and repay $100 at the end of the six years. The transactions could be recorded as:

|  |  | $ |
|---|---|---|
| Cash | Dr. | 98 |
| Bond Payable | Cr. | 98 |

Although the net value of the bond is only $98 — the company could buy them (or their equivalent) back at this price — it is more informative to record the transaction as:

|  |  | $ |
|---|---|---|
| Cash | Dr. | 98 |
| Bond Discount | Dr. | 2 |
| Bond Payable | Cr. | 100 |

The Bond Discount is amortized over the six years on either a straight line or (preferably) compound interest basis, as an addition to the $7 interest expense. Effectively, the company is paying $7 per annum on $98 borrowed, plus an additional $2 interest at the end of year 6. This is an effective interest rate of 7.43 per cent per annum.[2] The bond discount ought to be deducted from the bond payable in the balance sheet to show its net discounted value; however, in Australia the usual practice is to show the discount as a long-term intangible asset for the reason that it is analogous to prepaid interest. If the amount involved is significant, this practice results in overstatement of both assets and liabilities.

### 4. Liability under Lease Contracts

An increasingly popular method of financing the acquisition of assets is for the firm to lease rather than to buy them. The firm may either contract to rent the asset (e.g., car) for some period of time from the owner (an "operating lease"); or arrange for a finance company to buy a fixed asset (e.g., plant) on its behalf and then lease the plant from that finance company, generally for the effective working life of the plant (a "financial lease"); or sell its own asset (generally premises) to a finance company for cash and lease it back (a "sale and leaseback" agreement). In all cases the firm (i.e., the lessee) obtains sole rights to use the asset during the lease period and thereby avoids having to find the cash for an outright purchase. Leasing is similar to renting except that there are normally future contractual commitments in the lease which require the firm to make regular payments irrespective of whether or not it still wants to use the asset. This is always the case for the "financial" and "sale and leaseback" types of agreement, but it need not be for "operating leases", where the period of the lease is generally fairly flexible. Essentially, leasing lies somewhere between the two extremes of straight rental and outright purchase, and the methods of accounting for leases reflect these two extremes.

Leasing in effect is another form of debt finance which can increase a firm's debt capacity and asset base. If the firm borrowed the money and bought the asset, the additional liability and asset would be shown in the balance sheet. This affects its financial position and structure, and creditors and investors desire to know this. The same thing happens in effect with leasing. Although the firm does not buy the property in the asset, it buys the use of the asset. It incurs an obligation to make regular payments to a lessor in much the same way as for the repayment of loans.

Under the conventional method of accounting for leases (the rental method), the lease transaction is not regarded as an accounting event and no asset or liability is recognized at the time the contract is signed. Rather, the only record is made when the payments either fall due or are made. They are recorded analogously to rent commitments, and are treated primarily as expenses (with an appropriate adjustment for prepayments where required at the year's end).

Thus, no information is provided about the asset (i.e., the right to use the asset in the future) or the liability (the future contractual payments under the lease agreement). So assets and liabilities are both understated, and the firm's disclosed financial structure is misleading.

The extent to which the firm uses debt finance is understated, and consequently the measures of financial risk are unreliable. The rental method is justified on the grounds of simplicity and because it does not affect expense recognition, and therefore profits and owners' equity, as the asset and liability cancel out.

The alternative method of leasehold accounting which is now gaining favour is to capitalize all lease payments as the measure of both the asset and the liability and to amortize the lease asset over its life.[3] This method informs the users of financial reports about the lease commitments and enables a more accurate measure of the firm's financial position and structure. The value of the lease liability is the sum of the future lease payments discounted for time at the rate of interest implicit in the lease contract. This rate of interest is that which equates the present value of the stream of lease payments to the present total cash price of buying the asset. For example, if a machine can be bought for $1,006 cash now, or leased for five years at a cost of $300 per annum payable at the end of each year, then the effective rate of interest implicit in the lease terms is 15 per cent, i.e.,

$$1,006 = \sum_{t=1}^{5} \frac{300t}{(1.15)^t}$$

The present value of the lease liability at the start of the contract is $1,006, and likewise for the present value of the leasehold asset. At the end of each year, the lease values are as follows:

|        | $    |
|--------|------|
| Year 1 | 856  |
| 2      | 685  |
| 3      | 488  |
| 4      | 261  |
| 5      | —    |

The values are calculated from the above formula for each year.

### 5. Other Executory Contracts

The principle involved in lease capitalization can be applied to other executory contracts where both the payments are to be made and the services are still to be performed. Thus it can be applied to all contractual obligations covering the construction of new premises or any fixed asset, supply of raw materials or merchandise, employment of senior staff, and so on. Accounting in such a situation can become very complex, and it raises the issue of whether accounting ought to be historically based or relate to the future in order to best serve its functions. Future-based accounting is analyzed in the present value system later on in the course. One simple compromise which avoids the complexities of present value accounting for executory contracts is to account for them on a rental basis but to report the obligations under these contracts outside the balance sheet as contingent liabilities. Informed users can then adjust the apparent balance sheet measures of financial structure to suit their needs.

### 6. Deferred Company Income Taxes

The measure of taxable income on which company tax is levied will differ from the firm's measure of its net profit where it does not choose to follow some regulations in the tax code for the calculation of its own net profit. The main differences between accounting and tax treatments lie in the depreciation rates allowed on long-term assets, some expenditures in mining development, and in the recognition of profits on hire-purchase sales. The tax code allows reducing balance depreciation to be used in the tax return, at a rate exceeding the straight line rate, whereas the company may use the straight line method in its own accounts. Mining companies are allowed to treat some development expenditures as current expenses for tax purposes, though they are capitalized as assets and depreciated for their own accounting reports. Likewise the tax code allows the recognition of profits on the cash collection basis for hire-purchase sales in the tax return whereas the company may use the delivery basis in its own reports. These factors mean that, in an initial or growth phase of a company's operations, taxable income is less than accounting income; and hence that the tax assessable on the former is less than that calculated on accounting income. It is claimed by many accountants that the "true" tax charge for the period is that based on the accounting income, even though the tax assessment is calculated on taxable income, and that any "tax savings" in the current year will have to be repaid in the form of a higher tax bill in future years. Hence, the "savings" merely represent deferred taxes rather than tax reductions, and the deferred taxes should be shown as a liability.[4]

The deferred tax argument really reduces down to the proposition that annual taxes are levied on accounting and not taxable income, but that only the amount levied on the taxable income is payable in the current year. The remainder of the charge is deferred to an indefinite date in the future.

As an example of how the two measures of income and of taxes payable can arise, assume that a company's income before depreciation is $100, and it charges $20 straight line depreciation in its own accounts but is permitted to charge $30 reducing balance depreciation in its tax return, its accounting income is $80 while its taxable income is $70. At a rate of 40 cents in the dollar, the liability based on accounting income is $32, and that on taxable income is $28. The company only has to pay $28 in the coming year, and $4 is treated as a deferred tax liability. In later years when the straight line depreciation charge exceeds the reducing balance charge, accounting income is less than taxable income, with obvious consequences for the two measures of the current tax charge. The difference between the two measures of taxation is taken out of the deferred tax account.

It can be shown that, in some cases where a company takes advantage of tax concessions permitted by the tax code, future tax payments are increased; whereas in other cases they are not.[5] Essentially each position depends on a prescribed set of future operating conditions applying. However, in the case of a profitable, growing company, future tax payments are not increased by the fact of the company's having previously taken advantage of the tax concessions. The trend of professional opinion is to treat deferred taxes as a liability. In the opinion of this writer, they are at most a contingent liability dependent upon the existence of a particular set of future operating conditions. Furthermore, they scarcely satisfy the criteria of a liability — no legal liability exists at the present time, they may not involve liquidation at a later date, and the amounts and payment dates are very problematical. The logic in the argument that taxes are really levied on *annual* accounting profits because in the long run the sum of accounting profits may coincide with the sum of taxable income is questionable because it disregards the whole issue of periodicity which lies at the base of all measures of annual profits.[6]

### FURTHER READING

A.A.A., Committee to Prepare a Statement of Basic Accounting Theory. *A Statement of Basic Accounting Theory*. Evanston, Ill.: A.A.A., 1966. Pp. 32–35, on executory contracts and deferred income taxes.

Gordon M. J., and Shillinglaw, G. *Accounting: A Management Approach*. 4th ed. Homewood, Illinois: Richard D. Irwin, 1969. Chap. 13.

Henderson, M. S., "The Nature of Liabilities", *Australian Accountant*, July 1974.

Moonitz, M. "The Changing Concept of Liabilities". In Zeff, S., and Keller, W. *Financial Accounting Theory*. New York: McGraw-Hill, 1964.

### NOTES

1. See Moonitz, "The Changing Concept of Liabilities".

2. The effective rate of interest on the loan is calculated as follows:

$$\text{At } 7\% \quad \sum_{t=1}^{6} \frac{7}{(1.07)^t} + \frac{100}{(1.07)^6} = 100$$

$$\text{At } 8\% \quad \sum_{t=1}^{6} \frac{7}{(1.08)^t} + \frac{100}{(1.08)^6} = 95.376$$

By interpolation, the effective rate i lies between 7% and 8%.

$$i = 7\% + \frac{2}{4.62} = 7.43\%$$

(when $100 - 98 = 2$: $98 - 95.376 = 2.62$; $2 + 2.62 = 4.62$)

i.e.
$$\sum_{t=1}^{6} \frac{7}{(1.0743)^t} + \frac{100}{(1.0743)^6} = 98$$

3. A detailed analysis of accounting for leases is given in J. H. Myers, "Reporting of Leases in Financial Statements", *Accounting Research Study No. 4* (New York, A.I.C.P.A., 1962).

4. See for example, Moonitz, "The Changing Concept of Liabilities"; Institute of Chartered Accountants in Australia, Research Report, "Treatment of Income Tax in Accounts of Companies", *Chartered Accountant in Australia* (January 1970).

5. An analysis of these situations is contained in A. D. Barton, "Company Income Tax and Interperiod Allocation", *Abacus* (September 1970).

6. For a detailed analysis of the deferred tax issue, see Barton, ibid; R. J. Chambers, "Tax Allocation and Financial Reporting", *Abacus* (December 1968); Moonitz, "Income Taxes in Financial Statements"; *Accounting Review* (April 1957).

## QUESTIONS AND EXERCISES

1. Should the concept of liabilities be restricted to those which are legally payable, or is a broader concept desirable? What criterion is applied in deciding on the concept to be used?

2. What are contingent liabilities? How should they be shown in a balance sheet?

3. What basis of valuation should be used for the measurement of liabilities?

4. Describe how you would treat the following items, and give reasons for your answers:

    i.   The liability under a $1m. contract for the construction of new premises. The work is half completed at balance date, and $300,000 has been paid to date.

    ii.  The liability for $10,000 per annum interest payable on debentures over the next five years.

    iii. Management's decision to recommend payment of a $500,000 dividend for the year.

    iv.  The estimated cost of after-sales service on goods sold under warranty.

    v.   Future payments of $50,000 per annum for ten years under a lease contract.

    vi.  The company is being sued for damages, and

        a.   It appears likely to lose the case
        b.   It appears likely to win the case.

    vii. Reserve for depreciation (i.e., accumulated depreciation).

5. "As a minimum, all items which meet the legal tests for debt qualify without further ado also as liabilities. But the legal test does not establish the outer limits of the concept for accountants." M. Moonitz, "The Changing Concept of Liabilities".

   Discuss this statement, and illustrate your answer with some of the major borderline cases of liabilities.

6. Tax regulations normally require that the expense incurred in meeting warranty costs should be recognized when the repairs are made rather than when the products are sold. Is this treatment satisfactory for the measurement of periodic income?

7. Do you consider that the measure of a company's financial position should include the capitalized value of a non-cancellable lease? Give reasons for your answer.

8. How does a "liability for deferred income taxes" arise? Does this "liability" satisfy the accounting tests for a liability? How should this "liability" be disclosed in a company's balance sheet?

# Chapter 16
# Accounting for Shareholders' Equity

The final matter to be considered for the presentation of a company's annual report concerns accounting for the capital contributed to it by shareholders. Companies can be of several kinds, have several classes of shares, and the shares can be issued on various terms. These matters have various consequences for accounting.

A company, unlike a sole trader or partnership firm, has a separate legal entity distinct from that of its owners, and as a consequence it can own property, sue and be sued, be taxed separately, and so on. The broad administrative aspects of a company are governed by company law — for example, in New South Wales by the 1961 New South Wales Companies Act, as amended — and by two internal documents of the company — its Memorandum and its Articles of Association. The companies acts of all states are very similar.

The Memorandum of Association is a document which sets out the name and address of the company, the objects for which the company has been formed (for example, to carry on business as a retailer), the type of liability of its members (for example, that their liability is limited), the amount of its share capital and its division into shares of a fixed registered amount (for example, 1,000,000 ordinary shares of $1 each par value). The Articles of Association set out the rules governing the internal affairs of the company — rules for the appointment of directors and their powers, voting rights of members, conduct of meetings, and so on. Both documents must be registered with the appropriate statutory authority — for example, the Registrar of Companies — at the time of formation of the company. It is only upon the registration of these documents and the payment of the prescribed registration fees that the company is incorporated and comes into being as a legal body.[1]

## KINDS OF COMPANIES

Several kinds of companies can be formed according to the type of liability assumed by shareholders.

### 1.  Public Companies Having Limited Liability

The liability of the shareholders for the debts of a public company is limited to any unpaid amounts on the shares they hold. There must be at least five shareholders in a public company, and there can be no restrictions on the sale of shares by shareholders. If the company is sufficiently large, its shares may be quoted on the stock exchange.

Limited liability companies lie at the heart of the modern capitalist system. They enable the savings of persons and institutions in the community at large to be channelled into huge business units which can gain the economies of large-scale production and distribution, develop new production methods and products, and so forth. However, by investing in large companies, shareholders must sacrifice control over their funds and hence undertake enormous risks. The law grants them the privilege of limited liability and the power to elect directors as the managers of their funds in order to restrict the risks borne by shareholders. Furthermore, the law requires directors to act in the best interests of shareholders and to report back annually to them on the stewardship of their funds. This function forms the legal basis for the publication of the company's annual reports, the holding of annual general meetings, and auditing.

### 2.  Proprietary Companies Having Limited Liability

The liability of shareholders in proprietary companies is limited in the same way as for public companies. There need be only two shareholders, but no more than fifty shareholders, in a proprietary limited company. The rights of shareholders to sell their shares is restricted in some way — for example, they must obtain the permission of directors to do so. Shares in these companies cannot be quoted or traded in on the stock exchange. Proprietary limited companies may be essentially incorporated family firms or subsidiaries of public companies. The first type are known as exempt proprietary companies and there must be no ownership of shares in them by public companies. They are not subject to any compulsory audit requirement and do not publish their reports. The accounts of subsidiary companies must be audited and their reports published along with the parent company's reports, either in consolidated group form or separately. If the parent company is an overseas registered company, then the local subsidiary is classified as a foreign company, and it has to meet all the requirements of an Australian public company in terms of audits and the publication of results.

### 3.  No Liability Companies

No liability companies are confined by law to the mining industry. Shareholders cannot be sued for any amounts owing by them on the shares they hold. This special provision has been made in the Company's Act in order to encourage investment in the search for minerals. Such searches are normally extremely risky ventures and only a small proportion are successful. A shareholder forfeits his shares in the event of non-payment of calls made by the company and he cannot be paid dividends on any share for which there is a call in arrears.

### 4. Unlimited Liability Companies

The shareholder is liable for the debts of the company in the same way as the owner of an unincorporated firm is liable for the debts of the firm. Unlimited liability companies are not common in Australia and they are probably confined to non-trading companies whose risks are minimal and to some mutual fund investment companies. Unlimited liability companies are allowed to buy back their own shares, i.e., effect a return of capital to shareholders who desire to cash their shares, and this feature makes them attractive to mutual funds. They prefer to be incorporated bodies rather than partnerships so that there can be more than twenty owners (the legal limit to the number of partners). Limited liability companies are not allowed to purchase their own shares in Australia though they are allowed to do so in the U.S. Legal requirements for unlimited liability companies are relatively lax — for example, no annual meetings or statutory reports are required.

### 5. Companies Limited by Guarantee

Companies limited by guarantee are generally confined to non-profit-making organizations such as social and sporting clubs. The liability of members is limited to the amounts guaranteed by them in the event of the company being insolvent when it is wound up. Such companies do not have a share capital. They cannot pay dividends but must apply all their surpluses to the furtherance of the company's object.

The following table summarizes the number of New South Wales registered companies in each group in 1973 and indicates the relative importance of each group.[2]

Local companies limited by shares:

| | | |
|---|---|---|
| i. | Public | 1,869 |
| ii. | Proprietary — exempt | 100,027 |
| iii. | Proprietary — non-exempt | 11,110 |
| iv. | No liability | 195 |

| | |
|---|---|
| Local companies limited by guarantee | 2,072 |
| Foreign companies | 7,824 |
| Other (in liquidation, etc.) | 5,189 |
| Total number of companies on register | 128,286 |

## TYPES OF SHARES IN LIMITED LIABILITY COMPANIES

A company can issue several types of shares, the two main kinds being ordinary shares and preference shares. In addition, there can be subcategories of preference shares. The rights attaching to each class of share are contained in the Memorandum and Articles of Association. *Preference shares* entitle their owners to some special privileges such as preferential rights to dividends and frequently return of capital in the event of the company being liquidated. Preference dividends are normally paid at a fixed rate before any dividends are paid to ordinary shareholders. However, in exchange for this preferred treatment, the preference dividend rate is normally less than the ordinary dividend rate. Preference shareholders bear less risk than ordinary shareholders. Normally, the voting rights of preference shareholders are restricted — for example, they may have no voting rights unless their dividends are in arrears, the matter concerns their class of shares, and so on.

Several classes of preference shares may exist. First, they may be different dividend rates attaching to each class — for example, 7 per cent preference shares and 8 per cent preference shares — because the shares were sold in different years when different interest rates applied in the capital market. Secondly, preference shares may be cumulative or non-cumulative. Cumulative preference shares entitle their holders who receive less than the fixed dividend in any year to receive the arrears of the preferential dividend, plus the current year's dividend, before any ordinary dividend is paid. Non-cumulative preference shares do not have any rights of carry-forward attaching to their dividends. Thirdly, preference shares may be participating or non-participating. Normally they are of the latter type. Participating preference shares entitle their holders to participate in dividends additional to the fixed dividend rate in years of buoyant profits.

*Ordinary shares* entitle their holders to the residual equity in the company. Ordinary shareholders subscribe risk capital to the company, and their claims to profits and return of capital (in the event of liquidation) rank behind all other claimants. Ordinary dividend rates may fluctuate from year to year according to the size of residual profits (i.e., profits after taxes and preference dividends), and their payment is dependent upon the directors' annual recommendation. Ordinary dividends may be missed altogether in loss years, and there are no cumulative dividend rights attaching to the shares. However on average, the ordinary dividend rate should exceed preference rates to compensate ordinary shareholders for the additional risks norne by them. Because of their risky, junior position in their claims upon the company's profits and assets, ordinary shareholders usually have the main voting rights in the company — they have the power to elect the directors, etc. — and hence it can be argued that they exercise the ultimate control over the company's operation.

For accounting purposes, the main significance of the different classes of shares is that they must be accounted for separately and so different capital accounts must be kept for each class. They must be reported separately in the balance sheet.

## MATTERS CONCERNING THE ISSUE OF SHARES

A company cannot sell shares to the public unless it first issues a prospectus, a document inviting applications for the shares. Stringent legal requirements attach to the information which must be contained in the prospectus about the company's operations, and a copy of it must be lodged with the Registrar of Companies.

To ensure that the company raises the amount of capital required for its operations, it normally has its share issues underwritten by a firm of stockbrokers or a merchant bank who guarantee that the shares will be sold. For this service, underwriters charge a fee, normally in the range of from 1 per cent of the value of the issue for a soundly established profitable company to over 10 per cent for a new or risky company. The shares may be offered to the public at large (a public issue), or sold to a large financial institution (a placement), or sold to existing shareholders of the company of a pro rata basis (a rights issue).

They may be issued (i.e., sold) to investors at their registered or par value, or at a price above their par value. For example, shares with a par value of $1 may be sold for $3 each. The surplus of $2 is called a share premium. An established company can issue shares at a premium when their market price exceeds their par value. The difference, if any, between the market price and the issue price is the "rights value" of the shares. For example, if the current market price of the shares in the above illustration is $4.50 and it is a one-for-one rights issue, the shares have a "rights value" of $1.50 each attaching to them. However, there is no need to record this rights value in accounting — it is of significance for the shareholder's decision to buy his entitlement to the new issue. Secondly, the shares may be sold on the basis of full payment of the issue price on application or alternatively on an instalments basis. The instalments are referred to as application, allotment, and call monies. There may be several separate calls made. In practice however, most shares are payable in full on application.

Legally, shares are not issued to the public at the date of publication of the prospectus. Rather, the prospectus merely invites the public to make an offer for the shares, and this occurs when the investor applies for shares. The offer is accepted when the directors decide to allot the shares to applicants. All application moneys are kept in a trust account until this date.

## SHARE CAPITAL CONCEPTS USED

For each class of share, it is necessary to distinguish between the following capital concepts:

1. Registered, authorized, or nominal capital — the total capital for each type of share which the company is authorized to issue under its Memorandum of Association. It is the maximum potential capital of the company.

2. Unissued capital — the amount of registered capital which remains unissued.

3. Issued capital — the registered value of the shares which have been issued or allotted to shareholders.

4. Uncalled capital — the amount on issued shares which have not yet been called-up, i.e., which shareholders have not been asked to pay for.

5. Called-up capital — the amount on issued shares for which shareholders have been asked to pay.

6. Calls-in-arrears — the amount of calls made remaining unpaid.

7. Paid-up capital — the amount paid up on issued shares. It does not include share premiums paid.

8. Contributed capital — the sum of paid-up capital plus share premiums paid. This measures the amount actually paid by shareholders to the company.

The various concepts of capital and the accounts required are summarized in Figure 16—1.

| Action | Accounts Required | |
|---|---|---|
| 1. Register the company's capital potential | Unissued Capital<br>Registered Capital | Dr.<br>Cr. |
| 2. Decision to issue shares applied for | Uncalled Capital<br>Unissued Capital | Dr.<br>Cr. |
| 3. Decisions to request payment by investors (either in full on application, or by instalments—application, allotment, and calls) | Application<br>Allotment (if required)<br>Calls (if required)<br>Uncalled Capital<br>Share Premium Reserve<br>(if required) | Dr.<br>Dr.<br>Dr.<br>Cr.<br><br>Cr. |
| 4. Receive money from investors | Bank<br>Application<br>Allotment<br>Calls | Dr.<br>Cr.<br>Cr.<br>Cr. |

Figure 16—1. Accounting for Capital Issues

## AN ILLUSTRATION

The Bandewollop Co. Ltd. was incorporated on 1 July to carry on the business of retailing. Its registered capital comprised 1,000,000 8 per cent preference shares of $1 each par value and 9,000,000 ordinary shares of $1 each par value.

On 3 July the directors decided to invite offers from the public for all the preference shares and 5,000,000 ordinary shares to the public. A prospectus was prepared and the issue was underwritten by a firm of stockbrokers. The terms of issue were:

1. Preference shares — issued at par, payable $1 in full on application.

2. Ordinary shares — issued at par, payable:
   i.  40 cents per share on application
   ii. 40 cents per share on allotment
   iii. 20 cents per share on the first and final call.

The share issue was duly advertised and the shares were popular with investors. On 31 July the issue closed fully subscribed and all application moneys were received and paid into a trust account.

On 1 August the directors proceeded to allot the shares to applicants and the money received was transferred to the company's bank account. All allotment moneys on ordinary shares were received by 31 August. Expenses connected with the issue — costs of the prospectus, underwriting commission, and brokerage charges — amounting to $60,000 were then paid. On 1 December directors decided to make the first and final call on ordinary shares.

By 31 December, $8,000,000 had been received.

*Required:*
1. Record the above items in the general journal.
2. Post these entries to ledger accounts.
3. Prepare balance sheets as for the end of each stage of the process.

| | *General Journal* | | Dr. $ | Cr. $ |
|---|---|---|---|---|
| July 1 | Unissued Preference Capital | Dr. | 1,000,000 | |
| | Unissued Ordinary Capital | Dr. | 9,000,000 | |
| | Registered Capital | Cr. | | 10,000,000 |
| | Registered capital of Bandewollop Co. Ltd. comprising 1,000,000 8% preference shares of $1 each and 9,000,000 ordinary shares of $1 each | | | |
| July 31 | Bank | Dr. | 3,000,000 | |
| | Preference Application | Cr. | | 1,000,000 |
| | Ordinary Application | Cr. | | 2,000,000 |
| | Receipt of application money from share offer | | | |
| Aug.1 | Uncalled Preference Capital | Dr. | 1,000,000 | |
| | Unissued Preference Capital | Cr. | | 1,000,000 |
| | Decision to issue 1,000,000 preference shares applied for | | | |
| Aug. 1 | Uncalled Ordinary Capital | Dr. | 5,000,000 | |
| | Unissued Ordinary Capital | Cr. | | 5,000,000 |
| | Decision to issue 5,000,000 ordinary shares applied for | | | |
| Aug. 1 | Preference Application | Dr. | 1,000,000 | |
| | Uncalled Preference Capital | Cr. | | 1,000,000 |
| | $1 payable on application for preference shares | | | |

| | | | | |
|---|---|---|---|---|
| Aug. 1 | Ordinary Application<br>Uncalled Ordinary Capital<br>40 cents payable on application for<br>    ordinary shares | Dr.<br>Cr. | 2,000,000 | 2,000,000 |
| Aug. 1 | Ordinary Allotment<br>Uncalled Ordinary Capital<br>40 cents payable on allotment of<br>    5,000,000 ordinary shares | Dr.<br>Cr. | 2,000,000 | 2,000,000 |
| Aug. 31 | Bank<br>Ordinary Allotment<br>Receipt of allotment money | Dr.<br>Cr. | 2,000,000 | 2,000,000 |
| Aug. 31 | Preliminary Expenses<br>Bank<br>Payment of costs associated with<br>    share issue — prospectus costs,<br>    underwriting commission, and<br>    brokerage | Dr.<br>Cr. | 60,000 | 60,000 |
| Dec. 1 | Ordinary Call<br>Uncalled Ordinary Capital<br>Decision to call up 20 cents<br>    per ordinary share | Dr.<br>Cr. | 1,000,000 | 1,000,000 |
| Dec. 31 | Bank<br>Ordinary Call<br>Receipt of ordinary call money | Dr.<br>Cr. | 800,000 | 800,000 |

NOTE: 1.    The cash entries could be shown in the cash journals rather than in the general journal.
        2.    Two registered capital accounts could be used.

### *General Ledger*

Registered Capital Account

| | | Dr. $ | Cr. $ | Balance $ |
|---|---|---|---|---|
| July 1 | Unissued Preference Capital<br>Unissued Ordinary Capital | | 1,000,000<br>9,000,000 | 1,000,000 Cr.<br>10,000,000 Cr. |

Unissued Preference Capital Account

| | | | | |
|---|---|---|---|---|
| July 1 | Registered Capital | 1,000,000 | | 1,000,000 Dr. |
| Aug. 1 | Uncalled Preference Capital | | 1,000,000 | — |

Unissued Ordinary Capital Account

| | | | | |
|---|---|---|---|---|
| July 1 | Registered Capital | 9,000,000 | | 9,000,000 Dr. |
| Aug. 1 | Uncalled Ordinary Capital | | 5,000,000 | 4,000,000 Dr. |

### Uncalled Preference Capital Account

| Aug. 1 | Unissued Preference Capital | 1,000,000 | | 1,000,000 Dr. |
| | Preference Application | | 1,000,000 | — |

### Uncalled Ordinary Capital Account

| Aug. 1 | Unissued Ordinary Capital | 5,000,000 | | 5,000,000 Dr. |
| | Ordinary Application | | 2,000,000 | 3,000,000 Dr. |
| Aug. 1 | Ordinary Allotment | | 2,000,000 | 1,000,000 Dr. |
| Dec. 1 | Ordinary Call | | 1,000,000 | — |

### Preference Application Account

| Aug. 1 | Uncalled Preference Capital | 1,000,000 | | 1,000,000 Dr. |
| | Bank | | 1,000,000 | — |

### Ordinary Application Account

| Aug. 1 | Uncalled Ordinary Capital | 2,000,000 | | 2,000,000 Dr. |
| | Bank | | 2,000,000 | — |

### Ordinary Allotment Account

| Aug. 1 | Uncalled Ordinary Capital | 2,000,000 | | 2,000,000 Dr. |
| Aug. 31 | Bank | | 2,000,000 | — |

### Ordinary Call Account

| Dec. 1 | Uncalled Ordinary Capital | 1,000,000 | | 1,000,000 Dr. |
| Dec. 31 | Bank | | 800,000 | 200,000 Dr. |

### Preliminary Expenses Account

| Aug. 31 | Bank | 60,000 | | 60,000 Dr. |

### Bank Account

| Aug. 1 | Preference Application | 1,000,000 | | 1,000,000 Dr. |
| Aug. 1 | Ordinary Application | 2,000,000 | | 3,000,000 Dr. |
| Aug. 31 | Ordinary Allotment | 2,000,000 | | 5,000,000 Dr. |
| Aug. 31 | Preliminary Expenses | | 60,000 | 4,940,000 Dr. |
| Dec. 31 | Ordinary Call | 800,000 | | 5,740,000 Dr. |

*Balance Sheets as at:*

1. July 1 after incorporation of Company

| *Shareholders' Equity* | Ordinary $ | Preference $ | Total $ |
| --- | --- | --- | --- |
| Registered Capital | 9,000,000 | 1,000,000 | 10,000,000 |
| Less Unissued Capital | 9,000,000 | 1,000,000 | 10,000,000 |
| Paid-up Capital | — | — | — |

2. Aug. 1 after decision to issue shares

*Shareholders' Equity*

| | | | |
|---|---|---|---|
| Registered Capital | 9,000,000 | 1,000,000 | 10,000,000 |
| Less Unissued Capital | 4,000,000 | – | 4,000,000 |
| Issued Capital | 5,000,000 | 1,000,000 | 6,000,000 |
| Less Uncalled Capital | 3,000,000 | – | 3,000,000 |
| Called-up Capital | 2,000,000 | 1,000,000 | 3,000,000 |
| Less Application Money Owing | 2,000,000 | 1,000,000 | 3,000,000 |
| Paid-up Capital | – | – | – |

3. Aug. 1 after receipt of cash from issue

*Shareholders' Equity*
As above to Called-up Capital

| | | | |
|---|---|---|---|
| Called and Paid-up Capital | $2,000,000 | 1,000,000 | 3,000,000 |

*Assets*

| | |
|---|---|
| Bank | $3,000,000 |

4. August 31 after allotment of shares and receipt of cash

*Shareholders' Equity*
As above to Issued Capital

| | | | |
|---|---|---|---|
| Issued Capital | 5,000,000 | 1,000,000 | 6,000,000 |
| Less Uncalled Capital | 1,000,000 | – | 1,000,000 |
| Called and Paid-up Capital | $4,000,000 | 1,000,000 | 5,000,000 |

*Assets*

| | |
|---|---|
| Bank | 4,940,000 |
| Preliminary Expenses | 60,000 |
| | $5,000,000 |

5. December 31 after decision to make the call and receipt of cash

*Shareholders' Equity*

| | | | |
|---|---|---|---|
| Registered Capital | 9,000,000 | 1,000,000 | 10,000,000 |
| Less Unissued Capital | 4,000,000 | – | 4,000,000 |
| Issued and Called-up Capital | 5,000,000 | 1,000,000 | 6,000,000 |
| Less Calls in Arrears | 200,000 | – | 200,000 |
| Paid-up Capital | $4,800,000 | 1,000,000 | 5,800,000 |

*Assets*

| | |
|---|---|
| Bank | 5,740,000 |
| Preliminary Expenses | 60,000 |
| | $5,800,000 |

*Comments on the above:*

1. On registration of the company, a record is made of the potential asset, i.e., the right to issue shares, in the Unissued Capital account; and the potential equity in the Registered Capital account.

2. No entry is made on the decision to invite public offers for shares.

3. On the decision to issue shares, the issuing power is converted to a calling power by a transfer entry from Unissued to Uncalled Capital. Paid-up capital is zero at this stage.

4. As the decisions to ask for application, allotment and call moneys are made, transfers are made from the Uncalled Capital accounts to the Application, etc. accounts to record the conversion of uncalled capital into other potential assets. — the rights receive the moneys. Paid-up capital is still zero.

5. Receipt of cash from the trust account converts the potential assets into an actual one and the source accounts are credited. Paid-up capital is now a positive amount.

6. Balances in Unissued Capital accounts represent shares not yet issued; in Uncalled Capital accounts — moneys not yet asked for on issued shares; in Application, Allotment, or Call accounts — moneys asked for but not yet received.

7. Accounts are not required for issued, called-up capital, and paid-up capital as these amounts are obtained by deduction.

8. The limit to the shareholders' liability for the debts of the company in the event of its insolvency is shown by the amount of uncalled capital plus calls, etc. in arrears, i.e., by the difference between the par value of the share and the amount paid by the shareholder towards that par value.
For example on 31 December it is $200,000. Shareholders are not liable for any debts of the company once they have paid fully for their shares; nor are they required to take up unissued shares in the event of insolvency.

## OTHER MATTERS CONCERNING SHARE ISSUES

### 1. Non-Payment of Allotment or Call Moneys

The company normally has the power to forfeit the shares of a shareholder who fails to pay the amounts due on them, and to resell them. The amount already paid by the defaulting shareholder is transferred from paid-up capital to a Forfeited Shares Reserve account through a series of reversing entries. The resale of the shares is recorded in the usual way, but any loss on resale is debited to the Forfeited Shares Reserve account. This account is shown in the capital reserves part of shareholders' equity in the balance sheet.

### 2. Issue Oversubscribed

Where a share issue is oversubscribed, the allotment of the shares is at the directors' discretion. They may decide to allot them on a pro rata basis to applicants or to return the money to unsuccessful applicants. In the former case, excess application money (shown by a credit balance in the Application account) is transferred to the Allotment account (hence debit Application and credit Allotment accounts) and this reduces the allotment money owing by shareholders. In the event of the money being returned to shareholders, the entry is to debit Application account and credit Bank account. A credit balance in the Application account should be treated as a current liability.

### 3. Issue of Shares at a Premium

An established profitable company can frequently sell its shares at a premium above the par value. The excess is credited to a Share Premium Reserve account. This too is a capital reserve. Share premiums are payable on application for the shares. For example, if $1 par value shares are issued for $3.00, payable in full on application, the entries are:

|  |  |  | $ |
|---|---|---|---|
| i. | Uncalled Capital | Dr. | 1.00 |
|  | Unissued Capital | Cr. | 1.00 |
| ii. | Application | Dr. | 3.00 |
|  | Uncalled Capital | Cr. | 1.00 |
|  | Share Premium Reserve | Cr. | 2.00 |
| iii. | Bank | Dr. | 3.00 |
|  | Application | Cr. | 3.00 |

### 4. Issue of Shares at a Discount

Normally it is illegal for shares to be issued at a price below par value, i.e., at a discount, as this diminishes the stock of assets which should be kept intact for the protection of creditors.

This also means that in practice, a company cannot make a share issue when the market price of its shares falls below the par value. It cannot issue the shares at a discount, and investors will not buy new shares at a price equalling the par value when they can buy identical existing shares on the market at a lower price.

### 5. Shares Issued for Assets Other Than Cash

Shares may be issued for assets other than cash in the event of a company buying out another business. Instead of the company paying cash for the other business, it pays for the assets taken over by issuing its own shares. The share issue is recorded in the usual way except that asset accounts other than a bank account may be debited.

### 6. Bonus Share Issues

A variant of the above is for the company to make a bonus share issue. In effect this is a gift of new shares to existing owners made by transferring reserves to paid-up capital. Theoretically the company gives away nothing except a slip of paper (i.e., another share certificate) as the reserves belong to the shareholders in any case. Nevertheless, Australian shareholders appear to appreciate this worthless gesture. Bonus share issues are normally made "out of" share premium reserves or asset revaluation reserves (arising from upward revaluations of assets as their market prices appreciate), though they may be made from any type of reserve. For example, the entry to record a bonus issue of 1,000,000 fully paid $1.00 shares made from an asset revaluation reserve is:

|  |  | $ |
|---|---|---|
| Asset Revaluation Reserve | Dr. | 1,000,000 |
| Unissued Capital | Cr. | 1,000,000 |

This is purely a "book entry" and no funds are involved in the transfer. Its effect is to convert the asset revaluation reserve into paid-up capital.

### 7. Sale of Shares by a Shareholder

The sale of shares by a shareholder does not affect the company's paid-up capital and no entries are required in its general ledger accounts. The shares of large public companies are bought and sold every day on stock exchanges, and hence the identity of a company's owners can change rapidly. However, the sale is recorded in the company's share register (essentially the owners' subsidiary ledger), and on its share certificates. The new owner assumes all the rights and obligations of the previous owner.

### FURTHER READING

Mathews, R. L. *The Accounting Framework*. 3rd ed. Melbourne: Cheshire, 1971. Chap. 10, pp. 258–69.
New South Wales Government. *Companies Act* 1961. Parts III and IV.
New South Wales Government. *Report of the Corporate Affairs Commission* (latest).

### NOTES

1. The scale of fees payable in New South Wales in 1972 is as follows:

   i. *For registration of a local company:*                                          $
      a. Registered capital $10,000 or less                                         100
      b. For every $1,000 of registered capital from $10,000 to $200,000              2
      c. For every $1,000 of registered capital from $200,000 to $1,000,000           1
      d. For every $1,000 of registered capital over $1,000,000                    0.50

   ii. *For registration of a foreign company* − one half of the above fees

   iii. *For registration of annual reports*                                         12

   Thus for example it costs $1,280 to register a company with an authorized capital of $1,000,000.

2. Report of the Corporate Affairs Commission for the year ended 31 December 1973.

## QUESTIONS AND EXERCISES

[Solutions to problems marked * are given in Appendix 4.]

1. When a company is incorporated, it must register its Memorandum and Articles of Association with the appropriate statutory authority. What are these documents and why are they required?

2. What types of companies may be formed? What are the chief characteristics of each type and which types are the most important in industry?

3. Explain and illustrate the concept of limited liability of a company with reference to the following example:

   Par value of share — $1
   Issue price of share (including $2 share premimum) — $3
   Application money paid (including share premium) — $2.20
   Allotment money paid — 40 cents
   Call no. 1 made but not yet paid — 20 cents.

4. What is the reason for "limited liability" of companies? Why does the law permit companies to have liabilities which are limited when it does not extend the same privilege to its own citizens? What could be the consequences of abolishing limited liability for companies?

5. What are the major differences between ordinary and preference shares?

6. Explain the concepts of registered capital, issued capital, called-up capital, and paid-up capital.

7. What is a bonus share? Do bonus issues form part of paid-up capital? Does the company acquire any funds from a bonus issue? Why do companies issue bonus shares?

In the following problems, record all transactions in the general journal, post to the appropriate ledger accounts, and present a balance sheet as at the end of the problem.

*8. Adult Publications Limited is registered as a company on 1 January to engage in the publication of magazines. Its registered capital comprises 1,000,000 ordinary shares of $1 each. A prospectus is published and the shares are offered for sale to the public on 31 January at $1 each, payable in full on application. The issue was underwritten by a firm of stockbrokers for a fee of $30,000. The issue was fully subscribed by 28 February and the shares were then allotted. Registration costs of $2,000 were paid on 10 February, and the underwriting and prospectus costs were paid on 28 February.

9. Feb. 1. Green & Co. Ltd. was incorporated with a registered capital of $100,000, divided into 100,000 ordinary shares of $1 each.

   Feb. 15. Offered 60,000 ordinary shares of $1 each, payable 25 cents on application to and 25 cents on allotment to the public.

   Feb. 20. Application and allotment money paid in full and shares alloted to applicants.

   Mar. 31. Call of 40 cents per share made on all the issued shares.

   Apr. 30. Cash received in respect of Call no. 1 ordinary shares.

10. The Shareholders' Equity segment of the balance sheet of the Kuring-gai Co. Ltd. on 30 June 1972 was as follows:

|  |  | $ |
|---|---|---|
| Registered Capital 10,000,000 $1 ordinary shares | | 10,000,000 |
| Less Unissued Capital 4,000,000 $1 ordinary shares | | 4,000,000 |
| Paid-up Capital 6,000,000 $1 ordinary shares | | 6,000,000 |
| Retained Earnings | | 1,500,000 |
| | | $7,500,000 |
| *Assets* | | $7,500,000 |

On 31 July the directors decided to make a rights issue to shareholders of 3,000,000 shares. As the current market price of the shares was $4, the directors agreed to issue the new shares at a premium of $2 each. Terms of the issue were:

$2.50 on application, being $2 premium and 50 cents application money; 50 cents on allotment.

The issue was underwritten by the company's stockbrokers for a fee of $50,000, and this was paid on 31 August.

All application monies were received by 31 July, at which time the shares were allotted. All allotment monies were received by 31 August.

*11. Feb. 1. Endurance Motors Limited was incorporated with a registered capital of $200,000, divided into 70,000 preference and 130,000 ordinary shares of $1 par value.

Feb. 15. The directors invited the public to subscribe for 50,000 preference shares and 100,000 ordinary shares. The terms of the issue were:

*Preference Shares*

50 cents per share payable on application
25 cents per share payable on allotment
25 cents per share payable in calls as and when required.

*Ordinary Shares*

Issued at a premium of 50 cents per share. Amounts payable were:
75 cents per share payable on application (including the share premium)
25 cents per share payable on allotment
50 cents per share payable in calls as and when required.

Feb. 28. Application moneys were received for 80,000 preference shares and 120,000 ordinary shares.

Mar. 1. Allotted 50,000 preference shares and 100,000 ordinary shares on a *first-come first-served basis.* Application money was returned to the unsuccessful applicants.

Mar. 3. Paid brokerage of 5 cents per share on 75,000 shares; legal expenses of formation and registration of company, $1,200; and costs of prospectus, $1,000.

Mar. 31. Moneys due on allotment were received.

12. Da Costa Company Limited was registered on 1 April 1970 with a registered capital of $400,000 in shares of $2 each. It was proposed to offer to the

public 100,000 shares, payable 50 cents on application, 50 cents on allotment, 50 cents first call, and 50 cents second call.

The shares were offered on 1 May, and applications for the whole of the offered shares were received. The shares were allotted on 15 May and all allotment money was received.

On 1 June the first call was made. The amount was received in full.

On 1 November the second call was made. At 31 December this call had been paid on 80,000 shares.

13.   The Eldon Company Limited was registered on 1 April 1970 with a registered capital of $500,000 divided into: 400,000 $1 ordinary shares and 100,000 $1 preference shares (7 per cent). It was decided to offer for public subscription: 300,000 ordinary shares, payable 25 cents on application, 25 cents on allotment, 50 cents in two calls of 25 cents each as and when required; and 50,000 preference shares (7 per cent) payable 50 cents on application, 50 cents on allotment. In response to this offer of shares the public subscribed for the full number of ordinary shares. Applications were received for 150,000 preference shares. In each case application money forwarded was in accordance with the amount payable on the shares applied for.

The directors decided to:

i.   Allot the ordinary shares in accordance with the applications received

ii.   Allot the preference shares to certain applicants in the proportion of one share for every two applied for and apply the surplus application money on these shares to the amount due on allotment. They also decided to return the application money to applicants for 50,000 shares.

This decision was implemented and allotment moneys were received. It was afterwards decided to make a call of 25 cents on the ordinary shares (15 July). The amount due thereon was received, with the exception of the amount payable on 10,000 shares.

14.   On 1 March, Littleton Ltd., an existing public company, decides to raise funds by issuing 60,000 ordinary $1 shares at a premium of 50 cents per share. The terms of the issue are that:

i.   75 cents per share is payable on application (including the share premium)
ii.   25 cents per share is payable on allotment
iii.   50 cents per share is payable in calls to be made.

The Company has a registered capital of 500,000 ordinary shares of $1.00 each, of which 300,000 are issued and fully paid. Retained earnings are $54,000, and Sundry Assets are $354,000.

Mar. 26.   Application moneys received for 80,000 shares. The directors decide to allot the shares on the basis of 3 shares for every 4 applied for. Excess application moneys were to be applied towards moneys due on allotment.

July 16.   A call of 30 cents per share payable on 15 August was made.

Aug. 15.   Call moneys received in respect of 54,000 shares. The holders of 10,000 shares also forwarded an additional 20 cents per share in respect of calls to be made in the future.

15. The following items are included in the balance sheet of Macquarie Muddlers Limited.

|  | Ordinary $ | Preference $ | Total $ |
|---|---|---|---|
| Registered Capital ($1 shares) | 2,000,000 | 500,000 | 2,500,000 |
| Less Unissued Capital | 600,000 | 100,000 | 700,000 |
| Issued Capital | $1,400,000 | $400,000 | $1,800,000 |

The company decides, on 15 June, to issue 120,000 $1 ordinary shares at par and 60,000 $1 7 per cent preference shares at par, to finance planned expansion. The terms of the issue are as follows:

*Ordinary Shares*

50 cents per share payable on application
15 cents per share payable on allotment
35 cents per share payable in calls as and when required.

*Preference Shares*

20 cents per share payable on application
20 cents per share payable on allotment
10 cents per share payable on.a call to be made on 20 August.

The company incurred legal and other costs of $5,000 in respect of the proposed share issue. These amounts were paid on 1 July.

July    1.    Application moneys for 170,000 ordinary shares and 66,000 preference shares received.

July    4.    The directors decided to:

    i.    Refuse applications for 20,000 ordinary shares and 6,000 preference shares and returned application moneys to the unsuccessful applicants.

    ii.    Allot the preference shares, and allot the ordinary shares on the basis of 4 ordinary shares for every 5 applied for. Excess application moneys were to be applied towards money due on allotment.

July  13.    The allotment moneys due were paid in full. The holders of 20,000 ordinary shares also included a further 35 cents per share in respect of future calls to be made.

Aug. 20.    The directors made the preference call and a call of 15 cents per share on the ordinary shares. The calls were made payable on 15 September.

Sept. 15.    Call moneys were received in respect of 50,000 preference shares and 80,000 ordinary shares.

16. The Oxford Corporation Limited, requiring additional funds for expansion purposes, decided to raise the funds in two ways:

i.    The issue of 80,000 $1 ordinary shares at a premium of 25 cents per share

ii.    The issue of 20,000 $1 7 per cent preference shares at par.

The terms of the issue of the above were as follows:

*Ordinary Shares*

50 cents per share on application (including the premium)
50 cents per share on allotment
25 cents per share on a call one month after allotment.

*Preference Shares*

50 cents per share on application
25 cents per share on allotment
25 cents per share on a call one month after allotment.

Applications were received as follows:

Ordinary shares — for 105,000 shares
Preference shares — for 20,000 shares.

The directors allotted the preference shares in accordance with the applications. With the ordinary shares they decided:

a.   To refuse applications for 5,000 shares
b.   To allot 8 shares for every 10 applied for to the remaining applicants, the surplus application money being applied towards that due on allotment.

All money due on allotment was received — but the allotment money received for some preference shareholders was accompanied by $2,000 in advance on the call to be made.

The calls for both ordinary and preference shares were duly made. All call monies on preference shares was received. Calls on 3,500 ordinary shares were unpaid.

*Required:*

Record the above transactions in the accounting records of the company (journals and ledger).

17.   The directors of Expanda Limited decide to make a bonus share issue of 1 share for every 3 shares currently held by shareholders. The issue is to be made from the Share Premium Reserve. The balance sheet before the issue includes the following items:

|  | $ |
|---|---|
| *Shareholders' Equity* | |
| Registered Capital $1 ordinary shares | 10,000,000 |
| Less Unissued Capital | 4,000,000 |
| Issued and Paid-up Capital | 6,000,000 |
| Share Premium Reserve | 2,000,000 |
| General Reserve | 1,500,000 |
| Appropriation account | 500,000 |
| Total Shareholders' Equity | 10,000,000 |

*Required:*

Record the bonus issue in ledger accounts and show the revised balance sheet.

# Chapter 17
# Cash Flow Statements

Cash flow statements summarize the flow of cash into and out of the entity over a period of time. In other words, they are statements of cash receipts and cash payments in which all the cash transactions of the period are summarized. They may be prepared from the records of a firm which maintains only the cash basis of accounting, or from the cash records of firms using accrual accounting.

One form of cash flow statement for the Northside Trading Company Ltd. is given below:

Northside Trading Co. Ltd.

*Cash Flow Statement for the Year Ended 31 December 197X*

|  | $ | $ | $ |
|---|---|---|---|
| Bank Overdraft 1 Jan. |  |  | 15,000 |
| *Current Items* |  |  |  |
| *Cash Surplus from Current Operations* |  |  |  |
| Cash Receipts from Sales and Customers |  | 125,000 |  |
| Less Cash Payments for Inputs |  |  |  |
| Merchandise Purchases | 97,000 |  |  |
| Advertising | 3,500 |  |  |
| Sales Salaries | 6,000 |  |  |
| Office Salaries | 2,000 |  |  |
| Directors' Fees | 1,000 |  |  |
| Interest | 1,000 | 110,500 | 14,500 |
| Less Payments from Profits |  |  |  |
| Dividends Paid |  |  | 2,000 |
| Cash Surplus from Operations Available for "Capital" Uses |  |  | 12,500 |
| *Capital Items* |  |  |  |
| Add *New Cash Raised from* |  |  |  |
| Mortgage |  | 20,000 |  |
| Shareholders |  | 10,000 | 30,000 |
|  |  |  | 42,500 |

Less *Cash Spent on Long-term Assets*

|  |  |  |
|---|---|---|
| Shop Fittings | 4,500 | |
| Land and Buildings | 26,000 | 30,500 |
| *Excess of Cash Receipts over Payments for Year* | | 12,000 |
| Bank Overdraft 31 Dec. | | $3,000 |

## FORM AND CONTENT OF CASH FLOW STATEMENTS

The general format of a cash flow statement consists of the opening cash or bank balance of the firm, the cash inflows and outflows classified into significant groups, and the closing cash or bank balance. Cash transactions are generally classified into those concerning current operating and "capital" items, and the latter are further classified into short and long-term items. Current operating items relate to the firm's normal trading activities — cash sales plus collections from customers on account of credit sales, and cash purchases of inputs plus payments to trade creditors on account of credit purchases. In addition, it is useful to disclose separately payments from profits so that the cash surplus generated from current operating activities is measured. "Capital" items relate to all non-trading transactions — purchase and sale of long-term assets, short-term or long-term borrowing, new share issues, repayment of loans, and so on. However, it should be noted that the term "capital" when used in this sense is not the usual accounting or legal concept of the ownership equity; rather it is the economist's concept which has been accepted into normal business usage. "Capital" items are subclassified into short-term and long-term periods because the time element is crucial in cash flow analysis. All current operating items are of course short-term ones.

Other forms of presentation are possible and whichever one is adopted, plus the amount of detail shown, should be appropriate to the purpose for which the report is used. The accounting information standards should be applied in the presentation of the report. The statement may be prepared as a series of estimates for the coming year, that is, a *budget*. A cash budget shows the expected sources of cash for the coming year, and the expected cash outlays. Frequently the budget will be rearranged from the above form to answer questions such as how much additional borrowing and new share issues are required in order for the company to buy new shop fittings for $4,500 and new premises for $26,000, and to reduce its bank overdraft to $3,000 by the end of the year. The following problem illustrates its use as a budget, prepared in this case on a monthly basis.

Thistle and Co. Limited plans to buy additional premises to serve as a bulk store because of congestion in its existing retailing building. The premises will become available at the end of September, for $20,000 cash. However, because of a recent government announcement of credit restrictions, the bank has sent a request that the company's bank overdraft be reduced from the present $40,000 limit on 1 July to $30,000 by 30 September. After considering several financing alternatives, the management decides to raise additional share capital in September to finance both items to the extent necessary. It is expected that the $1 shares can be sold to existing shareholders at par. How much share capital should be raised, given that the cash inflows and outflows for the coming three months are expected to be as below?

|  | July $ | August $ | September $ |
|---|---|---|---|
| Sales and customer receipts | 50,000 | 55,000 | 66,000 |
| Payments for merchandise purchases | 24,000 | 30,000 | 32,000 |
| Payments for electricity used | 1,000 | 1,000 | 1,000 |
| Payments for rent | 4,000 | 4,000 | 4,000 |
| Payments for advertising | 4,000 | 6,000 | 7,000 |
| Payments for wages and salaries | 9,000 | 10,000 | 10,000 |
| Dividends payable | 6,000 | — | — |
| Company tax payable | — | — | 5,000 |

Thistle & Co. Ltd.

*Cash Budget for the Three Months July–September 197X*

|  | July $ | August $ | September $ |
|---|---|---|---|
| Bank Overdraft (start month) | −40,000 | −38,000 | −34,000 |
| Cash Surplus from Operations |  |  |  |
| Sales Receipts | 50,000 | 55,000 | 66,000 |
| Less Payments for Merchandise | 24,000 | 30,000 | 32,000 |
| Electricity | 1,000 | 1,000 | 1,000 |
| Rent | 4,000 | 4,000 | 4,000 |
| Advertising | 4,000 | 6,000 | 7,000 |
| Wages and Salaries | 9,000 | 10,000 | 10,000 |
|  | 42,000 | 51,000 | 54,000 |
| Cash Surplus from Operations | +8,000 | +4,000 | +12,000 |
| Bank Overdraft Balance | −32,000 | −34,000 | −22,000 |
| Profit Distribution |  |  |  |
| Dividends | −6,000 | — | — |
| Company Tax | — | — | −5,000 |
| Bank Overdraft Balance | −38,000 | −34,000 | −27,000 |
| Capital Outlays |  |  |  |
| Purchase of Premises | — | — | −20,000 |
| Capital Receipts |  |  |  |
| New Share Issue | — | — | +17,000 |
| Bank Overdraft (end month) | −38,000 | −34,000 | −30,000 |

Hence, a share issue of 17,000 shares at $1 each in September should enable the company's operating cash commitments to be met and enable purchase of premises and repayment of $10,000 to the bank.

NOTE:

1. One should work through the July budget to determine expected cash balance at 31 July, and then carry this balance up to 1 August; and so on.

2. Intervening lines for bank overdraft may be omitted – they are for arithmetical convenience only.

3. Concluding bank overdraft amount may be shown at the net figure without showing the $10,000 repayment as a specific outlay.

Although cash flow statements are most conveniently prepared directly from the firm's cash journals or bank account, it may be necessary for external analysts to prepare them from published income statements and balance sheets. In this case it is necessary to work backwards and reconstruct the accounts to calculate the cash flows for each item. For example, if the data are in the form: debtors 1 January $20,000, credit sales for year $260,000, debtors 31 December $35,000, then the cash collected from customers for the year is $245,000, calculated as follows:

Accounts Receivable Account

|  |  | $ | $ | $ |
|---|---|---|---|---|
| Jan. 1 | Balance |  |  | 20,000 Dr. |
| Dec. 31 | Credit Sales | 260,000 |  | 280,000 Dr. |
|  | Bank |  | 245,000 | 35,000 Dr. |

## A COMPARISON WITH THE INCOME STATEMENT

In any comparison of the current operating section of the cash flow statement with the income statement, it should be remembered that each is prepared for a different purpose and hence the contents are not strictly comparable. The differences between the two can be illustrated by comparing the income and cash flow statements for the Northside Trading Co. Ltd. [1]

1. The cash collected during the year on account of sales is not a measure of revenue earned – it includes cash collections relating to sales (as recognized on a delivery basis) of previous periods, but does not include the credit sales of the current period to the extent that the cash has not been collected. In the Northside Trading Co. Ltd., the gross sales revenue is $140,000, while the cash collected is $125,000. Consequently Accounts Receivable increased over the year. If the reverse position of cash collections exceeding sales applied, Accounts Receivable would be reduced.

2. Cash expenditures on current inputs are not measures of current expenses. The expenditure on merchandise purchased must differ from the cost of goods sold where the merchandise inventory and accounts payable balances change over the year. No allowance is made for accrued or prepaid expenses in the cash flow report, and all depreciation charges are omitted from it. For example, in this illustration the operating expenses are $117,000 while cash payments on operations amounted to $110,500.

3. Consequently, the cash surplus from operations (here $14,500) is not in any sense a measure of the profit earned (of $11,500). It is nothing more than its name implies. However, it is a very useful figure in its own right as it measures the contribution of operations to cash liquidity. After making payments from profits, this surplus is available for "capital" purposes – the purchase of long-term assets or repayment of loans – or merely to increase the firm's liquidity.

A misleading practice which is becoming popular in the published reports of some companies and which is used by some financial analysts and sharebrokers is that of using the cash flow from operations as a measure of the earning power of the firm. The cash flow is compared with profits, and, like profits, it is frequently expressed in terms of dollars per share. The implication is frequently made that the cash surplus is a superior measure of performance, partly because it is not subject to the arbitrariness involved in any measure of income. Furthermore, the term "cash flow" itself is abused in these contexts as in fact the data normally refer to "funds from operations" and not cash surplus from operations.[2] The figure is calculated as net profit plus depreciation, and hence includes credit items as in the income statement. The adding back of depreciation to net profit in this way is doubly misleading in that it conveys the impression that depreciation is an optional expense to be included or excluded at will, and that the depreciation charge is a source of cash! Cash flow information is useful and valid for an analysis of financial policy, but not for the measurement of historic earning capacity.

## USE OF CASH FLOW STATEMENTS

### 1. By Business

Cash flow statements are required for effective cash planning and control, and for investment project evaluation by management. In addition, outside users can obtain much useful information from them.

Effective cash planning and control are essential for the survival of the business and its financial efficiency. The business must always have cash available for its necessary commitments and, if possible, something in reserve. The quickest way for a firm to become bankrupt is for it to become short of cash. Cash which is surplus to immediate commitments represents an uncommitted resource – it gives command over goods and services in general, and it is therefore available for any use that management decides on. This gives management the means for some flexibility of future operations. To be liquid, a firm does not necessarily have to maintain cash on hand or at the bank; rather, most firms work on bank overdrafts, that is, they have drawing rights at the bank up to some agreed limit. Sufficient liquidity at all times is also necessary for financial efficiency, since short-term funds obtainable in an emergency are generally very costly because of the high risk element involved.

Likewise, non-payment of trade creditors within the discount period represents expensive financial accommodation as the effective annual rate of interest in the discount rate is generally very high, as does also purchase on hire-purchase terms. On the other hand, the financially efficient firm does not have excessive liquid resources available for long because idle cash can be invested either in expansion of the business or in external securities to earn profits, or used to repay loans and hence to reduce interest payments. Management must determine from its experience how much liquidity the firm needs.

Cash planning requires that a set of integrated budgets of operating activities and capital expenditures be prepared, and that the periodic cash receipts and payments associated with these activities are determined. Such cash budgets should be prepared on at least a monthly basis for the coming year, and even on a weekly basis for the immediate future in periods of low liquidity. The closer the future period in the analysis is to the present, for example, the coming month, the more refined is the budget. Where a cash deficit is expected in any period, arrangements should be made in advance of the deficit to overcome it, either through additional borrowing, a sales drive, collection of overdue debts, etc. to increase receipts, or by postponing some expenditures such as the purchase of new plant or building renovations.

Cash control comprises implementation of the cash budgets. Regular comparisons of budget data with actual results must be made, variances between the two analyzed, and causes of unfavourable variances corrected if possible. Proper administrative controls over cash are required to ensure that liabilities are paid by the firm on time and that debts are collected as they fall due. An accrual basis of accounting is needed for this.

Historical cash flow reports are necessary for the preparation of cash budgets, for control comparisons with the budget, and for an analysis of the firm's liquidity situation; however they have little managerial use for other purposes.

The task of the careful evaluation of alternative investment projects open to the firm and the selection of the most profitable is of major importance to management. The firm has to live through the future with the projects adopted and mistaken decisions can affect its profitability and risk for many years to come. Investment projects comprise any projects on which cash is spent now in anticipation of future benefits, for example, purchase of new plant or development of a new product. The profitability of investment projects is evaluated in terms of their expected cash flows, and hence, to evaluate a project, the cash receipts and outlays in each period of the asset's life must be estimated. However, because the flows stretch over some years, a straightforward comparison of absolute receipts and payments is not a reliable method of evaluation. Rather, the expected receipts and payments must be discounted to allow for the costs of finance over time, back to the current time to derive their "present values". The projects can then be easily ranked according to their expected profitability, and the less profitable ones rejected.

Outside users of accounting reports who have no access to the firm's budgets, particularly trade creditors, lenders, and shareholders, find historical cash flow reports useful as a basis for judging the firm's debt-paying capacity, its ability to meet large debt retirement commitments without having to raise more loans, and its ability to finance plant replacement or expansion without recourse to new loans or share issues. The size of the cash surplus on operations is particularly important here since it represents a regular inflow of cash to the firm which is available for capital uses. An inadequate cash operating surplus, and more particularly a cash operating deficit, indicates approaching financial problems for the firm if some plant replacement or debt retirement will soon be due. Although cash flow statements are not normally published, it is possible to derive them from a set of comparative final accounting reports.

### 2. By Government

Cash basis accounting and cash flow reports comprise the greater part of government accounting and reporting. Nearly all government financial reports — in particular, budgets and balance of payments reports — are cash flow statements. The Commonwealth Government's annual budget introduced in August of each year for the fiscal period 1 July to 30 June is the most important economic and accounting report prepared in the country. The budget, prepared in accordance with the government's economic and social objectives, summarizes its economic policies for the coming year. In accounting terms, the budget is a statement of:

i. Cash receipts from current sources (e.g., taxation, public enterprises such as railways and the post office, and interest and dividends from investments in securities or government business undertakings such as Trans Australia Airlines)

ii. Expenditure on current goods and services (e.g., defence, law and order, state government reimbursements) and social services

iii. The budget surplus in the political sense, i.e., the excess of current receipts over current expenditure

iv. Expenditures on capital items (e.g., public works projects)

v. Capital receipts (e.g., government borrowing from the public or overseas countries).

The volume and distribution of government receipts and outlays are of fundamental importance in macro-economic analysis. The cash receipts from domestic sources (current and capital) show the extent to which the government has reduced the spending power, and hence the level of economic activity, of the private sector of the economy. The domestic outlays (excluding social service transfer payments) show the government's direct contribution to the level of economic activity, that is, to the gross national product. In economic analysis, the budget surplus or deficit is the difference between total receipts and total outlays. In the simplest situation, the size of this surplus or deficit shows the extent of the government's contractionary or expansionary influence respectively on the economy. The government regulates this surplus or deficit in order to maintain the economy at full employment, to control balance of payments fluctuations and inflation, and to promote economic growth. The distribution of receipts and outlays in the budget reflects the government's income distribution and resource allocation policies.

Once the year is completed, the government publishes a statement of its actual cash receipts and expenditures for the year. The historical report should be compared with the budget, and differences noted and analyzed.

The government uses its budgets for planning and control in much the same way as private firms. It must, like private industry, have the cash available to meet its payment commitments. Because of the seasonal nature of some cash receipts, particularly company profits taxes which are mainly paid in the last quarter of the financial year, the government may encounter severe cash deficits during other parts of the year (mainly from December to March), and it must make arrangements in advance to bridge these deficits. It raises short-term loans, mainly through the sale of treasury bills to trading banks and other financial institutions; these bills are then redeemed in the months of cash surpluses.

## FURTHER READING

Commonwealth of Australia. *Treasury Information Bulletins.*
Mason, Perry. *Cash Flow Analysis and the Funds Statement.* Accounting Research Study No. 2. New York: A.I.C.P.A., 1961.

## NOTES

1. Chap. 6.
2. Chap. 18.

## QUESTIONS AND EXERCISES

[Solution to problem marked * is given in Appendix 4.]

1. Distinguish between "cash surplus from operations" and "historic cost income".

2. For what purposes is the measure of "cash surplus from operations" useful?

3. To what extent does cash basis accounting provide a good information system in business, and what are its major limitations?

4. From the trial balances extracted for the following problems in chapter 5 prepare cash flow statements:

    i.     R. Martin's milk bar
    ii.    Mick Slob's pie and soup kitchen
    iii.   Bob Marlin's submarine cruises.

5. Joe Daley, garage proprietor, wants to buy a new hoist for his garage. It will cost him $3,000, and, being a prudent man, he will buy it only when he has enough cash. He hopes to buy it early in February next. On 1 January he has $2,500 in the bank. He estimates his petrol sales for January will amount to $850, and revenue from car servicing will be $220. His expected outlays for the month are: employees' wages $100; petrol and lubricant purchases $600; electricity $30; sundry items $20; and personal wages $80.

    Prepare a cash budget for January to determine if Joe will have enough cash by 1 February to buy his new hoist.

*6. Angel Airlines Limited is due to take delivery of two new jet aircraft at the end of September 19X0. It paid $3m. deposit on each aircraft at the time of order, and the balance of $7m. each is due on delivery. The company's budgeted income and appropriation statements for the coming quarter 1 July — 30 September, contain the following projections:

|  | $ |
|---|---|
| Ticket sales (all cash) | 18m. |
| Purchase of fuel and supplies | 7m. |
| Salaries | 2m. |
| Airport taxes | 1m. |
| Depreciation of aircraft and facilities | 3m. |
| Income taxes payable | 4m. |
| Dividend payable | 2m. |

    The company pays for purchases of all goods and services at the end of each month.

    Its balance sheet on 30 June discloses that the company has $5m. invested in Commonwealth bonds and it has $2m. cash at bank.

    The finance director is about to negotiate a long-term loan from the Overseas Development Bank for the amount of cash needed by the company to pay for the aircraft. How much should be borrowed, given that the company plans to sell the bonds for $5m. and that it must maintain $1m. cash at bank for working capital purposes? Present your answer in the form of a cash budget.

7. Dowell and Company Limited

    On 1 June, Dowell and Co. Ltd. was requested by its bank manager to reduce its bank overdraft, currently at $100,000, to $60,000 by the end of July. The company must also pay the final instalment of $40,000 on the purchase of new premises by the end of July.

    The company's budgeted income statement for the two months shows the following data:

| | June | July |
|---|---|---|
| | $ | $ |
| Sales (all cash): | 70,000 | 80,000 |
| Purchases (all cash): | 40,000 | 45,000 |
| Sundry Cash Expenses: | 10,000 | 10,000 |
| Depreciation: | 2,000 | 2,000 |

How much additional finance should the company raise by the end of July in order to meet these commitments? Prepare your answer in the form of a cash budget.

8. Bunyip Corporation

The following information relates to the anticipated operations of the Bunyip Corporation for the month of September.

Sales: Estimated to be $50,000, 20 per cent of which are cash and the balance on terms of 2 per cent discount if paid within thirty days.

Bond interest of $750 will be received. Purchases for the month are estimated to be $16,800. Purchases are made on terms of 2 per cent discount if paid within thirty days.

In the past the receipts from credit sales and the payments for credit purchases have been finalized in the month following the original transaction.

Wages accrued, 1 September — $300. Estimated expense for wages during September is $7,500, of which $400 will remain unpaid at 30 September.

Other operating expenses for the month for which cash expenditure is necessary total $8,600.

The annual dividend of $4,000 will be paid during the month.

| | $ |
|---|---|
| Cash at Bank, 1 September | 3,200 |
| Debtors, 1 September | 32,000 |
| Creditors, 1 September | 15,000 |

*Required:*

Prepare a forecasted cash flow statement for September.

9. Hopeful Traders
[BOM = Beginning of Month; EOM = End of Month.]

The following information relates to the projected activities for Hopeful Traders for the month of September:

Anticipated Sales     5,000 fridgets @ $10 each
Anticipated Purchases     4,300 fridgets @ $6 each.

One fifth of sales are for cash.

Past experience has shown that all cash payments for purchases and all cash receipts from debtors have been finalized in the month following the original transaction.

| | $ |
|---|---|
| Accounts Receivable 31 August | 31,250 |
| Accounts Payable 31 August | 18,500 |

*Other Operating Data:*

|  |  | $ |
|---|---|---|
| i. | *Payroll:* | |
|  | Sales, Wages paid | 3,400 |
|  | Office, Wages paid | 1,350 |

ii. *Accruals:*

|  | BOM $ | EOM $ |
|---|---|---|
| Sales Salaries | 275 | 335 |
| Office Salaries | 105 | 80 |
| Rent | 100 | — |

iii. A three-month advertising contract of $4,800 will be paid in September.

iv. Inventories are valued on the FIFO basis.

Inventory    BOM    4,100 units @ $5.

v. A rental payment of $500 will be made to cover 5 months.

vi. Delivery costs incurred and paid are expected to be $1,400.

vii. The firm depreciates showroom fittings at the rate of 10 per cent per annum on the straight line basis. Original cost of showroom fittings $3,600.

viii. Bank overdraft, 31 August, $11,250.

*Required:*

A. Prepare:
    a.   A cash flow budget for the month of September
    b.   A budgeted income statement for the month of September

B. Explain the difference between the concepts of accounting profit and cash surplus from operations.

10. Discount Retailers Limited have embarked on an expansion programme in which they hope to increase sales by 30 per cent over the coming three months. The company trades on fine profit margins and it finds that it continually runs short of cash. It cannot obtain a bank overdraft at the moment because of stringent credit restrictions in the economy. All purchases of goods and services, and all sales, are made on a cash basis. A $30,000 loan is due for repayment at the end of the third month, and the company desires to strengthen its liquidity by building up its cash balance to $25,000 by then. Its balance at the start of the first month is $19,000.
Will the company be able to repay the loan and improve its cash balance from its trading activities, or should it begin now to seek additional loans or shareholder finance?
The expected cash receipts and payments for each month are as follows:

|  | Month 1 $ | Month 2 $ | Month 3 $ |
|---|---|---|---|
| Sales | 120,000 | 138,000 | 156,000 |
| Merchandise Purchases | 102,000 | 125,000 | 130,000 |
| Wages and Salaries | 9,000 | 9,000 | 9,000 |
| Rent | 2,000 | 2,000 | 2,000 |
| Advertising | 3,000 | 5,000 | 8,000 |

    i.    Prepare a cash budget, and advise the company.

    ii.   What significance is attached to the quantity, "Cash Surplus from Operations"?

11.   Bonza Traders Pty. Ltd. has retained the services of your firm of consultants. The bank has granted the firm a maximum overdraft limit of $20,000. Bank overdraft at 30 September was $18,925. The company provides you with the following data of activity for the December quarter:

| | October | November | December |
|---|---|---|---|
| Unit Selling Price: $ | 23 | 22 | 20 |
| Expected Sales (units): | 1,600 | 1,650 | 1,850 |
| Expected Purchases (units): | 1,600 | 1,900 | 2,300 |
| Unit Purchase Price: $ | 10 | 11 | 12 |

*Anticipated Cash Payments:*

| | October | November | December |
|---|---|---|---|
| Interest on Debentures | | | 430 |
| Dividends | | 3,800 | |
| Property Rates | 3,600 | | |
| Taxes | | | 8,200 |
| Advertising | 15,000 | | |
| Insurance and Registration | 720 | | |
| Delivery Expenses | 1,250 | 1,400 | 1,600 |
| Sales and Delivery Salaries | 6,630 | 6,950 | 7,210 |
| Office Salaries | 1,750 | 1,820 | 1,840 |
| Bank Charges | 35 | 32 | 28 |

*Other Information:*

    i.    All receipts from credit sales and payments for credit purchases are expected to be finalized in the month following the original transaction. This is normal practice for this firm.

| | $ |
|---|---|
| Accounts Receivable, 30 September | 31,000 |
| Accounts Payable, 30 September | 14,000 |

    ii.   No sales or purchase discounts are given or received.

    iii.  FIFO method of inventory valuation is used. There were 500 units of stock on hand at 30 September. Value of inventory $5,000.

    iv.  The advertising outlay is for a half-yearly contract.

    v.   The insurance premium is the annual insurance on delivery vehicles. The property rates are for the whole year. Interest on debentures covers a six-months period.

    vi.  One-third of all sales are on a cash basis.

    vii.  *Accruals:*

| | | October | November | December |
|---|---|---|---|---|
| | | $ | $ | $ |
| Sales Salaries | BOM | 350 | 430 | 535 |
| | EOM | 430 | 535 | 850 |
| Office Salaries | BOM | 120 | 135 | 115 |
| | EOM | 135 | 115 | 200 |

viii.  *Anticipated depreciation charges*

| | | | |
|---|---|---|---|
| Showroom Fittings | 100 | 125 | 150 |
| Delivery Vehicles | 240 | 240 | 240 |

ix.  Leasehold is amortized at the monthly rate of $760.

x.  Additional office and showroom equipment already ordered will be delivered and installed in November. The contract price is $5,750, due for payment in December.

*Required:*

The directors of Bonza Traders Pty. Ltd. request the preparation of budgeted income statements and cash flow statements:

a.  For each month
b.  For the quarter.

12.  The following information relates to Bazza Corporation Limited:

*Balance Sheet as at 30 June 197X (Working capital segment)*

| Current Assets | $ | Current Liabilities | $ |
|---|---|---|---|
| Cash at Bank | 40,000 | Creditors | 120,000 |
| Debtors | 160,000 | Loans Payable | 60,000 |
| Inventories | 120,000 | Dividends Payable | 30,000 |
| | | Tax Payable | 40,000 |
| | $320,000 | | $250,000 |

| | July | August |
|---|---|---|
| | $ | $ |
| Sales — Cash | 100,000 | 120,000 |
| — Credit | 260,000 | 300,000 |
| Purchases — Credit | 200,000 | 240,000 |
| Wages and Salaries Payable | 60,000 | 60,000 |
| Advertising Payable | 30,000 | 20,000 |
| Rates Payable | — | 40,000 |
| Depreciation | 20,000 | 20,000 |
| Dividends Payable | 30,000 | — |

*Other Information:*

| | | |
|---|---|---|
| Collections from debtors | $140,000 | $200,000 |
| Payments to creditors | 120,000 | 200,000 |
| Loans repayable | 40,000 | 20,000 |

The company must maintain a minimum balance of $30,000 at the bank at the end of each month for working capital purposes.

The company can raise loans through the short-term money market to meet temporary working capital deficits. How much might it have to borrow in July and in August to meet expected commitments?

Prepare your answer in the form of a cash budget for July and August.

# Chapter 18
# Funds Statements

The final accounting report which can be prepared from the transaction data of the firm is the funds statement. The funds statement is a summary of the entire financial activities of a firm over a period. It shows both the sources and types of funds used by the firm to finance its activities over the period, and the uses of those funds in its operating, investment, and debt redemption programmes. Finance, or funds, covers cash and all substitutes for cash; it represents general purchasing power. The funds statement must be distinguished from the three related final accounting reports (that is, the income and appropriation statements and balance sheet) and from the cash flow statement. Its nature, use, and presentation are similar to the cash flow statement, but the coverage of the funds statement is wider in that it embraces all types of credit as well as cash. The funds statement overlaps the three final accounting reports and uses the same basic external transaction data, but, because its purpose is to report on the financing activities of the firm and not to measure income or financial position, it does not include the host of non-financing events necessarily included in those final reports.

As outlined in chapter 5, all external transactions between the firm and its markets necessarily involve a financing aspect. The acquisition of resources by the firm must be financed from its cash resources, by borrowing or by the credit of its suppliers; and at a subsequent date creditors must be paid from the firm's cash resources. Likewise, the sale of goods and services to customers results in the receipt of cash or financial claims on customers, which are subsequently extinguished by a cash transfer. The source of finance for the acquisition of all resources was seen to result in a credit entry to the relevant source account, while the use to which the finance was put was debited to the appropriate use account. Hence the double-entry record for each external transaction of the firm records the source of finance involved in the transaction and the use to which the finance is put. The funds statement is a summary of the twofold effect of all such transactions entered into by the firm over the period which shows the total sources of finance for those transactions and the way in which those finances have been used. In other words, the funds statement summarizes the financing aspects of all external transactions of the firm. The statement can be classified in various ways to emphasize different aspects of the firm's financing operations.

Two criteria must be satisfied for an item to be recorded in the funds statement — it must involve an external transaction and it must involve resource flows. The funds statement includes all external transactions of the firm which involve the acquisition or disposal of resources. However it does not include any "transactions" or events which are internal to the firm and "transactions" with persons outside the firm which do not involve resources and hence funds. "Transactions" which are internal to the firm and which do not involve funds comprise items such as allocations of long-term asset costs as charges against revenue (that is, depreciation and amortization expense), allocations of "capitalized expenses" as charges against profits (for example, goodwill written off), transfers of profits to reserves, asset revaluations, "goodwill on consolidation" in consolidated holding company balance sheets, and losses incurred on the destruction of assets. The second type of "transaction" does affect the relationship of the firm with outsiders, but again no funds are involved at the time of the "transaction". Expected dividend and tax payments are recorded immediately at the end of the financial year as liabilities of the firm even though no funds are received from shareholders or the government to give rise to these particular liabilities. Arrangements concerning the registration of a company's share capital on its incorporation, and the decision to sell shares, are recorded as non-fund events. Issues of bonus shares and share splits likewise do not involve funds but must be recorded. All these items are relevant for income statements and/or balance sheets, but because they do not involve funds they are omitted from the funds statement.

The funds statement can be prepared from the records kept in the partial accrual basis of accounting, or from those kept in the full accrual basis. In the latter case, though, all events not involving funds must be eliminated from the data.

One form of funds statement is illustrated below:

Superior Trading Co. Limited

*Funds Statement for the Year Ended 31 December 197X*

*During the year additional funds were obtained from:*

|  | $ | $ |
|---|---|---|
| 1. Operations: | | |
|     Sales Revenue | 150,000 | |
|     Less Expenses Requiring Funds | 96,000 | 54,000 |

2. Short-Term Borrowing:

| | | |
|---|---:|---:|
| Accounts Payable | 21,000 | |
| Accrued Expenses | 1,000 | 22,000 |

3. Long-Term Borrowing:

| | |
|---|---:|
| Debentures Sold | 35,000 |

4. Shareholders' Funds:

| | |
|---|---:|
| Shares Sold | 20,000 |

5. Reduction of Investment in Short-Term Assets:

| | |
|---|---:|
| Accounts Receivable | 5,000 |

6. Reduction of Investment in Long-Term Assets:

| | |
|---|---:|
| Land Sold | 14,000 |

*Total Additional Funds Obtained* — $150.000

*These additional funds were used for:*

1. Payments from Profits:

| | | |
|---|---:|---:|
| Dividends Paid | 10,000 | |
| Company Tax Paid | 14,000 | 24,000 |

2. Investment in Short-Term Assets:

| | | |
|---|---:|---:|
| Cash | 2,000 | |
| Inventories | 18,000 | 20,000 |

3. Investment in Long-Term Assets:

| | | |
|---|---:|---:|
| Equipment | 10,000 | |
| Land and Buildings | 50,000 | 60,000 |

4. Repayment of Short-Term Loans:

| | |
|---|---:|
| Bank Overdraft | 16,000 |

5. Repayment of Long-Term Loans:

| | |
|---|---:|
| Mortgage | 30,000 |

*Total Funds Used* — $150,000

## CONTENT OF THE FUNDS STATEMENT

The funds statement normally shows all the sources and types of additional finance obtained by the firm during the accounting period, and how those funds were used in its activities. In most firms the major source of finance is its normal operating activities. The surplus of the inflow of funds from sales over those expenses requiring the use of funds is the measure of the *funds from operations.* All sales represent a source of cash or financial claims to the firm; however the net revenue rather than the gross revenue figure is used because the estimated credit losses, sales returns, etc. included in the gross figure are treated as cancellations of revenue and hence gross revenue is not the effective source of finance. *Funds-using expenses* comprise all those short-term resources used up by the firm during the revenue-earning period. However not all expenses of earning revenue require the use of funds during the current period. *Non-fund expenses* comprise those relating to the using up of the firm's own long-term assets. The purchase of these assets involves a financial transaction which is treated as a separate use of funds, and the expense of using them in the firm's operations is measured by a systematic process of allocating this purchase cost to the revenue-benefiting periods. Such long-term cost allocations (for example, depreciation or amortization of buildings) do not involve an external transaction and hence there is no financing aspect to them. Recognition of such expenses is necessary for income determination and asset valuation, but they are not relevant in the determination of funds from operations. Hence funds from operations represent the value of the *gross* financial resources obtained from the firm's operating activities. They do not include any allowance for the recovery of investment in long-term assets, and must *not* be confused with *net profit,* which represents the *net* financial resources obtained from operations and does include an allowance for the recovery of investment in long-term assets.

Funds earned from operations are shown as one figure, rather than sales being shown as the source of funds and expenses as a use of funds because of the importance of the net figure. The funds from operations represent additional resources available to the firm, to be used according to management's plans for the future. They represent the internal source of finance to the firm. Typically, in the established profitable business, funds from operations comprise the most important source of new finance. There are fewer restrictions on management's use of internal finance than where the funds have been borrowed from creditors (and hence have to be repaid) or raised from owners (and hence about which promises must be made concerning future use, and on which dividends must be paid). Management has more discretion about the use of internal funds than borrowed funds. Some of them are committed to the payment of dividends and taxation, but the remainder can be used as management decides. Undoubtedly some of the funds from operations will be used for the replacement of long-term assets as the need arises, but this may not materialize within the current year, and in the meantime such funds can be used for any purpose determined by management, for example, on expansion or diversification projects or for debt repayment. Moreover, it is not necessary for management to replace the specific assets which are scrapped – they may now be obsolete, the firm's trading interests may have changed because of better profit opportunities in other areas, and so on, and hence the "replacement funds", (that is, those required to replace long-term assets to maintain the firm's production capacity) become available for general planning purposes. Funds from operations normally exceed net profit since no charges are made in the funds statement for non-fund expenses of operations (that is, depreciation and amortization expenses). It should be noted that profits are not a source of finance to the firm – the source of finance in all cases is sales, but of course the sales revenue should include a profit component.

Payments from profits (that is, drawings and salaries of owners, dividends paid to shareholders, and company income tax payments) may be deducted immediately from funds from operations or shown separately as a use of funds. The former method highlights the funds which are retained from operations and hence available for gross investment purposes (that is, the actual amount of long-term resources purchased, irrespective of whether they represent replacement or additional resources), or for repayments of loans. Taxes and payments to owners are related to profits, and hence to funds from operations. Taxes are unavoidable commitments, while dividends up to some "normal" rate are almost unavoidable because, if a profit-earning public company does not pay a "normal" dividend rate, its share prices may fall and thereby make it an easy takeover prospect for another company. On the other hand, showing dividends and taxes as separate fund-using items emphasizes that the cash actually used to pay them comes from a general pool of finance to which all sources contribute, and that they are not necessarily paid for out of the cash actually received from operations. This approach emphasizes that the total funds which become available during the period can be used according to management's financial decisions.

The firm may also obtain additional finance during the period by direct borrowing on a short-term basis (for example, bank overdrafts, short-term deposits, and notes), or long-term basis (for example, mortgage, debentures, long-term notes, or deposits); and by increased buying on short-term credit (and hence an increase in accounts payable). It may raise additional capital from owners by the sale of shares.

Finally, the firm may obtain additional finance by liquidating some of its assets. It may either not replace some of its short-term assets as they are converted into cash in the normal course of events, or it may sell long-term assets. Current assets such as inventories and accounts receivable are in a continuing process of being converted into cash, and, if they are not fully replaced, the funds become available for other uses. Similarly, a reduction in cash balances means that the initial investment of funds in cash form is not replaced and hence that the funds have been made available for other purposes. The firm sells various long-term assets from time to time as it no longer needs them and such sales are a source of funds. In all these instances, the firm reduces its investment in the assets concerned and the funds are released for other uses. The change in the composition of assets is referred to as the redeployment of assets. Funds are redeployed by reducing investment in some assets and increasing investment in others.

The second part of the funds statement shows how the additional funds have been used during the period. In general, they may be used for payments from profits, or to purchase additional assets, or repay liabilities. Any unused funds will be reflected in an increase in the cash balance — this may be the result of a deliberate policy to increase liquidity, or it may represent an accumulation of funds temporarily not needed. The change in the cash balance is essentially the residual item in the funds statement.

## FORM AND CLASSIFICATION OF THE FUNDS STATEMENT

There is no fixed form of presentation and classification of the funds statement. Various alternatives are available and the one adopted should be tailored to satisfy the user's needs for financial information. The accounting information standards should be applied so that the statement is prepared in a form which is appropriate to its expected use, it should disclose significant financing relationships, and so on. The form illustrated above is a simple one; other forms which emphasize the use of funds retained from operations, the financing of additional working capital and long-term assets are illustrated below.

There is, however, one principle of presentation which should be adhered to in all funds statements. Because the element of time is crucial in all financial analysis, it is important that the funds statement always shows items classified into short-term and long-term periods. Funds are typically obtained from both short-term and long-term sources for investment in short and long-term assets. Balance sheet classification is based on this principle, and it is followed in the funds statement. The short-term, long-term classification of items helps in financial planning and control.

The funds statement should clearly present significant financing relationships occurring in the firm.[1] In determining financing policy, it is important to separate current assets into a permanent base level and a temporary fluctuating component, and to ensure that long-term funds are used to finance the permanent level of current assets plus the purchase of long-term assets. Long-term funds comprise all equity funds and long-term liabilities. Some permanent level of current assets is necessary for the continued operations of the firm. It is known as *working (or circulating) capital* because it represents investment in those resources which are used up or turned over regularly in the firm's daily trading activities, and is distinguished from fixed capital (comprising those resources which are used up slowly). Both terms came into accounting from economics. Any increases in current assets above this level are regarded as temporary increases and they can be financed from short-term sources — either loans (bank overdrafts, deposits, and notes) or trade credit (an automatic means of financing provided by suppliers — hence, as purchases increase, so do accounts payable). Liquidation of current assets in the near future provides the cash for repaying the loans or creditors — the assets themselves are not to be replaced. However, cash provided from liquidating current assets forming part of the permanent base level must be used to replace the assets disposed of; it cannot be used for paying debts. Hence it must come from long-term sources. Working capital refers to the funds that are more or less permanently available for financing a firm's daily operations (mainly its purchase of inventories, wage payments, and financing of credit sales). It represents the amount of short-term assets that are financed from long-term sources, and it is conventionally measured as current assets less current liabilities, i.e., net current assets. The working capital ratio is measured as current assets divided by current liabilities.

The appropriate proportion of short-term assets which can safely be financed from short-term sources varies substantially according to the trading and risk characteristics of the industry in which the firm operates. This appropriate proportion is known as the optimum working capital ratio. Thus firms which sell on long credit terms need more working capital than otherwise similar firms selling for cash only; firms whose inventories do not naturally turn over quickly (for example, inventories of durables) require more working capital than those handling merchandise with a rapid turnover (for example, perishables); firms in risky trading situations need more liquidity than those firms the demands for whose products are stable; retailers generally need a larger investment in inventories and accounts receivable than manufacturers; and so on. Basically, the firm must have a sufficient reservoir of working capital to ensure that the cash inflow on the product market side of the activity cycle diagram is sufficient to meet the cash outflow on the factor market side of the diagram. Creditors are interested in the amount of working capital as well as management because it indicates the short-term creditworthiness of the firm to them — their debts are normally paid from liquidated current assets.

As with working capital, long-term assets should not be financed from short-term sources because, when the loans fall due for repayment in the near future, the assets of the firm are not sufficiently liquid to enable repayment. Long-term assets are frequently not readily marketable — they (or their services) are far removed from the stage of conversion into cash. Long-term assets should be financed from long-term sources so that, over time, they generate sufficient funds from operations for use in repayment of the liability (if they are not financed by owners) and for replacement of the asset where necessary.

Because of the importance of the short and long-term classification and of working capital, funds statements are frequently arranged to show this information specifically. For example, the funds statement of the Superior Trading Co. Ltd. could be arranged in either of the following ways (detailed items are omitted for brevity):

Superior Trading Co. Ltd.

*Funds Statement for the Year Ended 31 December 197X*

|  | $ | $ | $ |
|---|---|---|---|
| Funds from Operations | | | 54,000 |
| Less Payments from Profits | | | 24,000 |
| | | | $30,000 |

Funds Retained from Operations available for Working Capital and Long-Term Assets, used as follows:

| | | | |
|---|---|---|---|
| 1. To finance an increase in Working Capital: | | | |
| Net Increase in Current Assets | | 15,000 | |
| Less Net Increase in Current Liabilities | | 6,000 | 9,000 |
| 2. To finance an increase in Fixed Capital: | | | |
| Net Increase in Long-Term Assets | | 46,000 | |
| Less Net Increase in Long-Term Liabilities | 5,000 | | |
| Less Increase in Paid-up Capital | 20,000 | 25,000 | 21,000 |
| | | | $30,000 |

This form of presentation shows how the funds retained from operations have been used to finance additional working capital and additional fixed capital.

Alternatively, it may be shown as:

| *Sources of Funds* | $ | $ |
|---|---|---|
| 1. Operations | 54,000 | |
| Less Payments from Profits | 24,000 | 30,000 |
| 2. Increased Long-Term Borrowing | | 5,000 |
| 3. Increased Paid-up Capital | | 20,000 |
| | | $55,000 |

| *Uses of Funds* | | |
|---|---|---|
| 1. Increased Investment in Working Capital | | 9,000 |
| 2. Increased Investment in Long-Term Assets | | 46,000 |
| | | $55,000 |

This form emphasizes the long-term finance obtained from each source and its investment in additional working and fixed capital.

By grouping current assets and current liabilities together, the change in working capital can be highlighted along with changes in the long-term financial structure of the company. The latter reflect important financial decisions of management which have long-term repercussions. Although the change in working capital is generally the significant figure in the short-term part of the statement rather than the changes in individual current assets and current liabilities (as these are the result of daily trading operations rather than management financing decisions), it is important nevertheless that the changes in individual current assets and liabilities are disclosed (in a schedule if necessary) for an accurate picture to be given. Frequently, the change in working capital is shown as a net figure only. However, this can hide important information about changes in component items; for example, a substantial increase in hire-purchase debtors compensated for by a reduction in cash does not affect net working capital; neither does a substantial increase in inventories offset by the same increase in accounts payable. Yet in both instances the financial position of the firm can be materially affected towards less liquidity.

A further matter of disclosure relates to long-term items. It is desirable to disclose gross changes in long-term items where they are significant rather than merely the net change, as is done with individual short-term items. Transactions involving long-term assets, liabilities, and capital are not everyday occurrences, and they can be sufficiently important to warrant separate disclosure in the funds statement. For example, the firm may make a new debenture issue to finance repayment of maturing debentures. There may be no net change, or even no cash involved if it is a straightforward conversion operation with existing debenture holders, yet such a transaction is important in financial analysis because the time span of the debenture liability has changed substantially, and there may be alterations in interest rates or debenture holders' legal rights. Similarly, the firm may replace some property during the year. This may not affect the firm's asset structure but it tells the user about the change in property owned. The new property may have different use characteristics or profit potential which investors want to know about. On the other hand, the composition of short-term items changes every day — inventories, debtors, and creditors are continually changing — and the individual changes in each item are of no significance for financial analysis. The net change is the important magnitude here.

The funds statement could be presented to show opening and closing balances of total funds on hand, by analogy with the cash flow statement. However, no purpose is served by such a procedure in the funds statement. In the cash flow report, the opening cash balance is shown because it is a general purpose resource and management's cash planning decisions are based on the cash balance plus cash inflow. But the sources of funds and the forms in which they are invested are not general purpose ones — they are specific to particular sources and uses, with the exception of cash itself. Management can plan uses with respect to the flow of funds only, and not to the total stock of funds. Most of the funds at a particular point of time are committed to specific uses (that is, they are invested in buildings, inventories, and so on), and it is only in respect of new funds coming into the firm that new decisions can be made. Moreover, the omission of an opening balance avoids thorny valuation problems caused by changes in market prices of particular assets and changes in the purchasing power of the dollar.

## USE OF THE FUNDS STATEMENT

In its historical form, the funds statement shows how the firm was financed over the period and how the funds were used; that is, it summarizes the financial history of the firm's activities. It is a report on the financial management of the firm. Answers to specific questions, such as where the profits went to (particularly when the firm finds itself short of cash), how debt retirement was financed, how plant expansion or replacement was financed, and so on, can be obtained by appropriately rearranging the items in the statement. It shows the extent to which short-term finance was used for short-term purposes and long-term purposes during the period, etc., and the extent to which internal funds were used to finance activities. If funds statements are extended back over some years, a more complete picture of financial patterns and trends can be seen. An investment analyst concerned with predicting future financial policies could ascertain the size, use, and frequency of debenture and share issues, the size and frequency of capital expenditure programmes, possible difficulties which could be encountered in repaying large loans, and so on. This historical information is very useful for predicting the firm's future financial policies and the likely effect of these on share prices. Long-term lenders can see whether the firm's operations generate sufficient funds to cover interest and loan repayments with safety, or whether the firm will have to raise replacement loans to repay its existing ones.

The funds statement is of most use to management in its budgeted form. Use of the funds budget is rather similar to that of the cash budget. Where management does not have perfect knowledge of the more distant future, long-term projections are normally made on a fund flow rather than a cash flow basis. Cash budgets are generally confined to the coming twelve months, whereas funds budgets may extend five or twenty years into the future. For example, in investment project evaluation, it is difficult enough to forecast sales for three or four years ahead, let alone the division of sales into cash and credit. In any case, the differences caused to the evaluation by using funds instead of cash estimates should be slight. Funds budgets are prepared to answer questions about financing into the distant future. For example, can debt retirement, plant replacement, or plant expansion in five years' time be financed from funds from operations, or will a new long-term loan or share issue be required; in determining the best period for a proposed long-term loan, can it be repaid from funds from operations in ten years' time or not until fifteen years; should short or long-term finance be used for a particular project? If plans are made on the basis of the funds budget, then as time progresses, sufficient resources should be coming into the firm from operations to avoid any awkward financial problems (assuming the estimates turn out to be reasonably reliable), and management can then see to it that the resources are put into cash form as the immediate need for the cash arises. Hence the funds budget is used for long-term financial planning, whereas the cash budget is used mainly for the immediate future to ensure that the cash, and not just resources in any form, is available to meet liabilities as they fall due. Similarly, large institutional investors, for example, life assurance companies, may require a long-term funds budget as a condition for making loans.

## PREPARATION OF FUNDS STATEMENTS

The funds statement can be prepared from comparative trial balances extracted from the ledger either after all financial transactions and financial adjustments have been recorded (as in the partial accrual basis of accounting) or after all transactions and events have been recorded (as in the full accrual basis of accounting). However, in the latter case all accounts which represent non-fund items must be disregarded. Either set of trial balances can be used since it is axiomatic that all financial transactions involve a debit and a credit entry to accounts recording a source or use of funds (that is, fund accounts), while all non-financial events must involve a debit and a credit to non-fund accounts. The comparative trial balances are those at the beginning and the end of the accounting period. However the opening trial balance will include only zero balances in revenue, expense, and loss accounts as these are begun afresh each year. The differences between the opening and closing balances in the funds accounts represent the flow of finance during the period. However this information should be supplemented by details about particular transactions involving long-term items or payments from profits as the account balances show only net changes.

The following example relates to the Northside Trading Co. Ltd., whose other reports were illustrated in chapters 6 and 17. The opening and closing trial balances (after all adjustments have been made except for those relating to the appropriation of profits) are shown. The fire loss of $6,000 relates to buildings destroyed and is added back to the Buildings account to show the gross value of buildings acquired; all non-fund accounts are marked with an asterisk and disregarded; two worksheet columns are added to the trial balances to facilitate preparation of the funds statement; and the Sales and Accounts Receivable accounts are shown at net balances in the funds statement columns. The debit colum in the funds statement shows the uses of funds and the credit column the sources of funds. A schedule of funds earned from operations is appended in order to relieve the funds statement of unnecessary detail.

Northside Trading Co. Ltd.

| | Trial Balances | | | | Funds Statements | |
|---|---|---|---|---|---|---|
| | 1 January | | 31 December | | Net Changes | |
| | Dr. $ | Cr. $ | Dr. $ | Cr. $ | Use-Dr. $ | Source-Cr. $ |
| Sales | | | | 140,000 | | |
| Estimated Credit Losses | | | 6,000 | | | 134,000 |
| Cost of Goods Sold | | | 100,000 | | 100,000 | |
| Advertising | | | 3,000 | | 3,000 | |
| Sales Salaries | | | 6,000 | | 6,000 | |
| Depreciation of Shop Fittings* | | | 1,000 | | | |
| Directors' Fees | | | 1,000 | | 1,000 | |
| Office Salaries | | | 2,000 | | 2,000 | |
| Depreciation of Buildings* | | | 3,000 | | | |
| Interest | | | 1,000 | | 1,000 | |
| Fire Loss* | | | 6,000 | | | |
| Dividends | | | 2,000 | | 2,000 | |
| Accounts Receivable | 20,000 | | 30,000 | | 9,000 | |
| Estimated Bad Debts | | 2,000 | | 3,000 | | |
| Merchandise Inventory | 34,000 | | 32,000 | | | 2,000 |
| Prepayments | 500 | | 1,000 | | 500 | |
| Shop Fittings | 7,500 | | 12,000 | | 4,500 | |
| Accumulated Depreciation of Shop Fittings* | | 2,000 | | 3,000 | | |
| Land and Buildings | 28,000 | | 54,000 (48,000) | | 26,000 | |
| Accumulated Depreciation of Buildings* | | 15,000 | | 18,000 | | |
| Goodwill 1 Jan.* | 8,000 | | 8,000 | | | |
| Bank Overdraft | | 15,000 | | 3,000 | 12,000 | |
| Accounts Payable | | 11,000 | | 12,000 | | 1,000 |
| Accrued Expenses | | 1,000 | | 1,000 | | — |
| Mortgage | | — | | 20,000 | | 20,000 |
| Paid-up Capital | | 40,000 | | 50,000 | | 10,000 |
| Reserves, 1 Jan.* | | 7,000 | | 7,000 | | |
| Retained Profs, 1 Jan.* | | 5,000 | | 5,000 | | |
| | $98,000 | $98,000 | $262,000 | $262,000 | $167,000 | $167,000 |

Northside Trading Co. Ltd.

*Funds Statement for the Year Ended 31 December 197X*

| During the year, additional funds were obtained from: | | $ |
|---|---|---:|
| 1. Operations | | 21,000 |
| 2. Short-Term Borrowing | | |
| Accounts Payable | | 1,000 |
| 3. Long-Term Borrowing | | |
| Mortgage | | 20,000 |
| 4. Shareholders | | |
| Paid-up Capital | | 10,000 |
| 5. Reduction of Investment in Current Assets | | |
| Merchandise | | 2,000 |
| *Total Additional Funds Obtained* | | $54,000 |

| These additional funds were used for: | | |
|---|---:|---:|
| 1. Payment of Dividends | | 2,000 |
| 2. Increased Investment in Current Assets | | |
| Accounts Receivable | 9,000 | |
| Prepayments | 500 | 9,500 |
| 3. Increased Investment in Long-Term Assets | | |
| Shop Fittings | 4,500 | |
| Land and Buildings | 26,000 | 30,500 |
| 4. Repayment of Short-Term Loans | | |
| Bank Overdraft | | 12,000 |
| *Total Additional Funds Used* | | $54,000 |

| Schedule of Funds Earned from Operations: | | |
|---|---:|---:|
| Sales Revenue | | 134,000 |
| Less Expenses Requiring Funds | | |
| Cost of Goods Sold | 100,000 | |
| Advertising | 3,000 | |
| Sales Salaries | 6,000 | |
| Directors' Fees | 1,000 | |
| Office Salaries | 2,000 | |
| Interest | 1,000 | 113,000 |
| Funds Earned From Operations | | $21,000 |

## OTHER MATTERS CONCERNING FUNDS STATEMENTS

The theory underlying funds statements, the concept of funds to be employed, the form of presentation of the statements and their uses are the subject of much controversy in accounting. The development of the topic above has not followed conventional lines. Some of the alternative methods used are now considered, together with the specific problem area concerning "non-fund" items.

## 1.  The Concept of Funds

By far the most common concept of funds employed in industry and in text-books is that of working capital, and the funds statement is confined to reporting changes in working capital. Working capital is defined as short-term assets less short-term liabilities, but it can be derived by corollary as the excess of long-term liabilities and proprietorship over long-term assets. Hence there are two ways of arriving at changes in working capital — to report the changes in short-term assets and liabilities; or the changes in long-term assets, liabilities, and proprietorship. Both methods are used in practice, and the result is that only one segment of the funds statement is reported. Hence only part of the total financial operations of the company is reported upon, and any significant changes in components of the unreported part are simply not disclosed. Such statements are inadequate for purposes of financial analysis and the non-disclosure of relevant information can cause wrong decisions to be made. They do not comply with the communication guidelines required for a good information system and it is difficult to see what useful purpose they serve.

Similar criticisms can be applied to other concepts of "funds" sometimes used, such as cash plus marketable securities, or net monetary assets (cash, debtors, and marketable securities).

## 2.  Preparation of the Funds Statement from Comparative Balance Sheets

Funds statements are invariably prepared from comparative balance sheets. Historically, this method is due to the fact that funds statements were first prepared by external investment analysts. Because published balance sheets were the only sources of data on financing activities of companies available to them, they had to work back to get the information for funds statements. This method of preparation was adopted by accountants when subsequently they recognized the usefulness of funds statements. However, as they have direct access to the basic data, there is no need to work back to get the funds statement. In itself, their preparation from comparative balance sheets is satisfactory so long as additional information on non-fund items and gross changes in long-term items is available. The balance sheet in its simplest form is a statement showing the sources of finance on a particular date, and the investment of that finance in specific assets. Changes in financing and investment over a period can be determined by comparing the start-of-year balance sheet with the end-of-year one, and, with the addition of net profit and non-fund item data, a funds statement can be derived.

However, several reservations about this approach may be noted. First, a funds statement prepared from comparative balance sheets tends to be both prepared and interpreted as a statement of balance sheet changes — it may do no more than list increases and decreases in assets, liabilities, and proprietorship. The funds statement can degenerate into a mere reconciliation between opening and closing balance sheets which serves no useful purpose to management, investors, creditors, and shareholders. Instead, the funds statement must be presented to inform the user that it is reporting on the flow of finance into the firm during the period and on the spending of that finance, and that this results from all the external transactions engaged in by the firm. It summarizes the history of the firm's financial activities over the period. Comparative trial balances prepared after all financial transactions have been recorded are the immediate sources of data for funds statements.

Secondly, although the historical cost balance sheet in its simplest form is a statement of the sources and uses of funds on a particular date, the modern balance sheet is rarely such a statement. Typically, it incorporates a host of non-fund items — asset revaluations, accumulated depreciation, bonus share issues, reserves, expected future liabilities, and so on — and "adding back" adjustments must be made to eliminate them from the funds statement data. Although none of these items involves funds, they appear in the funds statement as a "source" or "use" of funds if the balance sheet figures are included in the statement, and tend to cause confusion.

Thirdly, the method does not highlight the main source of funds for virtually all firms, namely sales. Funds from operations are calculated by adding back non-fund expenses to net profits, although none of these items is a source of funds, and none of them results from an external transaction of the firm. This negative way of calculating the figure again tends to cause confusion and to lead to the belief that depreciation is not a necessary expense of operations and furthermore that it is even a source of funds.

### 3. Non-Fund Items

Where funds statements are prepared from other reports which include non-fund items as well as transactions which involve the use of funds, a whole series of adjustments is necessary to eliminate the effects of the non-fund items from the account balances. The main non-fund items are listed below:

i. *Depreciation and amortization expenses,* that is, allocations of the costs of long-term assets to the periods in which they are used. Depreciation is a necessary expense item in income calculation, but it is not an expense involving the purchase of resources from outside the firm, and hence does not require the use of any funds. Purchase of the long-term resource requires the use of funds, and is shown as such in the period of its purchase. Regrettably, depreciation is added back to net profit as a "source" of funds in the typical funds statement, notwithstanding that accountants never fail to emphasize that depreciation does not require the use of funds, and that expenses can never be a source of funds anyway. This practice has caused endless confusion amongst business managers, investment analysts, and economists.

To demonstrate that depreciation is *not* a source of funds, consider the North-side Trading Co. Ltd. Its Funds from Operations are $21,000 (i.e., sales $134,000 less expenses requiring funds $113,000). Its Net Operating Profit is $17,000 after charging depreciation of $4,000. If the depreciation charge were increased to, say $6,000, Funds from Operations remain at $21,000 as expenses requiring funds are not affected. Alternatively, on the "working back" calculation, the increase in depreciation reduces Net Operating Profit to $15,000, so that Funds from Operations are: Net Operating Profit $15,000 plus Depreciation $6,000 equals $21,000, as before.

ii.   *Bad debts.* No adjustments for anticipated bad debts are required if sales revenue and accounts receivable are valued at the net amounts after allowing for the possibility that some credit sales are made to uncreditworthy customers; and bad debts written off are then a non-fund charge to the estimated bad debts account. However, bad debts recovered are shown as a source of funds as they involve an external transaction and an inflow of cash.

iii.  *Amortizations of "capitalized" expenses* such as goodwill, patents, preliminary expenses, and debenture discount. The costs of these items are amortized over several accounting periods in a manner similar to the depreciation of other long-term assets, but for various reasons the amortization may be treated as a profit allocation and not as an expense of earning revenue. Again, such amortizations do not affect cash or credit or involve an external transaction, and hence are not relevant in a funds statement.

iv.   *Provisions for future dividends and taxation.* They should not be included in the current year's funds statement, but in that for the following year in which they are paid. They do not involve an external transaction and they are not a source of finance for the firm. Payment of taxes and dividends is shown as a use of funds in the year in which the payments are made.

v.    *Asset revaluations* to bring historic values into equality with current market values do not involve external transactions and hence funds. They are adjustments of asset values which are internal to the firm. They are relevant for the determination of the firm's current financial position, but not to a record of its past financing activities.

vi.   *Transfers of profits to reserves* do not involve the use of funds and are not relevant in a funds statement. They are internal reallocations of retained profits between accounts of different names but which are essentially of the same type. No external transaction is involved.

vii.  *Bonus share issues* alter the paper titles to shareholders' existing property, and do not involve any funds. The firm does not acquire funds from a bonus issue of shares, as it does from the sale of shares. No financial transaction occurs, and bonus share issues should not be included in the funds statement.

## 4.   Funds from Operations and Net Income

The practice referred to in chapter 17 of confusing cash flow from operations with net income occurs as well with funds earned from operations. Funds from operations are *not* a measure of *income*-earning capacity, but of *funds*-earning capacity from the firm's everyday trading activities, i.e., of the *gross* contribution of operations to the firm's stock of resources as distinguished from the net contribution (i.e., income). Although credit transactions are included in the calculation, all depreciation and amortization charges necessary for income determination are excluded from the measure.

### FURTHER READING

Carrington, A. S.; Battersby, G. B.; and Howitt, G. *Accounting: An Information System*. Christchurch: Whitcombe and Tombs. 1975. Chap. 4.

Mason, Perry. *Cash Flow Analysis and the Funds Statement* Accounting Research Study No. 2, A.I.C.P.A., 1961, Pp. 47–91.

Mathews, R. L. *The Accounting Framework*. 3rd ed. Melbourne: Cheshire, 1971. Chap. 4.

### NOTE

1. These relationships are examined in chap. 26, and a brief explanation of some of the principles of sound financial policy is given in Appendix 1.

### QUESTIONS AND EXERCISES

[Solutions to problems marked * are given in Appendix 4.]

1. Explain the concept of "funds" as used in funds statements.

2. Distinguish between "funds from operations", "cash surplus on operations", and "historic cost income".

3. What is the distinction between "fund-using expenses" and "non-fund expenses"? Are non-fund expenses optional ones for purposes of measuring income?

4. What criteria are applied in determining whether an item is to be recorded in the funds statement? Using these criteria, state whether the following would be included in the funds statement, and whether they represent a source or a use of funds.

   i.     Credit sales of merchandise
   ii.    Wages owing
   iii.   Depreciation of shop premises
   iv.    Goodwill written off
   v.     Transfer to general reserve
   vi.    Net profit
   vii.   An increase in cash at bank
   viii.  Revaluation of land
   ix.    Income tax paid
   x.     Income tax payable
   xi.    Dividend payable
   xii.   Increase in share premium reserve
   xiii.  Issue of bonus shares
   xiv.   Increase in retained earnings.

5. Do depreciation charges provide funds to a business? Illustrate your answer by using the following information: sales $300,000, cost of sales $220,000, wages $30,000, depreciation $20,000. To provide more funds for the business, the owner recommends increasing the depreciation charge to $30,000.

6. Explain the nature and uses of a funds statement.

7. Explain the uses and limitations of the partial accrual basis of accounting as an information system in business.

8. Distinguish between "fixed capital" and "working capital". Give illustrations.

9. Prepare funds statements from the trial balances extracted for:

   i.   R. Davis
   ii.  F. James
   in Questions and Exercises for chapter 5, nos. 9 and 10.

For Problems 10–16, prepare a funds statement worksheet and a suitably classified final funds statement showing total sources and total use of funds for the year.

10. Reg Higgins and Co.

*Trial Balances*

|  | 1 Jan. | | 31 Dec. | |
|---|---|---|---|---|
|  | Dr. $ | Cr. $ | Dr. $ | Cr. $ |
| Sales |  |  |  | 76,000 |
| Cost of Merchandise Sold |  |  | 52,000 |  |
| Salaries |  |  | 8,000 |  |
| Rent. |  |  | 10,000 |  |
| Drawings |  |  | 4,000 |  |
| Cash at Bank | 8,000 |  |  | 3,000 |
| Accounts Receivable | 23,000 |  | 16,000 |  |
| Merchandise Inventory | 9,000 |  | 20,000 |  |
| Shop Premises | 30,000 |  | 45,000 |  |
| Accounts Payable |  | 12,000 |  | 17,000 |
| Short-Term Deposits |  | 5,000 |  |  |
| Mortgage |  | 20,000 |  | 26,000 |
| Capital |  | 33,000 |  | 33,000 |
|  | $70,000 | $70,000 | $155,000 | $155,000 |

11.   Hughes & Co. Ltd.

*Trial Balances*

|  | 1 Jan. Dr. $ | 1 Jan. Cr. $ | 31 Dec. Dr. $ | 31 Dec. Cr. $ |
|---|---|---|---|---|
| Bank | 14,000 | | 17,000 | |
| Accounts Receivable (Net) | 32,000 | | 38,000 | |
| Merchandise Inventory | 26,000 | | 22,000 | |
| Prepayments | 1,000 | | — | |
| Shop Fittings | 10,000 | | 14,000 | |
| Buildings | 50,000 | | 80,000 | |
| Accounts Payable | | 17,000 | | 20,000 |
| Accrued Expenses | | 1,000 | | 2,000 |
| Long-Term Notes | | 15,000 | | 25,000 |
| Paid-up Capital | | 100,000 | | 110,000 |
| Sales (Net) | | | | 120,000 |
| Cost of Goods Sold | | | 72,000 | |
| Salaries | | | 14,000 | |
| Advertising | | | 6,000 | |
| Directors' Fees | | | 2,000 | |
| Interest | | | 1,000 | |
| Income Taxes Paid | | | 5,000 | |
| Dividends Paid | | | 6,000 | |
| | $133,000 | $133,000 | $277,000 | $277,000 |

*Additional Information:*

During the year, the long-term notes matured, and a new issue of $25,000 was successfully made.

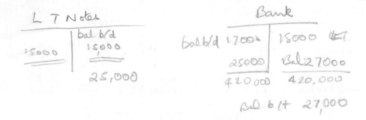

12. Bellbird Corporation Limited

*Trial Balances*

|  | 1 Jan. 1968 | | 31 Dec. 1968 | |
|---|---|---|---|---|
|  | Dr. $ | Cr. $ | Dr. $ | Cr. $ |
| Bank | 24,000 |  | 21,000 |  |
| ✓ Accounts Receivable (Net) | 34,000 |  | 48,000 |  |
| ✓ Merchandise Inventory | 42,000 |  | 36,000 |  |
| ✓ Premises | 100,000 |  | 150,000 |  |
| Accum. Depreciation Premises |  | 25,000 |  | 30,000 |
| ✓ Accounts Payable |  | 27,000 |  | 32,000 |
| ✓ Debentures |  | 40,000 |  | 60,000 |
| ✓ Paid-up Capital |  | 80,000 |  | 90,000 |
| General Reserve, 1 Jan. |  | 15,000 |  | 15,000 |
| Appropriation, 1 Jan. |  | 13,000 |  | 13,000 |
| ✓ Sales (Net) |  |  |  | 330,000 |
| ✓ Cost of Goods Sold |  |  | 280,000 |  |
| ✓ Salaries |  |  | 24,000 |  |
| Depreciation of Premises |  |  | 5,000 |  |
| ✓ Dividends Paid |  |  | 6,000 |  |
|  | $200,000 | $200,000 | $570,000 | $570,000 |

13. B. Moore & Company **Limited**

*Trial Balances*

|  | 1 Jan. | | 31 Dec. | |
|---|---|---|---|---|
|  | Dr. $ | Cr. $ | Dr. $ | Cr. $ |
| Sales |  |  |  | 50,000 |
| Cost of Merchandise Sold |  |  | 30,000 |  |
| Wages |  |  | 8,000 |  |
| Advertising |  |  | 4,000 |  |
| Company Income Tax |  |  | 2,000 |  |
| Dividends |  |  | 3,000 |  |
| Cash at Bank | 2,000 |  | 3,500 |  |
| Accounts Receivable | 5,500 |  | 8,500 |  |
| Merchandise Inventories | 8,000 |  | 6,000 |  |
| Delivery Vans | — |  | 5,000 |  |
| Land and Buildings | 14,000 |  | 21,000 |  |
| Accounts Payable |  | 4,500 |  | 7,000 |
| Notes Payable |  | 2,000 |  | — |
| Debentures |  | 8,000 |  | 12,000 |
| Capital |  | 15,000 |  | 22,000 |
|  | $29,500 | $29,500 | $91,000 | $91,000 |

*Additional Data on Long-Term Transactions:*
Previous premises sold and new ones purchased.

14. Entity Corporation Limited

*Trial Balances*

| | 1 Jan. | | 31 Dec. | |
|---|---|---|---|---|
| | Dr. $ | Cr. $ | Dr. $ | Cr. $ |
| Sales (Net) | | | | 125,000 |
| Cost of Goods Sold | | | 81,000 | |
| Advertising | | | 5,000 | |
| Sales Salaries | | | 14,000 | |
| Depreciation | | | | |
|    Shop Fittings | | | 3,000 | |
|    Office Equipment | | | 1,000 | |
| Office Salaries | | | 6,000 | |
| Directors' Fees | | | 1,000 | |
| Interest | | | 6,000 | |
| Accounts Payable | | 8,400 | | 12,700 |
| Accounts Receivable (Net) | 13,500 | | 22,500 | |
| Bank Overdraft | | 6,200 | | 8,700 |
| Notes Payable | | 3,000 | | — |
| Mortgage | | 30,000 | | 35,000 |
| Land | 65,000 | | 78,000 | |
| Shop Fittings | 20,000 | | 22,000 | |
| Office Equipment | 12,000 | | 12,000 | |
| Accumulated Depreciation | | | | |
|    Shop Fittings | | 3,000 | | 6,000 |
|    Office Equipment | | 2,000 | | 3,000 |
| Merchandise | 42,100 | | 25,900 | |
| Paid-up Capital | | 100,000 | | 100,000 |
| Dividends Paid | | | 6,000 | |
| Income Tax Paid | | | 7,000 | |
| | $152,600 | $152,600 | $290,400 | $290,400 |

15. Keller Company Limited

*Trial Balances*

|  | 1 Jan. | | 31 Dec. | |
|---|---|---|---|---|
|  | Dr. $ | Cr. $ | Dr. $ | Cr. $ |
| Sales |  |  |  | 100,000 |
| Cost of Sales |  |  | 55,000 |  |
| Expenses (Excluding Depreciation) |  |  | 10,500 |  |
| Depreciation |  |  | 7,500 |  |
| Plant | 50,000 |  | 102,000 |  |
| Land and Buildings | 15,000 |  | 36,000 |  |
| Shop Fittings | 4,000 |  | 4,000 |  |
| Office Equipment | 1,000 |  | 2,000 |  |
| Accumulated Depreciation |  |  |  |  |
|   Plant |  | 16,000 |  | 19,000 |
|   Shop Fittings |  | 1,000 |  | 1,300 |
|   Office Equipment |  | 600 |  | 800 |
| Investments | 58,000 |  | 19,250 |  |
| Merchandise | 20,000 |  | 26,250 |  |
| Taxation Paid |  |  | 7,700 |  |
| Dividends Paid |  |  | 4,800 |  |
| Accounts Payable |  | 7,500 |  | 10,000 |
| Accounts Receivable (Net) | 28,250 |  | 32,500 |  |
| Prepayments | 750 |  | 600 |  |
| Accrued Expenses |  | 900 |  | — |
| Appropriation |  | 6,000 |  | 6,000 |
| Debentures |  | 65,000 |  | 10,000 |
| Paid-up Capital |  | 75,000 |  | 125,000 |
| Share Premium Reserve |  | 5,000 |  | 15,000 |
| Asset Revaluation Reserve |  | — |  | 21,000 |
|  | $177,000 | $177,000 | $308,100 | $308,100 |

*Additional Information:*

i.  During the year the company's land and buildings were revalued at $36,000.

ii. During the year the company sold obsolete plant for $11,000. This plant originally cost $15,000 and had been depreciated *by* $4,000 at the time it was sold.

*16.  Fuddy Duddy Company Limited

*Trial Balances*

|  | 1 Jan. | | 31 Dec. | |
|---|---|---|---|---|
|  | Dr. $ | Cr. $ | Dr. $ | Cr. $ |
| Cash at Bank | 29,000 | | 16,000 | |
| Accounts Receivable (Net) | 47,000 | | 61,000 | |
| Merchandise Inventory | 78,000 | | 69,000 | |
| Prepayments | 2,000 | | 3,000 | |
| Shop Fittings (at Cost) | 14,000 | | 22,000 | |
| Accumulated Depreciation of Shop Fittings | | 6,000 | | 8,000 |
| Shop Premises (at Cost) | 70,000 | | 115,000 | |
| Accumulated Depreciation of Premises | | 22,000 | | 30,000 |
| Accounts Payable | | 23,000 | | 25,000 |
| Notes Payable | | 12,000 | | — |
| Mortgage | | 35,000 | | 50,000 |
| Paid-up Capital | | 100,000 | | 110,000 |
| Share Premium Reserve | | 30,000 | | 35,000 |
| Retained Earnings, 1 Jan. | | 12,000 | | 12,000 |
| Sales (Net) | | | | 280,000 |
| Cost of Goods Sold | | | 190,000 | |
| Salaries | | | 25,000 | |
| Advertising | | | 15,000 | |
| Depreciation of Shop Fittings | | | 2,000 | |
| Depreciation of Premises | | | 8,000 | |
| Dividends Paid | | | 14,000 | |
| Income Tax Paid | | | 10,000 | |
|  | $240,000 | $240,000 | $550,000 | $550,000 |

*Additional Information:*

With the purchase of additional premises, the previous mortgage had to be repaid and a new mortgage arranged with another finance company.

*17. *Brian Jones* owns a pharmacy. He is told by his accountant that the funds earned from current operations for the year were $14,000, but he is perturbed by the low state of his bank balance. During the course of the year, he had withdrawn $7,000 as a personal salary. He had hoped to take an overseas trip in the near future and had planned to withdraw $10,000 for the purpose, but he now finds that not sufficient cash is available. He wishes to know "where the money has gone". He realizes that his premises were extended during the year, but claims that this expenditure was more than covered by a mortgage.

Prepare a funds statement in an appropriate form to answer his question.

*Trial Balances*

|  | 1 Jan. | | 31 Dec. | |
|---|---|---|---|---|
|  | Dr. $ | Cr. $ | Dr. $ | Cr. $ |
| Sales |  |  |  | 64,000 |
| Cost of Goods Sold |  |  | 38,000 |  |
| Salaries |  |  | 12,000 |  |
| Cash | 7,000 |  | 1,000 |  |
| Debtors | 4,000 |  | 6,000 |  |
| Merchandise Inventory | 8,000 |  | 13,000 |  |
| Premises | 24,000 |  | 30,000 |  |
| Fixtures and Fittings | 3,000 |  | 6,000 |  |
| Creditors |  | 6,000 |  | 1,000 |
| Mortgage |  |  |  | 8,000 |
| Capital |  | 40,000 |  | 40,000 |
| Drawings |  |  | 7,000 |  |
|  | $46,000 | $46,000 | $113,000 | $113,000 |

18. *Ebert* is a sole trader and presents the following trial balances to you for analysis. His business has earned a profit during the year and he is concerned that he cannot withdraw funds without worsening the liquidity position of the business.

Ebert — Sole Trader

*Trial Balances*

|  | 1 Jan. | | 31 Dec. | |
|---|---|---|---|---|
|  | Dr. $ | Cr. $ | Dr. $ | Cr. $ |
| Sales |  |  |  | 70,000 |
| Cost of Sales |  |  | 25,000 |  |
| Expenses (Including Depreciation) |  |  | 19,000 |  |
| Plant | 20,000 |  | 25,000 |  |
| Land | 17,000 |  | 30,000 |  |
| Vehicles | 10,000 |  | 10,000 |  |
| Accumulated Depreciation |  |  |  |  |
| Plant |  | 4,000 |  | 5,500 |
| Vehicles |  | 2,000 |  | 3,000 |
| Debtors (Net) | 10,250 |  | 13,750 |  |
| Merchandise | 9,000 |  | 12,650 |  |
| Bank | 1,250 |  |  | 2,750 |
| Creditors |  | 14,500 |  | 8,400 |
| Mortgage |  | 10,000 |  | 12,000 |
| Drawings |  |  | 3,250 |  |
| Capital |  | 37,000 |  | 37,000 |
|  | $67,500 | $67,500 | $138,650 | $138,650 |

Prepare a report explaining why he is unable to withdraw further funds.

19. From the following trial balances, prepare a suitably classified report showing where the *Gunardoo Company Ltd.* obtained its funds from over the year and how it utilized those funds.

Gunardoo Company Ltd

*Trial Balances*

|  | 1 Jan. | | 31 Dec. | |
|---|---|---|---|---|
|  | Dr. $ | Cr. $ | Dr. $ | Cr. $ |
| Bank | 27,000 | | 7,000 | |
| Accounts Receivable | 40,000 | | 56,000 | |
| Inventory | 66,000 | | 78,000 | |
| Delivery Vehicles | 30,000 | | 38,000 | |
| Accumulated Depreciation Vehicles | | 16,000 | | 21,000 |
| Shop Premises | 140,000 | | 220,000 | |
| Accumulated Depreciation of Premises | | 55,000 | | 70,000 |
| Goodwill | 27,000 | | 27,000 | |
| Accounts Payable | | 20,000 | | 24,000 |
| Notes Payable | | 24,000 | | – |
| Dividend Payable | | 7,000 | | – |
| Tax Payable | | 9,000 | | – |
| Accrued Expenses | | 1,000 | | 2,000 |
| Mortgage | | 70,000 | | 85,000 |
| Registered Capital | | 200,000 | | 200,000 |
| Unissued Capital | 110,000 | | 70,000 | |
| Asset Revaluation Reserve | | – | | 30,000 |
| Appropriation, 1 Jan. | | 38,000 | | 38,000 |
| Sales | | | | 360,000 |
| Cost of Goods Sold | | | 240,000 | |
| Salaries | | | 36,000 | |
| Advertising | | | 22,000 | |
| Interest | | | 8,000 | |
| Depreciation of Delivery Vehicles | | | 14,000 | |
| Depreciation of Premises | | | 15,000 | |
| Profit on Sale of Vehicles | | | | 1,000 |
| | $440,000 | $440,000 | $831,000 | $831,000 |

*Additional Information:*

1. During the year, vehicles which had cost $12,000 and had been depreciated to $3,000 were sold for $4,000 cash.

2. The company's premises were revalued upwards by $30,000, and extensions costing $50,000 were added to them, during the year.

3. The company repaid its old mortgage and renegotiated a new one with another finance company.

20. Use the following data to explain the distinction between the concepts of:

i. Cash surplus from operations
ii. Funds flow from operations
iii. Accounting net income.

A. M. Sales Pty. Ltd.
Information extracted from the records of A. M. Sales Pty. Ltd. for month of May:

|  | $ |
|---|---|
| Sales: | |
| Credit | 40,000 |
| Cash | 35,000 |
| Purchases: | |
| Cash | 18,500 |
| Credit | 21,500 |
| Merchandise Inventory: | |
| BOM | 3,500 |
| EOM | 4,500 |
| Assets of the firm include: | |
| Buildings (net) | 40,000 |
| Plant (net) | 25,000 |
| Other Equipment (net) | 9,000 |

These assets are depreciated on the basis of net book values at the following rates:

Plant 24 per cent per annum
Buildings 6 per cent per annum
Other 12 per cent per annum

| *Expenses* | $ |
|---|---|
| Accrued Expenses: | |
| BOM | 1,500 |
| EOM | 3,300 |
| Prepaid Expenses: | |
| BOM | 1,800 |
| EOM | 1,500 |
| Expenses paid during month: | 10,675 |

NOTE: May is the first month in which the firm has made sales and purchases on credit terms.

21. The following trial balances of the *Swivel Corporation Limited* relate to the beginning and the end of the financial year 1 January — 31 December 19X7:

Swivel Corporation Limited

*Trial Balances*

|  | 1 Jan. Dr. $ | 1 Jan. Cr. $ | 31 Dec. Dr. $ | 31 Dec. Cr. $ |
|---|---|---|---|---|
| Cash at Bank | 6,000 |  |  | 8,000 |
| Accounts Receivable | 29,000 |  | 37,000 |  |
| Merchandise Inventory | 19,000 |  | 32,000 |  |
| Prepayments, 1 Jan. | 1,000 |  |  |  |
| Delivery Vehicles (Cost) | 15,000 |  | 24,000 |  |
| Accumulated Depreciation of Vehicles, 1 Jan. |  | 4,000 |  | 4,000 |
| Premises (Cost) | 60,000 |  | 100,000 |  |
| Accumulated Depreciation of Premises, 1 Jan. |  | 12,000 |  | 12,000 |
| Accounts Payable |  | 15,000 |  | 19,000 |
| Accrued Expenses, 1 Jan. |  | 2,000 |  |  |
| Mortgage |  | 30,000 |  | 40,000 |
| Paid-up Capital |  | 60,000 |  | 90,000 |
| General Reserve, 1 Jan. |  | 5,000 |  | 5,000 |
| Appropriation, 1 Jan. |  | 2,000 |  | 2,000 |
| Sales |  |  |  | 190,000 |
| Cost of Goods Sold |  |  | 130,000 |  |
| Salaries |  |  | 16,500 |  |
| Interest |  |  | 3,000 |  |
| Advertising |  |  | 8,500 |  |
| Rates |  |  | 2,000 |  |
| Taxes Paid |  |  | 7,000 |  |
| Dividends Paid |  |  | 10,000 |  |
|  | $130,000 | $130,000 | $370,000 | $370,000 |

*Additional Data:*

i. Depreciation to be charged on delivery vehicles $3,000, and premises $6,000.
ii. Salaries owing $1,500, advertising $500.
iii. Rates paid in advance $1,000.
iv. Transfer $3,000 to General Reserve.

*Required:*

a. Prepare a funds statement for the year.

b. Prepare an income statement, appropriation statement, and balance sheet.

c. Comment briefly on the difference between the measure of "funds from operations" and net profit.

22. From the following trial balances, for Cartray Limited, prepare:
    i.   A funds statement
    ii.  An income statement, appropriation statement, and balance sheet.

Cartray Limited

*Trial Balances*

|  | 1 Jan. | | 31 Dec. | |
|---|---|---|---|---|
|  | Dr. $ | Cr. $ | Dr. $ | Cr. $ |
| Accounts Receivable | 46,000 | | 54,000 | |
| Accounts Payable. | | 22,000 | | 28,000 |
| Accumulated Depreciation of Delivery Vehicles | | 12,000 | | 12,000 |
| Advertising | | | 11,000 | |
| Appropriation | | 16,000 | | 16,000 |
| Asset Revaluation Reserve | | | | 25,000 |
| Bank | 25,000 | | 20,000 | |
| Cost of Goods Sold | | | 246,000 | |
| Debentures | | 20,000 | | 35,000 |
| Delivery Vehicles | 40,000 | | 40,000 | |
| Dividend | | | 8,000 | |
| Directors' Fees | | | 5,000 | |
| General Reserve | | 25,000 | | 25,000 |
| Goodwill | 20,000 | | 20,000 | |
| Interest | | | 3,000 | |
| Merchandise Inventory | 54,000 | | 82,000 | |
| Office Expenses | | | 5,000 | |
| Office Salaries | | | 8,000 | |
| Paid-up Capital | | 130,000 | | 150,000 |
| Premises | 40,000 | | 100,000 | |
| Sales | | | | 334,000 |
| Sales Returns | | | 4,000 | |
| Salesmen's Salaries | | | 19,000 | |
|  | $225,000 | $225,000 | $625,000 | $625,000 |

*Additional Data:*

i.   Depreciation to be charged on delivery vehicles at 20 per cent on cost
ii.  Provide for final dividend $7,000 and taxation $10,000
iii. Write $6,000 off goodwill
iv.  Salesmen's salaries owing on 31 December $1,000
v.   The company's existing premises were revalued upwards by $25,000 early in the year.

23. The following balance sheet relates to the *Winray Co. Ltd.* on 1 January, 19X8.

Winray Company Limited

*Balance Sheet as at 1 Jan. 19X8*

| Current Assets | $ | $ | Current Liabilities | $ | $ |
|---|---|---|---|---|---|
| Cash at Bank | 8,000 | | Accounts Payable | 19,000 | |
| Accounts | | | Dividends Payable | 5,000 | |
| Receivable | 22,000 | | Taxes Payable | 3,000 | 27,000 |
| Inventories | 30,000 | 60,000 | | | |
| | | | | | |
| *Long-Term Assets* | | | *Shareholders' Funds* | | |
| Plant | 60,000 | | Paid-up Capital | 50,000 | |
| Less Accumulated | | | Retained Earnings | 13,000 | 63,000 |
| Depreciation | 30,000 | 30,000 | | | |
| | | $90,000 | | | $90,000 |

At present, the company is renting its premises and they have been offered for sale to it at a price of $60,000. The company has decided to buy them, and it can arrange mortgage finance of $50,000 for a ten-year, fifteen-year, or twenty-year period. It has decided to raise immediately $10,000 additional capital to help finance the purchase.

Which mortgage period should the company select if it wishes to repay the mortgage from internal sources as soon as it has the ability to do so and having regard to the fact that its plant will need replacing in five year's time?

The outlay on the new plant is expected to be $70,000, and its salvage value zero. The company would make a new share issue to the extent necessary to finance the plant replacement.

Assume that no growth in its business is expected, that the existing levels of current assets and current liabilities at each budget date are maintained, that the annual dividend and tax payments are maintained at the levels shown in the balance sheet, and that Funds from Operations remain constant at $18,000 each year.

To help in the selection of the appropriate mortgage period, prepare budgeted funds statements covering the periods up to the time:

i. Immediately after the purchase of the building to show how its purchase is to be financed

ii. Immediately after the plant replacement to show how it is to be financed

iii. Immediately after repayment of the mortgage to show when it can be repaid.

*24. *The Bushwacka Trading Co. Ltd.,* of Sydney, is planning to establish a major new branch in the booming mining township of Deadhorse Creek. The management estimates that the cost of establishing the new store would be $3,000,000; and that it could not embark on the project for another two years. It is currently examining the financing of the new store.

The balance sheet of the company at 31 December 19X1 is as follows:

| Current Assets | $ | $ | Current Liabilities | $ | $ |
|---|---|---|---|---|---|
| Debtors (Net) | 1,400,000 | | Bank Overdraft | 800,000 | |
| Inventories | 700,000 | 2,100,000 | Creditors | 400,000 | |
| | | | Tax Payable | 200,000 | |
| | | | Dividends Payable | 100,000 | 1,500,000 |
| *Long-Term Assets* | | | *Long-Term Liabilities* | | |
| Government | | | Notes Payable | | 600,000 |
| Bonds | 700,000 | | *Shareholders' Equity* | | |
| Motor Vehicles | | | | | |
| (Net) | 60,000 | | Paid-up Capital | 2,000,000 | |
| Premises (Net) | 1,500,000 | 2,260,000 | Retained Profits | 260,000 | 2,260,000 |
| | | $4,360,000 | | | $4,360,000 |

The following operating results are expected for the next two years:

| | 19X2 | 19X3 |
|---|---|---|
| | $ | $ |
| Net Sales | $3,400,000 | $4,000,000 |
| COGS | 2,200,000 | 2,600,000 |
| Wages and Salaries | 500,000 | 600,000 |
| Advertising | 100,000 | 100,000 |
| Depreciation | 140,000 | 140,000 |
| Dividends | 100,000 | 100,000 |
| Company Tax | 200,000 | 250,000 |

The figures for tax and dividends are the expected payments for each year.

Other transactions planned for the period are:

i.   Additional motor vehicles to be bought in 19X2 at a cost of $60,000
ii.  The long-term notes are due for repayment in December 19X3
iii. The level of inventories is to be raised to $900,000 by December 19X2
iv.  The bank overdraft is to be reduced to $600,000 by December 19X2
v.   Assume no changes occur in the remaining assets and liabilities.

The company would be prepared to sell its government bonds if the money is required for the Deadhorse Creek project. They would be sold at face value.

How much money does it appear that the company will have to raise about the end of 19X3 to finance the new store?

Prepare your answer in the form of a budgeted funds statement for the two years.

# Chapter 19
# The Pure Historic Cost Valuation System Reviewed

We have now covered accounting for the firm's transactions and the preparation of the major financial reports in the pure historic cost valuation system. This system is the simplest one and it is the one from which the more complex ones are developed. All transactions between the firm and its markets are recorded, and they are recorded in the dollar values applying at the time of the transaction. We now review the system, and in particular examine the relationships between the various reports; the concepts of income, capital maintenance and assets; and how well it fulfills the objectives of a financial information system plus its major limitations.

## RELATIONSHIP BETWEEN THE MAJOR ACCOUNTING REPORTS

The economic activity of the firm involves a flow of resources between the firm and its factor markets and between the firm and its product markets, offset by reverse flows of finance and ultimately of cash. (chapter 5). The current operating segments of the three flow reports (cash, funds, and income statements) would all be identical over the life of the firm since all credit transactions would have been liquidated and all operating assets used up or sold. However, because of the need to determine the economic results of the firm periodically (chapter 3), the continuous flow of activity is divided up into accounting periods (chapter 4) and summaries are prepared of the cash inflows and outflows, sources and uses of funds and income earned during the period, inter alia (chapters 6, 17, and 18). However, the cycles involving the three flows of cash, funds, and income do not coincide *within each period* where credit transactions occur and long-term assets are used, so that three flow reports are necessary to report on all aspects of current operating activity.

Fundamentally, the funds statement and the income statement are closely allied to the cash flow statement, but not necessarily to the cash flow statement of the *same period*. Thus all items in the funds statement which have not passed through the current period's cash flow statement (i.e., unliquidated credit transactions) must have passed through a previous cash statement *or* will go through a future one. The same applies to the income statement – it may be viewed as a cash flow statement adjusted for time leads and lags. Current revenue, for example, must be recorded in a cash statement of a past, current, or future period. For every revenue recognized in the current period but not received in cash, a financial claim asset of equal value is recorded. All expenses must similarly be recorded – for example, expenses paid this year for the benefit of next year's operations are recorded as prepayments, those paid for next year in respect of this year's operations are accrued expenses, and long-term asset expenditures are merely lump-sum payments covering several years' expenses.

In fact the criterion of the amount of revenue or expense to recognize in an accounting period is the amount of cash ultimately to be received or paid out on operations. Over the life of the firm, therefore, all revenue recorded in the funds and income statements must be recorded as cash received from operations, while all expenses incurred must be recorded as cash payments for operations.

In a comparison of the major reports for a particular period, it can be seen that the major difference between the cash flow and funds statements lies in the first one being restricted to external cash transactions only whereas the funds statement embraces all cash and credit transactions. The cash surplus on operations shows the amount of cash generated from current trading, and this is reflected by an increase in the cash asset in the balance sheet. The funds earned from operations are reflected in an increase in gross assets in the balance sheet. The income statement encompasses all items in the current operating segment of the funds statement and includes as well events internal to the firm (to recognize the using up of its own long-term assets). Income from operations is therefore reflected by an increase in net assets in the balance sheet. The appropriation statement overlaps part of the cash and funds flow statements where some profits have been paid out over the period, while the other appropriations appear in the balance sheet (for example, provisions made for dividends and tax, and transfers to reserves). Finally the balance sheet incorporates all the "capital" segments of the cash and funds flow statements involving assets and liabilities on hand at the end of the period, plus the residual equity.

Although each accounting report contains a substantial overlap with other accounting reports because of time leads and lags in different aspects of transactions, each one is important in its own right because it summarizes those different aspects of transactions. Many claims have been made in the past about the relative merits of each report. In particular one school of thought argues that the income statement is pre-eminent, while another that the balance sheet is. But such arguments are really futile – each report is important for its own end use. If the user wants detailed information about the firm's cash situation, the cash flow statement is the appropriate report; if he wants to know how the firm's operations were financed, the funds statement is most useful; if he wants to know how the profit was earned, the income statement is relevant; and so on. Accounting reports are the *joint* output of the information processing system, and each has an important role in the financial information system.

## THE HISTORIC COST CONCEPTS OF INCOME AND ASSETS

The historic cost concept of income is likewise based upon the notion of the ultimate cash surplus on operations — over the life of the firm, profit is the excess of cash revenue over cash expenses; and within any one period it is the excess of revenue ultimately to be received in cash over expenses ultimately involving cash outlays. For any one period, it is the surplus of the inflow of assets over the outflow of assets caused by current trading activity. The historic cost concept of periodic income is based upon maintaining intact the initial monetary investment in the firm. Income is the surplus generated from operations after maintaining intact this initial investment, and it is reflected by the increase in the net assets of the firm as valued at their transaction prices (less amortizations where applicable). The matching principle is used to measure periodic profit, and it is basically a process of recovering monetary expenditures from revenue before a profit is deemed to be earned. By charging the cost of goods sold, wages, depreciation, and so on as expenses of earning revenue, the firm is recovering the expenditures on these resources from the cash inflow from sales. Profit results only if revenue provides more than sufficient cash (ultimately) to recover the cash outlays on the resources consumed in the revenue-earning process. For example, if the cost of goods sold is $1,000, then no profit is made until this $1,000 is recovered (along with other expenses of the period), from the revenue of the period. Only by first recouping these expenses from revenue can the initial investment be maintained intact; that is, the investment in the resources used up must be replaced from revenue. However this does not mean that within any *particular* period the firm necessarily recovers from revenue received in cash form all the expenses paid for in cash in that same period. A profit-making firm can incur a cash deficit on operations in a period (for example, where credit sales are growing); conversely, a firm can incur a net loss in a period, yet still have a cash surplus during the period (for example, where credit sales are falling). Likewise, recovery of the money spent on resources in earning the period's revenue does not mean that *cash* is available to replace those resources in the same period. The recovery is of resources in general, and not of cash in particular. The funds statement can be arranged to show the form of the resources recovered. The financial manager should arrange the affairs of the firm in such a way that sufficient of its resources are converted into cash when needed.

The above results always apply in the historical cost system even though there are many different methods of recovering historical outlays on inventories and fixed assets. The use of different historical cost allocation methods causes the pattern of cost recovery to differ over time (for example, the use of FIFO versus LIFO, or straight line versus reducing balance depreciation), but all methods are based on recovery of initial investment of resources consumed in earning revenue; that is, they are all based on the concept of maintaining intact the initial monetary investment.

The most accurate description of assets and expenses in the pure historical cost system is that contained in Gilman's *Accounting Concepts of Profit*.[1] Gilman defines expenses as the historical outlays on resources which are to be currently charged against revenue. He defines and classifies assets as:

1. Cash and claims to cash, for example, cash on hand and at bank

2. Deferred claims to cash; for example, accounts receivable, investments in securities

3. Deferred charges to future revenue; for example, inventories (charged as cost of goods sold), plant and buildings (charged as depreciation), and prepaid expenses (amortized on a strict time basis).

This classification of assets is superior, from an analytical point of view, to the conventional "liquidity plus intended use basis". It reflects the position of assets with respect to the cash cycle — some assets are already in cash form, others are in the final stage of conversion into cash, while the third group can be converted into cash only by passing through the revenue-earning process by contributing to revenue and being recovered as expenses from that revenue. Thus the net balance sheet values of inventories, plant, buildings, and so on refer to the amounts of expenditures on these assets which have still to be recovered from future revenues or resale of the assets.

Gilman's classification is not used in practice because it does not convey the picture that the balance sheet is a statement of financial position; rather, it shows the balance sheet to be the vehicle for storing up expenditures until they can be expensed against revenue. Financial position refers to the firm's ability to meet its financial commitments, and it is assessed by comparing the current market values of assets and their liquidity with the size and repayment dates of liabilities. Assets described in the Gilman manner are meaningful as part of the measure of financial position only if their historic cost values in fact coincide with their current market values. The historic cost balance sheet is not primarily intended as a statement of financial position, and it will only be a reliable one in the idealized conditions analyzed in chapter 21.

### THE REALIZATION CONCEPT

Implicit in the historic cost system is the notion that an economic event must involve realization for it to be recognized in the accounts. Realization in this context means that cash or financial claims must be obtained. The concept of realization is tied to the notion of a transaction — the event cannot be regarded as a transaction unless realization is involved. It is claimed that adherence to the realization concept is necessary for objective measurement of profits and asset values, as there is then evidence of the amount involved in the transaction. Only realized profits can be recognized.

Application of the realization concept means that all accounting records must be kept in terms of historic transaction prices and that subsequent changes in market prices of assets are disregarded. Other valuation systems are precluded by its use.

### THE HISTORIC COST SYSTEM AS A FINANCIAL INFORMATION SYSTEM

The usefulness of any accounting system must be judged by the extent to which it fulfills its main functions in satisfying the requirements of users for information. These requirements and information standards were analyzed in chapter 3. Users want to know how relevant, reliable, and so on the information is for such purposes as measuring profit performance and financial position, as a basis for forecasting future performance and position, as a basis for decision-making and control, and for reporting on the stewardship of funds.

#### Advantages of the Historic Cost System

In terms of the functions to be served by accounting data, it would appear that the historic cost value system serves some well but not others. Because it is primarily concerned with cash flows resulting from the transactions of the firm (with appropriate adjustments for accruals and deferrals in income and financial position measurement), the historic cost system serves the *stewardship function* very well, that is, of managers reporting back to owners of funds on their custodianship of such funds. The historic exchange price property of the dollar is the relevant dimension to measure for stewardship purposes. The historic cost system provides a summary of all transactions involving either cash or credit. The cash flow statement is fully objective and verifiable. But it is not as comprehensive a stewardship report as the funds statement, which reports on *all* external transactions of the firm involving funds. Furthermore, the funds statement is almost fully objective (very few assumptions are required in its preparation) and it is not cluttered up with non-fund items which are irrelevant to the stewardship function. It does not try to measure the satisfaction of other objectives such as profit performance for which it is ill-equipped.

Sound stewardship of funds is essential in any modern economy, be it capitalist or socialist. Funds are entrusted to professional managers by private investors and governments for use in business or government operations, and the economic system would break down if these funds were subject to substantial embezzlement or crass mismanagement. The stewardship function of management is the basis of company and other parts of business law, and it is a primary reason for the compulsory audit of the accounts of public companies and governments. Auditors are appointed by the shareholders of a company or by the government for its own operations to check on the stewardship of funds and on the reliability of its financial reports. Auditors are often likened to the watchdogs of shareholders' interests, and, when the occasion demands, to bloodhounds. (Unfortunately in some instances they appear to play the role of pet poodles to management.)

By basing the measure of income on maintaining the owners' initial monetary investment intact in the firm, the historic cost system helps to ensure the maintenance of a minimum level of assets for the *protection of creditors*. Creditors can normally rely on the firm maintaining this minimum level of assets so that, when their claims are not met voluntarily, they have recourse to these assets. The legal concept of distributable profits of companies is closely allied to this notion of capital maintenance. It is a serious offence for companies to pay dividends out of capital as this impairs the stock of assets that must be kept intact for the protection of creditors. But unfortunately this whole principle can be reduced to a farce by the use of "$2 proprietary limited companies". Here, the company needs only to maintain assets costing $2, i.e., the value of its paid-up capital, to satisfy legal requirements, and creditors can be unaware of this small asset backing because the company is a proprietary one. (This is of course a criticism of the inadequate disclosure requirements for proprietary limited companies and not of the historic cost system.)

A third advantage of the historic cost system is that it is necessary for all types of *administrative control*. Records must be kept of all cash receipts and payments to ensure cash control, of all debtors and creditors to ensure that financial claims are settled by the due dates, and so on. It provides management with information to ensure that sufficient cash is kept on hand to meet commitments. It provides a useful basis for comparisons by management of forecasted actions with actual actions and consequently for the analysis of variances between the two. This comparison must be made to ensure achievement of the firm's objectives and plans, and to ensure efficiency of operations.

Fourthly, the system provides a necessary basis for *forecasting future events*. An analysis of historical events is generally the best single basis for forecasting, though normally it must be supplemented by additional information.

Next, the historic cost system is generally favoured for *taxation* purposes because it provides verifiable evidence about transactions. Administrative expediency and verifiability are important in any tax scheme so as to minimize costs of administering the scheme and the scope for tax avoidance.

Finally, it can provide a reasonable measure of a firm's *short-term financial position* for the benefit of short-term creditors and management. Short-term liabilities and monetary assets are already in current terms; if the estimate of bad debts is reliable and the debtors are short-term ones, and if the inventories have been recently acquired, it is likely that their values will be reasonably good measures of the resources available to meet the firm's current liabilities.

### Deficiencies of the System

While the historic cost system serves some uses fairly well, it does not satisfy some other requirements of an information system nearly as fully. It can be particularly faulty with respect to long-term decision-making and the measurement and analysis of profit performance and long-term financial position, because it omits *necessary information* about changes in market prices of the firm's assets away from their historic costs, changes in the purchasing power of the dollar, and changes in expectations about the future.

*1. The historic cost system disregards changes in asset prices and inflation*

Where inflation is occurring and the value of the dollar is declining, it is likely that the market prices of some assets change substantially away from their historic costs. Both factors affect measurement of the long-term financial position and performance of firms. Properties of the dollar other than historic exchange prices are more relevant for these purposes in an inflationary period. Analysis of a firm's profit performance, financial structure, and financial position is misleading unless all financial reports are based on current market prices of assets and liabilities. Only then are the dollar figures of assets, expenses, revenues, and liabilities comparable. All these price changes are disregarded in the historic cost system. As a consequence, this means in particular that:

i. Capital gains and losses resulting from changes in the market prices of assets are not recorded as they arise but only as they are realized. Hence reported capital gains and losses for any one period are incomplete (as they are not recognized until the asset is sold) and net profit for the period can be understated. But against this, some capital gains and losses of former periods may be recognized in the current period when assets are sold, and current profits are overstated to this extent. This adherence to the realization concept offends the timeliness standard for information and can distort the comparability of periodic profits. It also enables management in some circumstances to sell assets and hence realize capital gains or losses according to the time they wish to disclose them. A further consequence of the non-recognition of unrealized capital gains and losses is that current market values of assets are not reported in the balance sheet. The balance sheet is not a statement of current financial position in these circumstances.

"The Fable of the Two Investment Trusts" provides a memorable example of the distortions to periodic income and asset measurement caused by the realization principle in a period of changing prices.[2] Each trust began with $1,000 for investment in securities, and one bought stock A while the other bought stock B. By the end of the year both stocks had doubled in price and paid dividends of $100. The first trust sold its stock for $2,000 on 31 December, and re-invested the proceeds immediately in stock B. In its final reports it shows assets of $2,100 and income of $1,100. The second trust likewise adheres to historic cost principles but it reports assets of $1,100 and income of $100 because the stock price appreciation is unrealized. Yet both trusts are in an identical situation at the end of the year!

Because changes in asset prices are ignored, the financial reports may not, therefore, reliably indicate a firm's long-term debt-paying capacity, the protection afforded to creditors, the risks undertaken by owners, and the rewards available to them. Such reports may lead to unsound lending by creditors, and unsound financial structure decisions by management, investment decisions by shareholders, and so on.

ii. There is no recognition of changes in the general price level and thus no separation of real and monetary elements in reported profit figures and no reliable statement of real net worth in the balance sheet. Such a statement is necessary if real capital is to be maintained intact, for measurement of economic performance of the firm and for sound long-term financing decisions.

iii.The income concept employed is based on maintaining money capital intact and not either physical or real capital intact, and this can cause subsequent financial problems in the replacement of assets used up in operations during an inflationary period. The amount of expenses recovered from revenue does not enable all assets to be replaced and this gives rise to problems of "capital erosion". Only past outlays are recovered, and if asset prices have risen in the meantime the funds recovered from operations are not sufficient to replace the resources consumed. For example, if the historical cost of goods sold is $1,000 and the firm recovers that amount, it may find that $1,200 is now required to replace the same quantity of inventories, i.e., to maintain its physical capital intact. This means that historic cost income is overstated in terms of current or real income, and the rates of return on investment arc exaggerated because the numerator in the formula can be overstated and the denominator understated. This can lead to inappropriate investment decisions by management and shareholders, cause share prices to be overstated, and so on.

## 2. Expectations of future trading conditions are disregarded

Even though they are the most important determinant of the firm's economic value, future trading conditions are ignored as the system is backward looking. Firms typically experience cycles of growth and recession — the current situation embodied in recent historical reports does not fully repeat itself into perpetuity. Information about future events and prospects is necessary for all decisions about future action by management, shareholders, creditors, and so forth.

## 3. A very wide choice of measurement rules is permitted

The historic cost system provides for a large number of options in the methods of cost allocation, and hence in the measurement of profits and asset values. It has been calculated that for a manufacturing company applying the rules permitted by the generally accepted principles of accounting (G.A.A.P.), there are 108 different methods of inventory valuation, 24 methods of fixed asset valuation, and 48 methods available for the valuation of security investments.[3] For a company with a wide spread of assets, there are 108 x 24 x 48 = 124,416 methods available for the valuation of assets! This can provide enormous scope for variations in financial reports of a company prepared according to G.A.A.P. and it becomes exceedingly difficult to interpret them and to compare them over time or between companies. It is no wonder that balance sheets used to be generally defined by professional bodies as the list of ledger account balances remaining open at the end of the year. In this definition there is no pretence that the balance sheet is a useful financial report.

On the other hand it should be noted that, although this vast array of options is available to the accountant in measuring income and financial position, in many cases the same measures will be obtained whether one or another rule is used; that the rules envisage certain important departures from historical cost (as discussed in chapter 20); and that the choice of rules to apply can be substantially constrained by (a) applying sensible guidelines to their selection — e.g., long-term asset costs to be allocated over the expected revenue-producing periods in a systematic manner and according to expected benefit flows, and FIFO to be used in inventory valuation; and by (b) the use of consistent methods over time and between firms. While such rules may not be perfect, they can be sensible and yield results which are in accord with other indicators of performance, such as the firm's volume of activity or its ability to pay its debts.

### 4. No external verification of the results of its measurements is possible

It is frequently claimed that the historic cost system is objective as compared with alternative accounting systems. However, this claim overlooks the distinction between the basic transaction data and process of converting those data into measures of historic cost income and financial position, i.e., between the inputs into the information system and their transformation into financial information. The transaction data themselves and the cash and funds statements summarizing them are objective (or nearly so). But many assumptions must be made about future events and a choice must be made from a myriad of rules in the transformation process to measure periodic income and financial position, such that these concepts are not capable of objective measurement except in highly idealized circumstances.

The major conceptual weakness of the historic cost system of periodic income measurement and asset valuation is that there is no provable basis for determining the portion of any given investment which has been used up in earning the revenue of that period, i.e., the expense (and which therefore must be recovered in that period to maintain capital intact); and by corollary, the amount which is still to be used up, i.e., the asset (and recovered in future years as expense charges or from the resale of the asset). There is no reference to external market prices of assets at the balance sheet date to establish the validity of the amended historic cost values. One cannot prove that the historic cost of inventories on hand is $10,000, that the historic cost value of depreciated plant is $20,000, and so on, except in the idealized conditions of the stationary state. The historic cost system concentrates on the objectivity of the inputs to the information system rather than the outputs from the system.

In summary then, the historic cost system fulfills some but not all requirements for information. Other valuation systems which take account of changes in asset prices, inflation, and expectations must be used to satisfy these requirements. In terms of the standards for accounting information, the system scores well on the standards of relevance, verifiability, and so on for such purposes as stewardship and administrative control, but it cannot always be rated highly for other purposes such as the measurement of economic performance and financial position, and for decision-making.

In fact no one valuation system can provide complete information for all purposes. The historic cost valuation system is the starting point for the more sophisticated systems — it is a necessary but not sufficient information system.

## FURTHER READING

A.A.A. "The Realization Concept." *Accounting Review* (April 1965).

Chambers, R. J. "Financial Information and the Securities Market." *Abacus* (September 1965).

Gilman, S. *Accounting Concepts of Profit*. New York: Ronald Press Co., 1939, Chap. 19.

MacNeal, K. *Truth in Accounting*. Philadelphia: University of Pennsylvania Press, 1939. Chap. 1.

Nelson, G. K. "Current and Historical Costs in Financial Statements." *Accounting Review* (January 1966).

Storey, R. K. "Cash Movements and Periodic Income Determination." In Zeff, S., and Keller, W. *Financial Accounting Theory*. New York: McGraw-Hill, 1964.

## NOTES

1. Gilman, *Accounting Concepts of Profit*, p. 300.
2. "The Fable of the Two Flour Mills", and "The Fable of the Two Investment Trusts", are told in MacNeal, *Truth in Accounting*, chap. 1.
3. Chambers, "Financial Information and the Securities Market", p. 16.

## QUESTIONS

1. Consider the following items and their dates.
   For each one, specify for the dual aspects of the transaction or event:

   i.    The accounting reports in which it is included
   ii.   The accounting periods in which it is included.

   All accounting periods follow the calendar year.

   Set out your answer in the form of a table as follows:

| Years | Income Statement | Balance Sheet | Cash Flow Statement | Funds Statement |
|-------|------------------|---------------|---------------------|-----------------|
|       |                  |               |                     |                 |

   a.   Merchandise purchased November 1972 on credit, to be paid for in January 1973

   b.   Merchandise purchased for cash November 1972

   c.   Merchandise sold for cash November 1972

   d.   Merchandise sold on hire purchase November 1972, repayment spread over two years, first payment November 1972

   e.   Repayments on the above sale

   f.   Rates paid January 1972 for one year in advance

   g.   Rates paid October 1972 for one year in advance

   h.   Plant purchased on credit December 1972, to be paid for in February 1973, estimated life three years

   i.   Annual depreciation on the above plant

   j.   Three-year loan raised June 1972, interest payable in June of each year

k.    Wages paid in December 1972 for work done

l.    Wages accrued end December 1972, to be paid in January 1973.

Comment in general on the above with respect to which reports the items are included.

2.    Explain the relationship between the cash flow, funds, and income statements in terms of leads and lags in cash flows.

3.    Explain the statement that the historic cost income statement is a period-adjusted cash flow statement.

4.    Explain and compare the following concepts:

i.     The cash surplus on operations
ii.    Funds from operations
iii.   Historic cost net operating income.

For what purpose is each concept required? Does the sum of each over the "long-run" tend to equality?

5.    Explain Gilman's concept and classification of assets.

6.    Critically examine whether profits should be realized, i.e., available in cash or financial claims, before being recognized as having been earned. Illustrate your answer with respect to "The Fable of the Two Flour Mills".

7.    For the purposes of:

i.     assessing the stewardship of company management

ii.    assisting in the administrative control of a company

iii.   measuring the profit performance and current financial position of a company

iv.    deciding as a shareholder whether to buy or sell your shares in the company

how would you rate the financial reports prepared under historic cost accounting against each of the standards for accounting information? Give a brief reason for each answer, and assume that there is inflation in the economy.

8.    Critically examine the claim that historic cost income statements and balance sheets are "objective".

9.    Critically examine the major advantages and limitations of historic cost accounting for the measurement of income and financial position during a period of inflation.

10.   "The historic cost system provides a measure of periodic income which cannot be distributed to shareholders without causing capital erosion." Discuss.

# Chapter 20
# External Influences on Accounting

The historic cost system as outlined to date is not applied in its pure, rigid form in the business world. An analytical approach has been adopted here, whereas the profession adopts a pragmatic one. In reality, many ad hoc modifications to a pure historic cost system are made to accommodate the inherent conservatism of the accounting profession and various external pressures on accounting.

These outside influences arise mainly from three sources — management, taxation, and law — and in practice they often dominate accounting measurements and published reports. The modifications sometimes involve departures from historic cost and at other times involve distorted allocations of historic costs of assets between periods. Accounting in reality is very pragmatic and is little concerned with logical precision or consistency. Particular problems are considered in isolation, and they are not examined within the context of an overall logically consistent accounting theory. For example, the problem of inventory valuation may not be considered as an aspect of income determination; likewise the problem of long-term asset valuation; the connection between income measurement and asset valuation is not always recognized; current replacement costs or realizable values are used for some assets but not for others, and there is no recognition of the need for consistency in the use of valuation bases; and so on. This piecemeal approach often results in logically inconsistent practices being applied; practices moreover which are virtually dictated to the accountant by these outside influences which have ends to satisfy other than those of accounting. Much of the current confusion in accounting practice and criticism of the profession arises from the use of inconsistent or irrelevant accounting procedures.

## THE DOCTRINE OF CONSERVATISM

Some of the most important influences on accounting are embodied in the *doctrine of conservatism*. Different aspects of conservatism are reflected in the accounting reports because of management policies, law, and the desire of accountants to be "on the safe side" in all matters where judgment is involved. An accounting doctrine is "a belief generally held and advocated by accountants as to what accounting practices ought to be".[1] It is a statement of policy objectives, whereas the conventions of accounting are rationalizations of generally adopted practices. Some company managements apply the doctrine of conservatism in their accounting and disclosure policies in such a way as always to portray the company's results in what they consider to be the most favourable light. Periodic accounting reports are distorted to suit these objectives.

The basic objectives of the doctrine of conservatism have changed over time. Initially, it began in the nineteenth century in owner-controlled firms in which owners knew the current values of their assets, and a conservative or cautious valuation of these assets was appreciated by lending institutions as a basis for making loans. Such conservatism added to the banker's security for the loan — it was the sign of prudent financial management of the firm. The policy was not applied to manipulate the firm's results or to mislead users of accounting reports.

However during the 1920s the doctrine of conservatism came to be abused and it was deliberately used to distort the firm's profit and financial position for motives both proper and improper. Here, we shall define the doctrine as a policy of deliberate understatement of profits and asset values, and overstatement of liabilities. It causes the presentation of results that are normally more pessimistic than justified. The doctrine does not appear to be applied as excessively nowadays as it has been in the past, though it still seems to be applied on a moderate scale by a large segment of industry.

The doctrine can be applied in many ways, the most important of which are as follows:

1. Inconsistent application of the realization concept. The realization concept is adhered to when it suits the accountant to do so, but is departed from in other circumstances indicated below.

   i. The use of inconsistent bases for recognizing revenues and expenses. Thus revenues are recognized only when realized, but expenses are provided for as soon as there is any possibility that they may be incurred. The policy here is one of never anticipating revenues, but always anticipating expenses.

   ii. The use of inconsistent bases for recognizing capital gains and losses. As in (i), capital gains are not recognized and recorded until they are realized on the sale of the asset, whereas capital losses are recognized immediately a reduction in market prices occurs. Moreover the lower of market replacement cost or selling value is used. Firms do not hesitate to write down the values of their assets, but they are reluctant to record appreciations in value. This "principle" is embodied in the so-called golden rule of inventory valuation, "cost or market, whichever is lower" (or COMWIL), which has almost universal application in industry. In the interpretation of this rule, several meanings may be attached to "market" value. It may mean replacement cost, or it may mean selling price less normal profit margin (net selling value). Hence, if the selling price is reduced, the value of the inventory is reduced below historical cost to the lower of the replacement cost or the "net selling value". To illustrate the rule in its simplest form, consider the following example. An item of merchandise costs $10, and normally sells for $15. The profit margin is 1/3 of the selling price, or conversely, cost is 2/3 of the selling price. If the replacement cost of the item declines to $9, and the selling price to $12, the inventory is valued at the lowest of historical cost ($10), replacement cost ($9), and net selling value (2/3 of 12 = $8), that is at $8. Hence the current period bears the "loss" which, through the reduction in the value of the balance sheet inventory, automatically increases the charge for the cost of goods sold of the current period. The COGS comprises both the historical COGS and the reduction in value of the balance sheet inventory, and the two amounts are not distinguished from each other in the accounting report. This raises the question of whether the *cost* of goods sold should include the *"loss"* on *goods not yet sold*. But conversely, if either the selling price or replacement cost rose, inventories would still be valued at the $10 historical cost.

2. Expenses are overstated wherever possible by anticipating future expenses, and by charging long-term expenditures to current revenue, for example, through the inappropriate use of accelerated depreciation methods, charging long-term maintenance and replacement outlays to current expense, and charging all research and development expenditures as current expenses.

3. Long-term intangible assets are written off as quickly as profits permit, to reduce the size of retained earnings.

4. All estimates are deliberately biased to suit the required end result by overstating expenses or losses (for example, through excessive estimates for bad debts, underestimates of long-term asset lives so as to increase the periodic depreciation charges, use of reducing balance depreciation when other methods would be more appropriate); by understating asset values (by the means listed immediately above, plus those in (2) and (3)), and overstating liabilities (particularly taxation).

5. Incorrect balance sheet classifications, such as showing proprietorship reserves as liabilities.

The effects of these procedures are to understate net income, assets, and proprietorship, and overstate liabilities. Hence, where the doctrine is applied, the firm's income, assets, and proprietorship are greater than the amounts disclosed, and its liabilities are less. The net amount of understatement is embodied in *secret reserves*, that is, financial resources of the firm which are not disclosed in the balance sheet. However it must be understood that secret reserves are not undisclosed hordes of cash. The term is a technical accounting one which means that the values of assets which cannot be subjected to complete verification (as can cash), i.e., all those values where assumptions and estimates are involved, are understated with respect to the pure historic cost system.

In general, the motives prompting the application of the doctrine of conservatism are honourable though misguided. The firm has 'hidden strength' which it can call upon in emergencies. Investors, creditors, and financiers can rely on the firm's net worth as disclosed in its balance sheet as being below the current market value of its assets, and this provides them with an extra cover for security. The firm's performance as indicated by its disclosed profits is normally not an outstanding one in terms of profit rates on investment and profit growth, but stability of disclosed profits helps foster the feeling of security in the firm. One of the objectives in applying the doctrine is to smooth out fluctuations in periodic profits in order to create the impression that the firm can successfully combat depressed trading conditions and hence that its management is exceptionally good. This consideration is an important one for financial institutions which rely on the public's confidence in them for their survival. The use of LIFO, optional depreciation charges, optional expensing of major repair costs, optional writing-off of intangible assets, and so on enable disclosed profits to become extremely stable.[2] Another motive for applying the doctrine is that it helps to account for future uncertainty and rises in replacement costs of assets. By understating profits and by building up secret reserves, the firm is better able financially to withstand the effects of possible future difficult trading conditions or capital losses, and to finance the replacement of assets at prices which exceed their historical cost (on which expense determination and recovery have been based). The understatement of profits may limit demands by labour unions for higher wages and by shareholders for higher dividend payments. The apparent dividend payout ratio (that is, dividends/net profit after tax) is higher where profits are understated. However it should be noted that the dividend recommendation rests with directors, as shareholders are legally prevented from proposing an increase above the rate recommended by directors. Theoretically, of course, shareholders can elect other directors who favour higher dividend rates, but in practice this is virtually impossible. Finally, it is maintained that losses ought to be recognized immediately they can be anticipated in order that future periods will not be burdened by them. Those periods will have to bear their own anticipated and actual losses.

Hence, in general, the better motives for the application of the doctrine revolve around the desire of management to protect the security of the shareholder's investment, and to protect the shareholder from himself. It is essentially a very paternalistic approach, or a "we know what's best for you" one.

Application of the doctrine of conservatism in the measurement of periodic income and balance sheet valuation is generally supported by the doctrine of conservatism in reporting to shareholders. Not only are periodic results distorted, but only the legal minimum of information is published for shareholders. The Companies Act specifies what information must be published, and companies are free to publish further information.[3] Some companies publish much more than the legal minimum, but most do not. In general, the amount of detail to be published in the balance sheet is substantial, but only a few items from the income and appropriation statements need be published. Publication requirements are briefly considered in the section below on Company Law.

### Objections to the Doctrine

The objections to the use of the doctrine of conservatism centre around the presentation of distorted and unreliable information to users, particularly external users, and that the whole rationale behind the doctrine is misguided. Its use means that the criteria of a good information system, particularly verifiability, freedom from bias, consistency, and reliability are not satisfied, and hence the information is either of limited value to users or is misleading and therefore causes incorrect decisions to be made. Even though external users can detect the application of the doctrine, they cannot estimate the actual extent of its application and hence cannot accurately allow for its distorting effects.

If the balance sheet is scarcely a statement of financial position under the pure historic cost system, it is likely to be even less so after its distortion through the doctrine of conservatism. External users must have reliable information on which to make decisions, and they are better judges of what is in their own interests than company management. Moreover, it is likely that many of the company's own managers will be misled by the distorted information, and hence make incorrect planning, control, and evaluation decisions. Frequently it is only the most senior executives who are informed of the "true" position.

The smoothing out of fluctuations in periodic income is an undesirable practice from the viewpoint of long-term creditors and shareholders as it hides some of the risk inherent in their investment in the company. It is essential that long-term investors, and shareholders in particular as they provide the risk capital for the company, are given reliable information on which to assess the risks inherent in a company's income stream. These risks determine the investment quality of the income stream and hence they affect the compensating rewards required by the investor and the company's share prices.

Although application of the doctrine reduces apparent profits, it cannot do this consistently in so far as periodic allocations are concerned. Thus, for example, if accelerated depreciation is unjustly used, the profits of the early years are understated, but those of later years must be overstated when the asset is still in use but has no unamortized cost remaining. Hence profits over time cannot be compared with reliability.

Sometimes the motive for applying the doctrine can be to protect the existing management rather than shareholders. Inefficiency and inadequate profits or losses can be hidden through undercharging expenses after some years of excessive charges. Use of the doctrine can delay the necessary reorganization of the firm's operations to make it more efficient. Access to secret reserves can be abused, and there have been some cases of fraud occurring in this way.

Excessive application of the doctrine can depress prices of the company's shares and make it an attractive takeover proposition for another company.[4] Understatement of profits and asset values reduces disclosed profits per share and net assets per share, with consequential effects on the share price. Existing shareholders may sell their shares before the takeover bid is announced and hence sell their shares at a price well below their "true" worth. Likewise, the predator company need offer only some small margin over the existing share price to succeed in the bid, and again this price may be much less than the share's "true" worth, as based on the current market values of the firm's assets and its profit prospects. In these cases, application of the doctrine is not in the interests of existing shareholders.

Similarly, its application in reporting negates some of the criteria of good communication of information to users. Significant relationships in the data may not be determinable, there may be lack of uniformity of the data within the firm and comparability over time, and the data cannot be reliably compared with those from other firms.

Use of the doctrine of conservatism in accounting results from a confusion between the roles of accounting measurement, disclosure of results, and financial policies. Accounting is basically an information collection and communication system, and by itself it cannot provide safeguards against future uncertainty, price changes, instability, financial crises, and so on. Prudent financial policies, cautious but informed and honest estimates of future magnitudes, measurement of income on a basis which allows for maintaining real capital intact and so on, are always highly desirable and necessary to facilitate the survival, growth, and profitability of the firm. The firm must always adopt financial policies which safeguard its short-term and long-term liquidity to help ensure its survival and guard against future uncertainty. But these policies can, and should, be adopted without at the same time resorting to the doctrine of conservatism. In fact, such policies can be formulated more effectively if the doctrine is not applied because they will then be based on more reliable information, for example, on a measure of income related to a concept of maintaining real capital intact, and on a balance sheet which is a statement of financial position. Similarly, use of an accounting system based on current market prices throughout enables a more accurate and comprehensive measure of the effects of rising replacement costs on the need to conserve existing financial resources, as compared with the piecemeal and secret approach applied through the doctrine of conservatism. The arguments in favour of the doctrine are, therefore, unsoundly based. Financial prudence is not a corequisite of accounting conservatism.

It scarcely needs mentioning that if one cannot satisfy the requirements of a good information system, deliberate understatement of profits and assets is preferred to deliberate overstatement of profits and assets. No justifications can be advanced for the latter.

## ASSET REVALUATION

In an inflationary period substantial increases can occur in the current market prices of long-term assets, particularly land, buildings, and share investments. Managements of progressive companies tend to recognize such appreciations in value and revalue their assets to bring their stated balance sheet values more into line with current market values.[5] The appreciation is recognized as an unrealized capital gain which is not included in income and has no direct implications for dividend policy. While in a few cases revaluations are made annually, the typical situation is for them to occur at much longer intervals, such as every five or ten years.

The entry to record the revaluation is:

|  |  | $ |
|---|---|---|
| Land and Buildings | Dr. | 1,000,000 |
| Asset Revaluation Reserve | Cr. | 1,000,000 |

The Asset Revaluation Reserve is a capital reserve included in Shareholders' Equity in the balance sheet. Frequently bonus share issues are made from asset revaluation reserves, and this has the effect of converting the reserve into paid-up capital. The entry to record such a bonus issue is:

|  |  | $ |
|---|---|---|
| Asset Revaluation Reserve | Dr. | 1,000,000 |
| Unissued Capital | Cr. | 1,000,000 |

The revaluation of assets represents a departure from the pure historic cost system and with it a relaxation of the realization concept. Progressive managements recognize the irrelevance of out-dated historic cost asset values for many purposes and the revaluation of assets represents a move towards the use of a current value system.

The non-recognition of substantial increases in asset values has been a feature of many company takeovers in Australia.[6] Predator companies analyze the financial reports of prospective victims and the current market values of their assets to determine whether a takeover bid is worth making. The predator may intend to expand his own operations, in which case he is interested in the price he has to pay for the victim's net assets compared with the prices he would have to pay for the purchase of similar assets on the open market. Alternatively, he may intend to sell up the victim's assets and make a quick capital gain — here, he is interested in the current realizable value of its assets. So long as the victim's share price is significantly below its net assets per share (valued at current prices), the predator has sufficient scope for making a successful takeover bid as he normally has to offer a price which is only marginally above the current share price.

Non-progressive and conservative companies are generally reluctant to revalue assets upwards. Their managements adhere to the doctrine of conservatism. In many cases asset revaluation would depress the rate of return on investment to unacceptably low levels and this could react against the existing management. Non-revaluation might enable an existing inefficient management to survive for longer.

## COMPANY LAW

Many accounting practices are governed by law, particularly company law in the case of normal business operations.[7] Aspects of accounting practice which have been influenced most by company law comprise the basic nature of accounting as a historic cost valuation system to serve the stewardship function of accounting, the entity concept in the case of companies, the accounting concept of profit, and the disclosure of accounting information in published reports. The first two aspects have been analyzed previously and discussion is now devoted to the remaining ones. In addition, the compulsory audit requirements for public companies normally ensure that proper accounting records are kept and this has undoubtedly raised the general standards of accounting practice.

### The Profit Concept Used in Accounting

The concept of profit employed in accounting owes much to the legal concept of divisible profits, i.e., those profits which can legally be distributed as dividends.[8] A basic principle of company law is that dividends may only be paid out of profits. They must not be paid out of capital as this would constitute a return of capital to shareholders, and the law requires special procedures to be followed for the return of capital. The Companies Act does not define the concept of profits or the maintenance of capital — rather there is only a general requirement that the final reports in which profit is measured give a "true and fair" result. It is the responsibility of the courts to interpret this requirement in a particular situation, and hence we must examine some case law to determine what constitutes distributable profit. However, court judgments on this topic are very infrequent as the courts prefer to leave profit determination to a company's management — they will not interfere except on special grounds.

The leading cases are British ones and all date back to the last century. They were concerned with specific issues rather than the general principle of what should constitute profits and there is no general statement about profit determination in them. The court decisions owe much to the writings of the classical economists on the distinction between circulating (i.e., working) capital and fixed capital, and to the need for companies to maintain sufficient assets for the protection of creditors. Trade creditors supply goods to the company and lenders supply money to it on the faith that its capital will be maintained intact. Because a company has limited liability and a legal personality separate from that of its owners, creditors have no recourse to the personal assets of owners and hence they must rely on the company's maintaining a fund of assets. The courts have insisted that companies maintain capital intact for the protection of creditors.

However, this rule is not free from ambiguity as it depends upon the method of determining the fund of net assets represented by paid-up capital. A series of leading British cases endeavoured to clarify the principles involved in the late nineteenth century. In *Lee* v. *Neuchatel Asphalte Company* (1889), it was held that a company need not make up the capital lost through a decline in the value of its assets. Dividends could be paid out of profits calculated by established business principles (which at the time neglected such reductions in asset values). The rule was modified in *Verner* v. *General and Commercial Investment Trust* (1894) to take account of the division between circulating and fixed capital, and it was held that losses or reductions in value of circulating capital must be made good, whereas those in fixed capital need not be. In other words it is required that losses on inventories be recognized but that losses on fixed assets need not be, and depreciation does not have to be charged to maintain capital intact. The question of losses of prior years arose in the *National Bank of Wales Case* (1899) — should operating losses of previous years be recouped in this year's profit calculation before a distributable profit is made? The court held that they need not be — each year's profit calculation is considered to be a separate matter. Hence a company can pay dividends out of current profits even though it has accumulated losses and has not therefore maintained its capital intact. In a recent case, *Dimbula Valley (Ceylon) Tea Company* v. *Laurie* (1961), it was ruled that a bonus share issue could be made from an unrealized appreciation in fixed assets, and the judge expressed the opinion that a cash dividend could likewise be made from an unrealized profit on fixed assets.

This appears to be the situation as it exists in Australia today and in the United States as well. If the management does not want to do so, it is not necessary for companies to charge depreciation on fixed assets, recognize losses of fixed assets in the measure of distributable profit, or make up the accumulated trading losses of previous years. Conversely, there is no legal obligation on them to recognize capital gains on fixed assets, but, if they do so, such gains can form part of distributable profits. These legal principles provide the reason for many companies' not charging depreciation on buildings, although they charge depreciation on most other fixed assets because it is allowed for tax purposes.

The approach adopted by the courts of relying on currently accepted business practice and avoiding any definition of business income means that they provide little guidance as to what the concept of income for use in accounting ought to be. Accountants cannot seek answers to their problems from the courts where they in turn rely on current practice for their judgments.

### Disclosure in Published Reports

The Companies Act stipulates the minimum disclosure requirements for public companies and overseas companies operating in Australia.[9] Proprietary limited companies are not required to publish their reports unless they are foreign companies or are owned by other companies, in which case they have the option of either separate publication or consolidation with the reports of the holding company group. Invariably this latter method is adopted. Public companies must publish their reports annually. In addition the stock exchanges require quoted public companies to publish their profits for the past six months in interim reports.

The legal requirements for disclosure of operating performance and financial position represent a minimum in terms of the standards for good information. In general, they are dominated by the stewardship function of accounting and not by the need for information serving other purposes, particularly evaluation of economic performance and long-term decision-making. Many of the requirements have resulted directly from major fraud cases and company collapses rather than from an evaluation of what information is required by major users of company reports.

Publication requirements are confined to historical reports (i.e., no budgets are required), and to the income and appropriation statements and balance sheets (i.e., no cash flow or funds statements are required). While the majority of companies do not go beyond the legal minimum requirements, there is an increasing number who recognize the need for more detailed information and publish much more than is required.

In addition to the detailed items which must be disclosed in the reports, there is a general requirement that the income statement should give a "true and fair view of the profit or loss of the company for the financial year", and the balance sheet a "true and fair view of the state of affairs of the company as at the end of the financial year".

Directors must attest to this in their report, as must the accountant and the auditor (unless the latter gives a qualified report). The concepts of a "true and fair view" of profits and of the state of affairs of a company are not defined in the statutes, and it is the responsibility of the courts to determine what they mean in a particular case. Directors must publish a report (the director's report) about the company's operations for the year which is in addition to the financial reports, and it may contain further useful information for users. For example, directors must indicate whether operating results have been substantially affected by items of an unusual nature, and, if so, give particulars of the item. This provision includes in its ambit any changes in accounting principles employed and changes in the basis of inventory valuation. They must state whether all bad debts have been written off and whether the estimate of bad debts deducted from debtors in the balance sheet is adequate; whether current assets (other than debtors) could not realize their balance sheet values in the ordinary course of business; and whether long-term assets are valued at a sum exceeding their replacement cost as at the end of the year in the case of a going concern.

Publication requirements for the income statement are fairly sparse, and major items such as sales, cost of goods sold, and other major expenses do not have to be disclosed. Items which must be specified include net profit or loss, bad debts written off, doubtful debts, profit or losses on sale or revaluation of long-term assets, profits or losses arising otherwise than in the ordinary course of business, interest, dividends, directors emoluments, depreciation, income tax, audit fees, transfers to and from reserves and provisions, balances of unappropriated profits, plus a few other sundry items. An explanation must be given where the tax charge for the year differs by more than 15 per cent from the amount of tax that would be levied on the net profit as disclosed.

Publication requirements for the balance sheet are much more extensive and include most items which ought to be shown, for example, authorized and paid-up capital, share premium reserves, reserves, all types of loans and creditors, debtors, inventories, loans to directors, loans to and from subsidiaries, goodwill, patents and trade marks, preliminary expenses, fixed assets, and so on. In particular it is required that all provisions (for doubtful debts, depreciation, current tax liability and future tax liability) are shown separately and as deductions from the related account where appropriate. Contingent liabilities must be disclosed. Valuation clauses require disclosure of current market value of investments quoted on the stock exchange; the methods of valuing inventories and fixed assets; the dates at which fixed assets were valued if not at cost, and whether they were valued by the company or an independent valuer.

In general, the provisions of the 1971 Companies Act have considerably strengthened the publication requirements and they represent a substantial improvement over what had been required earlier. Nevertheless, the requirements still fall short of the standards for good accounting information. The balance sheet is still not necessarily a statement of current financial position because, e.g., asset values may comprise a combination of historic costs and of valuations applying to various time periods, thereby depriving the aggregate figure of unambiguous meaning; and liabilities such as leasehold obligations do not have to be disclosed. Important items in the income statement are not required to be disclosed and this complicates the task of investors in analyzing reasons for changes in profits, in assessing whether the company is making effective use of its gross assets and individual assets, in forecasting profit trends and the likelihood of new share issues. Funds statements are not required. Investors are given virtually no information about the company's plans and prospects for the future. No information about major divisions of a conglomerate company group is provided and investors cannot ascertain whether each division is being soundly operated and achieving a good financial performance. There are still no publication requirements for proprietary limited companies. Company law still concentrates on the stewardship function of management to the neglect of the broader economic issues which are concerned with the use of published company reports to provide relevant information to investors so as to facilitate the efficient operation of the capital market, i.e., to allocate scarce capital resources according to where they can be used most profitably.

## INCOME TAX LAW

The final major external influence on accounting is exerted by company income tax law.[10] All companies which earn a taxable income must pay tax on it, and the tax legislation (like company law) requires that proper accounting records be kept.

Before considering the impact of tax law on the measure of accounting profit, it is useful to consider the nature of taxable income. There is no concept of taxable income as such. Instead, the Income Tax Assessment Act prescribes what items must be included in assessable income, what items are allowable deductions therefrom, and what special concessions are available to the company. The net balance is what can loosely be called "taxable income". In determining whether a receipt should be included in assessable income, tax law generally lays great stress on the intention of the taxpayer in acquiring the asset — was it purchased for resale at a profit, or as a capital asset for use within the business? Profits on the sale of a capital asset are not part of assessable income (though they may be subjected to a separate capital gains tax). The calculation of assessable income is based on actual transactions — realization is a necessary attribute and the historic cost basis of valuation is used. The prescriptions of the Act incorporate the various economic, political, and social objectives of the government and they are often designed to be capable of easy administration and enforcement. Verifiability of data is of prime importance for this. Taxable income is not intended to be a good measure of a company's economic performance. Hence, because the purposes behind the determination of accounting and taxable incomes differ, there is no necessary identity between the two measures.

Various types of differences occur between taxable and accounting income. First, there are differences in the timing of items in each measure. For reasons of administrative expediency, the tax act tends to adhere to a cash basis of accounting for many items, whereas the accrual basis is used for accounting profit. Thus, for example, revenues received in advance and expenses paid in advance are included in the current year's tax assessment, not the revenues earned or expenses incurred; only warranty expenditures actually incurred, long-service leave and superannuation payments actually made in the year are allowable deductions in that year; and so on. Doubtful debts cannot be charged as a deduction − only the bad debts written off can be. The company need include only cash received from sales and customers during the year as revenue and not the total of cash and credit sales. In these parts of the tax calculation, taxable income approximates the cash surplus on operations rather than accounting income. From a liquidity viewpoint, the company is best able to pay the tax when it has a cash surplus.

A second set of timing differences between the two measures occurs with non-cash charges such as depreciation. To limit the discretion of companies in claiming deductions for items for which no verifiable evidence is possible, the act specifies what assets are subject to depreciation and what rates can be charged. Only the straight line and reducing balance methods can be used, and the rates for the latter are 50 per cent greater than the straight line rates. From the company's viewpoint the reducing balance method is preferable for tax purposes because it results in postponing some tax payments, even though the straight line method may be more appropriate for accounting purposes.

Although timing differences cause divergences between accounting and taxable income on a year-by-year basis, in the long run the sum of the two measures of income would be equal. The existence of these timing differences has led to the development of tax-effect accounting under which the tax charge shown in the income or appropriation statement is calculated on accounting income but the current liability is calculated on taxable income; the surplus tax charge is credited to a Provision for Future Income Tax and it is shown as a long-term liability. Doubt as to the validity of this procedure was mentioned in chapter 15.

A third set of differences between accounting and taxable income occurs for reasons of government policy. Some items, justifiably included in the determination of accounting income, are excluded from the tax measure. Depreciation cannot be charged for tax purposes on some assets such as buildings and social infrastructure items. Dividends received by a company (other than an investment company) are included in its accounting income but not in its taxable income (so as to avoid double taxation). Part of the interest earned on government bonds is tax exempt. A company might base its cost of goods sold and depreciation charges on current replacement cost for accounting purposes but the tax law allows only historical cost for tax purposes. Realized gains on fixed assets may be treated as capital gains in accounting but assessed as part of taxable income in the tax return.

Conversely, some items may be deducted in the tax return but would not be in the measure of accounting income. Special concessional allowances such as investment allowances are granted by the government to promote its economic policies — in this instance, fixed asset formation by industry to foster economic growth. They reduce taxable income but do not enter into the calculation of accounting profit.

The third set of factors causes permanent differences between the two measures of income.

Subject to the constraints imposed by company law, tax law has a major influence on accounting practice. Many companies follow aspects of tax law rather than accounting principles in their measurement of periodic accounting profit. They justify a particular practice according to whether it is permitted by tax law rather than accounting principle. Thus they adhere somewhat too closely to the cash basis of accounting for recognizing revenues and expenses, do not charge depreciation on buildings, and so on. Although this approach has the advantage of expediency, it can mean that accounting reports may not satisfy the information requirements of users other than the tax department. Tax reports are best regarded as special purpose reports and not as general purpose ones for the use of creditors and shareholders. Tax law should not be used as a justification for an accounting practice because the purposes it serves differ somewhat from the other ones of accounting.

## FURTHER READING

### Doctrine of Conservatism

Fitzgerald, A. A. *The Analysis and Interpretation of Operating and Financial Statements.* Melbourne: Butterworth. Chaps. 2 and 3.

Hepworth, S. "Smoothing Periodic Income" In Zeff, S., and Keller, W. *Financial Accounting Theory.* New York: McGraw-Hill, 1964.

MacNeal, K. "What's Wrong with Accounting?" In *Studies in Accounting Theory,* edited by W. T. Baxter and S. Davidson. London: Sweet and Maxwell, 1962.

Mathews, R. L. *The Accounting Framework.* 3rd ed. Melbourne: Cheshire, 1971. Chap. 6.

### Company Law

Yamey, B. S. "The Case Law Relating to Company Dividends." In *Studies in Accounting Theory,* edited by Baxter and Davidson.

## NOTES

1. Fitzgerald, *Analysis and Interpretation of Operating and Financial Statements*, p. 18.
2. Hepworth, "Smoothing Periodic Income".
3. A. D. Barton, "Company Takeovers in Australia, 1957–62", *Australian Accountant* (February, 1964).
4. Ibid.
5. For example a survey of 1,354 companies in Australia and New Zealand over the period 1950–60 revealed that 591 had revalued their assets at least once during the period. Quoted in R. J. Chambers, "Financial Information and the Securities Market", *Abacus* (1965). In the U.S., the S.E.C. prohibits the inclusion of asset revaluations in published company reports.
6. In a survey of public company takeovers in Australia 1957–62, it was found that 70 per cent of predator companies had revalued their assets within the previous six years, but that only 30 per cent of victim companies had done so. See A. D. Barton, "Company Takeovers in Australia 1957–62". There have been many recent examples of takeovers where the undervaluation of assets has been an important feature, including the Slater Walker Ltd. takeover of Drug Houses of Australia Ltd., Colonial Sugar Refining Company Ltd. takeover of Wunderlich Ltd., and Turinga Securities Ltd. takeover of Angus and Robertson Ltd.
7. See the 1961 Companies Act of each state and the 1971 Companies (Amendment) Act of New South Wales, Victoria, and Queensland.
8. See T. R. Johnston and M. O. Jager, *Company Accounting* (Sydney: Law Book Co., 1971), chap. 7, and B. S. Yamey, "The Case Law Relating to Company Dividends", in Baxter and Davidson, eds., *Studies in Accounting Theory*.
9. See New South Wales Government, *Companies (Amendment) Act, 1971*, Part VI and the Ninth Schedule.
10. Commonwealth Government, *Income Tax Assessment Act* (latest).


## QUESTIONS AND EXERCISES

1.   Explain the concept of an accounting doctrine. Give examples of such doctrines.

2.   Many firms adopt one realization assumption for gains and another for losses. Can a realization assumption of this type be justified?

3.   Is the application of the doctrine of conservatism consistent with the matching principle of income determination? Discuss.

4.   i.    Determine periodic income and value closing inventories for the the Reactionary Company under:

   a.   The pure historic cost system
   b.   Cost or market whichever is lower (COMWIL) system.

   *Transactions data for the period:*

   Purchased 100 fridgets @ $15 each.
   Sold 80 fridgets @ $25 each.

   *Additional data:*

   No opening inventories:
   Selling price has declined to $20:
   Replacement cost has declined to $11.

   ii.   Determine periodic income and value closing inventories under:

   a.   the pure historic cost system, and
   b.   cost or market whichever is lower (COMWIL) system

   in the circumstances where the selling price of fridgets has increased to
   $30 and the replacement cost has increased to $18.

iii.   Critically examine the results obtained under each method. Do you
       consider that they arise from the consistent application of logical
       procedures? Explain.

5. Witches Britches specializes in fashion jeans. Its inventory on June 30 comprised the following lines:

   | Line | Quantity | Orig. Cost | Rep. Cost | Exp. Slg. Val. |
   |------|----------|-----------|-----------|----------------|
   | A | 600 units | $6,000 | $7,200 | $12,000 |
   | B | 300 | $3,600 | $3,300 | $ 7,200 |
   | C | 400 | $8,000 | $8,000 | $12,000 |

   The business operates on a normal profit markup of 50% on selling price.
   Line C jeans have been selling slowly and their price has been marked down
   to clear the stocks.

   At what value should the total inventory be valued in the final reports under
   the COMWIL rule?

6. Explain the nature of secret reserves. For what purposes are they created?
   Does the existence of secret reserves mean that there is a "pot of gold" buried
   away somewhere?

7. For what reasons do company managements adopt the doctrine of conservatism?

8. Is there a conflict between adherence to the doctrine of conservatism and
   satisfying the standards for accounting information? Which standards might
   the doctrine conflict with? Discuss.

9. Distinguish between the adoption of prudent financial policies and the
   doctrine of conservatism in accounting. Do the two necessarily go hand in
   hand?

10. Are published financial reports which have been affected by the doctrine of
    conservatism likely to be very useful to investors? Discuss.

11. Why do some companies revalue their fixed assets periodically in a period of
    inflation and others not do so?

12. What are the major influences of company law on accounting practice?

13. What does the legal requirement that published reports should give "a true
    and fair view" mean?

14. Critically examine the publication requirements for the annual financial
    reports of companies. To what extent do you think they are satisfactory:

    i.    For the needs of investors to make informed investment decisions?

    ii.   For the needs of the economy in promoting efficiency in the capital
          market?

15. What are the major influences of income tax law on accounting practice?

# Part 3
# Alternative Valuation Systems

# Chapter 21
# The General Theory of Income Measurement and Balance Sheet Valuation

Several valuation and income measurement systems which are alternatives to the pure historic cost system are examined in the following chapters. These alternative systems have been advocated as a means of overcoming various defects of the historic cost system for purposes of measuring income and financial position, particularly in a period of inflation. Although they have not generally been used in practice as complete systems (if at all for some of them), nevertheless some of their features are commonly applied in accounting for particular expenses, assets, or liabilities. In real-world accounting, parts of these different valuation systems are generally mixed up together. This causes considerable confusion and published accounting reports are extremely difficult to interpret as a consequence – it is difficult to determine what the figures for income, assets, liabilities, and capital really mean in such cases. Secondly, several systems which incorporate the effects of inflation and/or changing asset prices into the measurement of income and financial position are under considerable discussion and experimentation at the current time.

In the real world the concepts of income, capital, financial position, and value are somewhat nebulous, and this accounts for much of the confusion in their use. Some of the problems in measuring income and capital can be illustrated in the following way. A plot of land is bought on 1 January for $1,000. On 31 December, the owner receives $200 rent; the price of land has risen to $1,600; and the general price level has risen by 10 per cent over the year. What income has been earned from the ownership of the land for the year and what is the value of capital on 31 December? Some of the possibilities are:

| | Value of Total Assets $ (Including $200 cash) | Capital $ | Income $ |
|---|---|---|---|
| 1. | 1,200 | 1,000 | 200 |
| 2. | 1,300 | 1,100 | 200 |
| 3. | 1,800 | 1,600 | 200 |
| 4. | 1,800 | 1,000 | 800 |
| 5. | 1,800 | 1,100 | 700 |

Each answer is correct according to the definition of income and capital employed.

## THE GENERAL NATURE OF INCOME

Income lies at the heart of business operations and financial accounting. Income provides the primary incentive for people to work and to invest in business, and firms would not exist but for the prospects of earning income. It is the criterion by which most business decisions concerning the mode and scale of operations are primarily determined. The measurement of income is one of the most basic functions of financial accounting.

Unfortunately, income is a difficult concept to define and measure, and there has been little agreement about the concept ever since Adam Smith began writing about it in his book, *The Wealth of Nations,* in 1776. There are substantial differences about income in ordinary business usage, the law, economics, and accounting. Part of the problem is that income is an abstract notion which results from applying various measurement procedures to transactions and/or to assets and liabilities. Income does not necessarily take the form of any particular asset acquired, such as cash, and hence it cannot always be separately identified and proved.

In general terms, the notion of business income is that of the net incoming of wealth arising from being in business. Income is in some sense the *gain in wealth* from being in business. It is the amount which can be spent without encroaching on the initial wealth of the firm, so that, if total income for a year is spent, the firm is just as well off at the end of the year as it was at the beginning. Wealth is the net stock of assets owned by the firm. More specifically, wealth can be defined as the monetary measure (i.e., the "value") of the firm's own economic resources after deducting the financial obligations to outsiders (excluding owners). Economic resources comprise all those assets having a market price, and this requires that they are capable of rendering future services (i.e., have a productive potential) and/or that they can be converted into cash. Because shareholders own the residual equity of the firm, net assets must always equal the residual equity in the firm, i.e., its capital in accounting terminology.

When seen in its most basic format, the problem of measuring income for a period, i.e., the gain in wealth over the period, is reduced to two matters:

1. How to measure the stock of assets and liabilities at two dates, i.e., the valuation of wealth problem

2. How to divide the wealth at the later date into its two notional parts – the base, initial capital component and the incremental, income component. This is the capital maintenance problem.

A firm's net stock of assets at the end of a period differs physically from its stock at the beginning of the period as a consequence of trading with its factor and product markets and using up its own assets; and secondly there may be changes in factors external to the firm which affect the monetary measure of its assets (for example, changes in asset prices, the purchasing power of the dollar, expectations of future trading conditions, and the rate of interest).

The situation is illustrated in terms of a wealth diagram in Figure 21−1.

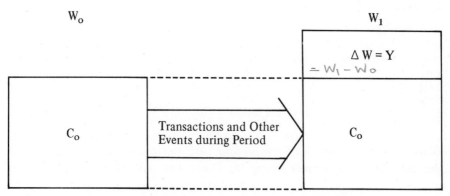

**Figure 21−1.** Relationship between capital and income

Where $C_0$ = $W_0$ = net assets, capital or wealth at start of period

$W_1$ = $C_1$ = net assets, capital, or wealth at end of period, as affected by transactions and exogeneous factors;

$Y$ = $\triangle W$ = income = increase in wealth or net assets.

The assumption is made throughout that there are no additional capital contributions by owners during the period, nor payments made to them. (These can be easily allowed for where they do in fact occur.)

In terms of the balance sheet equation, income is measured as the increase in net assets over a period as follows:

$$(A_1 - L_1) = P_1$$
Less $\quad(A_0 - L_0) = P_0$

$$\overline{\triangle (A - L) = \triangle P = Y}$$

In order to solve the valuation of wealth problem, information is required on:

1. The physical quantities of assets and liabilities

2. The measurement property of the dollar being used to express these quantities in monetary terms

3. The basis for valuing individual assets and liabilities so as to express them in monetary terms.

The capital maintenance problem involves an examination of capital maintenance benchmarks and the criteria which can be used to separate the increment in net assets from the base level. We shall examine these problems in turn.

## THE VALUATION OF WEALTH

### 1.  Quantities of Assets and Liabilities

These can be established by defining assets and liabilities precisely and determining their existence through a physical inventory of items and auditing the records of past transactions and management decisions.

### 2.  Measurement Properties of the Dollar

The two properties of the dollar which can be used for financial measurements comprise the medium of exchange property and the general purchasing power property. These were considered in chapter 4.

### 3.  Asset Valuation Bases

Typically an asset can have several values simultaneously and each one can be used as a basis for accounting reports. The several values arise from changes in price over time, differences between buying prices and selling prices, and private expectations of future usefulness. The major valuation bases comprise:

i.    The historic transaction prices used in the acquisition of each asset or liability, less depreciation charges where appropriate.

ii.   The current market buying prices of similar assets. These will differ from historic purchase prices of assets if there have been price changes in the meantime.

iii.  The current market selling prices of assets. These will differ from historic purchase prices if there have been price changes since the date of purchase and/or if there is a profit margin difference between buying and selling prices.

iv.   The present values of assets and liabilities. Present values are based on expected future cash receipts and outlays associated with the asset or liability, as discounted for time and uncertainty. They are personal, subjective values placed upon assets and liabilities.

### 4.  Wealth and Income Measurement Systems

A number of wealth and income measurement systems can be obtained by combining the measurement properties of the dollar with the asset valuation bases, as illustrated in Figure 21–2.

| Net Asset Valuation Bases / Measurement Property of Dollar | Medium of Exchange (No. of Dollars) | General Purchasing Power (No. of Purchasing Power Units) |
|---|---|---|
| Historic Transaction Prices | Historic Cost System | Constant Dollar Value System |
| Current Buying Prices | Current Value (Current Cost) System | Real Value (Current Cost) System |
| Current Selling Prices | Current Value (Selling Price) System | Real Value (Selling Price) System |
| Present Values | Present Value System | Real Present Value System |

Fig. 21−2. Wealth and income measurement systems

Each system can form an accounting system. The major ones are:

i. The historic cost system which combines historic transaction prices with the medium of exchange property of the dollar.

ii. The constant dollar value system. This combines historic transaction prices with the general purchasing power measurement property of the dollar. All dollars recorded in transactions are converted into units of equivalent general purchasing power as of the current time where there has been inflation in the meantime.

iii. The current value (current cost) system. Current market buying prices of the firm's assets are combined with the medium of exchange property of the dollar. Non-monetary assets are revalued at their current market buying prices for the measurement of wealth.

iv. The current value (selling price) system. As in iii, only current selling prices of assets are used.

v. The real value (current cost) system. Current buying prices of assets are combined with the general purchasing power property of the dollar.

vi. The real value (selling price) system. Current selling prices of assets are combined with the general purchasing power property of the dollar.

vii. The present value system. Prices associated with expected future transactions are combined with the medium of exchange property of the dollar, and the values are discounted back to the current date for time and uncertainty.

viii. The real present value system. Present values are combined with the number of general purchasing power units to determine real present values.

Each system can give a different measure of wealth and income for the same physical stock of assets and liabilities in typical business environments. This is another reason for the complexity and lack of agreement on income measurement. The conditions under which all systems give the same measure of wealth and hence of periodic income are highly untypical of reality, and they are examined later in this chapter.

## MAINTAINING CAPITAL INTACT

Once the firm's wealth at each date has been determined, the next problem is to divide the end-of-period wealth into the base component (the capital maintenance part) and the incremental component (the income for the period). The benchmark for the division of end-of-period wealth between the initial capital base and the increment is called the concept of maintaining capital intact. The value of all resources used up or dissipated in the period's operations must be a first charge on the resource inflows (principally from sales) to enable replacement of their value before any increment or surplus can be reckoned. In other words, there must be a recovery of capital used up so as to maintain in monetary terms a constant net stock of resources. In order to keep capital intact, any item in the stock of net assets that is sold or used up in operations must be replaced by an item of equivalent monetary value. In the context of the analogy sometimes made in which capital is likened to a lake, output is measured by the flow of water from the lake, and that volume of water must be replaced from the inflow before the lake begins to rise. Income is then the increase in the level of the capital lake.

The concept of capital maintenance does *not* imply the *actual replacement* of *each asset* used up in the period; rather, it means that there are items of the same *aggregate value* in the net stock at the end of the period. It simply means that the capital at the end of the period *can* be exchanged for the capital at the start, not that it *will* be. Capital and the maintenance of capital have reference only to a monetary valuation placed upon a collection of heterogeneous assets, and the maintenance of capital does not refer to the replacement of any specific asset in that collection. The firm is not committed to replacing assets used up with identical items, or even to replacing any assets. Asset purchase decisions are management decisions which have nothing to do with the accounting processes employed for the measurement of income. The adoption of any particular capital maintenance concept does not necessarily imply anything about the future action of the firm.

The recovery of capital is the basis of the matching principle of income determination: capital is recovered through the process of deducting all expenses (i.e., resources consumed in operations) from revenue (i.e.. resources gained from operations). As we saw in the pure historic cost system, the main problems here concern the measurement of the resource inflows from sales and measurement of the firm's own resources (inventories and fixed assets) used up in the process. However, there are normally difficult problems concerned with the precise interpretation of the concept of maintaining capital intact. If the stock of assets were homogeneous like water and consisted of a single type of article, the quantity of capital would be unambiguous and the number of units to be replaced before the stock was increased would be a straightforward calculation. Here, capital is maintained intact where the physical inventory of items remains constant. But the stock of assets is invariably heterogeneous (consider the usual range of assets in the balance sheet) and each asset must be measured in dollars to put them all onto a common basis for comparison; and, as we have seen above, there is more than one basis for valuing assets. Secondly, it is important that the same property of the dollar is used for the measurement of the beginning and end-of-period net assets so that the two magnitudes are directly comparable, and the gain can be established. The specific interpretations of the concept of capital maintenance vary according to the valuation system used, and they are considered subsequently in the context of each valuation system.

### Other Criteria for the Division between Income and Capital Maintenance

In addition to measuring income as the gain in wealth over a period after maintaining capital intact, several other criteria are frequently used to separate income from capital maintenance. These criteria can give a third component of wealth, viz., capital gains – which are neither income nor capital maintenance. If applied, the measure of income is not an all-inclusive gain in wealth and it can become incredibly complicated. These criteria are all somewhat arbitrary and they are not always applied consistently. They are not relevant for the all-inclusive measure of income except in so far as they affect the valuation of wealth itself.

### 1.  Income and Capital Must Be Separated

This idea was embodied in the writings of early classical economists such as Adam Smith, and came into accounting usage through business practice and several leading court decisions on distributable profits during the late nineteenth century. It is also embodied in current tax law. Thus there is considered to be a capital "fund" and an income "fund" which are separate from each other. The capital "fund" is represented by fixed assets, and the income "fund" by working capital.

Any increase in the value of the capital fund from natural growth or price increases is treated as a capital gain and not income. This appreciation is often called a holding gain since it arises from holding assets over time rather than from their utilization. Growth in the working capital fund may be treated as income. However, where this growth proceeds from the fixed capital, e.g., the fruit on a tree, the wool on a sheep, the crop on the land, interest on a bank deposit, it must be severed from the base property for it to be recognized. It is held that income must be detached from capital; otherwise it is capital appreciation.

### 2. Realization May Be Necessary

Before a capital gain (or loss) can be recognized, or income from trading recognized, a transaction must have occurred so that the gain (or loss) is offset by cash or financial claims. No unrealized items are recognized. If income and capital are thought of as belonging to separate funds, then profits (losses) on the sale of fixed assets are treated as realized capital gains (losses) which are not part of income. Thus the profit realized on the sale of sheep, the orchard, or the land and its crop is a capital gain; likewise the interest on a bank account not withdrawn. However, if the wool is shorn, the fruit picked, or the crop harvested, and is sold, the proceeds of the sale are recognized as income; likewise interest withdrawn. The requirement of realization can be applied separately to each fund.

### 3. Intention in Acquiring the Asset

This criterion is closely associated with the classification of assets between working capital and fixed capital. Assets acquired with the intention of reselling at a profit are part of the working capital fund, and realized holding gains and losses thereon are part of income. Assets acquired for long-term use within the firm are part of the fixed capital fund and realized holding gains and losses on them are capital items.

### 4. Expectations May Be Relevant

In some concepts of income, the state of expectations is held to be important in distinguishing between income and capital. All expected changes in value are part of income; whereas unexpected changes in value are windfall items which are treated as capital gains or losses.

### DIFFERENT CONCEPTS OF INCOME

Some of the main concepts of business income either used or advocated for use in accounting are outlined below. They comprise only a small proportion of the concepts contained in the writings of accountants and economists, but they are the ones most relevant for our purposes.

### 1. Pure Historic Cost Income

Income is the increase in net assets over the period, where all liabilities and all assets are valued at historic transaction prices less amounts amortized and the medium of exchange measurement property of the dollar is applied. Unrealized capital gains and losses are not recognized as part of wealth and hence income, but realized gains and losses are recognized and included in income (although perhaps as non-operating items). Maintenance of capital is based on recovery of initial monetary outlays from resource inflows so as to maintain the initial money investment intact. Income and capital are integrated as parts of wealth. In the land example, income is $200, capital maintenance is $1,000. If the land were sold for $1,600, income would be $800.

### 2. Constant Dollar Value Income

This is pure historic cost income adjusted for general price-level changes. Income, capital, and wealth concepts are as in section 1 above (Pure Historic Cost Income), except that they are measured in terms of the general purchasing power property of the dollar. Changes in the general purchasing power of the dollar are allowed for by adjusting historic costs with a general price-level index. The adjustment may take the form of converting beginning-of-year (BOY) dollar values to end-of-year (EOY) dollar values, or the reverse of this. Capital maintenance is based on preserving the general purchasing power of the initial investment. In terms of EOY dollar values in the land example, wealth is $1,300, capital maintenace is $1,100 (comprising initial investment $1,000 plus price-level adjustment $100), and income is $200. If the land is sold, the $600 holding gain is recognized, and total income is $700 in EOY dollar values.

### 3. Current Income (Current Cost)

Income is the increase in net assets over the period, after maintaining intact the net stock of monetary and physical assets. All assets are valued at end-of-year costs and the measurements use the medium of exchange property of the dollar. All realized and unrealized holding gains and losses are recognized as they occur and remain as part of capital. Maintenance of capital is based on preserving a net stock of monetary and physical assets intact, and capital recovery charges are based on the current cost of acquiring asset services. Capital and income are integrated. In the example, wealth is $1,800, holding gain is $600 (whether the land is sold or not), capital maintenance is $1,600, and income is $200.

### 4.   Current Income (Selling Price)

This is similar to current income (current cost) concept, except that current selling prices are used instead to value assets, and the capital maintenance concept is based on preserving the money selling value of the initial net assets intact. Holding gains (whether realized or not) form part of income. In the example, wealth is $1,800, capital maintenance is $1,000, and income is $800.

### 5.   Real Income (Current Cost)

Real income is current income adjusted for general inflation. The general purchasing power property of the dollar is used. Real income is therefore the increase in net assets over the period, after maintaining real capital intact. Real capital maintenance preserves intact the sum of the general purchasing power of net monetary assets plus the stock of physical assets. In EOY purchasing power dollars in the example, real income is $200, and capital maintenance is $1,600 (comprising initial investment $1,000, price-level adjustment $100, and real holding gain $500).

### 6.   Real Income (Selling Price)

Real income is the current income (selling price) adjusted for general inflation. The measurements are based on the general purchasing power property of the dollar. Real income is the increase in net assets over the period after maintaining intact the general spending power of initial capital. In the example, real income is $700 (comprising rent $200 and real holding gain $500), and the capital maintenance is $1,100 (i.e., the initial investment plus price-level adjustment $100) in terms of EOY dollars.

### 7.   Present Value Income

Present value income may be defined in terms of the total income expected up to the firm's time horizon, or of periodic expected income. Total income is defined as the excess of the present value of a firm over the investment in its net assets, valued at current market prices. Periodic income is defined as the increase in a firm's present value over a period. Present value income is based entirely on the size and timing of expected cash flows in the future, and on the discount rate used to reduce them to their present value. The concept of capital maintenance is that of maintaining intact the present (discounted) value of the existing investment in net assets. Changes in present values caused by changes in expectations or the discount rate may be treated as windfall capital gains or losses, or as part of income. Realization is not required as everything in the system relates to the future.

### 8. Real Present Value Income

This is present value income adjusted for general inflation. This may be done by adding the expected inflation rate to the discount rate in each future period so as to express all present values in terms of the current purchasing power of the dollar.

### 9. Historic Cost Income Modified by Doctrine of Conservatism

Income is the increase in net assets over the period valued at historic transaction prices less amounts amortized and less unrealized capital losses where not excessive. Unrealized holding gains are not recognized, and realized holding gains are treated as capital appreciation. Unrealized holding losses are recognized as income reductions where moderate and as capital losses where substantial. Essentially, capital and income are treated as separate unless the losses are relatively small. There is no easily definable or consistently applied capital maintenance concept. The example does not apply to this situation because the land price has risen. But, if its price had fallen to, say, $750, the $250 loss would be recognized whether realized or not as either a capital loss or reduction in income.

### 10. Historic Cost Income Modified by Asset Revaluation

Income is the increase in net assets over the period valued at adjusted historic transaction prices less amounts amortized. Realized and unrealized holding gains and losses are recognized from time to time (but not annually) as capital gains and losses. Maintenance of capital is based on recovery of initial balance sheet values from resource inflows. Capital and income are separate. In the example, income is $200, capital gain is $600 if the land is revalued or zero if it is not, and capital maintenance is $1,000.

### 11. Legal Income[1]

Income is the amount which may be legally distributed to shareholders. No precise concept is available and court judgments indicate that normal current business practice is acceptable. There tends to be a distinction between a working capital fund and a fixed capital fund; adherence to the realization concept and to historic cost valuation except when the firm wishes to depart from it. Gains and losses recognized on fixed capital (whether realized or not) are capital gains and not income, while those on working capital are part of income; and working capital must be maintained intact in the measure of income, while fixed capital need not be.

### 12. Taxable Income[2]

Income is the amount on which tax must be paid. Again no concept is given and tax legislation prescribes what must be included in assessable income and what items are allowable deductions. Tax acts tend to adhere to cash flows and historic costs. A sharp distinction is generally drawn between capital items and income items, which distinction is often based on the taxpayer's intended use for the items — is the asset acquired for the purpose of resale at a profit or for use within the business? Likewise, expected gains are included in income whereas windfall items are excluded. Realized capital gains are either not taxed at all or taxed separately as capital gains.

It is evident that there is no shortage of income concepts, that they can become very complex indeed, and that this complexity is compounded as the number of net asset valuation bases and criteria for the division of wealth between income and capital maintenance are increased. Moreover, this complexity is accentuated by arbitrariness where income is not an all-inclusive concept. It would be advantageous to discard the arbitrary division criteria between capital and income and to use a comprehensive income concept defined as the increase in net wealth after maintaining capital intact. This would eliminate capital gains as a separate segment of wealth. Additional information about how the income was earned, whether it was expected or otherwise, realized or not, and so on, could then be shown as components of net income. The concept of income is an abstraction, but this ought not to make it totally nebulous and incapable of rigorous explanation.

Furthermore, it should be recognized that in realistic circumstances there is no universally correct measure of periodic income. A limited number of answers is possible according to the specific valuation principles and dollar measurement properties. The choice between the income concepts to be measured should depend on the purpose for which the measurement is required. But, whatever the concept used, it is essential that the income and capital maintenance concepts are mutually consistent and that they sum to a particular wealth concept, of which they are both parts — i.e., the concepts must be articulated. To show how unrealistic the desire for the one and only measure of income is, it is instructive to consider the conditions which must hold for there to be a unique measure of income.

## CONDITIONS NECESSARY FOR UNIQUE INCOME MEASUREMENT

The only situations in which a unique income measure can be obtained, and hence true and correct income statements can be prepared, are:

1. When the life of the firm is terminated, all assets are sold and all liabilities repaid, and the purchasing power of money has remained constant throughout. Here, profit can be determined as the increment in cash held by the firm above the amount contributed by owners, and after allowing for withdrawals by them. In simple algebraic form, profit is:

$$
\begin{aligned}
\text{Cash } t_n &= \text{Proprietorship } t_n \\
\text{Less Cash } t_o &= \text{Proprietorship } t_o \\
\hline
\Delta \text{ Cash} &= \Delta \text{ Proprietorship} = \text{Profit}
\end{aligned}
$$

where $t_n$ is time at the end of the firm's life; and
$t_o$ is time at the formation of the firm.

Since Proprietorship equals Net Assets, Profit is the increase in Net Assets of the firm. In other words, it represents the value of the assets acquired over time by the firm after replacing the value of the assets consumed during that time; that is, after maintaining intact the value of the firm's net assets, which equals proprietary capital. Hence income of a period is defined as the increase in the value of the firm's assets over the period, assuming no proprietary contributions or withdrawals during the period, or alternatively as the maximum amount of assets which the firm could distribute while maintaining its capital intact. In the case of the terminated firm there is no problem in asset valuation because cash is the only asset.

However, for the reasons discussed earlier, users of accounting reports cannot wait until the end of a firm's life for measures of income, assets, and financial position, and periodic measurements of these magnitudes are required.

2. Where the firm is still carrying on its business activities, a unique measure of periodic income can be obtained if it is operating in the ideal conditions of the stationary state. The stationary state is a theoretical economic model of an economy in perpetual equilibrium and without growth or technical progress. It does not purport to be realistic. In the stationary state there is no inflation (hence there is only the one measurement property of the dollar) and no changes in market prices over time (and hence current market prices always coincide with historic cost). The following assumptions are necessary for the model.[3]

i. Identity of cost and market values is maintained throughout. The cost of anything purchased always equals its current market value, and the sum of production costs, including normal profit, equals its market selling value. The present market prices of assets equal their historic costs — thus there can be no price changes over time. Perfect competition throughout all industry must exist to maintain this identity and to ensure that no pure profits occur. Hence investors earn just their required rate of return and there can be only the one discount rate in the market which never changes. This in turn ensures that periodic income never changes and that historically based measures of income, assets, liabilities, and capital always coincide with their valuations on a discounted cash flow basis.

ii. The unit of monetary measurement is stable; that is, the price level remains constant. Hence all dollars are homogeneous in terms of general purchasing power value. The value of the 1900 dollar equals that of the 1974 dollar, and the two dollars can be added together to give the sum in terms of current dollar values. It is irrelevant therefore whether some land was, acquired forty years ago, and some yesterday, as the dollar values placed on each are comparable. The identity of cost and market values throughout ensures that no inflation occurs.

iii. Certainty. Only if the future is known with certainty can the allocation of costs and revenues among past, present and future periods be accurately done in a continuing firm. Certainty implies perfect knowledge of all future events, the absence of risk in all business operations, and the need for only one rate of interest in the economy. Hence losses will never be incurred and no reward for risk-taking is required.

Where any one of these conditions does not hold, periodic accounting reports cannot be unique and be the only true and correct reports possible. For example, if condition i. does not hold, historic and current market values diverge and several balance sheets can be prepared. If condition ii. is not fulfilled, dollars of different vintages cannot be summed together without some price level adjustment being made. If condition iii. does not hold, the future is not known with certainty and various assumptions about future events must be made. Periodic reports therefore require some estimates to be made. Mistakes will be made in forecasting and *exante* reports will differ from *expost* reports. The firm requires compensation for risk-taking and the normal rate of profit will exceed the pure rate of interest in the market.

It is because these conditions do not hold in reality that various valuations can be placed upon assets and liabilities and the dollar has two measurement properties, and consequently that several concepts of periodic income can be developed. Thus if they did occur, then there would be no scope for applying the doctrine of conservatism (everyone knows what is happening and results cannot be distorted), there can be no asset revaluations or holding gains, and there can be no general price level adjustments. Hence pure historic cost income, current income, real income, and present value income all coincide. Capital maintenance likewise would be unique because there is never any change in the composition, technology or prices of assets and those used up in operations are replaced with identical items and at the same price.

### FURTHER READING

Kerr, J. St.G. "Three Concepts of Business Income." *Australian Accountant* (April 1956). Reprinted in Davidson, S., et al., eds. *An Incomes Approach to Accounting Theory*. Englewood Cliffs, N.J.: Prentice-Hall, 1964.

## NOTES

1. For a detailed explanation of legal income, see T. R. Johnston and M. O. Jager, *Company Accounting* (Sydney: Law Book Co., 1971), chap. 7.
2. Some features of taxable income in Australia are explained in K. Ryan, *Manual of Income Tax Law in Australia* (Sydney: Law Book Co.).
3. See E. O. Edwards and P. W. Bell, *Theory and Measurement of Business Income* (Berkeley California: California University Press, 1961), chap. 1.

## QUESTIONS AND EXERCISES

1. Explain in general terms, the concepts of wealth, income, and capital maintenance.

2. What criteria have been used for the division of end-of-period wealth between capital maintenance and income? Which ones, if any, would you *not* include? Are there other tests you would like to include?

3. Examine the case for including

   i.   intention
   ii.  realization

   as tests for the recognition of income.

4. You buy a parcel of shares in X Ltd. on 1 January for $100. At 31 December following, the current market price of the shares is $500. Would you treat the gain in market value for the year as part of income, of capital, or just not recognize it, in each of the following circumstances —

   i.   Assume the shares are not sold.

      a.   The shares were bought with the intention of earning dividend income and not for resale at a profit.

      b.   The shares were bought with the hope of obtaining capital gains as well as dividends.

   ii.  Assume the shares are sold for $500 — does this affect your answer to a. and b.?

   iii. Assume the general price-level index doubled over the year. How does this fact affect your measure of income?
      Justify your answer in each case with reference to a concept of income.

5. What reasons permit more than one measure of periodic income to be normally possible?

6. "It is evident that there is not one concept of income which is suitable for all purposes or which could be claimed to be the "true" income for the period. It must be recognized that for different purposes we need different concepts of income, and in each case a choice must be made as to the concept which is relevant to the use to be made of the income determination. It is the suitability of the concept for the purpose which should be the decisive factor in any choice of a concept of income." (Kerr, "Three Concepts of Business Income".)
   Explain and illustrate this conclusion.

7. Consider the view that reductions in the market values of a firm's non-monetary assets are "paper losses" that do not really affect shareholders' wealth.

8. Should profits on the sale of shares by an investment company be treated as operating income or capital gains?

9. i. An investment company receives dividends of $1,000,000 for the year on the shares it owns, incurs operating expenses of $700,000, and declares a profit of $300,000. The market value of its portfolio (which was unchanged over the year) fell from $12,000,000 to $8,000,000 over the year. How much profit do you consider was made? Would it make any difference to your answer if the entire portfolio were sold for $8,000,000 at the end of the year?

   ii. Suppose that the market value of the portfolio rose to $14,000,000 by the end of the year, what would be your answer? Would realization affect it?

10. Critically examine the following accounting practices:

    i. A company declares a net profit of $5,000,000 determined according to accepted accounting principles

    ii. In addition it recognizes a $3,000,000 reduction in the market value of part of its investment portfolio and writes off this amount against revenue reserves

    iii. An appreciation of $2,000,000 in other portfolio investments is reported in a footnote in the published reports but is not recorded in the accounts

    iv. Losses on the sale of fixed assets of $10,000,000 are incurred and charged to share premium reserves.
    How would you have accounted for these items?

11. In a double entry recording system, demonstrate that income is the increase in net assets from trading activities by using the following items. Set out your answer in the following tabulation:

| Income Statement Account | Dr. or Cr. | $ | Balance Sheet Account | Dr. or Cr. | $ |
|---|---|---|---|---|---|

|  |  | $ |
|---|---|---|
| i. | Cash sales | 8,000 |
| ii. | Credit sales | 20,000 |
| iii. | Cost of goods sold | 17,000 |
| iv. | Wages paid | 5,000 |
| v. | Wages accrued at EOY | 200 |
| vi. | Advertising paid | 1,000 |
| vii. | Depreciation of buildings | 1,500 |
| viii. | Cash collected from customers | 18,000 |

There were no other expenses for the year. Net assets at the start of the year were $30,000.

Is it possible to break the connection between the income statement and the balance sheet?

# Chapter 22
# Constant Dollar Value System

We have seen that most of the major limitations of historic cost accounting as a financial information system arise from its disregard of inflation and of changes in current market prices of assets. These limitations can be overcome through adjusting historic cost data for the effects of inflation and revaluing non-monetary assets. Although these two problems are generally interrelated – prices of most assets rise during periods of general inflation – it is not true of all cases, and the two phenomena can occur independently at the firm level. Thus while there is general inflation and the majority of asset prices rise, it can still happen that the market prices of some assets fall, and the prices of others remain constant for a long time. Where asset prices increase, it is generally the case for most firms that some asset prices rise at a slower rate than inflation, some rise at the same rate, and others appreciate at a far greater rate. Conversely some asset prices rise during a period of declining general price levels. There are thus two categories of price changes that can be isolated and accounted for – changes in the general level of prices, and changes in the market prices of specific assets; and these two can be then combined to account for changes in asset prices relative to general price level changes.

Here, we shall examine the price-level problem first and make adjustments to the historic cost reports for inflation; secondly, examine the asset price change problem and make appropriate adjustments for it; and, finally, combine the two systems to account for relative price changes. It does not particularly matter which set of adjustments is made first to the accounts so long as both sets of adjustments are ultimately made. The first system is known as *price-level accounting* (PLAC), current purchasing power accounting (CPPA) or the *constant dollar value system*, the second one as the *current value system*, and the third one as the *real value system*.

## THE GENERAL NATURE OF PRICE-LEVEL ACCOUNTING

Increases in the general level of prices throughout the economy, i.e., inflation, mean that the purchasing power of the dollar declines. The measure of the change in purchasing power is merely the reciprocal of the measure of the average price increase; for example, if the general level of prices rises by 10 per cent, then the purchasing power of the dollar has fallen by 10 per cent. In other words $1.10 is now required on average to buy the quantity of goods and services that $1 would acquire previously. Most countries have experienced more or less continuous inflation for many years. For example, in Australia the Gross Domestic Product Implicit Price Deflator has risen from 83.3 in June 1960 to 183.4 in June 1975, indicating a rise in the general price level of approximately 120 per cent over the period and an average price rise of almost 5½ per cent per annum.[1] In other words the purchasing power of the dollar has declined at this rate.

The historic cost system uses the medium of exchange property of the dollar as its relevant measuring rod. The measurement of results is based on the number of dollars required to complete transactions. In price-level accounting, all transaction prices are restated to allow for changes in the general purchasing power of the dollar so that the results are measured in terms of a dollar of constant general purchasing power. The general purchasing power of the dollar is held to be the significant measurement property of the dollar in this system. Where general purchasing power is the significant property of the dollar and there has been inflation, it is no more meaningful to add a 1960 dollar to a 1970 dollar to get the result of two dollars than it is to add a 1960 and a 1970 model Ford car together when model properties are relevant. In essence the price-level accounting system corrects for a dollar measuring rod of variable length. The dollars used in the historic cost system are not homogeneous with respect to their general purchasing power and the aggregate dollar measures of income, assets, liabilities, and equity have little meaning in terms of their current worth. An analogy is that of measuring distances with an elastic tape. The constant dollar value system corrects for this deficiency in the dollar measuring rod by adjusting the yardstick with an index of general purchasing power so as to keep it constant. Price-level adjusted dollars are dollars of *constant* general purchasing power or exchange value. All financial results are then measured in terms of these constant general purchasing power units. The only method of making this conversion is to do so with a price index. All historic transaction dollars are adjusted by the index to restate them in terms of the general purchasing power of the dollar as of a given date. The restatement of historic cost dollars to constant purchasing power dollars is of the same form as, for example, the conversion of distances from feet to metres — the conversion factor is consistently applied to all items and no relativities are disturbed. But in all other respects the system retains the characteristics of the historic cost system — it is still based on historic transaction prices and the realization convention. It is the historic cost system restated in terms of constant dollar purchasing power.

## WEALTH, INCOME, AND CAPITAL CONCEPTS

If price-level adjustments are made to the pure historic cost system, then the concepts measured are very similar. Wealth is the sum of the net assets valued at historic purchase prices as adjusted for changes in the general purchasing power of the dollar since acquisition. Capital maintenance refers to maintaining intact the pool of general purchasing power provided by the owners' opening investment, (the general purchasing power capital maintenance concept). Constant dollar income $(Y_D)$ is the gain in general purchasing power over the period accruing from operating transactions. Thus,

$$A_1 - L_1 = P_1$$
$$\text{Less} \quad A_0 - L_0 = P_0$$
$$\overline{\Delta (A - L) = \Delta P = Y_D}$$

where all beginning-of-year assets, liabilities, and capital, and all end-of-year non-monetary assets owned from the start of the year, are restated in terms of end-of-year dollar purchasing power; and all other end-of-year items are shown at their (recent) transaction prices.

## PRICE-LEVEL ACCOUNTING

There are two alternatives which may be used in the restatement of historic cost reports to incorporate general price-level changes — all data may be converted back to the purchasing power of the dollar applying at an earlier date, e.g., start of the year, or all historic data may be converted forward to the current time, e.g., end of year. The second alternative is generally preferred as users of financial statements are more familiar with current purchasing power than with that of some time ago.

In analyzing the effects of price-level changes on a firm's income and financial position, it is useful to separate monetary from non-monetary assets because the effects of inflation on each differ. Monetary assets are claims to a fixed number of dollars, and they remain unchanged in dollar terms irrespective of changes in the purchasing power of the dollar. For example, if customers owe the firm $100, that is all they are required to pay whatever the amount of inflation. The main examples are cash and financial claims. Likewise liabilities are normally claims to fixed numbers of dollars and they do not vary with the inflation. However, deferred performance liabilities which represent obligations to provide goods or services in the future (e.g., advances received on sales contracts and estimated warranty costs on products sold) are non-monetary items. Non-monetary assets comprise all assets which are not claims to a fixed number of dollars. They include all physical assets, prepayments, leasehold assets, intangible assets and share investments.

Inflation affects monetary and non-monetary items differently. It reduces the purchasing power of cash invested in monetary assets, and hence the firm suffers a purchasing power loss on these assets. But, conversely, it reduces the amount of purchasing power to be repaid to creditors, and hence firms make a purchasing power gain on liabilities. If monetary assets exceed liabilities (i.e., there are positive net monetary assets), the firm suffers a price-level loss; while it makes a price-level gain if monetary assets are less than liabilities (i.e., if net monetary assets are negative).

Non-monetary assets can benefit from inflation because there is a general tendency for their prices to rise. This is part of the process of inflation — prices rise. They have market prices which can change from the original transaction price measuring the cash invested in them. Hence a firm does not necessarily incur a purchasing power loss on its investment in non-monetary assets — it does so only if an asset's price does not appreciate to the same extent as the general price level. In many cases asset prices rise by more than the general price level, and here the firm makes a net gain in terms of general purchasing power.

Generally, constant dollar income will be less than accounting income during a period of inflation because of the higher charges for depreciation and cost of goods sold occasioned by the price-level adjustment, and by the price-level loss incurred on holding net monetary assets. However, for those firms with substantial net liabilities which make price-level gains on net monetary liabilities, constant dollar income can exceed historic cost income.

The effect of general price-level changes on a firm's balance sheet can be illustrated as follows.[2] Assume a very simple situation in which a firm has only two classes of assets — one monetary and one non-monetary — the liabilities are netted out against the monetary assets, and the net monetary assets are positive. Secondly, assume that the prices of all non-monetary assets increase at the same rate as the general price level. At the beginning of the year, the balance sheet is expressed as:

$$M_0 + N_0 = P_0 \qquad \text{......(i)}$$

where $M_0$ are the net monetary assets
$N_0$ are the non monetary assets
$P_0$ is the owners' equity.

Restatement of these same assets at the end of the year after an inflation rate of r per cent gives:

$$M_0(1+r) + N_0(1+r) = P_0(1+r) \qquad \text{......(ii)}$$

Since the number of dollars in net monetary assets remains fixed and prices of non-monetary assets are assumed to rise by r, equation (ii) can be rearranged in a more meaningful form as:

$$M_o + N_o (1 + r) = P_o (1 + r) - Mr \qquad ......(iii)$$

$N_o(1 + r)$ is the opening balance of non-monetary assets restated in terms of the end-of-year dollars; $P_o(1 + r)$ is the opening balance of owners' equity restated in terms of end-of-year dollars — it is the capital maintenance amount; and Mr measures the price-level loss incurred on the holding of net monetary assets. The amount by which opening owners' equity is restated upwards, i.e., Pr, is a straight price-level adjustment to put the dollars in opening owners' equity into the same purchasing power terms as the closing owners' equity, and similarly for Nr relating to non-monetary assets. Pr is not a gain or loss to the firm — it does not represent increased command over goods and services. It is in effect a transformation from one measuring unit to another. Pr is the price-level adjustment made to opening capital to maintain intact the general purchasing power of that initial investment, and it is credited to an account titled Price-Level Adjustment account or Capital Mainten- ance Adjustment account. It shows the extra funds that must be retained in the firm to maintain intact the general purchasing power of the initial investment. The restatement of non-monetary assets (Nr) is debited to the appropriate asset accounts. The price-level loss (Mr) is the measure of the extent to which the firm has suffered a loss in general purchasing power from its holding of net monetary assets and it is debited to a Price-Level Loss account rather than to the monetary asset accounts. It is a genuine loss of purchasing power rather than a mere restatement of monetary magnitude and consequently the price- level loss is deducted in the income statement to arrive at constant dollar income. The reverse procedure is followed where the firm has net monetary liabilities — the Price-Level Gain account is credited and the Price-Level Adjustment account is debited. The price-level gain is then added to profit in the income statement. The total debits to the net asset accounts must equal the credit to the Price-Level Adjustment account, i.e., Mr + Nr = Pr.

After a year's transactions (excluding changes in direct proprietary investment) the end-of-year balance sheet can be stated as:

$$M_1 + N_1 = P_1 \qquad ......(iv)$$

where all N assets owned from the beginning-of-year are measured at their inflation restated values, and all assets acquired during the year are measured at their (recent) transaction prices.

Constant dollar income for the year $(Y_D)$ is then equation (iv) minus equation (ii), i.e.,

$$Y_D = [M_1 - (M_0 + Mr)] + [N_1 - (N_0 + Nr)] = P_1 - (P_0 + Pr)$$
$$......(v)$$

$$\therefore Y_D = (M_1 - M_0) + N_1 - (N_0 + Nr) - Mr = P_1 - (P_0 + Pr)$$
$$......(vi)$$

Constant dollar income is thus the increase in net monetary assets plus the increase in non-monetary assets valued at constant dollars, less the price-level loss on initial net monetary assets; or, alternatively, the increase in proprietorship after maintaining intact the general purchasing power of initial proprietorship. In the income statement, constant dollar income is determined as revenue less expenses less price-level loss, where all asset consumption charges (cost of goods sold and depreciation) are based on the end-of-year constant dollar values of those assets.

The capital maintenance and income concepts used in the constant dollar value system can be illustrated in the wealth diagram as follows:

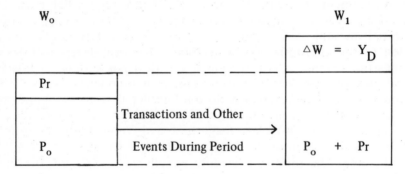

**Figure 22−1** Constant dollar system wealth diagram where all items are measured as in the equations above.

## AN ILLUSTRATION OF PRICE-LEVEL ACCOUNTING[3]

As an illustration of price-level accounting, suppose that on 1 January the Inflationary Co. Ltd. balance sheet prepared on a historic basis shows the following data:

|  | $ |  | $ |
|---|---|---|---|
| Cash | 100 | Creditors | 80 |
| Inventories | 100 | Paid-up Capital | 400 |
| Plant (New) | 300 | Retained Earnings | 20 |
|  | $500 |  | $500 |

Its historic cost income statement for the year ended 31 December is:

| | $ | $ | $ |
|---|---|---|---|
| Sales | | | 2,000 |
| Less Cost of Sales | | | |
| Opening Inventory | 100 | | |
| Purchases | 1,630 | 1,730 | |
| Less Closing Inventory | | 120 | 1,610 |
| Gross Profit | | | 390 |
| Less Cash Operating Expenses | | 300 | |
| Depreciation | | 40 | 340 |
| Historic cost income | | | $50 |

The historic cost balance sheet on 31 December is:

| | $ | $ | | $ | $ |
|---|---|---|---|---|---|
| Cash | | 240 | Creditors | | 150 |
| Inventories | | 120 | Paid-up Capital | 400 | |
| Plant | 300 | | Retained Earnings | 20 | |
| Less Accumulated | | | Net Income | 50 | 470 |
| Depreciation | 40 | 260 | | | |
| | | $620 | | | $620 |

No dividends were paid during the year. The historic cost income of $50 is represented by the additional net assets owned at the end of the year (i.e., 470 − 420). The opening inventories were all sold and the closing inventory comprises recently purchased merchandise. The general price level rose by 10 per cent over the year.

In order to convert the historic cost reports into a set of constant dollar value statements, the following adjustments are made to the January balance sheet to restate it in terms of end-of-year purchasing power dollars:

*Balance Sheet of 1 January restated in December Dollars*

| | $ | | $ | $ |
|---|---|---|---|---|
| Cash | 100 | Creditors | | 80 |
| Inventories | 110 | Paid-up Capital | 400 | |
| Plant | 330 | Retained Earnings | 20 | |
| | | Price-Level | | |
| | | Adjustment | 42 | |
| | | Price-Level Loss | (2) | 460 |
| | $540 | | | $540 |

The journal entry recording the adjustments is:

| | | $ | $ | | |
|---|---|---|---|---|---|
| Inventories (10% on 100) | Dr | 10 | | Nr | = 40 |
| Plant (10% on 300) | Dr | 30 | | | |
| Price-Level Loss on Net Mty Assets (10% on 100–80) | Dr | 2 | | Mr | = 2 |
| Price-Level Adjustment (10% on 420) | Cr | | 42 | Pr | = 42 |

Non-monetary asset accounts are debited with the inflation factor adjustment and the Price-Level Adjustment account is credited. The same principle is applied to monetary items but the procedure is to debit the Price-Level Loss account instead of the asset account and credit the Price-Level Adjustment account, and vice versa for liabilities. The Price-Level Loss is then temporarily shown as a deduction in owners' equity in the beginning-of-year balance sheet, and is subsequently deducted from net operating income in the income statement at the end of the year. The capital maintenance amount is now $462 in terms of EOY dollars. The inflation restated balances in the non-monetary asset accounts owned for the year are carried forward to the EOY balance sheet, and all asset consumption charges for the year (i.e., cost of goods sold and depreciation) are based on these restated values.

The constant dollar income statement for the year becomes:

| | $ | $ | $ |
|---|---|---|---|
| Sales | | | 2,000 |
| *Less* Cost of Sales | | | |
| Opening Inventory (+10) | 110 | | |
| Purchases | 1,630 | 1,740 | |
| *Less* Closing Inventory | | 120 | 1,620 |
| Gross Profit | | | 380 |
| *Less* Cash Operating Expenses | | 300 | |
| Depreciation (+4) | | 44 | 344 |
| Net Operating Income | | | 36 |
| *Less* Price-Level Loss on Net Mty Assets | | | 2 |
| Constant Dollar Income | | | $34 |

Finally, the constant dollar balance sheet of 31 December stated in December dollars is:

|  | $ | $ |  | $ | $ |
|---|---|---|---|---|---|
| Cash |  | 240 | Creditors |  | 150 |
| Inventories |  | 120 | Paid-up Capital | 400 |  |
| Plant | 330 |  | Retained Earnings | 20 |  |
| Less Accumulated |  |  | Price-Level |  |  |
| Depreciation | 44 | 286 | Adjustment | 42 |  |
|  |  |  | Constant Dollar |  |  |
|  |  |  | Income | 34 | 496 |
|  |  | $646 |  |  | $646 |

Constant dollar income for the year, after maintaining intact the general purchasing power of the initial capital at $462, is $34. It is the increase in net assets stated in end-of-year dollars after deducting the price-level loss on initial net monetary assets (i.e., 496 −462). In fact it is is the historic cost net income ($50), less the additional cost of goods sold ($10) and depreciation ($4) and price-level loss ($2). If the firm paid out its total historic cost income as dividends, it would deplete its capital by $16 in terms of end-of-year purchasing power.

In this illustration, it can be seen how the Price-Level Adjustment account covers the restatement of all assets and liabilities in end-of-year dollars. It is a capital maintenance account showing the additional funds which must be retained in the firm to preserve the general purchasing power of the opening capital. In fact it is the restatement of opening capital by the inflation factor $(420 \times \frac{110}{100} = 462)$. The Price-Level Loss account is not a capital maintenance account but a genuine loss of purchasing power attributable to holding net monetary assets in an inflationary period.

The procedures for adjusting the income statement are derived from the formulae above. The method illustrated above recognizes only the inflation that has occurred over the whole year, and all intra-year inflation is disregarded in the adjustments. All the inflation adjustments are confined to the opening balance sheet items. It is the simplest of the several methods that can be used to account for the effects of inflation on a firm's income and financial position, and it would provide suffic-ient accuracy where the inflation is but a mild one. In calculating cost of goods sold, the opening inventory is converted by the December index number, purchases are treated in the same way as currently incurred expenses, and no adjustment is required to closing inventory (if valued on a FIFO basis). Fixed assets (and their related accumulated depreciation accounts) must be listed in an ageing schedule and the relevant year's index is applied to the assets acquired in each year. Depreciation is then charged on the restated values according to the normal historic cost methods. Where beginning-of-year fixed assets are already stated on a price-level adjusted basis, their opening balances (together with their respective accumulated depreciation accounts) are merely restated for the current year's inflation rate.

More accurate methods of measuring the impact of general inflation on a firm's income and financial position involve adjusting all transaction data for the year (except that occurring around the end of the year) as well as the opening balance sheet items. The adjustments become much more numerous and complex, and the additional costs incurred in ensuring greater accuracy must be assessed against the added benefits obtainable from the information. The method generally recommended where inflation is occurring at a moderate rate requires adjusting all income statement items which have occurred throughout the year for the last six months' inflation and beginning-of-year items for the year's inflation, while items occurring around the last part of the year are not adjusted. This method centres the continuing items of revenue and expenses at the mid-year and adjusts them for the last six months' inflation to put them into end-of-year dollars so that they are compatible with the closing balance sheet items. Similar adjustments are made to movements in net monetary items over the year to calculate the price-level loss. Fixed assets purchased during the year are adjusted for inflation for the number of months owned. The method assumes that activity and inflation take place at a fairly uniform rate over the year.

This method may be applied to the Inflationary Company as follows. Assume that the General Price Level Index was 100 on January 1, 104 on June 30, and 110 on December 31, and that FIFO inventory costing is used.

*Income Statement for the Year ended 31 December*

|  | Hist. Cost $s | Conversion Factor | P–L Adjusted $s |
|---|---|---|---|
| Sales | 2,000 | AOY 110/104 | 2,115 |
| *Less* Opening Inventory | 100 | BOY 110/100 | 110 |
| Purchases | 1,630 | AOY 110/104 | 1,724 |
|  | 1,730 |  | 1,834 |
| *Less* Closing Inventory | 120 | EOY — | 120 |
| Cost of Goods Sold | 1,610 |  | 1,714 |
| Gross Profit | 390 |  | 401 |
| *Less* Cash Operating Expenses | 300 | AOY 110/104 | 317 |
| Depreciation | 40 | BOY 110/100 | 44 |
| Total Expenses | 340 |  | 361 |
| Net Operating Income | 50 |  | 40 |
| *Less* Price-Level Loss on M | — |  | 6 |
| Net Income | $50 |  | $34 |

*Comments*:

1. Sales, purchases and recurring cash operating expenses are assumed to occur fairly evenly over the year and hence their values are centred on the average purchasing power of the dollar for the year, i.e., that holding in June when the index was 104. These items are inflated for the inflation occurring in the second half year (i.e., by the factor 110/104) to restate them in December purchasing power dollars.

2. Beginning-of-year items such as opening inventories and depreciation are restated for the year's inflation factor (i.e., 110/100) to express them in December purchasing power dollars.

3. End-of-year items do not require any restatement. The age of closing inventories should be checked by the turnover rate for inventories (i.e., COGS/Average Inventory). Here it is 1630/110 equals 14.6 times p.a., i.e., the inventories are on hand for less then 4 weeks on average, and hence their prices are expressed in end-of-year dollars. If, however, the inventories had been on hand for, say, six months, then they would be restated for the past six months inflation.

4. Any irregular or infrequent operating expenditures (e.g., interest, dividend and tax payments) may be adjusted separately for the period between their payment and the end of the year.

5. The price-level loss on holding net monetary assets is calculated in two parts:

   a. The price-level loss on opening net monetary assets is determined for the year, i.e., $(100 - 80). \dfrac{10}{100} = 2.$

   b. The price-level loss on the increased holding of net monetary assets over the year is determined as the net change times the second half year inflation rate, i.e., closing balance $(240 - 150 = 90)$ less opening balance $(100 - 80 = 20) = 70. \dfrac{6}{104} = 4.04.$

   Total price level loss is $(2 + 4.04) = 6.04$.

6. The journal entry to record the above price-level adjustments is:

| | | | |
|---|---|---|---|
| Inventories | Dr | 10 | |
| Plant | Dr | 30 | |
| Price-Level Loss on M | Dr | 6 | |
| Purchases | Dr | 94 | |
| Cash Operating Expenses | Dr | 17 | |
| Sales | Cr | | 115 |
| Price-Level Adjustment | Cr | | 42 |

7. The simple method involving adjustments to beginning-of-year items only and the more complex method illustrated here will not necessarily give the same net income figure or price-level adjustment figure.

High rates of inflation may require the use of still more detailed methods, such as subdividing the year into shorter periods, e.g., quarters, and adjusting the items on a quarterly basis using methods similar to those for annual adjustments. The results for each quarter are then compounded forward to the end of the year at the quarterly inflation rates to derive the annual results in terms of end-of-year dollars.

When comparisons over several years are required, the constant dollar incomes of each year and balance sheet items at the end of each year are converted by the ratio of the current index number to the index number of each year to restate all data of previous years into current dollars.

## PRESENTATION OF FINAL REPORTS

Price-level adjusted results are best presented along with a firm's historical results so that the impact of inflation on its income and financial position can be highlighted. This can be accomplished by adding Price-Level Adjustment columns to the historic cost reports or by the presentation of supplementary reports; and secondly by using a Price-Level Adjustment account as part of owners' equity to show the extra funds to be retained in the firm for capital maintenance, and a Price-Level Loss account in the income statement to show the loss in purchasing power of net monetary assets. The dual presentation of results complies with an important standard for the communication of financial information, viz., the presentation of relevant environmental data.

## CHOICE OF INDEX NUMBER SERIES[4]

The general level of prices is not a physical phenomenon whose height can be measured directly as can, say, the level of water in a lake, and consequently the measurement of changes in it is subject to many assumptions and approximations. Changes in the general price level can be measured only in terms of price index numbers, and several different indexes have been advocated.

The Gross Domestic Product Implicit Deflator is recommended here as being the most appropriate measure of changes in the general purchasing power of the dollar. The GDP Implicit Deflator is the most comprehensive price index available. It embraces almost all goods and services produced in the economy, and encompasses the various sectional indexes. It measures (subject to the limitations in all index numbers and the quality of the information collected by the Commonwealth statistician) the weighted average change in the prices of all goods and services occurring in all sectors and in all parts of the country, i.e., the changes in the general price level which by definition are the reciprocal of the general purchasing power of the dollar.

The index does not measure changes in the actual purchasing power of the dollar in the hands of person A or person B; or its purchasing power in Melbourne or in Sydney; or the power of the dollar to buy consumer goods or investment goods, etc. It is a population-wide, nationwide, sector-wide index and it will measure personal, geographical, or sectoral changes only if they happen to coincide with the weighted average of all price changes occurring everywhere in the economy. The weightings in the index are automatically kept up to date as expenditure patterns change in the economy. The index is prepared by the government to convert the GDP in money terms to real terms so that reliable measures of growth in real national output can be ascertained. Conversion of accounting data by the index is appropriate where changes in the general purchasing power of the dollar are to be removed from that data.

The Consumer Price Index is frequently advocated as the one to use in accounting. However. it is a sectional index which covers consumer goods only and thereby leaves out investment goods and government services. It measures changes in the ability of the dollar to buy consumer goods and is not a measure of the change in the general price level. Where it is applied to accounting reports, initial capital investment is restated in terms of its ability to buy consumer goods at the end of the year, and the capital maintenance concept is that of shareholder consumer purchasing power. The aim of the concept is to preserve intact the shareholder's ability to spend money on consumer goods and services. The index is not recommended here because it omits the entire range of investment goods from its ambit and hence is of restricted relevance to a firm having substantial investment in fixed assets. It is more relevant for the personal accounts of shareholders as consumers rather than as investors.

Nevertheless, use of the Consumer Price Index may be justified on practical grounds. The CPI is published monthly whereas the information for the GDP Implicit Deflator is published quarterly, and then only after some time lag.[5] Firms, therefore, do not have to wait so long for the CPI to adjust their accounts for inflation and they do not have to balance at the end of a quarter. Secondly, the CPI is a more reliable index than the Deflator and it is subject to less revision. Finally, the two series are highly correlated as consumption expenditures typically account for over two-thirds of gross domestic expenditure.

An index of investment goods prices in general, or of limited ranges of investment goods, is likewise advocated. Use of these indexes is based on the aim of maintaining intact the investment purchasing power of the firm. They do not really aim to correct for changes in the general price level, and are more appropriately used as surrogates for current market prices in the current value and real value accounting systems.

## ADVANTAGES AND LIMITATIONS OF THE CONSTANT DOLLAR VALUE SYSTEM

Because the constant dollar value system has all the basic characteristics of the historic cost system, with one exception, it has the advantages attributed to that system. It is based on historic cost and on the realization test for transactions, and is therefore claimed to be objective. It corrects a serious and widely acknowledged weakness of the pure historic cost system, viz., the variable purchasing power of the dollar over time. After adjustment by the price level index, all dollars are now homogeneous in terms of general purchasing power, and the laws of mathematics concerning addition of unlike units are not now infringed. The relative magnitudes of all assets and all liabilities are not disturbed, as they are all adjusted by the same percentage. Given the publication of a suitable price index by an independent authority, the method can be objectively applied. Consequently, the system enjoys the support of professional accounting bodies in some countries.

Furthermore, the system reports some additional information to management and investors. It shows some effects of inflation on the measure of operating income, the additional resources which must be kept within the firm to maintain intact the purchasing power of the owners' initial investment, and the purchasing power losses incurred on net monetary assets or gains derived from net liabilities. This is useful information for management in determining dividend and financial policy and in making forecasts of the future. Management and shareholders can see some additional benefits from the use of debt finance (its real cost is reduced by inflation) and that there are losses to be incurred on holding excessive monetary assets (whose real value is also reduced by inflation). This is part of the explanation for companies in general tending to be more highly geared during an inflation and for companies in the finance industry (whose major assets are monetary ones) using a very high proportion of debt finance compared with other industries.

As compared with the historic cost system, the constant dollar value system normally affords greater protection to creditors since firms are likely to retain additional funds in the business for the maintenance of owners' purchasing power. While it does not add anything to the stewardship or administrative control functions of management, it does not interfere with them either.

Hence one can conclude that *price-level accounting* or the *constant dollar value system* has some clear advantages over the pure historic cost system. Unfortunately, however, while it does possess these advantages, price-level accounting still suffers from all the other defects of historic cost accounting as it is really just the historic cost system restated in terms of constant dollar purchasing power. Thus changes in the prices of individual assets are not recognized as they occur, and this can have profound effects on operating efficiency, in allowing real capital erosion to occur surreptitiously, in encouraging takeover bids, and so forth — matters which are examined in the *current* and *real value systems* following. The assumption underlying the system that the prices of all non-monetary assets rise at the general inflation rate is a false one for most assets. The general inflation rate is a weighted average of price changes for all goods and services, and typically the prices of individual assets owned by a firm rise at other rates — some higher and some lower. Consequently, the system does not report on the income that can be distributed without impairing the firm's real productive capacity, nor on its current financial position in terms of the current market prices of its assets, nor on the rate of return earned on current investment. If the whole of the price-level adjusted profit is to be distributed and the firm's non-monetary assets have risen in price at a greater rate than general inflation, the cost of goods sold and depreciation charges will be insufficient to enable replacement of the assets used up. The firm will have to run down its operating ability or borrow additional funds to meet the dividend payment. In other words, a firm's productive capacity can be eroded if it distributes constant dollar income. For example, in the Inflationary Company's reports, $1,714 does not necessarily measure the cost of replacing the goods sold to maintain the same level of inventories without additional investment in the Company, and $44 does not necessarily recover sufficient funds from revenue to enable replacement of the plant services used up over the year. Distribution of the $34 constant dollar income in dividend and the tax payments could cause an erosion of the Company's stock of net assets. If, for example, the 31 December buying price of closing inventories is $130 and not $120, and the cost of equivalent new plant is $350 and not $330, it is shown in Chapter 23 that only $23 could be distributed without eroding the stock of net assets. Similarly, the current value balance sheet shows that the total assets are $673 at current market prices, and given the liability of $150, the shareholders net investment in assets is $523. The rate of return on investment is only 4.4. per cent in current value terms (i.e., 23/523), as compared with 6.85 per cent in constant dollar value terms (i.e., 34/496). Similar results will always occur where the rate of price increase in the firm's physical assets exceeds the general inflation rate and where the firm has positive net monetary assets. The opposite situation occurs where the general inflation rate exceeds the rate of price increase in the firm's physical assets.

It is frequently claimed that price-level accounting enables the maintenance of the general purchasing power of owners' initial investment.[6] However, this result will not occur unless all asset selling prices rise at the general inflation rate and the firm has zero net monetary assets.[7] For example, assume that an investor buys a parcel of shares on 1 January for $10,000, and by 31 December the selling value of the shares rises to $11,500, and the general price-level had risen by 20 per cent. A dividend of $2,000 is received on 31 December. Under the constant dollar value system, the investor's 1 January balance sheet is restated in 31 December dollars as:

|  | $ |  | $ |
|---|---|---|---|
| Shares | 12,000 | Capital | 10,000 |
|  |  | Price-Level Adj. | 2,000 |
|  | $12,000 |  | $12,000 |

The 31 December balance sheet in 31 December dollars is:

|  | $ |  | $ |
|---|---|---|---|
| Cash | 2,000 | Capital | 10,000 |
| Shares | 12,000 | Price-Level Adj. | 2,000 |
|  |  | Constant Dollar |  |
|  |  | Income | 2,000 |
|  | $14,000 |  | $14,000 |

But in reality the shares are worth only $11,500, and the balance sheet overstates the income and financial position of the investor. To maintain intact the general purchasing power of the initial investment, net assets of $12,000 must be preserved so that the gain in wealth, i.e., income, is only $1,500. The 31 December balance sheet should be shown as:

|  | $ |  | $ |
|---|---|---|---|
| Cash | 2,000 | Capital | 10,000 |
| Shares | 11,500 | Price-Level Adj. | 2,000 |
|  |  | Income | 1,500 |
|  | $13,500 |  | $13,500 |

Income comprises the $2,000 dividend less the $500 loss in the purchasing power of the shares. The constant dollar value system does not necessarily maintain the general purchasing power of initial capital intact because it simply restates historic cost capital for general inflation rather than revalues assets according to the impact of inflation on the particular asset holdings of the firm.

A further deficiency of the system is that the price-level adjusted values attached to non-monetary assets can be difficult to compare and to aggregate meaningfully, and hence to interpret. If the firm purchases several units of the same type of asset at different times and prices, the aggregate price-level adjusted value has little meaning. For example, if the firm buys 100,000 shares in company X for $100,000 on 1 January, and again buys another 100,000 shares in company X on 31 December for $200,000, the total cost of the shares is $300,000, and they would be shown at this value in a historic cost balance sheet. However, if the general price level had risen by 15 per cent over the year, the shares would be stated at $315,000 in a constant dollar value balance sheet, being the number of December purchasing power units expended on them. Yet one parcel would be valued at $115,000 while the other identical parcel would be valued at $200,000. Can the two values be meaningfully compared and aggregated when two different values are placed upon identical assets? The aggregate value bears no relationship to the $400,000 current market value of the shares. This type of situation is compounded in the balance sheet of a typical business which acquires a wide range of different assets at different dates. Here, the problem of interpreting the meaning of the price-level adjusted values is hidden because the assets themselves are different but nevertheless the problem of the meaningful additivity of price-level adjusted outlays on assets still remains.

Furthermore, the system does not enable reliable comparisons to be made of key items for one firm over time or for comparisons between firms. For example, price-index adjusted sales do not show the growth in sales volume over time because sales values are not adjusted by the firm's own price changes; the system does not show growth in the general purchasing power of profits over time because individual expenses for asset consumption have not been adjusted by the changing costs of using the particular assets of the firm; it does not show the growth in plant capacity because plant investment is not adjusted by plant prices; and so on. The only complete adjustments made are those to monetary items. Similarly, the system does not facilitate making reliable interfirm comparisons except in relation to monetary items. Price-level adjusted values are not comparable between firms for the same reason that they are not comparable within firms. The price behaviour of specific assets owned by each firm does not necessarily follow the general inflation rate. For example, if firm A buys some land in Sydney for $100,000 and firm B buys land in Adelaide also for $100,000 in 1970, and there has been 50 per cent general inflation from 1970 to 1976, then both firms would show their land at $150,000 in the 1976 constant dollar value balance sheet. This would be the case even though the 1976 market price of the Sydney land is $500,000 and the Adelaide land is only $80,000. No reliable interfirm comparisons of price-level adjusted asset values can be made; and as a consequence, neither can reliable interfirm comparisons be made of financial position, profits or the rate of return on investment.

When assessed by the standards for good information, the constant dollar value system cannot be rated highly for purposes of performance and financial position measurement and for decision-making. Information on the price-level adjusted cost of goods sold, depreciation, non-monetary asset values and so on is of little relevance for decision-making by management and shareholders. The system does not provide relevant, reliable, or comparable information on the current financial position of firms and their earning power; it does not normally maintain intact the operating capacity of the firm or the general purchasing power of owners' investment. Its only major advantage over the historic cost system for decision-making purposes derives from the measurement of price-level losses or gains on net monetary assets or liabilities, and the implication this has for financial planning and dividend policy. However, the system does this at the great risk that the uninformed reader will believe that *all* effects of inflation including changes in asset prices have been allowed for; and that real income and current financial position are being measured; and that valid interfirm comparisons of the data can be made. Price-level accounting will show these matters only if the firm's asset prices change at the same rate as general inflation, and this is likely to be a rare occurrence. It is inevitable that the price-level adjusted values of many assets, and to a lesser extent of total assets of a firm, will be overstated in relation to their current market prices, and this can have serious consequences for the measure of financial position. For example, consider the situation that arises where the price-level adjusted historic cost of an asset is $1,000,000 but its current market price is $700,000. Because of this, a "lower of price-level adjusted cost or market value" rule has bee proposed.[8] But such a rule offends against the accounting standards of consistency and freedom from bias – downward asset revaluations are allowed but not upward ones. Application of the rule would flaunt the objectivity standard claimed for the system by its proponents. Furthermore, the rule would require extensive revaluation of assets at current market prices to determine whether these prices were less than the price-level adjusted costs and the system is supposed to avoid asset revaluations. For a large firm with a wide variety of assets, it should be expected that up to one half of the price-level adjusted values will exceed current market prices. Finally, the aggregate value of assets obtained by applying the rule would be difficult to interpret; and along with it, the measures of financial position and rate of return on investment.

Thus while price-level adjusted information represents a definite improvement on historic cost reports for some purposes in a period of inflation, it is most important that the accounting system does not end with it. Changes in asset prices typically have far more impact on the firm than general inflation because they are specific to the firm and not an overall average of everything in which price rises and falls tend to cancel out. Specific changes in asset prices must be accounted for along with inflation to yield a meaningful accounting system, and this is done in the *current* and *real value systems* to which we now turn.

## FURTHER READING

Institute of Chartered Accountants in Australia and Australian Society of Accountants, Preliminary Exposure Draft, "A Method of Accounting for Changes in the Purchasing Power of Money", December 1974.

Gynther, R. S., "The First Preliminary Exposure Draft: A Method of Accounting for Changes in the Purchasing Power of Money", *Australian Accountant*, (September 1975).

Lemke, K. W., "Capital Maintenance and Confusion", *Abacus* (June 1974).

Mason, P. *Price-Level Changes and Financial Statements — Basic Concepts and Methods.* Columbus, Ohio: A.A.A., 1956.

Mathews, R. L. *The Accounting Framework.* 3rd ed. Melbourne: Cheshire, 1971. Chap. 8.

Moonitz, M. "Price-Level Accounting and Scales of Measurement." *Accounting Review* (July 1970).

## NOTES

1. Australian Bureau of Statistics, *Australian National Accounts, National Income and Expenditure* (Canberra: Government Printer, 1975).
2. This analysis is based on R. J. Chambers, *Accounting, Evaluation, and Economic Behavior* (Englewood Cliffs, N.J.: Prentice-Hall, 1966), chap. 10.
3. Detailed illustrations of price-level accounting are given in P. Mason, *Price-Level Changes and Financial Statements.* Accounting Research Study No. 6, *Reporting the Financial Effects of Price-Level Changes.* New York: A.I.C.P.A., 1963; and A.P.B. *Financial Statements for General Price-Level Changes.* Statement No. 3. New York: A.I.C.P.A., 1969.
4. Most of the official index number series are published in the *Monthly Review of Business Statistics, Australian National Accounts, National Income and Expenditure* (quarterly), *Labour Report* (annual), and Reserve Bank of Australia statistical bulletins (monthly).
5. Actually, the GDP Implicit Deflator is not published as an index. It must be calculated from the statistics of GDP at current prices in any given year and the GDP for that same year measured at the 1966–67 base year prices. For example, the 1974–75 Australian GDP at 1974–75 prices was $59,000m, and at 1966–67 prices it was $32,000m; hence the Deflator for 1974–75 is 183 (i.e., $\frac{59,000}{32,000}$ on base 1966–67 = 100.
6. ICA and ASA, Preliminary Exposure Draft, "A Method of Accounting for Changes in the Purchasing Power of Money", December 1974.
7. Lemke, K. W., "Capital Maintenance and Confusion", *Abacus* (June 1974).
8. ICA and ASA, Preliminary Exposure Draft, "A Method of Accounting for Changes in the Purchasing Power of Money", December 1974.

## QUESTIONS AND EXERCISES

[Solution to problem marked * is given in Appendix 4.]

1. Explain the concepts of wealth, income, and capital maintenance in the constant dollar value system.

2. What is the relationship between inflation and the general purchasing power of the dollar?

3. What property of the dollar is used as the unit of measurement in the constant dollar value system?

4. Why are the effects of inflation on monetary and non-monetary assets likely to differ?

5. Explain the notion of a price-level loss on holding monetary assets and a price-level gain on liabilities.

6. Distinguish between a revaluation of assets and a restatement of assets in terms of dollars of constant purchasing power. Does the amount of the restatement form part of income or capital?

7. If the entire constant dollar value income for a year were distributed, would this necessarily preserve intact a firm's initial stock of assets?

8. What price index do you consider to be most appropriate for use in price-level accounting?

9. What are the major advantages of the constant dollar value system as compared with the pure historic cost system?

10. Critically assess the merits of the constant dollar value system in terms of the standards for accounting information.

11. i. An investor bought debentures for $10,000 on 1 January, on which the rate of interest was 8 per cent. He duly received the interest payable on 31 December. The general price level index rose from 120 to 126 over the year and the market price of the debentures remained constant. What income did the investor earn over the year?

    ii. Assume the 31 December market price of the debentures was $9,700. What income did the investor earn over the year? At what figure would you show the debentures in his balance sheet?

12. A firm owns two identical blocks of land which have a current market price of $50,000 each on 31 December 1973. Block A was bought on 1 January 1960 for $8,000, and block B on 31 December 1966 for $20,000. The general price-level index was 100 on 1 January 1960, 130 on 31 December 1966, and 180 on 31 December 1973. Using constant dollar value accounting, at what values would each block be shown in the December 1973 balance sheet? What does the aggregate value shown for land mean?

13. A firm bought a new building for $100,000 on 1 January 1970. Its current market price remained constant for the next three years. The general price-level index at the purchase date was 150, and on 31 December 1973 was 200. At what figure would the building be shown in the 1973 balance sheet in the constant dollar value system? Comment on the result. Show the journal entry for the price-level adjustment.

14. A firm bought a block of land on 1 January for $200,000 which it immediately leased to a parking station operator for $30,000 rent, payable on 31 December. The operator is responsible for all rates and taxes on the land. The general price level index rose from 140 to 160 over the year.

    What is the constant dollar income for the year, in end-of-year dollars? If this income is wholly paid to the owner, has the general purchasing power of his initial investment been maintained intact if:

    a. The selling value of the land on 31 December is $210,000?
    b. The selling value of the land on 31 December is $250,000?

*15. The balance sheet of the PQ Company, prepared according to the constant dollar value accounting system, on 1 January was:

|  | $ | $ |  | $ |
|---|---|---|---|---|
| Debtors |  | 200 | Creditors | 100 |
|  |  |  | Debentures | 400 |
| Plant | 600 |  | Capital | 1,000 |
| Less Accumulated |  |  |  |  |
| Depreciation | 100 | 500 | Price-Level Adjustment | 100 |
| Premises |  | 900 |  |  |
|  |  | $1,600 |  | $1,600 |

At 31 December, its balance sheet before the year's adjustments for inflation is:

|  | $ | $ |  | $ |
|---|---|---|---|---|
| Cash |  | 100 | Creditors | 60 |
| Debtors |  | 300 | Debentures | 400 |
| Plant | 600 |  | Capital | 1,000 |
| Less Accumulated |  |  | Price-Level Adjustment |  |
| Depreciation | 200 | 400 | (1 Jan.) | 100 |
| Premises |  | 900 | Retained Profits | 140 |
|  |  | $1,700 |  | $1,700 |

The general price level index rose from 120 to 130 over the year. No dividends were paid during the year.

*Required:*

i. Recast the 1 January balance sheet in terms of end-of-year dollars, and show journal entries for the adjustments.

ii. What is the historic cost income for the year?

iii. What is the constant dollar value income for the year?

iv. Comment on the significance of the results of the conversion into end-of-year dollars. Explain the significance of the price-level adjustment and the price-level gain amounts.

16. The Caper Corporation Limited have been using constant dollar value (or price-level adjusted) accounting for several years. Their balance sheet on December 31, 1974 (in Dec. 31, 1974 purchasing power dollars) is as below:

| | $ | $ | | | $ | $ |
|---|---|---|---|---|---|---|
| *Current Assets* | | | *Current Liabilities* | | | |
| Bank | 46,000 | | A/cs Payable | 84,000 | | |
| A/cs Receivable | 120,000 | | Tax Payable | 40,000 | | |
| Inventories | 74,000 | 240,000 | Dividend Payable | 30,000 | 154,000 | |
| *Long Term Assets* | | | *Long Term Liabilities* | | | |
| Plant | 240,000 | | Debentures | | 200,000 | |
| *Less* Accumm. | | | | | | |
| Depreciation | 40,000 | 200,000 | *Shareholders Equity* | | | |
| Buildings | 200,000 | | | | | |
| *Less* Accumm. | | | Paid up Capital | 300,000 | | |
| Depreciation | 30,000 | 170,000 | Share Premium | | | |
| Land | | 150,000 | Reserve | 60,000 | | |
| Goodwill | | 40,000 | 560,000 | General Reserve | 30,000 | |
| | | | Price Level Adj. | 50,000 | | |
| | | | Ret'd Earnings | 6,000 | 446,000 | |
| | | $800,000 | | | $800,000 | |

The transactions summary for the year ended December 31, 1975 shows the following information:

| | |
|---|---|
| Sales (all credit) | $1,200,000 |
| Purchases (all credit) | 798,000 |
| COGS (based on FIFO) | 780,000 |
| Wages paid | 160,000 |
| Other cash operating costs | 66,000 |
| Interest paid (June 30, $10,000; Dec. 31, $10,000) | 20,000 |
| Cash paid to creditors | 780,000 |
| Cash received from customers | 1,166,000 |
| Tax paid (June 30) | 40,000 |
| Dividends paid (Jan. 31) | 30,000 |

In measuring the year's income, depreciation is to be charged at 10% on gross value (i.e., price level adjusted cost) of plant and at 5% on gross value of buildings.

The year's income is to be appropriated to:

Company tax  — 50% of taxable income
Dividends    — 10% on paid up capital

Transfer to general reserve — $22,000

Company tax is levied on historic cost income. The historic cost of plant is $220,000, and 10% straight line depreciation is allowed. Buildings are not depreciable for tax purposes.

The general price level index on Jan. 1, 1975 is    140
                                June 30, 1975    150
                                Dec. 31, 1975    168

*Required:*

i.   An income and appropriation statement measuring constant dollar income for 1975 in end-of-year purchasing power units.

ii.  A balance sheet as at December 31, 1975, in end-of-year purchasing power units.

iii. Journal entries recording all price-level adjustments made.

iv.  All balance sheet ledger accounts.

Set out your accounting reports showing: Unadjusted Amounts, Conversion Factor, Price Level Adjusted Amount.

17. The Withit Corporation Ltd desires to publish a set of general price level adjusted historic cost financial reports along with its traditional historic cost reports.

   a.  Its historic cost balance sheet on 31 December 1974 is as follows:

| *Current Assets* | | $ | *Liabilities* | $ |
|---|---|---|---|---|
| Bank | | 40,000 | Creditors | 50,000 |
| Accounts Receivable | | 100,000 | Tax Payable | 35,000 |
| Inventories | | 60,000 | Dividend Payable | 25,000 |
| | | | Debentures | 120,000 |
| | | 200,000 | | 230,000 |
| *Long Term Assets* | | | *Shareholders Equity* | |
| Buildings | 300,000 | | Paid up Capital | 250,000 |
| *Less* Accum. Deprecn. | 120,000 | 180,000 | Reserves | 50,000 |
| Land | | 120,000 | Retained Earnings | 20,000 |
| Goodwill | | 50,000 | | |
| | | 350,000 | | 320,000 |
| | | $550,000 | | $550,000 |

   b.  Transactions during 1975 were:

| | $ |
|---|---|
| Sales (all credit) | 1,000,000 |
| Purchases (all credit) | 640,000 |
| Cash Operating Expenses | 280,000 |
| Interest paid (31 Dec. 1975) | 12,000 |
| Dividends paid (30 June 1975) | 25,000 |
| Tax paid (30 June 1975) | 35,000 |
| Cash paid to creditors | 620,000 |
| Cash collected from debtors | 950,000 |

   c.  Other items to be included in the reports:

   Depreciation on buildings: 4% on historic cost.
   Inventories 31 December 1975 (FIFO cost) $70,000.

Company tax at the rate of 50% on taxable income is to be provided for. Taxable income coincides with historic cost income except for depreciation on buildings being non-tax-deductible.

A 10% dividend on paid up capital is to be provided for.

d. The buildings, land, and goodwill were all purchased on 31 December 1964.

e. The general price level index numbers at each relevant date are:

| | |
|---|---|
| 31 Dec. 1964 | 80 |
| 31 Dec. 1974 | 160 |
| 30 June 1975 | 170 |
| 31 Dec. 1975 | 180 |

*Further Information:*

i. Set out the income statement showing columns for Historic Cost, Conversio. Factor, Price Level Adjusted Amount; and the balance sheet showii. Historic Cost and Price Level Adjusted Amount.

ii. Use the mid-yeai compromise for trading transactions and assume all transactions occurred at a fairly uniform rate throughout the year, except where otherwise indicated.

iii. Show all necessary calculations and specify all assumptions made in the course of your calculations.

*Required:*

i. A general price level adjusted (or constant dollar value) balance sheet as at 31 December 1974.

ii. An historic cost and a gener l price level adjusted income statement in EOY purchasing power units for 1975.

iii. An historic cost and a general price level adjusted balance sheet as at 31 December 1975.

iv. The Price Level Adjustment ledger account.

# Chapter 23
# Current Value Accounting Systems

In this chapter we shall extend the analysis to take absolute changes in the current market prices of assets into account. The system is known as the *current value accounting system,* and the measure of income as *current income.* To some extent the current value system involves a departure from the use of historic transaction prices for the measurement of expenses and valuation of assets, and the realization convention is not adhered to throughout. Changes in market prices of assets are recognized as they occur rather than when they are realized, and the implications of these changes for income measurement and financial position determination are recorded. However, the system does not report the impact of general inflation on the firm's results.

Significant and frequent changes in prices of some assets between the times of purchase and of completed use are a fact of business life in most advanced countries. They occur for a variety of reasons – general inflation, technical progress and obsolescence, changes in consumer tastes, taxes, and other supply and demand conditions in the market in which the firm operates. Proponents of current value accounting believe that these price changes should be recognized as they occur, whereas historic cost supporters believe that they should be neglected until and if embodied in a market transaction.

The problem of asset price changes is confined to severable, non-monetary assets – primarily physical assets (e.g., such as inventories, plant, and premises) and marketable securities. With physical assets there is a time lag between their purchase and their complete utilization, such that the current market prices of these assets can diverge from their historic cost or unexpired cost. Monetary assets are not affected as they remain at their stated dollar values, and likewise all liabilities. Intangible assets such as preliminary expenses, research and development costs, and goodwill are not affected because they normally have no existence separate from that of the firm and cannot be sold as separate assets.

Current value accounting is based on the use of current market prices of non-monetary assets for the measurement of periodic income and financial position. All changes in the market prices of assets are recognized in the year in which they occur — realization is not necessary — and all measures of asset usage are based on these prices. Current market prices are a measure of the market opportunity costs of assets, and these form part of the basis for all rational decisions about the purchase, use, and sale of assets at the current time. In general terms, opportunity cost is the value of the most attractive alternative that is sacrificed by taking a proposed action. In terms of asset values, opportunity cost may be stated as the least costly sacrifice avoided by owning an asset. It is always the lower of the top two values under consideration as the opportunity cost shows the sacrifice incurred in taking the better alternative. The system is very easily applied where current market prices are readily available and there is only the one price ruling in the market at any time. These prices are substituted for historic costs in the asset accounts in a manner similar to that used for asset revaluations in the modified historic cost system. For upward revaluations, the asset account is debited and an Asset Revaluation Reserve or Holding Gains account is credited; the reverse applies to downward revaluations. The credit account is part of owners' equity. All charges for asset usage, i.e., cost of goods sold and depreciation, are then based on the current prices of assets in order that sufficient funds are deemed to be recovered from revenue to maintain capital intact. All other expenses for wages, power, etc. are charged as in historic cost accounting as there is not much time lag, if any, between acquisition and utilization.

Complications in current value accounting are encountered where there are market imperfections causing more than one price to exist for the same assets. Frequently the buying price of an asset differs from the price at which the firm could sell it because the firm buys and sells in different markets. The two prices approach each other as the new and secondhand markets become more competitive, as the costs directly attaching to the transaction are reduced, and as transport and installation costs become negligible; while they can diverge sharply in the case of specialized assets, where there is no active secondhand market or where transport and installation costs become significant.

A current value system can be based on either asset buying prices (i.e., current costs) or on asset selling prices (i.e., current cash equivalents), and ideally information from both systems is required where buying and selling prices differ significantly. We shall refer to them as *current value (current cost)* and *current value (selling price)* respectively, and to the income concepts as *current income (current cost)* and *current income (selling price)*, and analyze them in turn. The current value (current cost) system is also known as the current replacement cost system. Where no suffixes are used, the statements apply generally to both versions of current value accounting. The interpretations of the results and the uses of each system differ somewhat; however, the recording procedures are identical throughout both systems. The medium of exchange measurement property of the dollar is used in current value accounting.

## CURRENT VALUE (CURRENT COST) SYSTEM

### WEALTH, INCOME, AND CAPITAL MAINTENANCE CONCEPTS

In current value (current cost) accounting, *wealth* is the aggregate value of the firm's net assets, and *income* is the increase in that wealth over a period after maintaining intact the initial stock of net assets of the firm, where all non-monetary assets are valued at end-of-year buying prices in the market.

The precise nature of the concepts of income and capital maintenance can be illustrated by extending the algebraic analysis of chapter 22. Let the firm's initial balance sheet be stated as:[1]

$$M_0 + N_0 = P_0 \qquad \qquad \text{......(i)}$$

where      $M_0$ represents the net monetary assets held
$N_0$ represents the non-monetary or physical assets held, valued at beginning-of-year buying costs
$P_0$ represents the proprietorship.

If the current purchase costs of similar physical assets rise by c per cent over the year, the initial balance sheet may be restated in end-of-year buying cost terms as:

$$M_0 + N_0 \, (1 + c) = P_0 + Nc \qquad \qquad \text{......(ii)}$$

The term $N_0 (1 + c)$ represents the initial physical assets at end-of-year prices; Nc represents the appreciation in the prices of physical assets over the year; and $(P_0 + Nc)$ is the measure of the firm's productive capacity which is to be maintained. Where the prices of the physical assets change at different rates over the year, a separate c term is required for each asset. Here it is assumed that all asset prices rise at the same rate for simplicity of exposition. No adjustment is made to the values of monetary assets or liabilities — they are valued at their nominal dollar amounts in the usual way.

At the end of the year, the firm's balance sheet may be stated as:

$$M_1 + N_1 = P_1 \qquad \qquad \text{......(iii)}$$

The physical assets are valued at end-of-year buying costs. It is assumed that no proprietor's contributions or withdrawals are made over the year. Current income (current cost) $(Y_c)$ is then:

$$Y_c = [M_1 - M_o] + [N_1 - N_o (1 + c)] = P_1 - (P_o + Nc) \quad \ldots\ldots(iv)$$

Thus, current income is the gain in net assets over the year, where physical assets are valued at end-of-year buying prices throughout. Alternatively, it may be defined as the maximum amount that can be distributed without encroaching upon the opening stock of net assets.

*Current income (current cost)* measures the increase in wealth generated from operations after maintaining intact the aggregate *stock* of net monetary assets and physical assets (as distinct from the original money investment in its physical assets). Because physical assets provide the firm with its basic operating capacity and net monetary assets with the financial resources to enable utilization of the physical assets in a monetary economy, this concept of capital maintenance is often called the maintenance of operating capacity concept. Maintenance of operating capacity means that the service potential of the stock of net assets is preserved and hence that the firm's ability to supply goods and services in the future is maintained. Capital is considered to be a pool of operating capacity and, as the physical assets are gradually converted into funds through operating activity, some of the funds are required to replace the assets and maintain operating capacity, and the surplus remaining is income. In terms of the matching principle, current income is revenue less the current purchase costs of related inputs; and operating capacity is maintained by basing the charges for asset consumption (i.e., cost of goods sold and depreciation) on the amounts required to replace at the end of the period the goods sold or the fixed asset services used up. Thus the amounts recovered from revenue before a profit is struck are sufficient to replace the assets used up, so long as they are replaced immediately while their current market prices last. For example, if the historic cost of goods sold is $1,000 and their cost of immediate replacement is $1,400, then $1,400 is charged against revenue so that the same volume of inventories can be kept on hand for the next period without having to finance an additional outlay on inventories from new equity or debt funds. The whole of current income (current cost) can be distributed without impairing the volume of physical assets and net monetary assets owned by the firm at the beginning of the year, and it is all realized as all profit accrued at the point of sale. By valuing opening and closing assets at the same set of prices, all price variations are removed from the comparison of the stocks of opening and closing net assets. Hence an increase in the *value* of net assets over the year must represent an increase in the *volume* of the net assets on hand. Current income measures this increased volume of net assets. As compared with historic cost income, (which measures the cash surplus on operations in the long run for a firm where the surplus is based on maintaining the original money investment intact), current income measures the cash surplus in the long run for the going concern where the surplus is based on maintaining the original stock of net assets intact.

The *capital maintenance* benchmark used is that of the stock of net assets of the firm rather than initial money investment or the general purchasing power of that investment. Management finds this a useful benchmark to use as it enables the firm to conserve its physical and financial resources without having to raise additional funds to finance a given volume of operations during a period of changing asset prices. For the firm to remain as an effective going concern and to achieve its profit objective, to repay its debts as they fall due and so on, it must normally maintain the volume of its assets so as to maintain its physical level of operations. The determination of current income (current cost) helps thereby to guard against the problem of physical capital erosion in which there is a gradual running down of the firm's volume of assets (and hence its size), even though the initial dollar capital has been maintained intact. Use of the maintenance of operating capacity as the benchmark for measuring current income does not necessarily imply that assets used up are replaced with other identical assets, or indeed with any physical assets at all. It merely means that assets used up *can* be replaced from the funds recovered from revenue if need be, and not that they *will* be. Capital and the maintenance of capital have reference only to a general property of a collection of assets (dollar investment, constant purchasing power, productive capacity, and so on); and the maintenance of capital does not mean the maintenance of any specific asset. Under all valuation systems, some benchmark has to be adopted to measure this increment in wealth that is defined as income, whether that benchmark be nominal dollars, or something else.

Benchmarks are general reference points (either internal to the firm or external) used for measurement purposes and they do not necessarily imply anything about future action. Measurement processes are not concerned with specific ends. The choice of a benchmark should be determined by what is useful in terms of the general financial information provided. The decision to replace or not replace an asset used up in operations is a subsequent investment decision to be made by management and it should be assessed according to the alternative investment options open to the firm at the time. Indeed it might be preferable not to replace a specific asset in the process of maintaining overall physical capital intact because investment in that particular asset is no longer profitable. Furthermore the decision to maintain intact operating capacity is a separate managerial decision, and management may decide to reduce or increase the size of the firm rather than leave it at a constant size. There is nothing inconsistent about a firm measuring income on a current cost basis and deciding to reduce the scale of its operations. It is better that the management does this explicitly than that it should occur by default through inappropriate income measurement procedures. In the same way, the measurement of income does not imply that the whole of that income should be distributed – the question of income distribution is separate from (though influenced by) the problem of income measurement. It merely shows the maximum "value" of resources that can be distributed without impairing "capital" (according to which valuation concepts are used).

The relationship between the several concepts is illustrated in Figure 23−1 below.

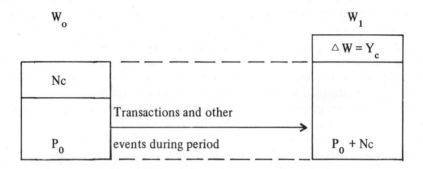

**Figure 23−1** Current Value System Wealth Diagram
where all items are measured as in the equations above.

The treatment of *net holding gains* on non-monetary assets in the current value system is the subject of much contention. Some authors treat them as part of current income and others regard them as part of capital maintenance. Here, it is argued that net holding gains on the physical assets which form the firm's basic productive capacity are part of capital maintenance, whereas those on marketable securities and assets held for speculative purposes are part of current income.

The classification of net holding gains depends upon the capital maintenance concept adopted. Where the object of income measurement is to measure the surplus which can be distributed without impairing the firm's stock of net assets, any fluctuation in the current market prices of the assets making up that stock remain as part of the capital base. The opening stock of assets is revalued at current market prices so that the charges for their use in operations are based on their current buying costs, and the balance sheet shows the current market value of the funds tied up in the assets. The net holding gains on these assets show the extent to which their prices have changed over the year and they are a capital maintenance adjustment. They show the additional funds which must be kept within the business to allow for the increased money investment in a given stock of inventories and fixed assets. They do not show an increase in wealth as measured in terms of an increased command over assets of the type used by the firm. These net holding gains could not be distributed without reducing the stock of physical assets or the monetary assets, i.e., without impairing operating capacity.[2] While it is also the case that most of the net holding gains for the year may be unrealized and their distribution could cause financial problems to the firm, the realization question is not relevant to the issue of whether they form part of income or capital maintenance in current value accounting. Net holding gains are a capital maintenance adjustment because of the concept of capital maintenance adopted in the current value (current cost) system. They represent the increased market value of the funds committed to maintaining the firm's existing operating capacity. The name "holding *gains*" is in fact misleading in this context – rising replacement costs of assets are more likely to be a burden than a benefit to the firm. Higher expense charges must be made against revenue for asset consumption if the firm is to remain a viable long run entity. If the increased costs cannot be passed on in higher selling prices, its profits and rate of return on investment are depressed. The term "asset revaluation reserve" is preferred as it does not signify that rising replacement costs necessarily confer benefits on the firm.

There are, however, two circumstances in which it is possible to convert net holding gains into income. First, the firm may be able to convert to another set of assets which enables the same volume of business to be maintained but at a lower cost. It may switch from high to low cost inventory lines, it may move to another locality where it can obtain premises providing similar facilities at a lower price, and so on. The surplus so created is released from the firm's investment in its physical capacity and it can be distributed as income while maintaining intact its productive capacity. Secondly, the firm may sell all its assets, repay all liabilities, and leave the industry. Here, there is no need for the concept of operating capacity, and wealth would be assessed on a monetary basis. However, the relevant market prices here are selling rather than buying prices.

## AN ILLUSTRATION OF CURRENT VALUE ACCOUNTING

The example of the Inflationary Company in chapter 22 can be modified to illustrate the application of current value (current cost) accounting. In addition to the historic cost information previously given, the following information is provided.

| i. | Valuation data | Hist. Cost $ | Current Cost $ |
|----|----------------|--------------|----------------|
| | Inventories 1 Jan. | 100 | 100 |
| | Plant       1 Jan. | 300 | 300 |
| | Inventories 31 Dec. | 120 | 130 |
| | Plant       31 Dec. | 300 | 350 |

ii. The same quantity of inventories was hold on both dates.

iii. Plant is depreciated at 13.3 per cent on cost.

iv. EOY plant and inventory values are to be used in the income statement.

*Income Statement for the year ended 31 December*

| | | Hist. Cost $ | | Current Cost $ | |
|---|---|---|---|---|---|
| Sales | | | 2,000 | | 2,000 |
| *Less* Invent 1 Jan. | 100 | | | 130 | |
| Purchases | 1,630 | | | 1,630 | |
| | 1,730 | | | 1,760 | |
| *Less* Invent 31 Dec. | 120 | | | 130 | |
| Cost of Goods Sold | | | 1,610 | | 1,630 |
| Gross Profit | | | 390 | | 370 |
| *Less* Cash Operating Costs | 300 | | | 300 | |
| Depreciation | 40 | | 340 | 47 | 347 |
| Net Income | | | $50 | | $23 |

*Balance Sheet as at 31 December*

| | | Hist. Cost $ | | Current Value $ |
|---|---|---|---|---|
| Cash | | 240 | | 240 |
| Inventories | | 120 | | 130 |
| Plant | 300 | | 350 | |
| *Less* Accum. Deprecn. | 40 | 260 | 47 | 303 |
| | | $620 | | $673 |
| Creditors | | 150 | | 150 |
| Capital | 400 | | 400 | |
| Retained Earnings | 20 | | 20 | |
| Income | 50 | 470 | 23 | |
| Asset Revaluation Reserve | | | 80 | 523 |
| | | $620 | | $673 |

## Comments

i.  End-of-year values are used for inventories (both opening and closing balances) in the income statement. As the volume of inventories is unchanged over the year, COGS coincides with purchases in the current value income statement. Use of historic cost inventory values in the historic cost report causes the appreciation in the value of opening inventories to the closing value (i.e., $20) to be included in gross profit. This is the reason for the difference between the two gross profit measures.

ii.  The depreciation charge is based on the EOY plant value of $350.

iii.  No adjustments are required to the other items in the reports.

iv. The Asset Revaluation Reserve account summarizes all revaluations of assets and it shows the additional investment in net assets in terms of current costs required to maintain the stock of net assets at a constant level.

v. Current income of $23 could be distributed while maintaining the initial stock of net assets intact. It is $27 less than historic cost income because the unrealized profit on opening inventories ($20) is eliminated and because of the higher depreciation charge ($7).

vi. The income statement measure of current income agrees with the balance sheet measures, i.e.,

$$Y_c = (M_1 - M_0) + N_1 - (N_0 + Nc) = P_1 - (P_0 + Nc)$$

$$= (90 - 20) + (433 - 480) \qquad = 523 - (420 + 80)$$

$$= 70 - 47 \qquad\qquad\qquad = 523 - 500$$

$$= 23 \qquad\qquad\qquad\qquad = 23$$

vii. The journal entry to record the revaluation adjustment is:

| Inventories $(100 \rightarrow 130)$ | Dr | 30 | | $\Big\}$ Nc |
| Plant $\qquad(300 \rightarrow 350)$ | Dr | 50 | | |
| Asset Revaluation Reserve | Cr | | 80 | Nc |

Revaluation of initial assets at EOY buying prices.

viii. The problem could be solved by basing the inventory figures on middle-of-year (MOY) values of $115 in the calculation of COGS, and by calculating depreciation on the MOY value of plant of $325, giving $43 depreciation. In this case, $4 backlog depreciation on plant for the second half-year must be recorded. Current value income statements may be centred on middle-of-year values as in the constant dollar value system. This increases their accuracy as well as their complexity.

In the presentation of current value results, it is probably best to show them along with historic cost results at least for a transitional period. The reporting of both sets of results highlights the impact of asset price changes on the firm's performance and financial position. Furthermore, a current value firm will not then be disadvantaged in comparisons with historic cost firms whose income and rates of return become exaggerated in an inflationary period. There is a risk that if a firm publishes only current value results when its competitors publish historic cost results its performance will be judged as poor, and its share price will be depressed in relation to those of its competitors.

## PROBLEMS ENCOUNTERED IN CURRENT VALUE ACCOUNTING

The major problems encountered in applying current value accounting are concerned with obtaining current market prices of assets, obsolescence and technical progress in products and in production methods, and backlog depreciation allowances.

### 1.  Obtaining Current Market Prices of Assets

The ease with which current buying prices can be obtained varies considerably according to the nature of the markets for different assets. The sources from which the prices of typical assets can be obtained and the problems which can be encountered are indicated below. Where current market prices are not readily available, surrogate measures such as indexed historic costs and depreciated values of new fixed assets rather than secondhand market values must be used. In all cases the lowest price which need be paid to acquire the asset at the current time is the relevant price for current value accounting.

### *Inventories*

In retailing there are generally active markets in merchandise, and buying or selling prices are easily obtained from transactions or price lists. The merchandise should be valued at the prices payable for quantities normally traded in where prices are functionally related to volume.

In the case of a manufacturer, current purchase prices of raw material inventories are generally available. The current costs of finished goods inventories are readily ascertainable from current manufacturing costs. The current costs of party processed inventories can be ascertained from current manufacturing costs, with due allowance being paid to the stage of manufacture reached.

### *Motor Vehicles*

Both new and secondhand markets are fairly active and prices can be readily ascertained for most vehicles according to their existing condition. Where secondhand prices are readily available, depreciation can be measured directly from the market as the reduction in the purchase cost of an asset owned for the period. For example, the depreciation on a car in its first year is the EOY new purchase price less the EOY purchase price of a one-year-old car, where the model has not changed significantly.

### *Plant and Equipment*

There are generally list prices available for all new items of plant and equipment not made to special order. Values for used assets can be readily obtained if there are active secondhand markets. The major difficulties are encountered with custom-made plant as there are no quoted market prices for it and the cost of replacement must be estimated in some way. Prices of similar equipment may be available and these could be translated into the current cost of the firm's equipment as new. Alternatively, an index of plant prices may be applied to the historic cost of plant to update it to current cost. The index may be constructed by the firm itself where it is a large one which buys equipment regularly, or it may be an official one. For example, in Australia, the Gross National Expenditure price deflator for the "all other" category of private gross fixed capital expenditure can be used. This index covers expenditure on all types of plant and equipment in Australia. Due allowance for the used condition of the existing equipment can be made by applying the index to both the cost of plant as new and to the accumulated depreciation account.

## Land and Buildings

The market for land and buildings tends to be very active in urban growth areas so that current buying and selling prices for similar properties are readily obtainable. Where special features attach to a particular site or building which are not duplicated elsewhere, or where the property market is not active, an appraisal by a qualified property valuer may be necessary. Essentially the valuer determines what the most likely price would be if the property were to come onto the market. Alternatively an index of building costs and of land values may be used to adjust historic cost up to a current cost approximation. In addition, official valuations of the unimproved value of land are made by the Valuer-General every few years for rating purposes.

## Marketable Securities

There is no difficulty in obtaining current market prices of securities for which there is an active market as they are quoted daily on the stock exchanges.

### Specific Price Indexes

Specific indexes may be used to approximate current market prices for some physical assets whose current market prices are difficult to obtain. A specific price index covers a limited range of goods only and its purpose is to measure proportionate changes in the prices of those goods rather than changes in the general purchasing power of the dollar.

The Commonwealth government publishes a number of specific

price indexes relating to basic raw materials, building materials, wage rates, wool prices, and other items.[3] In addition a range of indexes — the implicit deflators — can be calculated from the GDP and GNE statistics at current year and at constant 1966—67 prices.

The narrower the range of goods and services covered by a specific price index, or the more nearly that prices of all items move together, the more closely is the index-adjusted historic cost likely to approximate the current cost of the item. A broadly based index of, for example, construction costs, may bear little relationship to price changes for an office desk.

The use of specific price indexes should be justified on the grounds that they enable approximations to the current costs of assets for which current market prices are not readily available, rather than that they have any intrinsic merits in themselves, e.g., of objectivity, or that they correct for deficiencies in the dollar measuring rod.

Hence, although there can be many practical difficulties in the way of obtaining reliable current market price data, these difficulties can easily be exaggerated for the typical firm. For the retailer, current market prices of all assets are likely to be readily available; and the same is likely to be true for manufacturers not engaged in highly specialized industries. It would appear that in reality many progressive companies, including the largest and most complex ones, do revalue their assets systematically every year or two, even though the results are not incorporated in the accounting system or included in published reports. Many firms consider it prudent to keep their asset valuations up to date for fire insurance purposes at least, and it is often a condition for secured loans that disaster insurance be based on current replacement costs.

The use of current market prices in itself does not mean that current value balance sheets are less objective than those based on historic cost. Indeed the reverse applies where current market prices of all assets are readily available and can be independently verified, and where many assumptions are required for the preparation of historic cost reports. But they may be less objective where current market prices are difficult to determine. This fact should be made explicit by using a range of asset values in the balance sheet, and there should be explanatory notes as to causes of difficulty and proper interpretation of items.

### 2. Technical Progress and Obsolescence

Current value accounting is fairly straightforward where physical assets do not change form over the year as the replacement assets take the same form as those used up. EOY prices can be obtained for the initial set of assets and the capital maintenance amount unambiguously determined. Even though the composition of the total asset stock changes, it is easy in these circumstances to measure the capital maintenance amount in terms of the prices holding at the end of the year. But in reality products change over time – new models are brought out each year in many industries, fashion goods come and go, and there are changes in consumer tastes – and firms frequently do not replace inventories sold with identical lines. Similarly, technical progress causes new capital equipment to be superior to existing machines and the firm replaces its equipment with the new types. Because the assets are superseded, EOY prices cannot be obtained for them and hence it is difficult to determine the capital maintenance amount.

The problems vary according to the nature of the change that has occurred. In retailing, the problem is typified by fashion goods for which the demand has passed by the end of the year. Such inventories are no longer in production and they do not have a current cost. They should be valued at their net realizable values as this is now their current market opportunity cost.

In the case of fixed assets such as plant, there are several ways of approximating the current cost of existing plant used by the firm where that plant has been superseded by technically superior models, though not made obsolete. Fixed assets are owned for the services they provide, and the services of new equipment are in many cases very similar to those provided by the existing equipment. The service capacity of the new equipment can be related to the existing equipment and its cost can be prorated on this basis. For example, if the new equipment is twice as productive, the current cost of the existing equipment as new is taken to be one half that of the new equipment. This method, however, can be used only if the operating costs of each are similar, as the depreciation charge relates to the cost of new superior equipment and the operating costs to the existing equipment. Another method is to estimate the current reproduction cost of the existing plant. A third method is to index the historic cost of the existing plant.

Next, the partly used condition of the firm's plant is recognized by adjusting its new cost for the proportion of its service potential already used. Where straight line depreciation is charged, the current value of used plant can be determined as:

$$\text{Current cost (as new)} \times \frac{\text{remaining life in years}}{\text{total life}}$$

Likewise the revalued accumulated depreciation is:

$$\text{Current cost (as new)} \times \frac{\text{expired life}}{\text{total life}}$$

The periodic depreciation charge is calculated as:

$$\frac{\text{Current cost}}{\text{Total life}}$$

In estimating the current cost of depreciable assets, the remaining lives of the assets should be appraised in the light of changing technology and consumer tastes so that realistic economic lives of assets are used in the measurement of periodic depreciation and net asset values. This problem of course is not confined to current value accounting.

Where existing plant is already obsolete, i.e., its continued use is uneconomic, then it should be valued at its net realizable value as this is the measure of its current market opportunity cost.

While technical progress and obsolescence create problems for the measurement of capital maintenance, net assets, and income, the magnitude of these problems must not be exaggerated. Although these types of changes are forever occurring in a progressive firm adapting to a changing market environment, it should be noted that they are typically changes at the margin of its operations and they do not involve the firm as a whole in suddenly switching from one set of assets to another of a rather different type. Consequently the overall effect on the measurement of its expenses and assets for one year is likely to be small. Where however the firm does make a substantial switch in its total operations, income measurement should be based on the maintenance of operating capacity up to the switch, and a separate income measurement based on the new measure of capital should be made after the switch, as if it were two separate businesses. Change is a fairly evolutionary process, and while the nature of the assets of a progressive firm may completely change between, say, 1920 and 1970, there is likely to be only a moderate change between 1960 and 1970, and an infinitesmal one between 1969 and 1970 — the major concern for periodic income measurement.

### 3.   Backlog Depreciation

When fixed asset prices keep on rising, a problem appears to arise from the inadequacy of funds retained in the business from the accumulated depreciation charges to replace the asset. Current cost depreciation charges are based on the cost of acquiring the asset at the end of each year, and if this cost continues to rise, the depreciation charges of earlier years are less than those of later years. Hence the accumulated depreciation account (which sums the funds retained within the firm on account of depreciation charges) is less than the final replacement cost, i.e., there is a shortfall in the accumulated depreciation account. This shortfall is known as backlog depreciation. The shortfall is not due to errors in determining the annual depreciation charge but to subsequent increases in the cost of the asset. For the accumulated depreciation account (plus salvage value if any) to equal the ultimate replacement cost, the annual depreciation charges would have to be based on that cost. It appears, therefore, that current cost depreciation charges do not enable the stock of fixed assets, and hence the operating capacity of the firm, to be kept intact.

The problem arises in this way. Assume that a machine is bought on 1 January for $1,200; it lasts three years, has no scrap value, and its new price rises by $300 each year. Straight line depreciation is to be charged. The depreciation charges for the three years sum to $1,800, as follows:

|  | Depreciation $ | Backlog $ | Accum. Deprecn. $ |
|---|---|---|---|
| Year 1 | 500 (1/3 of 1,500) | – | 500 |
| 2 | 600 (1/3 of 1,800) | 100 | 1,200 |
| 3 | 700 (1/3 of 2,100) | 200 | 2,100 |
|  | $1,800 | $300 |  |

They fall short of the replacement cost of $2,100 by $300. One solution is to revise the balance in the accumulated depreciation account each year to make up the backlog. Thus, in year 2, $600 current depreciation and $100 backlog depreciation caused by the inadequate charge in year 1 is credited to the accumulated depreciation account. The backlog depreciation is debited to the asset revaluation reserve account to reflect the current value of the used machine – as a new machine now costs $1,800 and 2/3 of its service potential has been used, its net book value should be 1/3 of its current cost, i.e., $600. Similarly in year 3, $700 current depreciation and $200 backlog depreciation caused by the inadequate charges in years 1 and 2 should be credited to the accumulated depreciation account. The net book value of the machine is now zero – its total service potential has been used up.

However, the debit entry to the asset revaluation reserve account does not cause extra funds to be retained in the business to finance the replacement of the machine. The firm must refrain from distributing its total current income in each year if the machine is to be replaced without recourse to borrowing or capital raising. This can be accomplished by debiting retained earnings (to which the profit is transferred) and crediting an asset replacement reserve account, or by simply restricting the dividend payment to leave a sufficient balance of retained earnings to cover the backlog. The alternative method which is sometimes advocated of adding the backlog charge to the current depreciation charge is not recommended as the backlog depreciation is not an expense of the current period — it is an extra-periodic item caused by a delay in replacing the asset being used.

It was hinted above that backlog depreciation may not be a real problem — it only appears to be a problem for a single asset situation in which the replacement expenditure occurs only intermittently. Where the funds retained from revenue on account of current cost depreciation are reinvested before the next round of price increases, no shortfall in funds required for asset replacement is experienced. For example, if the firm above had 3 identical machines, and 1 falls due for replacement in each year, then the total depreciation charges in each year recover sufficient funds from revenue for the purchase of 1 machine. Thus in year 1, the $1,500 depreciation charge enables 1 machine to be bought; in year 2 the $1,800 share does likewise; and similarly for the $2,100 charge in year 3. Thus, if there is *no reinvestment lag*, current cost depreciation does provide a sufficient charge to enable maintenance of the stock of net assets. This result always holds in more complex situations where there is a variety of depreciable assets and where asset prices rise fairly uniformly, so long as the funds recovered on account of depreciation charges for the year are spent on new fixed assets during the year.

Thus the problem of financing fixed asset replacements from current cost depreciation charges does not arise where the firm immediately reinvests its "depreciation funds". Neither will it arise in a growth situation where the firm's stock of fixed assets is increasing. No retention of current income is required, and neither is an asset replacement reserve account with its related debit to retained earnings. However the backlog depreciation entries to the asset revaluation reserve and accumulated depreciation accounts are still required to maintain the correct valuations of used assets in the balance sheet. The apparent problem of backlog depreciation arises from a reinvestment lag rather than the inadequacy of current cost depreciation charges. There can be many good reasons for a firm not wishing to replace its assets immediately, or not at all. But this is a problem of investment policy and not one of income measurement. Current cost accounting merely provides the profitable firm which distributes its entire income with a sufficient funds recovery from revenue to replace the assets used up over the year if it so desires to replace them.

## ADVANTAGES OF CURRENT VALUE (CURRENT COST) ACCCOUNTING

### The General Case for the System

The broad need for current value accounting arises from the economics of business operations. Firms are generally established in the hope that they will have a long and profitable life and that they will remain as going concerns into the indefinite future. This is particularly true of large public companies. The complex nature of modern business operations in most industries forces firms to adopt a long run approach to policy formulation. Many of their fixed assets are long-lived ones designed to perform highly specific production tasks and they have negligible realizable values; large expansion projects typically take at least several years to implement; new products take several years to design and test; and there can be substantial expenditures on intangibles such as research and development, staff training and organizational structures which have no realizable values. These expenditures can only be recovered from sales revenue over a long period — they cannot be recovered from selling the assets. Moreover, firms invariably finance a significant part of their assets from long term debt funds and they must remain profitable to be able to meet periodic interest payments and repayment of the principal. These considerations force management to adopt planning periods of at least three to five years, with ten years being common for very large projects.

Another consideration encouraging a long-run approach is that firms are substantially locked into their existing industries by their management expertise, technology, customer relationships, and scale of operations. The management may build up substantial expertise in running the firm in its particular industry. This requires a detailed technical knowledge and the development of good industrial relations with employees and trading relationships with suppliers and customers. The economies of large scale operations are important in most modern industries and a firm must operate on a large scale in order to be efficient and to compete with other firms in the industry. These considerations make it difficult for a firm to leave an industry voluntarily, and conversely to start up operations in another industry.

Thus, firms typically are confined to their existing industries and they make large expenditures on nonvendible assets and intangibles. The only way they can recover these expenditures and be profitable is to remain operating in the industry as an efficient, progressive entity for many years into the future. If sufficient profits cannot be made in the long run, the firm is likely to become bankrupt and incur substantial losses on the liquidation of its nonvendible assets. Creditors and owners may lose their investment, and employees their jobs.

For a firm to survive in the long run, it must earn at least a normal rate of profit on investment. A normal rate of profit is one which just enables a firm to recover from sales revenue all operating costs and replace its physical assets as they are used up, to pay its interest commitments on debt finance, and to pay sufficient dividends to owners such that they are willing to invest their funds in the business. In other words, a normal profit must cover the supply price of risk funds invested in the business, and this is governed by the rewards which investors can obtain from alternative investment of their funds.[4] A firm is a viable going concern in the long run only if it can earn at least a normal rate of profit, as cash receipts from sales are then sufficient to cover the supply prices of all resources used up in operations and service the funds invested in the business. Where cash receipts in the long run do not cover the supply prices of resources used and the required servicing of investment funds, the firm is not viable and must eventually collapse as it cannot fully replace assets used up. Its dismal profit record reacts against both its ability to raise additional finance and its incentive to reinvest in replacement assets. Investors become wary of lending on a fixed interest basis because of the declining income cover for interest payments and the low realizable value of its assets, and they require higher interest rates as compensation for the additional risk undertaken. Likewise investors become reluctant to invest further equity funds in the business when its earnings per share are falling and the risk of loss increasing. These factors cause its share price to fall, and this again deters equity investors. Once the process continues for some time and the share price falls below its par value, the company cannot normally make a new share issue because it is illegal to issue shares at a discount and investors will not purchase new shares at par when they can buy existing shares at a lower price in the share market. Unless profits return to a normal rate of return on investment, the firm cannot survive. It either runs out of cash or it is taken over by another, stronger firm.

Thus the ability to earn a normal rate of profit on investment in the long run is a survival condition for any firm. This does not mean that a firm has to earn a profit in each and every year, but that it does so on average. A normal rate of profit on investment is determined after all operating costs, based on the current supply prices of factor inputs, (including physical assets) have been recovered from revenue. A firm earning a normal rate of profit is able to refinance its continuing operations, including the replacement of physical assets used up, from revenues without having to obtain additional funds from lenders or owners or to retain profits. Its continuing operations at the existing scale of output are self-financing, and it does not suffer from physical capital erosion. Thus normal profit is determined on the basis that the firm can maintain its stock of net assets or its operating capacity intact. Current income is the cash surplus on operations in the long run after the firm has maintained its stock of net assets intact, i.e., it is the measure of income relevant for determining whether or not a firm is earning a normal rate of return on investment, and hence whether the firm is viable in the long run. Current value accounting provides management and investors with necessary information to determine whether the firm should be continued in the long run for the making of long run policy decisions.

The profitability of Australian companies in the 1970's has shown an alarming decline and the continued existence of many companies must be in doubt. Although rate of return on investment data cannot be obtained because there are no reliable statistics on the current value of net assets in industry, the trend in the rate of return is apparent from the information on total profitability. The following table shows the historic cost and current incomes earned by the non-finance company sector in Australia for the years 1970–75, plus the forecast data for 1976.

*Profits of Non-Finance Companies in Australia 1970–76*

$m, years ended 30 June

|  | 1970 | 1971 | 1972 | 1973 | 1974 | 1975 | 1976 |
|---|---|---|---|---|---|---|---|
| Hist. Cost income | 3,118 | 3,166 | 3,425 | 4,157 | 5,085 | 4,705 | 4,930 |
| *Less* Inventory Appreciation | 185 | 333 | 478 | 521 | 989 | 1,820 | 1,400 |
| *Less* Extra Depreciation | 228 | 267 | 421 | 475 | 610 | 1,090 | 1,480 |
|  | 413 | 600 | 899 | 996 | 1,599 | 2,910 | 2,880 |
| Current Income | 2,705 | 2,566 | 2,526 | 3,161 | 3,486 | 1,795 | 2,050 |
| *Less* Tax | 1,353 | 1,365 | 1,448 | 1,851 | 2,305 | 2,100 | 2,100 |
| Current Income a/t | 1,352 | 1,201 | 1,078 | 1,310 | 1,181 | −305 | − 50 |
| *Less* Dividends | 719 | 763 | 803 | 894 | 884 | 900 | 920 |
| Savings | 633 | 438 | 275 | 416 | 297 | −1,205 | −970 |

Source: Based on "Company Profits and Finance", Tables 2A and 2B, *The Australian Economic Review*, 3rd Quarter 1975.

The statistics show that the gap between historic cost income and current income is widening as inflation has accelerated from around 3 per cent p.a. in the early 1970s to rates in the range of 13–15 per cent p.a. in the mid 1970s; while the trend in historic cost income is upwards, that for current income is downwards (notwithstanding the additional net investment in industry over most of the period); the effective tax rate on current income has increased substantially, with a rate of 115 per cent being reached in 1975 when tax collections exceeded current income; dividends have been paid out of capital in 1975 and will probably be so again in 1976; and company savings which are available to finance industrial growth have declined from a modest sum to a substantial dissaving, reflecting considerable physical capital erosion in industry. With the substantial decline in current income after tax, the rate of return on investment in industry must have declined markedly as well.

The statistics help to explain the malaise in Australian industry in the mid 1970s. Much of industry is unprofitable, it cannot finance its current level of operations from current revenues, and it is suffering from physical capital erosion. The ability and willingness of industry to raise additional external finance is severely circumscribed by business and investor uncertainty about the profitability of future operations and by high interest rates. The lack of investment in industry in turn reacts upon the G.N.P. and employment, and this reacts upon the level of effective demand, and hence business revenue. And so the vicious inflationary spiral with substantial unemployment and business bankruptcy continues. The statistics indicate another powerful reason for the use of current value accounting, namely to provide the government with relevant statistics on company profits for the purpose of macroeconomic policy formulation. Historic cost income data disguises the real trends in company profitability and can be most misleading in a period of strong inflation.

Furthermore, it has been noted how historic cost income exaggerates both profits and losses over the trade cycle of boom and slump. Studies in the United States, United Kingdom, and Australia indicate that, as compared with current income, historic cost income exaggerates the profits earned by companies in boom periods and thereby accelerates the boom; while conversely it overstates losses in a depression and thereby extends it.[5] Moreover, a high proportion of losses in a depression are in holding activities rather than operating activities, and likewise for profits in a boom. This exaggeration of profit data can have a marked effect on business confidence and the trade cycle. The universal use of current income has a dampening effect on company profits and it should, therefore, reduce the amplitude of the trade cycle.

### Specific Advantages of Current Value Accounting

The above analysis of current value accounting concerned the general need for the system. As well current value accounting has many specific uses and advantages for the individual firm.

### 1. To Maintain the Firm's Operating Capacity

The need for the firm to maintain its physical operating capacity intact to facilitate continued operation into the future, and to avoid financial problems in replacing assets used up in operations, has already been discussed. If the firm's scale of operations is to be reduced, this should be done as a matter of deliberate managerial policy rather than surreptitiously through "capital erosion". As well as shareholders and management being concerned with this matter, long-term creditors are concerned to see that the firm's operating capacity is maintained intact as this helps ensure the safety of their loans.

## 2.  To Provide Reliable Measures of Profit Performance and Financial Position

The concepts of current income, rate of return on investment, and financial position have a useful meaning for the purposes of evaluating the firm's economic performance. In the determination of current income (current cost), all expenses are measured in terms of the current cost of resource inputs and related to revenue, which is necessarily in current terms too. Hence income is measured entirely in current dollars. Fictitious inventory gains arising from charging lower historic costs in the cost of goods sold are eliminated from profits. Furthermore, all factors affecting profits during the period (other than inflation) are embodied in the measure of income, and no events from other periods (especially price changes in them) are included in it. It is a measure of profit which is insulated from extra-periodic events. Current income (current cost) is one of the best measures of the performance of the firm as a going concern because of the above reasons and its being based on maintaining operating capacity intact.

In addition to income, all assets and liabilities are measured in current dollar values, and hence net equity in the firm. The measures of gross and net investment in assets are meaningful ones. The current value balance sheet shows the investment in gross and net assets at their current market prices, and hence what it would currently cost to acquire that set of assets. The rate of return on owner's equity is therefore a reliable measure of the effectiveness with which their funds are invested by management. The current value (current cost) system does not cause overstatement of profit, understatment of asset values, and exaggeration of the rate of return on investment as does the historic cost system in a period of inflation. Income and the rate of return on investment are two of the most crucial figures required by management and investors for the evaluation of performance, selection of business policies, and investment projects to be adopted, and for their effect on share prices. Investors and management require current rates of return to determine the firm's status as a going concern and hence whether to continue its operations in the long run.

Similarly, the measure of financial position under current value accounting is a meaningful one. The current market values of assets are disclosed and they can be matched against the current market values of liabilities to judge the firm's financial position. So long as the physical assets are rationally owned, their aggregate current cost value indicates to creditors that the firm expects them to generate future cash flows greater than their current value, and it is from these future cash flows that long-term creditors are normally repaid.

Because of all the above reasons, current income and financial position provide a more informed basis for management to forecast future events and plan business operations, and for investors to forecast future performance and financial position, than does historic cost accounting.

Furthermore, reliable comparisons of performance and financial position of firms in the same industry can be made. Such comparisons ought to be made by management to see what they can learn from competitors, and by investors to see which companies have achieved the better performance and hence which are more likely to provide the better investment prospects. Socially, this helps to improve upon the allocation of resources in industry generally, as scarce new investment funds are channelled into the more profitable uses, as indicated by the rate of return on an investment. It indicates the areas where new investment is needed, either by existing firms or by potential entrants.

### 3. To Promote Efficiency of Operations and Regular Adaptation to Changing Factor Market Conditions

A firm is an economic entity engaging in a stream of transactions with its factor and product markets with a view to making profits, as outlined in chapter 5. In a competitive market environment a firm must operate efficiently and it must regularly adapt to changes in its economic environment in order to sell its output and earn a profit. If it does not do this, then it cannot survive for long.

Market forces operate on both sides of the firm, i.e., in the factor markets as well as in the product markets. Pressures for adaptation to changes in product markets are readily recognized from declining sales or profits. For example, if competitors reduce prices, the firm must normally do so as well to maintain sales; if they introduce successful new products, it must endeavour to do likewise; if customers' tastes change, product quality and range must be adjusted to the new requirements; and so on. In other words the firm adjusts its marketing strategies to counter competitors' actions and exogenous changes in the market.

Similar types of changes occur also in the factor markets. Suppliers change their prices, wage rates rise, and the current prices of many fixed assets change. The firm must adjust its operations to comply with changes in factor market supply prices, or market opportunity costs. For factor inputs, market supply prices are the minimum prices which must be paid to acquire inputs, i.e., current buying prices; and for outputs they are the minimum prices for which the firm or its competitors are willing to sell the product. The firm must pay at least the current prices to obtain factor inputs because other firms are willing to pay them. It is irrelevant to the measure of market opportunity cost if the firm already owns the resource and had acquired it earlier at a lower price, as other firms are willing to purchase it at the current market price.

Optimum operating efficiency occurs where a given volume of output is produced at the minimum total market opportunity cost of the factor inputs. For this measure, current buying prices of factor inputs and not their historic costs are relevant. If the market price of a factor rises appreciably, then the firm should amend its operating methods and use less of that factor, and endeavour to increase output. For example, if wage rates rise, more capital intensive methods of production are required so as to reduce labour input for a given level of output; if the market price of the firm's premises rises substantially, they should be used more intensively or the management should consider whether similar services could be rendered more cheaply in another location.

The process of adjustment to changing factor supply prices is analyzed in economic theory in terms of isocost and isoproduct functions. Assume an elementary situation in which the firm has two factor inputs (labour and premises) and one product. The firm owns the premises and the annual opportunity cost of using them is most conveniently measured by the rent it would have to pay in the event of non-ownership. The isocost function $(l_1 r_1)$ shows the total outlays on labour (up to $ol_1$ if the entire expenditure is on labour) and on premises (up to $or_1$ if all money is spent on rent), and its slope is determined by the relative price of labour to premises. The isoproduct function shows the various combinations of workers and building usage which are required to produce a given output X, and its slope at any point is given by the relative marginal productivities of each factor.

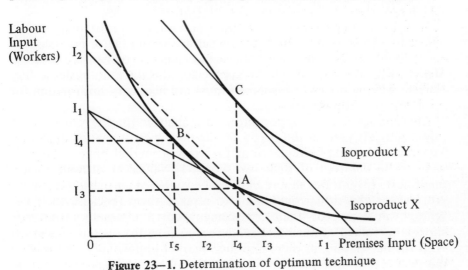

**Figure 23–1.** Determination of optimum technique

At the initial wage rates and rents, the optimum combination of workers and premises occurs at point A at which the two functions are tangential. Here, the labour cost is $ol_3$ and rent cost $or_4$, and the total cost of achieving output X is minimized.

If the current market price of the firm's premises doubles, the annual rent charge doubles and the isocost function tilts against rent — for the same outlay, only one half of the premises can now be rented ($or_2$) — and the new isocost function is $l_1 r_2$. The firm must increase its total outlay to maintain output constant at X, and the revised isocost function ($l_2 r_3$) has the same slope as $l_1 r_2$ because it is based on the same relative factor prices.

The new least-cost combination of factors occurs at B at which $ol_4$ labour and $or_5$ premises are used. This position embodies more intensive utilization of premises for a given output. In reality it means that the firm should rent out part of the building (i.e., use smaller premises itself); or move to another location where property values are lower; or use its existing premises more intensively by employing more workers and expanding output, i.e., move up to point C on a higher isoproduct function Y. Greater output is necessary to justify retention of the now dearer premises.

If the firm does not recognize the appreciation in market price and retains its premises at historic cost and consequently does not modify their use (i.e., it remains operating at point A), it is in effect operating along the dotted isocost function passing through A. The extent of its inefficiency in producing X at point A is shown by the difference between the dotted isocost function and $l_2 r_3$. Pursuit of this policy in the long run must encourage takeover attempts by other companies which recognize the current market price of its premises.

It is just as important for the firm's survival and profitability that it adjust its production methods to changes in current factor prices as it is for it to adjust its marketing policies to changes in demand conditions. Many firms do not appear to appreciate this fact of business life. Current buying prices of resource inputs are necessary information for economic operating efficiency.

The implications of opportunity cost analysis for the valuation of physical assets used in the firm's production cycle is that all long-term assets which would be replaced at the current market price if the firm were to be deprived of their use should be valued at current replacement cost. Inventories should likewise be valued at current replacement cost where the firm would want to replace them (because their net selling value exceeds their replacement cost). Obsolete inventories should be valued at their net selling value. The firm is not concerned with further trading in them and their market opportunity cost is what the firm can dispose of them for. Obsolete plant should be valued at its net selling value if positive, or written off completely. There need be no inconsistency in adding current costs and current selling values together — they both use the same measurement property of the dollar. The difference between these two values is the profit margin on the asset in a market transaction, and here the relevant question is whether to recognize that profit or not before the point of sale. The answer to this question should depend on the critical event in the circumstances of the asset. Both values can be measures of current opportunity cost. Opportunity cost is always the lower of the two values involved in the final decision about which action to take as it shows the sacrifice incurred in taking the preferred alternative.

## 4. Pricing and Output Policy

Current income (current cost) indicates whether current prices are sufficient to cover the current supply prices of the firm's products. Current supply price is that price necessary to induce the supply of a product, and for continuing supply it is measured by the current buying prices of resource inputs embodied in a firm's output. All firms in the industry must normally pay the ruling buying prices for their inputs, and a rise in them affects all firms in the industry and raises the supply prices of their outputs.

Firms can be divided into two classes according to their market power. Firms in highly competitive industries have little market power and have to accept ruling selling prices. However, such "price-takers" are free to vary the amount they sell, and they must determine how much merchandise they are willing to sell at the existing selling price. This output decision should be based on the current costs of its inputs. Optimum output policy can be formulated only with respect to current supply prices.

Similarly, "price-makers", who have some ability to influence the prices charged for their products, must base their prices on current supply prices for an optimum pricing policy. Normally price-makers in an uncertain market base their prices on operating costs as well as on demand conditions. This pricing practice is called the (misnamed) "full-cost principle", and most large firms use some variant of it. The costs which are relevant as the cost base upon which a profit margin is added are the current costs of all resource inputs as these measure the supply price of the finished product.

## 5. Recognition of Holding Gains and Losses As They Occur

Use of current value accounting requires that all holding gains and losses on assets are recognized in the year of occurrence rather than later on when the asset is sold. This removes any discretion from management in deferring realization of assets, and hence reporting of these gains and losses, to a period when it suits management. Furthermore, it improves the comparability of results between firms and over time. Recognition of holding gains and losses only at the time of realization distorts periodic results in that gains accruing in earlier periods are disregarded and they are all recognized in the final period. In addition, in historic cost accounting only the holding gains on some assets are separately reported, and the major part of them is hidden in the lower historic charges for inventory and fixed asset usage which result in the inflated historic cost profit figure. Thus these holding gains are automatically included in income, and the question of whether they ought to be so included is evaded. In other words, current value accounting overcomes the limitations attaching to the realization concept. Furthermore, an important economic feature of the firm's factor markets is recognized as it occurs, and so the information is timely. Asset price change data are relevant to the needs of management in devising optimum operating policies with respect to the use of assets, pricing, and so on; to shareholders as they ultimately reap the rewards; and to shareholders and long-term creditors because of the improved measure of current financial position provided from these policies to them.

Another advantage is that the separate reporting of holding gains can enable more accurate assessments of managerial operating performance to be made as operating performance is separated from asset holding performance. From an investment point of view, holding gains on physical assets can be interpreted as cost savings from the early purchase of assets at prices lower than current ones. They show the amount of cash saved thereby. Had the assets not been bought earlier, owners would have had to invest more cash to achieve a business of the same size. Net holding gains show this one aspect of investment performance (though there are other aspects to be considered as well). Holding performance can be an important part of overall investment performance − it saves on direct ownership investment and thereby increases the discounted cash flow rate of return, and it can add to net wealth in terms of general purchasing power in some circumstances as does income. Conversely, holding losses can bankrupt firms just as easily as operating losses where creditors and shareholders see their security being eroded, and they call in their loans or sell their shares. Holding losses indicate that excessive investment expenditures may have been made and that it would have been better for the firm to have postponed asset purchase, and in the meantime made other arrangements such as short-term leasing or buying in the asset's services. Investors and top management need information on this aspect of investment performance which is reported separately from operating performance.

Finally, the separate reporting of holding gains and operating performance enables more accurate budgeting of future operations. The two components depend on different factors and they ought to be predicted separately. In addition, it facilitates predictions of the future as asset values are closer in terms of time to the future.

### 6. Other Advantages

Current value (current cost) accounting confers other important advantages as a financial information system for the formulation of prudent financing and dividend policies. These matters are closely linked to the *real value system* and their consideration is postponed till the following chapter.

Finally it possesses advantages for various types of decision-making with respect to the uses of assets, asset replacement, and company takeovers; these matters are considered in chapter 25 on the *present value system*.

## CURRENT VALUE (SELLING PRICE) SYSTEM

### Wealth, Income, and Capital Maintenance Concepts

In *current value (selling price)* accounting, all assets and liabilities are valued at their current realizable prices, i.e., at the prices at which assets could be converted into cash and liabilities discharged. For this reason, the more embracing term "current cash equivalent" is often used as an alternative name for the system as it readily includes monetary assets and liabilities which do not have selling prices as such.[6] The selling prices used relate to disposal of assets in the normal course of business rather than what could be fetched in a forced liquidation sale, i.e., they are normal prices and not liquidation prices. The firm's initial non-monetary assets are valued at the selling prices ruling at the start of the period, while the closing ones are valued at end-of-period prices. No distinction between physical assets and marketable securities is necessary in this system as both are valued on the same basis throughout. Monetary assets and liabilities are valued at their current cash equivalent or realizable values. The use of selling prices does not imply that the assets are to be sold and the firm liquidated – it is a means of valuing assets according to the external market environment. Again, as with the use of current buying prices of assets, the valuation basis does not necessarily imply anything about future action by the firm. The basis is used because it provides useful information, and not just because the assets may be sold.

Again, the precise nature of current income (selling price) and capital maintenance can be indicated by resorting to the algebraic analysis used previously. Let the initial balance sheet be stated as:

$$M_o + N_o = P_o \qquad \qquad ......(i)$$

where  $M_o$ represents the net monetary assets held
$N_o$ represents the non-monetary assets held, valued at beginning-of-year prices
$P_o$ represents proprietorship.

If the current selling prices of similar assets rise by s per cent over the year, the initial balance sheet may be restated in end-of-year selling prices as:

$$M_o + N_o (1 + s) = P_o + Ns \qquad \qquad ......(ii)$$

The term $N_o (1 + s)$ represents the revalued non-monetary assets, and Ns the holding gain on initial non-monetary assets. The capital maintenance term is simply $P_o$, since holding gains are not included in capital maintenance in this system.

The end-of-year balance sheet, after a year's transactions, but before any proprietary contributions or withdrawals, may be stated as:

$$M_1 + N_1 = P_1 \qquad \qquad ......(iii)$$

where $N_1$ are valued at end-of-year selling prices. Current income (selling price) $(Y_s)$ is then:

$$Y_s = [M_1 - M_o] + N_1 - [N_o (1 + s) - Ns] = P_1 - P_o \qquad ......(iv)$$
$$= [M_1 - M_o] + [N_1 - N_o] = P_1 - P_o \qquad \qquad ......(v)$$

The holding gains on initial net assets cancel out, leaving the initial assets valued at the beginning of year selling prices. They are of course implicit in the increment in non-monetary assets when valued at the opening and closing selling prices. Thus the basis of asset valuation in this system is simply the selling prices of assets at the two dates. This is a fortunate result because, for reasons indicated below, holding gains are frequently difficult to isolate in the current value (selling price) system. In addition, their separation is not necessary for the measure of income because they form part of income and not capital maintenance.

Current income (selling price) is the increment in net assets over the period accruing from both operating activities and asset holding activities, where assets are valued at the appropriate current selling prices as indicated above. All holding gains are included in income as they represent an increment in current spending power over goods and services in general. Capital is considered to be a pool of financial resources which is best valued at its current cash equivalent, i.e., it is essentially a fund of cash which can be available for any future use. Hence capital maintenance refers to maintaining intact the current cash equivalent of the begining-of-period capital, or the money investment in net assets valued at their current cash equivalents. Income is therefore the maximum amount the firm could pay in dividends for the period without impairing this initial capital. This measure of income does not necessarily maintain physical capital intact; rather the realizable value of initial net assets is maintained intact. The medium of exchange property of the dollar is used as the unit of measurement.

### Obtaining Current Selling Prices of Assets

In those highly competitive markets in which transaction costs and transport and installation costs are negligible, current selling prices of assets tend to coincide with their buying prices and so there is little to choose between the two current value systems. The important cases, however, occur where there is a significant gap between the two prices because in these situations the results of each system can differ substantially.

Current selling prices for finished goods inventories are generally available, as are those for most raw materials. However, there can be complications in using market selling prices for raw materials as they are frequently perishable or transport costs are high, and their selling value to the firm may be but a fraction of their cost. A similar complication occurs with works-in-progress inventories. There is normally no market for partly made products — they may be of no use to another manufacturer or to consumers — and hence their current selling price may be zero or even negative when disposal costs are deducted. General-purpose plant for which there are many uses frequently has established new and secondhand market prices, and likewise motor vehicles. Specialized and custom-made plant, however, may have no established market prices, and secondhand values for highly expensive plant can be negligible because there is no market for it. Resort cannot be had to specialized price indexes in these cases as such indexes are based on purchase costs. Normally current market selling prices of land and general-purpose buildings are readily obtainable; however, where land and buildings are isolated geographically, their selling value may be negligible. Current market prices of marketable securities are normally obtainable.

In general then, there are more difficulties encountered in obtaining realistic selling prices of some assets than there are in obtaining purchase costs because many assets, particularly in manufacturing industries, are non-marketable. Specialized assets acquired for use within the business are frequently of little or no use to any other firm, or else disposal costs preclude their transfer to another firm. The use of the current cash equivalent system can mean that these assets are shown at negligible or zero values in a balance sheet.

### Some Special Features of the Current Value (Selling Price) System

A fundamental characteristic of the current cash equivalent system is its complete rejection of the realization concept for the measurement of periodic profits. In principle, all non-monetary assets are revalued at their current selling prices on acquisition, plus those obtaining at any later date should selling prices subsequently change. (In practice, though, they may not be revalued till their disposal or until the end of the year). This means that holding gains or losses are recognized on the acquisition of assets rather than on their disposal; the critical point in the operating cycle is held to be acquisition and not disposal. The sale of assets (including inventories) is regarded as the process of exchanging a non-monetary asset for a financial asset of *equal* value. Thus all profit would be recognized before the point of sale (except where there is a last-minute change in selling prices). This is in contrast to the current cost system wherein *no* operating profit is recognized until the assets are sold.

Because of the recognition of holding gains and losses immediately as they occur on or after acquisition of assets, it is difficult to separate out net holding gains from operating income in current cash equivalent accounting. Indeed, the distinction does not have much meaning for operating assets. For example, is the profit margin on merchandise inventories a holding gain or part of normal operating income? Retailers only trade in merchandise which offers the prospects of a profit margin, and thus the holding gains form their operating income. To what extent is the reduction in the selling price of a fixed asset over the year depreciation or a holding loss caused by obsolescence? As net holding gains are included in income in this system, their separate measurement is not critical to the measurement of income. In the current cost system, however, net holding gains on operating assets are part of capital maintenance and they must therefore be separated from operating income. Because holding gains are part of income in the current cash equivalent system, opening assets are valued at beginning-of-year prices rather than at end-of-year prices (as in the current cost system).

In accounting for merchandise inventories, opening inventories would be valued at selling prices then applying; closing inventories would be valued at end-of-year selling prices; and the "cost of goods sold" would in fact be *cost of goods bought* for the period at historic cost. With respect to income measurement, there is no difference between goods actually sold to customers and goods unsold at the year's end (as these are valued at selling price). Unless there has been a subsequent price increase, no profit on the sale of opening inventories is recognized in the current period – it would all have been recognized in previous periods. Losses would be recognized on non-disposable raw material and works-in-process inventories at the end of the period even though they are to be fully used in the subsequent period; on the other hand opening inventories of such items may be "free" to this period's operations.

Accounting for fixed assets and depreciation pose further problems. Depreciation plus holding loss caused by obsolescence is measured by the reduction in the selling price of the asset over the period. Unless there is an active secondhand market for a fixed asset, the two components cannot be separated. But, where there is a market which provides selling prices for each condition of a used fixed asset, the holding loss (or gain) could be measured as the change in selling price of an asset in the same used condition at the year-end as at its start, e.g., the change in the secondhand price of a two-year-old lathe over the year. Depreciation of the lathe would then be the total reduction in its selling price over the year, less the holding loss. Where there is no effective secondhand market for fixed assets, the greater part of the purchase cost would be recognized as depreciation in the year of purchase, and the remaining balance sheet value of the asset would be small.

The concept of wealth or assets in the current value (selling price) system encompasses only those assets having a market resale value. The assets must be severable from the firm and have a positive selling value to be recognized as assets. Otherwise, they do not add to the stock of cash that could be called upon for future use. This criterion normally means that all intangible assets are excluded from the balance sheet as they cannot be sold as individual, separate assets. Rather, if they have any value, this value can only be realized through the sale of the firm as a whole. However, a possible exception concerns patents — these would appear as an asset if they could be separately sold or franchised to other firms. But in general, all expenditures on intangible assets are treated as sunk costs and are charged against the current period's revenue. The application of the criterion to specialized fixed tangible assets means that they are not included in the assets of the firm either, if they have no separate resale values. Such resources have no capacity to add to the stock of cash by sale, even though they can be very valuable resources which provide the firm with its operating capacity and profit potential. A substantial proportion of specialized fixed assets used in manufacturing industry have no secondhand markets in a small economy such as Australia and hence they would not appear as assets in the balance sheets of the firms owning them. As with intangible assets, expenditure is treated as depreciation in the year of acquisition. Depreciation is measured as the cost of new plant less its resale value at the end of year one. This treatment of nonvendible fixed assets differs markedly from that in the current cost system wherein vendibility is not a criterion for an asset, and such resources are recognized as assets and valued at their current purchase cost in each year of their working life. The nonvendibility of some raw material and works-in-process inventories is the reason for their valuation at zero values, mentioned above.

### Uses of Current Value (Selling Price) Accounting

In situations where current buying and selling prices reasonably coincide, all the reasons for using each system coincide and the measures of income and financial position are much the same. The complete set of uses therefore applies to either system. The special advantages of the selling price valuation basis as listed below apply to the situation wherein the two sets of prices diverge significantly.

### 1. Measure Financial Adaptability of the Firm

A primary function of the current cash equivalent system is to indicate the total capacity of a firm to adapt its assets to another use by selling off its existing assets and purchasing another set, i.e., an asset-switching situation. The need for this measure of the financial capacity to adapt arises out of the uncertainties of future operations and constantly changing market environments (factor and product) in which the firm operates. The firm must be ready to adapt its asset situation to comply with these market factors if it is to survive and prosper. Where the current cash equivalent value of a firm's assets is low in relation to their current cost, the firm has limited financial capacity to adapt; whereas, where their value is relatively high, the firm has a substantial adaptive capacity. Compare, for example, the abilities of a firm in the iron and steel industry (whose fixed assets are highly expensive, specialized, and immobile and the selling value of which may be negligible) and that of an investment company (whose assets consist of readily marketable securities and real estate) to dispose of their existing assets and acquire a new set.

### 2. Measure of Risk of Investment in Assets

A matter closely related to the above concerns asset risk. The financial risk incurred in investing in assets which are not readily marketable at a reasonable price is substantial compared with that of investing in readily realizable assets. Again, compare the iron and steel firm with the investment company. Two measures of financial risk in assets are the ratio of historic cost to current cash equivalent in the case of assets acquired for resale, and the ratio of current replacement cost to current cash equivalent in the case of assets acquired for use within the firm.[7] Financial risks are high where the ratios are high. In the second case, management must feel fairly confident about the flow of cash surpluses from using the asset before the asset will be acquired; otherwise the asset may have to be sold and heavy holding losses realized. All long-term investors, and particularly creditors, are concerned with such risks in asset cover. Asset cover is measured by the ratio of total assets (at current values) to liabilities and is an indication of the security afforded to creditors.

### 3. Indicate Liquidity of Assets

Current realizable values of assets are relevant in determining what assets additional to the normal cash cycle should be converted into cash required for the everyday operations of the firm. Obviously assets with a low liquidity value in relation to their replacement costs will not be converted into cash, except by compulsion.

### 4. For Decisions Concerning Use or Sale of Assets

The current cash equivalent values of all assets are necessary information for the very basic decisions of whether to retain an asset in use or sell it. They are crucial to many company takeover decisions. Current selling prices of assets measure the opportunity costs of their continued retention and use by the firm — by retaining the assets, the firm forgoes the cash that could be obtained from their sale. It must compare this with the cash surpluses expected from their continued use, and unless the expected cash surpluses (suitably discounted for time) exceed the current cash value of the asset, the asset should be sold. These retain or sell decisions are analyzed in chapter 25 as they involve the *present value system* of accounting.

### 5. For Decisions Concerning the Continued Operations of the Firm

Where the firm is not a viable going concern in the long run, the question arises as to whether it should continue operations or terminate them and sell the assets. The same form of analysis that applies to individual assets also applies to the whole set of assets owned by the firm. Because the current resale values of assets measure their market opportunity cost in the short run, the firm could earn a profit Ri by selling the assets and investing the funds elsewhere, where R is the realizable value of the net assets and i is the rate of return on the alternative investment. The firm should only continue its current operations if $Y_s > Ri$, i.e., if its current income exceeds the alternative income sacrificed by maintaining investment in its existing assets. This rule is the periodic counterpart of that given in chapter 25, i.e., that $P_F > R_F$.[8] The analysis is similar to that in the economic theory of the firm wherein the firm should continue to operate in the short run if price exceeds average variable cost but is less than average total cost (including fixed costs and normal profit). The excess of price over average variable cost shows the gain per unit of output from continued operations over temporary cessation of activities.

### 6. *Measure Income, Financial Position, and Rate of Return on Investment*

For the terminating firm or the sick firm whose future existence is doubtful, asset selling values are relevant for the measurement of income and financial position. The existing assets may have to be sold fairly soon to repay the firm's liabilities and the firm may be wound up. Creditors cannot rely upon the generation of future cash surpluses from operations and the existing assets may have to provide directly the financial pool from which the debts are repaid.

In the case of the profitable firm whose continuing existence well beyond balance date is not in doubt, there is some choice between the use of either current value system. Current cash equivalent appears at first sight to be the more appropriate valuation basis for the measurement of financial position because it shows the cash which could be realized by selling the assets (and hence used to repay liabilities). But this approach is too simplistic for most firms. In using the concept of financial position in its context of the ability of the firm to meet its financial commitments as they fall due, the value and liquidity of assets should be judged in relation to the value and maturity dates of liabilities. Because some liabilities are due for payment in the near future and others are not normally repayable until the distant future, separate measures of short term and long term financial position are required. The current cash equivalent balance sheet provides the appropriate measure of the firm's ability to repay creditors in the short run from its existing resources whereas the current value balance sheet based on current cost provides the relevant measure of the ability to meet financial commitments over the long run for the going concern. In the continuing firm the existing stock of assets normally do not provide by direct realization the pool of cash from which long term debts are repaid — rather they are normally repaid from funds generated from operations or from new debt. The cash flow ratio rather than the asset cover is the more significant indicator of long run solvency.[9] So long as the firm is a genuine going concern, valuation of its non-monetary assets at current cost is an appropriate measure of its long run financial position because the future cash surpluses generated by the assets should exceed current costs, and this information is, therefore, indicative of minimal debt repayment capacity.

Similarly, in analyzing the financial structure aspects of a firm's financial position, the sources of finance must be assessed in relation to the investment of funds in assets.[10] Where expenditure on nonvendible assets is substantial, the exclusion of these assets from the balance sheet can seriously distort the analysis of financial structure. The firm's financial position could appear pitiful where large liabilities helped finance the new nonvendible assets — sufficient assets just do not appear in the balance sheet because much of the expenditure on them has been written off as a sunk cost. Long term creditors may be worried by the low asset cover provided for their loans, debenture trust deeds regarding asset cover may be breached, and share prices depressed by the seemingly large losses in years of asset growth, high debt/equity ratio, and low asset backing per share. All these factors could jeopardize the firm's future existence by encouraging foreclosure by creditors or takeover bids by predator companies, even though the expenditures promise to be highly profitable ones and the risk of non-repayment of liabilities is negligible.

Likewise, current income measures based on current cost rather than selling price provide a better measure of profit for the going concern. Recognition of profit at the point of purchase of finished goods inventories rather than at the point of sale transfers the profit from around the end of the economic cycle to around its start. This is a risky procedure to adopt when the sale of the products is not assured. A buildup in the stocks of finished goods inventories creates an increase in reported profits even though the buildup is an involuntary one caused by a slackening market demand. In the current cost system, income is measured on the basis of maintaining productive capacity intact and this is a better managerial guideline than the maintenance of money capital. Where secondhand values are negligible in relation to new or used asset costs of expensive fixed assets, the measure of income based on selling prices could be dominated by the pattern of capital expenditure. In years of high capital expenditure substantial losses could be reported because of the recognition of heavy losses on new fixed assets; in effect, much of the cost of new fixed assets would be charged as depreciation in the year of acquisition, whereas there would be small depreciation charges in subsequent years and hence high incomes, even though the level of production and merchandise selling prices have remained fairly constant. Thus there could be little comparability in the annual income data for a firm or in results between it and other firms. Finally, the rate of return on investment is better measured in the current cost system for the going concern. The understatement of investment in nonvendible assets and the variability of current income (selling price) with expenditures on finished goods inventories and nonvendible assets could cause the rate of return on investment to be a rather capricious figure. In years of substantial expenditure on nonvendible assets (and hence growth of the firm), income is seriously depressed, investment in assets is understated, and the rate of return on investment is understated; whereas in other years of low capital expenditure, income is overstated, investment in assets is understated, and the rate of return is exaggerated. Under the current value (selling price) system, it would appear that the solution to low profitability of a growth firm is to cease growing. Rates of return on investment as calculated under this system for the going concern owning nonvendible assets are not comparable for the one firm over time or for intercompany comparisons. They do not provide shareholders and investors with relevant information for the appraisal of profit performance of a going concern. Rates of return on investment based on current selling prices of assets are inappropriate for resource allocation questions because assets are resource inputs rather than outputs and the relevant information must encompass factor supply prices.

A further reason for preferring the current cost to the current selling price version of current value accounting is that the current cost system is likely to be more objective where markets for secondhand assets are not active. It is generally easier to obtain buying prices than selling prices in secondhand industrial markets, with the result that the current cost system can be based on more reliable information.

## CONCLUSIONS ON CURRENT VALUE ACCOUNTING

It is evident that most of the reasons for the use of current value accounting as a financial information system are concerned with various facets of management's planning and control functions designed to keep the firm as an effective operating entity; and for the evaluation of financial results of operations. While good management is always in the interests of investors in that it increases the security and profits of the firm, current value accounting in addition confers direct informational benefits to long-term creditors and shareholders in that it gives them information about income and financial position which satisfies accounting information standards better than historic cost or price-level adjusted historic cost data. It thereby enables them to make more rational investment decisions.

Both current value systems are necessary for total financial information where market buying and selling prices differ. The current cost system is appropriate for some uses and the current cash equivalent system is appropriate for other purposes in the going concern. The current cash equivalent system provides relevant information for short run decisions relating to the existing stock of assets and operations of the firm — how liquid it is, how financially adaptable it is, whether it should keep using assets or sell them, whether it should continue operations or sell up, and so on. On the other hand, the current cost system provides relevant information for long run decisions — maintenance of the firm's operating capcity into the future, determination of the most efficient methods of operating, prudent dividend and financing policies, optimum pricing and output policies where the scale of operations can be changed, and so on. Hence, the two systems provide complementary information to management, creditors, and investors. Where the two systems clash as in the measurement of income and financial position one must investigate the results given by each to assess which one gives the more useful results. The current cash equivalent system alone is relevant for the terminating or sick firm.

Rejection of the realization concept for the recognition of holding gains and losses in current value accounting, and for income measurement in the current cash equivalent system, is not a major limitation as is sometimes claimed. Realization is basically a financial matter rather than a matter of success or the measure of investment in assets, and the appropriate financial reports for it are the cash flow and funds statements. The extent to which holding gains or income have been realized can be shown in these statements.

When assessed against the standards for accounting information, it is apparent that for many purposes — measurement of income and financial position, interfirm comparisons, and decision-making — current value accounting ranks high in terms of the provision of relevant and timely information measured according to a consistent valuation basis. The objectivity standard would be compromised where current market values are difficult to obtain but not otherwise. The major objections to current value accounting relate to its lack of objectivity in some circumstances, to the extra costs it imposes on the firm in obtaining current price data and putting it through the accounting system, and to its neglect of the general inflation problem. Management will have to judge whether the benefits outweigh the additional costs of current value accounting. Simultaneous presentation of historic and current value results satisfies all standards for financial information, and particularly that for the presentation of environmental factors affecting the firm's operations.

## FURTHER READING

### General

Walker, R. G. *Takeover Bids and Financial Disclosure.* Accounting Research Study No. 4. Melbourne: Accounting Research Foundation, 1973.

### Current Value (Current Cost) System

A.A.A., Committee to Prepare a Statement of Basic Accounting Theory. *A Statement of Basic Accounting Theory.* Evanston, Ill.: A.A.A., 1966. Chaps. 3 and 4, Appendices A and B.

Barton, A. D., "Why Use Current Value Accounting?" *Australian Accountant* (September 1975).

Edwards, E., and Bell, P. *The Theory and Measurement of Business Income.* Berkeley, Calif.: University of California Press, 1961. Chaps. 3–7 (very advanced).

I.C.A. and A.S.A., "A Method of Current Value Accounting". Preliminary Exposure Draft (June 1975).

Mathews, R. L. *The Accounting Framework.* 3rd ed. Melbourne: Cheshire, 1971. Chap. 9.

Popoff, B., "The Effects of Inflation and Price Changes on Business Enterprises: An Accounting Dilemma". *Australian Accountant* (October 1975).

Stamp, E. "Income and Value Determination and Changing Price Levels: An Essay Towards a Theory." *Accountant's Magazine* (June 1971).

### Current Value (Selling Price) System

Chambers, R. J., "Accounting for Inflation", Exposure Draft. University of Sydney (September 1975.)

————.*Accounting for Inflation: Methods and Problems,* University of Sydney, August 1975.

Chambers, R. J. *Accounting, Evaluation, and Economic Behavior.* Englewood Cliffs, N.J.: Prentice-Hall, 1966. Chaps. 5, 9, and 10 (very advanced).

Edwards and Bell, *The Theory and Measurement of Business Income.* Chaps. 3–7 (very advanced).

## NOTES

1. Another category of assets can be added in this formulation — marketable securities and speculative assets. These assets are bought for a number of reasons such as to use up temporary cash surpluses or because of the expectation of a good profit on resale, and are outside the firm's normal sphere of operations. They are not regarded by management as forming part of its operating capacity. They are omitted at this stage of the analysis in order to keep the explanation simple. These assets are best valued at their selling prices at the beginning and end of the year and the holding gains can be included in current income.

2. If total current income is distributed, the value of the net stock of assets at the end of the year is the same as at the beginning of the year, hence:

$$[M_1 - M_0] + [N_1 - (N_0 + Nc] - Y_c = 0$$

If net holding gains were included in income and distributed, the value of the net stock of assets at the end of the year must be less than the opening stock by Nc, i.e.,

$$[M_1 - M_0] + [N_1 - (N_0 + Nc)] - [Y_c + Nc] = -Nc$$

3. Commonwealth of Australia, *Monthly Labour Reports, Monthly Bulletin of Business Statistics, National Income and Expenditure*; Reserve Bank of Australia, *Statistical Bulletins* (Canberra: Commonwealth Government Printer, latest issues).

4. A firm is a going concern if its current income exceeds or equals the alternative income which could be earned by investing its funds elsewhere, i.e., if $Yc \geqslant iC$,
   where i is the rate of return which investors can earn on alternative investments; and
   C is the current value of the firm's net assets.

   Alternatively the condition may be expressed as $P_F \geqslant C_F$,
   where $P_F$ is the present value of expected cash surpluses from future operations of the firm; and
   $C_F$ is the current value of the firm's net assets.

   This requirement is further discussed on pages 425–26 below.

5. See data given in Edwards and Bell, *The Theory and Measurement of Business Income*, chapts. 1 and 7, for the U.S.; K. Lacey, "Profit Measurement and the Trade Cycle: , *Economic Journal* (December 1947), for the United Kingdom; and R. L. Mathews and J. McB. Grant, *Inflation and Company Finance*, 2nd ed. (Sydney: Law Book Company, 1962), p. 94, for Australia.

6. The use of this term is advocated by Chambers, *Accounting Evaluation and Economic Behavior.*
7. See p. 502.
8. See p. 426.
9. See p. 457.
10. See pp. 457–60.

## QUESTIONS AND EXERCISES

[Solution to problem marked * is given in Appendix 4.]

1. Are changes in the prices of non-monetary assets frequently important in reality? Give illustrations. If important, do you consider there is a good case for incorporating them in a firm's accounting system?

2. Explain the concept of opportunity cost. Why do current market prices measure opportunity cost?

3. What are the major characteristics of current value accounting as compared with (a) historic cost accounting, and (b) constant dollar value accounting. .

4. Explain the concepts of wealth, capital maintenance and income used in

    i.    Current value (current cost) accounting
    ii.    Current value (selling price) accounting.

5. Does the use of replacement cost accounting require that the firm replace all its physical assets as they are used up with identical assets?

6. What property of the dollar is used as the unit of measurement in current value accounting?

7. Should net holding gains (losses) on assets be treated as part of income or capital? Justify your answer. Why is it advocated that holding gains on physical assets used within the business be treated as part of income in the current value (selling price) system and as part of capital maintenance in the current value (current cost) system?

8. Is current value accounting practicable for most businesses? What are the major obstacles to use? Why do not most companies use it now?

9. Should current value reports be in place of, or additional to, historic cost reports?

10. What are the major advantages and disadvantages claimed for current value (current cost) accounting?

11. What are the major advantages and disadvantages claimed for current value (selling price) accounting?

12. How would you rate—

    i.    current value (current cost) accounting
    ii.    current value (selling price) accounting

against the standards for accounting information for purposes of:

a. stewardship?
b. management decision-making?
c. measurement of profits and financial position?
d. forecasting of future events?

13. Explain the relationship between the two current value systems. Are they basically competitive or complementary accounting measurement systems?

14. Explain the notion of unrealized gains on inventory holdings. How do they arise? Should they be included in income or capital maintenance?

15. To what extent does the charging of current replacement cost depreciation recoup sufficient funds to enable a fixed asset to be replaced?

16. Distinguish between backlog depreciation and the financial shortfall in funds available for asset replacement. Are the two necessarily equal at all times? How should each be recorded?

17. i. You bought a house for living in during 1960 for $10,000. Because of a change in your employment, you find it desirable to move to another location nearer your new job. After investigation you ascertain that you could sell your present house for $25,000, but that it would cost you $25,000 for another similar house. How much better off, if at all, are you if you make the housing transfer?

ii. Suppose that the cost of a similar house in the other locality is $30,000, what is your answer?

iii. Suppose that the cost of a similar house is only $20,000, what is your answer?

18. i. From the following information prepare an income statement showing historic cost income and current income:

| | | |
|---|---|---|
| Sales for year | 50,000 units at $10 each | |
| Purchases for year | 48,000 " | " $ 8 " |
| Opening inventories | 12,000 " | " $ 6 " |
| Cash operating costs | | $54,000 |

Depreciation on plant to be charged at 10% on cost.
Its historic cost was $200,000 while its current cost is $400,000.
Income tax at the rate of 45% of historic cost income is to be charged.
A dividend of $25,000 is to be provided for.
The FIFO method of inventory valuation is used in the HCS.

ii. Provide a statement reconciling $Y_H$ with $Y_C$.
iii. Comment on the results.

*19.   A company's balance sheet on 1 January at the current market prices then prevailing is as follows:

|  | $ | $ |  | $ |
|---|---|---|---|---|
| Cash |  | 100 | Creditors | 50 |
| Inventories |  | 300 | Capital | 1,000 |
| Buildings | 1,000 |  | Net Holding Gains | 150 |
| Less Accumulated |  |  |  |  |
| Depreciation | 200 | 800 |  |  |
|  |  | $1,200 |  | $1,200 |

Revalued at 31 December prices, the 1 January balance sheet is:

|  | $ | $ |  | $ |
|---|---|---|---|---|
| Cash |  | 100 | Creditors | 50 |
| Inventories |  | 400 | Capital | 1,000 |
| Buildings | 1,200 |  | Net Holding Gains | 410 |
| Less Accumulated |  |  |  |  |
| Depreciation | 240 | 960 |  |  |
|  |  | $1,460 |  | $1,460 |

On 31 December, its assets and liabilities comprised: cash $300, inventories — current cost $660, selling value $1,000, buildings $1,200, accumulated depreciation $260, and creditors $120.

i.   Show the journal entries to record the asset price changes.

ii.   What is the company's current income (replacement cost) for the year? What is the capital maintenance amount?

iii.   What is current income (selling price) for the year, and the capital maintenance amount?

(Assume buying and selling prices are identical for the buildings.)

20.   On 1 January 1973 a firm commenced business with cash $500, inventories which cost $1,500, and premises which cost $10,000. Sales for the year were $20,000, cost of sales $12,000, depreciation on buildings $500, and other operating expenses $4,000. At 31 December, the same quantity of inventories are held, their FIFO cost is $2,200, and their current replacement cost is $2,500. The current market price of similar premises had increased by 10 per cent over the year. No dividends were paid during the year. All transactions were made in cash.

Prepare income statements and balance sheets on the basis of:

i.   Historic cost accounting
ii.   Current value (replacement cost) accounting.

Comment on the two sets of results.

21.   The Doodaa Corporation Limited has traditionally maintained its accounting system on a historic cost basis, but because of continuing inflation, it has decided to prepare its financial reports as well on a current value basis. Its historic cost balance sheet on 31 December 1974 is:

*Current Assets*

| | | |
|---|---|---|
| Bank | 46,000 | |
| Inventories | 172,000 | |
| Accounts Receivable | 112,000 | 330,000 |

*Long Term Assets*

| | | | |
|---|---|---|---|
| Motor Vehicles (At cost. Acquired Jan. 1973) | 85,000 | | |
| *Less* Accum. Deprecn. (20% p.a. straight line) | 34,000 | 51,000 | |
| Plant (At cost. Acquired Jan. 1971) | 188,000 | | |
| *Less* Accum. Deprecn. (10% p.a. straight line) | 75,200 | 112,800 | |
| Buildings (At cost. Acquired Jan. 1965) | 220,000 | | |
| *Less* Accum. Deprecn. (2% p.a. straight line) | 44,000 | 176,000 | |
| Land (at cost. Acquired Jan. 1965) | | 160,000 | |
| Goodwill (At cost. Acquired Jan. 1965) | | 40,000 | 539,800 |
| | | | $869,800 |

*Current Liabilities*

| | | |
|---|---|---|
| Accounts Payable | 110,000 | |
| Tax Payable | 60,000 | |
| Dividend Payable | 50,000 | 220,000 |

*Long Term Liabilities*

| | |
|---|---|
| Debentures | 250,000 |

*Shareholders Equity*

| | | |
|---|---|---|
| Paid up Capital (300,000 shares of $1 par val.) | 300,000 | |
| Share Premium Reserve | 50,000 | |
| General Reserve | 40,000 | |
| Retained Income | 9,800 | 399,800 |
| | | $869,800 |

The Company has its assets valued at their current buying prices on 31 December, 1974, with the following results:

| | $ |
|---|---|
| Inventories | 182,000 |
| Motor Vehicle (as new) | 115,000 |
| Plant (as new) | 260,000 |
| Buildings (as new) | 400,000 |
| Land | 380,000 |

As goodwill is not separately purchaseable, it has no current buying price.

The transactions summary for 1975 is:

|  | $ |
|---|---|
| Sales (all credit) | 2,330,000 |
| Purchases (all credit) | 1,490,000 |
| Wages paid | 461,000 |
| Other cash operating costs | 227,000 |
| Interest paid | 25,000 |
| Cash paid to creditors | 1,444,000 |
| Cash received from debtors | 2,259,000 |
| Tax paid | 60,000 |
| Dividend paid | 50,000 |
| Plant purchased for cash (30 June) | 70,000 |
| Motor vehicles purchased for cash (30 Dec.) | 30,000 |
| Share issue for cash: 100,000 shares at a premium of 20 cents (30 June) | 120,000 |

### Additional Information

1. The new motor vehicles and plant are subject to the same straight line depreciation rates as the existing ones.

2. Company tax is to be provided for at 50% of taxable income (based on historic cost and excluding depreciation of buildings).

3. Dividends of 15% on the par value of shares (including the new issue) are to be provided for.

4. The historic cost of 31 December inventories is $236,000.

5. The 31 December buying prices of equivalent physical assets owned by the Company are:

|  | $ |
|---|---|
| Inventories | 284,000 |
| Motor Vehicles. As new, incl. new vehicles | 160,000 |
| Plant. As new. Owned on 1 January | 294,000 |
| Purchased in June | 75,000 |
| Building. As new. | 420,000 |
| Land | 400,000 |

6. The 30 June buying price of 1 January inventories was $204,000, while the 30 June buying price of 31 December inventories was $220,000.

### Required

1. A current value balance sheet on 31 December, 1974.

2. Journal entries to record the conversion from historic cost to current values in balance sheet accounts in December 1974 and for 1975.

3. Balance sheet ledger accounts based on current values

4. Final reports for 1975 based on historic cost and current values

### NOTE:

1. The current value income statement should be centred on June values, and the

balance asset should be based on December values. Unless otherwise stated, assume that physical asset prices rose at a constant rate over the year.

2. Backlog depreciation is to be charged, but no additional charges are to be made against retained earnings.

3. List any assumptions made for your calculations.

22. Joe Smog takes out a lease on a new service station, to be called Smoggie's Service Station P/L, on 1 January. He leases it from the Nogo Oil Company Ltd, and rent is payable in advance on the first of each month. After the initial purchase, all petrol is bought for cash on the last day of the month, and Joe's policy is to buy sufficient to fill up his storage tanks which have a capacity of 50,000 gallons. He invests $50,000 in the business to provide adequate working capital. Joe decides to withdraw each month's profits on the first day of the following month as his personal salary, and he feels secure in the belief that he is maintaining his business capital intact. His business income is subject to a 50% tax rate, and the tax is payable immediately at the end of each month. The tax is levied on historic cost income.

Joe employs 2 attendants who are paid at the end of each month. Petrol is subject to price control, and the profit margin is fixed at the current whole- sale price + 10 cents. The Nogo Oil Company increases the wholesale regular- ly on the first day of each month.

*Joe's transactions are as follows:*

1 Jan.  Invests $50,000 in the business; obtains monthly lease of service station for $2,000; buys 50,000 gallons of petrol at 50 cents per gallon to fill his tanks: $25,000.

Jan.  Sells 36,000 gallons at 60 cents per gallon: $21,600;
Buys 36,000 gallons at 50 cents per gallon: $18,000;
Pays attendants wages $1,200; and other sundry expenses $300;
Pays tax.

Feb.  Withdraws January profits net of tax;
Sells 40,000 gallons at 70 cents per gallon: $28,000;
Buys 40,000 gallons at 60 cents per gallon: $24,000;
Pay wages $1,200, other sundry expenses, $300,
lease $2,000 and tax.

Mar.  Withdraws February profits net of tax.
Sells 40,000 gallons at 80 cents per gallon: $32,000;
Buys 40,000 gallons at 70 cents per gallon: $28,000;
Pays wages $1,400, sundry expenses $300, lease $2,000,
and tax.

Apr.  Withdraws March after-tax profits;
Sells 37,000 gallons at 90 cents per gallon: $33,300;
Buys 37,000 gallons at 80 cents per gallon: $29,600;
Pays wages $1,400, sundry expenses $400, lease $2,000,
and tax.

May  Withdraws April after-tax profits;
Sells 35,000 gallons at $1.00 per gallon: $35,000;
Buys 35,000 gallons at 90 cents per gallon: $31,500;
Pays wages $1,600, sundry expenses $400, lease $2,000,
and tax.

June   Withdraws May after-tax profits.
Sells 36,000 gallons at $1.10 per gallon: $39,000;
Buys 36,000 gallons at $1.00 per gallon: $36,000;
Pays wages $1,600, sundry expenses $400, lease
$2,000 and tax.

1 July   Withdraws June after-tax profits. Pays lease $2,000.

*Required:*

i.    A set of historic cost income statements and balance sheets for each month. (Use FIFO inventory valuation.)

ii.   A cash flow statement for each month.

iii.  A set of current value income statements and balance sheets for each month. Use end-of-month inventory valuations for the determination of COPS (cost of petrol sold).

iv.   A balance sheet on 1 January (after purchase of petrol and lease), and on 1 July. Compare Joe's financial position as at the two dates. Why is Joe so perplexed about his financial position on 1 July after he has followed conventional accounting principles so scrupulously and withdrawn only the profits of the business?

23.   The balance sheet of the Raymond Corporation Ltd on 1 January 1976 prepared according to the historic cost system and the current value (selling price) system is:

|  |  | *Historic Cost $* |  | *Current Value $* |
|---|---|---|---|---|
| Cash |  | 48,000 |  | 48,000 |
| Debtors |  | 60,000 |  | 60,000 |
| Inventories (14,000 units at cost $4 each) |  | 56,000 |  | 112,000 |
| Plant (Purchased 1975) | 200,000 |  |  |  |
| Accum. Deprecn. Plant (1 year at 20%) | 40,000 | 160,000 |  | 80,000 |
| Premises (Purchased 1975) |  | 200,000 |  | 240,000 |
|  |  | $524,000 |  | $540,000 |
| Creditors |  | 54,000 |  | 54,000 |
| Tax Payable |  | 46,000 |  | 46,000 |
| Debentures |  | 150,000 |  | 150,000 |
| Paid Up Capital | 250,000 |  | 250,000 |  |
| Undistributed Profits | 24,000 | 274,000 | 40,000 | 290,000 |
|  |  | $524,000 |  | $540,000 |

Transactions during 1976 comprized:

| | $ |
|---|---|
| Credit Sales 100,000 units at $8 each | 800,000 |
| Credit Purchases 106,000 units at $5 each | 530,000 |
| Cash paid to creditors | 524,000 |
| Cash received from debtors | 784,000 |
| Cash operating costs | 120,000 |
| Taxes paid | 46,000 |
| Plant purchased on 3 January for cash | 100,000 |

Resale values of physical assets at 31 December 1976 are:

| | |
|---|---|
| Inventories at $8 each | |
| Plant | 70,000 |
| Premises | 285,000 |

FIFO inventory valuation is used in the historic cost system. Income tax at the rate of 50% on historic cost income is to be provided for.

*REQUIRED:*

i. The financial reports for 1976 prepared according to each system.

ii. The Plant and Net Holding Gains ledger accounts for the CV(SP) system.

iii. Demonstrate that net income is the increase in net assets after maintaining capital intact in each system.

iv. Comment on the difference in the methods used to prepare the CV(SP) reports.

# Chapter 24
# Real Value Systems

We are now in a position to bring together the *constant dollar value* and *current value systems* into a combined *real value system*. The real value system corrects the deficiencies in each of the other systems — in effect it incorporates current market prices of assets into the former one or adjusts the latter one for general inflation. The constant dollar value and current value systems are thus shown to be complementary rather than alternatives. In the real value system, adjustments are made to correct for the variable measuring rod of the dollar caused by changes in the general level of prices and to recognize changes in current market prices of assets owned by the firm. Either buying or selling prices may be used, according to the circumstances of the firm and the use to be made of the information. The general purchasing power property of the dollar is used in the system. It is the most comprehensive of the historically based income measurement systems. The term "real" in this context refers to the general purchasing power property of the dollar rather than the money value of the dollar, and its use does not imply that other measures are "unreal" or false.

## REAL VALUE (CURRENT COST) SYSTEM

### WEALTH, INCOME, AND CAPITAL MAINTENANCE CONCEPTS

In general terms, all assets and liabilities are valued at current market prices and adjusted for inflation for the measurement of wealth, income, and capital maintenance. Wealth is the current market value of net assets where all non-monetary assets are valued at end-of-year buying prices or at their lower resale prices in the case of superceded assets; it is the same concept as in the current value system. *Real capital maintenance* refers to maintaining intact the sum of the initial stock of non-monetary assets plus the general purchasing power of net monetary assets. Alternatively it could be described as the preservation of the ability of initial capital to buy the same types of physical assets and maintain the same general purchasing power of net monetary assets.

*Real income* is the gain in wealth after maintaining real capital intact.

The nature of the combined adjustments can be illustrated by extending the algebraic formulations of chapters 22 and 23. No new procedures in addition to those of the two previous systems are required in real value accounting. The initial balance sheet can be stated as before:

$$M_o + N_o = P_o \qquad \qquad \text{......(i)}$$

where     M is the net monetary asset
            N are the non-monetary assets valued at the buying costs applying
            at that date
            P is the owners' equity.

Restatement of this balance sheet at the end of the year after a general inflation rate of r per cent and a price increase of c per cent in the current costs of physical assets gives:

$$M_o (1+r) + N_o [(1+r) + (c-r)] = P_o (1+r) + N_o (c-r)$$
$$\text{......(ii)}$$

The term (1+r) represents the price-level restatement and (c-r) represents the relative price changes in non-monetary assets. Thus the term $N_o [ (1+r) + (c-r) ]$ shows the opening value of non-monetary assets restated for the year's inflation and revalued at end-of-year prices. Equation (ii) can be restated as:

$$M_o + N_o + Nc = [P_o + Pr + N_o (c-r)] - Mr \qquad \text{......(iii)}$$

Nc is the total money holding gain on initial non-monetary assets; $[P_o + Pr + N_o (c-r)]$ is the capital maintenance term; Pr is the price-level adjustment to initial capital (or net assets); $N_o (c-r)$ is the real holding gain on non-monetary assets; and Mr is the price-level loss on initial monetary assets. If asset market prices rise by more than the inflation rate (i.e., $c > r$), there is a real holding gain; if by less (i.e., $c < r$), there is a real holding loss; and if they rise at the same rate as general inflation (i.e., $c = r$), there is neither a gain nor a loss. It should be noted that the general inflation term, r, cancels out on non-monetary assets in equation (iii), and hence they are simply revalued at end-of-year prices.

After a year's transactions (which do not include any proprietor's contributions or withdrawals), the end-of-year balance sheet can be depicted as:

$$M_1 + N_1 = P_1 \qquad \qquad \text{......(iv)}$$

where $N_1$ are valued at end-of-year costs. Real income (current cost) $(Y_{RC})$ is then:

$$Y_{RC} = P_1 - [P_0 + Pr + N_0 (c - r)] \qquad ......(v)$$

Real income is the increase in proprietorship after maintaining intact the general purchasing power and operating capacity of net assets. Capital maintenance here includes the general price-level adjustment and the real holding gains. This measure of income can be shown to be equal to:

$$Y_{RC} = [M_1 - M_0] + [N_1 - (N_0 + Nc)] - Mr \qquad ......(vi)$$

where N are valued at end-of-year costs. That is, real income is the gain in the stock of net assets valued throughout at end-of-year purchase prices, less the inflation loss on net monetary assets. Thus it equals current income (current cost), less the inflation loss on net monetary assets.

The only differences between the current and real value systems are that the real value system takes account of the general price-level loss or gain on net monetary assets and that the changes in asset prices are separated between the general price-level component and the relative price change in the capital maintenance adjustment accounts. These differences arise because of the inclusion of the general price-level adjustment in the system. The price-level loss or gain affects the measure of real income. However, as equations (iii) and (iv) above show, the assets and liabilities are the same in both systems, i.e., they are shown at end-of-year values. The asset revaluation credit is separated between the general price-level change and the relative price change in the capital maintenance adjustment accounts, and as a consequence holding gains are divided into these two components. The first is regarded as a fictional holding gain (it is really the price-level restatement which does not increase the firm's general purchasing power) and only the second as a real holding gain. For example, if the current market price of land rises from $100,000 to $140,000 over the year, and there was 8 per cent general inflation, $8,000 of the monetary holding gain of $40,000 represents the general inflation effect (the "fictitious gain") and the real gain in the relative price change of $32,000. The entry to record such events is:

|  |  | $ |
|---|---|---|
| Land | Dr. | 40,000 i.e., Nc |
| Price-Level Adjustment | Cr. | 8,000 i.e., Nr |
| Asset Revaluation Reserve | Cr. | 32,000 i.e., N(c−r) |

The relationship between the wealth, income and capital maintenance terms in the system can be depicted as follows:

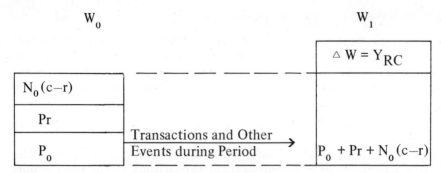

**Figure 24–1.** Real Value System Wealth Diagram where all items are measured as in the equations above.

### Illustration of Real Value (Current Cost) Accounting

To illustrate the type of adjustment needed to convert historic cost records to the real value (current cost) system, suppose that the firm's balance sheet on 1 January shows:

| | $ | $ |
|---|---|---|
| Plant | 1,000 | |
| Less Accumulated Depreciation | 400 | 600 |

The gross value of plant is the current cost of similar though new plant on 1 January. The plant has an expected life of ten years, and straight line depreciation is being charged based on the assumption of zero scrap value. This method is being used because secondhand market prices are not readily available. By 31 December the price level had risen by 10 per cent, and the current cost of similar new plant has risen to $1,250.

i. The price-level adjustments entry is:

| | | $ | $ |
|---|---|---|---|
| Plant (+ 10%) | Dr. | 100 | |
| Accumulated Depreciation (+ 10%) | Cr. | | 40 |
| Price-Level Adjustment | Cr. | | 60 |

ii. The revaluation of plant at December prices is recorded as:

| | | $ | $ |
|---|---|---|---|
| Plant (+ 15%) | Dr. | 150 | |
| Accumulated Depreciation (+ 15%) | Cr. | | 60 |
| Asset Revaluation Reserve | Cr. | | 90 |

iii. Depreciation based on the January price is:

| | | $ | $ |
|---|---|---|---|
| Depreciation | Dr. | 100 | |
| Accumulated Depreciation | Cr. | | 100 |

iv. Additional depreciation based on the December price is:

| | | $ | $ |
|---|---|---|---|
| Depreciation (10% of 250) | Dr. | 25 | |
| Accumulated Depreciation | Cr. | | 25 |

In the December balance sheet, the items are:

| | | $ |
|---|---|---|
| Assets: | Plant (CC of new plant at 31 December) | 1,250 |
| | Less Accumulated Depreciation (5 years @ 10% p.a.) | 625 |
| | Estimated CC of 5-year-old plant | 625 |
| Equity: | Asset Revaluation Reserve | 90 |
| | Price-Level Adjustment | 60 |

Thus the current year's depreciation charge is based on the current new cost of the plant; and the net balance sheet value for the five-year-old plant is half its current new cost (in the conditions assumed). The Price-Level Adjustment account shows the general price level change in the value of plant (the "fictitious" component) while the Asset Revaluation Reserve account shows the relative cost increase in plant (the "real" component).

A more detailed illustration of the system can be obtained by combining the constant dollar and current value reports for the Inflationary Company Ltd which were given in chapters 22 and 23. The real value reports may either neglect intra-period inflation and incorporate the adjustments to the beginning-of-year balance sheet items only (the simple method), or include the intra-period inflation adjustments in addition to the beginning-of-year balance sheet adjustments. In the simple method using BOY adjustments only, the real value income statement is the same as the current value income statement up to the calculation of current income, and the only amendment required is the deduction of the price-level loss on net monetary assets from current income. Thus, the income statement on page 364 is amended as follows:

| | $ |
|---|---|
| Current Income | 23 |
| Less Price-Level Loss on M | 2 |
| | $21 |

The Price-Level Loss on M of $2 is based on BOY net monetary assets and its calculation is explained on page 340. The real value balance sheet is identical with the current value balance sheet on page 364 for all assets and liabilities; however the capital maintenance accounts now comprise both a Price-Level Adjustment account and an Asset Revaluation Reserve account to reflect the general inflation adjustment to net assets (i.e., 420 x $\frac{10}{100}$) and the relative cost increases on non-monetary assets. The shareholders equity under each system appears as:

|  | Current Value $ | Real Value $ |
|---|---|---|
| Paid-up Capital | 400 | 400 |
| Retained Earnings | 20 | 20 |
| Price-Level Adjustment |  | 42 |
| Asset Revaluation Reserve | 80 | 40 |
| Income | 23 | 21 |
|  | $523 | $523 |

In the more complex method incorporating intra-period inflation adjustments, EOY physical asset values are again used for the measure of asset consumption charges (and not MOY values as in this method in the current value system), and all income statement items occurring throughout the year are adjusted for the inflation occurring in the second half year to restate them from average MOY values to EOY prices and general purchasing power units. The income statement would be:

|  | Hist. Cost $ | Current Value $ | Adjustment Factor | Real Value $ |
|---|---|---|---|---|
| Sales | 2,000 | 2,000 | MOY 110/104 | 2,115 |
| Less Opg. Invent. | 100 | 115 | EOY value | 130 |
| Purchases | 1,630 | 1,630 | MOY 110/104 | 1,724 |
|  | 1,730 | 1,745 |  | 1,854 |
| Clg. Invent. | 120 | 115 | EOY value | 130 |
| COGS | 1,610 | 1,630 |  | 1,724 |
| Gross Profit | 390 | 370 |  | 391 |
| Cash Opg. Costs | 300 | 300 | MOY 110/104 | 317 |
| Depreciation | 40 | 43 | EOY value | 47 |
| Total Expenses | 340 | 343 |  | 364 |
| Net Opg. Income | 50 | 27 |  | 27 |
| Less P-L Loss on M | – | – |  | 6 |
| Net Income | $ 50 | $ 27 |  | $ 21 |

Real income is still current income less the price-level loss on M in this system. However, the makeup of the figures may differ slightly from those derived in the simpler method; for example the current income measure is based on MOY values, and the price level loss covers the loss on the initial net monetary assets plus the loss on the increase in them over the year, as explained on page 343. The balance sheet remains the same as that for the simpler method.

The journal entries recording the conversion from historic cost data to real values are as follows:

|    |    |    | $ | $ |
|----|----|----|----|----|
| i. | Inventories | Dr. | 20 | |
|    | Price-Level Adjustment | Cr. | | 10 |
|    | Asset Revaluation Reserve | Cr. | | 10 |

Revaluation of opening inventories at EOY historic cost, incorporating 10 per cent P-L adjustment and $10 relative price increase.

|     |    |    | | |
|-----|----|----|----|----|
| ii. | Inventories | Dr. | 10 | |
|     | Asset Revaluation Reserve | Cr. | | 10 |

Revaluation of closing inventories at EOY buying prices.

|      |    |    | | |
|------|----|----|----|----|
| iii. | Plant | Dr. | 50 | |
|      | Price-Level Adjustment | Cr. | | 30 |
|      | Asset Revaluation Reserve | Cr. | | 20 |

Revaluation of plant at EOY cost, incorporating 10 per cent P-L adjustment and $20 relative cost increase.

|     |    |    | | |
|-----|----|----|----|----|
| iv. | Purchases | Dr. | 94 | |
|     | Cash Operating Costs | Dr. | 17 | |
|     | Price Level Loss on M | Dr. | 6 | |
|     | Sales | Cr. | | 115 |
|     | Price-Level Adjustment | Cr. | | 2 |

Restatement of operating items from MOY purchasing power to EOY purchasing power units.

## REAL VALUE (SELLING PRICE) SYSTEM

This system, which is also known as continuously contemporary accounting (or COCOA), incorporates both the revaluation adjustments and the general inflation adjustment as does the real value (current cost) system. However, here the revaluations are based on the current selling prices of assets. *Wealth* is the current cash value of the net assets or the amount of cash the owners could obtain if the firm's assets were to be sold in the normal course of business. *Real capital maintenance* refers to maintaining the general purchasing power of the cash value of initial net assets, or capital, intact. *Real income* is the gain in general purchasing power accruing from the period's activities and events, or the increased command over goods and services in general, or the maximum amount that could be distributed without impairing real spending power.

The analysis for the real value (selling price) system is similar to that for the other real value system, except that the real holding gains form part of income and assets are valued at selling prices. Let the initial balance sheet be as before, i.e.,

$$M_0 + N_0 = P_0 \qquad\qquad\qquad (i)$$

where the non-monetary assets are valued at BOY selling prices.

After a year of inflation at the rate r per cent, this balance sheet can be restated as:

$$M_0(1+r) + N_0(1+r) = P_0(1+r) \qquad\qquad (vii)$$

$M_0(1+r)$ shows the general purchasing power of initial net monetary assets and $N_0(1+r)$ the general purchasing power of the non-monetary assets, while $P_0(1+r)$ shows the general purchasing power of opening capital – it is the capital maintenance term. Because real holding gains are included in income, the balance sheet is not restated for the asset revaluations over the year.

The end-of-year balance sheet is simply:

$$M_1 + N_1 = P_1 \qquad\qquad\qquad (viii)$$

Real income (selling price) $(Y_{RS})$ is then:

$$Y_{RS} = P_1 - [P_0 + Pr] \qquad\qquad ......(ix)$$

That is, real income is the increment in price-level adjusted proprietorship, after maintaining intact the general purchasing power of opening proprietorship. This measure of income can be shown to be equal to:

$$Y_{RS} = (M_1 - M_0) + N_1 - (N_0 + Nr) - Mr \qquad ......(x)$$

Real income is the increment in price-level adjusted net assets, less the price-level loss on net monetary assets, where the initial non-monetary assets are valued at beginning-of-year selling prices and closing non-monetary assets are valued at end-of-year selling prices. In the context of the income statement, real income (selling price) is measured as: Revenue less expenses, plus net holding gains on non-monetary assets (or less net holding losses), and less the price-level adjustment on initial net assets, i.e., as current income (selling price) less the price-level adjustment.

**Illustration of Real Value (Selling Price) Accounting**

The balance sheet of the Excelsior Company Ltd. on 1 January is as follows:

| | $ | | $ | $ |
|---|---|---|---|---|
| Cash | 150 | Debentures | | 250 |
| Inventories | 140 | Paid-up Capital | 300 | |
| Vehicles | 80 | Price-Level Adj. | 80 | |
| Premises | 300 | Retained Earnings | 40 | 420 |
| | $670 | | | $670 |

All assets are valued at their 1 January selling prices. The Company made the following transactions during the year:

| | $ |
|---|---|
| Cash sales | 1,000 |
| Cash purchases | 650 |
| Cash operating costs | 200 |
| Vehicles purchased (March) | 30 |

On 31 December, the current resale values of its physical assets are:

| | |
|---|---|
| Inventories (cost 110) | 170 |
| Vehicles | 70 |
| Premises | 340 |

Over the year, the general price-level index rose from 180 to 200.

The Company's income statement for the year could be presented as:

| | $ | $ |
|---|---|---|
| Sales | 1,000 | |
| Closing inventories | 170 | |
| Holding gain on premises | 40 | 1,210 |
| *Less* Opening inventory | 140 | |
| Purchases | 650 | |
| Cash operating costs | 200 | |
| Deprecn. on vehicles (or holding loss) | 40 | 1,030 |
| Current income | | 180 |
| Less Price-level adjustment | | 47 |
| Real income | | $ 133 |

Its balance sheet on 31 December would be:

| | $ | | $ | $ |
|---|---|---|---|---|
| Cash | 270 | Debentures | | 250 |
| Inventory | 170 | Paid-up Capital | 300 | |
| Vehicles | 70 | Price-Level Adj. | 127 | |
| Premises | 340 | Retained Earnings | 173 | 600 |
| | $850 | | | $850 |

*Comments*

i.  Other forms of presentation of the income statement could be used. For example, if only the real holding gains (and losses) on the non-monetary assets are included in income, then only the purchasing power loss on net monetary assets would be deducted rather than the total price-level adjustment. The fictional holding gains (i.e., the Nr term) is common to both the money holding gains on non-monetary assets and the total price-level restatement and hence may be omitted from the statement.

ii.  Real income calculated in the income statement agrees with that calculated in the balance sheet, i.e.,

$$Y_{RS} = P_1 - (P_0 + Pr)$$

$$= 600 - (420 + 47)$$

$$= 133$$

It could all be distributed without impairing the general purchasing power of opening net assets.

iii.  There are no adjustments made to sales and other operating items occurring throughout the year for intra-period inflation, as all items are automatically measured in EOY dollars because of the purchasing power adjustment and the valuation of all assets and liabilities at EOY selling prices.

iv.  The journal entry to record the net holding gains on the revaluation of EOY assets at 31 December selling prices is:

|  |  | $ | $ |
|---|---|---|---|
| Inventories $(110 \rightarrow 170)$ | Dr | 60 | |
| Premises     $(300 \rightarrow 340)$ | Dr | 40 | |
| Vehicles     $(80 + 30 \rightarrow 70)$ | Cr | | 40 |
| Income | Cr | | 60 |

v.  The journal entry to restate BOY net assets into equivalent EOY purchasing power units is:

|  |  | $ | $ |
|---|---|---|---|
| Income | Dr | 47 | |
| Price-Level Adjustment $(420 \times \dfrac{20}{180})$ | Cr | | 47 |

## ADVANTAGES OF THE REAL VALUE SYSTEMS

As the real value systems are the most sophisticated of the histor-ically based accounting systems, they satisfy the standards of a good financial information system better than any other system. They have worthwhile advantages of both constant dollar and current value systems without their particular disadvantages because they encompass both changes in current market prices and the general price-level. Each real value system should be used in the context appropriate for its related current value system.

### 1. Decision-Making

Data on real profits and on real financial position do not add anything in most decision-making in business to what is already provided by the current value systems. For example, in determining the optimum combinations of factor inputs, or size of output, current buying prices are required; in retain or sell decisions, current selling prices are required, and so on. Nevertheless real data are useful for some forms of management decision-making, particularly for financing questions. A firm may desire to maintain its real capital intact, and real profit then provides a better basis for formulating prudent dividend policies. It is helpful in determining an optimum financial structure for a company as it shows how the real cost of debt finance is progressively reduced by inflation. Conversely, it is useful for working capital management because it shows the purchasing power losses on money asset holdings and hence emphasizes the need to avoid carrying surplus cash or overdue accounts receivable.

### 2. Measures of Financial Performance and Position

The major advantage of the real value systems arise from their pro-vision of the most comprehensive measures of financial performance and financial position, and hence rates of return on investment. They overcome one major defect of current income, in that they include the inflationary loss on money assets in their ambit, and this loss is a genu-ine loss of purchasing power which should be disclosed. They also show to what extent net holding gains are real. Asset price rises which do not at least outpace inflation confer no net benefit on the firm, and fiction-al holding gains can be quite delusory. Real holding gains are relevant as part of the information for assessing management's asset purchase policy. When compared with the constant dollar value system, they have significant advantages in the recognition of holding gains as they occur and in the measurement of asset consumption at current asset prices. Similarly, the real value systems confer substantial balance sheet advantages. They have all the advantages of the current value balance sheets in showing current financial position (as the assets and the liabilities are the same for each balance sheet); and in addition show the cumulative effects of inflation on the firm's capital maintenance requirements. The real value (current cost) balance sheet shows as well the additional funds which must be retained within the firm to maintain intact its real productive capacity. Finally, the measures of the rate of return on investment are the best obtainable. This measure is the acid test of management performance.

### 3.  Inter-firm Comparisons of Performance and Position

Although current value balance sheets are good for inter-firm comparisons in the same industry, real value balance sheets are preferable for inter-industry comparisons. Financial structures and asset composition between monetary and non-monetary assets can vary substantially between industries and as the real value balance sheets incorporate the effects of inflation on net monetary assets, inter-industry comparisons are more reliable.

### 4.  Comparisons of a Firm's Performance over Time

Better assessment of real growth in profits and size of the firm is made possible by real value data. The inflation effects on profits and assets are removed by converting the current value data for previous years up to the current time. Figures for several years are then all expressed in dollars of current purchasing power.

### 5.  Forecasting

The real value systems provide more detailed and segregated information about current profits, extent and effects of asset price changes, and extent and effects of inflation on a firm's current operations and financial position. Consequently they provide a better basis for forecasting future movements in these variables than is provided by other systems which furnish part only of the information, or scramble it together. Each variable can be subject to different influences and should be predicted separately. Improved forecasting makes possible better planning of future operations and consequently higher future profits and sounder financial positions.

### CONCLUSIONS

We have now completed the analysis of historically based or ex post concepts and measurement of income and financial position. The complexities in income measurement are all too apparent and it is important that the concepts be carefully defined before the measurement process is begun. Income is an abstract concept which is not capable of isolation and separate measurement — it must be measured indirectly through the measurement of transactions and relevant economic events, and/or through the measurement of asset changes. Firms operate in a complex economic environment involving uncertainty of the future (and indeed of many aspects of current operations), changing asset prices and inflation, and unique measures of income and financial position are just not possible. There are countless approaches to the measurement of periodic income and financial position used in practice or advocated in the literature, and only a few of them have been analyzed here. There is not much agreement on the grey areas of the topic. Neither the analysis presented here, nor any other analysis presented elsewhere can claim to represent a generally accepted approach — there is as yet insufficient agreement on any one method for such a claim to be made. The approach adopted here is a flexible one in that it recognizes that no one income measurement and asset valuation system can suit all types of decision-making, measurement of financial performance and position, stewardship purposes, etc; and that the system adopted should be tailored to suit the end uses of the information. Each system should be judged against the standards for accounting information for the broad categories of end-uses which it serves. Nevertheless, there is a strict limit to the amount of flexibility which can be permitted by the rules of logical analysis and relevance. Finally, a couple of important practical matters should not be overlooked. It must be recognized that information costs money to obtain and that all systems should be subject, at least implicitly, to cost-benefit analysis to help ensure that the information is worth obtaining; and that many approximations to the logically correct data will have to be made in reality.

## FURTHER READING

As for chapter 23, plus:

Parker, R. H., and Harcourt, G. C. eds. *Readings in the Concept and Measurement of Income* Cambridge; Cambridge University Press, 1969. Chap. 1.

## QUESTIONS AND EXERCISES

[Solutions to problems marked * are given in Appendix 4.]

1. Explain the concepts of wealth, income, and capital maintenance in:
   i.  The real value (current cost) system
   ii. The real value (selling price) system.

2. What are the basic characteristics of real value accounting?

3. What are the advantages of real value accounting over current value accounting?

4. Distinguish between "fictitious" holding gains and "real" holding gains on non-monetary assets. Give illustrations.

5. Assess the merits of the each value system for the measurement of financial performance and position against the standards for accounting information.

6. A firm's balance sheet on 1 January shows:

| | $ |
|---|---|
| Plant | 20,000 |
| Less Accumulated Depreciation | 4,000 |
| | $16,000 |

$20,000 is the current cost of similar new plant on 1 January. The plant has an expected life of five years and zero scrap value, and straight line depreciation is charged on it. By 31 December, the general price-level had risen by 4 per cent and the current cost of new similar plant to $22,000. Show the journal entires to record the holding gains and plant depreciation for the year.

7. The current cost of a two-year-old machine on 1 January is $5,000. On 31 December following, the current cost of an identical two-year-old machine is $5,500, and on a three-year-old machine is $4,000. The general price level rose by 3 per cent over the year. Show the journal entries to record the price-level adjustment and holding gain on the machine, and the depreciation for the year.

*8. The current cost of inventories on hand on 1 January is $20,000. At 31 December prices, the same set of inventories would cost $26,000 to replace. During the year, merchandise costing $180,000 was purchased, and merchandise on hand on 31 December had a current cost of $34,000. The general price level rose by 5 per cent over the year. Show the journal entries to record the holding gain and price-level adjustment on inventories, and show the calculation of current cost of goods sold for the year.

9. i. Rework Question 20, chapter 23, for the real value system, with the additional information that the general price level rose by 6 per cent over the year.
   ii. Record the adjustments in journal entries.
   iii. Compare the results with those obtained under current value accounting and interpret the differences.
   iv. Demonstrate that real income is the increase in net assets for the year, after maintaining real capital intact.

*10. The balance sheet of Abington Co. Limited, based on the real value system, on 1 January is:

|  | $ | $ |  | $ |
|---|---|---|---|---|
| Cash |  | 5,000 | Creditors | 10,000 |
| Debtors |  | 30,000 | Capital | 100,000 |
| Inventories (CC) |  | 40,000 | Price-Level Adjustment | 6,000 |
| Plant (CC equivalent |  |  | Asset Revaluation Reserve | 9,000 |
| new) | 80,000 |  |  |  |
| Less Accumulated |  |  |  |  |
| Depreciation | 30,000 | 50,000 |  |  |
|  |  | $125,000 |  | $125,000 |

At 31 December prices, the current replacement costs of the initial set of inventories is $44,000, and of similar new plant is $86,000. The general price level rose by 5 per cent over the year. No dividends were paid during the year nor was any additional capital contributed.

Its assets and liabilities at 31 December, based on end-of-year purchase prices, comprise:

|  | $ |  |
|---|---|---|
| Cash |  | 12,000 |
| Debtors |  | 41,000 |
| Inventories |  | 58,000 |
| Plant | 86,000 |  |
| Less Accumulated |  |  |
| Depreciation | 43,000 | 43,000 |
| Creditors |  | 6,000 |

i.   Show journal entries to record the price-level adjustments and holding gains on January assets.

ii.  Prepare a 1 January balance sheet restated in end-of-year prices and dollar values.

iii. Prepare the 31 December balance sheet and show in it the current income and real income for the year.

11. Rework Question 21, chapter 23 (Dooda Corporation Ltd.) with the additional information that the general price-level index was 150 on 1 January 1975 and 160 on 31 December 1975.

12. Rework Question 23, chapter 23 (Raymond Corporation Ltd.) with the additional information that the general price level index rose from 120 to 135 over the year.

# Chapter 25
# Present Value Accounting

So far, we have considered only historically based accounting systems in which actual transactions of the firm were recorded and the results of operations were measured according to several valuation systems. Although some estimates of future events were necessary for the measurement of historic income and financial position, these estimates all related back to past transactions where whole transaction cycles had not been completed — the life of long-term assets acquired, the likely collections from debtors, and so on. The measures of income and financial position concerned what the firm had achieved from its operations over specified periods and where it stood financially at specified dates in the past. The present value (or discounted cash flow) system on the other hand concerns only the future. It encompasses only those transactions which are expected to occur in the future, i.e., those transactions included in the firm's budgets. However, the present value system is more than just a series of budgets in that the results of the expected transactions are evaluated in terms of profit or loss as at a point of time, e.g., now, and all assets and liabilities are valued according to their expected cash flows.

The relationship between the present value system and historically-based systems can be illustrated as in Figure 25−1.

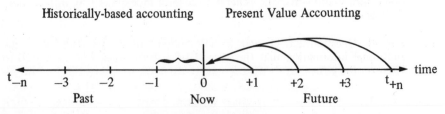

**Figure 25−1.** Time path

In the historically based accounting systems, the historic life of the firm is divided into periods, and measurements of income, profit appropriations, fund and cash flows over the period, and financial position at the end of the period, are made. In the present value system, future transactions are estimated up to the time horizon of the management $(t_n)$, which may be any number of years ahead, and their cash dimensions are brought back to the present time to evaluate the expected profit or loss. There is no measurement of periodic income — rather, total income up to the horizon is evaluated. The present value system may be supplemented by a series of budgeted periodic income statements and balance sheets, prepared in a similar manner to the historically based ones, but these statements are outside the present value system itself and are prepared at a subsequent stage.

To understand the nature of present value accounting, one must first appreciate the role of management in business operations. Management must make decisions now about what the firm is to do in the future — expand plant, set up a new shop, introduce new products, scrap existing plant, change prices, raise more finance, and so on. However, management is fairly uncertain of future market events and rational decisions are difficult to make in the face of uncertainty. Consequently all types of predictions and judgments about the future must be made. We saw that one of the basic functions of historical accounting systems is to facilitate this process of forecasting. If the objective of management is to do the best it can, it should aim to maximize the present value of the firm. (This aim is the dynamic counterpart of the static profit maximization objective generally made in elementary economics.) To maximize present value, management should search around for various means of achieving this goal and evaluate each one in terms of its net present value, and select those yielding positive net present values. It then prepares detailed budgets for its proposed operations and puts the plans into action. In this way it hopes to convert its profit expectations into actual profits as evidenced by an increase in net tangible assets. Detailed comparisons of actual results with budgets are made as operations continue including the measurement of periodic results, and all budget variances are progressively analyzed to determine whether the plans for the future need modification, or whether closer control is warranted over actual operations. This is essentially a process of learning from experience and of adapting the firm's planned operations to changing market conditions as the need for change becomes evident. Firms can survive only by operating in this way where they do not have perfect knowledge of the future. This method of approach should enable management to convert expected profits into maximum actual profits in each period and thereby to maximize the firm's share market value. This in turn is what owners desire as it maximizes their wealth and gains from investment.

In terms of the management information flow chart in chapter 3, present value accounting applies to stages 3 and 4 of the Planning phase (i.e. the evaluation and selection of policies to follow); budgeting to stage 5 of the Planning phase (i.e., coordination of plans and detailed planning requirements for the policies that have been selected); and historically based accounting systems to stages 6 and 7 (i.e., implementation of plans, control, and measurement and evaluation of performance and position). The historically based systems measure the *consequences* of the decisions that were taken some time before in the present value system.

Hence, in the overall cycle of business operations, it can be seen how the functions served by present value accounting differ entirely from those of historically based systems. Present value accounting is required purely for decision-making or planning purposes and in particular for decisions having long-term consequences. It involves the stages of evaluating and selecting alternative future courses of action, and thereby enables management, shareholders, and long-term investors to make rational decisions about which ones to adopt. It is axiomatic that all decisions about future action must logically be based on future data because decisions can only relate to the future and never the past, and secondly that such future data must be estimates. The *net* present value (which is a combination of present value and current values) of the expected consequences of any decision indicates to the decision-maker whether the decision is expected to be a profitable one or not, and the extent of such profit or loss; i.e., it provides the basis for choice between alternative actions.

It should be noted that all future transactions are completely hypothetical, and hence we cannot measure their financial attributes in any objective way. Rather, we can only guess or estimate them, and *evaluate* the results of these estimates. The confidence to be placed on such estimates depends upon our ability to forecast the future. Where the future course of events is known with certainty, as in the ideal state, reliable estimates can be made. However, in the typical situation of some uncertainty, there is always the risk that some estimates will turn out to be wrong. Predictions of the future typically run the whole gamut from absolute certainty to complete ignorance, according to what is being forecast. For example, management may have no doubt that it will repay its debentures, but have no idea as to how successful a new product will be.

### ELEMENTS OF THE PRESENT VALUE SYSTEM

Decisions about future courses of action to follow should be evaluated in terms of their effects on net cash inflow. The cash surpluses (or deficit) consequent upon a decision measure the net gain to the firm. However, net cash flows are likely to differ in amounts, timing, and duration according to each prospective venture, and it is necessary to put them on to a comparable basis for a decision to be made. This is done by discounting the prospective cash flows back to the present time.[1]

The discounting process overcomes the problem that a dollar expected to be received in one year's time is not worth a dollar now. Rather, cash tied up over time has a cost, and this cost must be allowed for. The cost of cash is the reward — interest, dividends, and so on — that must be paid to investors to induce them to lend their money, and it is measured by the rate of return required by investors. Discounting is based on the formula:

$$P_o = \frac{F_n}{(1+r)^n} \qquad \qquad ......(i)$$

where     $P_o$ is the present value of the cash flow
          $F_n$ is the future value of the cash flow at time n
          r is the rate of return, or the cost of cash
          n is the number of time periods involved.

For example, if F = \$110, r = 10%, and n = 1 year, then

$$P_o = \frac{110}{(1+0.10)^1} = 100$$

i.e., the present value of \$110 to be received in a year's time when the rate of interest is 10 per cent per annum is \$100.

Where a series of future cash receipts and payments are involved at discrete time intervals, the formula becomes:

$$P_o = \frac{(R-E)_1}{(1+r)^1} + \frac{(R-E)_2}{(1+r)^2} + ...... + \frac{(R-E)_n}{(1+r)^n} \qquad ......(ii)$$

Let $(R - E) = S$

$$P_o = \frac{S_1}{(1+r)^1} + \frac{S_2}{(1+r)^2} + ...... + \frac{S_n}{(1+r)^n} \qquad ......(iii)$$

$$= \sum_{t=1}^{n} \frac{S_t}{(1+r)^t} \qquad \qquad ......(iv)$$

where     $P_o$ is the gross present value of the cash surpluses
          $R_t$ are the cash receipts in each period t
          $E_t$ are the cash expenditures in each period t
          $S_t$ are the cash surpluses in each period t
          $t = 1 ... n$ are the time periods involved.

The net present value ($NP_o$) of the stream of expected cash flows is the gross present value less the initial cash outlay ($C_o$) required on the project, i.e., the cost of the investment project.

$$NP_o = P_o - C_o \qquad \qquad ......(v)$$

It is the measure of the surplus or pure profits expected from the project calculated after all cash costs have been recovered from the cash inflows. The process of discounting is in fact no more than a short-cut mathematical method of taking out the financing costs on the money tied up in the cash flows. By removing the financing costs for the time involved, the cash flows for all future courses of action are put onto a comparable basis, and they can be added up for each proposed venture to get its net result. The firm can then rank the proposed ventures according to their net present values, and select the profitable ones.

The cash flows included in the evaluation comprise all the operating (i.e., non-financing) cash receipts and payments beyond the initial investment outlays (which are included in $C_o$). Receipts ($R_t$) include all receipts from sales of merchandise and other assets, but not from any loans or capital. Expenditures ($E_t$) comprise all payments made for operating expenses, and taxes and subsequent purchases of fixed assets (for either replacement or expansion purposes), but not interest or dividends (which are taken account of in the discount rate) or repayments of loans or capital. The financing items are removed so that it can be ascertained if the project is likely to be profitable, and hence whether it is worthwhile to raise the finance for the investment expenditures to be made. It is fundamental that financing cash flows are excluded from the operating cash flows in the evaluation — for example, receipt of loan money does not increase the profitability of a project nor does the repayment of a loan reduce its profitability.

The discount rate used in the determination of present values varies from situation to situation. In the case of loans, it is the effective rate of interest payable on the loan. The interest rate comprises a reward to the investor for waiting for the return of his money, plus a reward for any risk that he takes with respect to payment of interest and repayment of the principal. The longer the time period or the greater the risk, the higher is the rate of interest required by the investor. Calculation of the cost of equity capital is not always an easy matter. Share investors have the opportunity to invest their funds in a large variety of ways, and if a company wants to attract their funds it must pay the going market rate (just as it does for the purchase of any other resource). This rate is determined by the yield investors are obtaining from shares in other companies possessing similar investment risk characteristics. Although ultimately the cost of equity capital to the company is its dividend cost, in the shorter term it need not be, as companies retain funds to finance expansion and this should lead to larger future dividends, they make bonus and rights issues of shares and so on, which disguise the effective dividend return to shareholders. These matters can make the cost of equity capital to the company difficult to calculate. Although it is an identifiable outlay cost in the long run, in the short run it need be only an opportunity cost which is being measured. In the case of proposed ventures by a firm, the discount rate to be used is the weighted average cost of all finance used by the firm, i.e., its weighted average cost of capital. Firms normally obtain finance in a variety of forms — bank overdrafts, term loans, debentures, share issues, funds retained from operations, and so on — and these funds are merged together in its operations. The weighted average cost of finance is not always easy to calculate because of problems involved in determining the cost of equity funds.

If the public had no preferences for current money over future money, the rate of interest would be zero and money for investment purposes would be freely available. In this case it would not be necessary to discount future returns and the profitability of projects would be measured by the absolute cash surplus.

## APPLICATION OF THE PRESENT VALUE SYSTEM IN DECISION-MAKING

The present value system can be understood most easily by considering a simple illustration. Suppose a retailer has the opportunity to lease a new shop for three years, with the right of renewal. The cost of the lease is $30,000, payable immediately; and the cost of finance to the firm is 10 per cent per annum. The expected cash receipts from sales and cash costs are as follows:

|  | Cash Receipts | Cash Costs | Cash Surplus |
|---|---|---|---|
|  | $ | $ | $ |
| Year 1 | 80,000 | 70,000 | 10,000 |
| Year 2 | 100,000 | 85,000 | 15,000 |
| Year 3 | 110,000 | 90,000 | 20,000 |

Should the shop be leased? (Assume year-end cash flows and no taxation.)

The proposal can be evaluated as follows:

$$NP_0 = -30,000 + \frac{10,000}{(1.1)^1} + \frac{15,000}{(1.1)^2} + \frac{20,000}{(1.1)^3}$$
$$= -30,000 + 9,090 + 12,390 + 15,020$$
$$= +6,500$$

Hence on the basis of current expectations, it is profitable to lease the shop. The firm recovers the $30,000 cost of the lease, all cash operating costs, the 10 per cent cost on the funds tied up in the lease (which covers its normal profit requirement), and makes a pure profit whose present value is $6,500. In fact, the firm could pay $36,500 for the lease and still make a normal profit.

Other proposals for future action should be evaluated on a similar basis, and they should all be ranked according to their net present values. For a firm whose aim is to maximize profits and which suffers from no physical restrictions on its ability to accept all profitable ventures (for example, inadequate finance or management capacity), the decision rules are as follows:

1. If $NP_0$ is positive (i.e., where $P_0 > C_0$), accept the venture
2. If $NP_0$ is negative (i.e., where $P_0 < C_0$), reject the venture
3. If $NP_0$ is zero (where $P_0 = C_0$), the venture just pays for itself, and it could be accepted.

Where the net present value is zero, the firm should earn just sufficient cash from the venture to recover all funds invested in it, and also pay all interest charges on debt finance and return a normal rate of profit to owners. The normal rate of profit is measured by the rate of return the firm must pay its owners (in dividends, etc.) for them to provide risk capital. The concept of normal profit differs from accounting profit in that the latter measures the total return to owners, and not just the necessary cost of equity capital. Accounting profit covers both normal and pure profits.

Where the net present value is positive, the firm should recover all funds invested in the ventures together with the costs of providing the funds, and earn economic pure profits as well. An economic loss would be incurred where the net present value is negative, with the result that the firm would not recover both the funds invested in the venture and the cost of providing the funds.

The same form of analysis should be applied to all long-term asset purchase, replacement, hold or disposal decisions. The *economic value of an asset* to a firm is the gross present value of the cash surplus generated from its use. This value is frequently called its internal value, value in use, or subjective value. In the present value system, assets are recognized explicitly as bundles of future services and are valued by capitalizing (i.e., discounting) the net cash surpluses expected to be generated by the asset. So long as the asset's internal value ($P_0$) exceeds its market purchase price ($C_0$), it is profitable to acquire the asset because its generates more cash surpluses than its cost, and therefore the firm more than recovers the funds invested in it, and the cost of financing it. Similarly, an asset due for retirement should be replaced if the gross present value of the new asset exceeds its current replacement cost. Gross present values and current replacement costs are relevant for all asset purchase or replacement decisions. In the case of an asset already owned by the firm, the asset should be kept in use while its gross present value exceeds its current realizable price ($R_0$); and it should be sold when its realizable price exceeds its gross present value. Here, continued use of the asset is not economically justified and the firm gains more by selling it. Gross present values and current realizable prices of assets are relevant for all holding or disposal decisions.

Thus it can be seen that both an asset's gross present value and its current market value are relevant for all decisions concerning it.[2] The decision rules for particular long-term assets can be summarized as:

1. If $P_o \geqslant C_o$, purchase the asset
2. If $P_o < C_o$, do not purchase the asset
3. If $P_o \geqslant R_o$, continue using the asset
4. If $P_o < R_o$, sell the asset
5. If $R_o < P_o < C_o$, continue using the asset but do not replace it
6. If $P_o > R_o > C_o$, buy the asset for use in the normal course of business but it can be resold at a profit if necessary
7. If $P_o > C_o > R_o$, buy the asset for use in the normal course of business and avoid being forced to liquidate it.

The same rules apply to inventories if the proceeds from their sale in the normal course of operations are included in P, and not in R. They are included in R only in the event of stock liquidation.

Moreover, the same type of analysis should be applied to the operations of the firm as a whole. The *going concern value of a firm* is the gross present value of its net assets, i.e., the gross present value of its expected cash surplus stream from continued operations.[3] The aim of the firm should be to maximize its going concern value, and all policies should be formulated to achieve this objective. Maximization of the going concern value is the time and risk-adjusted version of the static profit maximization concept. Those policies which increase the firm's going concern value should be adopted, while those which reduce it should be discarded. In a well-informed capital market, maximization of the firm's going concern value as perceived by its management will concurrently maximize the company's share market value and its share prices (for a given number of shares).

The decision rules with respect to the firm as a whole are formally the same as those applying to individual assets. The firm should continue operations as a going concern so long as its going concern value $(P_F)$ as perceived by management exceeds or equals the current replacement cost of its net assets $(C_F)$, and it should replace its individual assets as required. This is a decision to continue operations in the long run. Where its going concern value exceeds the current replacement costs of its net assets, the firm is earning pure profits; it is earning normal profits where the two are equal.

At the other end of the spectrum, the firm's operations should be terminated where its going concern value as perceived by management is less than the current realizable value of its net assets $(R_F)$. Here, the firm should be liquidated and its assets sold. For the in-between situation of the going concern value being less than the current replacement cost of its net assets but exceeding their current realizable value, the firm should continue operating until the going concern value sinks down to the realizable value, and then wind up its activities and sell its assets. In other words it is profitable to continue operations in the short run but not in the long run.

Again it can be seen how current values and present values are necessary information for decisions concerning the future life of the firm as a whole. Historic costs and price-level adjusted costs are not relevant for this purpose.

The decision rules with respect to the firm's operations can be summarized as:

1. If $P_F \geqslant C_F$, continue operations and replace assets
2. If $P_F \geqslant R_F$, continue operations with existing assets
3. If $R_F < P_F < C_F$, continue operations with existing assets but do not replace them
4. If $P_F < R_F$, cease operations and sell the assets

   where $P_F$ is the going concern value of the firm
   $C_F$ is the current replacement cost of the firm's net assets
   $R_F$ is the current realizable value of the firm's net assets.

It is assumed that $C_F > R_F$ throughout.

Another way of explaining the same analysis is in terms of *subjective goodwill*. Subjective goodwill is the difference between the firm's going concern value and the aggregate market price of its net assets, i.e., it is the *net* going concern value. It is the present value of the expected *pure* profit stream. The aim of the firm can be restated as the maximization of subjective goodwill. Subjective goodwill may be defined with respect to either current replacement costs (i.e., $SG_c = P_F - C_F$) or to current realizable values (i.e., $SG_R = P_F - R_F$) of the firm's net assets. Where $SG_c > O$, the firm is expected to earn pure profits in the long run. The firm should be operated as a going concern and its assets replaced as required. Pure profits may result from superior management, products, efficiency, and so on, or simply from monopoly power in the market. If the firm is sold as a going concern, prospective buyers are willing to pay for a stream of pure profits above the current cost of its net assets. The price they pay is termed *"objective goodwill"*. (Both these concepts should be distinguished from book value goodwill in historic cost accounting; such goodwill is the excess of the price paid for a firm over the book value of its net assets.) Where $SG_c = O$, the firm is expected to earn only a normal profit in the long run. It should be operated as a going concern and its assets replaced as required. The firm has no subjective goodwill and buyers would be prepared to pay only the current market price of its net assets for it. Where $SG_c < O$, the firm is expected to earn less than normal profits or even incur losses, and it should not be operated in the long run. The short-run decision rules in terms of $SG_R$ should now be applied. If $SG_R > O$, the firm should continue operating with its existing assets and terminate operations when its subjective goodwill becomes zero (e.g., when major asset replacement becomes necessary). If $SG_R < O$, the firm should terminate operations now and sell up its assets.

*Company takeover proposals* are assessed according to these decision principles. Takeover bids are frequently made for public companies (the victim) where another company (the raider) observes that it is not making effective use of its assets, or is understating its assets or profits.[4] The adoption of such policies depresses a company's share prices, and hence its total share market value ($M_F$). The share price is determined in the capital market according to the company's disclosed financial performance and position and its future prospects. In fact the share price is the present value of the future benefits expected by investors at large to accrue to each share. The total share market value of a company is simply the number of shares times the share price, and it summarizes investors' expectations of the company's future profit prospects and ultimate realizable value of its net assets. The raider perceives the value of the victim's net assets (either present value and/or current value) as exceeding its share market value. This situation provides the raider with the opportunity to bid for the victim's shares at a price marginally above its current share price. The majority of existing shareholders normally take advantage of the higher share price and sell to the raider, who thereby gains control of the victim company. Four types of policies make a company an attractive takeover proposition:

1. Where a company continues operating even though the current realizable value of its net assets exceeds its share market value (i.e., $R_F > M_F$); or in other words, where the net tangible asset backing per share (measured by realizable values) exceeds the share price. This situation commonly arises because of appreciation in the market prices of the victim's assets without a corresponding increase in its profits to push up its share price, and the victim does not recognize this adequately (whereas the raider does); or because the victim refuses to recognize a subnormal profit situation and wind up its activities. This is the case of the "sick company" which is worth more dead than alive. In these situations, the raider does what should have been done by the previous management and sells up the victim's assets, keeping the capital profits (generally tax free) for himself. This type of raider is referred to as the "asset stripper" and the victim as an "asset rich" company.

2. Where a raider thinks that he can make more profitable use of another company's net assets, the going concern value of the firm to the raider ($P_{FR}$) exceeds its current share market value (i.e., $P_{FR} > M_F$). This can happen even though the victim company is a profitable one and is justified in continuing its operations. However, it probably has not adapted sufficiently to changing economic conditions, including changes in its long-term asset prices, and is not maximizing its going concern value. It can also happen where a company keeps on retaining profits year after year without adequate justification in terms of profitable use of them. This is case of the somewhat sick company which can benefit from some doctoring.

   In this case the raider does not liquidate the victim's assets but reorganizes its operations to trade more profitably. Frequently some aspects of the first situation will apply as well, and the raider sells off surplus assets. This in turn helps to pay for the takeover.

3. Where a company intent on expansion can acquire the assets of another company more cheaply than it would cost to buy a similar set of assets in the normal markets because its share market value is less than the current replacement costs of its assets (i.e., $C_F > M_F$), that is, where net tangible assets per share (valued at current replacement cost) exceed the share price. The takeover is

a cheaper form of expansion for the raider. Again this situation is likely to result from the victim's not recognizing rising replacement costs of its assets, and failing to adapt its operations to take account of this.

4. Where a company substantially understates its disclosed profits through applying the doctrine of conservatism and causes its share prices to be depressed (i.e., $P_F > M_F$).

   Here the raider need only adopt more objective disclosure policies after the takeover to avoid being placed in a similar situation himself.

There are, of course, other factors prompting company takeovers; however, those above are important in the business world and they are the ones which have most significance for accounting.

## APPLICATION OF THE PRESENT VALUE SYSTEM TO ACCOUNTING

Present value accounting is often regarded as the ideal system as it provides all users with the information they want about the firm's future. Hence creditors can immediately see whether they will be repaid; debenture holders can see that the firm will pay interest and repay the principal on schedule; investors can determine which shares to buy and what the returns will be; and management will always make the optimum decisions about prices to charge, output to produce, products to make, and so on. Moreover, the system avoids all the arbitrary interperiod allocations of the historic cost system — and hence problems in the measurement of periodic depreciation, etc. — because there are none in it. Only external cash transactions are relevant to it. The need for interperiod allocations is removed by discounting all future cash flows back to the present time. Outlays on long-term assets — whether for the initial asset or for its replacement — are included in these cash flows and so these expenditures are recovered along with all other outlays from the present value of the cash receipts.

### Concepts of Income and Maintaining Capital Intact

The concepts of income and capital maintenance in the present value system differ from those in the historically based systems. First, the net present value concept of income is not primarily a concept of *periodic income* — rather it is the *total income* expected to be earned up to the time horizon of the firm (when the data relate to the firm as a whole) or the total income expected to be earned over time consequent upon a particular decision being made (for example, to introduce a new product). It is not just the income to be earned next year. Net present value income is the present value of expected futʳre pure profits, and is in fact what we have called subjective goodwill above. It is also called subjective income or economic income. Secondly, the measure of income is made up of two components — the income implicit in the discount rate (normal profits and interest), and the surplus income (or deficit) shown by the net present value figure (pure profits or losses). The income implicit in the discount rate can readily be converted into an absolute income figure by applying the discount rate to the investment in the firm in each period and the pure profits or losses can be added to derive total income. In fact this figure is none other than the undiscounted surplus of cash receipts over payments on operations for the remaining perceived life of the firm. This procedure merely reverses the discounting process and is illustrated in Case B.[5] It exactly parallels the determination of historic income in the completed firm as the excess of all cash receipts over payments for the life of the firm, determined after all assets have been liquidated, all liabilities repaid, and all profit payments to owners have been added back. Thirdly, the income figure so derived is the sum of profits plus interest, and the interest component must then be taken out to reconcile it with accounting income.

Because net present value income is primarily a measure of *total* income, it is not directly comparable with measures of *periodic* historic income. The relevant comparison for historic cost income is the budgeted income for the same period — budgeted income is an estimate of periodic income which is prepared on the same accounting principles as historic income. Nevertheless, calculations of periodic *ex ante* income are made, and (wrongly) compared with historic income. Periodic present value income calculations are made in either of two ways. First, it may be determined from the change in gross present value of net assets over the next year, i.e., $P_1 - P_0$, where $P_1$ is the present value at the end of the year 1 and $P_0$ is the current present value; and assuming no payments to or by owners. This is illustrated in Cases A and B in note 5. This method requires that all pure profits are recognized at the date of perception and as a result they are all included in year 1 income, assuming constant expectations. Future years earn only normal profits on the investment at the start of each year, i.e., $rC$.[6]

Alternatively, it may be assumed that the firm earns a constant rate of profit on investment each year (notwithstanding fluctuations in the absolute levels of cash flows), and the constant rate of profit can be determined and applied to the investment figure. This is illustrated in Case C in note 5. Calculation of the rate of profit is formally similar to the determination of net present values, but, instead of an external cost of capital being used as the discount rate, the discount rate is the variable solved for in the equation so as to bring the net present value to zero. This discount rate is known as the internal rate of return, and is $r^*$ in the following equation:

$$O = -C + \sum_{t=1}^{n} \frac{S_t}{(1+r^*)^t} \qquad \qquad \dots\dots(vi)$$

However it should not be overlooked that the assumption of a constant rate of profit earned on investment in each year is an arbitrary one, and other assumptions giving varying periodic rates of profit may equally be made. The two measures give different annual income figures except where the external cost of capital equals the internal rate of return, i.e., where only normal profits are earned. This can be seen by comparing Cases B and C in note 5.

Neither of these concepts of periodic income is comparable with a historically based measure of income unless the firm is in a stationary state where expectations, prices, and periodic activity remain constant throughout and where only normal profits are earned. The assumption of a constant rate of profits per period is realistic in this situation, as trading conditions remain constant throughout. It is only in the ideal conditions outlined in chapter 21 that a unique measure of periodic income can be determined.

The concept of maintaining capital intact in the present value system likewise differs from those in historically based systems. Capital is measured by the gross present value of net assets at the current time and maintaining capital intact does not refer to maintaining a stock of resources intact in terms of investment outlays or productive capacity but to maintaining them intact in terms of their future income-generating power. Maintaining capital intact means the retention of sufficient resources to maintain the future income stream intact. In the stationary state, the concepts coincide. The differences become apparent, however, when we consider effects of changes in expectations or the discount rate. Suppose that, initially, the net present value of the firm's profit prospects is zero and its cost of finance is 10 per cent (for example, case A in note 5). If expectations of profitability increase (for example, because of higher sales prices), the net present value of profits becomes positive and the gross present value of net assets is increased even though the stock of assets on hand or their current market prices have not altered in any way (for example, Case D in note 5). Some resources (i.e., investment) can be returned to owners to reduce the present value of net assets back to the initial amount and the net present value of profits back to zero. At this figure, the income stream is maintained intact while the physical volume of resources or capital has been reduced. If, on the other hand, profit prospects are reduced (for example, because of rising replacement costs for long-term assets), additional investment is required now to keep the income stream constant at zero net present value. Secondly, any change in the discount rate alters the net present value of the profit stream. Thus, if the cost of finance falls below 10 per cent, the net present value of the profit stream becomes positive and some capital can be returned to owners (for example Case E in note 5); and conversely where the cost of finance rises. It should be noted that changes in expectations or the discount rate change net present value income, even though not one transaction affecting income has as yet occurred.

### Income Statements and Balance Sheets in the Present Value System

There is no formal income statement in the present value system. Income is the net present value of all future cash flows which are recorded in the sequence of cash budgets (pure profit) plus the normal income implicit in the external discount rate. There is no distinction between income statement and balance sheet items, and there are no credit transactions or interperiod allocations in these budgets. The measure of income is total income up to the time-horizon of the firm, unless an arbitrary periodic allocation is made.

The balance sheet still remains in the system however. A forward-looking balance sheet can be prepared for all the firm's existing assets and liabilities. The value of each item is the present value of the future cash flows attributable to it. Thus, with assets, cash on hand or at the bank is shown at its face value; accounts receivable are shown at their gross value, less estimated bad debts, less the interest cost on the investment in them till repayment; investments in securities and other assets held for resale are shown at their current realizable value (which should equal their discounted cash flow value); and finished goods inventories are shown at their realizable prices, less costs of disposal, and less interest on investment in them up to the date of sale. Leases are valued at the present value of the rental services to be yielded by the asset; this figure equals the present value of the lease liability where future payments are required. All other assets would normally be shown as one figure only. These assets are not for resale but are used jointly within the firm to generate future cash operating surpluses, and their value is the gross present value of these cash surpluses. Their individual values are likely to be meaningless for balance sheet purposes as they are not separately used to generate separate cash flow streams. It may be difficult to attribute cash flows to one asset or another where they are used together. But, even if separate identification is possible, the separate values of each asset can be misleading for balance sheet purposes (though not necessarily for decision-making purposes) because the assets are frequently more productive as a group than when used separately. In this situation, the present value of the group exceeds the sum of their individual present values. The whole rationale for using assets in combination is that they are more productive this way – they can be more specialized and larger and hence take advantage of the economies of continuous processing and large-scale production. It may well be that a large portion of the value of this asset group is subjective goodwill. Liabilities, like monetary assets, are shown at the amounts to be repaid, including interest, and discounted from their maturity dates back to the present time. Owners' equity then remains as the difference between the gross present value of assets and of liabilities, i.e., as the gross present value of net assets. Given a share market well informed about the future prospects of the firm, the owners' equity calculated in this way would equal the total share market value of the company, i.e., share price times the number of shares. There is no distinction between contributed capital and retained earnings in the present value balance sheet. Thus the focus of a present value balance sheet is on the valuation of the firm as a whole rather than on the valuation of its components.

A present value balance sheet, based on the assumption that the time-horizon of the firm is only three years hence, that the cost of finance is 10 per cent per annum, and that the cash flows occur at the end of each year, is shown below. Only assets and liabilities of the firm existing on 1 January 1974 are shown in it. Future assets and liabilities to be created in future operations are encompassed in the cash flow generated by the firm's "all other assets" group.

Futuristic Corporation Ltd.

*Present Value Balance Sheet as at 1 January 1974, for the Three Years to 31 December 1976*

| | Expected Cash Receipts or Payments | | | | Total PV |
|---|---|---|---|---|---|
| Date | 1 Jan. 1974 | 31 Dec. 1974 | 31 Dec. 1975 | 31 Dec. 1976 | 1 Jan. 1974 |
| Discount Factor @ 10% | 1.0 | 0.909 | 0.826 | 0.751 | |
| *Assets* | $ | $ | $ | $ | $ |
| Cash | 3,000 | — | — | — | 3,000 |
| Accounts Receivable (Net) | 2,000 | 2,000 | 1,000 | — | 4,644 |
| Merchandise Inventory | 5,000 | 2,000 | 500 | — | 7,231 |
| Leasehold Premises | — | 1,000 | 1,000 | 1,000 | 2,486 |
| All Other Assets | — | 6,000 | 7,000 | 8,000 | 17,244 |
| Total PV of Assets | 10,000 | 11,000 | 9,500 | 9,000 | 34,605 |
| Less *Liabilities* | | | | | |
| Accounts Payable | 500 | 500 | — | — | 955 |
| Bank Overdraft | 1,000 | — | — | — | 1,000 |
| Income Tax Payable | — | 400 | — | — | 364 |
| Debentures 10% | — | 500 | 500 | 5,500 | 5,000 |
| Lease Liability | — | 1,000 | 1,000 | 1,000 | 2,486 |
| Total PV of Liabilities | 1,500 | 2,400 | 1,500 | 6,500 | 9,805 |
| *Owners' Equity* (12,400 shares @ $2 each market price)[7] | | | | | $24,800 |

The value of subjective goodwill can be included in the balance sheet if the "All Other Assets" group is not valued at its internal value but instead each asset is valued at its current market price. For example, if the separate market prices of the assets in this group amount to $15,000, the value of subjective goodwill is $2,244. It represents the excess (18 cents) of the market price of each share ($2) over the net tangible assets per share ($1.82), or, in other words, the premium paid by investors over the current market value of assets per share for the prospects of future pure profits.

## AN ILLUSTRATION OF PRESENT VALUE ACCOUNTING

Lucky Co. Limited was established on 1 January 1974, with a registered capital of 1,000,000 shares of $1 each par value, to operate as a retailer. Its stockbrokers had advised that shareholders in retailing companies require a 10 per cent dividend yield for them to buy and hold shares in the company. Lucky's promoters believed that the company would earn at least 10 per cent rate of profit on investment, and the shares were duly sold for $1 each. The company was fortunate to acquire good premises in the suburb of Concordia for $600,000 cash. It purchased merchandise costing $300,000 and kept the remaining cash as part of its working capital. When it was ready to commence business on 31 January, its historical cost balance sheet was as follows:

| Assets | $ | Equity | $ |
|---|---|---|---|
| Cash | 100,000 | Paid-up Capital | 1,000,000 |
| Merchandise Inventories | 300,000 | | |
| Premises | 600,000 | | |
| | $1,000,000 | | $1,000,000 |

The management adopted a policy of selling only for cash, paying all expenses as they were incurred and replacing merchandise as soon as it was sold. All profits are to be paid out as dividends at the end of each year, and there are no company taxes. Operations for the year were as forecast and the historic cost accounting reports on 31 December 1974 were as follows:

*Income Statement for 1974*

| | $ |
|---|---|
| Sales | 3,000,000 |
| Less Operating Expenses | 2,900,000 |
| Net Profit | 100,000 |
| Less Dividends | 100,000 |
| Retained Earnings | – |

*Balance Sheet as at 31 December 1974*

| Assets | $ | Equity | $ |
|---|---|---|---|
| Cash | 100,000 | Paid-up Capital | 1,000,000 |
| Merchandise Inventory | 300,000 | | |
| Premises | 600,000 | | |
| | $1,000,000 | | $1,000,000 |

Its balance sheet prepared according to present value accounting is formally similar:

| Assets | $ | Equity | $ |
|---|---|---|---|
| Cash | 100,000 | Share value 1,000,000 | |
| Merchandise Inventory | 300,000 | shares @ $1 | 1,000,000 |
| Premises | 600,000 | | |
| | $1,000,000 | | $1,000,000 |

Present value income for the year is 10 per cent on $1,000,000, i.e., $100,000.

On 1 January 1975, the company was delighted to learn that the government planning authority had just rezoned Concordia to become a major regional shopping centre. Property values in the area immediately boomed and sales increased many fold. Nevertheless, the company found that its existing working capital was adequate to support the higher levels of activity.

Its historic cost income statement for 1975 was as follows:

| | $ |
|---|---|
| Sales | 8,000,000 |
| Less Operating Expenses | 7,500,000 |
| Net Profit | 500,000 |
| Less Dividends | 500,000 |
| Retained Earnings | — |

Its historic cost balance sheet as at 31 December 1975 remained unchanged from the previous year.

However, the sharp increase in earnings and dividends per share which were expected to be permanent, boosted Lucky's share price to $5. (This is derived as dividends per share discounted at 10 per cent in perpetuity, i.e., 50 cents per share /.10).

Lucky's present value balance sheet reflects this increase in profit prospects, and it becomes as follows:

*Present Value Balance Sheet as at 31 December 1975*

| Assets | $ | Equity | $ |
|---|---|---|---|
| Cash | 100,000 | Share Capital (1m. x $5) | 5,000,000 |
| Merchandise Inventory | 300,000 | | |
| Premises | 600,000 | | |
| Subjective Goodwill | 4,000,000 | | |
| | $5,000,000 | | $5,000,000 |

Its subjective income for the year can be measured as the increment in the present value of the company's net assets, i.e., $(5,000,000−1,000,000) = $4,000,000. It is also the increase in subjective goodwill over the year, by definition. Subjective goodwill at the end of 1974 was zero as the company earned only a normal rate of profit of·10 per cent.

Subjective income is the present value of Lucky's future income prospects, and, as such, it has not yet been earned. (The company earned only $500,000 profit for the year.) The company's total *ex ante* income for the year is its subjective income plus the dividend paid of $500,000 (which equals 10 per cent of the revalued investment). The going concern value of the company is now $5,000,000.

An alternative treatment is to add subjective goodwill to the value of the assets to which it attaches, if any. Here, it attaches essentially to the site, and the premises could be revalued at $4,600,000. Given Lucky's profit prospects it could sell its premises for this sum. The replacement costs of inventories and the buildings are assumed to have not altered.

Lucky's shareholders' good fortunes are still not at an end because, on 1 January 1976, the Aggressive Company Limited which operates next door to Lucky made a takeover bid. Aggressive's management considered that, by merging the businesses, more effective use could be made of the premises of each company and some price competition could be eliminated. They calculated that Lucky's net profit could be boosted to $700,000 per annum, determined as follows:

*Budgeted Income Statement for 1976*

|  | $ |
|---|---|
| Sales | 9,000,000 |
| Less Operating Expenses | 8,300,000 |
| Net Profit | $ 700,000 |

On this basis, Lucky's shares would be worth (70 cents per share /.10) = $7 each.

Its budgeted present value balance sheet on 31 December 1976 would be:

| Assets | $ | Equity | $ |
|---|---|---|---|
| Cash | 100,000 | Share Capital (1m. @ $7) | 7,000,000 |
| Merchandise Inventory | 300,000 | | |
| Premises | 600,000 | | |
| Subjective Goodwill | 6,000,000 | | |
| | $7,000,000 | | $7,000,000 |

The subjective income expected for 1976 is $(7,000,000−5,000,000) = $2,000,000 and its total income is $2,700,000.

Naturally Aggressive's management did not intend to pay the full going concern value of $7,000,000 for the Lucky Company, and it decided to offer Lucky share-holders $5.50 for each of their shares, this figure being 50 cents greater than the current share price. Hence a total outlay of $5,500,000 was required to buy the company. Lucky shareholders duly accepted this offer, and the company continued its operations as a subsidiary of Aggressive in the same mode as before.

Unfortunately for the Aggressive Company, conditions in the capital market for the retailing industry deteriorated because of a massive mining boom elsewhere in the country. Investors began switching their funds to mining, where rates of return were higher. Share prices of retailers fell so as to yield a 15 per cent rate of return on their shares and this became the new equilibrium yield.

Although Lucky's operating performance did achieve the budgeted level and a net profit of $700,000 was earned in 1976, Aggressive's management were unhappy with their purchase. Lucky's shares were now worth only $4.667 each (70 cents per share /.15).

In these changed circumstances Lucky Company's present value balance sheet on 31 December 1976 is:

| Assets | $ | Equity | $ |
|---|---|---|---|
| Cash | 100,000 | Share Capital (1m. x | |
| Merchandise Inventory | 300,000 | $4.667) | 4,667,000 |
| Premises | 600,000 | | |
| Subjective Goodwill | 3,667,000 | | |
| | $4,667,000 | | $4,667,000 |

The going concern value of Lucky had been reduced from $7,000,000 to $4,667,000 by the higher cost of equity capital, and Aggressive Company had suffered a loss of $833,000 on its purchase ($5,500,000 purchase price, less present value of $4,667,000), i.e., subjective income for 1976 is —$833,000. It had hoped for a subjective income of $2,500,000 (i.e., $7,000,000 expected going concern value, less $5,500,000 purchase price). An alternative way of portraying goodwill in the balance sheet is to show it as:

| | $ |
|---|---|
| Objective Goodwill | 4,500,000 |
| Less Subjective Loss | 833,000 |
| Subjective Goodwill | $3,667,000 |

Although this illustration is highly simplified and unrealistic, it does illuminate the basic nature of present value system as a system related to future events only. In particular, it can be seen that there is no simple relationship between historic periodic income (whether historic cost or current income) and net present value income when calculated for a period; and secondly how changes in expectations or the discount rate affect the measure of subjective income.

## EVALUATION OF PRESENT VALUE ACCOUNTING

Although it is often held to be the ideal accounting system, the present value system should not be regarded as an alternative to a historically based system for several reasons. Present value accounting is of an entirely different type and fulfills different functions from those of historical accounting, and *both* are required in a comprehensive information system. To begin with, present value accounting relates only to the future — not one of the transactions to which it relates has as yet occurred. It does not report on actual operations or measure the achieved performance and current market position of the firm — only a historical system can do this. It can never satisfy the stewardship or legal functions of historical accounting. Secondly, until the time of perfect knowledge is reached, historical accounting will always be required to assist in predictions of the future and the preparation of forecasts which form the basis of present value accounting. Thirdly, because it must be based on forecasts throughout, present value accounting is almost completely subjective and many of the items in it cannot be verified at the present time. Present value accounting cannot satisfy any of the objectivity standards for accounting information. Cash is the only item which is objectively valued. The valuation of the other items will typically range from those for which management is reasonably certain of their cash flow (for example debtors and creditors) to those for which the cash flow is highly debatable. Present value accounting could not possibly be used in audited published reports. Moreover, in situations where the future is highly uncertain, present value accounting is just impracticable. Fourthly, treating the two systems as alternatives confuses the information required for decisions with the realized consequences of those decisions, i.e., it confuses expectations of the results of the future with actual achievements to date. Present values are necessary (though not sufficient) information for all long-term decisions, whereas historic systems measure the consequences of those decisions after they have been put into effect. Both current values of assets and present values from their use are required for rational decisions to be made, as is evident from the decision rules given earlier. Finally, present value accounting is subject to frequent changes as forecasts of the future and operating plans are revised in the light of current experience; hence, present value results are likely to be unstable.

The present value system, therefore, should be regarded as complementing the ex post systems rather than replacing them in conditions where perfect knowledge does not exist. Present value accounting refers to the future, whereas ex post accounting relates to current and past periods, and the functions of each system are totally different. It is in the area of management decision-making that the present value system has its role to play. Present values are always relevant (along with current values) for any decision having long-term implications — continue operations or liquidate, buy or sell plant, takeovers, introduce new products, and so on. Present value accounting also satisfies the consistency standard (as all cash flows are discounted to make them comparable over time) and the timeliness standard (as the cash flows are reported in advance of events) of a good information system.

In so far as published reports are concerned, present value reports are not appropriate for publication. They summarize *management*'s expectations of future prospects of the firm and are appropriate for management decisions about future action. However, *shareholders* provide the risk capital to the firm and they bear the ultimate risks of loss or benefit from profits. They should assess the prospects from, and risk of, investment in the company's shares for themselves. But they must be provided with good quality information on the company's past economic performance and current financial position so that they can make informed judgments about the company's future prospects and the risks likely to be incurred. In addition, they would be assisted by information on the goals of management, major expansion and diversification programmes planned, new share issues plans, and so forth.

Nevertheless, some parts of present value accounting are applied in historical accounting, either because it overlaps the historical system or to remedy some defects in it. Thus, for short-term financial assets and liabilities, the two systems tend to coincide, as both show these items at their realizable (i.e., cash) values and the interest component is negligible. Long-term debtors (e.g., for hire-purchase sales) are shown at their gross value, less estimated bad debts and accrued interest. This valuation should approximate what the debtors' accounts could be sold for to a factoring firm. Long-term creditors are likewise shown at their immediate repayment value. The bankruptcy of companies with long-term lease commitments undisclosed in the balance sheet has led to reconsideration of the conventional method of accounting for those leases where the lessee makes periodic payments for the hire of assets. The old-fashioned method was to treat the annual lease payments as expenses in the same way as a rental payment, and not to recognize the legal liability for future lease payments, nor the leasehold asset owned by the firm. The A.I.C.P.A. recommends that all future lease obligations should be capitalized and shown as a long-term liability, with the equal present value of their rental services shown as a long-term asset. The same principle can be applied to all other executory contracts in which the firm is committed to future payments for future services to be rendered. The capitalization method is fully consistent with historical cost accounting — the full liability is recognized at the time of the transaction, as is the complementary asset of the leasehold rights. Annuity depreciation is sometimes used in historical accounting in place of the conventional straight line or reducing balance methods. The annual depreciation charges follow an increasing pattern in this method, and this is normally hard to justify in terms of the exhaustion of benefits. Annuity depreciation is really concerned with accumulating funds sufficient to replace the asset at the current cost of finance, and it adds an imputed financing charge to the usual depreciation charge. This is not done with the other assets, and it is really irrelevant in a historical system where the financing charge is part of the profit stream that is to be measured. The effect of charging all assets, including working capital assets, with their financing costs is to allocate a share of normal profit to each asset. Such an allocation serves no useful purpose and it requires a large amount of tedious work. The method originated around the time when the nature of depreciation charges was not clearly understood and they were confused with the need to accumulate funds for replacement. The method is frequently integrated with the use of a sinking fund for financing asset replacement by government enterprises. Finally present value accounting is applied to the valuation of subjective goodwill when the firm is being valued for sale as a going concern. Some authors advocate that subjective goodwill be included in all published balance sheets.

### FURTHER READING

Gordon, M. J., and Shillinglaw, G. *Accounting: A Management Approach*. 4th ed. Homewood, Illinois: Richard D. Irwin, 1969. Chap. 9.
Mathews, R. L. *The Accounting Framework*. 3rd ed. Melbourne: Cheshire, 1971. Chap. 7.

### NOTES

1. For details of the financial mathematics required for present value accounting, see Mathews, *The Accounting Framework*, Appendix to chap. 7.

2. Refer back to chap. 23 on current value accounting.

3. This concept of going concern value should not be confused with the bogus "going concern value" concept in the historic cost system.

4. A. D. Barton, "Company Takeovers in Australia 1957–62", *Australian Accountant* (February 1964).

5. Determination of total and periodic net present value income. Assume an asset generates the following end-of-year cash flows: 200, 300, 200, 400; that the cost of capital is 10 per cent per annum, and that cash surpluses are distributed each year.

*Case A*   Cost of asset $(C_0)$ 853.

| | | Year 1 Income $Y_1$ | | Year 2 Income $Y_2$ | | Year 3 Income $Y_3$ | | Year 4 Income $Y_4$ | |
|---|---|---|---|---|---|---|---|---|---|
| Years | Year Surplus S | Discount Factor @10% D.F. | Present Value $P_0$ | D.F. | $P_1$ | D.F. | $P_2$ | D.F. | $P_3$ |
| 1 | 200 | .9091 | 181.8 | — | | — | | — | |
| 2 | 300 | .8265 | 247.8 | .9091 | 272.7 | — | | — | |
| 3 | 200 | .7513 | 150.2 | .8265 | 165.2 | .9091 | 181.8 | — | |
| 4 | 400 | .6830 | 273.2 | .7513 | 300.4 | .8265 | 330.4 | .9091 | 363.6 |
| | | | 853.0 | | 738.3 | | 512.2 | | 363.6 |

$$Y_1 = P_1 + S_1 - P_0$$
$$= 738.3 + 200 - 853$$
$$= 85.3$$
$$= 10\% \text{ on } P_0$$

$$Y_2 = P_2 + S_2 - P_1$$
$$= 512.2 + 300 - 738.3$$
$$= 73.9$$
$$= 10\% \text{ on } P_1$$

$$Y_3 = P_3 + S_3 - P_2$$
$$= 363.6 + 200 - 512.2$$
$$= 51.4$$
$$= 10\% \text{ on } P_2$$

$$Y_4 = P_4 + S_4 - P_3$$
$$= 0 + 400 - 363.6$$
$$= 36.4$$
$$= 10\% \text{ on } P_3$$

Net present value of income $(P_0 - C_0) = 0$.
Aggregate income over 4 years         = 247.
Aggregate cash surplus over 4 years   = $(1,100 - 853) = 247$.

*Case B*    Cost of asset 761.
Net present value of income $= (853 - 761) = 92$.
$Y_1 = 92 + 85.3 = 177.3$ i.e., all pure profits included in first year's income.
$Y_2 \ldots Y_4$ as in Case A, i.e., normal profits earned in subsequent years.
Aggregate income over 4 years $= 339$.
Aggregate cash surplus over 4 years $= (1,100-761)$
$\qquad\qquad\qquad = 339$.

*Case C*    Cost of asset 761.
Internal rate of return is 15 per cent.
Pure profit spread over the 4 years at the internal rate of return.

| | | Year 1 | Income $Y_1$ | Year 2 | Income $Y_2$ | Year 3 | Income $Y_3$ | Year 4 | Income $Y_4$ |
|---|---|---|---|---|---|---|---|---|---|
| Years | S | Discount Factor @15% | $P_0$ | D.F. | $P_1$ | D.F. | $P_2$ | D.F. | $P_3$ |
| 1 | 200 | .8696 | 173.9 | | | | | | |
| 2 | 300 | .7561 | 226.8 | .8696 | 260.9 | | | | |
| 3 | 200 | .6575 | 131.5 | .7561 | 151.2 | .8696 | 173.9 | | |
| 4 | 400 | .5718 | 228.7 | .6575 | 263.0 | .7561 | 302.4 | .8696 | 347.8 |
| | | | 761.0 | | 675.1 | | 476.3 | | 347.8 |

$Y_1 = P_1 + S_1 - P_0$
$\quad = 675.1 + 200 - 761$
$\quad = 114.1$
$\quad = 15\%$ on $P_0$

$Y_2 = P_2 + S_2 - P_1$
$\quad = 476.3 + 300 - 675.1$
$\quad = 101.2$
$\quad = 15\%$ on $P_1$

$Y_3 = P_3 + S_3 - P_2$
$\quad = 347.8 + 200 - 476.3$
$\quad = 71.5$
$\quad = 15\%$ on $P_2$

$Y_4 = P_4 + S_4 - P_3$
$\quad = 0 + 400 - 347.8$
$\quad = 52.2$
$\quad = 15\%$ on $P_3$

Aggregate income over 4 years = 399.
Aggregate cash surplus over 4 years = 339.

*Case D*    Same as for Case A, except that expected cash surplus for year 1 is raised by 100.
Present value of cash surplus stream is now 943.9.
Net present value of income is increased by 90.9.
This can be paid to investors and capital maintained intact at 853 to yield the 10 per cent income stream each year.

*Case E*    Same as for Case A except that the cost of capital falls to 8 per cent.
Present value of cash surplus stream is raised to 895.12.
Net present value of income is 42.12. This can be paid to owners and capital maintained intact at 853 to yield the 10 per cent income stream each year.

6. Note that the statement in Mathews's chapter 7 that this method is circular applies only in the two situations envisaged in his analysis, viz., where the discount rate is a rate of return expected to be earned or where it is the internal rate of return. The circularity of the measure does not apply where the cost of capital to the firm is used as the discount rate.

7. This equality between the company's share market value and its present value as perceived by management is not a necessary result in reality. It is a consequence here of the assumption of a rational and well-informed capital market. Divergence between the two values provides scope for profitable share-trading. For example, where the present value as perceived by management exceeds the share market value, and management's expectations are being realized, it pays to buy the shares in anticipation of an appreciation of their price; and, conversely, where the share market value exceeds the management's present value, shareholders will avoid a loss by selling their shares.

## QUESTIONS AND EXERCISES

[Solutions to problems marked * are given in Appendix 4.]

1.   Explain the relationship between present value accounting and historically

based accounting systems. Should they be regarded as complementary or alternative systems?

2. What are the main functions served by present value accounting? How are they related to the functions served by historically based accounting?

3. Explain the concept of present value.

4. Why are all accrual and depreciation items left out of present value calculations; i.e., why are only cash items relevant?

5. What discount rate should be used in present value calculations?

6. List and explain the decision rules about investment proposal acceptance.

7. Explain the concepts of:

   i. The economic value of an asset
   ii. The going concern value of a firm
   iii. Subjective goodwill
   iv. Objective goodwill.

8. Can the economic value of a single machine which is part of an integrated production line be defined and measured? Is it possible that the sum of the economic values of all machines on such a production line exceeds the economic value of the line as a whole? If so, how should the group of machines be valued?

9. Explain the conditions under which a firm should continue operations:

   i. In the long run
   ii. Only in the short run.

   When should it cease operations and liquidate its assets?

10. What is meant by a company takeover? What factors can encourage company takeover bids to be made?

11. Explain the concepts of income and capital maintenance in the present value system.

12. What are the major differences between the contents of a present value balance sheet and an ex post balance sheet?

13. Evaluate the present value system according to the standards for accounting information for purposes of:

   i. Decision-making by management
   ii. Measurement of income and financial position
   iii. Stewardship
   iv. External reporting by management to shareholders.

14. What are the major obstacles to the adoption of a present value system?

---

The following financial mathematics table shows the present value of $1 if received at the end of year one .... year five, where the discount rate is 10 per cent per annum; i.e., it is the $\left[\dfrac{1}{(1+i)^n}\right]$ table where $i = .10$. Use it to solve the following problems in which the rate of discount is 10 per cent throughout.

| Year | Amount $ |
|------|----------|
| 1 | 0.909 |
| 2 | 0.826 |
| 3 | 0.751 |
| 4 | 0.683 |
| 5 | 0.621 |

15. You have been left an endowment of $5,000 to be received in five years' time. What is the present value of the endowment?

16. You have just purchased a new car on hire purchase on the following terms: $1,000 deposit, plus $500 to be paid at the end of each year for four years. What is the cash purchase price of the car?

*17. A firm can buy a machine for $20,000 which is expected to generate the following cash surpluses on operations over the next five years:

$6,000, $5,000, $4,000, $3,000, $3,000.

The machine's realizable value at the end of year five is expected to be $2,000.

i. What is the gross present value of the machine?
ii. What is the net present value of the machine?
iii. Should the firm buy it? Explain the reason for your answer in layman's language.

18. The management of the Black and White Company is prepared to accept all investment proposals which return 10 per cent or more on investment. Which of the following proposals should it accept and which should it reject? Assume all outlays would be made on 1 January 1974, and all net receipts occur at the end of each year indicated.

i. Outlay $76,000. Receipts $35,000 for three years.
ii. Outlay $28,000. Receipts 1974: $12,000; 1975: $11,000; 1976: $10,000; 1977: $8,000.
iii. Outlay $110,000. Receipts 1974: $20,000; 1975: $23,000; 1976: $25,000; 1977: $25,000; 1978: $20,000. Expected realizable value December 1978: $4,000.
iv. Outlay $150,000. Receipts $40,000 for four years. Expected realizable value December 1977: $20,000.

*19. The current selling price of a firm's existing plant and equipment (which is four years old) is $100,000. It is expected to generate operating cash surpluses of $30,000 each year for the next four years and to have a scrap value then of $3,000. Should the firm keep operating the assets or sell them?

20. Two years previously, the P.H.B. Company built a blast furnace costing $20,000,000. The current realizable value of the furnace is $500,000. It is expected to generate operating cash surpluses of $3,000,000 each year for the next five years, and to have a salvage value of $400,000 at the end of that period. Should the company keep on operating the furnace or scrap it now?

21. The following valuations apply to a company's net assets on 30 June. What is the subjective goodwill in each case. Should it continue operations or sell up its assets in each case? Justify your answers.

i. Total current replacement cost $6,500,000; current realizable value $3,200,000; present value from continued use $8,000,000.

ii.    Total current replacement cost $14,000,000; current realizable value $10,000,000; present value $11,000,000.

iii.    Total current replacement cost $9,000,000; current realizable value $6,000,000; present value $5,000,000.

22.    The following valuations apply to a company and its net assets on 30 June. Indicate whether the company should continue operating under its existing management or liquidate its assets; and whether there is risk of a takeover bid being made by a raider, and what action he might take if he makes a successful bid at a price exceeding the current share market value of the company by $1m. in each case. Justify your answer in each case.

|  | CRC of Net Assets | CRV of Net Assets | PV of Company under Existing Management | Share Market Value of Company | PV of Company under Raider |
|---|---|---|---|---|---|
| i. | $20m. | $17m. | $19m. | $14m. | $16m. |
| ii. | 6 | 4 | 7 | 8 | 6 |
| iii. | 12 | 9 | 12 | 12 | 14 |
| iv. | 30 | 24 | 27 | 25 | 32 |
| v. | 18 | 14 | 12 | 10 | 10 |

# Part 4
# Analysis and Interpretation of Financial Reports

# Chapter 26
# Analysis of Financial Statements

The information value of financial reports can be improved substantially by the calculation of various financial ratios which highlight significant relationships in the data. The classification of accounting reports should always enable the calculation of any significant structural relationships in the data. This requirement is one of the most important standards for the communication of accounting data to users and it is essential in any good information system. The ratios relate to the two major aspects of the information requirements of users:

1. Measures of earning power and operating performance
2. Measures of financial structure and financial risk of investment in the company.

Some general points about the use of ratios should first of all be noted. The validity of ratios depends entirely on the reliability of the valuations employed in the balance sheet and on the accuracy of the classification of items. It is essential that current values are used throughout if all data refer to the one date, or real dollar values are used where comparisons over time are made, in order that the measurements are made in homogeneous dollars. The use of historic cost values where these are no longer current values vitiates the analysis. Subjective goodwill must not be included in assets for the purpose of calculating ratios as it is not an asset used to generate profits and it has normally no separate market value to assist in meeting debt repayments. Rather, it is a summary of future profit prospects. Its inclusion would reduce all rates of return to the normal rate and thereby hide all pure profits. The ratios must be interpreted in the light of economic conditions applying to the firm and the industry in which it operates; and rules-of-thumb guides which are claimed to apply to all firms and all industries simultaneously are most misleading. Ratios do not show causal relationships — only correlative ones — and it is necessary to analyze the background economic environment to determine what factor caused subsequent changes to occur. This applies in particular to those ratios which have to add up to 100 per cent — the mere fact that one ratio rises must cause others to fall, and vice versa. Ratios should be used to highlight significant features in the financial reports which are not otherwise apparent and it is easy to confuse the picture by the presentation of too many ratios at once. Most ratios fall into complementary groups and some ratios in the group are more basic than others. If the subsidiary ratios merely confirm what a basic ratio has indicated then it is better to leave them out of the final ratio report — they should be used only when they indicate something which is not already apparent. Nevertheless the analyst should check them first before discarding them as adding nothing to the analysis.

Accounting reports should be analyzed with the information requirements of users in mind as these ought to govern the form and content of the reports. Readers should refer back to this subject and the standards for accounting information in chapter 3. The methodology applied in the book should also be noted — we are now seeing to what extent the information needs of users are being met by accounting reports, i.e., whether the objectives of the accounting system are being fulfilled.

## 1. MEASURES OF EARNING POWER AND OPERATING PERFORMANCE

Measures of earning power all concern the relationship of profits to some basis of comparison so that the many aspects of performance can be viewed. Virtually all users of financial reports are interested in a company's profits, and, in particular, investors and management. Profits measure achieved success and are a necessary indicator of the firm's future prosperity, growth, and financial position. Some subsidiary measures of operating performance (expense ratios and asset turnovers) are useful in that they provide additional information about reasons for changes in profits and some aspects of financial position. Profits can be related to several bases for measures of performance — shares, investment, and sales.

### i. Share Basis

### a. Earnings per Ordinary Share (EPS)

$$\frac{\text{Net profit after taxes and preference dividends (E.A.)}}{\text{Number of ordinary shares}} = x \text{ cents per share}$$

The numerator shows the earnings available for ordinary shareholders. (EA) The ratio measures the earnings of ordinary shareholders' investment on a per share basis and it indicates the company's capacity to pay dividends on its shares. Earnings per share is a major determinant of the share price. Shares are frequently valued according to their expected future earnings stream, i.e.,

$$P_o = \sum_{t=o}^{n} \frac{E_t}{(1+r)^t}$$

where  $E_t$ is expected earnings per share in each period t
r is the appropriate rate of discount which takes account of the risk factor, or the earnings yield on the share.
$P_o$ is the current share price.

This information is required by shareholders, investors generally, and by financial management. The potential effect on EPS is always a dominant consideration in the decision to make a new issue of shares, to undertake a major investment programme or to take over another company.

### b. Dividends per Share (DPS)

$$\frac{\text{Ordinary dividend payout}}{\text{Number of ordinary shares}} = y \text{ cents per share}$$

This measures the income received by shareholders on each share owned. It is normally less than earnings per share because of profit retention by the company. It can be a major determinant of share prices. The excess of EPS over DPS is often called the dividend cover, and it serves as a measure of potential growth in the company and security afforded to the shareholder. Dividends per share are likewise sometimes used to value shares, i.e.,

$$P_o = \sum_{t=o}^{n} \frac{D_t}{(1+r)^t}$$

where  $D_t$ is the expected dividend in each period
r is the appropriate discount rate, or the dividend yield on the share.

However a variant of this formula which allows for dividend growth per share is generally preferred.

### c. Earnings Yield on Shares (E%)

$$\frac{\text{Earnings per ordinary share (EPS)}}{\text{Current share price}} \times 100 = x\%$$

This ratio measures the earnings yield which a new investor would receive from the purchase of shares in the company at their current market price, or an existing shareholder earns by retaining his shares. It is relevant for shareholders' decisions to buy, hold, or sell shares in the company. This yield should be compared with the yields on alternative investments for any decision to be made. As well, the yield on government bonds forms a useful basis for comparison because it represents the price that currently must be paid for money to which no risks attach, i.e., it is a pure rate of interest paid to reward investors for waiting on liquidity. Yields on shares should exceed the bond rate by a risk premium in order to compensate investors for the risks undertaken. The earnings yield may be used as a measure of the company's cost of equity capital (the price paid for risk`funds) and as such is a relevant part of the discount rate to be used in appraising the profitability of all investment decisions by management. It is used as the discount rate in valuing shares according to earnings per share. It is a useful index of the regard with which the company is held by investors at large − it is used to judge the quality of an investment. As earnings per share rise and/or become more reliable, the company's share price rises because investors' confidence in the company's profit-generating capacity and security of operations is increased. The increase in the share price may push down the yield on the share. A low yield is said to indicate a high quality or safe investment (the premium for risk required by investors above the pure rate of interest need only be small), whereas a high yield indicates a low quality or risky investment (the required risk premium is substantial).

Frequently the earnings yield is quoted in its reciprocal form as the *price-earnings ratio,* i.e., share price/EPS. This measure shows the number of times earnings per share can be divided into the share price, or the number of "years' " earnings paid for in the share price. A low earnings yield means a high price earnings ratio, and vice versa.

### d. Dividend Yield (D%)

$$\frac{\text{Dividends per ordinary share (DPS)}}{\text{Current share price}} \times 100 = y\%$$

The dividend yield shows the cash rate of return received by existing shareholders, or which would be received by new shareholders. It will be less than the earnings yield if the company retains some profits. It has the same uses as the earnings yield and, where the dividend payout remains a fairly uniform proportion of after-tax profits, it generally varies with the earnings yield. It is used as the discount rate where shares are valued according to an expected dividend stream. The dividend yield is likewise a measure of the quality of an investment − a low yield signifies a safe stock and a high yield a risky one.

The dividend yield should be interpreted in conjunction with the earnings yield and share prices. For example, a moderate dividend yield together with a similar earnings yield signifies that the market judges the investment to be an income stock with little growth potential and possessing some risk; a low dividend yield plus a low earnings yield on high-priced shares are indications of a safe growth stock for which there is the expectation of growth in dividends and earnings per share, and bonus and rights issues. Low yields on low-price shares indicate meagre profit prospects or losses; and a low dividend yield together with a high earnings yield indicates a risky investment having growth potential. Essentially, in these interpretations, earnings yields indicate the quality (or, in reverse form, the risk) of the income stream, and income retention (E%–D%) indicates growth in per share returns so long as the funds are invested profitably.

Dividend yields can be calculated for preference shares in a manner similar to the above.

### ii.  Investment Basis:

### a.  Return on Paid-up Ordinary Capital

$$\frac{\text{Net profit after taxes and preference dividends (EA)}}{\text{Paid-up ordinary capital}} \times 100 = x\%$$

The primary emphasis in rates of return is always given to the ordinary capital since this is the residual equity, or the risk capital of the company, where preference shareholders have prior rights to dividends and capital return. This measure is always calculated by companies but it is a most misleading measure of performance – it is based on the par value of shares and it neglects the other sources of owners' funds, e.g., share premium reserves and retained profits. The rate of return on paid-up capital ought to rise each year where the company has retained some profit from the previous year. This may give the impression that management is doing a better job for shareholders, whereas in fact the rate of return on total shareholders' funds may be declining.

### b.  Return on Total Ordinary Shareholders' Funds

$$\frac{\text{Net profit after taxes and preference dividends (EA)}}{\text{Average total ordinary shareholders' funds}} \times 100 = x\%$$

This ratio measures the effectiveness with which shareholders' funds have been used over the year, or the profitability of their total investment. It should always be used in preference to ii.a above. It is a critical ratio for management in planning the operations of the company and for shareholders. The ratio summarizes in one figure the annual profitability of shareholders' investment in the company. Ordinary shareholders' funds are calculated as total shareholders' funds less paid-up preference capital. An average is taken of the beginning and end-of-year balances to get a more typical volume of shareholders funds for the year; obviously not all the funds of a profitable company on hand at the year's end were available earlier in the year.

As an alternative, ii.a. and ii.b. may be calculated with respect to ordinary and preference capital combined, in which case the numerator is net profit after tax.

c.   *Return on Total Assets*

$$\frac{\text{Net profit before interest and taxes (EBIT)}}{\text{Average total assets}} \times 100 = x\%$$

This ratio measures the profitability of the total investment in the company by shareholders and all creditors, or the return on total funds employed. It is of more relevance to operating management than ii.b. above because the influence of leverage (i.e., debt finance) in the company's financial structure is removed by taking earnings before interest. Although the numerator can be after tax, the pre-tax figure is preferred because it is not then distorted by the effect of the tax deductibility of interest on profits. The performance of companies with different financial structures can be more easily compared with this measure than with ii.b. The earning rate on total assets is generally less than that on total shareholders' funds because debt finance is cheaper than equity finance, owing to the secured position of the former. The difference between the two rates of return (after allowing for company tax) shows the extent to which shareholders benefit by the company's using some debt finance. They should relate this extra benefit to the additional financial risks that they consequently bear. These additional returns and risks affect the share price. The average figure is preferred for the asset base.

d.   *Turnover of Assets*

$$\frac{\text{Gross sales}}{\text{Average total assets}} = x \text{ times p.a.}$$

This ratio indicates how effectively assets are being utilized in generating revenue. A low turnover can indicate excessive investment in assets in relation to activity, and therefore the existence of excess capacity. It may be calculated with respect to major fixed assets, e.g., to plant and equipment, and to buildings, as well to give some indication of the effectiveness of their use. The asset turnover ratio is of course affected by the accounts receivable and inventory turnover rates, and a variation in it should be analyzed by components to establish the reasons for the variation. It is an important managerial ratio.

The asset turnover rate forms part of the return on investment formula, i.e., ii.c. above:

$$\text{Return on total assets} = \frac{\text{EBIT}}{\text{Sales}} \times \frac{\text{Sales}}{\text{Average Total Assets}}$$

$$\text{which reduces to} \quad \frac{\text{EBIT}}{\text{Average total assets}}$$

In other words the return on investment arises from the profit margin on sales *and* the intensity of asset utilization.

The average level of assets is included to give a more accurate measure of assets used over the year. Some intangible assets, such as goodwill and preliminary expenses, may be omitted from the base, but not others such as patents.

### iii. Sales Basis
### a. *Return on Sales*

$$\frac{\text{Net operating profit before interest and taxes (EBIT)}}{\text{Net Sales}} \times 100 = x\%$$

This ratio shows the share of profits in each dollar of revenue, or the profit margin on sales from which all non-operating items, interest, and profits taxes must be met. Earnings before interest and taxes (i.e., net operating profit before interest) are used so that non-operating items (which are not related to current sales) and interest (which reflects financial structure) and company taxes (which reflect government policy) are excluded. However, as an alternative the ratio can be calculated as net profit after taxes and interest to sales to emphasize the ultimate profit in each dollar of revenue.

The measure is important to general management in determining sales policy and to an analysis of the profitability of operations.

### b. *Gross Profit on Sales*

$$\frac{\text{Gross profit}}{\text{Net Sales}} \times 100 = x\%$$

Management requires to know the average gross profit margin on sales because it affects their merchandising decisions — higher profit lines are normally preferred to lower ones — and it is the margin from which all operating expenses must be recovered before a net operating profit can be made. It should be used in conjunction with the return on sales ratio as part of the explanation for changes in the latter — e.g., is a higher net profit margin due to a higher gross profit margin or better operating expense control?

### c. *Expense Ratios to Sales*

$$\frac{\text{COGS}}{\text{Net sales}} \times 100 \qquad \frac{\text{Selling expense}}{\text{Net sales}} \times 100 \qquad \frac{\text{Administrative expense}}{\text{Net sales}} \times 100$$

$$\frac{\text{Finance expense}}{\text{Net sales}} \times 100$$

These ratios complement the gross and net profit ratios and should be used in conjunction with them for purposes of explanation. They show the proportion of the sales dollar absorbed by each category of expense, and are important for managerial planning and control. For example, is the reduction in the net profit margin due to higher selling or administration expenses? Is there need for greater control over these expenses, or the use of alternative lower cost methods?

## 2. MEASURES OF FINANCIAL POSITION AND FINANCIAL RISK

These ratios are mainly calculated from the balance sheet. They attempt to summarize a company's short-term financial position, its long-run financial structure, and the financial risks incurred by investors and creditors. In other words, they are meant to indicate a company's ability to repay debts and pay interest, and the security afforded to long-term investors.

### i. Liquidity Ratios

These ratios attempt to show a company's short-term financial position, i.e., its ability to repay its short-term debts.

### a. Quick Asset Ratio or Acid Test

$$\frac{\text{Quick assets}}{\text{Quick liabilities}} = \text{\$x of quick assets per \$1 of quick liability}$$

This ratio is intended to measure the company's immediate ability to repay its short-term liabilities. Quick assets comprise cash plus those current assets that can be converted into cash fairly quickly. Conventionally these are considered to be net debtors plus marketable securities but not inventories. Debtors are at the net amount to show the expected cash collection from them. Long-term hire-purchase debtors may, however, be excluded. Quick liabilities comprise current liabilities, possibly excluding a bank overdraft if it is a fairly secure loan. The ratio shows the liquidity cover given to the immediate liabilities.

However, the ratio suffers from several grave defects. It is essentially a stock measure (stock of quick assets compared with the sum of quick liabilities) which is applied to a situation for which a flow measure is more appropriate — will cash on hand plus the expected inflow of cash (from cash sales, customer collections, etc.) exceed the expected need for cash (to repay maturing liabilities and to pay for the continuing stream of new commitments for wages and purchases of all types which are not yet included in quick liabilities). The cash budget is the report containing this information and management should have no need for the quick asset ratio. However, outsiders normally have to use the ratio as a second-best guide to liquidity. Other defects of the ratio concern its composition. Debtors are included but inventories are excluded for the reason that they must be replaced. But the same situation applies to debtors if the company sells on credit. In any case the same level of debts or inventories may not have to be maintained and some funds can be released from them in such a case. The ratio omits unused borrowing facilities such as the unused part of its overdraft or its ability to borrow on the short-term money market, and these affect its debt-paying capacity. Finally, the ratio disregards any differences between the rate at which quick assets are converted into cash and the maturity dates of quick liabilities; e.g., assets may take several months for conversion, whereas the liabilities may all mature within a month.

### b. Working Capital or Current Asset Ratio

$$\frac{\text{Current assets}}{\text{Current liabilities}} = \$x \text{ of current assets per } \$1 \text{ of current liability}$$

The working capital ratio shows the amount of short-term assets available to meet short-term liabilities and provides an indication of the safety margin afforded to current creditors. It is intended as a measure of the not-so-immediate liquidity of the company. It suffers from much the same limitations as the quick asset ratio and management ought to use a cash budget in its place.

The working capital ratio should be supplemented by the debtors and inventory turnover ratios, as both these ratios provide a measure of the liquidity of the two major current assets. For a given investment in debtors and inventories, a company with high turnover rates is much more liquid than another with low rates. Also, the working capital ratio may be supplemented by the proportion of debtors in current assets and the proportion of inventories in current assets. The working capital of a company may be constant but a reduction in the inventory ratio offset by an increase in the debtors ratio can increase its liquidity.

The working capital ratio is a difficult one to interpret accurately. A high ratio may indicate good liquidity, or low liquidity (where turnover rates for inventories and debtors are low) and low profitability (because investment in these assets is excessive). A slowdown in these turnover rates increases the working capital ratio but reduces effective liquidity and profitability. On the other hand, a low ratio may indicate either poor liquidity (where current asset turnover rates are low), good liquidity (where they are high), or lost profit opportunities (where inadequate assets are kept). The ratio should not be used without the turnover rates for inventories and debtors. The optimum ratio necessarily involves a balancing between liquidity and profitability, and universal rule of thumb ratios such as 2:1 can be very misleading.

### c. Turnover of Accounts Receivable

$$\frac{\text{Gross credit sales}}{\text{Gross accounts receivable}} = \text{x times p.a.}$$

This measures the number of times debtors are "turned over" each year, or the average time taken by debtors to pay their bills. The result should be compared with the credit terms granted. Thus, if debtors are turned over six times per annum, this means they take on average two months to pay up. If the credit period is only one month, there is laxity in the credit collection department. The measure should also be compared with the ageing schedule of debtors to ascertain where the problem, if any, is located. The ratio can be calculated separately for classes of debtors (according to age, geography of customers and shops, etc.).

Gross rather than net figures are used so as not to eliminate the problem customers from the data — it is these customers who cause the turnover to slacken. Most good customers pay their bills on time, so the turnover of good debtors (calculated from net figures) should always approximate the credit period granted. Cash sales are excluded from sales because they do not give rise to debtors. The end-of-year debtors figure is used in preference to the average figure because beginning-of-year debtors relate to sales of previous years.

Financial management requires debtors' turnover data to help assess credit and collection policies. The ratio indicates the liquidity of debtors and it is an important part of the financial position assessment.

### d. Turnover of Inventories

$$\frac{\text{COGS}}{\text{Average inventory}} = \text{x times p.a.}$$

The inventory turnover ratio shows the number of times finished goods inventories are "turned over" each year, i.e., the average time an item of merchandise remains in inventory before sale. This should be compared with desired turnover rates. It may be calculated separately for each class of inventory carried. The merchandising manager should know this ratio. Slow turnovers can indicate that excessive inventories or poor selling lines are being carried and very high turnover rates can indicate that inadequate levels of inventories are maintained, with consequent loss of sales caused by merchandise not being available to meet customers' requests. The ratio indicates the liquidity of inventories and hence is an important part of financial position assessment.

The ratio is measured in cost terms — inventory is valued at cost, and this is related to the cost of goods sold. Relating it to sales is incorrect because sales include the gross profit margin. The average inventory carried is used as a more accurate measure of inventory levels during the year than just the closing balance.

*e.   Cash Flow Ratio*

$$\frac{\text{Total debt}}{\text{Cash surplus on operations after tax p.a.}} = \text{x years}$$

This ratio indicates the number of years required for total debt to be repaid from the cash surplus generated from the company's own operations, assuming that cash surpluses are used only for this purpose. It shows the company's ability to meet its fixed financial commitments from its own resources without having to liquidate its existing assets for the purpose. The ratio should be interpreted as an index of liquidity rather than an absolute measure of repayment ability, as normally the cash surplus will be used for more than just debt repayment. The ratio is a very good indicator of long-term liquidity and hence of the vulnerability of the company to unforeseen difficulties in the capital market. The company should not have any liquidity problems where the ratio is low as it can then avoid having to raise additional loans to meet its repayment obligations. The cash budget is again the better source of information about future liquidity if it is available. For long period analysis, the ratio may be applied as funds from operations to total debt. Long-term lenders would be very interested in this ratio as it indicates the company's ability to repay loans without recourse to refinancing.

The cash surplus from operations after tax comprises the cash generated from the company's own operations and it excludes all non-cash expenses. It is available for the company to use as it wishes. It could be taken after dividends where they are regarded as a normal long-run outlay. The total debt commitments exclude all operating charges as these are included in the cash surplus calculations.

### ii.   Financial Structure Ratios

These ratios summarize a company's long-term financial position, i.e., its ability to meet commitments for all debt repayment in the long run. They are concerned with the sources of funds employed by the company judged in relation to their investment in assets. The balance sheet is viewed as an accumulated sources and uses of funds statement.

a.   Short-term sources of funds   i.e.,

$$\frac{\text{Short-term sources of funds}}{\text{Total funds}} \quad \text{i.e.,} \quad \frac{\text{Current liabilities}}{\text{Total liabilities and shareholders' funds}}$$

b.

$$\frac{\text{Long-term sources of funds}}{\text{Total funds}} \quad \text{i.e.,} \quad \frac{\text{Long-term liabilities and shareholders' funds}}{\text{Total liabilities and shareholders' funds}}$$

c.

$$\frac{\text{Current assets}}{\text{Total assets}}$$

d.

$$\frac{\text{Long-term assets}}{\text{Total assets}}$$

The ratio of current liabilities shows the proportion of short-term debt used in a company's financial structure. This ratio should be compared with that for investment in current assets. Essentially it indicates the working capital ratio. The ratio of long-term finance to total funds indicates the proportion of long-term funds used by the company. This ratio should similarly be compared with the investment in long-term assets. It too indicates the working capital ratio as the surplus of long-term funds over long-term assets must provide the working capital of a company. Interpretation of changes in these ratios is facilitated by the funds statement as this report shows the sources of new funds and their deployment over the year.

e.  Internal financing ratio

$$\frac{\text{Increase in gross assets}}{\text{Funds from operations after tax}} = \text{x years}$$

This ratio supplements those above. It indicates the extent to which expansion can be financed from internal sources (assuming all such funds are used for this purpose) and hence the extent to which new equity or debt funds must be raised. A high ratio (i.e., exceeding 1) signifies that the company cannot finance its existing growth from internal sources and hence must rely on external finance to some extent; whereas a low ratio indicates that it can finance its growth from internal sources. Investors interested in new share issues are interested in this ratio, but for management purposes the funds budget is the appropriate source of information. The ratio also indicates the period for which debt finance may be required; e.g., if the ratio is three years and no expansion beyond that date is currently planned, medium term loans could be the appropriate form of debt finance. Again, the ratio should be interpreted as an index number for use in comparative situations rather than as an absolute measure of internal financing ability.

As with the cash flow ratio, funds from operations could be after dividends where it is normal to pay them. The increase in gross assets (i.e., before depreciation) is used in the numerator rather than increase in total assets (i.e., after depreciation) as it measures total expenditure on new assets. The figure is derived from the funds statement.

### iii. Financial Risk Ratios

Several ratios can be calculated to provide measures of the financial risk borne by creditors, i.e., the probability of non-payment, and secondly by shareholders, i.e., the increment in risk of loss of capital and income resulting from their surrendering prior rights to outsiders for the payment of interest and repayment of debt. They are the gearing or leverage ratios which measure a company's reliance on debt finance in its financial structure, and the net tangible assets per share. Financial risk borne by shareholders is additional to business operating risk which arises from the economic characteristics of the industry in which the company operates. Shareholders require higher earnings and dividends to compensate them for this additional risk.

The higher earnings are expected to accrue from investment of borrowed funds in the company's operations to yield a rate of profit exceeding the rate of interest on those funds.

In addition to these ratios, the liquidity and financial structure ratios are also relevant in the assessment of financial risk.

### a. Financial Leverage Ratio

$$\frac{\text{Debt Funds}}{\text{Total Funds}} \quad \text{i.e.,} \quad \frac{\text{Current and long-term liabilities}}{\text{Total liabilities and shareholders' funds}}$$

This measures the extent to which the company is financed by external debt finance. The higher the ratio, the greater the financial risk borne by the creditors and hence the greater the care they should exercise in lending to the company.

Since total funds equal total assets, its reciprocal provides a measure of the asset cover, i.e., security, afforded to creditors. The lower this ratio is, the lower the asset cover and the greater the risk borne by creditors.

### b. Proprietary Ratio

$$\frac{\text{Proprietorship}}{\text{Total funds}}$$

The proprietary ratio is the complement of the financial gearing ratio above. It highlights gearing from the shareholders' viewpoint. As the gearing ratio rises, the proprietary ratio falls and the risk of loss of control by owners rises. However, at the same time, the size of the potential loss borne by the shareholders in a limited liability company declines because an increasing proportion of funds and therefore the loss are borne by creditors. This is the reason for the prevalence of so many "$20 companies" (i.e., those with an issued capital of only $20).

### c. Times-Interest-Earned Ratio

$$\frac{\text{Net profit before interest and taxes (EBIT)}}{\text{Annual interest charges}} = x \text{ times p.a.}$$

This measures gearing in the income stream, i.e., the ability of the company to meets its interest charges from income. It measures the income cover afforded to creditors. A company with a stable income stream can safely accommodate a higher gearing than one with a fluctuating or risky income stream.

### d.   Fixed-Financial-Charges Ratio

$$\frac{\text{Net profit before interest and taxes (EBIT)}}{\text{Annual fixed financial charges}} = \text{x times p.a.}$$

This ratio extends iii.c. above to include all fixed financial charges in the denominator. The main additional charge is the annual lease payment. Where leases are not capitalized in the balance sheet, the company may appear to have a modest gearing, whereas the same does not apply if they are so capitalized. Lease payments involve a fixed, and often preferential, charge each year, and this ratio shows the capacity of the company to meet them along with its interest commitments. It is a better ratio to use than iii.c.

### e.   Net Tangible Assets per Share

$$\frac{\text{Total assets less LT intangibles less liabilities}}{\text{Number of shares}} = \$ \text{ x per share}$$

This provides a measure of the asset backing per share, and hence of the profit or loss which could be incurred by shareholders in the event of liquidation (where assets are valued at current selling prices). It may be calculated separately for preference shares and for ordinary shares. Long-term intangible assets are excluded where they have no separate realizable value or where it is difficult to estimate.

Shareholders are particularly interested in the asset cover per share because firstly it helps to indicate the safety of their investment according to whether their funds are being invested in assets having good market values or in ones having negligible market values in comparison with their costs. Secondly, shareholders and management should regularly compare the net tangible assets per share with the share price, as the two figures effectively summarize management's investment policies. Net assets per share show the market value of the assets acquired by management with the shareholder's money, and the share price measures investors' expectations of the profits to be generated from those assets according to the risk perceived. If management makes good forecasts and rational investment decisions, it will not invest shareholders' funds unless the present value of profit prospects exceeds or equals the cost of the assets acquired. If investors are well informed about the company's past profit performance and future prospects, the share price should not fall below the net assets per share. The difference between the two figures is, consequently, a crucial figure for decision-making. An excess of net assets (valued at current selling prices) over the share price can indicate that the company ought to be wound up and its assets liquidated. Likewise the company can be an attractive takeover proposition in this situation, or where its net assets (at current cost) exceed its share price. On the other hand, a healthy surplus of share price over net assets indicates that profitable future operations are expected and the company ought to continue its operations. The premium indicates what investors are currently willing to pay for the expected stream of pure profits per share.

## PRESENTATION OF THE RATIOS

Ratios may be shown in separate ratio statements or in additional columns added to the income statement and balance sheet where appropriate. In this way they can emphasize the structural relationships in the financial reports.

The following example relates to the Northside Trading Company Limited, whose final reports were shown in chapter 6, cash flow statement in chapter 17, and funds statement in chapter 18.

*Additional Information:*

1. The company's share price on 31 December was $1.50.
2. Total assets at 1 January $69,000, inventory $34,000.
3. Assume all sales during the year were on credit.

1. *Earning Power and Operating Performance*

| | |
|---|---|
| Earning per Share (after tax) | 6,000/50,000 = 12 c per share |
| Dividends per Share | 4,000/50,000 = 8 c per share |
| Earnings Yield | .12/1.50 = 8% |
| Dividend Yield | .8/1.50 = 5.3% |
| Return on Paid-up Capital | 6,000/50,000 = 12% |
| Return on Shareholders' Funds | 6,000/62,000 = 9.7% |
| Return on Total Assets | 17,000/.5 (69,000 + 105,000) = 19.5% |
| Turnover of Assets | 140,000/.5 (69,000 + 105,000) = 1.6 times per annum or once every 7.5 months |

Return on Sales:

### Profit and Loss Statement

| | $ | % |
|---|---|---|
| Net Sales | 134,000 | 100 |
| Cost of Goods Sold | 100,000 | 74.6 |
| Gross Profit | 34,000 | 25.4 |
| Selling Expenses | 10,000 | 7.5 |
| Administration Expenses | 6,000 | 4.5 |
| Finance Expenses | 1,000 | .7 |
| Total Operating Expenses | 17,000 | 12.7 |
| Operating Profit | 17,000 | 12.7 |
| Non-operating Expenses | 6,000 | 4.5 |
| Net Profit | $11,000 | 8.2% |

2. *Measures of Financial Position and Financial Risk*

   i.  Liquidity

| | |
|---|---|
| Quick Asset | 28,000/20,000 = 140% or $1.40 of quick assets per $1.00 quick liability |
| Current Asset (or Working Capital) | 60,000/23,000 = 261% or $2.61 of current asset per $1.00 of current liability |
| Turnover of Debtors | 140,000/30,000 = 4.67 times per annum or about one every 11 weeks, i.e. average credit period taken is 11 weeks |
| Turnover of Inventories | 100,000/.5 (34,000 + 32,000) = 3.03 times per annum or about once every 17 weeks |
| Cash Flow Ratio | 43,000/14,500 = 2.97 years |

  ii.  Financial Structure

Source of Funds

| | $ | % | | $ | % | % |
|---|---|---|---|---|---|---|
| Current Assets | 60,000 | 57 | Current Liabilities | 23,000 | 22 | 22 |
| Long-Term Assets | 45,000 | 43 | Long-Term Liabilities | 20,000 | 19 ) | |
| | | | Total Liabilities | 43,000 | 41 | |
| | | | Shareholders Equity | 62,000 | 59 ) | 78 |
| | $105,000 | 100% | | $105,000 | 100% | 100% |

| | |
|---|---|
| Short-Term to Total Finance | 23,000/105,000 = 22% or 22c. of short-term finance in each $1.00 of total finance |
| Long-Term to Total Finance | (20,000 + 62,000)/105,000 = 78 % or 78c in each $1.00 of total finance |
| Short-Term to Total Investment | 60,000/105,000 = 57% or 57c investment in current assets in each $1.00 of total investment |
| Long-Term to Total Investment | 45,000/105,000 = 43% or 43c investment in long-term assets out of each $1.00 |
| Internal Financing Ratio | 38,000/16,000 = 2.375 years |

 iii.  Financial Risk

| | |
|---|---|
| Gearing or Leverage | 43,000/105,000 = 41% or 41c. of external finance in each $1.00 of total finance |
| Proprietary | 62,000/105,000 = 59% or 59c in each $1.00 of total finance |
| Times — interest-earned | (17,000 + 1,000)/1,000 = 18 times |
| Fixed Financial Charges | (17,000 + 1,000)/1,000 = 18 times |
| Net Tangible Assets per Share | (105,000 − 6,000 − 43,000)/50,000 = $1.12 per share |

## TREND ANALYSIS AND TREND STATEMENTS

In addition to the structural ratios calculated for a given year or date, trends in data over time can also be ascertained. Trends can be established for individual items (e.g., sales, gross profit, net profit, current assets, total assets, and so on) by obtaining growth rates over a base period, and for structural ratios (e.g., earning power, working capital) by comparing the ratio over time. The analysis of trends in the data can add much insight to the analysis and interpretation of financial reports by users, particularly where the company is either growing or struggling. Investors are in a better position to predict a company's future profits and financial position if they have analyzed recent trends in its financial data, and management is in a better position to plan its future. Normally data for at least four or five years are required to establish any reliable trends.

It is advisable to interpret trend data along with statements which explain what has happened in each period, i.e., the income, cash flow, and funds statements. For example, an increase in the net profit to shareholders' funds ratio could be due to higher gross profit margins, better expense control, lower income tax rates, higher turnover rates for debtors, inventories, or total assets, or any combinations of the above. Similarly, an increase in the working capital ratio could be due to repayment of short-term debt, injection of extra long-term funds into working capital, build-ups of inventories or debtors because of increased sales or because of obsolete stock and delinquent debtors. The cash flow, funds, and income statements are necessary for the explanation and evaluation of such changes.

Trends in the data may be shown in a variety of ways — for example, in special index statements summarizing income and financial position statement data, in graphs, in bar charts, and so on.

Trends may as well be determined by analyzing various ratios on a marginal basis. All the ratios have been calculated on an average basis to date, but, while they give the overall picture, the marginal ratios are more sensitive to change, they indicate the current direction of change, and they can help explain changes in the average ratio over time. For example, the calculation of performance ratios based on sales can indicate whether the company is pursuing sales growth for its own sake or whether the increase in sales is justified in terms of investment and profits. In particular:

1. $\Delta$ profits/ $\Delta$ sales indicates whether the increase in sales generated additional profits. This ratio can assist in explaining changes in the net profit/sales ratio over time.

2. $\Delta$ sales/ $\Delta$ total assets indicates whether an increase in gross investment has resulted in an increase in sales. If not, the additional assets would appear to be lying idle and the investment not justified. It helps to explain changes in the asset turnover ratio.

3. $\Delta$ sales/ $\Delta$ shareholders' funds indicates whether new shareholders funds, particularly retained earnings, have been put to work.

4. $\Delta$ profits/ $\Delta$ shareholders' funds indicates whether additional shareholders' investment has been justified in the short run. Ratios 2 and 4 assist in explaining changes in the rate of profits earned for shareholders.

5. $\Delta$ Share price/ $\Delta$ retained earnings per share indicates whether the retention of earnings has been profitable for shareholders. Unless the share price rises at least by the amount of retained earnings per share, shareholders lose and the retention is not justified in the short run.

6. $\Delta$ share price/ $\Delta$ net assets per share indicates whether increases in net assets are reflected in an increase in the share market value of the company. If the share price fails to rise with net assets per share, the company becomes an "asset rich" one which incurs the risk of being taken over. Ratios 5 and 6 indicate whether additional shareholder investment in the company is reflected in a sufficient appreciation in its share market value.

It is likewise informative to calculate many other ratios on a marginal basis.

A further set of useful indicators can be calculated from long-term data with respect to profitability and risk. Management and shareholders are concerned with the effective rate of return over time on shareholders' investment, growth in returns, and the risk in the income stream. The average long-term return on investment is best measured by the internal rate of return on the investment. This is that rate of interest which discounts the selling price of the share at some date in the future plus all dividends received in the meantime down to equal the initial buying price. It is that rate of interest r in the formula which equates both sides in the equation:

$$P_o = \sum_{t=o}^{n} \frac{D_t}{(1+r)^t} + \frac{P_n}{(1+r)^n}$$

where
$P_o$ is the initial share price
$P_n$ is the share price on ultimate sale in period n
$D_t$ is the dividend received in each period
$t = o \ldots n$ are the periods for which the share is owned.

This measure of the rate of return includes both dividends received and capital gains on the share. It is called the *investor return* or yield. Separate measures can be calculated for each component in the return, i.e., the dividend return and the capital gains return, as these have important implications for personal income taxation and risk. Shareholders should compare this rate of return with the yield on alternative investment options, e.g., government bonds and shares in other companies. For a given degree of risk, the return on their shares should be at least equal to the yields on alternative investments.

The effective rates of growth in earnings per share and in dividends per share are of interest to shareholders. They can be calculated by removing all bonus and rights issues from the share base. Where bonus issues result in an increase in the total dividend payout, the dividends are related back to the pre-bonus shares to determine the increase in dividends per share. The effect of rights issues is removed by assuming that the shareholder sells all his rights and uses the cash to buy old shares. This increases the number of his old shares without any further investment on his part, and increases his dividend income and the value of his shareholding. The compound rate of growth in earnings and dividends per share can then be calculated with respect to a fixed initial number of shares. Rates of growth in these variables are important determinants of share prices − are the current low earnings and dividend yields (i.e., high share prices) justified in terms of growth potential?

Finally, some useful measures of risk can be calculated from data over time. Measures of volatility about the trend in sales, earnings before interest and taxes, net profit available for ordinary shareholders, earnings per share, and dividends per share indicate the degree of stability in the company's revenue, income, and dividend streams, and hence the extent to which shareholders incur risk of loss. One measure of risk is the coefficient of variation V:

$$V = \frac{\text{standard deviation of the series}}{\text{mean of the series}}$$

The standard deviation measures the average amount of variation about the trend in the series of, for example, earnings before interest and taxes. By dividing the average into it, a measure of relative dispersion is obtained. The relative volatilities in the earnings streams of different companies can then be readily compared. For example, suppose that the income streams of two companies, A and B, have the following characteristics:

| | | |
|---|---|---|
| Company A | EBIT average for 5 years | $90,000 p.a. |
| | Standard deviation | $30,000 p.a. |
| Company B | EBIT average for 5 years | $160,000 p.a. |
| | Standard deviation | $40,000 p.a. |

$$V_A = \frac{30,000}{90,000} = .33$$

$$V_B = \frac{40,000}{160,000} = .25$$

The income stream for Company A is relatively more risky than that for Company B.

## LIMITATIONS OF RATIO ANALYSIS

Ratio analysis can be invaluable in gleaning important information from financial reports. However it can be no more reliable than the primary data from which it is derived. Some of the main dangers in it arise from:

1. Faulty classification of data. Consider the effects on the financial position ratios of classifying all long-term debtors as current assets when they ought to be shown as long-term assets; of classifying provision for depreciation as a liability instead of as an asset deduction.

2. Inconsistent classification of data over time.

3. Bases of asset valuation. It is essential that all assets at one date are shown in current values, and that all comparisons over time are made in terms of real dollar values, so that comparisons are meaningful. The dollar measuring unit must be homogeneous for purposes of financial analysis. Comparisons of 1900 dollars spent on land with 1974 dollars tied up in debtors are meaningless.

4. Bases of liability valuation. Again, there must be a consistent basis of valuation applied to liabilities, i.e., current values.

5. The same current value basis must be applied to the measurement of income. Otherwise the figure for income cannot be related to an asset base. For example, the use of historical cost valuation causes income to be overstated and assets to be understated in terms of current values, and hence the rate of profit on total or net assets is overstated.

6. Accounting principles must be applied consistently throughout, e.g., a change in the basis of revenue recognition can have substantial effects on revenue, profits, debtors, and inventory values.

7. Application of the doctrine of conservatism vitiates ratio analysis.

8. Intercompany comparisons are valid only if the same accounting principles and valuation bases are applied by all companies in the same group.

9. Lack of published data for use by persons outside the company.

## INTERPRETATION OF FINANCIAL REPORTS

There are many difficulties encountered in interpreting accounting reports which are prepared according to the highest theoretical standards of accounting. For example, an increase in the working capital ratio, in stock turnover, in leverage, etc. may be a good or a bad change. These ratios need to be compared with an optimum measure for any reliable assessment of the change to be made. There are no such things as reliable general purpose optima such as 2:1 working capital ratios. Optimum ratios must be calculated to suit the economic conditions of each firm and mostly they involve a compromise between risk and profits. The determination of optimum ratios lies in the provinces of finance theory and operations research and are beyond the scope of accounting as such. However, much can be learned from comparisons of ratios between firms in the industry as a second-best solution.

From a management point of view, all the ratios concerned with working capital are second-best ratios. A cash budget is the best measure of expected short-term debt-paying capacity. The optimum holdings of cash and inventories ought to be calculated according to the factors which affect their usage, the cost of holding them, and the need to maintain minimum safety levels. The optimum level of debtors depends upon the credit terms which competitors force the company to offer. The appropriate proportions of debt and equity finance depend upon the relative after-tax costs of each, the stability of the income stream and asset values, and the rate of inflation. Equity funds are dearer than debt funds because dividend payments are not tax deductible as are interest payments and because shareholders have to be compensated for the provision of risk capital. However, excessive reliance on the cheaper debt funds depresses a company's share prices and raises the cost of equity funds. The optimum proportions of short-term and long-term finance depend mainly upon the asset structure of the company and the relative costs of each source. In general, long-term assets should not be financed from short-term sources so that no immediate repayment problem is involved; the assets can generate sufficient funds from operations in the long run to repay the debt. On the other hand, temporary holdings of current assets can safely be financed from short-term sources since the assets will shortly be liquidated and the cash is therefore available to repay the debt. A company desires to use as much short-term finance as is safe because it is cheaper than long-term finance.

A brief review of some of the main principles of finance theory is given in Appendix 1 to assist the reader in interpreting accounting reports. However, it must be recognized that interpretation is a complex matter which demands a lot of experience. Furthermore, accounting reports can only be interpreted accurately in the light of knowledge about the economic characteristics of the industry in which the company operates.

Unfortunately one can have very little, if any, confidence in the interpretation of accounting reports prepared according to "the generally accepted principles of accounting" and published according to the Ninth Schedule of the Companies Act. The most fundamental defect of current accounting practice is that it is not designed as a financial information system for the purposes of decision-making and evaluation, and as a consequence it lacks direction.

## FURTHER READING

Carrington, A. S.; Battersby, G. B.; and Howitt, G. *Accounting: An Information System*. Christchurch: Whitcombe and Tombs, 1975. Chap. 10.

Gordon, M. J., and Shillinglaw, G. *Accounting: A Management Approach*. 4th ed. Homewood, Illinois: Richard D. Irwin, 1969. Chap. 8.

Mathews, R. L. *The Accounting Framework*. 3rd ed. Melbourne: Cheshire, 1971. Chap. 14.

## QUESTIONS AND EXERCISES

1. What are the main measures of earning power of a company?

2. Explain the concept of financial position. What are the main measures of financial position?

3. Explain the concept of financial risk. What are the main measures of financial risk?

4. Examine the view that published financial statements are of little use to the investor in assessing the investment worth of a company because they relate to the past and he wants to know about the future.

5. You own 1,000 shares in the Shangrila Corporation Limited, a public company whose shares are listed on the stock exchange. What information would you require to make a rational decision about whether to keep or sell your shares? To what extent do Shangrila's financial reports, which are prepared according to generally accepted accounting principles, aid you in making this decision? (Assume inflation has been occurring for a long time.)

6. Why are intangible assets generally excluded from the calculation of most financial ratios?

7. Critically examine the return on paid-up capital as an index of profit performance. Suggest reasons why directors frequently highlight this ratio in their annual reports.

8. How would you interpret the following share yield data:

    i.   Dividend yield 1 per cent, earnings yield 6 per cent
    ii.  Dividend yield 12 per cent, earnings yield 14 per cent
    iii. Dividend yield 3 per cent, earnings yield 12 per cent
    iv.  Dividend yield 7 per cent, earnings yield 8 per cent

    Assume that the yield on long-term Commonwealth bonds is 7 per cent.

9. Company A earns 20 per cent rate of profit on sales but only 5 per cent total investment. Company B earns a 2 per cent profit on sales but 10 per cent on investment. Explain why these results are possible.

10. A company grants thirty days credit to its customers. Its turnover of accounts receivable is once every two months. What does this indicate?

11. A company turns over its inventories once every three months. Its main competitors have a monthly turnover. What are the major implications of this?

12. Critically examine the usefulness of working capital and quick asset ratios as measures of short-term liquidity.

13. A company has a working capital ratio of 3:1, a quick asset ratio of 1:1, a debtors' turnover rate of six times a year, and an inventory turnover rate of eight times a year. How will each of the following transactions affect the ratios?

    i. Purchase of merchandise for cash
    ii. Purchase of merchandise on credit
    iii. Sale of merchandise for cash
    iv. Sale of merchandise on credit
    v. Cash collections from debtors
    vi. Repayment of creditors

14. What are the possible advantages and disadvantages of a company increasing its proportion of debt finance from 20 per cent of total funds to 60 per cent of total funds from the viewpoint of:

    i. Debenture holders?
    ii. Unsecured creditors?
    iii. Shareholders?

15. Company X has a rate of growth in total assets of 20 per cent per annum and an internal financing ratio of 90 per cent. Company B has likewise a 20 per cent growth rate but an internal financing ratio of 30 per cent. What does this mean with respect to probable new share or debenture issues by each company?

16. A company proposes to finance the purchase of expensive new plant by obtaining a bank overdraft. Its current financial position is moderately healthy and its gearing is normal for the industry. Would you advise the company to use this form of finance?

17. A company with a very unstable earnings stream is proposing to finance a major expansion programme largely from a debenture issue so that it can obtain the benefit of the tax remission on interest payments. The fixed assets to be purchased are highly illiquid. The company's current gearing is appropriate for its operations. What would be your advice about its financing plans?

18. A company regularly transfers about 50 per cent of its net profits after tax to general and special reserves for purposes of improving its financial position and financing expansion. The company's sales have grown at a somewhat slower rate than its net assets, and its profits at a much slower rate. Its gearing has declined over the years and the company is very liquid. Its share price has remained fairly constant for some years. Comment on the management's dividend policy and its effects on the company. Do they appear to be running the company in the shareholders' interests?

19. The net tangible assets per share, at book value, of a company are shown at $1. The share price is 90 cents. However, the net tangible assets per share at current realizable values are $3. Comment on this situation.

20. A company shows a rate of profit on total shareholders' funds of 10 per cent in its published reports. However, this rate is reduced to 4 per cent when its assets are valued at their current replacement costs. Comment on this situation.

21. Analyze the following information relating to a firm and indicate briefly the significance of the relationships which can be derived therefrom:

*As at 30 June*

| | 19X5 | 19X6 | 19X7 |
|---|---|---|---|
| | $ | $ | $ |
| Cash at Bank | 3,200 | 400 | — |
| Debtors | 5,300 | 5,300 | 5,200 |
| Stock (at Cost) | 12,700 | 12,600 | 10,500 |
| Plant | 8,800 | 9,200 | 10,800 |
| Buildings | 5,000 | 7,500 | 9,500 |
| Creditors | 7,600 | 5,400 | 6,500 |
| Bank Overdraft | — | — | 300 |
| Mortgage on Buildings | — | 2,000 | 2,000 |
| Paid-up Capital | 25,000 | 25,000 | 25,000 |
| Reserve | 2,000 | 2,000 | 2,000 |
| Appropriation Account (Cr.) | 400 | 600 | 200 |

*Year ended 30 June*

| | 19X5 | 19X6 | 19X7 |
|---|---|---|---|
| | $ | $ | $ |
| Cash Sales | 5,000 | 4,600 | 6,000 |
| Credit Sales | 14,500 | 13,100 | 10,800 |
| Cost of Goods Sold | 14,300 | 13,900 | 12,700 |
| Selling Expenses | 2,200 | 2,400 | 2,500 |
| Administrative Expenses | 1,200 | 1,100 | 1,000 |
| Net Profit | 1,800 | 300 | 600 |
| Stock at 1 July 19X4 (at Cost) | 11,500 | | |

22. W. Smith operates a wholesale delicatessen business and has found that, despite increasing turnover, he is running into financial difficulties. The profit has fallen and his cash position has deteriorated.

*Relevant information for the last two years:*

| | 19X1 | 19X2 |
|---|---|---|
| | $ | $ |
| Sales (All Credit) | 30,000 | $36,000 |
| Cost of Goods Sold | 20,000 | 28,000 |
| Operating Expenses | 4,000 | 5,000 |
| Net Profit | 6,000 | 3,000 |
| Drawings | 6,000 | 3,000 |
| Bank | 3,000 (Dr.) | 2,000 (Cr.) |
| Debtors | 4,000 | 6,000 |
| Stocks (at Cost) | 12,000 | 18,000 |
| Fixed Assets (at Cost) | 12,000 | 12,000 |
| Accumulated Depreciation on Fixed Assets | 3,000 | 4,000 |
| Creditors | 5,000 | 7,000 |
| Capital | 23,000 | 23,000 |
| Stocks at 1 July 19X0 (at Cost) | 8,000 | |

Write a report to Mr. Smith giving the reasons for the changed results. Your report should include an analysis and interpretation of appropriate financial relationships and a statement showing sources and uses of funds.

23. The following are extracts from the accounting reports of J. Burton, Wholesaler:

### Balance Sheet Items as at 30 June

|  | 19X3 | 19X4 |
|---|---|---|
|  | $'000 | $'000 |
| Accounts Receivable | 15 | 22 |
| Inventory | 20 | 25 |
| Cash | 5 | 3 |
| Fixtures and Fittings | 10 | 9 |
| Vehicles | 5 | 4 |
| Premises | 25 | 27 |
|  | 80 | 90 |
| Accounts Payable | 25 | 20 |
| Accrued Expenses | 5 | 5 |
| Mortgage on Premises | 15 | 20 |
| Capital | 35 | 45 |
|  | 80 | 90 |

### Summary of Income Statements for Years Ended 30 June

|  | 19X3 | | 19X4 | |
|---|---|---|---|---|
|  | $'000 | $'000 | $'000 | $'000 |
| Sales (All Credit) | | 100 | | 110 |
| Less Cost of Goods Sold | | | | |
| Inventory at Beginning | 10 | | 20 | |
| Purchases | 85 | | 95 | |
|  | 95 | | 115 | |
| Less Inventory at End | 20 | 75 | 25 | 90 |
| Gross Profit | | 25 | | 20 |
| Less | | | | |
| Selling Expenses | 5 | | 7 | |
| Administrative Expenses | 10 | 15 | 2 | 9 |
| Net Profit | | 10 | | 11 |

On 15 August 19X3, Mr. Burton made application to his bank for an overdraft of $20,000 to enable him to expand his business activities. In support of his application he presented his audited balance sheet as at 30 June 19X3. A condition of bank accommodation is a minimum current ratio of 2:1 and a minimum liquid ratio of 1:1. As neither of these required ratios was reached, Mr. Burton's application was rejected.

On 1 August 19X4, he again made application to the bank for the overdraft, supporting his application with his audited balance sheet as at 30 June 19X4 and advice that he had raised his net profit by $1,000 per annum. As the required minimum ratios had now been achieved, his application was successful.

*Required:*
i.  Calculate the following:
    a.  Current (or working capital) ratio at 30 June 19X3 and 30 June 19X4
    b.  Liquid (or quick asset) ratio at 30 June 19X3 and 30 June 19X4
    c.  Turnover of stocks
    d.  Turnover of debtors.
ii.  Comment on the financial position of the business, including in your answer a critical discussion of the bank's requirement of minimum current and liquid ratios, before the accommodation is granted.
iii.  Comment on the apparent improvement in profitability.

24.  The following information has been obtained from the books of a company for the past three years:

*Year Ended 30 June*

|  | 19X6 | 19X7 | 19X8 |
|---|---|---|---|
|  | $ | $ | $ |
| *Equities* |  |  |  |
| Trade Creditors | 6,410 | 14,160 | 28,877 |
| Bills Payable | 2,280 | 5,876 | 9,215 |
| Bank Overdraft |  | 4,285 | 9,340 |
| Paid-up Capital | 70,000 | 70,000 | 70,000 |
| Profit and Loss Appropriation |  |  |  |
| Account | 7,300 | 8,020 | 17,825 |
|  | 85,990 | 102,341 | 135,257 |
| *Assets* |  |  |  |
| Cash in Hand | 10 | 15 | 10 |
| Cash at Bank | 2,200 |  |  |
| Sundry Debtors | 7,124 | 12,886 | 16,744 |
| Inventory | 26,156 | 25,440 | 43,103 |
| Plant and Machinery | 42,000 | 54,000 | 63,400 |
| Freehold Premises | 8,500 | 10,000 | 12,000 |
|  | 85,990 | 102,341 | 135,257 |
| *Other Information* |  |  |  |
| Sales (Credit) | 78,210 | 101,000 | 104,000 |
| Gross Profit | 26,070 | 26,600 | 41,000 |
| Net Profit | 12,950 | 13,900 | 24,000 |
| Dividends Paid during Year | 7,000 | 12,780 | 14,195 |

Inventory at 1 July 19X5 was valued at $17,300.

*Required:*

Write a report to the directors and comment on:
i.  The financial state of the business as shown by movements in balance sheet figures
ii.  The possible causes for fluctuations in the profits
iii.  Any indicated weaknesses in management control
iv.  The policy you suggest the company should follow in the future.

25. Extracts from the latest published accounts of two companies in the "quick-food" industry are set out below. You are employed as the accountant of Burger Foods Ltd; the directors want you to prepare a report on comparative efficiency, as far as it is possible, with the published accounts of their chief competitor Aussie Pies Ltd. Because both companies completed mergers during the year, you decide to base your ratios on the final balance sheet figures and not on averages. For this reason only final balance sheet figures are shown below.

|  | Burger Foods Ltd. | Aussie Pies Ltd. |
|---|---|---|
|  | $ | $ |
| Sales | 3,250,000 | 3,000,000 |
| Net Profit after Tax | 260,000 | 300,000 |
| Owners' Equity | 1,260,000 | 1,450,000 |
| Fixed-Term Borrowings | 800,000 | 650,000 |
| Creditors | 390,000 | 700,000 |
| Bank Overdraft | 60,000 | 200,000 |
| Fixed Assets (Book Value) | 1,610,000 | 1,650,000 |
| Stock | 300,000 | 800,000 |
| Other Current Assets | 600,000 | 550,000 |

*Share Capital*

Burger Foods Ltd.   1,000,000 fully paid $1 ordinary shares
Aussie Pies Ltd.    800,000 fully paid $1 ordinary shares

*Required:*

i. Prepare a statement of figures and comparative ratios suitable for presentation to the directors, showing tests for profitability, liquidity, and solvency.

ii. Write a report to the directors summarizing the conclusions you draw from your statement of comparative ratios.

26. The installation manager of Slick Oil Co. Ltd., which is presently erecting a $8,000,000 refinery, is considering letting a contract for the erection of part of the plant. This section of the work is anticipated by Slick to cost approximately $500,000 and the erection schedule calls for the completion of this section within four months to avoid delaying the rest of the project. Five firms have tendered prices as follows:

|  | $ |
|---|---|
| Colossal Constructions Ltd. | 492,000 |
| Installation Engineers Ltd. | 449,998 |
| Chemical Plant Suppliers Ltd. | 449,998 |
| Sunrise Overseas Enterprises Pty. Ltd. | 449,750 |
| Lightning Fabricators Ltd. | 440,000 |

Four of the firms are local (Australian) and the other, Sunrise Overseas Enterprises Pty. Ltd., is a wholly owned subsidiary of a large overseas corporation. At present the local establishment of this company is an Australian manager with a design office. The firm has stated its intention of sending the necessary resources to complete the work if it gains the contract.

The installation manager has asked you to obtain and study the latest balance sheets of each of these firms with a view to making a recommendation as to their possible reliability.

The balance sheets and additional information obtained are as follows:

Colossal Constructions Ltd.

### Balance Sheet as at 30 June 19X1

| | $ | | $ |
|---|---|---|---|
| Sundry Debtors | 2,000,000 | Bank Overdraft | 500,000 |
| Stock in Trade | 500,000 | Trade Creditors | 2,000,000 |
| Contracts in Progress | 4,000,000 | | 2,500,000 |
| | 6,500,000 | Debentures (Maturing | |
| Motor Vehicles | 160,000 | 30 June 19X8) | 2,000,000 |
| Plant and Equipment | 8,000,000 | | |
| Land and Buildings | 4,000,000 | | 4,500,000 |
| | | *Owners' Equity* | |
| | | Paid-up Capital | 6,000,000 |
| | | Reserves | 6,000,000 |
| | | Profit and Loss | |
| | | Appropriation | 2,160,000 |
| | $18,660,000 | | $18,660,000 |

| | |
|---|---|
| Turnover for year ended 30 June 19X1 | $11,000,000 |
| Profit from trading year ended 30 June 19X1 | $ 1,500,000 |
| Dividend for year ended 30 June 19X1 | 10% |

Installation Engineers Ltd.

### Balance Sheet as at 30 June 19X1

| | $ | | $ |
|---|---|---|---|
| Sundry Debtors | 2,000,000 | Bank Overdraft | 750,000 |
| Stock in Trade | 500,000 | Trade Creditors | 2,000,000 |
| Contracts in Progress | 3,000,000 | | 2,750,000 |
| | 5,500,000 | *Owners' Equity* | |
| Motor Vehicles | 160,000 | Paid-up Capital | 4,000,000 |
| Plant and Equipment | 6,000,000 | Reserves | 2,000,000 |
| | | Profit and Loss | |
| | | Appropriation | 2,910,000 |
| | $11,660,000 | | $11,660,000 |

| | |
|---|---|
| Turnover for year ended 30 June 19X1 | $12,000,000 |
| Profit from trading for year ended 30 June 19X1 | $ 1,200,000 |
| Dividend paid for year ended 30 June 19X1 | 15% |

Chemical Plant Suppliers Ltd.

### Balance Sheet as at 30 June 19X1

| | $ | | $ |
|---|---|---|---|
| Cash at Bank | 100,000 | Trade Creditors | 3,500,000 |
| Accounts Receivable | 1,900,000 | *Owners' Equity* | |
| Stock in Trade | 1,000,000 | Paid-up Capital | 6,000,000 |
| Contracts in Progress | 4,000,000 | Reserves | 4,000,000 |
| | 7,000,000 | Profit and Loss | |
| Motor Vehicles | 160,000 | Appropriation | 1,660,000 |
| Plant and Equipment | 6,000,000 | | |
| Land and Buildings | 2,000,000 | | |
| | $15,160,000 | | $15,160,000 |

| | |
|---|---|
| Turnover for year ended 30 June 19X1 | $12,000,000 |
| Profit from trading for year ended 30 June 19X1 | $ 1,700,000 |
| Dividend paid for year ended 30 June 19X1 | 15% |

Sunrise Corporation Ltd.*

### Balance Sheet as at 30 June 19X1

| | | | |
|---|---|---|---|
| Cash at Bank | 500,000 | Accounts Payable | 9,000,000 |
| Debtors | 10,000,000 | Bills Payable | 11,000,000 |
| Raw Material Stock | 6,000,000 | | 20,000,000 |
| Contracts in Progress | 24,000,000 | Debentures (Maturing | |
| | 40,500,000 | 30 June 19X4) | 16,000,000 |
| Rolling Stock | 1,000,000 | | 36,000,000 |
| Plant and Equipment | 40,000,000 | *Owners' Equity* | |
| Land and Buildings | 16,000,000 | Paid-up Capital | 40,000,000 |
| | | Reserves | 10,000,000 |
| | | Profit and Loss | |
| | | Appropriation | 11,500,000 |
| | 97,500,000 | | 97,500,000 |

| | |
|---|---|
| Turnover for year ended 30 June 19X1 | 72,000,000 |
| Profit for year ended 30 June 19X1 | 8,000,000 |
| Dividend paid for year ended 30 June 19X1 | 10% |

\* This information pertains to the parent company which owns Sunrise Overseas Enterprises Pty. Ltd. It is expressed in beams, the current exchange rate for which is 5 beams to $1 Australian.

Lightning Fabricators Ltd.

*Balance Sheet for Year Ended 30 June 19X1*

|  | $ |  | $ |
|---|---|---|---|
| Sundry Debtors | 1,000,000 | Bank Overdraft | 200,000 |
| Stock in Trade | 1,000,000 | Trade Creditors | 1,800,000 |
| Contracts in Progress | 2,000,000 |  | 2,000,000 |
|  | 4,000,000 | Debentures (Maturing |  |
| Motor Vehicles | 160,000 | 30 June 19X3) | 1,000,000 |
| Plant and Equipment | 2,000,000 |  | 3,000,000 |
| Goodwill | 1,000,000 | *Owners' Equity* |  |
|  |  | Paid-up Capital | 3,000,000 |
|  |  | Reserves | 200,000 |
|  |  | Profit and Loss |  |
|  |  | Appropriation | 960,000 |
|  | $7,160,000 |  | $7,160,000 |

| Turnover for year ended 30 June 19X1 | $6,000,000 |
|---|---|
| Profit for year ended 30 June 19X1 | $  300,000 |
| Dividend paid for year ended 30 June 19X1 | 10% |

*Required:*

Make a recommendation specifying the firm to which you would award the contract. State your reasons for the selection of this firm and the rejection of others.

27.   The directors of Cabanosi Ltd. are concerned about the company's profitability and financial position. Although sales volume has increased according to plan, profits and financial position are unsatisfactory. The following information is made available:

i.        *Income Statements for the Years Ended 30 June*

|  | 19X1 | | 19X2 | |
|---|---|---|---|---|
|  | $'000 | % | $'000 | % |
| Credit Sales | 240 | 100 | 300 | 100 |
| Less Cost of Sales | 192 | 80 | 250 | 83.3 |
| Gross Profit | 48 | 20 | 50 | 16.7 |
| Less Expenses | 33.6 | 14 | 35 | 11.7 |
| Net Profit before Tax | 14.4 | 6 | 15 | 5 |
| Less Provision for Tax | 5 |  | 6 |  |
| Net Profit after Tax | 9.4 |  | 9 |  |
| Less Provision for Dividends | 7 |  | 8 |  |
| Retained Profits | 2.4 |  | 1 |  |

ii.

*Balance Sheets as at 30 June*

| | 19X1 | | | 19X2 | | |
|---|---|---|---|---|---|---|
| | $'000 | $'000 | $'000 | $'000 | $'000 | $'000 |
| *Owners' Equity* | | | | | | |
| Paid-up Capital | | | 100 | | | 104 |
| Reserves | | | 20 | | | 21 |
| | | | 120 | | | 125 |
| *Long-Term Liabilities* | | | | | | |
| 8% Debentures | | | 12 | | | 25 |
| | | | 132 | | | 150 |
| | | | | | | |
| Represented by: | | | | | | |
| | | | | | | |
| Long-Term Assets | | | 100 | | | 140 |
| *Working Capital:* | | | | | | |
| *Current Assets* | | | | | | |
| Bank | 2 | | | — | | |
| Debtors | 20 | | | 30 | | |
| Stocks | 40 | 62 | | 30 | 60 | |
| | | | | | | |
| *Less Current Liabilities* | | | | | | |
| Bank Overdraft | — | | | 20 | | |
| Provision for Tax | 5 | | | 6 | | |
| Provision for Dividends | 7 | | | 8 | | |
| Creditors | 18 | 30 | 32 | 16 | 50 | 10 |
| | | | 132 | | | 150 |

iii. Stock on hand 1 July 19X0   $44,000
The terms of credit for both purchases and sales were 10 days.

iv.     *Funds Statement for the year Ended 30 June 19X2*

| | $'000 | |
|---|---|---|
| *Sources of Funds* | | |
| Revenue from Sales | 300 | |
| Use of Cash Funds and Bank Overdraft | 22 | |
| Issue of Shares | 4 | |
| Issue of Debentures | 13 | |
| Stock Rundown | 10 | 349 |
| | | |
| *Application of Funds* | | |
| Purchases of Merchandise for Sale | 250 | |
| Expenses (excluding deprecn. $5,000) | 30 | |
| Fixed Assets Acquired | 45 | |
| Taxes Paid | 5 | |
| Dividends Paid | 7 | |
| Additional Credit Allowed to Debtors | 10 | |
| Reductions in Amounts Owing to Creditors | 2 | 349 |

Write a report:

a. Suggesting reasons for the failure of profits to increase
b. Setting out the trend in the financial position and the apparent cause of any trends revealed
c. Giving your recommendations for future management action.

28. N. Borsari conducts a wholesale grocery business. He asks you to explain why the profit of the business has fallen during the past year despite increased sales, and why the liquid position of the enterprise has deteriorated to the extent that a substantial bank balance at 30 June 19X2 has been replaced by an overdraft at 30 June 19X3.

Your investigation reveals the following information:

| | Year Ended 30 June | |
| --- | --- | --- |
| | 19X2 | 19X3 |
| | $ | $ |
| Sales (All Credit) | 15,000 | 16,000 |
| Cost of Goods Sold | 10,000 | 11,500 |
| Selling and Administrative Expenses | 2,000 | 2,500 |
| Net Profit | 3,000 | 2,000 |
| | As at 30 June | |
| | 19X2 | 19X3 |
| | $ | $ |
| Bank | 3,250 Dr. | 1,000 Cr. |
| Debtors | 5,000 | 6,500 |
| Stocks (Cost) | 10,000 | 14,000 |
| Fixed Assets (Cost) | 7,500 | 7,500 |
| Accumulated Depreciation of Fixed Assets | 750 | 1,000 |
| Creditors | 4,000 | 5,000 |
| Proprietor's Capital | 21,000 | 21,000 |
| Stock 1 July 19X1 (Cost) $6,000 | | |

You are required to write a report to Borsari, showing the reasons for the changed results. Your report should incorporate:

i. An analysis of the above information whereby significant income statement, balance sheet and inter-statement relationships are revealed

ii. A funds statement showing the purposes for which new funds were required and the sources of the funds.

29. Alpha Ltd. and Beta Ltd. are two public companies engaged in the same industry. The following information relates to their performance in the financial years ended 30 June 19X3 and 30 June 19X4.

|  | Alpha Ltd. | | Beta Ltd. | |
|---|---|---|---|---|
|  | 19X3 | 19X4 | 19X3 | 19X4 |
|  | $'000 | | $'000 | |
| Sales | 250 | 270 | 300 | 330 |
| Cost of Sales | 175 | 216 | 210 | 264 |
| Gross Margin | 75 | 54 | 90 | 66 |
| *Operating Expenses* | | | | |
| Selling | 20.5 | 24 | 30 | 36 |
| Administrative | 14 | 15 | 11 | 13 |
| Finance | 0.5 | 1 | 9 | 12 |
| Total Operating Expenses | 35.0 | 40 | 50 | 61 |
| Net Profit | 40 | 14 | 40 | 5 |
| Estimated Taxation | 20 | 7 | 20 | 2.5 |
| Net Profit after Tax | 20 | 7 | 20 | 2.5 |
| Dividends Proposed | 10 | 4 | 10 | 1.5 |
| Retained Profit | 10 | 3 | 10 | 1.0 |

*Other Information:*

a. *Capital*:
   Alpha Ltd.   100,000 $1 ordinary shares fully paid.
   Beta Ltd.     75,000 $1 ordinary shares fully paid.

b. *Share prices:*             19X3        19X4
   Alpha Ltd.                  1.20        1.30
   Beta Ltd.                   1.33        0.80

c.          *Balance Sheets 19X3 and 19X4 ($'000):*

|  | Alpha Ltd. | | Beta Ltd. | |
|---|---|---|---|---|
|  | 19X3 | 19X4 | 19X3 | 19X4 |
| *Assets* | $'000 | | $'000 | |
| *Short-Term* | | | | |
| Debtors (Net) | 30 | 38 | 40 | 46 |
| Merchandise | 36 | 44 | 44 | 56 |
| Other | 23 | 18 | 20 | 12 |
|  | 89 | 100 | 104 | 114 |
| *Long-Term* (Net) | 94 | 95 | 105 | 106 |
| Total Assets | 183 | 195 | 209 | 220 |
| *Liabilities* | | | | |
| *Current* | | | | |
| Overdraft | 10 | 25 | 11 | 32 |
| Estimated Tax Payable | 20 | 7 | 20 | 2.5 |
| Proposed Dividend | 10 | 4 | 10 | 1.5 |
| Other | 23 | 36 | 24 | 39 |
|  | 63 | 72 | 65 | 75 |
| *Long-Term* | – | – | 60 | 60 |
|  | 63 | 72 | 125 | 135 |
| *Owners' Equity* | | | | |
| Paid-up Capital and Reserves | 120 | 123 | 84 | 85 |
|  | 183 | 195 | 209 | 220 |

d.    *Merchandise 1 July 19X2:*
       Alpha Ltd.      $24,000
       Beta Ltd.       $36,000

e.    *Depreciation charged on long-term assets was:*

|  | 19X3 | 19X4 |
|---|---|---|
| Alpha Ltd. | $6,000 | $7,000 |
| Beta Ltd. | 7,500 | 9,000 |

f.    Each company paid taxation ($20,000) and dividends ($10,000) during 19X4.

*Required:*

(1) Prepare a report evaluating the performance of Alpha Ltd. and Beta Ltd. with respect to

     (i)     the profitability
     (ii)    the efficiency in the use of funds
     (iii)   the financial structure and risk
     of the two companies.

(2) Prepare a funds statement for each company for 19X4 and explain any significant factors that are revealed.

30. The final accounting reports of the Charlton Emporium Ltd., are summarized below:

*Income and Appropriation Statements for the Year Ended 31 December 19X1*

|  | $ |
|---|---|
| Sales (All Credit) | 3,200,000 |
| Cost of Goods Sold | 2,000,000 |
| Gross Profit | 1,200,000 |
| Operating Expenses | 600,000 |
| Interest | 100,000 |
| Net Profit | 500,000 |
| Company Tax | 200,000 |
| Dividends | 200,000 |
| Retained Profit | $100,000 |

*Balance Sheet as at 31 December 19X1*

| | $ | $ | | | $ |
|---|---|---|---|---|---|
| *Current Assets* | | | *Current Liabilities* | | |
| Bank | | 110,000 | Accounts Payable | | 600,000 |
| Accounts | | | Tax Payable | | 200,000 |
| Receivable | 800,000 | | Dividends Payable | | 200,000 |
| Less Estimated | | | | | 1,000,000 |
| Bad Debts | 50,000 | 750,000 | *Long-Term Liability* | | |
| Inventories | | 440,000 | Debentures | | 1,500,000 |
| | | 1,300,000 | *Total Liabilities* | | 2,500,000 |
| *Long-Term Assets* | | | *Shareholders' Equity* | | |
| Plant | 600,000 | | Paid-up Capital | | 1,000,000 |
| Less Accumulated | | | Share Premium | | |
| Depreciation | 200,000 | 400,000 | Reserve | | 300,000 |
| Premises | 2,400,000 | | Retained Profits | | 200,000 |
| Less Accumulated | | | | | 1,500,000 |
| Depreciation | 400,000 | 2,000,000 | | | |
| Goodwill | | 300,000 | | | |
| | | 2,700,000 | | | |
| | | | *Total Liabilities and* | | |
| *Total Assets* | | $4,000,000 | *Equity* | | $4,000,000 |

*Additional Data:*

| | | $ |
|---|---|---|
| Inventories | 1 January 19X1 | 360,000 |
| Total Assets | 1 January 19X1 | 3,200,000 |
| Shareholders' Equity | 1 January 19X1 | 1,400,000 |

The paid-up capital comprises 1,000,000 shares of $1 each.
Share price 31 December 19X1 — $2.20.
Credit terms granted to customers — maximum 60 days.
The industry norm for inventory turnover is 8 times per annum.

*Required:*

Prepare a report of the profitability, liquidity, financial structure, and financial risk of the company.

*31. An inspection of recent accounting reports of the Boomer Company Ltd. revealed the following information.

| | 19X8 | 19X9 |
|---|---|---|
| | $ | $ |
| *Income and Appropriation Statements* | | |
| Sales (All Credit) | 200,000 | 320,000 |
| Cost of Goods Sold | 160,000 | 256,000 |
| Gross Profit | 40,000 | 64,000 |
| Other Expenses | 8,000 | 10,000 |
| Net Profit | 32,000 | 54,000 |
| Company Tax | 10,000 | 18,000 |
| Net Profit after Tax | 22,000 | 36,000 |
| Dividends | 8,000 | — |
| Retained Profit | 14,000 | 36,000 |
| *Balance Sheet* | | |
| *Current Assets* | | |
| Accounts Receivable | 40,000 | 168,000 |
| Inventories | 40,000 | 100,000 |
| | 80,000 | 268,000 |
| *Long-Term Assets* (Net) | 80,000 | 92,000 |
| Total Assets | $160,000 | $360,000 |
| *Current Liabilities* | | |
| Bank Overdraft | 8,000 | 72,000 |
| Accounts Payable | 20,000 | 100,000 |
| | 28,000 | 172,000 |
| *Long-Term Liabilities* | | |
| Debentures | 20,000 | 20,000 |
| *Total Liabilities* | 48,000 | 192,000 |
| *Owner's Equity* | | |
| Paid-up Capital ($1 Shares) | 80,000 | 100,000 |
| Retained Profits | 32,000 | 68,000 |
| | 112,000 | 168,000 |
| *Total Liabilities and Owners' Equity* | $160,000 | $360,000 |

*Additional Data:*

| Opening Inventories | 19X8 | $40,000 |
|---|---|---|
| Opening Total Assets | 19X8 | $140,000 |
| Opening Owners' Equity | 19X8 | $98,000 |

*Other Information:*

Share price 19X8 – $1.80; 19X9 – $2.00.

*Required:*

Report on the profitability, financial position, and financial structure of the company, and the changes therein, as revealed by the above information. Include a brief explanation of each ratio used in your answer.

*32. The following accounting reports were recently published by Turramurra Traders Ltd., a firm of general retailers.

### Year ended December 31

|  | 19X6 | 19X7 |
|---|---|---|
|  | $'000 | $'000 |
| *Income and Appropriation Statements* |  |  |
| Sales | 9,000 | 10,000 |
| Cost of Sales | 6,000 | 6,800 |
| Gross Profit | 3,000 | 3,200 |
| Operating Expenses | 2,400 | 2,560 |
| Net Profit | 600 | 640 |
| Income Tax | 300 | 320 |
| Net Profit after Tax | 300 | 320 |
| Dividends | 100 | 100 |
| Retained Profits | $200 | $220 |

### Balance Sheets as at December 31

|  | 19X6 | 19X7 |
|---|---|---|
|  | $'000 | $'000 |
| *Current Assets* |  |  |
| Debtors | 1,500 | 2,000 |
| Inventories | 2,000 | 2,600 |
|  | 3,500 | 4,600 |
| *Long-Term Assets* |  |  |
| Shop Fixtures (at Cost Less Accumulated Depreciation) | 500 | 450 |
| Premises (at Cost Less Accumulated Depreciation) | 2,500 | 2,250 |
| Goodwill | 500 | 500 |
|  | 3,500 | 3,200 |
|  | $7,000 | $7,800 |

*Current Liabilities*

| | | |
|---|---|---|
| Creditors | 1,000 | 1,200 |
| Bank Overdraft | 300 | 660 |
| Income Tax Payable | 300 | 320 |
| Dividends Payable | 100 | 100 |
| | 1,700 | 2,280 |

*Long-Term Liabilities*

| | | |
|---|---|---|
| Debentures | 2,000 | 2,000 |

*Shareholders' Equity*

| | | |
|---|---|---|
| Paid-up Capital ($1 Shares) | 2,000 | 2,000 |
| General Reserve | 1,000 | 1,000 |
| Retained Earnings | 300 | 520 |
| | 3,300 | 3,520 |
| | $7,000 | $7,800 |

*Additional Data:*

i.   Inventories on hand 1 January 19X6, $2,000,000.

ii.  All sales are made on thirty days credit terms.

iii. Company policy is to provide for bad debts only when they are declared to be bad. No bad debts were recognized in the two years.

iv.  The premises were recently revalued by the Valuer-General at $10,000,000 for rating purposes.

v.   The company's share price has remained around $1.50 throughout 19X7; and it has exhibited no significant growth for several years.

vi.  In their report for the year, the directors have commented favourably on the company's progress over the year in terms of the growth in sales, net profits, and return on paid-up capital.

vii. The industry norm for inventory turnover rates is six times a year.

As an investment analyst, you are asked to prepare a report on the company's profit performance, financial position, and financial policy for the two years. In your report, refer to the directors' report analysis.

33. The final accounting reports, prepared according to the pure historic cost system and the real value system, of the Gog Magog Corporation Limited, are shown below:

*Income Statements for the Year Ended 31 December 19X5*

| | Historic Cost | Real Value |
|---|---|---|
| | $ | $ |
| Sales | 58,500,000 | 58,500,000 |
| Less Cost of Goods Sold | 42,000,000 | 42,900,000 |
| Gross Profit | 16,500,000 | 15,600,000 |
| Less Depreciation | 460,000 | 575,000 |
| Other Operating Expenses | 12,040,000 | 12,040,000 |
| | 12,500,000 | 12,615,000 |
| Net Income | 4,000,000 | 2,985,000 |
| Less Income Tax 40% | 1,600,000 | 1,600,000 |
| Net Income after Tax | 2,400,000 | 1,385,000 |
| Less Price Level Loss on Net Monetary Assets | | 344,000 |
| Real Income | | 1,041,000 |
| Less Dividends | 1,400,000 | 1,400,000 |
| Income Retained | $1,000,000 | $ (359,000) |

*Balance Sheets as at 31 December 19X5*

| | Historic Cost | | Real Value | |
|---|---|---|---|---|
| | $ | | $ | |
| *Current Assets* | | | | |
| Cash | 1,700,000 | | 1,700,000 | |
| Debtors | 7,600,000 | | 7,600,000 | |
| Merchandise Inventories | 8,400,000 | 17,700,000 | 8,400,000 | 17,700,000 |
| *Long-Term Assets* | | | | |
| Plant and Equipment | 2,400,000 | | 3,000,000 | |
| Less Accumulated Depreciation | 1,300,000 | | 1,625,000 | |
| | 1,100,000 | | 1,375,000 | |
| Buildings | 4,000,000 | | 5,000,000 | |
| Less Accumulated Depreciation | 2,800,000 | | 3,500,000 | |
| | 1,200,000 | | 1,500,000 | |
| Land | 5,000,000 | 7,300,000 | 11,000,000 | 13,875,000 |
| | | $25,000,000 | | $31,575,000 |
| *Current Liabilities* | | | | |
| Creditors | 3,200,000 | | 3,200,000 | |
| Tax Payable | 1,600,000 | | 1,600,000 | |
| Dividends Payable | 1,400,000 | 6,200,000 | 1,400,000 | 6,200,000 |

*Shareholders' Equity*

| | | | | | |
|---|---|---|---|---|---|
| Paid-up Capital | | | | | |
| (15m. Shares) | 15,000,000 | | 15,000,000 | | |
| General Reserves | 2,000,000 | | 2,000,000 | | |
| Retained earnings, | | | | | |
| 1 Jan. | 800,000 | | (780,000) | | |
| Income Retained for | | | | | |
| Year | 1,000,000 | | (359,000) | | |
| Price-Level | | | | | |
| Adjustment, 1 Jan. | — | | 3,400,000 | | |
| Price-Level | | | | | |
| Adjustment for | | | | | |
| Year | — | | 2,200,000 | | |
| Real Holding Gains, | | | | | |
| 1 Jan. | — | | 2,614,000 | | |
| Real Holding Gains, | | | | | |
| for Year | — | 18,800,000 | 1,300,000 | 25,375,000 | |
| | | $25,000,000 | | $31,575,000 | |

*Additional Data:*

i.   Share price 31 December 19X5, $1.20. The share price has fluctuated around this figure throughout the year.

ii.  The general price level has increased by 10 per cent over the year. This is a much higher rate than has been experienced in recent years.

iii. The price-level adjustments and real holding gains for the year are shown in the reports.

*Required:*

Prepare a report for the directors appraising the financial performance and position of the corporation. In the report pay particular attention to the effects of inflation and increasing asset prices on the corporation.

34. As an investment analyst, you are asked to analyze the published reports of several prominent companies in each of the merchandise retailing, manufacturing, and finance industries. Consider the reports in terms of the standards for accounting information and guidelines for the communication of information for investors. Pay particular attention to the presentation of the reports (including classification of items and clarity), the meaningfulness of the measures of income and financial position, the methods of financing used by the company, and the behaviour of its share prices. Compare the results of each company in the same industry. Would you recommend the purchase of the shares in one company as against the other?

# Chapter 27
# Overview of Financial Accounting

In this final chapter we shall review the development of the course so as to highlight the general framework of analysis used and the reasons for it, and the major difficulties encountered in obtaining useful financial information.

## THE NATURE OF ACCOUNTING

We began the study by asking what accounting ought to be about, and chose the definition of accounting advocated in *A Statement of Basic Accounting Theory:* accounting is "the process of identifying, measuring and communicating economic information to permit informed judgements and decisions of users of the information". This definition stresses the purpose of accounting and covers the major functional areas of accounting. Several categories of people who require financial information and the reasons for which they require it were examined so as to establish the general objectives of the accounting system. The processes of identifying the information required, measuring it in terms of sales, expenses, income, assets, and so on, and communicating it in financial reports have formed the bulk of the course. Alternative methods of measuring the information were examined and the results assessed according to some standards for accounting information in order to determine which measurement systems provided the "best" information for particular users. The accountant has a fundamental role to play in the firm's financial information system because he controls the transformation system from the raw data input stage to the financial information output stage, and frequently designs the whole system as well. In order to perform this function effectively, he must understand the raw data inputs and the information output requirements so that the system can effectively convert the one into the other.

The primary input for the information system comprises the transaction data. Transaction data merely show what the firm does in its everyday business operations — it buys or hires a wide range of factor inputs and sells finished goods and services to customers. Transactions are recorded in ledger accounts and periodically summarized, so that progress measurements of operations and financial position can be made.

## MAJOR PROBLEMS IN THE TRANSFORMATION PROCESS

However, many difficulties are encountered in transforming these raw transaction data into the appropriate types of financial information required by a wide range of users for many different purposes. The major problems arise from the interrelated sources of time, uncertainty, and changing measurement properties of the dollar; from the complex nature of some of the key concepts being measured; and from the need for information about the future when the basic data all relate to the current and past periods. *Time lags* between purchase, payment, and use of resources give rise to the problems of accruals and prepayments; of determining the periodic charges for using up the firm's own resources and the value remaining on hand at the period's end; and of revenue recognition and doubtful debts. They create the need for several sets of reports emphasizing different aspects of operations over time — for reports on cash flow, funds, income, and financial position. The measurement of *periodic* results for income and financial position generally requires that some estimates of future events be made for items such as plant life and the creditworthiness of customers, and these estimates might well be wrong. A further perplexing problem arising from time lags is that the measurement properties of the dollar, and market prices of assets, change over time. The accountant has to be careful in defining precisely what attributes of the dollar he is concerned with in his measurement processes, and he must adhere rigidly to these attributes and not mix them up, otherwise the reports may not be meaningful. Because asset values and the measurement properties of the dollar typically change over time, several measures of income and financial position for the same period can be prepared. Only in highly unrealistic conditions is a unique measure of periodic profit and financial position possible. The choice between the reports has then to be based on which measurement system is most appropriate to the financial information needs of users.

The complex nature of some of the key concepts measured adds to the difficulties. Wealth, financial position, income, and capital maintenance are difficult concepts in the typical business environment, and they have been the subject of controversy for several hundred years at least. Various sets of concepts were examined and, while there is general agreement about the basic nature of income as the gain in wealth over a period, and financial position as a measure of wealth, there are many thorny problems encountered in the valuation of assets and liabilities, the treatment of abnormal items, the role of expectations in determining values, the treatment of inflation, and the role of realization in recognizing value changes.

The final problem in providing useful financial information occurs because all decision-making by creditors, investors, and management of necessity requires information about the future as well as about the present. Yet *ex post* accounting provides only information about the past and current periods, i.e., it provides only one half the information required. Information about the future can only take the form of estimates and these can range from being highly informed estimates to sheer guesses. It is entirely subjective and *ex ante*. Then, to put this information into a form usable for most decision-making, the effects of time and costs of financing operations over time have to be removed from the present forecasts by converting them into present value equivalents. This can be a tricky operation.

## OUTLINE OF BOOK

We began the study of accounting by examining the requirements of various parties for financial information in order to establish objectives for accounting processes. We saw that accounting is multifunctional and a range of accounting reports tailored to suit the different requirements of users is required; and that, for them to be useful, the reports must satisfy certain standards of quality. Cash flow reports are required to report on the use of cash over the period for purposes of cash control, and cash planning and budgeting by management. Funds statements which summarize the entire financial activities of the firm associated with external transactions over the period are required for stewardship and to assist in long-range forecasting for financial and investment planning. Income statements are required to summarize total operating activity for the period and the net gain in resources from operations. Balance sheets are required to summarize the firm's financial position at a point of time – the value of the resources it owns and its liabilities, and its owners' equity. These two reports are needed for a wide range of stewardship, forecasting, planning, and evaluation purposes by creditors, owners, and management. The basic nature of the firm and its operations were then examined, and techniques for recording transactions were developed.

In Part II, the simplest of the financial information systems – the historic cost measurement system – was developed and appraised according to the information quality standards. Cash flow and funds statements were prepared directly from the transaction data for the period. Various adjustments to the transaction data were necessary for the preparation of periodic income statements and balance sheets to take account of time leads and lags in revenue and expense recognition, and in the measurement of assets and liabilities. All the reports were found to be useful for some purposes, particularly stewardship. However, there were some serious deficiencies in the income statement and balance sheet arising from the omission of changes in asset prices and inflation, in relation to some information requirements. Some modifications made to the pure historic cost system in reality, partly to overcome these limitations and partly because accounting is subject to some powerful external influences, were next examined. It was found that they did not overcome the major limitations of the historic cost system, and in some respects they actually reduced the quality of the information by distorting income measurement and asset valuation and hiding sources of risk to investors.

Alternatives to the historic cost measurement system which aimed at remedying its defects were examined in Part III. Adjustments to the historic cost system to eliminate the effects of inflation on the dollar measuring rod were explained and considered in the constant dollar system. However, while the quality of accounting reports was improved in some respects, they still suffered from many of the limitations of the historic cost reports. The use of current market prices of assets as the basis for measuring income and financial position was then studied. The current value system was found to improve the quality of financial reports substantially when current market prices are readily available, but there are difficulties in obtaining market prices in some cases and the system still neglects the problem of general inflation. The real value system in which account is taken of both inflation and changing asset prices is the most comprehensive alternative to the historic cost system and the one which satisfies the standards for accounting information best for most purposes for which *ex post* information is relevant – the measurement of income and financial position, the formulation of optimum current operating policies, and as a basis for predicting the course of future events. Nevertheless, the real value system is still not a total financial information system because it does not provide sufficient information for decision-making by management and investors and the formulation of long-term policies. Information about the future course of events is required as well for this. In a world of future uncertainty, the future course of events can be notoriously difficult to predict and forecasts must be based in large part on a detailed analysis of recent history. The real value system provides the best basis for forecasting because it reports separately on different aspects of the firm's past operations and market environment – its transactions, changes in asset prices as they occur, and general inflation – and the effects of each on its income and financial position. The forecasts are converted into present values and compared with current values so that rational decisions can be taken. All decision rules about long-term operating policies involve the interaction of current values with present values, of contemporary data with prospective data. In some conditions the current values refer to asset buying prices and in other cases to selling prices. Once the long-term operating decisions are taken, the appropriate long-term financial and dividend policies can be devised.

Finally, various ratios which emphasize different aspects of financial performance over a period, financial position at the end of the period, and risk, were studied so as to provide greater insight into the information contained in the financial reports.

## ECONOMIC THEORY OF THE FIRM

The approach adopted in this accounting course has been based on various parts of economic theory relating to firm behaviour. It involves an integration of parts of the behavioural theory of the firm with the marginal theory. The behavioural theory of the firm is concerned with the analysis of goal formation under conditions of uncertainty, the need for management to learn from experience, the decision-making and forecasting processes used within the firm, and the need for policies to be continually adapted to changing market conditions and prospects. The marginal theory of the firm analyzes the nature of the information required and provides the rules for rational decision-making about economic resources use once sufficiently reliable information about the alternatives is available. The firm is viewed as an economic entity generally controlled by a professional management and operating in an economic environment which is subject to change and uncertainty. It cannot survive unless it makes sufficient profits to attract and retain its share capital. These profits must be adequate in the eyes of the investors to compensate them for the risks involved in advancing their money to the firm. The modern corporation is frequently very large and the providers of risk capital cannot manage its operations so they delegate the management function to full-time executives. The professional management have special legal obligations imposed on them, particularly those of honest stewardship, and they must perform sufficiently well in terms of maintaining liquidity, profits, and financial position to avoid being dislodged from their jobs. Shareholders cannot have access to detailed information about the firm's operations and the law requires that directors inform all shareholders of certain financial matters about the company. They must rely on this published information for their share investment decisions. The firm generally has some long-term commitments arising from its use of long-term debt and investment in illiquid fixed assets, and management must formulate many of its policies on a long-term basis. Generally management will endeavour to maintain the firm as an effective going concern so that it can at least survive for long enough to recoup outlays on fixed assets and make a profit and protect its own employment. In addition to the maintenance of its physical and financial capacity, this requirement has other implications as well, such as the preservation of its staff, market shares, and customer and supplier relationships. The safest goal for management to adopt, subject to the constraints imposed by the law and competitors, is to maximize its share market value as this goal protects their own jobs, makes new finance for expansion easier to raise, maximizes profitable growth of the firm, protects it from unwanted takeover bids, reduces the effect of mistaken forecasts, and so on. But this goal requires that management adopt optimal investment and financial policies, produce wanted products efficiently, and so forth, and for this it must have good quality information on the firm's activities and its prospects. The environment in which the firm operates is subject to change — changes in technology, products, factor prices, product prices, and so on; and to uncertainty of the future course of market events. Information which highlights the need for change and which enables the greater confidence in forecasts of the future is invaluable to management in all aspects of policy formulation and control as it minimizes mistakes and encourages management to keep on adapting policies and operations to conform with changing conditions. Management must keep on learning from its experience and adapt the firm's operations and goals appropriately.

The accounting system must be designed to provide management with useful information; otherwise management cannot hope to perform its complex functions effectively. Any information is required which improves their forecasting ability and indicates the need for closer control of operations, for the revision of goals and forecasts, for adaptation in operations, for more cash, and so on. Periodically, the firm's profit performance and financial position must be measured as accurately as possible in the light of current market conditions, so that management can see how far its goals are being achieved and how much subjective goodwill has been converted into actual assets, to assist in further forecasts and long-range planning, and to assist in the formulation of its various operating, financial, and dividend policies. Periodic measurements, but not necessarily of the same type, must also be taken to satisfy the various statutory requirements. Essentially, management requires all the data contained in the real value and present value systems for its own use, and all that in historic cost reports for statutory purposes.

Shareholders, as the owners of the firm and the providers of its risk capital, require reliable information on the firm's profit performance and financial position in real value terms, and on the risks incurred by the firm. They must decide whether their investments are worth maintaining in the firm and they must be provided with sufficient information to make informed forecasts of its future performance so as to judge whether the prospective returns compensate them adequately for the risks undertaken. Although the present value reports of management would appear to be the obvious information for them, publication of these reports is not practicable at the current time (because of their subjective and confidential nature) and shareholders should make their own judgments of the future prospects and risks involved in their investments. They provide the risk capital to the firm and bear the risks from its future operations. It is investors who value the whole firm (but not its assets) as a going concern through determining its share prices, and management requires this information for planning purposes if its goals include share price maximization. Policies which should increase the share market value are the ones to be adopted while those which could reduce it should be rejected. There would be circularity of reasoning if investors were to be provided with, and adopt, management's own assessments of future prospects, as summarized in present value data. Management must adapt its policies to suit capital market conditions and these include investors' willingness to buy shares and take risks. Investors stand to gain or lose from the firm's future operations and they must bear the ultimate responsibility for risk-taking. Nevertheless, shareholders could be provided with far more relevant information than they now obtain, both about the company's past operations and its goals and general policies for the future, to assist them in their role.

It can therefore be appreciated that the modern corporation and its operations are very complex matters, and the accounting system required is necessarily complex and versatile. A range of accounting reports — income, cash flow, funds, and financial position — are required, and several systems of valuation are necessary (but they must not be mixed), and both *ex post* and *ex ante* reports are required. No one set of reports can satisfy all the functions of accounting data. There can be no unique measures of periodic income and financial position in realistic conditions, and all measures of periodic results are based on some assumptions and estimates. Only a few of the basic complexities of accounting have been covered in this course; there are still many more remaining in, for example, the areas of manufacturing and mining operations, government accounting, and the accounting for conglomerate and multinational enterprises. Moreover, the analysis conducted here is inevitably an unfinished story because a continually changing business environment throws up new problems for accounting.

## ACCOUNTING METHODOLOGY

Finally, it is worth recalling the methodology adopted throughout the development of this book. Most accounting theory to date has been built up from current practice and has served to justify and rationalize it. However, the theory has not been particularly successful in reducing the number of conflicting and roundabout practices adopted, in providing a logical analysis of problems and solutions of them, in making accounting useful or in handling new problems. The alternative approach of developing a systematic framework of analysis has been adopted here because it promises to be a more fruitful one in an area as complex as accounting. A theoretical approach is necessary to develop the processes by which the objectives of accounting can be achieved from the mass of transaction and market data. It is the route map of accounting developed according to an ends-means-constraints framework of analysis which cuts off all irrelevant and trivial sidetracks. A theoretical approach concentrates on what ought to be done and in this way it provides a valuable standard by which to assess and if necessary improve existing practices. It is required to give accounting the discipline which it currently lacks.

After defining accounting in terms of its being a financial information system, the objectives of accounting were examined (i.e., to provide good quality information to various users), and the processes by which this information could be provided were studied. This involved an examination of the information requirements of users; the definition of all key concepts (income, financial position, etc.), specification of simplifying assumptions (going concern, accounting period, point of revenue recognition, and so on); the derivation of rules to record transactions (debit inflows to the firm and credit outflows); and the specification of dollar measurement properties to form a coherent theory of income and financial position determination. Several theories of income and financial position were examined in turn, and each was assessed according to the objectives of accounting as providing good-quality information to users. Rules covering the detailed procedures for applying each theory were readily devised. The need for consistency in using the measurement properties of the dollar and asset valuation bases was stressed so that meaningful measures of income and financial position could be obtained. The many problems which have plagued the profession for generations — inventory valuation, bad debts, depreciation, goodwill, and so on — were analyzed in the context of theories of income and financial position determination rather than as a series of seemingly unrelated problems, and solutions to them were obtained.

The only major gap in the development of the theories expounded in this book relates to their application in practice and in determining whether they represent an improvement on traditional practices. This of course cannot be done in the classroom. However, the author believes that many progressive companies already apply to some extent most of the suggestions contained herein in their own internal accounting systems. Unfortunately they regard this information as confidential so that it is difficult to judge the extent to which such practices represent improvements over traditional ones.

The development of a scientific approach to accounting appears to be the major means by which the profession can solve the host of problems facing it. The traditional approach has had a long run without bringing much success, and it is now time to try the analytical approach.

# APPENDIXES

APPENDIXES

# Appendix 1
# Some Principles of Prudent Financial Management

An understanding of some of the principles of sound financial management is necessary for informed interpretation of financial reports. Companies invariably raise finance from a variety of sources so as to spread financial risks and repayment dates and to raise funds in the cheapest way possible. It is crucial for a company's continued existence that its financial structure is efficient and is appropriate for the economic characteristics of its operations. A company is said to have an *optimum financial structure* when its overall financing costs are minimized and its sources of finance exhibit risk characteristics similar to those of its income stream and asset structure.

In determining an optimum financial structure, regard must be had to the objectives of the company, economic conditions in the capital market, and the company's own economic characteristics.

## COMPANY OBJECTIVES

It is generally advocated that a company's ultimate objective should be to maximize the economic well-being of its owners, and that the maximization of share prices is one method of achieving this. Share price maximization requires that it maximize profits, produce efficiently, optimize its financial structure, and a few other things. As well as benefiting shareholders, the objective is in the company's best interests as it enables the company to raise finance more easily, and it facilitates takeovers by the company itself but discourages other companies from trying to take it over except at a high price.

## CAPITAL MARKET CONDITIONS

Economic and legal factors at work in the capital market, i.e., the market in which companies obtain their funds, must be considered in arranging a company's financial structure. These factors determine the supply of each type of funds available and their costs. Moreover, large companies must consider foreign capital markets as well as the domestic one as it can be cheaper for them to raise finance overseas.

In general, the cost of finance varies inversely with its risk and time of repayment. The cost of finance is measured by the yield (or the effective rate of interest) on that finance. The greater the security afforded to a creditor, the cheaper the finance is; the greater the risk undertaken by a provider of finance, the dearer the finance is.

Similarly, loans repayable in the short run carry low rates of interest, whereas long-term loans require a higher rate of interest. Equity capital is the riskiest form to investors and requires the highest yield; conversely, it is the safest for the company and the most expensive source of finance. The index of security to the lender is the measure of risk to the company in the case of long-term finance. A very general ranking of funds according to their repayment dates, risks, and costs is given in Figure A. 1−1.

| Type of Finance: | Repayment Date | Risk to Lender | Risk to Company | Cost to Company |
|---|---|---|---|---|
| Trade Credit | Soon | Low | Low | Negligible |
| Bank Overdraft | | | | |
| Unsecured Loan | | | | |
| Secured Loans and | | | | |
| Debentures etc. | | | High | |
| Ordinary Equity | Never | High | Safe | Expensive |

**Figure A. 1−1.** Ranking of funds

The relative costs of finance are further affected by income tax laws. Interest payments on debt finance are deductible from revenue in determining taxable income, whereas dividend payments are not. Hence, for a profitable company which pays income tax the effective cost of debt finance is the after-tax cost i.e., $(1 - t) r$, where $t$ is the company tax rate and $r$ is the rate of interest. For example, the after-tax cost of 10 per cent debentures is only 6 per cent where the company tax rate is 40 per cent on profits. The tax law provides a strong incentive for companies to use as much debt finance as is consistent with financial security in order to minimize overall financing costs.

Inflation likewise affects the relative costs of finance by lowering the real costs of long-term debt finance.

The capital market comprises many types of investors. Some want secure returns of income and capital; others are prepared to take risks in return for a higher rate of return; others are prepared to lend money for a short period only, while others want to invest their funds on a long-term basis. A company can take advantage of this diversity of investors' interests by splitting up its business operating risks into various segments and by raising its finance according to various maturity terms. One measure of business operating risk is given by the volatility of its stream of earnings before interest and taxes. By giving secured creditors prior rights to the payment of interest and repayment of the principal sum ahead of other creditors and shareholders, the company shifts their share of risk to unsecured creditors and to shareholders. Secondly, by giving unsecured creditors rights to interest payments and principal repayment ahead of shareholders, their risks are again transferred to shareholders. Thus by giving prior rights to outside providers of finance, the entire business operating risks can be transferred to shareholders. However, equity investors want to bear these risks as they are the providers of risk capital. This additional risk resulting from the financial structure of the company is called financial risk, and one measure of it is the volatility of the earnings available for ordinary shareholders. Shareholders require an additional return as compensation for this added risk. The degree of risk inherent in a company's shares is indicated by the yield on its shares – high risks require a high yield, and low yields indicate fairly safe shares.

## COMPANY CHARACTERISTICS

A company's financial structure should contain a mix of finance such that it is consistent with:

1. The size and stability of its income stream (EBIT)
2. Its asset structure and the liquidity of its assets
3. Retention of control by the existing owners.

### Income Stream

Where the income stream is unstable, interest costs should not exceed profits before interest and taxes in lean years. Creditors (particularly secured creditors) may have the right and ability to terminate the company's life in the event of non-payment of interest payments in a year of loss. A company's credit standing is likely to be very low in such a period and additional borrowing might be impossible. Fixed interest commitments should be avoided where losses are likely. On the other hand, companies with stable income streams can safely use a relatively high proportion of fixed interest finance. A measure of gearing in the income stream (i.e., the proportion of fixed financial charges in it) is given by the times-interest-earned and fixed financial charges ratios. A company with an unstable income stream should avoid much gearing in its income stream, whereas one with a stable stream can have a highly geared income stream. The diagrams in Figures A. 1–2 and A 1 –3 illustrate the situation.

The incentive for companies to use debt finance arises from its cheapness – its use reduces overall financing costs. But against this, every increase in the gearing transfers more risk to shareholders and increases the risk of bankruptcy. The company must be prepared to trade off some risk for continuing profits. Increases in gearing increase

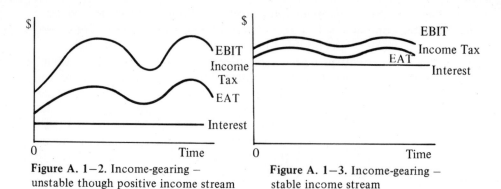

**Figure A. 1–2.** Income-gearing – unstable though positive income stream

**Figure A. 1–3.** Income-gearing – stable income stream

earnings per share (so long as the debt funds earn a rate of profit exceeding the after-tax interest cost) and likewise other shareholder profitability measures, and, other things being equal, this increases the share price. But conversely the risk to the earnings per share is increased and this reduces the quality of the earnings stream, raises the discount rate, and depresses the share price. The company should endeavour to balance the two opposing forces so as to maximize share prices.

The use of debt finance is often called "trading on the equity" and its effects on earnings per share should be determined. For example, a company may consider using two different financial structures. In situation A it uses equity finance only, whereas in B one-half of its finance is provided by 8 per cent debentures. The company tax rate is 40 per cent of net profit after interest. The shares are $1 each.

| | A $ | B $ |
|---|---|---|
| Total debt | — | 500,000 |
| Total equity | 1,000,000 | 500,000 |
| Total funds | $1,000,000 | $1,000,000 |
| | | |
| Earnings before interest and tax | 200,000 | 200,000 |
| Interest | — | 40,000 |
| Net profit before tax | 200,000 | 160,000 |
| Tax 40% | 80,000 | 64,000 |
| Net profit after tax | 120,000 | 96,000 |
| Earnings per share | $\dfrac{120,000}{1,000,000} = 12\text{c}.$ | $\dfrac{96,000}{500,000} = 19.2\text{c}.$ |

The effects on EPS of increasing the proportion of debt finance in a company's financial structure are illustrated in Figure A.1–4.

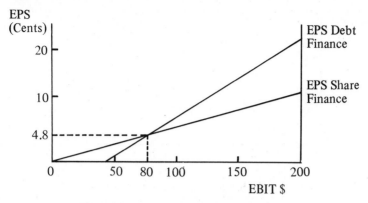

Figure A.1—4. Earnings per share chart

The EPS Debt function shows EPS for each level of EBIT from $0 to $200,000 if debentures are used to finance the company's operations. The EPS Equity function shows the EPS for each level of EBIT over the same range if equity finance is used. If EBIT is only $40,000, then EPS are zero if debentures are issued — the entire EBIT is absorbed by interest payments and no tax is payable. The EPS are equal at 4.8 cents whether debt or equity finance is used where EBIT is $80,000 — this is the break-even point on EPS. Below EBIT of $80,000, the use of debt finance depresses EPS, while above it EPS are raised. A company should only use debt finance in the range of EBIT wherein EPS are raised by its use. However, it should not aim to maximize EPS as this may increase the risk to shareholders to an excessive degree. Rather, it should use debt finance only up to that point at which the increase in EPS no longer raises share prices. The determination of this optimum is not, however, a simple matter.

The increasing financial risk borne by the shareholders because of higher gearing in the income stream can be indicated by the coefficient of variation. If, in the above example, the standard deviation in the EBIT stream is $50,000, the coefficients of variation in the earnings available for shareholders in each situation are:

$$VA \quad \frac{50,000}{120,000} = .42$$

$$VB \quad \frac{50,000}{96,000} = .52$$

Since the standard deviation in EBIT is the same for both situations, the relative dispersion in earnings available for ordinary shareholders is greater in B. Figure A.1—5 illustrates the probability distributions for each situation.

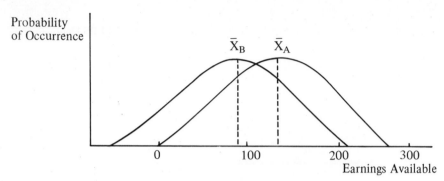

**Figure A.1—5.** Probability distributions of earnings available

### Asset Structure

It is desirable that the sources of finance suit the liquidity and risks involved in the company's assets. The liquidity of assets is determined by the rate at which they are converted into cash, while their risks are indicated by the potential for capital losses, e.g., as indicated by the ratio of their current replacement costs (for assets used in the business) or historical costs (for monetary assets and securities) to their current selling price. A high ratio signifies that the investment in such assets is risky.

Although current assets are in a continuous cycle of conversion into cash, those forming the minimum desired level of working capital must be continually replaced. The funds invested in them cannot be used for other purposes such as debt repayment without affecting the daily operations of the company. On the other hand, cash received from current assets which are above the minimum base level are available for general use and can be used for debt repayment. Such assets are self-liquidating. Long-term assets are not normally self-liquidating and outlays on them must be recouped gradually over time from the cash surpluses generated from operations. Apart from temporary current assets, then, it is desirable to finance the "permanent" level of current assets and long-term assets from long-term sources so as to avoid recurring repayment problems. Short-term sources of finance are generally cheap but they must be repaid regularly, and in a time of financial stringency this may impose strains on the company. So long as they have been used only to finance temporary current assets required for seasonal peaks of activity, there should be no major problem in repaying short-term debts. For example, a build-up in inventory balances in November in preparation for the Christmas selling period may be financed initially on trade credit. If the merchandise is sold for cash, the cash is then available to pay the suppliers; if sold on short-term credit, a bank overdraft could be used to pay the suppliers and then the overdraft is repaid progressively as customers pay their accounts. The cash is not required to replace the inventories. Long-term sources of finance are dearer but the repayment problem occurs much less frequently (for debt) or never (for equity), and they are appropriate for the financing of working capital assets and fixed assets. Hence the liquidity of assets should help determine the ratio of short-term to long-term funds, i.e., the liquidity of liabilities.

Similarly, where there is significant risk of capital loss on assets in the event of forced liquidation, it is desirable use a higher proportion of risk finance (i.e., equity) than otherwise, so as to minimize any repayment problem.

However, although the use of long-term finance alleviates temporary financing problems, it is not appropriate to use such finance only. Long-term finance is more expensive than short-term finance, and excessive use of it reduces earnings per share and the rate of return on equity. As with the use of debt or equity finance, there is again the need for some trade-off in the financial structure between long-term financial security (facilitated by the use of long-term funds) and profits (facilitated by the use of cheap short-term funds). The short-term — long-term financing situation can be illustrated as in Figure A.1−6.

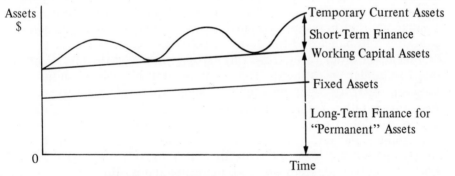

**Figure A.1−6.** Financial structure analysis

The ratios relevant for the analysis of asset structure comprise the liquidity and financial structure ratios.

### Retention of Control

There is a natural desire of existing owners and/or management to retain effective control of the company's operations. Their ability to control the company depends to a large extent on the proportion of finance provided by them. While it would be the normal case that effective control can be maintained if owners contribute more than one-half of the total funds, there are important exceptions to the case, for example in banking, finance, and insurance companies, where a much lower proportion of equity finance suffices.

The ratios relevant for the assessment of shareholder control comprise the financial leverage ratios — proportion of debt to total funds, proprietorship to total funds, times interest earned, and fixed financial charges ratios — and to a lesser extent, the liquidity ratios. The balance sheet ratios indicate the asset cover provided for creditors and hence their security. So long as creditors are paid interest on time and repaid on maturity, they have no legal powers to interfere in the operations of the company. But, if the company should default in its payments at any time, then they may have very extensive powers of interference. Secured creditors in particular generally have the legal right to assume complete control of the company and they can wind it up if they so desire. The income statement ratios indicate the ability to meet fixed financial commitments from current revenue, or the income cover for creditors. The liquidity ratios indicate whether the issue of creditors' interference will ever arise — so long as the company always remains sufficiently liquid to meet its debts, creditors cannot intervene.

The retention of control is obviously closely related to the characteristics of the company's income stream and the effects of the use of debt finance on the division of that stream between creditors and shareholders.

Again, in considering the optimum ratio of debt to total funds, there is some conflict between maximizing ownership control by the owners' providing all finance and the desire to use some cheaper external sources of finance in order to increase earnings per share and the rate of return on shareholder investment. The company must reach a compromise between security and profitability such that its share prices are maximized. Other things being equal, a company can use a higher proportion of debt finance than otherwise, if its income stream is healthy and stable, its fixed assets are readily realizable without risk of substantial capital losses, and its liabilities are dispersed with respect both to individual creditors and maturing dates. But, if its income stream and asset structure are risky, then it should minimize its use of debt finance.

## FURTHER READING

Peirson, G., and Bird, R. *Business Finance*. Sydney: McGraw-Hill, 1972. Chap. 17.

# Appendix 2
# Some Empirical Data

Some examples of accounting practices adopted by prominent Australian companies in recent years are given in this Appendix. They serve to illustrate many of the issues raised in the determination of periodic income and financial position, and the diversity of current practice. They illustrate inadequacies in accounting for doubtful debts and in the preparation of consolidated financial reports; the different approaches adopted in the treatment of items as income or capital gains; and the valuation of assets. The examples should not be construed as meaning that the company concerned is "good" or "bad" for adopting the particular practice.

The examples relating to Reid Murray Holdings Limited are taken from the report of the Australian Society of Accountants on "Accounting Principles and Practices Discussed in Reports on Company Failures" (January 1966). The other examples are taken from financial press comments on the annual reports of the companies concerned, on information released by companies as a consequence of takeover battles, and from the annual reports of companies. Many of these battles revolved around questions of the "true" values of companies and their assets (particularly real estate investments), and directors frequently issued information about the current market prices of their assets and profits which were at variance with the information given in their annual reports. The names of the particular newspapers are not cited in each case as similar information was generally given in several papers at about the same time. The papers used were the *Australian Financial Review*, the *Sydney Morning Herald*, and the *Australian*.

The classification of subject areas is somewhat arbitrary as many of the illustrations relate to several topics simultaneously — for example, all matters of asset valuation affect profit determination.

## PERIODIC INCOME DETERMINATION

*Reid Murray Holdings Ltd.*

The Reid Murray group of companies, engaged in a wide range of merchandise retailing, electrical appliance retailing, land development and house-building, and finance activities, collapsed in 1961—62 and incurred substantial losses. An official investigation into the affairs of the company revealed many inadequate accounting practices. In particular, the absence of adequate provisions for doubtful debts on hire-purchase sales (combined with the lack of good credit control) caused substantial overstatement of profits and debtors. In some cases where provisions were made they were shown in the appropriation statement so as not to reduce disclosed profit. Other incorrect asset valuations and profit overstatements were caused by excessive capitalization of interest, administration, and development costs into the cost of land held for subdivision; and by showing losses as assets. Profit on the sale of houses was recorded before the houses were built. Some known liabilities were not recorded, borrowed money was treated as revenue and repayments as expenses, no liability was recognized until a repayment was made to the lender, and contingent liabilities were not disclosed. Consolidation practices were highly deficient, and instances were found of the inclusion in consolidated net profits of pre-acquisition profits of subsidiary companies, profits earned by subsidiaries after the parent company's balance date; the extent of intercompany shareholdings was not always disclosed; intercompany transactions were not always recorded by both companies; and subsidiary company debts were included with customers' debts.

### H. G. Palmer (Consolidated) Ltd.                              13 December 1967

The company, a major retailer of domestic appliances, crashed in October 1965, at which stage it had liabilities to debenture holders of $41.7m. and to creditors of $18.8m. By March 1972 its accumulated losses had grown to $53.5m. The entire shareholders' funds of $18.6m. had been lost, creditors were not repaid anything, and debenture holders were repaid about 87.5 cents in the dollar. The major part of the operating losses consisted of bad debts resulting from poor credit control. Inadequate allowances had been made for doubtful debts during its period of operations.

### Rothmans of Pall Mall (Australia) Ltd.                        4 February 1971

The half-yearly profit for December 1970, which grew by almost 19 per cent over the previous second half-year profit, was determined after charging the costs of developing new brands of cigarettes and after a special provision (net after tax) of $400,000 for future sales promotion expenditure. Directors say this provision is available to minimize fluctuations in future profits whenever there may be exceptional expenditures on brand promotions.

### Martin Corporation Ltd.                                      11 December 1971

The company, a merchant bank, reported a loss of $3.6m. for the fourteen months ended 31 August 1971. The figure included the reduction in the value of its portfolio investments of $3.4m. All investments at balance date were valued at the lowest of cost, market value, or directors' valuation. Losses recognized included an investment of $1,327,299 in a mining company written down to the directors' valuation of $1; a loss of $1,049,374 on the sales of listed securities; $802.053 representing the write-down from cost to market value of listed investments, and $266,867 representing provision for further reduction in market values to 25 November 1971.

### North Broken Hill Ltd.                                       19 October 1971

The company (a large mining and investment company) reported a net profit of

$6.2m. for 1970–71. A profit of $520,808 on the sale of shares was not included in the net profit, but was credited to general reserves. The market value of its investment portfolio dropped by more than $9m. to $52m. over the year.

### *Castlereagh Securities Ltd.*         18 October 1971; 31 March 1972

The 30 June 1971 balance sheet of this mining investment company showed its investment portfolio at cost of $18.8m. The market value of the portfolio was $10.5m. Net profit for the year was stated to be $12,500.

In March 1972 directors announced that they had recognized a reduction in the market value of the portfolio and wrote off $12.9m. against capital on 31 December 1971. This "paper loss" represented almost 70 per cent of the funds raised from a share issue in the previous year. The company reported a loss of $594,594 for the six months.

### *Slater Walker Australia Ltd.*         23 April, 1971; 14 April, 1972

Slater Walker Australia (at one stage known as Austim Ltd.) is a large conglomerate investment company established by a similarly named United Kingdom company. Both companies had grown rapidly from a series of successful takeover bids.

Profit for the year ended 31 December 1970 was reported as $434,000 (compared with $3,806,000 in 1969). The calculation included $961,000 losses on share-trading during the year. It did not include a loss of $954,000 on the sale of former subsidiaries, a loss of $201,000 on the sale of investments, a provision of $200,000 for retiring allowances, other write-offs of $141,000, and a profit on the sale of fixed assets of $578,000. In addition, net tangible assets were written down by $20m. from $44.7m. to $24.9m. As a consequence, net tangible assets per share fell from $1.94 to $1.13, and the company's share price fell from a high of $5.50 in 1970 to around $1 in April 1971.

The following April the company reported growth in net profit to $2m. for the year ended 31 December 1971. The net profit did not include the following items:

1. A loss of $53,000 on extraordinary items

2. The sum of $1,920,000 was written off against reserves for "strategic" investments whose market value had fallen below cost

3. An appreciation of $3,178,000 in the market value of other investments over their cost was reported but not recognized in the accounts

4. Non-trading losses of $4,000,000 were incurred on the sale and/or write down of investments in subsidiary companies. These were charged against a capital loss account.

Shareholders were asked to approve the cancellation of $27.11m. of the share premium reserve no longer represented by available assets. Most of the loss had occurred in previous years. It was stressed that this was a result of a change in the method of accounting and that it would not affect net tangible assets per share.

## ASSET VALUATION

### *The Hydro (Medlow Bath) Ltd.*         12 November 1968

The company operated a guest hotel in a holiday resort near Sydney. The 30 June 1967 balance sheet showed:

|  | $ |
|---|---|
| Freehold Premises (at 1958 valuation) | 368,760 |
| Additions at Cost | 173,687 |
|  | $542,447 |

The Valuer-General's department valued the premises at $275,000. The company does not charge depreciation on buildings for the reasons that profits are rising, the buildings are maintained at a high standard of repair, depreciation is not an allowable tax deduction, and it is not a necessary charge under accepted accounting conventions.

*Bank of New South Wales Ltd.*                                    17 February 1970

The bank, Australia's largest commercial bank, transferred some freehold premises to a subsidiary company, Wales Properties Ltd., so that the latter company could make a debenture issue on the security of the properties for the purpose of expanding the bank's facilities. The current value of the five properties transferred was $33m. The balance sheet value before the transfer of the bank's enormous net work of "premises, sites, furniture and equipment", was shown at $60.7m.

*North Broken Hill Ltd.*                                    26 September 1970

The company announced a three-for-one bonus issue which quadrupled its issued capital from $18.2m. to $72.8m. The bonus issue was "financed" from a $56.8m. revaluation of the company's portfolio investments. Total investments had been shown in the June 1969 balance sheet at the cost figure of $38.9m. This included shares and debentures in listed companies ($21.2m.) and investments in other companies ($17.7m.). The market value of the shares in listed companies at 30 June, 1969 was $56.9m. The company previously made a nine-for-one bonus issue in 1960 which raised its issued capital from $700,000 to $7m.

Directors stated that listed shares had been revalued at two-thirds of their current stock exchange price. They observed that "the Company's investments, under current conditions, have been very conservatively valued and . . . give little indication of the real value of these assets".

The company also revalued its fixed assets by $68.2m. to reflect current replacement costs, and credited the increase to an asset revaluation reserve account.

*Broken Hill Proprietary Company Ltd.*                                    17 August 1968

The fixed assets of the company (a giant steel manufacturer and fabricator) were revalued by $165m. to a figure nearer the current replacement cost of the assets, and the amount was credited to an Asset Revaluation Reserve account. Directors pointed out that the revised asset values were still below current replacement cost because of their limited earning capacity.

In August 1969 the directors announced that the annual revaluation of fixed assets was to become regular policy. Changing replacement costs, asset lives, and technology are taken into account in the revaluation. A "suitable index" is used for the purpose. Depreciation is to be charged on current replacement costs and renamed "fixed asset utilization" charge. The additional charge is credited to a reserve account in shareholders' equity.

*John Lysaght (Australia) Ltd.*                                    8 May 1970

The company, engaged in steel fabrication, announced that fixed assets were revalued from a written-down historical cost of $65.1m. to a written-down replacement cost of $93.7m. The revaluation was made after a survey of assets based on current replacement costs and estimated remaining lives of assets. Depreciation is to be charged on the replacement costs on a straight line basis.

*Tooth and Company Ltd.*                                          6 April 1970

A one-for-two bonus issue (the first since 1955) was announced by the company, a brewery, in April 1970, and a further one-for-one issue was announced in April 1972. This second issue doubled paid-up capital from $32.4m. to $64.9m. Assets were revalued for the purpose of "financing" the bonus issues, and the effective dividend rates were increased on the enlarged capital. Some assets were, however, retained at 1962 valuations. There had been rumours in the sharemarket that a takeover bid might be made by a large overseas brewing group.

*McDonald Industries Ltd.*                                              1971

The company, engaged in the building and construction industry, crashed in 1971. The receivers valued its assets on a going concern basis at $7.7m., and on a forced liquidation basis at $5m.

*Federated Industries Ltd.*                                  18 December 1970

The company, a manufacturer of industrial plant, crashed in 1969 following a substantial loss for the year. Its assets in December 1969 were $16.3m. at cost or book value; they were expected to realize $6.2m. Creditors amounted to $12.9m.

*Rex Aviation Ltd.*                                            16 April 1971

A takeover bid was made for the company, a distributor of light aircraft, after several years of loss operations. The net asset backing per share was 52.5 cents on a going concern basis, and 15 cents on a forced realization basis. The bidder paid 20 cents per share.

## COMPANY TAKEOVERS

*Official Land Valuations in North Sydney Commercial Area*     1 September 1971

Real estate is revalued each five years in the state of New South Wales by the Valuer-General's department for rating purposes. The revaluations are based on current land prices of the time. The following examples illustrate the extent of land price appreciation in part of Sydney.

|        | *Unimproved Capital Values* | | |
|--------|-----------|-----------|------------|
|        | *1966*<br>$ | *1971*<br>$ | *% Increase* |
| Site 1 | 775,000   | 7,150,000 | 920        |
| Site 2 | 245,000   | 1,300,000 | 536        |
| Site 3 | 97,500    | 700,000   | 715        |
| Site 4 | 235,000   | 1,300,000 | 553        |

*Takeover of Drug Houses of Australia Ltd., by Slater, Walker Securities (Australia) Ltd.*                                                       November—December 1968

D.H.A. was an old-established manufacturer and distributor of pharmaceuticals. Slater Walker Securities was a recently established investment conglomerate which had made rapid progress from takeover activities. In November 1968 Slater Walker made a bid worth $27.2m. for D.H.A., the consideration being approximately equal parts of Slater Walker shares and debentures. The bid was worth $2.26 per D.H.A. share at the ruling Slater Walker share price. D.H.A. shares had been trading around $1.80 before the bid. The net tangible assets of D.H.A. were $26.5m. in 1966, and the N.T.A. per share were $2.22. The balance sheet value of its premises was $10.3m., virtually all at 1956 valuation.

D.H.A. directors rejected the bid. Active Slater Walker buying of their shares on the market at around $2.40 each soon gave them majority ownership. D.H.A. directors eventually extracted a higher bid price of about $2.40 for the remaining shares and recommended its acceptance. The final takeover price was about $30m.

The takeover raised the net tangible asset backing of Slater Walker shares by 40 per cent and earnings per share by 30 per cent. During the following year, Slater Walker sold off surplus D.H.A. assets for over $11m. and used the proceeds to repurchase the debentures. A reorganization of the D.H.A. operations enabled its profits to be increased from the much smaller asset base.

*Takeover of Wunderlich Ltd. by Colonial Sugar Refining Co. Limited*
                                                              July—September 1969

The Colonial Sugar Refining Company Ltd., a conglomerate engaged in sugar, mining, chemicals, and building materials industries, made a takeover bid for the old-established building materials company, Wunderlich Ltd., in July 1969. The value of the bid in terms of C.S.R.'s current share price was $17.5m. (or $4.57 per Wunderlich share). Wunderlich's current market value was approximately $10m. (or $2.50 per share). An alternative lower cash bid for $4 per share was made by C.S.R. as well as a combination of the two sets of consideration. Wunderlich had just announced its intention to issue 500,000 shares to Comalco, a large aluminium producer, at $2.20 per share. The net tangible assets of the company were shown at $11m. in its 1969 balance sheet, and N.T.A. per share were $2.64. Its assets included $3.4m. premises at 1955 valuation, $2m. premises at cost, and $11.9m. plant at 1946 book values, plus additions at cost. Wunderlich directors rejected the bid for the reason that it was far too low. They had the company's net tangible assets revalued by professional valuers at $24.3m., and they valued its goodwill at over $7m., and claimed the company was worth over $31m. as a going concern (or nearly $8 per share). They announced a one-for-four bonus issue and promised to maintain the same dividend rate on the increased capital. (This higher dividend payment would have absorbed almost the entire year's disclosed profit.)

The C.S.R. bid succeeded after several months of battle.

*Takeover of The Hotel Metropole Ltd. by Parkes Development Pty. Ltd.*
                                                               June 1968—May 1969

The Hotel Metropole occupied a valuable site in Sydney which led to a series of takeover bids for the site itself and for the company by property development companies. The balance-sheet value of the premises and all equipment was approximately $2.2m., its other net assets were negligible, and profits were stated at around $200,000.

The first bid, worth $4.5m. was made in June 1968 by the Hooker Corporation Limited for the company's shares, and was rejected by directors. This bid valued the site at $175 per square foot. A higher bid, worth more than $5m., was then made. Directors rejected the bid and, in return, made their own successful bid of

$1.7m. for a small motel chain, and made a one-for-four bonus issue. The Hooker bid failed.

In March 1969 two other development companies, Parkes Development Pty. Ltd. and Lend Lease Corporation Ltd., made separate cash bids for the site only, for nearly $6.5m., and promised to provide hotel facilities in a new building elsewhere in the city. These bids valued the site at $230 per square foot, and caused the share price to rise to around $4.15 and the total share market value of the company to $8m. Again, the directors rejected the bids. The company's rate of profit on this value for the hotel site would have been reduced to 3.6 per cent.

In May, Lend Lease Corporation made a new bid for all shares in the company at $4.15 per share, worth $8m. in total. This left the site valued at about $6.5m. in the bid. Directors again rejected the bid and shortly afterwards another bid from Parkes Development was received for $4.40 per share. This bid valued the company at $8.36m. and the site at $7m. (or $252 per square foot). No provision was to be made for hotel facilities in the new bid. Directors recommended the new bid, and it succeeded.

### Takeover of Angus and Robertson Ltd. by IPEC Insurance Company Ltd.
June 1970

A successful takeover bid was made by IPEC Insurance Company, an investment and operating conglomerate, for the old-established and ailing publishing and bookselling firm of Angus and Robertson Ltd. The bid comprised $3.8m. cash, plus 1,282,640 shares in IPEC. The Angus and Robertson share price was around $1.60, but the IPEC share price was difficult to establish as there had been no trading in its shares for some time. There were sellers of the shares at $2.80 but no buyers. At this price the total bid would be worth somewhat less than $7.4m., and the offer price less than $1.85 per Angus and Robertson share. Directors recommended the bid.

By December, IPEC had partly reorganized the business and sold off three city properties for over $3m., reputedly at a large profit. Many valuable properties were still retained by the company. Profits and sales of the bookselling business rose in the following year.

### Takeover of Mark Foys Ltd. by McDowells Ltd.
February—May 1968

McDowells, a Sydney retailer, made a successful cash bid of $4.5m. for the shares of Mark Foys, an ailing competitor. The book value of the Mark Foys real estate was shown at about $2m. (at 1962 valuations, plus additions at cost), and net assets at $3.3m. The premises had been valued, just before the takeover bid was made, at almost $7m. but the directors did not divulge this information to shareholders until after the bid (which they recommended) was successful. McDowells sold the major properties shortly afterwards and made a profit of nearly $3m. (stated as a capital profit of $1.75m after deducting $1.2m. paid in excess of book value for the shares and other expenses involved in the takeover).

### Attempted Takeover of McDowells Ltd.
June 1970

An unsuccessful takeover bid was made for all McDowells' shares for $1.60 cash. The total bid was worth $6.24m. McDowells share price was around $1.20, and net tangible asset backing $1.87. Directors rejected the bid and claimed the company was worth at least $11.7m., or $3 per share. They disclosed that the company's main city site had been valued recently at $8m. In the following month the company announced that it had sold the city site for about $9m., that it was returning $5.8m. cash to shareholders (equivalent to three times the par value of their shares), and retaining $3m. to finance expansion in suburban retailing.

*Takeover of McDowells Ltd. by Waltons Ltd.*                November–December 1971

A series of takeover bids for McDowells was initiated in November by another Sydney-based retailer, Waltons. McDowells had made a highly profitable takeover of Mark Foy's Limited in 1970, sold its own city property for a substantial profit, relocated its retailing in less expensive suburban areas, and returned $5.8m. to shareholders. Its sales and profits increased substantially in 1971 (22 per cent and 39 per cent respectively). Its share price was currently around $1.50 and its net tangible assets per share were $2.83 (at current values). Waltons initial bid was worth $4.75m., or $2.04 per McDowell share on Waltons' current share price of $1.14. The offer comprised 90 cents cash plus one Walton share for each McDowell share.

The following week another large Sydney-based retailer, David Jones Ltd., made a counter bid worth $5.18m. for McDowells.

Waltons quickly retaliated with a new bid worth $5.82m. or $2.50 a share, comprising one Walton share plus $1.36 cash for each McDowell share. David Jones followed up with a second counterbid worth $6.20m., in shares and cash. Waltons thereupon raised their own bid to $6.6m., or $2.86 per share, comprising $1.70 in cash and one Walton share. The McDowell directors recommended this bid and it was successful. In less than a month of rivalry the bid price had risen by nearly $2m. up to the current market value of McDowell's net assets.

*Takeover attempt by Concrete Industries (Monier) Ltd., of Rocla Industries Ltd.*
April–June 1972

In April 1972, Monier bid $18.7m. or $2.50 per share (comprising one Monier share plus $1.25 cash) for the entire capital of Rocla Ltd. The companies had complementary interests – Monier being a large manufacturer of building materials and cement products in Australia and the United Kingdom, and Rocla a large manufacturer of concrete and clay pipes in both countries. Monier claimed a merging of their operations would yield substantial operating economies (rationalization of properties and plant, research and development, etc.), and increase profits by $600,000, while the sale of suplus assets would provide funds for expansion. Rocla shareholders would get a substantial capital gain, and 90 per cent increase in income from the takeover. Rocla shares were selling for around $1.83 prior to the bid.

Rocla directors rejected the bid, claiming that it did not reflect the true value of the company. The directors forecast substantially higher profits and dividends for the year, announced a revaluation of assets by $5.3m., and a one-for-one bonus issue, and made their own (unsuccessful) takeover bid for a small company.

Monier countered with a new bid of $21.9m. or $2.93 per share (comprising 1¼ Monier shares plus $1.25 cash). Rocla directors again rejected it and, by late June, Monier had few acceptances so it withdrew the offer.

In August, Rocla announced an 85 per cent increase in profits, and a change in the method of depreciation which reduced the charge. (This probably meant a reversion to historic cost depreciation as the company had been charging depreciation on the current replacement cost of its fixed assets.) Dividends at the rate of 26 per cent on the old capital were to be paid (as against 16 per cent previously).

## CONSOLIDATED REPORTS

*M.L.C. Insurance Company Ltd. and H. G. Palmer Ltd.*                1 May 1969

The M.L.C. Insurance Company Ltd., which had taken over H. G. Palmer in 1963, announced that it had sold its majority interest in the company to two nominee companies for the nominal amount of $4. While the M.L.C. believed that the Palmer shares were valueless, they nevertheless secured an option to repurchase the shares for $1,000, if they so desired. By this process of "deconsolidation", the M.L.C. avoided the requirement to consolidate the enormous losses of Palmers with its own results.

## BALANCE SHEET AND SHARE MARKET VALUATIONS

The following table shows the balance sheet values placed on the net assets of a few prominent companies, and the values placed on these companies as going concerns by investors, as at 30 June 1972.

| Company | Balance Sheet Value of Net Assets | Share Market Value of Company | SMV / BSV |
|---|---|---|---|
| | $ | $ | % |
| Adelaide Steamship Co. Ltd. | 22,170,000 | 20,423,000 | 92 |
| Australian Consolidated Industries Ltd. | 162,283,000 | 170,050,000 | 105 |
| Broken Hill Proprietary Co. Ltd. | 1,103,962,000 | 2,043,000,000 | 185 |
| Cyclone Co. Ltd. | 19,223,000 | 13,234,000 | 69 |
| Conzinc Rio Tinto Ltd. | 362,273,000 | 1,125,170,000 | 311 |
| Henry Jones Ltd. (IXL) | 34,567,000 | 26,023,000 | 75 |
| Myer Emporium Ltd. | 168,350,000 | 303,763,000 | 180 |
| David Jones Ltd. | 97,130,000 | 82,705,000 | 85 |
| Grace Bros. Ltd. | 48,927,000 | 79,530,000 | 163 |
| Woolworths Ltd. | 89,502,000 | 118,778,000 | 133 |

## CURRENT VALUE RESULTS

| | B.P. Co. of Aust. Ltd. | | Shell Aust. Ltd. | |
|---|---|---|---|---|
| | 1974 $m | 1975 $m | 1974 $m | 1975 $m |
| Sales | 522.7 | 652 | 671.3 | 831.8 |
| Expenses | 517.6 | 605.8 | 632.1 | 759.6 |
| Hist. Cost Income b/t | 5.1 | 46.2 | 39.2 | 72.2 |
| Tax | 7.6 | 24 | 23.4 | 37.6 |
| Hist. Cost Income a/t | ( 2.5) | 22.2 | 15.8 | 34.6 |
| Additional current COGS charge | 42.8 | 18.5 | 38 | 21 |
| Additional current Deprecn. charge | 8.3 | 10 | 10 | 10 |
| | 51.1 | 28.5 | 48 | 31 |
| Current Income a/t | ( 53.6) | (6.3) | ($32.2m) | $ 3.6m |
| Add Price Level-Gain on Net Mty. Liabilities | 7 | 8.4 | | |
| Real Income a/t | ($46.6m) | $ 2.1m | | |

Net Assets 31 Dec. 1974 at HC $200.5 m
Net Assets 31 Dec. 1974 at CC $446.5 m

# Appendix 3
# Linear Algebra for Computerized Accounting

**PROLOGUE**

*The Calf-Path*

Sam Walter Foss

Each day a hundred thousand rout
Followed this zigzag calf about
And o'er his crooked journey went
The traffic of a continent.
A hundred thousand men were led
By one calf near three centuries dead.
They followed still his crooked way,
And lost one hundred years a day;
For thus such reverence is lent
To well established precedent.

A moral lesson this might teach
Were I ordained and called to preach;
For men are prone to go it blind
Along the calf-path of the mind,
And work away from sun to sun
To do what other men have done,
They follow in the beaten track,
And out and in, and forth and back.
And still their devious course pursue,
To keep the path that others do.
They keep the path a sacred groove,
Along which all their lives they move;
But how the wise old wood-gods laugh,
Who saw the first primeval calf,
Ah, many things this tale might teach —
But I am not ordained to preach.

*The Calf-Path Revisited*

Deryl Hedley Street

Yet wait! do not all academics preach
Ordained by mottos, "And Gladly Teche"?
And thus ought not to go it blind

Along the calf-path of the mind,
But strive from sun to sun to sun
To do what others have not done.
To seek unbeaten tracks to tread
So that their students might be led
To find new paths by which men move
Towards their sacred destiny —
　　unfettered and ungrooved.
Then would the wise old wood-gods smile
To see the primeval calf's first child,
Born once more from the original womb
Buried by men in a five centuries' tomb;
For thus such reverence is lent
To well established precedent.

Thus will I attempt to undo
The lost one hundred years a day that flew
When a hundred thousand men were led
By that prime calf revered as dead.
For this no mean a task I've used
The recent developments by that womb pursued,
And thereby straighten out the rout
Which followed that zigzag calf about;
And hopefully o'er this journey new
Will move the continental traffic true.
Ah yes, for this bold task was I ordained to preach
And with your help will I gladly teach.

## MATHEMATICS, COMPUTERS, AND ACCOUNTING

When Pacioli (1494) formally introduced the academic and business communities of his day to the techniques of double-entry bookkeeping, he chose as the medium a treatise on mathematics wherein he summarized the most recent advances in the field of mathematics.[1] In this Appendix we demonstrate how one modern advance in mathematics — viz., linear algebra — can be applied in processing accounting data. The flow approach to recording transactions of the firm can be analyzed graphically and applied as a form of linear algebra. The ledger can be formulated as a matrix and this facilitates the conversion of accounting data processing to computers.[2] All financial reports can be quickly prepared by the computer. Furthermore, the computerized accounting system can be integrated with other segments of the firm's management information system to form a "total information system".

The analysis in this Appendix will be restricted to a demonstration of how all the transactions of the firm with its external environment can be recorded and processed and a set of integrated financial reports produced, by applying linear algebra — that is, to what is traditionally known as financial accounting.

First-year accounting students require a logical framework to support their introduction to new ideas. The framework to be used in this Appendix will be taken from a recent article by Professor John E.

Butterworth.[3] This framework is clumsy and time-consuming to use manually on a problem as small as the illustration supplied in this Appendix. However, linear algebra was designed to overcome the problems of size and complexity found in real-world situations.

## INFORMATION FLOWS, COMMUNICATION, AND NETWORKS

In order to make a decision, facts bearing upon the decision are required. These facts are called "information", because they (hopefully) make known something that was previously unknown about the environment in which the decision must be made. The decision-maker ought then be able to reach decisions which will enable him to achieve more quickly the ends being sought.

For example, the information that six apples plus six apples equal twelve apples will enable a decision-maker to determine correctly how many apples to purchase in order to provide two groups of six boys with one apple each. Whenever interaction takes place between two or more people, facts or information may be conveyed from one person to another. This communication may be transmitted in a variety of ways. For example, one person may say to another:

> "Hey! Joe! Did you know that six apples plus six apples equal twelve apples? You did!! A bloody smart bastard aren't you?!"

Alternatively such information may be conveyed by means of a formal written communication such as:

> Dear Sirs,
>     In reply to your written communication of the 7th inst. you are informed that a newly discovered fact, which intelligent decision-makers should use, is that six apples plus six apples equal twelve apples.
>
> > Your Knowledgeable Informer,
> > The Rt. Hon. Cogitatio Cogitationis

Other means of conveying facts, believed to be relevant to the receiver by the sender, are available (e.g., mental telepathy) but are not frequently used in the world of business!

Since facts (which, in their initial impact, may be called knowledge) are the external expressions of the intellectual efforts of rational beings, the minimum requirements needed for the generation and communication of information would appear to be:

1. An ideas man

2. An idea considered worthy to be shared

3. A needy man

4. A means of converting the idea into a form capable of being recognized by the needy man as the idea generated and transmitted by the ideas man

5. A form or method by which the translated idea may be conveyed or transmitted to the needy man and retranslated into the form recognizable by the needy man.

The total activity set out in a highly simplified form above has been given the formal name of an information and communication system. When many ideas and needy men are involved, the activity becomes complexly interlaced like a finely woven filigree pattern. When this happens the communication system may be called a network system.[4]

The economic activities of the firm may be viewed as comprising physical and financial resource flows between the firm and its factor and product markets. The well-defined channels through which such flows take place may be described as the network channel system of the firm. The term "network" is most apt to describe how physical and financial resources flow vertically, horizontally, and diagonally through the various hierarchical levels of responsibility of the firm. Simultaneously with such movements, information concerning the flows is carried as well. It is with one property of such information flows that this Appendix is primarily concerned.

The financial aspect of information flows throughout the communication channel of the firm can be represented very readily (for simple examples) by means of a graph. A graph may be considered to be the arrangement of a given set of points, called nodes, according to some predetermined plan. The plan in the example we are about to discuss will normally be determined by the accountant (who may be called the information processor) in accordance with the information he desires the graph to produce. The shape of the graph is given by the lines, called arcs, joining the various members of this set of points.

Whenever the set of points are arranged in order to direct attention to one particular point, that particular point is called the apex or vertex of the graph. In the case of a graph representing financial information flows through a firm, the vertex of the graph will be the firm itself. The reason for this is twofold. First, the accounting system (and indeed the total information system) of the firm is designed to portray the results of the firm's economic activities for a given period from the point of view of the firm. Second, all flows through the entity have their culmination (or apex) in the provision of information to the entity (or its representatives) to enable correct decisions to be made about future courses of action in market places.

The example of the Westside Retailers Ltd., used to demonstrate the handwritten approach to ledger account recording in chapter 5, is used to illustrate the graphical or network approach to recording financial information flows through an entity.

In Figure A.3—1 each account is a node of the graph and the apex (or vertex) is represented by the entity itself. The income statement is represented as a subsection on the right-hand side of the graph (the "sub-tree"). It is a sub-set of owners' equity for the result of a firm's activities for a period is represented by an increase or decrease in owners' equity (assuming no dividends to or additional contributions from owners).

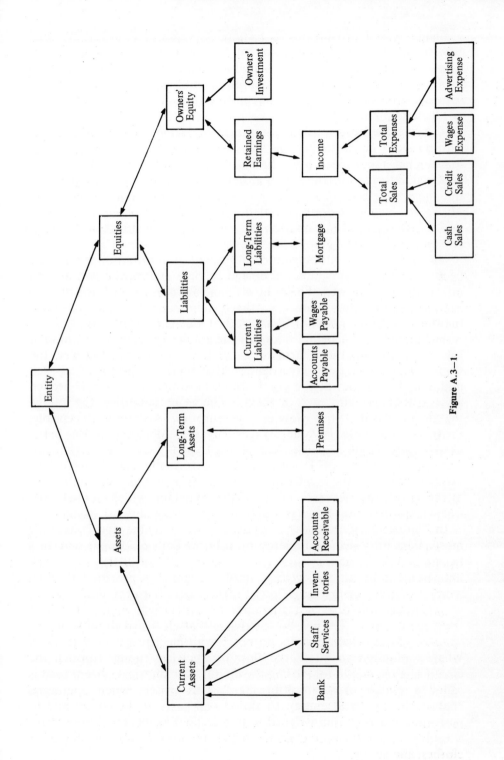

Figure A.3–1.

Figure A.3–1 provides for the complete range of financial information required for the preparation of the balance sheet, income statement, appropriation statement, funds statement, and cash flow statement. Thus the totals of assets, liabilities, and owners' equity are points (or nodes) on the graph even though traditional accounting systems do not include these.

As mentioned previously, ideas (or information) flow from the ideas (information) generator to the ideas (information) receiver. A similar transference takes place when financial information flows. This flow of financial information through and between the various participants of the financial information system is represented in the graph in Figure A.3–1 by means of double-headed arrows. The double-headed arrows imply that financial information may flow in either direction between any two nodes of the graph.

Up to the present, discussion of this financial information system has been in static terms which are devoid of time and movement, and no information has flowed. To see how financial information flows may be initiated within the system (i.e., the system made dynamic), we must first investigate the graph of Figure A.3–1 a little more closely.

The majority of labelled nodes of the graph of Figure A.3–1 have at least two double-headed arrows associated with them. However, the student will notice upon investigation that there is a group of labelled nodes at the bottom of the graph which have only *one* double-headed arrow associated with each of them.[5] The group comprises the following nodes: Bank, Staff Services, Inventories, Accounts Receivable, Premises, Accounts Payable, Wages Payable, Mortgage, Cash Sales, Credit Sales, Wages Expense, Advertising Expense, Owners' Investment. This particular set of labelled nodes is formally called the set of *pendant* nodes (from the Latin, *pendere* = to hang) and the individual members of the set are, in fact, the dynamos which activate the financial information flows through the accounting network system.

In the field of physics, a dynamo is a machine for converting mechanical into electrical energy by rotating coils of copper wire in a magnetic field. Such a conversion, however, is of little use in the improvement of human welfare until a channel is provided through which electrical energy may flow. Furthermore, the provision of a network circuit still does not guarantee that electrical energy will flow from the dynamo. The reason for this is that electrical circuits may be *open* or *closed*. Open circuits do not permit electrical energy to flow. What is required to allow the flow of electrical energy through the circuit is a *technique* for *closing* the circuit. The physical system used is called a switch or a circuit-breaker.[6] This switch, when operating, enables the electrical energy to flow to all parts of the circuit and to perform the many tasks assigned to it, e.g., light an electrical bulb, drive a motor which turns a cylinder which revolves a tub which washes clothes, and so on.

In a similar manner, human energy is converted into ideas, which, in turn, are translated into very many human activities. One of these activities is called, very broadly, commercial activity and enables very many human wants to be satisfied. To ensure that these wants are being satisfied in the desired manner, observation of the results of commercial activity is required.

However, in complex situations direct observation is not feasible, given the time constraints and the finite intellects available. The results of commercial activity must then be *fed back* to the ideas generator in some acceptable manner. The *value* of the information obtained from the feedback will normally be a function of the effort put into setting up a reliable and efficient feedback observation post.[7] This is analogous to the increase in the intensity of light obtained when a cyclist works his pedal-driven dynamo faster.[8] The result (or information) which most succinctly sums up the success or otherwise of commercial activity is the *financial* result. The *channel* through which the financial information flows is the accounting network circuit described in Figure A.3−1. The switch (or circuit-breaker) which closes the network and enables the financial information to flow is a *link* between any two of the *pendant nodes* of the network circuit of this figure. The link is represented by a single-headed arrow and is formally called an *arc*. Further, just as in an electrical circuit (for example, the direct current system of a motor car) the direction of the electrical current traditionally depends upon the red and black wires, so too is the *direction* of the financial information flow given by the *position* of the arrow head between any two pendant nodes.

An example from the Westside Retailers Ltd. will help to make these ideas a little clearer.

In Figure A.3−2 a single-arrow head (an arc) is shown as joining the two pendant nodes, Accounts Payable and Inventories. Since the arrow head is adjacent (next) to the pendant node, Inventories, we may interpret the direction of the financial information flow as being from Accounts Payable to Inventories. Thus, the commercial activity whose financial aspect is being recorded is that of purchasing merchandise (inventories) on credit.

This activity has been initiated between the firm and the outside commercial world. The firm is represented by the pendant node labelled Inventories, and the external participant by the pendant node labelled Accounts Payable. The arc has directed the flow so that a path may be traced from Accounts Payable to Inventories to Current Assets to Total Assets to the vertex of the graph in Figure A.3−2. This flow, in fact, represents the flow of information back to the ideas generator concerning the movement of merchandise into the firm.

As the merchandise was purchased on credit, the supplier of the merchandise was given a financial claim against the firm. The flow of financial information which represents the movement of this claim

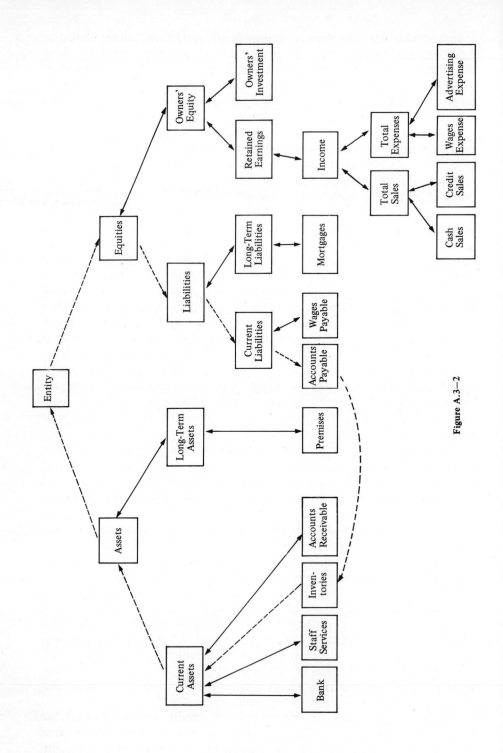

**Figure A.3—2**

from the firm to the supplier of merchandise is traced out by the path from the Entity (or vertex of the graph) to Equities to Liabilities to Current Liabilities to Accounts Payable. In Figure A.3−2 these two paths are illustrated by the broken lines with single arrow heads. Because the flow of financial information may be traced from the pendant node which represents the source of the financial information flow around the network and back to that same pendant node (source), the path traced out is called formally a *loop* (which is obvious upon reflection). This is analogous to the flow of electrical energy through a circuit from its source back to that same source.

As may be quickly realized, very many financial flows may take place through just one loop over a given period of time. Now, because of its finiteness, the human mind attempts to group its experiences according to several common characteristics. It will, therefore, attempt to classify all information in an aggregative or abstract form as often as is practical. This is done in order to minimize the time and effort needed to obtain relevant information concerning the results of some particular activity. For example, the common characteristics of a human being are abstracted and stored by the human mind to enable us to quickly recognize another human being, or, more importantly, to recognize when some being is *not* human. We humans very often base decisions as to future action upon the negative of the facts we need. For example, the decision concerning productive capacity may be based upon the premise that future demand is *not* expected to increase.

Likewise, aggregation of like facts is useful when information concerning absolute size is relevant to a particular decision. (For example, the *total* sales of a firm for period 2 as compared with period 1). One very convenient method for aggregating financial information flows, through the network described in Figure A.3−2, is to assign the symbol + 1 to represent all flows towards the vertex of the graph (or network) from a particular source, the symbol −1 to represent all flows from the vertex of the graph to this same source, and the symbol 0 when financial information flows do not occur.[9]

When it is realized that a loop can be formed between any two pendant nodes of the graph and that hundreds of pendant nodes are possible in a real-life situation, it can be seen that a graphical method of representation is inadequate. An adequate form of representation is available but it entails the use of a branch of mathematics called linear algebra − more specifically, vectors and matrices. As an introduction to these topics the student's knowledge of "sets" will be refreshed.

## SETS

Imagine a field of ripe wheat in which the millions of grains of wheat are identical in all respects and imagine a situation in which the users of the wheat grains have decided that minus quantities of wheat grains and fractions of a wheat grain have no significant or relevant meaning for all practical purposes and may be ignored. Given this collection of definite and well-defined grains of wheat, we may say that in this field we have a *set* of wheat grains. If, next, we label each grain of wheat, we are able to arrange these labelled grains in a definite order. For example, we could take the wheat grains labelled 1 and 2 and arrange them as (1,2). The result of this ordering is that the grain of wheat labelled 1 is placed in the first position (we will assume that the positions are determined from left to right) and the grain of wheat labelled 2 is placed in the second position. This pair of wheat grains is given the formal name, *ordered pair.* (The parentheses indicate that the grains of wheat, or the elements enclosed therein, are ordered.)

Next, assume that we possess another field of wheat in which the grains are identical in all respects with those in the first field. Let us name this field B and the first field A. It would now be possible for us to group together the wheat grain from set A labelled 1 with the wheat grain from set B which is also labelled 1, to form an ordered pair. We could do this with every labelled wheat grain taken from the two sets. For example, we could associate 2 from A with 3 from B to form (2,3). Whenever there exists such a sub-set of ordered pairs taken from the two sets of wheat grains, A and B, the sub-set is given the formal name, *Cartesian Product.*

Now, if we are asked to determine which ordered pairs, taken from the Cartesian Product, makes the following statement (or number sentence) true, viz.,

$x + y = 6$

We could say:

(5,1) where 5 is taken from set A (represented by x)

and 1 is taken from set B (represented by y)

as well as:

(4,2), (3,3), (2,4), (1,5)

These five ordered pairs also form a set of elements (viz., ordered pairs from the Cartesian Product) and are given the formal name, *relation* — because the ordered pairs are related in such a manner as to make the statement: $x + y = 6$, true.

So far we have assumed that every wheat grain in set A is able to be associated (i.e., paired) with every wheat grain in set B. If, however, set A contained more wheat grains than set B, there would be some wheat grains unpaired in set A after the pairing had been carried out. This activity of pairing or associating a grain of wheat from set B with a grain of wheat from set A is given the formal name, *mapping* (because one is able to represent this association in very great detail on a graph). In the first case, where every grain of wheat in set A is associated with every grain of wheat in set B, set B is said to have been *mapped onto* set A. In the latter case, where some wheat grains of set A are left unpaired, set B is said to have been *mapped into* set A.

We could approach this problem of associating the larger field of wheat grains, A, with the smaller field, B, in a slightly different way. We could decide that all the grains of wheat in field B are unique in that there may be associated (i.e., paired) with them *more than* one wheat grain from field A. For example, the wheat grains of set B may be *twice* as large as the wheat grains of set A but identical in all other respects. Whenever we are able to discover a sub-set of ordered pairs in which one or several grains of wheat from field A are associated with *only one* grain of wheat from field B, we may say that a *function* exists. Thus a function is a relation whereby to each wheat grain of set A there is associated a *unique* wheat grain from set B. In other words, a function is, in reality, a rule of mapping which describes the conditions under which the mapping takes place. The uniqueness of a wheat grain from set B is denoted by the number sentence: $y = f(x)$; where the symbol "f" denotes the existence of a function.

To make this a little clearer, note that a grain of wheat depends upon (is a function of) the amount of sun, water, fertilizer, soil, minerals, and time applied. The result is a *unique* grain of wheat. The situation is *not* reversible. Thus the statement that $y = x^2$ *is a function*, because x = +4 or −4 gives $y = 16$. However, the statement that $y^2 = x$ *is not a function* (as we have defined it above), because the value x = 4 is associated with either y = −2 or +2. Thus y is *not* unique. To make y unique we would have to restrict the values of y to $y \geqslant 0$.[10]

Whenever we have two sets of wheat grains, identical in *all* respects (including the number and size of the wheat grains), and we associate the wheat grains of one (set A) to the wheat grains of the other (set B), we may describe this mapping by saying that set A is being *mapped into itself.* This statement underlies the definition of a *graph* which we discussed previously. A graph may be formally defined as a set of points (symbolized by S) and a function (symbolized by F) which maps S into itself.

## VECTORS

Let us return once more to our field of millions of identical grains of wheat, in which negative and fractional grains of wheat are excluded for all practical purposes. If we labelled all these wheat grains with integer (whole) numbers, we could describe this set just as efficiently and effectively by the set of numbers which we have assigned. Let us do this from now on.

If we now add[11] together the elements 1 and 2 of this set we obtain the number 3 and we discover that this result is a member of the set of numbers as well. If we take the number 4 from the number 6 we obtain the number 2, which is also a member of this set. When we multiply the number 3 by the number 6 the product of 18 is also a member of this set. When we divide the number 20 by the number 10 the result of 2 is also a member of this set. (Dividing by 0 has no meaning in this context and is excluded from this discussion.) Further, the following statements about this set are also true:

(a)    $3 + 2$       $=$       $2 + 3$ or $(3x2)$   $= (2x3)$

(b)    $3 + (2+4)$  $= (3+2) + 4$ or $(3x2)4 = 3(2x4)$

(c)    $3(2+4)$     $= (3x2) + (3x4)$

The set of numbers complying with the above properties is formally called a *field*.

When we are able to discern an *ordered* set of numbers in this field of numbers[1][2] which enables us to determine a given point or direction on, say, a graph, we have what is formally called a *vector*. A vector is an ordered set of numbers taken from some field of numbers. It is *not* a number in and of itself. Vectors may be written as a row, e.g., $(a_1, a_2, a_3)$, or as a column, e.g., $\begin{pmatrix} a_1 \\ a_2 \\ a_3 \end{pmatrix}$. As in the case of numbers, we may add, subtract, and multiply vectors together. Addition and subtraction are carried out by associating the elements in the same positions of each vector. Thus vectors A $(a_1, a_2)$ and B $(b_1 b_2)$ when added give:

$$A + B = (a_1 + b_1, a_2 + b_2)$$

The product of two vectors can only be obtained[1][3] from the multiplication of a row vector and a column vector and when both vectors contain the same number of elements. Thus:

$$A\,B = (a_1, a_2)\begin{pmatrix} b_1 \\ b_2 \end{pmatrix} = (a_1 b_1 + a_2 b_2).$$

Further, the row vector must be placed to the left of the column vector.

Note that the method of multiplying the two vectors is to multiply the first element of vector $A(a_1)$ by the first element of vector $B(b_1)$, and then add to this result the product of the second element of vector $A(a_2)$ times the second element of vector $B(b_2)$. The result is, in fact, a *number, not* a vector, and is called formally the *inner product* of the two vectors. This property will be of great use to us when we return shortly to our accounting problems.

Because vectors are ordered sets of numbers which may be used to convey direction, magnitude, and dimension, vectors are excellent vehicles for conveying the ideas of information flows through the accounting (and in fact the total) information network system examined previously.

## MATRICES

If we now arrange a number of vectors according to some predetermined plan, we have what is formally called a *matrix*. Thus a matrix is an *ordered set* of vectors (ordered according to rows or to columns) and looks like an array of numbers. There may be any number of rows and columns in a matrix. In fact, a row vector may be considered to be a matrix of one row and N columns (where the symbol N gives the number of columns in the matrix), whilst a column vector may be thought of as a matrix of N rows and one column (where the symbol N gives the number of rows in the matrix). We are able to add and subtract like elements of two matrices and we can multiply two matrices together provided we follow the same steps that we followed in order to obtain the inner product of two vectors. Thus:

$$A \begin{pmatrix} a_{11}, a_{12} \\ a_{21}, a_{22} \end{pmatrix} \times B \begin{pmatrix} b_{11}, b_{12} \\ b_{21}, b_{22} \end{pmatrix} = A B \begin{bmatrix} (a_{11}b_{11} + a_{12}b_{21}), & (a_{11}b_{12} + a_{12}b_{22}) \\ (a_{21}b_{11} + a_{22}b_{21}), & (a_{21}b_{12} + a_{22}b_{22}) \end{bmatrix}$$

where the parentheses in AB are only used to separate out the four elements of the new matrix.[14]

## MATRIX ACCOUNTING

With this very elementary introduction to linear algebra, let us now return to the accounting problem we left on page 488 and translate into vectors the information loops formed by the activities initialized by any two of the pendant nodes of the graph, and then translate these vectors into a matrix. The transactions of Westside Retailers Ltd. are used to illustrate the procedures required. They are reproduced below.

Feb.  1.  50,000 shares of $1 each in the company offered to the public.
     10.  50,000 shares in the company fully subscribed and the cash received.
     12.  Employed five sales staff for $60 each weekly.
     15.  Purchased premises for $30,000 of which $20,000 was paid in cash and the remainder borrowed on mortgage.
     18.  Purchased merchandise $12,000 on credit.
     20.  Paid salaries $300; advertising $1,000.
     23.  Sales: cash $2,000; credit $3,000.
     24.  Sales: cash $2,500; credit $4,000.
          Purchased merchandise for cash $3,000.
     27.  Sales: cash $2,000; credit $3,500.
          Salaries paid $300; Creditors paid $10,000.
     28.  Sales: cash $3,000; credit $4,500.
          Purchased merchandise on credit $2,500.
          Cash received from debtors $7,000.

For convenience of exposition assume that the company has decided to divide the month of February into two accounting periods ending on 23 February and 28 February, respectively. Before undertaking the translation of the above data into vectors, several important points must be noted:

1. Each information loop relates to a *single activity only*. Thus every daily state-ment listed above must be broken down into individual activities. For example, the statement on 15 February consists of two activities:
   i.  Put a down payment on premises $20,000 cash.
   ii. Raised a mortgage for the balance $10,000.

2. The traditional accounting method described in textbooks records (for expediency) the services rendered by employees as *expenses* when salaries are paid. Thus the activity of 12 February is ignored. This is not correct. An *asset* is acquired on 12 February and should be recorded as such. If this is done, the added work at balance date of recording *prepayments* and of carrying out adjust-ing, closing, and reversing entries with respect to this type of asset is avoided. The correct method will be used in this illustration. To reduce the size of the example, the correct method is not illustrated in the case of advertising.

In Figure A.3–2 the financial flow aspects of the commercial activity, "Feb. 18. Purchased merchandise $12,000 on credit", were illustrated. The financial information flow was directed around this loop in a definite order. Now a vector (which we previously defined to be an *ordered* set of numbers) is ideally suited to represent this ordered flow of financial information around loops. And as we have already decided to use the symbol +1 to indicate financial information flows through arcs and nodes towards the vertex of the graph, the symbol −1 to indicate flows from the vertex of the graph through arcs and nodes,

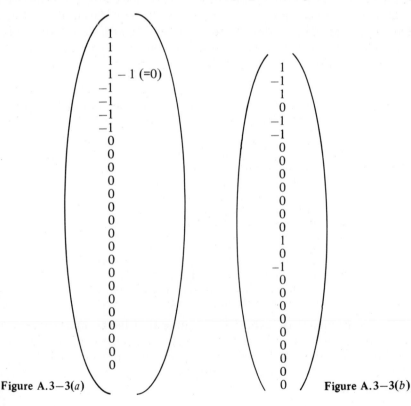

Figure A.3–3(*a*)

Figure A.3–3(*b*)

and the symbol 0 to indicate the absence of information flows, the vector representation of the commercial activity "Purchased merchandise $12,000 on credit", is that given in Figure A.3—3($a$) and ($b$). (The parentheses are used to indicate that the numbers represent a vector or matrix.)

Figure A.3—3($a$) illustrates the strict representation, in vector form, of the verbal description of the financial information flows associated with the commercial activity, "Purchased merchandise $12,000 on credit". Note that both the effect and the direction of the financial information flow through each node (or account) of Figure A.3—2 is given by the ordered set of +1, −1, and 0 of the vector of Figure A.3—3($a$).

An examination of Figure A.3—3($a$) discloses that the fourth node of this loop is represented by both +1 and −1. This node is in fact the vertex of the graph of Figure A.3—2. Because the representation of *every* activity in which the firm engages (both internally and externally) will include the vertex node and will show flows both to and from the vertex, the sum total of *all* such flows through the vertex must equal 0. Accordingly, it is convenient to leave the representation of this node out of every vector. Further, in order to make the transference to the computer mode of operation more effective and efficient, it will be convenient to rearrange the order of the vector elements. This is possible because the original order of the financial information flows is preserved by the +1, −1, and 0. The result for our purposes is Figure A.3—3($b$). The reason for this is explained later.

Because a matrix is defined as an ordered set of vectors, we can use it to represent effectively *all* the vector loops which, in turn, represent the financial information flows of each and every commercial activity of the firm. The *order* of the vectors is determined by the date of the first transaction in each class of commercial activity in our illustration. This is shown by the columns of Figure A.3—4($a$).

The matrix of Figure A.3—4($a$) has 25 rows and 13 columns and does, in fact, completely represent the accounting system of the Westside Retailers Ltd. and the financial information flows generated by the commercial activities of the company for the month of February.

An important point to note is that vectors duplicating the same type of financial information flows are *not* included in the matrix. For example, column 5 represents the flow of financial information concerning the commercial activity, "Feb. 18:   Purchased merchandise $12,000 on credit". This vector loop will also satisfactorily represent the flow of financial information for *every* action of purchasing "merchandise on credit" throughout the month, quarter, year, or life of the company. The same reasoning applies with respect to the repetition of *every other* commercial activity of the firm. A shorthand notation,

**Transactions Vector (t¹)** — by activity:

|  |  |
|---|---|
| 1. Issued Capital | 50,000 |
| 2. Hired Staff | 300 |
| 3. Premises for Cash | 20,000 |
| 4. Premises through Mortgage | 10,000 |
| 5. Merchandise on Credit | 12,000 |
| 6. Wages Paid | 300 |
| 7. Advertising Paid | 1,000 |
| 8. Cash Sales | 2,000 |
| 9. Credit Sales | 3,000 |
| 10. Wages Expense | 300 |
| 11. Merchandise for Cash | 0 |
| 12. Creditors Paid | 0 |
| 13. Cash from Debtors | 0 |

**Matrix S (Activities × Accounts) and Balance Vector (b¹):**

| Row | Accounts (Nodes) | 1 | 2 | 3 | 4 | 5 | 6 | 7 | 8 | 9 | 10 | 11 | 12 | 13 | Balance Vector |
|---|---|---|---|---|---|---|---|---|---|---|---|---|---|---|---|
| 1 | Assets | 1 | −1 |  | 1 | −1 | −1 | −1 | −1 | −1 | −1 |  | −1 |  | 75,700 |
| 2 | Equities | −1 | −1 |  | −1 | −1 | −1 | −1 | −1 | −1 | −1 |  | −1 |  | −75,700 |
| 3 | Current Assets | −1 | −1 | −1 |  | −1 | −1 | −1 | −1 | −1 | −1 |  | −1 |  | 45,700 |
| 4 | Long-Term Assets |  |  | 1 | 1 |  |  |  |  |  |  |  |  |  | 30,000 |
| 5 | Liabilities |  | −1 |  | −1 | −1 | −1 |  |  |  |  |  | −1 |  | −22,000 |
| 6 | Current Liabilities |  | −1 |  | −1 | −1 | −1 |  |  |  |  |  | −1 |  | −12,000 |
| 7 | Long-Term Liabilities |  |  |  | −1 |  |  |  |  |  |  |  |  |  | −10,000 |
| 8 | Owners' Equity | −1 |  |  |  |  |  |  | −1 | −1 |  |  |  |  | −53,700 |
| 9 | Owners' Investment | −1 |  |  |  |  |  |  |  |  |  |  |  |  | −50,000 |
| 10 | Retained Earnings |  |  |  |  |  |  | 1 | −1 | −1 | −1 |  |  |  | −3,700 |
| 11 | Bank | 1 |  | −1 |  |  | −1 | −1 | 1 |  |  | −1 | −1 | 1 | 30,700 |
| 12 | Staff Services |  | 1 |  |  |  |  |  |  |  | −1 |  |  |  | 0 |
| 13 | Inventories |  |  |  |  | 1 |  |  |  |  |  | 1 |  |  | 12,000 |
| 14 | Accounts Receivable |  |  |  |  |  |  |  |  | 1 |  |  |  | −1 | 3,000 |
| 15 | Premises |  |  | 1 | 1 |  |  |  |  |  |  |  |  |  | 30,000 |
| 16 | Accounts Payable |  |  |  |  | −1 |  |  |  |  |  |  | 1 |  | −12,000 |
| 17 | Wages Payable |  | −1 |  |  |  | 1 |  |  |  |  |  |  |  | 0 |
| 18 | Mortgage |  |  |  | −1 |  |  |  |  |  |  |  |  |  | −10,000 |
| 19 | Income |  |  |  |  |  |  |  | −1 | −1 | −1 |  |  |  | −3,700 |
| 20 | Total Sales |  |  |  |  |  |  |  | −1 | −1 |  |  |  |  | −5,000 |
| 21 | Cash Sales |  |  |  |  |  |  |  | −1 |  |  |  |  |  | −2,000 |
| 22 | Credit Sales |  |  |  |  |  |  |  |  | −1 |  |  |  |  | −3,000 |
| 23 | Wages Expense |  |  |  |  |  |  |  |  |  | 1 |  |  |  | 300 |
| 24 | Advertising Expense |  |  |  |  |  |  | 1 |  |  |  |  |  |  | 1,000 |
| 25 | Total Expenses |  |  |  |  |  |  | 1 |  |  | 1 |  |  |  | 1,300 |

Activities (columns): 1 Issued Capital; 2 Hired Staff; 3 Premises for Cash; 4 Premises through Mortgage; 5 Merchandise on Credit; 6 Wages Paid; 7 Advertising Paid; 8 Cash Sales; 9 Credit Sales; 10 Wages Expense; 11 Merchandise for Cash; 12 Creditors Paid; 13 Cash from Debtors.

Blank = 0

Fig. A.3–4(a)   Fig. A.3–4(b)   Fig. A.3–4(c)

which may be used to represent this accounting network system in matrix form, is to use the symbol S.

We have set up the matrix S by using columns of vectors. The *rows* of this matrix S are also vectors, and, in this particular matrix have the useful property that they show the effect of the financial information flows related to each and every commercial activity (in order of those activities) upon the account (node) which the particular row vector represents.

Thus, for example, row vector no. 4 shows that the account, Long-Term Assets, will be affected by the financial information flows from the two commercial activities: (a) purchasing premises for cash, and, (b) purchasing premises through a mortgage. In summary, long-term assets have been increased by purchasing premises by means of making a cash down-payment and raising a mortgage.

In contrast, the columns of matrix S show which accounts are affected by the financial information flows related to a particular commercial activity. Thus vector column no. 11 shows that the commercial activity, Purchasing Merchandise for Cash, affects the accounts (or nodes): (a) Bank (which is decreased), and (b) Inventories (which is increased). In summary, the column vectors show how the accounting system is affected by each and every commercial activity.

## IDEAS AND SYMBOLS

In our previous discussion of information and communication we said that we need some means of (or language for) communicating an idea from the sender (the ideas generator) to the receiver (the ideas acceptor). Apart from mental telepathy, the most effective and efficient means yet devised by human beings is to use *words* — both written and spoken. It is, therefore, of the utmost importance that the *word* used to communicate an idea be carefully and accurately defined.

For the sender can *never* be certain that the receiver has received that idea (symbolized by the word) which the sender is transmitting. Even the subsequent actions of the receiver will not reveal whether the idea which was sent was correctly received. These actions may be identical with those actions which the sender would undertake, based upon the idea. However, the receiver may have decided upon his actions as a result of a set of ideas which included an idea *incorrectly* derived from the symbol (or word) received from the sender. The best that the sender can do (if his purpose in transmitting the idea is to help the receiver make correct decisions about future actions) is to define the symbol (or word), which acts as a surrogate for the idea, as accurately and as carefully as possible.

The symbol used to communicate financial information is, by consensus, the monetary symbol of the country in which the communication takes place. In the case of Australia the monetary symbol is the *dollar.*

## TRANSACTIONS VECTOR

The monetary symbolization of the financial information related to every commercial activity of the Westside Retailers Ltd. may be completely and effectively represented in vector form. The *order* of the vector elements is the same as that of the vectors of the accounting system matrix S. This is shown in Figure A.3–4(*b*). As *one* vector of the matrix S represents the financial information flow related to *every* repetition of a particular commercial activity, the vector *element* representing the monetary symbolization of the financial information for any such activity must be the *sum* of every repetition related to that activity. Thus, for example, vector element no. 2 (viz., $300) of Figure A.3–4(*b*), is the sum five (5) amounts of $60 – representing the hiring of the services of five (5) employees.

## MATRIX MULTIPLICATION

Given the vector of monetary symbols representing financial information [Fig. A.3–4(*b*)], we now need some technique whereby we are able to record the effects of such information upon the accounts of the accounting network system (matrix S). The technique is given to us by a property of vectors which we discussed on page 491. Thus, when we multiply two vectors together we obtain a *number* which we called the *inner product* of the two vectors. The technique consists of multiplying the like elements of the two vectors together and summing the resultant series of products.

Let us take an example from our matrix S (viz., the first row vector), which we represent by the small symbol $s_1$, and multiply this by the vector of monetary symbols, which we will call the "transactions vector" and represent by the small symbol $t^1$. (The *superscript* [1] signifies that we are summarizing the financial information of the first period. Any *subscripts* would refer to the individual elements of the transactions vector and rows of the matrix S.)

This multiplication is illustrated graphically in Figure A.3–5.

The first element of $s_1$ is multiplied by the first element of $t^1$ and added to the product of the second element of $s_1$ and the second element of $t^1$ and so on. This gives:

$(1)(50,000) + (1)(300) + (0)(20,000) + (1)(10,000) + (1)(12,000) +$
$(-1)(300) + (-1)(1,000) + (1)(2,000) + (1)(3,000) + (-1)(300) +$
$(0)(0) + (-1)(0) + (0)(0) = \$75,700.$

This *number* represents the *total* effect of *all* the commercial activities of Westside Retailers Ltd. for period 1, upon the account, Total Assets. It does, in fact, provide the company with the financial information that the total assets of the company have a monetary price of $75,700 at the end of period 1.

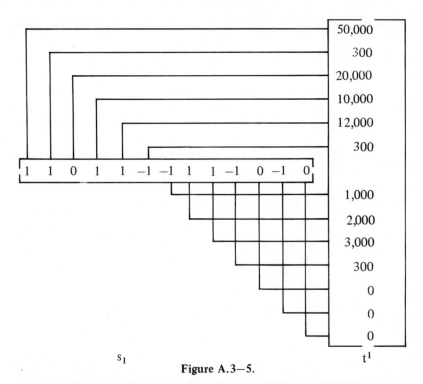

**Figure A.3—5.**

## BALANCE VECTOR AND FINANCIAL ACCOUNTING REPORTS

The result of multiplying *every row* vector of matrix S by the *transaction* vector is the production of another vector — a *column* vector. The elements of this column vector are the *balances* of the accounts of (in the same *order* in which these accounts are arranged in) the matrix S. This vector is shown as Figure A.3—4(*c*); it will be called the *balance* vector and will be assigned the small symbol $b^1$. (Again, superscripts indicate aggregate amounts for the first period and subscripts individual elements.) Thus:

$$b_1^1 = \$75,700$$

is the representation for the balance of the first account (Assets) for the first accounting period.

Symbolically this multiplication may be given as

$$St^1 = b^1$$

The effect of all financial information flows upon each account is given by the *multiplication*. Whether the account is an Asset, Liability, or Owners' account is determined by the *sign* in the various row vectors of S. This sign determines the direction of the flow of financial information through the accounting network system. Normally, a *positive* number indicates an asset or expense account, whilst a *negative* number represents a Liability, Owners', or Revenue account.

A closer examination of the balance vector [Fig. A3–4(c)] will reveal that this vector contains all the data required to prepare the traditional income, appropriation, and balance sheet statements. These statements are illustrated in Figures A.3–6(a), A.3–6(b), and A.3–6(c). Note how this *one* column vector (and the previous vector multiplication) suffices to record the effects of all financial information flows upon the accounting network system of Westside Retailers Ltd. for period 1. Compare this with the amount of detailed recording required under the traditional accounting bookkeeping system explained in all introductory accounting textbooks.

Westside Retailers Ltd.

### Income Statement for Period 1

|  | $ | $ |
|---|---|---|
| *Sales* |  |  |
| Cash | 2,000 |  |
| Credit | 3,000 |  |
| Total |  | 5,000 |
| *Expenses* |  |  |
| Wages | 300 |  |
| Advertising | 1,000 |  |
| Total |  | 1,300 |
| *Income* |  | $3,700 |

**Figure A.3–6(a)**

Westside Retailers Ltd.

### Appropriation Statement for Period 1

|  | $ |
|---|---|
| Retained Earnings at Beginning of Period | 0 |
| Income for Period | 3,700 |
| Retained Earnings at End of Period | $3,700 |

**Figure A.3–6(b)**

Westside Retailers Ltd.

### Balance Sheet as at End of Period 1

|  | $ | $ |  | $ | $ |
|---|---|---|---|---|---|
| *Current Assets* |  |  | *Current Liabilities* |  |  |
| Bank | 30,700 |  | Accounts Payable | 12,000 | 12,000 |
| Inventories | 12,000 |  |  |  |  |
| Accounts Receivable | 3,000 |  | *Long-Term Liabilities* |  |  |
|  |  |  | Mortgage | 10,000 | 10,000 |
| Total |  | 45,700 |  |  |  |
|  |  |  | *Total Liabilities* |  | 22,000 |
| *Long-Term Assets* |  |  |  |  |  |
| Premises | 30,000 | 30,000 | *Owners' Funds* |  |  |
|  |  |  | Owners' Investment | 50,000 |  |
|  |  |  | Retained Earnings | 3,700 |  |
|  |  |  | *Total* |  | 53,700 |
| Total Assets |  | $75,700 | Total Equities |  | $75,700 |

**Figure A.3–6(c)**

## PERIODIC FLOWS AND VECTORS ONCE AGAIN

In the traditional accounting bookkeeping system the Revenue and Expense accounts are closed off to the Profit and Loss and Retained Earnings accounts, and are then available for recording the financial results of the subsequent period. In the system described above the financial results for an accounting period are automatically and continuously recorded in the Retained Earnings account and in the Income account. *No closing* entries are required, but some method for clearing the Revenue and Expense accounts is needed.

One solution to this problem is to make use of two special types of vectors: (a) the *unit* vector, which is a vector containing *only one* positive element, viz., 1, in an *ordered* position, and *zeros* in all other positions of the vector; (b) the *zero* vector, which contains *zeros* in all ordered positions of the vector.

If we order this set of vectors so that the unit vectors are arranged first, with the positive elements (viz., 1) ordered so that they appear in the rows representing the balance sheet accounts, and the zero vectors are arranged to coincide with the rows representing the income statement accounts, we will have acquired the technique we need. This matrix is given as Figure A.3–7(a) and the symbol representing the matrix will be the capital E.

Looking at column 1 of matrix E, we can see that it contains a 1 in the first position and zeros in all other positions. (Blank equals zero in Figures A.3–7(a) and A.3–7(c). This has been done both here and in Figure A.3–4(a) to make it easier to read and understand the matrices.) Further, the positive element 1 is in the same row as the account, Assets. Again, note that the positive element 1 of the vector in column 18 is in ordered position no. 18, which is in the same row as the account, Mortgage (no. 18). On the other hand, row no. 19 (account, Income) has a *zero* in this same ordered position in column vector no. 19. The same situation holds for *all* vectors of the ordered set of vectors of matrix E [Fig. A.3–7(a)].

If we next multiply matrix E by the balance vector $b^1$ [which is reproduced as Figure A.3–7(b)], we will have effectively performed the same operation of clearing the Revenue and Expense accounts as is performed by the closing entries of the traditional (accounting) bookkeeping system.

Thus, if we multiply row vector 19 by column vector $b^1$ we obtain the number 0 in ordered position no. 19 of the column vector illustrated in Figure A.3–7(e), labelled $b^{11}$.

(0) (75,000) + (0) (−75,700) + (0) (45,700) + (0) (30,000) + (0) (−22,000) +
(0) (−12,000) + (0) (−10,000) + (0) (−53,700) + (0) (−50,000) + (0) (−3,700) +
(0) (30,700) + (0) (0) + (0) (12,000) + (0) (3,000) + (0) (30,000) + (0) (−12,000) +
(0) (0) + (0) (−10,000) + (0) (−3,700) + (0) (−5,000) + (0) (−2,000) + (0) (−3,000) +
(0) (300) + (0) (1,000) + (0) (1,300) = \$0

$E$    Figure A.3–7(a)

$b^1$    Figure A.3–7(b)

$S$    Figure A.3–7(c)

$t^2$    Figure A.3–7(d)

$b^{11}$    Figure A.3–7(e)

$b^{12}$    Figure A.3–7(f)

$b^2$    Figure A.3–7(g)

$b^1 + S = b^{11}$ ; $b^{11} + b^{12} = b^2$

| $b^1$ | $t^2$ | $b^{11}$ | $b^{12}$ | $b^2$ |
|---|---|---|---|---|
| 75,700 | 0 | 75,700 | 11,700 | 87,400 |
| -75,700 | 300 | -75,700 | -11,700 | -87,400 |
| 45,700 | 0 | 45,700 | 11,700 | 57,400 |
| 30,000 | 0 | 30,000 | 0 | 30,000 |
| -22,000 | 2,500 | -22,000 | 7,500 | -14,500 |
| -12,000 | 300 | -12,000 | 7,500 | -4,500 |
| -10,000 | 0 | -10,000 | 0 | -10,000 |
| -53,700 | 7,500 | -53,700 | -19,200 | -72,900 |
| -50,000 | 12,000 | -50,000 | 0 | 0 |
| -3,700 | 300 | -3,700 | -19,200 | -22,900 |
| 30,700 | 3,000 | 30,700 | 1,200 | 31,900 |
| 0 | 0 | 0 | 0 | 0 |
| 12,000 | 10,000 | 12,000 | 5,500 | 17,500 |
| 3,000 | 7,000 | 3,000 | 5,000 | 8,000 |
| 30,000 | | 30,000 | 0 | 30,000 |
| -12,000 | | -12,000 | 7,500 | -4,500 |
| 0 | | 0 | 0 | 0 |
| -10,000 | | -10,000 | 0 | -10,000 |
| -3,700 | | 0 | -19,200 | -19,200 |
| -5,000 | | 0 | -19,500 | -19,500 |
| -2,000 | | 0 | -7,500 | -7,500 |
| -3,000 | | 0 | -12,000 | -12,000 |
| 0 | | 0 | 0 | 0 |
| 300 | | 0 | 300 | 300 |
| 1,000 | | 0 | 0 | 0 |
| 1,300 | | 0 | 300 | 300 |

Blanks = 0

C = Columns

R = Rows

This, of course, is the balance in the income account at the beginning of the next period (in this case, 2).

In the case of the product of row vector no. 18 with column vector $b^1$, we obtain:

(0) (75,000) + (0) (−75,700) + (0) (45,700) + (0) (30,000) + (0) (−22,000) +
(0) (−12,000) + (0) (−10,000) + (0) (−53,700) + (0) (−50,000) + (0) (−3,700) +
(0) (30,700) + (0) (0) + (0) (12,000) + (0) (3,000) + (0) (30,000) + (0) (−12,000) +
(0) (0) + (1) (−10,000) + (0) (−3,700) + (0) (−5,000) + (0) (−2,000) + (0) (−3,000) +
(0) (300) + (0) (1,000) + (0) (1,300)  = − \$10,000

which is the balance of the Mortgage account shown under Long-Term Liabilities in Figure A.3−6(c).[15] The result of multiplying every row vector of matrix E by the balance vector $b^1$ is shown as the column vector $b^{11}$ [Fig. A.3−7(e)].

If we possess the transactions vector for the second (or subsequent) period we are able to produce the income, appropriation, and balance sheet statements for period 2. The reason should be obvious. The results for period 2 will be the sum of the financial results of those commercial activities for the second period and the balances of Assets, Liabilities, and Owners' accounts carried forward from the first period. This has been done and is illustrated in Figures A.3−7 (a)−(g)

Figure A.3−7(a) is the clearing matrix E.

Figures A.3−7(b) and A.3−7(c) are the balance vector $b^1$ and accounting system matrix S, reproduced from Figure A.3−4.

Figure A.3−7(d) is the transactions vector $t^2$ for period 2.

Figure A.3−7(e) is the product of matrix E, times vector $b^1$, and symbolized as $b^{11}$. (That is, the balances of Assets, Liabilities, and Owners' accounts at the *beginning* of period 2.)

Figure A.3−7(f) is the result of multiplying matrix S by transactions vector $t^2$ and symbolized as $b^{12}$. (That is, it shows the results of engaging in commercial activities during period 2.)

Figure A.3−7(g) is the balance vector for period 2, and symbolized as $b^2$. Thus: $b^2 = b^{11} + b^{12}$.

In symbolic form, the result of engaging in commercial activities over the first two periods would be given at the *end* of period 2 by:

$$b^2 = St^2 + Eb^1$$
$$= b^{12} + b^{11}$$

The result for period 3 would be given by:

$$b^3 = St^3 + Eb^2$$
$$= b^{13} + b^{22}$$

Therefore, the result for period n would be given by:

$$b^n = St^n + Eb^{n-1}$$

where n symbolizes the period for which financial results are being summarized.

The income, appropriation and balance sheet statements of the West-side Retailers Ltd. for period 2 are shown in Figures A.3−8(a), A.3−8(b), and A.3−8(c).

Westside Retailers Ltd.

*Income Statement for Period 2*

|  | $ | $ |
|---|---:|---:|
| *Sales* | | |
| Cash | 7,500 | |
| Credit | 12,000 | |
| Total | | 19,500 |
| | | |
| *Expenses* | | |
| Wages | 300 | |
| Total | | 300 |
| *Income* | | $19,200 |

**Figure A.3−8(a)**

Westside Retailers Ltd.

*Appropriation Statement for Period 2*

|  | $ |
|---|---:|
| Retained Earnings at Beginning of Period | 3,700 |
| Income for Period | 19,200 |
| Retained Earnings at End of Period | $22,900 |

**Figure A.3−8(b)**

Westside Retailers Ltd.

*Balance Sheet as at End of Period 2*

| | $ | $ | | $ | $ |
|---|---:|---:|---|---:|---:|
| *Current Assets* | | | *Current Liabilities* | | |
| Bank | 31,900 | | Accounts Payable | 4,500 | 4,500 |
| Inventories | 17,500 | | | | |
| Accounts Receivable | 8,000 | | *Long-Term Liabilities* | | |
| *Total* | | 57,400 | Mortgage | 10,000 | 10,000 |
| | | | Total Liabilities | | 14,500 |
| *Long-Term Assets* | | | | | |
| Premises | 30,000 | 30,000 | *Owners' Funds* | | |
| | | | Owners' Invesment | 50,000 | |
| | | | Retained Earnings | 22,900 | |
| | | | *Total* | | 72,900 |
| Total Assets | | $87,400 | Total Equities | | $87,400 |

**Figure A.3−8(c)**

Having now set out the basic discussion of the application of linear algebra to accounting network systems, we might profitably explore some of the properties of this new system a little more deeply, especially if we hope to integrate on a computer the accounting information system within the total information system of the firm.

One of the problems of computer programmes is that they are time-consuming and very expensive things to write. The result of this is that accounting systems (once placed on computers) tend to become very rigid and seldom changed. It would be a very useful property of a computerized accounting system if whenever needed, accounts could be added, which would be fully integrated within the existing accounting information system. The system discussed above does possess this property. However, in order to fully understand this property we must delve further into the subject matter of vectors.

## VECTORS – STILL MORE VECTORS AND VECTOR SPACES

The earth we live on occupies a definite position in the space (which we define as "the arrangement matter makes to spread its parts in") which is our galaxy. It is possible to locate the earth by reference to, say, the sun as the central (or pivot) point[16] and to the relative distance of the earth from the sun, the stars, and the other planets. Similarly, the position of Australia on the earth can be obtained from its longitude and latitude in relation to the pivot (or central) points of Greenwich and the equator. Inside Australia the positions of cities, towns, and streets (within cities or towns) can be obtained by using given reference points relative to some central (or pivot) point.

In like manner, we may think of vectors as occupying positions in a given space. The position of the vectors is given by certain reference points. These reference points are the coordinate axes and the origin (or central or pivot point) of this coordinate system. (A coordinate system is a system of magnitudes used to fix the position of a point, line, or plane.) In the case of a system of vectors the origin will be given by the *zero* (or null) vector and the coordinate axes by the *unit* vectors – both of which we have discussed previously.

With the origin and the coordinate axes available, we are able to locate the position of every vector in the given system of vectors. In fact, it can be demonstrated[17] that every vector in the given system of (or space containing) vectors can be reduced to the coordinate axes (i.e., the unit vectors) and to the origin (i.e., the zero vector).

Now we have already discovered above that a vector is an ordered set of numbers taken from some field of numbers. Whenever we consider a number, taken from this field of numbers, in isolation (i.e., as a number), we formally call that number a *scalar*. Given these two facts, we may now set out another property of vectors viz., that the product of a vector with a scalar is defined as $ka = \{ka_1, ka_2\}$, where k is the scalar and a is the vector containing two (2) ordered elements.

With all the properties of vectors which we have discovered to date we may now define a *vector space* to be a *set* of vectors such that the sum of every two vectors and the product, ka, for every vector, a, in the set with a scalar, k, taken from the field (F) of numbers, *are in* the *set*.[18]

However, given that we possess some workable definition of a vector space, how do we determine its limits, i.e., what is the dimension of this vector space? To discover this we must make use of the notions of an origin and of a set of coordinate axes of the coordinate system of vectors.

### Linear Combinations and Independence

If we possess a set of scalars $(k_1, k_2, ..., k_n)$ taken from some field of numbers and a set of vectors $(a_1, a_2, ..., a_n)$ and we combine them in the following manner:

$$b = k_1 a_1 + k_2 a_2 + ... + k_n a_n$$

the resultant vector, b, is said to be a *linear combination* of the given vector, a, and scalars, k.[19]

Now, whenever a vector taken from a set of vectors is able to be written as a linear combination of a group of other vectors taken from this set, that vector is said to be *linearly dependent* on that group. In addition, we say that the *set* of vectors which contains these linear combinations is a *linear dependent set*.

A more general definition of the linear dependence of a set of vectors may be given as: A set of vectors $(a_1, a_2, ..., a_n)$ is said to be *linearly dependent* if there exists a set of n scalars $(k_1, k_2, ..., k_n)$, not all zero, such that: $k_1 a_1 + k_2 a_2 + ... + k_n a_n = 0$, where 0 is the *zero* (or null) vector.

If no such set of scalars exists, the vectors $(a_1, a_2, ..., a_n)$ are said to be linearly independent.

The set of vectors which demonstrates this property of linear independence most clearly is the set of *unit* vectors.

Thus given the set of vectors $\begin{pmatrix} 1 & 0 \\ 0 & 1 \end{pmatrix}$, we are required to find a set of scalars, k, such that:

$$\begin{matrix} k_1(1) + k_2(0) \\ k_1(0) + k_2(1) \end{matrix} = \begin{matrix} 0 \\ 0 \end{matrix}$$

This set of simultaneous equations will be true if, and only if, $k_1 = 0$ *and* $k_2 = 0$. Therefore, we may say that this set of unit vectors $(1,0)$ and $(0,1)$ is *linearly independent*.

### Basis of a Vector Space

With this information we are now able to determine the limits (the boundary, the dimension) of a given vector space.

A set of vectors $(a_1, a_2, ..., a_n)$ from a given vector space is said to generate (or to span) that vector space if every *other* vector in the vector space is able to be written as a linear combination of that set of $a_1, a_2, ..., a_n$ vectors.

The set of vectors which we need to generate (or span) the vector space ought to be the smallest possible set of vectors and is given the formal name of the *basis* of the vector space. It can be proved very easily[20] that the set we are after is the set of linearly independent vectors taken from this vector space. This set is, in fact, the set of unit vectors which we have decided to use as the coordinate axes of the system.[21]

Thus we may define the *basis* of a vector space to be that set of *linearly independent* vectors which *generates (or spans)* the entire vector space. Accordingly, we are able to determine the dimension (or the limits or boundary) of a given vector space by defining it to be the *maximum* number of *linearly independent* vectors in that vector space.

With this additional information about vectors let us return to the accounting problem we left on page 503 and re-examine the matrix S, illustrated in Figure A.3—4(*a*).

## BASIS FOR MATRIX  S

The set of vectors which constitute the matrix S form a vector space. In order to make use of the properties of sets of vectors which we have discovered above, let us first determine the basis of this vector space. As we saw above, the set of linearly independent vectors which spans the entire vector space is the basis of that vector space. Now, as we have also seen, the set of unit vectors is a linearly independent set and thus forms a basis for the vector space. It also happens to be one of the easiest sets to obtain in any vector space and may be used to quickly determine the set of linearly independent vectors of the vector space.[22]

In the case of matrix S of Figure A.3—4(*a*), the set of unit vectors turns out to be a set taken from the row vectors formed by the set of *pendant nodes.* In fact the *basis* for the vector space is *one less* than the *maximum number* of row vectors formed by the set of pendant nodes of Figure A.3—2.[23] In our example the maximum number of linearly independent unit vectors is twelve and this also gives the *dimension* of the vector space and what is called formally the *rank* of the matrix S.

If one reflects upon Figure A.3—2 and Figure A.3—4(*a*), it is obvious that the basis for this vector space must come from the set of pendant nodes of Figure A.3—2. The vectors of Figure A.3—4(*a*) (matrix S) represent the ordered flows of financial information through loops formed by the commercial activities reflected in any two pendant nodes of Figure A.3—2. Thus the limit to the size of the vector space representing flows of financial information must be given by the number of pendant nodes in the financial network system.[24] The reason why the maximum number of linearly independent vectors is *one less* than the maximum number of pendant nodes is the twofold aspect of financial information classification, wherein both the physical and the financial aspects of every commercial activity are recorded.[25]

Given the determination of the *basis* of matrix S, we may say that every other vector in matrix S is a *linear combination* of some of these twelve basis vectors. Let us demonstrate this fact by reproducing the relevant part of matrix S illustrated in Figure A.3–4(*a*).

Figure A.3–9 reproduces the thirteen row vectors formed from the set of pendant nodes of Figure A.3–2. Remember that a vector was said to be a linear combination of a given set of vectors when the following condition held:

$$b = k_1 a_1 + k_2 a_2 + ... + k_n a_n$$

Now let $k_1 = k_2 = ... = k_{12} = -1$.

And from Figure A.3–9 let:

$a_1$ = row vector 11

$a_2$ = row vector 12, and so on

until $a_{12}$ = row vector 24.

Let $b$ = row vector 9.

When we add vectors we have already discovered that we must add like elements, that is,

$a_{11} + a_{21} + a_{31} + ...$ (where the first subscript represents the row, and the second, the column of the matrix; e.g., $a_{31}$ is the element in the *third* row and *first* column).

Further, as the scalar $-1$ is the same for *all* vectors, we may either multiply each element of each vector by the scalar $-1$ and then add the new vectors, *or* we may add the vectors together first and *then* multiply the result by the scalar $-1$. To simplify the illustration, let us use this latter method.

The result of adding the twelve vectors is given at the foot of Figure A.3–9.

| Rows \ Columns | 1 | 2 | 3 | 4 | 5 | 6 | 7 | 8 | 9 | 10 | 11 | 12 | 13 |
|---|---|---|---|---|---|---|---|---|---|---|---|---|---|
| 9 Owners' Investment | −1 | | | | | | | | | | | | |
| 11 Bank | 1 | | −1 | | | −1 | −1 | 1 | | | −1 | −1 | 1 |
| 12 Staff Services | | 1 | | | | | | | | −1 | | | |
| 13 Inventories | | | | | 1 | | | | | | 1 | | |
| 14 Accounts Receivable | | | | | | | | | 1 | | | | −1 |
| 15 Premises | | | 1 | 1 | | | | | | | | | |
| 16 Accounts Payable | | | | | | −1 | | | | | | 1 | |
| 17 Wages Payable | | −1 | | | | | 1 | | | | | | |
| 18 Mortgage | | | | −1 | | | | | | | | | |
| 21 Cash Sales | | | | | | | | −1 | | | | | |
| 22 Credit Sales | | | | | | | | | −1 | | | | |
| 23 Wages Expense | | | | | | | | | | 1 | | | |
| 24 Advertising Expense | | | | | | | 1 | | | | | | |
| Sum of Row Vectors 11−24 | 1 | 0 | 0 | 0 | 0 | 0 | 0 | 0 | 0 | 0 | 0 | 0 | 0 |

Blanks = Zero

**Figure A.3–9**

Thus: b = (−1)  [1,0,0,0,0,0,0,0,0,0,0,0,0]
      = [−1,0,0,0,0,0,0,0,0,0,0,0,0]
      = row vector 9

Having determined that row vector 9 is a linear combination of these twelve basis vectors, it can be easily demonstrated that the remaining row vectors of matrix S are linear combinations of some of these twelve basis vectors.[26] Thus we may assert that these twelve vectors do indeed form a basis[27] for the vector space which is matrix S, and that the set of vectors of matrix S is a linearly dependent set of vectors.

We may now use this property of linear dependence to extend the matrix S so that additional information, which the accountant may deem useful, is able to be produced.

## WORKING CAPITAL POSITION

The *working capital* position of a firm has traditionally been an important piece of financial information supplied to decision-makers by the accountant. The matrix S of Figure A.3–4($a$) does not directly provide this information. It can, however, be adjusted to provide this information directly by adding another row vector. This is done by obtaining a *linear combination* of the *relevant* vectors. Let us call the new row vector, $s_{26}$. The small s indicates a row of the set of row vectors which is matrix S.

*Either:* $s_{26} = s_3 + s_6$   $(k_1 = k_2 = 1)$
$= 1,0,-1,0,0,0,-1,1,1,-1,0,0,0$

*or:*   $s_{26} = s_{11}+s_{12}+s_{13}+s_{14}+s_{16}+s_{17}$   $(k_1 = k_2 = \,,,\, = k_6 = 1)$
$= 1,0,-1,0,0,0,-1,1,1,-1,0,0,0$

We see that we may form this new linear combination by combining *either* other linear combinations (because these linear combinations are ultimately formed from linear combinations of some of the *basis* vectors) *or* some of the basis vectors themselves.

When this new row vector is multiplied by the transactions vector for period 1 ($t^1$) the amount of \$33,700 is obtained.[28] This is the same figure as that obtained by subtracting Current Liabilities from Current Assets in Figure A.3–6($c$).

## CASH FLOW STATEMENT

We claimed previously that all the traditional financial accounting statements could be obtained from the accounting network system discussed above.

For example, multiplying the row vector 11 (Bank) of matrix S [Fig. A.3–4($a$)] by the transactions vector will give the *cash flow* statement of the firm for a given period. Thus in period 1 cash was received from: (a) the owners, (b) cash sales, and (c) debtors (accounts receivable), whilst cash was paid out to (a) put a deposit on premises, (b) pay salaries, (c) pay for advertising, (d) pay for merchandise bought on credit (accounts payable) and (e) purchase merchandise for cash.

## FUNDS STATEMENT

In order to obtain a *funds statement* from matrix S [Fig. A.3—4(*a*)], other row vectors are required.

When the "all purchasing power" concept of funds is used, we are concerned with accounting for the *total* movement of funds between the firm and the external environment in which the firm operates. Which node (account) of Figure A.3—2 succinctly summarizes the flows of funds to and from the firm? It is the vertex (or apex) of the accounting network system. This node represents the firm itself. Therefore, we must use the row vector associated with this node to determine the sources and uses of funds for any given period. This, however, appears to pose an insoluble problem, for all the elements of this row vector are zero. (This was the reason for excluding this node from the matrix illustrated in Figure A.3—4(*a*).)

In vector terms what is this vector of zeros? It is the origin of the vector space formed by the vectors representing the financial information flows associated with the commercial activities of the firm. As *all* commercial activity *originates* with the firm, it is obvious that the origin of the vector space of financial information flows must be the vertex of the graph representing this network of financial information flows. The dimension of this vector space is determined by the expected range of commercial activities entered into by the firm over its life-cycle. (Hence the importance of determining this expected range at the time of initiating the accounting network system. Any subsequent enlargement would be time-consuming and expensive, as changes in the coordinate axes of the system of vectors are involved. This is not as simple as adding linear combinations of existing basis vectors.)

As the flow of funds to and from the firm must be equal, the individual vector elements representing these flows to and from the firm must also sum to zero. (This fact was demonstrated in the illustration in Figure A.3—3(*a*).) The illustration of Figure A.3—3(*a*) provides us with the solution to the problem of formulating a row vector representing the sources and uses of funds. We take the zero row vector associated with the vertex of the graph illustrated in Figure A.3—2 and separate each element of the vector into its two components — thereby forming two row vectors called by us "sources" and "uses". (This is not sleight of hand, as may appear on first reading. The vertex node is always represented by both +1 and −1 in every vector column representing the flow of financial information around a loop of the accounting network system. As these two numbers sum to 0, we use the number 0 to conveniently represent the effects of the two directional flows through the vertex node.) This has been illustrated in Figures A.3—10(*a*) and A.3—10(*b*). The summation of the selected components of the individual row vectors is given at the bottom of both Figure A.3—10(*a*) and Figure A.3—10(*b*). When the two new row vectors ("sources" and "uses") are added together, we obtain the zero vector associated with the vertex of the graph illustrated in Figure A.3–2.

The observant student will have noticed that only twelve of the row vectors associated with the set of pendant nodes have been used to form the two new row vectors. Row vector 23 has been ignored. Further column vector 10 has been represented in both Figures A.3–10(a) and A.3–10(b) by zeros. Why? The answer lies in the type of information required from funds statements.

| Row \ Column | 1 | 2 | 3 | 4 | 5 | 6 | 7 | 8 | 9 | 10 | 11 | 12 | 13 |
|---|---|---|---|---|---|---|---|---|---|---|---|---|---|
| 9 | -1 | | | | | | | | | | | | |
| 11 | | | -1 | | | -1 | -1 | | | | -1 | -1 | |
| 14 | | | | | | | | | | | | | -1 |
| 16 | | | | | -1 | | | | | | | | |
| 17 | | -1 | | | | | | | | | | | |
| 18 | | | | -1 | | | | | | | | | |
| 21 | | | | | | | | -1 | | | | | |
| 22 | | | | | | | | | -1 | | | | |
| Sources | -1 | -1 | -1 | -1 | -1 | -1 | -1 | -1 | -1 | | -1 | -1 | -1 |

Blanks = 0

**Figure A.3–10(a)**

| Row \ Column | 1 | 2 | 3 | 4 | 5 | 6 | 7 | 8 | 9 | 10 | 11 | 12 | 13 |
|---|---|---|---|---|---|---|---|---|---|---|---|---|---|
| 11 | 1 | | | | | | | 1 | | | | | 1 |
| 12 | | 1 | | | | | | | | | | | |
| 13 | | | | | 1 | | | | | | 1 | | |
| 14 | | | | | | | | | 1 | | | | |
| 15 | | | 1 | 1 | | | | | | | | | |
| 16 | | | | | | | | | | | | 1 | |
| 17 | | | | | | 1 | | | | | | | |
| 24 | | | | | | | 1 | | | | | | |
| Uses | 1 | 1 | 1 | 1 | 1 | 1 | 1 | 1 | 1 | | 1 | 1 | 1 |

Blanks = 0

**Figure A.3–10(b)**

The accounting network system (illustrated in Figure A.3–2) represents not only the flow of financial information associated with movements of physical and financial resources to and from the firm, but also the flow related to movements of financial information *within* the firm itself. Row vector 23 and column vector 10 represent the flow of financial information associated with the determination of wages *expense* for the given period. For income statement purposes, *all* asset *expirations* (expenses) incurred in deriving income must be calculated — hence the presence of these two vectors. For funds statement purposes, only those vectors associated with movements of funds between the firm and its external environment are required. The column of zeros [column vector 10 in Figures A.3–10(a) and A.3–10(b)] fully represents the *absence* of any movement (external to the firm) associated with this expense and enables the vector associated with the vertex to be correctly determined. If the vector associated with the purchase of the asset, advertising, had been properly shown in matrix S [Fig. A.3–4(a)] (this was not done, because of the need to reduce size of illustration), there would have been two columns with zero elements in the row vectors used to represent the funds statement.

The multiplication of these two row vectors [Figs. A.3-10(a) and A.3–10(b)] by the transactions vector for period 1 produces the total funds utilized by the Westside Retailers Ltd. for period 1. The individual elements of each row vector provide the details necessary to determine the components of the sources and uses of funds for the period.

According to the traditionally determined funds statement [Fig. A.3–11(a)], the total sources of funds for period 1 amounted to $77,000. However, using the method described above we see that the firm utilized a total of $98,600 during period 1 [Fig. A.3–11(b)]. What is the explanation of this difference?

Westside Retailers Ltd.

### Traditional Funds Statment – Period 1

|  | $ | $ | $ |
|---|---|---|---|
| *Sources of Funds* | | | |
| Short-Term | | | |
| Sales for Period | | 5,000 | |
| Increase in Accounts Payable | | 12,000 | 17,000 |
| | | | |
| Long-Term | | | |
| Increase on Mortgage | | 10,000 | |
| Increase in Owners' Investment | | 50,000 | 60,000 |
| *Total Sources* | | | $77,000 |
| | | | |
| *Uses of Funds* | | | |
| Short-Term | | | |
| Cash Operating Expenses | | | |
| Wages | 300 | | |
| Advertising | 1,000 | 1,300 | |
| | | | |
| Increase in Current Assets | | | |
| Bank | 30,700 | | |
| Inventory | 12,000 | | |
| Accounts Receivable | 3,000 | 45,700 | 47,000 |
| | | | |
| Long-Term | | | |
| Increase in Long-Term Assets | | | |
| Premises | | 30,000 | 30,000 |
| *Total Uses* | | | $77,000 |

Figure A.3–11(a)

Westside Retailers Ltd.

## Improved Funds Statement – Period 1

|  | $ | $ | $ |
|---|---|---|---|
| *Sources of Funds* | | | |
| Short-Term | | | |
| Sales for Period | | 5,000 | |
| *Decreases* in Current Assets | | | |
| Bank | | 21,300 | |
| *Increases* in Current Liabilities | | | |
| Accounts Payable | | 12,000 | |
| Wages Payable | | 300 | 38,600 |
| | | | |
| Long-Term | | | |
| Increases in Mortgage | | 10,000 | |
| Increase in Owners' Investment | | 50,000 | 60,000 |
| *Total Funds Available for Period* | | | $98,600 |
| | | | |
| *Uses of Funds* | | | |
| Short-Term | | | |
| Cash Operating Expenses | | | |
| Advertising | | 1,000 | |
| Increases in Current Assets | | | |
| Bank | 52,000 | | |
| Staff Services | 300 | | |
| Inventories | 12,000 | | |
| Accounts Receivable | 3,000 | 67,300 | |
| Decreases in Current Liabilities | | | |
| Wages Payable | 300 | 300 | 68,600 |
| | | | |
| Long Term | | | |
| Increases in Long-Term Assets | | | |
| Premises | | 30,000 | 30,000 |
| Total Uses to Which Funds Have Been Put during Period | | | $98,600 |

**Figure A.3–11(b)**

## Velocity of Circulation of Funds

The economic activity of the firm is affected not only by the *absolute amount* of funds acquired by it during a given period, but also by the number of times that the firm *turns over* these funds during that period. Let us call this turnover of funds the *velocity of circulation* of funds.[29] The *additional* funds utilized by the Westside Retailers Ltd. as a result of the positive velocity of circulation of funds is reflected (together with the absolute quantity of funds acquired) in the information provided by the row vectors of Figures A.3–10(a) and A.3–10(b).

Decisions by management about future courses of action in market places must take into account not only the absolute amount of funds at its disposal during a given period, but also the expected velocity of circulation of such funds. The more rapidly management is able to recirculate this given supply of funds, the more profitable (presumably) is the firm. The firm benefits not only from sales of its products but also from reductions in its financing costs. The more "work" that a firm is able to get out of a given quantity of funds, the lower ought to be its financing costs for a given period.

The funds statement illustrated in Figure A.3–11(b) shows the *total* funds available to the Westside Retailers Ltd. for period 1. This total fund includes the *additional* funds made available by the recirculation of the given quantity of funds acquired by the firm during period 1.[30]

The funds statements for period 2 set out the differences between these two statements more clearly and highlight the netting effect of the traditional funds statement. According to Figure A.3–11(c), only $19,500 of funds were available during period 2 and the only sources of those funds were the sales for the period. This, of course, is quite clearly incorrect, as Figure A.3–11(d) demonstrates. Funds were obtained from credit granted to the firm by: (a) the suppliers of merchandise, and (b) the firm's employees. Both of these sources are ignored in the traditional funds statement.

Westside Retailers Ltd.

*Traditional Funds Statement – Period 2*

|  | $ | $ | $ |
|---|---|---|---|
| *Sources of Funds* | | | |
| *Short-Term* | | | |
| Sales for Period | | | 19,500 |
| *Total Sources* | | | $19,500 |
| | | | |
| *Uses of Funds* | | | |
| *Short-Term* | | | |
| Cash Operating Expenses | | | |
| Wages | | 300 | |
| Increase in Current Assets | | | |
| Bank | 1,200 | | |
| Inventories | 5,500 | | |
| Accounts Receivable | 5,000 | 11,700 | |
| | | | |
| Decrease in Current Liabilities | | | |
| Accounts Payable | | 7,500 | 19,500 |
| *Total Uses* | | | $19,500 |

**Figure A.3–11(c)**

Hence, in the case of the traditional funds statement of the Westside Retailers Ltd. for period 2, funds obtained from suppliers of merchandise and from employees are ignored. Likewise, the funds made available from decreases in the accounts "Bank" and "Accounts Receivable" are not included because of the netting effect of the classification and summarization of financial information related to these particular commercial activities. (This is an obvious example of the *loss of information* that occurs when aggregation, for decision-making purposes, takes place.)

As can be seen from Figure A.3–11(*d*), the total funds available to the Westside Retailers Ltd. during period 2 were $42,600, not $19,500 as suggested in Figure A.3–11(*c*). The knowledge that the firm had $42,600 available to it during period 2 ought to be important knowledge to the management of Westside Retailers Ltd. when it

Westside Retailers Ltd.

*Improved Funds Statement – Period 2*

|  | $ | $ | $ |
| --- | --- | --- | --- |
| *Sources of Funds* | | | |
| *Short-Term* | | | |
| Sales for Period | | 19,500 | |
| Decreases in Current Assets | | | |
| Bank | 13,300 | | |
| Accounts Receivable | 7,000 | 20,300 | |
| Increases in Current Liabilities | | | |
| Accounts Payable | 2,500 | | |
| Wages Payable | 300 | 2,800 | 42,600 |
| *Long-Term* | | | 0 |
| *Total Funds Available for Period* | | | $42,600 |
| *Uses of Funds* | | | |
| *Short-Term* | | | |
| Increases in Current Assets | | | |
| Bank | 14,500 | | |
| Staff Services | 300 | | |
| Inventory | 5,500 | | |
| Accounts Receivable | 12,000 | 32,300 | |
| Decreases in Current Liabilities | | | |
| Accounts Payable | 10,000 | | |
| Wages Payable | 300 | 10,300 | 42,600 |
| *Long-Term* | | | 0 |
| *Total Uses to Which Funds Have Been Put during Period* | | | $42,600 |

Figure A.3–11(*d*)

compares profitability in relation to total assets (or to owners' contributions, as is popularly done by financial analysts). The velocity of circulation of funds, as well as the quantity of funds available, affect the profitability of the firm for a given period.

## APPROPRIATION STATEMENT

As was illustrated in Figure A.3–6(*b*) and A.3–8(*b*), an appropriation statement may also be derived from the matrix S of Figure A.3–4(*a*). However, if the opening balance of retained earnings is required to be shown separately, this figure must be kept separately outside the matrix system. The reason for this can be seen from Figure A.3–2. The balance of the Retained Earnings account is continuously cumulated over the life of the firm and contains only the most recently updated balance.

## ANALYSIS AND INTERPRETATION OF ACCOUNTING INFORMATION

As was discussed in the chapter on the analysis of financial statements, the information value of financial reports can be improved substantially by the calculation of various financial ratios which highlight significant relationships in the data. Thus the proper classification of all the transaction data of a firm's economic activities is required if any significant structural relationships, implicit in the data, are to be produced. These relationships form one of the guidelines for the communication of accounting data and are essential to any good information system.

Apart from the problem of ensuring that the correct valuation basis and measurement techniques are being used, the proper interpretation of any relationships obtained must be carried out in the light of economic conditions applying to the firm and to the industry in which the firm operates. These calculations and interpretations must be carried out outside the traditional accounting bookkeeping system. It would seem to be an advantage from the view point of a decision-maker (in terms of cost and time) if such information could be produced automatically by the accounting system at the same time as the financial reports.

The accounting network system we have been discussing is, in fact, a subsystem of the *total* information system of the firm. From this total system both *financial* and *non-financial* information flows may be obtained. It is possible for this total system to include data concerning the economic conditions applying to both the firm and the industry in which the firm operates, as well as other environmental data, which will permit an interpretation of the current results of the firm's commercial activities to be automatically carried out. This interpretation would draw upon the results (and their interpretations) of past years which are stored in the firm's total information system. Such is the power of modern computers.[31]

However, the efficient and effecfive use of modern computer-based information systems requires the elimination of all duplications of information acquisition. This may be carried out by storing all the relevant properties of every commercial activity entered into by the firm during a given period in a single "data bank" — to which every decision-making body of the firm has access.

One method of setting up this data bank is to make use of the *transactions* vector which we have discussed previously. This transactions vector is, in reality, a *matrix of vectors.* Each element of the transactions vector may be considered to be the *first* element of a *vector,* with all the remaining zero elements suppressed.[32] It is feasible to use all the remaining elements of each vector member of this transactions matrix.

A simplified illustration of the advantage of such a total system is the production of the number of physical units of products sold by the firm during a given period. This information may be utilized by the accounting, marketing, finance, and production departments to produce (hopefully) *data relevant to* (that is, further information for) the input function of a decision-maker's decision rule.

For example, the element in position number 8 of the transactions vector of the Westside Retailers Ltd. for period 2 [Figure A.3–7($d$)] represents the cash sales made during this period. This element is a vector summarizing the financial flows for the following days:

$$t_8{}^2 = \text{24 February} + \text{27 February} + \text{28 February}$$
$$= \$2{,}500 \quad\quad + \$2{,}000 \quad\quad + \$3{,}000$$
$$= \$7{,}500$$

Use may be made of the remaining elements of this vector to provide the following information for period 2:

1. Total number of physical units sold for cash

2. The dollar cash sales for product (1...n) in territory (1...n) by salesmen (1...n)

3. The physical units sold for cash of product (1...n) in territory (1...n) by salesmen (1...n).

This break-down may be extended to include every property of cash sales considered relevant[33] to future courses of action by the decision-making bodies of the firm.

If one product, two territories, and three salesmen were used, the relevant section of the expanded transactions vector would appear as in the illustration of Figure A.3–12.[34] By multiplying the appropriate section of the total information matrix of the firm by the relevant column of the transactions matrix, any desired information may be obtained without the duplication normally associated with extant information systems of firms and without the necessity to go outside the formal information system itself.

| Label | Cash Sales |
|---|---|
| Territory 2 Salesman 3 Physical Units | 100 |
| Territory 2 Salesman 2 Physical Units | 400 |
| Territory 2 Salesman 1 Physical Units | 300 |
| Territory 1 Salesman 3 Physical Units | 600 |
| Territory 1 Salesman 2 Physical Units | 400 |
| Territory 1 Salesman 1 Physical Units | 700 |
| Territory 2 Salesman 3 Dollar Amount | 300 |
| Territory 2 Salesman 2 Dollar Amount | 1,200 |
| Territory 2 Salesman 1 Dollar Amount | 900 |
| Territory 1 Salesman 3 Dollar Amount | 1,800 |
| Territory 1 Salesman 2 Dollar Amount | 1,200 |
| Territory 1 Salesman 1 Dollar Amount | 2,100 |
| Salesman 3 Physical Units | 700 |
| Salesman 2 Physical Units | 800 |
| Salesman 1 Physical Units | 1,000 |
| Salesman 3 Dollar Amount | 2,100 |
| Salesman 2 Dollar Amount | 2,400 |
| Salesman 1 Dollar Amount | 3,000 |
| Territory 2 Physical Units | 800 |
| Territory 1 Physical Units | 1,700 |
| Territory 2 Dollar Amount | 2,400 |
| Territory 1 Dollar Amount | 5,100 |
| Total Physical Units | 2,500 |
| Total Dollar Amount | 7,500 |
| Transaction Vector (t²) Position Number | 8 |

Figure A.3–12

## MODEL EXTENSIONS

The information which management needs to plan the future operations of the manufacturing department of the firm (if one exists) may also be obtained from the system outlined in the above discussion. A matrix of information flows associated with the manufacturing operations of a firm may be set up as a subsystem of the total accounting network system of the firm.[35] From this matrix system management would be able to obtain the budgeted costs of operations and a variance analysis when budgeted and actual costs of operations are compared. The evaluation of investment opportunities could be integrated within the system described above and the financing decisions of management treated as a mathematical programming problem. All short-term decision problems of management are amenable to analysis within this system.

Finally, the student should realize that it is possible to conceive of vector loops of information flows which represent not only the formal organizational responsibilities associated with the managerial hierarchy of a firm, but also the *interactional energy flows* between employees caused by the motivational impact of duties and responsibilities assigned to the firm's employees.[36]

## NOTES

1. Pacioli, *Summa de arithmetica, geometria, proportioni et proportionalita.*

2. A major criticism which can be raised against management's use of computers in businesses at present is that they regard computers as superefficient accounting machines only. The modern computer ought to be considered a co-information processor and decision-maker within the integrated total information system of the firm — an extension of the human mind — albeit a lowly one.

3. J. E. Butterworth, "The Accounting System As an Information Function", *Journal of Accounting Research* 10, no. 1 (Spring 1972): 1–27.

4. It is hoped that students may be encouraged by this fragmented description of information and communication to undertake a deeper study of this very complex, yet highly important area of man's endeavours. In fact this writer ventures to suggest that most of man's misunderstanding of man throughout the world is due to the failure (or inability) of man to communicate effectively ideas to other men so that the desired message is understood.

5. They are *hanging*, as it were, like apples on strings which one finds at fairs and which one must attempt to eat whilst both hands are held behind one's back.

6. This is basically a moveable piece of metal which, when moved in a certain direction, comes in contact with the *two* remaining unconnected ends of the circuit — thus permitting a complete path (or better still a *loop*) to be formed.

7. In a world where uncertainty and imperfections exist, some feedback is necessary to signal when corrections of deviations from plans should be initiated.

8. This is not to argue that the cost and value of information are equal. Presumably, the value obtained from increasing the light being directed on the road in front of him more than compensates the cyclist for the increased muscular strain imposed by the need to move the pedals of his bicycle faster. In like manner, the cost and time involved in initially setting up an efficient and reliable feedback system is more than offset by the value of the information fed back to the ideas generator on the result of the firm's commercial activities. Further, this system, once established, needs only the minimum control; in a manner analogous to the case of the cyclist who needs to pedal on a well-lit road only fast enough to ensure that sufficient light is available to comply with the traffic regulations concerning headlights and tail-lights (assuming, of course, the cyclist is in no hurry to reach his destination).

9. This rule is analogous to the rule given in chapter 5.

10. The student is advised that multiple-valued functions exist. For an excellent discussion of sets, vectors, and matrices, the following texts are highly recommended:

   D. E. James and C. D. Throsby, *Introduction to Quantitative Methods in Economics* (Sydney, N.S.W.: John Wiley & Sons Australasia Pty. Ltd., 1973).
   G. Hadley, *Linear Algebra* (Reading, Mass.: Addison-Wesley Publishing Co. Inc., 1961).
   S. Lang, *A Second Course in Calculus* (Reading, Mass.: Addison-Wesley Publishing Co. Inc., 1964).
   S. G. Hanna and J. C. Saber, *Sets and Logic* (Homewood, Illinois: Richard D. Irwin Inc., 1971).

11. The purists will object to the switch from the property of order of numbers to the property of quantity. To be logically consistent in the development one would have to write a book not an appendix.

12. We have limited our discussion to the field of integers, rational numbers and real numbers. Accountants (theoretically) do not manipulate imaginary numbers! For a discussion of such numbers and for a treatment of the theory of numbers the student is advised to consult any recognized textbook on mathematics. Note that some mathematicians prefer to call integers (positive and negative), rational numbers (fractions), and real numbers (such as, $\sqrt{2}$) by the single name of *real numbers.*

13. Cross products exist as well as scalar products. The interested student should consult the references given in note 10 above.

14. The student is warned against assuming that AB = BA where A and B are symbols for two matrices. *In general* AB $\neq$ BA. For a full discussion of matrix multiplication and other properties of matrices, the student is advised to consult the references given in note 10 above.

15. The elements of the column vectors of matrix S were arranged in a special order, as we demonstrated in Figure A.3−3($b$). This was done to facilitate the conversion of this matrix system to a computer programme. If, for example, FORTRAN was the programming language being used, the matrix E could be reduced to *one very* simple arithmetic statement.

16. Astronomers may object to using the sun as the pivot point to locate the earth, as the sun is on the outer edge of our galaxy which is only one member of the group of seventeen galaxies called the Local Group. In fact our earth is 30,000 light years from the centre of our galaxy, which in turn has a diameter of 100,000 light years. (One light year is about *six* trillion miles!!) Other visual clusters may contain up to five hundred galaxies!! However, given the magnitude of the distances involved, the use of the sun as the pivot point will be accurate enough for our purposes.

17. Refer to the textbooks listed in note 10 above, for proof.

18. Although it is true that the notions of distance, length, and angle are required to completely define what is known as an euclidean vector space, the above definition is sufficiently accurate for the purposes of this introductory discussion.

19. The word *linear* implies that only *single* numbers are used to combine the vectors, i.e., the *power* of the scalar is unity viz., $k^1$ — in contrast to *non-linear* scalars where the power may be $k^2, k^3, \ldots$ and so on. Formally, this equation is said to be an equation of the *first degree*.

20. See textbooks such as those referred to in note 10 above, for proof of this statement.

21. This is not to assert that the set of unit vectors constitutes the only basis in $E^n$.

22. See textbooks such as those referred to in note 10 above, for the techniques involved in determining the set of unit vectors.

23. The discussion may have used column vectors instead of rows. However, rows were used to reduce the size of the illustration in Figure A.3–9.

24. In the traditional accounting bookkeeping system these pendant nodes are called the primary classification accounts.

25. It does not matter which twelve of the thirteen row vectors formed by the set of pendant nodes we use as our basis, because the double classification involved ensures no loss of relevant financial information.

26. The student should take all these other vectors of matrix S and prove for himself that they are indeed linear combinations of the selected twelve basis vectors.

27. The student is encouraged to satisfy himself that the set of vectors illustrated in Figure A.3–9 (below the broken line) is indeed a set of linearly independent vectors which span the entire vector space. That is, he ought to try and reduce this set to the set of *unit vectors*. To help him, the following elementary operations on rows of a matrix are given:

   i.   Two rows of a matrix may be interchanged without changing the matrix.
   ii.  The multiplication of any row by a non-zero number taken from the field of numbers, F, is permissible.
   iii. One may add k times one row to another row of the matrix, where k is a scalar (i.e., a non-zero number from the field of numbers).

   The result should be a set of twelve unit vectors with the positive element 1 in the ordered position down the main diagonal of the matrix, running from the top left-hand corner of the figure to the bottom right-hand corner. The student will also discover that there will be left over a row and a column of *zeros* — signifying that in Figure A.3–9 one row and one column were linear combinations of the twelve basis vectors.

28. The student ought to perform this multiplication to satisfy himself that this is the correct figure and to check that he understands the technique of matrix multiplication.

29. This is analogous to the notion of the velocity of circulation of money in economic literature, which must be considered along with the absolute quantity of money by the federal government when formulating monetary policy. Ignoring the velocity of circulation of funds used by firms may be one of the underlying causes of the economist's failure to measure the effects of monetary policy accurately.

30. The illustration in Figure A.3–11(*b*) is not wholly satisfactory because of the abridged form of matrix S [Fig. A.3–4(*a*)]. In Figure A.3–11(*b*) the asset services available from the purchase of advertising are not shown as a use of funds. Neither was the liability that was incurred shown as a source of funds. Instead, the *cash operating expense,* "advertising", is shown as a use of funds.

The funds statement, illustrated in Figure A.3–11($d$), demonstrates more accurately this suggested, improved form of funds statement.

31. This suggestion may not seem so "starry-eyed" when it is realized that "virtual memory" is already operational and that IBM consider that its present 370 series to be a *mere* third-generation machine compared with their plans for the late 1970s.

32. Incidentally, to further complicate matters one may conceive of *each* of these *first elements* of the transactions vector as being itself a vector representing the accumulation of (say) the daily financial information flows during the period of interest. Thus we possess a three-dimensional area within a n-dimensional vector space!

33. How properties are determined to be relevant raises interesting problems for the information processor.

34. It is not practical to try and represent on paper the three-dimensional aspect mentioned in note 32 above. However, the student should try and conceive of the vector ray extending out from the first element of the row vector illustrated in Figure A.3–12 containing the three elements shown in $t_8^2$ discussed on page 516.

35. The production system may be represented most effectively through the use of a linear programme. This requires a study of the relationship of linear programming to vectors and matrices and is beyond the scope of this Appendix.

36. These ideas are not as far out as may appear at first reading. The adverse motivational effects of automobile assembly lines (for example), well known for over fifty years, have recently caused a car manufacturer in Sweden to redesign parts of its assembly line into numerous self-contained units. It ought to be possible to programme into a computer model indices of organizational behaviour. The problem is one of measurement only — albeit an exceedingly difficult one.

# Appendix 4
# Solutions to Selected Problems

**FROM QUESTIONS AND EXERCISES, CHAPTER 5**

R. Martin's Milk Bar

**Problem 6**

### R. Martin Capital Account

|  |  | Dr. $ | Cr. $ | Bal. $ |  |
|---|---|---|---|---|---|
| July 1 | Bank |  | 8,000 | 8,000 | Cr. |

### Bank Account

|  |  | Dr. $ | Cr. $ | Bal. $ |  |
|---|---|---|---|---|---|
| July 1 | Martin Capital | 8,000 |  | 8,000 | Dr. |
|  | Lease of Shop |  | 2,000 | 6,000 | Dr. |
|  | Shop Equipment |  | 3,000 | 3,000 | Dr. |
|  | Merchandise |  | 500 | 2,500 | Dr. |
|  | Sales | 700 |  | 3,200 | Dr. |
|  | Drawings |  | 100 | 3,100 | Dr. |

### Shop Lease Account

|  |  | Dr. $ | Cr. $ | Bal. $ |  |
|---|---|---|---|---|---|
| July | Bank | 2,000 |  | 2,000 | Dr. |

### Shop Equipment Account

|  |  | Dr. $ | Cr. $ | Bal. $ |  |
|---|---|---|---|---|---|
| July | Bank | 3,000 |  | 3,000 | Dr. |

### Merchandise Account

|  |  | Dr. $ | Cr. $ | Bal. $ |  |
|---|---|---|---|---|---|
| July | Bank | 500 |  | 500 | Dr. |

### Sales Account

|  |  | Dr. $ | Cr. $ | Bal. $ |  |
|---|---|---|---|---|---|
| July | Bank |  | 700 | 700 | Cr. |

### Drawings Account

|  |  | Dr. $ | Cr. $ | Bal. $ |  |
|---|---|---|---|---|---|
| July | Bank | 100 |  | 100 | Dr. |

*Trial Balance as at 31 July*

|  | Dr. $ | Cr. $ |
|---|---|---|
| R. Martin Capital |  | 8,000 |
| Bank | 3,100 |  |
| Shop Lease | 2,000 |  |
| Shop Equipment | 3,000 |  |
| Merchandise | 500 |  |
| Sales |  | 700 |
| Drawings | 100 |  |
|  | $8,700 | $8,700 |

## Problem 11

B. Abel

*Trial Balance as at 18 March*

|  | Dr. $ | Cr. $ |
|---|---|---|
| Bank | 2,920 |  |
| B. Abel Capital |  | 3,000 |
| Rent | 80 |  |
| Purchases | 560 |  |
| Sales |  | 840 |
| Salaries | 120 |  |
| Advertising | 40 |  |
| Drawings | 120 |  |
|  | $3,840 | $3,840 |

## Problem 15

B. Quick

*Trial Balance as at 28 July*

|  | Dr. $ | Cr. $ |
|---|---|---|
| Bank | 1,490 |  |
| Quick Capital |  | 2,000 |
| Purchases | 870 |  |
| Rent | 120 |  |
| Wages | 160 |  |
| M. Last |  | 120 |
| Sales |  | 740 |
| J. Docker | 60 |  |
| B. James | 160 |  |
|  | $2,860 | $2,860 |

**Problem 19**

Smith & Co. Ltd.

*Trial Balance as at End of Period*

|  | Dr. $ | Cr. $ |
|---|---|---|
| Cash at Bank | 12,000 | |
| Accounts Payable | | 30,000 |
| Mortgage | | 40,000 |
| Paid-up Capital | | 70,000 |
| Accounts Receivable | 24,000 | |
| Merchandise Inventory | 51,000 | |
| Delivery Vehicles | 10,000 | |
| Premises | 51,000 | |
| Sales | | 20,000 |
| Wages | 2,000 | |
| Rates | 5,000 | |
| Dividends | 5,000 | |
| | $160,000 | $160,000 |

## FROM QUESTIONS AND EXERCISES, CHAPTER 6

**Problem 14**

T. Bee — Pharmacist

*Profit and Loss Statement for Year Ended 31 December*

|  | $ | $ |
|---|---|---|
| Sales | | 18,000 |
| Less Cost of Goods Sold | | 10,300 |
| Gross Profit | | 7,700 |
| *Less Operating Expenses* | | |
| Advertising | 200 | |
| Interest | 150 | |
| Salaries | 2,400 | |
| Sundry | 360 | 3,110 |
| Net Profit | | $4,590 |

*Balance Sheet as at 31 December*

|  | $ | $ |
|---|---|---|
| **Current Assets** | | |
| Bank | 2,970 | |
| Accounts Receivable | 760 | |
| Merchandise Inventory | 1,260 | 4,990 |
| | | |
| **Long-Term Assets** | | |
| Shop Fittings | 1,600 | |
| Premises | 10,000 | 11,600 |
| | | $16,590 |
| | | |
| **Current Liabilities** | | |
| Accounts Payable | 900 | |
| Salary Accrued | 100 | 1,000 |
| | | |
| **Long-Term Liability** | | |
| Mortgage | | 4,000 |
| | | |
| **Total Liabilities** | | 5,000 |
| | | |
| **Capital** | | |
| Capital — T. Bee | 7,000 | |
| Net Profit | 4,590 | 11,590 |
| | | $16,590 |

## FROM QUESTIONS AND EXERCISES, CHAPTER 7

**Problem 7**

| Sales | Dr. $ | Cr. $ | Bal. $ |
|---|---|---|---|
| Jay | | 670 | 670 Cr. |
| Cash | | 480 | 1,150 Cr. |
| *Cash* | | | |
| Sales | 480 | | 480 Dr. |
| Sales Returns | | 40 | 440 Dr. |
| *Income Statement* | | | |
| Sales | | 1,150 | |
| Less Sales Returns | | 160 | 990 |

| Jay | Dr. $ | Cr. $ | Bal. $ |
|---|---|---|---|
| Sales | 670 | | 670 Cr. |
| Sales Returns | | 120 | 550 Cr. |
| *Sales Returns and Allowances* | | | |
| Jay | 120 | | 120 Dr. |
| Cash | 40 | | 160 Dr. |

**Problem 11**

Ajax Textile Co.

| Sales | Dr. $ | Cr. $ | Bal. $ |
|---|---|---|---|
| Accounts Receivable | | 650,000 | 650,000 Cr. |
| *Accounts Receivable* | | | |
| Sales | 650,000 | | 650,000 Dr. |
| Estimated Bad Debts | | 14,000 | 636,000 Dr. |

*Estimated Credit Losses*

| | Dr. $ | Cr. $ | Bal. $ |
|---|---|---|---|
| Estimated Bad Debts | 19,500 | | 19,500 Dr. |
| *Estimated Bad Debts* | | | |
| Estimated Credit Losses | | 19,500 | 19,500 Cr. |
| Accounts Receivable | 14,000 | | 5,500 Cr. |

## FROM QUESTIONS AND EXERCISES, CHAPTER 8

**Problem 12**

Hardware Department

(a) *Periodic Inventory System*
    *Stock on Hand Account*

| | Dr. $ | Cr. $ | Bal. $ | |
|---|---|---|---|---|
| Jan. Balance | | | 4,000 | Dr. |
| Jan. COGS | | 4,000 | — | |
| Mar. COGS | 2,960 | | 2,960 | Dr. |

*Purchases Account*

| | Dr. $ | Cr. $ | Bal. $ | |
|---|---|---|---|---|
| Jan. Accounts Payable | 4,800 | | 4,800 | Dr. |
| Feb. Accounts Payable | 3,200 | | 8,000 | Dr. |
| Mar. Accounts Payable | 2,800 | | 10,800 | Dr. |
| COGS | | 10,800 | — | |

*Accounts Payable Account*

| | Dr. $ | Cr. $ | Bal. $ | |
|---|---|---|---|---|
| Jan. Purchases | | 4,800 | 4,800 | Cr. |
| Feb. Purchases | | 3,200 | 8,000 | Cr. |
| Mar. Purchases | | 2,800 | 10,800 | Cr. |

*Sales Account*

| | Dr. $ | Cr. $ | Bal. $ | |
|---|---|---|---|---|
| Jan. Accounts Receivable | | 7,500 | 7,500 | Cr. |
| Feb. Accounts Receivable | | 10,500 | 18,000 | Cr. |
| Mar. Accounts Receivable | | 3,750 | 21,750 | Cr. |

*Accounts Receivable*

| | Dr. $ | Cr. $ | Bal. $ | |
|---|---|---|---|---|
| Jan. Sales | 7,500 | | 7,500 | Dr. |
| Feb. Sales | 10,500 | | 18,000 | Dr. |
| Mar. Sales | 3,750 | | 21,750 | Dr. |

*COGS Account*

| | Dr. $ | Cr. $ | Bal. $ | |
|---|---|---|---|---|
| Jan. Stock | 4,000 | | 4,000 | Dr. |
| Mar. Stock | | 2,960 | 1,040 | Dr. |
| Purchases | 10,800 | | 11,840 | Dr. |

(b) *Perpetual Inventory System*
    *Merchandise Inventory Account*

| | Dr. $ | Cr. $ | Bal. $ | |
|---|---|---|---|---|
| Jan. Balance | | | 4,000 | Dr. |
| Jan. Accounts Payable | 4,800 | | 8,800 | Dr. |
| COGS | | 4,000 | 4,800 | Dr. |
| Feb. Accounts Payable | 3,200 | | 8,000 | Dr. |
| COGS | | 5,600 | 2,400 | Dr. |
| Mar. Accounts Payable | 2,800 | | 5,200 | Dr. |
| COGS | | 2,000 | 3,200 | Dr. |
| Merchandise Leakage | | 240 | 2,960 | Dr. |

*COGS Account*

| | Dr. $ | Cr. $ | Bal. $ | |
|---|---|---|---|---|
| Jan. Merchandise Inventory | 4,000 | | 4,000 | Dr. |
| Feb. Merchandise Inventory | 5,600 | | 9,600 | Dr. |
| Mar. Merchandise Inventory | 2,000 | | 11,600 | Dr. |

| | | |
|---|---|---|
| Sales Account | ) | As in Periodic |
| Accounts Receivable | ) | System |
| Accounts Payable Account | ) | |

*Merchandise Leakage*

| | Dr. $ | Cr. $ | Bal. $ | |
|---|---|---|---|---|
| Mar. Merchandise Inventory | 240 | | 240 | Dr. |

Note that there is a shortage of six tool kits costing $240.

**Problem 20**

Shindig Company

*Accounts Receivable*

|  | Dr. $ | Cr. $ | Bal. $ |
|---|---|---|---|
| Balance |  |  | 800,000 Dr. |
| Sales | 1,000,000 |  | 1,800,000 Dr. |
| Bank |  | 500,000 | 1,300,000 Dr. |
| Bad Debts Recovered | 2,000 |  | 1,302,000 Dr. |
| Bank |  | 2,000 | 1,300,000 Dr. |
| Estimated Bad Debts |  | 12,000 | 1,288,000 Dr. |

*Estimated Bad Debts*

|  | Dr. $ | Cr. $ | Bal. $ |
|---|---|---|---|
| Balance |  |  | 30,000 Cr. |
| Accounts Receivable | 12,000 |  | 18,000 Cr. |
| Estimated Credit Losses |  | 10,800 | 28,800 Cr. |

*Bank*

|  | Dr. $ | Cr. $ | Bal. $ |
|---|---|---|---|
| Accounts Receivable | 500,000 |  | 500,000 Cr. |
| Accounts Receivable | 2,000 |  | 502,000 Cr. |

*Income Statement*

|  | $ |
|---|---|
| Sales | 10,000,000 |
| Less Estimated Credit Losses | 100,800 |
| Net Sales | 9,899,200 |
| Non-Operating Income |  |
| Bad Debts Recovered | 2,000 |

*Sales*

|  | Dr. $ | Cr. $ | Bal. $ |
|---|---|---|---|
| Balance |  |  | 9,000,000 Cr. |
| Accounts Receivable |  | 1,000,000 | 10,000,000 Cr. |

*Estimated Credit Losses*

|  | Dr. $ | Cr. $ | Bal. $ |
|---|---|---|---|
| Balance |  |  | 90,000 Dr. |
| Estimated Bad Debts | 10,800 |  | 100,800 Dr. |

*Bad Debts Recovered*

|  | Dr. $ | Cr. $ | Bal. $ |
|---|---|---|---|
| Accounts Receivable |  | 2,000 | 2,000 Cr. |

*Balance Sheet*

|  | $ |
|---|---|
| Accounts Receivable | 1,288,000 |
| Less Estimated Bad Debts | 28,800 |
| Net Accounts Receivable | 1,259,200 |
| Bank | 502,000 |

## Problem 16

Juggernaut Bus Co.

$$D = \frac{C - S}{n} \quad = \quad \frac{9,000 - 3,000}{3} \quad = 2,000$$

### Motor Bus Account

| | | Dr. $ | Cr. $ | Bal. $ |
|---|---|---|---|---|
| 1970<br>Jan. 1 | Cash | 9,000 | | 9,000 Dr. |
| 1972<br>Dec. 31 | Accumulated Depreciation<br>Cash<br>Loss on Sale | | 6,000<br>2,500<br>500 | 3,000 Dr.<br>500 Dr.<br>— |

### Accumulated Depreciation of Bus Account

| | | Dr. $ | Cr. $ | Bal. $ |
|---|---|---|---|---|
| 1970<br>Dec. 31 | Depreciation | | 2,000 | 2,000 Cr. |
| 1971<br>1972 | Depreciation<br>Depreciation<br>Motor Bus | 6,000 | 2,000<br>2,000 | 4,000 Cr.<br>6,000 Cr.<br>— |

### Depreciation on Bus Account

| | | Dr. $ | Cr. $ | Bal. $ |
|---|---|---|---|---|
| 1970<br>Dec. 31 | Accumulated Depreciation Bus<br>P & L* | 2,000 | 2,000 | 2,000 Dr.<br>— |
| 1971 | Accumulated Depreciation<br>P & L | 2,000 | 2,000 | 2,000 Dr.<br>— |
| 1972 | Accumulated Depreciation<br>P & L | 2,000 | 2,000 | 2,000 Dr.<br>— |

### Loss on Sale of Bus Account

| | | Dr. $ | Cr. $ | Bal. $ |
|---|---|---|---|---|
| 1972 | Motor Bus | 500 | | 500 Dr. |

*Optional.

**Problem 19**

Property Developments

*Flat Leasehold Account*

| Feb. 1 | Bank | 120,000 | | 120,000 Dr. |
|--------|------|---------|---|-------------|

*Accumulated Amortization of Lease Account*

| June 30 | Amortiza-tion of Lease | | 5,000 | 5,000 Cr. |
|---------|------|---|-------|-----------|

*Amortization of Lease Account*

| June 30 | Acc. Amort. | 5,000 | | 5,000 Dr. |
|---------|-------------|-------|---|-----------|

*Balance Sheet 30 June 1970*

| Flat Leasehold | $120,000 |
|----------------|----------|
| Less Accumulated Amortization | 5,000 |
| | $115,000 |

# FROM QUESTIONS AND EXERCISES, CHAPTER 9

**Problem 10**

Aphis Limited

| *Appropriation Account* | Dr. $ | Cr. $ | Bal. $ |
|---|---|---|---|
| Balance | | | 16,450 Cr. |
| Net Profit | | 100,000 | 116,450 Cr. |
| Dividends | 37,700 | | 78,750 Cr. |
| Formation Expenses | 2,750 | | 76,000 Cr. |
| Goodwill W/O | 3,000 | | 73,000 Cr. |
| Reserve | 3,000 | | 70,000 Cr. |
| Asset Replace-ment Reserve | 13,000 | | 57,000 Cr. |
| Tax | 39,000 | | 18,000 Cr. |

| *Dividend Account* | Dr. $ | Cr. $ | Bal. $ |
|---|---|---|---|
| Bank | 16,700 | | 16,700 Dr. |
| Dividends Payable | 21,000 | | 37,700 Dr. |

| *Tax Payable Account* | Dr. $ | Cr. $ | Bal. $ |
|---|---|---|---|
| Appropriation Balance | | 27,500 | 27,500 Cr. |
| Bank | 29,000 | | 1,500 Dr. |
| Appropriation | | 39,000 | 37,500 Cr. |

**FROM QUESTIONS AND EXERCISES, CHAPTER 10**

**Problem 3**

Fashion Retailers

*Profit and Loss Statement for the Year Ended 30 June 19X8*

|  | $ | $ | $ |
|---|---|---|---|
| Sales |  |  | 37,300 |
| Less Returns Inward |  | 620 |  |
| Less Estimated Credit Losses |  | 820 | 1,440 |
| *Net Sales* |  |  | 35,860 |
| Less Cost of Goods Sold |  |  | 19,200 |
| *Gross Profit* |  |  | 16,660 |
| Less *Selling Expenses* |  |  |  |
| Advertising | 2,960 |  |  |
| Travellers' Salaries | 3,300 |  |  |
| Travellers' Commission | 1,310 |  |  |
| Depreciation of Delivery Vans | 672 |  |  |
| Depreciation of Store Fixtures | 225 | 8,467 |  |
| Less *Administration Expenses* |  |  |  |
| Office Salaries | 1,820 |  |  |
| Office Stationery | 780 |  |  |
| Rent | 2,440 | 5,040 |  |
| Less *Finance Expenses* |  |  |  |
| Interest |  | 180 |  |
| *Total Operating Expenses* |  |  | 13,687 |
| *Net Profit* |  |  | $2,973 |

### Balance Sheet as at 30 June 19X8

| | $ | $ | $ |
|---|---:|---:|---:|
| **Current Assets** | | | |
| Debtors | 12,600 | | |
| Less Estimated Bad Debts | 760 | 11,840 | |
| Merchandise Inventory | | 8,860 | |
| Stock of Stationery | | 120 | 20,820 |
| **Long-Term Assets** | | | |
| Delivery Vans | 4,480 | | |
| Less Accumulated Depreciation | 1,492 | 2,988 | |
| Store Fixtures | 1,760 | | |
| Less Accumulated Depreciation | 485 | 1,275 | 4,263 |
| | | | $25,083 |
| **Current Liabilities** | | | |
| Bank Overdraft | | 5,500 | |
| Creditors | | 6,640 | |
| Accrued Expenses | | 210 | 12,350 |
| **Proprietorship** | | | |
| T. Bowman Capital | 12,000 | | |
| Add Net Profit | 2,973 | 14,973 | |
| Less Drawings | | 2,240 | 12,733 |
| | | | $25,083 |

## Problem 7

Nepean Co. Ltd.

| | $ | | $ |
|---|---:|---|---:|
| Gross Profit | 43,050 | Net Profit | 19,534 |
| Current Assets | 55,010 | Current Liabilities | 33,536 |
| Long-Term Assets | 48,860 | Long-Term Liability | 8,000 |
| | | Shareholders' Equity | 62,334 |

## Problem 11

Balaclava Battlers Ltd.

| | $ | | $ |
|---|---:|---|---:|
| Gross Profit | $81,300 | Net Profit | $22,100 |
| Current Assets | 135,200 | Current Liabilities | 49,400 |
| Long-Term Assets | 120,000 | Long-Term Liability | 35,000 |
| | | Shareholders' Equity | 170,800 |

**Problem 12**

Gold Coast Retailers Limited

*Income Statement for Year Ended 31 December 19X9*

|  | $ | $ | $ |
|---|---|---|---|
| Sales | | 250,000 | |
| Less Sales Returns | | 6,000 | 244,000 |
| Less Estimated Credit Losses | | | 4,480 |
| *Net Sales* | | | 239,520 |
| Less COGS | | | 156,000 |
| *Gross Profit* | | | 83,520 |
| Less *Selling Expenses* | | | |
| Advertising | 8,500 | | |
| Sales Salaries | 8,600 | | |
| Travellers' Salaries | 6,530 | | |
| Depreciation Travellers' Cars | 720 | 24,350 | |
| Less *Administration Expenses* | | | |
| Audit Fees | 2,500 | | |
| Directors' Fees | 1,800 | | |
| Office Expenses | 5,760 | | |
| Office Salaries | 7,070 | | |
| Rates | 1,600 | | |
| Depreciation Office Equipment | 440 | | |
| Depreciation Premises | 2,000 | 21,170 | |
| Less *Finance Expenses* | | | |
| Interest | | 3,000 | 48,520 |
| Net Profit | | | 35,000 |
| Less Income Tax | | | 14,000 |
| Net Profit after Tax | | | 21,000 |
| Less Dividends | | 12,000 | |
| Goodwill (Written Off) | | 4,000 | |
| Transfer to Reserve | | 6,000 | 22,000 |
| | | | (1,000) |
| Add Retained Profits 1/1 | | | 12,200 |
| Retained Profits 31/12 | | | $11,200 |

*Balance Sheet as at 31 December 19X9*

| | $ | $ | $ |
|---|---|---|---|
| **Current Assets** | | | |
| Bank | | 11,740 | |
| Accounts Receivable | 63,200 | | |
| Less Estimated Bad Debts | 3,000 | 60,200 | |
| Inventory | | 46,730 | |
| Prepaid Rates | | 480 | 119,150 |
| **Long-Term Assets** | | | |
| Office Equipment | 4,400 | | |
| Less Accumulated Depreciation | 2,040 | 2,360 | |
| Travellers' Cars | 7,200 | | |
| Less Accumulated Depreciation | 5,000 | 2,200 | |
| Premises | 50,000 | | |
| Less Accumulated Depreciation | 12,000 | 38,000 | |
| Goodwill | | 26,000 | 68,560 |
| | | | $187,710 |
| **Current Liabilities** | | | |
| Accounts Payable | | 15,090 | |
| Accrued Expenses | | 420 | |
| Tax Payable | | 14,000 | |
| Dividend Payable | | 7,000 | 36,510 |
| **Long-Term Liability** | | | |
| Debentures | | | 20,000 |
| **Total Liabilities** | | | 56,510 |
| **Shareholders' Equity** | | | |
| Paid-up Capital | | 80,000 | |
| Reserve | | 28,000 | |
| Share Premium Reserve | | 12,000 | |
| Retained Profits | | 11,200 | 131,200 |
| | | | $187,710 |

**Problem 15**

Pacific Retailers Ltd.

| | $ | | $ |
|---|---|---|---|
| Gross Profit | 154,600 | Net Profit before Tax | 23,800 |
| Current Assets | 101,500 | Current Liabilities | 60,500 |
| Long-Term Assets | 118,100 | Long-Term Liability | 40,000 |
| | | Shareholders' Equity | 119,100 |

## FROM QUESTIONS AND EXERCISES, CHAPTER 12

### Problem 12

Ryde Construction Co.

1. *Production Basis*

*Profit and Loss Statement*

| | $ |
|---|---:|
| Sales | 1,468,750 |
| Less Cost of Work Completed | 1,175,000 |
| Net Profit | $293,750 |

*Balance Sheet*

*Assets*

| | |
|---|---:|
| Inventory | — |
| N.S.W. Govt. − Debtor | 318,750 |

*Liabilities*

| | |
|---|---:|
| Bank | 25,000 |
| Equity | 293,750 |
| | 318,750 |

2. *Billing Basis*

*Profit and Loss Statement*

| | |
|---|---:|
| Sales | 1,150,000 |
| Less Cost of Work Completed | 920,000 |
| Net Profit | $230,000 |

*Balance Sheet*

*Assets*

| | |
|---|---:|
| Inventory | 255,000 |
| N.S.W. Government − Debtor | — |

*Liabilities*

| | |
|---|---:|
| Bank | 25,000 |
| Equity | 230,000 |
| | 255,000 |

## FROM QUESTIONS AND EXERCISES, CHAPTER 13

### Problem 4

| | *FIFO* | *Cost of Sales* | | | *LIFO* | *Cost of Sales* | |
|---|---|---|---|---|---|---|---|
| Jan. | Inventory | 100 x 30 | 30 | Mar. | Purchases | 140 x 60 | 84 |
| Jan. | Purchases | 120 x 40 | 48 | Feb. | Purchases | 110 x 50 | 55 |
| Feb. | Purchases | 110 x 50 | 55 | Jan. | Purchases | 120 x 40 | 48 |
| Mar. | Purchases | 70 x 60 | 42 | Jan. | Inventory | 30 x 30 | 9 |
| | | | 175 | | | | 196 |

| | | | | | | | |
|---|---|---|---|---|---|---|---|
| Sales | | 400 x 80 | 320 | Sales | | | 320 |
| Less COS | | | 175 | Less COS | | | 196 |
| Profit | | | 145 | Profit | | | 124 |
| Inventory | | 70 x 60 | 42 | Inventory | | 70 x 30 | 21 |

*Note:* COS plus inventory equals 217 in each case.

## FROM QUESTIONS AND EXERCISES, CHAPTER 14

### Problem 11

| | Asset Cost | Residual Value | Depreciable Cost | Estimated Life | Depreciation Rate | |
|---|---|---|---|---|---|---|
| | | | | | Reducing Balance | Straight Line |
| | $ | $ | $ | Years | % | % |
| (a) 1 | 1,000 | 400 | 600 | 2 | 36.8 | 30 |
| 2 | 1,000 | 400 | 600 | 3 | 26.3 | 20 |
| (b) 1 | 1,000 | 100 | 900 | 8 | 24.3 | 11.25 |
| 2 | 1,000 | 1 | 999 | 8 | 57.8 | 12.5 |

## FROM QUESTIONS AND EXERCISES, CHAPTER 16

### Problem 8

Adult Publications

*Ledger Accounts*

Registered Capital Account

| | | $ | $ | $ |
|---|---|---|---|---|
| Jan. 1 | Unissued Capital | | 1,000,000 | 1,000,000 Cr. |

Unissued Capital Account

| | | | | |
|---|---|---|---|---|
| Jan. 1 | Registered Capital | 1,000,000 | | 1,000,000 Dr. |
| Feb. 28 | Uncalled Capital | | 1,000,000 | — |

Uncalled Capital Account

| | | | | |
|---|---|---|---|---|
| Feb. 28 | Unissued Capital | 1,000,000 | | 1,000,000 Dr. |
| | Application | | 1,000,000 | — |

Application Account

| | | | | |
|---|---|---|---|---|
| Feb. 28 | Uncalled Capital | 1,000,000 | | 1,000,000 Dr. |
| Feb. 28 | Bank | | 1,000,000 | — |

Registration and Formation Costs Account

| | | | | |
|---|---|---|---|---|
| Feb. 10 | Bank | 2,000 | | 2,000 Dr. |
| Feb. 28 | Bank | 30,000 | | 32,000 Dr. |

Bank Account

| | | | | |
|---|---|---|---|---|
| Feb. 10 | Registration Costs | | 2,000 | 2,000 Cr. |
| Feb. 28 | Application | 1,000,000 | | 998,000 Dr. |
| | Formation Costs | | 30,000 | 968,000 Dr. |

*Balance Sheet as at 28 February*

| | $ |
|---|---|
| *Assets* | |
| Current | |
| Bank | 968,000 |
| Long-Term | |
| Formation Costs, etc. | 32,000 |
| | 1,000,000 |
| *Owners' Equity* | |
| Registered, Issued, and Paid-up Capital | 1,000,000 |

**Problem 11**

Endurance Motors Ltd.

*Balance Sheet as at 31 March*

| *Assets* | $ | $ | $ |
|---|---|---|---|
| *Current* | | | |
| Bank | | 131,550 | |
| *Long-Term* | | | |
| Formation Costs, etc. | | 5,950 | $137,500 |

*Owners' Equity*

| | *Ordinary* | *Preference* | *Total* |
|---|---|---|---|
| Registered Capital | 130,000 | 70,000 | 200,000 |
| Unissued Capital | 30,000 | 20,000 | 50,000 |
| Issued Capital | 100,000 | 50,000 | 150,000 |
| Uncalled Capital | 50,000 | 12,500 | 12,500 |
| Called-up Capital | 50,000 | 37,500 | 87,500 |
| Calls in Arrear | — | — | — |
| Paid-up Capital | 50,000 | 37,500 | 87,500 |
| Share Premium Reserve | | | 50,000 |
| Total Owners' Equity | | | $137,500 |

**FROM QUESTIONS AND EXERCISES, CHAPTER 17**

**Problem 6**

Angel Airlines Limited

*Cash Flow Statement for Period Ended 30 September 19X0*

|  | $ | $ | $ |
|---|---|---|---|
| Cash at Bank, 30 June |  |  | 2,000,000 |
| *Current Items* |  |  |  |
| Cash Flow from Current Operation |  |  |  |
| Cash Receipts from Ticket Sales |  | 18,000,000 |  |
| Less Cash Payments for Inputs |  |  |  |
|     Purchases | 7,000,000 |  |  |
|     Salaries | 2,000,000 |  |  |
|     Airport Taxes | 1,000,000 | 10,000,000 |  |
|  |  | 8,000,000 |  |
| Less Payments from Profits |  |  |  |
|     Income Tax | 4,000,000 |  |  |
|     Dividends | 2,000,000 | 6,000,000 |  |
| Cash Surplus from Operations Available for Capital Uses |  |  | 2,000,000 |
| *Capital Items* |  |  |  |
| Add Cash Raised from |  |  |  |
|     Sale of Commonwealth Bonds |  | 5,000,000 |  |
|     Reduction in Cash at Bank |  | 1,000,000 | 6,000,000 |
|     Cash Available |  |  | 8,000,000 |
|     Less Cash Spent on Aircraft |  |  | 14,000,000 |
| ∴ Loan required |  |  | $6,000,000 |

## FROM QUESTIONS AND EXERCISES, CHAPTER 18

### Problem 16

Fuddy Duddy Company Limited

*Funds Statement for Year Ended 31 December 1967*

|  | $ | $ | $ |
|---|---|---|---|
| *Sources of Additional Funds* | | | |
| 1. Funds from Operations | | | |
| Sales | | 280,000 | |
| Less Cost of Goods Sold | 190,000 | | |
| Salaries | 25,000 | | |
| Advertising | 15,000 | 230,000 | 50,000 |
| 2. Increase in Short-Term Borrowing | | | |
| Accounts Payable | | | 2,000 |
| 3. Increase in Long-Term Borrowing | | | |
| Mortgage | | | 50,000 |
| 4. Reduced Investment in Short-Term Assets | | | |
| Cash at Bank | | 13,000 | |
| Merchandise Inventory | | 9,000 | 22,000 |
| 5. Sale of Shares | | | |
| Paid-up Capital | | 10,000 | |
| Share Premium Reserve | | 5,000 | 15,000 |
| *Total Sources* | | | $139,000 |
| | | | |
| *Uses of Funds* | | | |
| 1. Payments from Profits | | | |
| Dividends | | 14,000 | |
| Tax | | 10,000 | 24,000 |
| 2. Increased Investment in Short-Term Assets | | | |
| Accounts Receivable | | 14,000 | |
| Prepayments | | 1,000 | 15,000 |
| 3. Increased Investment in Long-Term Assets | | | |
| Shop Fittings | | 8,000 | |
| Premises | | 45,000 | 53,000 |
| 4. Repayment of Liabilities | | | |
| Notes Payable | | 12,000 | |
| Mortgage | | 35,000 | 47,000 |
| | | | $139,000 |

**Problem 17**

Brian Jones' Pharmacy

*Funds Statement for the Year Ended 31 December 196X*

|  | $ | $ | $ |
|---|---|---|---|
| Sales |  |  | 64,000 |
| Less Expenses Requiring Funds |  |  |  |
| Cost of Goods Sold |  | 38,000 |  |
| Salaries |  | 12,000 | 50,000 |
|  |  |  | 14,000 |
| Add Additional Long-Term Funds Obtained |  |  |  |
| Mortgage |  |  | 8,000 |
| Total Funds Available |  |  | 22,000 |
| Less Funds Used for |  |  |  |
| 1. Additional Short-Term Assets |  |  |  |
| Debtors | 2,000 |  |  |
| Merchandise Inventory | 5,000 | 7,000 |  |
| 2. Repayment of Short-Term Liabilities |  |  |  |
| Creditors |  | 5,000 |  |
| 3. Purchase of Long-Term Assets |  |  |  |
| Premises | 6,000 |  |  |
| Fittings | 3,000 | 9,000 |  |
| 4. Personal Drawings |  | 7,000 | 28,000 |
| Reduction in Cash at Bank |  |  | $ 6,000 |

**Problem 24**

The Bushwacka Trading Co. Ltd.

### Expected Funds from Operations 19X2–X3

|  | 19X2 | 19X3 | Total |
|---|---|---|---|
|  | $ | $ | $ |
| Sales | 3,400,000 | 4,000,000 | 7,400,000 |
| COGS | 2,200,000 | 2,600,000 | 4,800,000 |
| Wages and Salaries | 500,000 | 600,000 | 1,100,000 |
| Advertising | 100,000 | 100,000 | 200,000 |
|  | 2,800,000 | 3,300,000 | 6,100,000 |
| Funds Surplus | $600,000 | $700,000 | $1,300,000 |

### Budgeted Funds Statement for 19X2–X3

|  | 19X2 | 19X3 | Total |
|---|---|---|---|
| Total funds Required for Project |  |  | $3,000,000 |
| *Sources of Funds* |  |  |  |
| Funds from Operations | 600,000 | 700,000 | 1,300,000 |
| *Uses of Funds* |  |  |  |
| Payment of Dividends | 100,000 | 100,000 | 200,000 |
| Payment of Tax | 200,000 | 250,000 | 450,000 |
| Repayment of Bank Overdraft | 200,000 | – | 200,000 |
| Repayment of Notes | – | 600,000 | 600,000 |
| Purchase of Vehicles | 60,000 | – | 60,000 |
| Extra Inventories | 200,000 | – | 200,000 |
|  | $760,000 | $950,000 | $1,710,000 |
| Expected Excess of Sources over Uses | −160,000 | −250,000 | −410,000 |
| Less Sale of Bonds | – | 700,000 | 700,000 |
|  | −160,000 | +450,000 | +290,000 |
| Additional Funds Required for Project |  |  | 2,710,000 |
| Total Funds Required |  |  | $3,000,000 |

## FROM QUESTIONS AND EXERCISES, CHAPTER 22

### Problem 15

P. Q. Company

i.

*Balance Sheet 1 January Restated in 31 December Dollars*

| | $ | $ | | | $ |
|---|---|---|---|---|---|
| Debtors | | 200 | Creditors | | 100 |
| Plant | 650 | | Debentures | | 400 |
| Less Accumulated | | | Capital | | 1,000 |
| Depreciation | 108 | 542 | Price-Level Adjustment | | 192 |
| Premises | | 975 | Price-Level Gain | | 25 |
| | | $1,717 | | | $1,717 |

Price-level gain: Net monetary liabilities = 500−200 = 300

$$300 \times \frac{130}{120} = 325$$

Gain = 325 − 300 = 25.

*Journal Entries*

| | | $ | $ | | | $ | $ |
|---|---|---|---|---|---|---|---|
| Plant | Dr. | 50 | | Premises | Dr. | 75 | |
| Accumulated | | | | Price-Level | | | |
| Depreciation | | | | Adjustment | Cr. | | 75 |
| Plant | Cr. | | 8 | | | | |
| P−L Adjustment | Cr. | | 42 | | | | |
| Price-Level | | | | | | | |
| Adjustment | Dr. | 25 | | | | | |
| Price-Level Gain | | | | | | | |
| (or P + L) | Cr. | | 25 | | | | |

ii. Historic cost income = Δ net assets = 1,240 − 1,100 = 140.

iii. *Balance Sheet 31 December Restated in 31 December Dollars*

| | | $ | | | $ |
|---|---|---|---|---|---|
| Cash | | 100 | Creditors | | 60 |
| Debtors | | 300 | Debentures | | 400 |
| Plant | 650 | | Capital | 1,000 | |
| Less Accumulated | | | | | |
| Depreciation | 217 | 433 | Price-Level | | |
| Premises | | 975 | Adjustment | 192 | |
| | | | Price-Level Gain | 25 | |
| | | | Net Operating | | |
| | | | Income | 131 | 1,348 |
| | | $1,808 | | | $1,808 |

Constant dollar income = 131 + 25 = 156
  or 1,348 (P₁) − 1,192 (Po + Pr) = 156

(Note: The reduction in Net Opg. Income is due to $9 additional depreciation charge.)

## FROM QUESTIONS AND EXERCISES, CHAPTER 23

**Problem 19**

ii.    *Balance Sheet as at 31 December at 31 December Replacement Costs*

| | $ | $ | | $ |
|---|---|---|---|---|
| Cash | | 300 | Creditors | 120 |
| Inventories | | 660 | Capital | 1,000 |
| Buildings | 1,200 | | Net Holding Gains | 410 |
| Less Accumulated | | | | |
| Depreciation | 260 | 940 | Current Income | 370 |
| | | $1,900 | | $1,900 |

iii.    *Balance Sheet 31 December at 31 December Selling Prices*

| | $ | $ | | $ |
|---|---|---|---|---|
| Cash | | 300 | Creditors | 120 |
| Inventories | | 1,000 | Capital | 1,150 |
| Buildings | 1,200 | | Current Income | 970 |
| Less Accumulated | | | | |
| Depreciation | 260 | 940 | | |
| | | $2,240 | | $2,240 |

| | |
|---|---|
| Ys comprises NHGs on initial assets | 260 |
| Yc | 370 |
| Unrealized profits on closing inventories | 340 |
| | 970 |

## FROM QUESTIONS AND EXERCISES, CHAPTER 24

**Problem 8**

| | | $ | $ |
|---|---|---|---|
| Inventories | Dr. | 6,000 | |
| Price-Level Adjustment (5%) | Cr. | | 1,000 |
| Real Holding Gain | Cr. | | 5,000 |

*Cost of Goods Sold*

| | |
|---|---|
| January 1 Inventories at 31 December CRC | 26,000 |
| Purchases | 180,000 |
| | 206,000 |
| Less 31 December Inventories at 31 December CRC | 34,000 |
| Cost of Replacing Goods Sold | $172,000 |

**Problem 10**

Abington Co.

*Balance Sheet 1 January Restated in December Dollars Plus CRCs*

|  | $ | $ | $ |
|---|---|---|---|
| Cash | 5,000 | | |
| Debtors | 30,000 | 35,000 | |
| Less Creditors | | 10,000 | |
| Net Monetary Assets | | | 25,000 |
| Add: Non-Monetary Assets | | | |
| Inventories | | 44,000 | |
| Plant | 86,000 | | |
| Less Accumulated Depreciation | 32,250 | 53,750 | 97,750 |
| Net Assets | | | $122,750 |
| | | | |
| Proprietorship | | | |
| Capital, 1 Jan. | | 100,000 | |
| Price-Level Adjustment (including | | | |
| 5% x 115,000) (6,000 + 5,750) | | 11,750 | |
| Real Holding Gains | | 12,250 | 124,000 |
| Less Price-Level Loss on Net | | | |
| Monetary Assets | | | 1,250 |
| | | | $122,750 |

| | | | | |
|---|---|---|---|---|
| 1. | Inventories | Dr. | 4,000 | |
| | Price-Level Adjustment (5%) | Cr. | | 2,000 |
| | Real Holding Gain | Cr. | | 2,000 |
| 2. | Plant | Dr. | 6,000 | |
| | Price-Level Adjustment (5%) | Cr. | | 4,000 |
| | Real Holding Gain | Cr. | | 2,000 |
| 3. | Price-Level Adjustment (5%) | Dr. | 1,500 | |
| | Real Holding Gain | Dr. | 750 | |
| | Accumulated Depreciation ($\frac{3}{8}$. 6,000) | Cr. | | 2,250 |
| 4. | Price-Level Loss (on net mty. assets) | Dr. | 1,250 | |
| | Price-Level Adjustment (5%) | Cr. | | 1,250 |

*Real Holding Gains Account*

| | | | |
|---|---|---|---|
| Balance | | | 9,000 Cr. |
| Inventories | | 2,000 | 11,000 Cr. |
| Plant | | 2,000 | 13,000 Cr. |
| Accumulated Depreciation | 750 | | 12,250 Cr. |

*Balance Sheet 31 December in CRCs*

|  | $ | $ | $ |
|---|---|---|---|
| Cash |  | 12,000 | 53,000 |
| Debtors |  | 41,000 | 53,000 |
| Less Creditors |  |  | 6,000 |
| Net Monetary Assets |  |  | 47,000 |
| Add Non-Monetary Assets |  |  |  |
|     Inventories |  | 58,000 |  |
|     Plant | 86,000 |  |  |
|     Less Accumulated Depreciation | 43,000 | 43,000 | 101,000 |
| Net Assets |  |  | $148,000 |

*Proprietorship*

|  | $ | $ |
|---|---|---|
| Capital 1 Jan. | 100,000 |  |
| Price-Level Adjustment | 11,750 |  |
| Real Holding Gains | 12,250 | 124,000 |
| Current Income (by Deduction) | 25,250 |  |
| Less Price-Level Loss on Monetary Assets | 1,250 |  |
| Real Income |  | 24,000 |
|  |  | $148,000 |

## FROM QUESTIONS AND EXERCISES, CHAPTER 25

### Problem 17

*Gross Present Value*

| Year | CS $ | PV $ |
|---|---|---|
| 1 | 6,000 | 5,454 |
| 2 | 5,000 | 4,130 |
| 3 | 4,000 | 3,004 |
| 4 | 3,000 | 2,049 |
| 5 | 3,000 | 1,863 |
| 5 | 2,000 | 1,242 |
|  | GPV   = | $17,742 |

NPV = $17,742 − $20,000 = $−2,258
Purchase is not warranted.

**Problem 19**

| Year | CS $ | | PV $ |
|------|------|---|------|
| 1 | 30,000 | | 27,720 |
| 2 | 30,000 | | 24,780 |
| 3 | 30,000 | | 22,530 |
| 4 | 30,000 | | 20,490 |
| 5 | 3,000 | | 2,049 |
| | | GPV   = | $97,119 |

NPV = $97,119 − $100,000 = $−2,811
Firm should sell the plant now.

## FROM QUESTIONS AND EXERCISES, CHAPTER 26

### Problem 31

Boomer Company Ltd.

| | Ratio | 19X8 | | 19X9 | |
|---|---|---|---|---|---|
| (i) | Current or Working Capital | $\dfrac{80}{28}$ | 2.86 | $\dfrac{268}{172}$ | 1.5 |
| (ii) | Quick Asset | $\dfrac{40}{20}$ | 2.0 | $\dfrac{168}{100}$ | 1.68 |
| (iii) | Short-Term to Total Funds | $\dfrac{28}{160}$ | 17.5% | $\dfrac{172}{360}$ | 48% |
| (iv) | Proprietary | $\dfrac{112}{160}$ | 70% | $\dfrac{168}{360}$ | 47% |
| (v) | Turnover of Debtors (times p.a.) | $\dfrac{200}{40}$ | 5 times p.a. | $\dfrac{320}{168}$ | 1.9 times p.a. |
| (vi) | Turnover of Inventories (times p.a.) | $\dfrac{160,000}{40,000}$ | 4 times p.a. | $\dfrac{256,000}{70,000}$ | 3.66 times p.a. |
| (vii) | Turnover of Assets (times p.a.) | $\dfrac{200,000}{\frac{1}{2}(140,000 + 160,000) = 150,000}$ | 1.33 times p.a. | $\dfrac{320,000}{\frac{1}{2}(360,000 + 160,000) = 260,000}$ | 1.23 times p.a. |
| (viii) | Before-Tax Return on Sales | $\dfrac{32,000}{200,000}$ | 16% | $\dfrac{54,000}{320,000}$ | 17% |
| (ix) | After-Tax Return on Owners' Equity | $\dfrac{22,000}{\frac{1}{2}(98,000 + 112,000) = 105,000}$ | 21% | $\dfrac{36,000}{\frac{1}{2}(112,000 + 168,000) = 140,000}$ | 25.7% |
| (x) | After-Tax Return on Total Assets | $\dfrac{22,000}{\frac{1}{2}(140,000 + 160,000) = 150,000}$ | 14,66% | $\dfrac{36,000}{\frac{1}{2}(160,000 + 360,000) = 260,000}$ | 13.85% |
| (xi) | Earnings Yields | $\dfrac{22,000}{144,000}$ | 15.3% | $\dfrac{36,000}{200,000}$ | 18% |
| (xii) | Earnings per Share | $\dfrac{22,000}{80,000}$ | 27.5 cents | $\dfrac{36,000}{100,000}$ | 36 cents |

*Comments:*

1. Liquidity, CA ratio ) All down — decreasing liquidity.
QA ratio )
Debtors' Turnover ) Substantial slowdown in debtors'
Inventories Turnover ) turnover — planned or unplanned?
Compare with credit period granted.
Sales expansion into less credit-
worthy customers? Potential bad
debts problem? Ageing schedule?
Credit control?

2. Financial structure:

   i. ST/Total Funds — risen substantially
   LT/Total Funds — fallen substantially
   c/f change in asset structure (calculation not required)

   $$\frac{CA}{TA}\ \frac{80}{160} = 50\%; \frac{268}{360} = 74\%$$

   Additional ST Asset (debtors) largely financed from ST Funds. Also
   helps explain reduction in WC%. Wise?

   ii. Gearing risen substantially; asset growth largely financed from debt
   sources — Current Liabilities. Wise? Conversely, Proprietary % down.

3. Performance:
   Return on sales and total assets relatively unchanged.

   Return on owners' equity up because of higher gearing; also EPS and
   earnings yield — higher risk?

   Asset turnover up — more effective utilization of LT Assets.

   But turnover of inventories and debtors down, indicating less liquidity
   and efficiency in use of working capital.

*Overall:*

Query ST financial structure and liquidity changes, and financing of growth from
ST sources, creditworthiness of debtors, and the system for control of credit.

### Problem 32

Turramurra Traders Ltd.

| Ratio | 19X6 | | 19X7 | |
|---|---|---|---|---|
| 1. After-Tax Return on Sales | $\dfrac{300}{9,000}$ | 3.3% | $\dfrac{320}{10,000}$ | 3.2% |
| 2. After-Tax Return on Paid-up Capital | $\dfrac{300}{2,000}$ | 15% | $\dfrac{320}{2,000}$ | 16% |
| 3. After-Tax Return on Shareholders equity | $\dfrac{300}{3,300}$ | 9.1% | $\dfrac{320}{3,520}$ | 9.1% |
| 4. Dividend Yield | $\dfrac{5 \text{ cents}}{1.50}$ | 3.3% | $\dfrac{5 \text{ cents}}{1.50}$ | 3.3% |
| 5. Working Capital | $\dfrac{3,500}{1,700}$ | $2.06 | $\dfrac{4,600}{2,280}$ | $2.02 |
| 6. Turnover of Debtors | $\dfrac{9,000}{1,500}$ | 6 times p.a. or every 2 months | $\dfrac{10,000}{2,000}$ | 5 times p.a. or every 2½ months |
| 7. Turnover of Inventories | $\dfrac{6,000}{2,000}$ | 3 times p.a. | $\dfrac{6,800}{2,300}$ | 2.96 times p.a. |
| 8. Sources of Funds | $\dfrac{1,700}{7,000}$ | 24% | $\dfrac{2,280}{7,800}$ | 29% |
| | $\dfrac{5,300}{7,000}$ | 76% | $\dfrac{5,520}{7,800}$ | 71% |
| | $\dfrac{3,500}{7,000}$ | 50% | $\dfrac{4,600}{7,800}$ | 60% |
| | $\dfrac{3,500}{7,000}$ | 50% | $\dfrac{3,200}{7,800}$ | 40% |
| 9. Leverage | $\dfrac{3,700}{7,000}$ | 53% | $\dfrac{4,280}{7,800}$ | 54% |
| 10. NTA per Share | $\dfrac{2,800}{2,000}$ | $1.40 | $\dfrac{3,020}{2,000}$ | $1.51 |
| 11. $\Delta$ Share Price/$\Delta$ RE per Share | | | $\dfrac{0}{220/2,000}$ | 0 |
| 12. $\Delta$ Share Price/$\Delta$ NTA per Share | | | $\dfrac{0}{220/2,000}$ | 0 |

13. NTA per Share after Premises Revaluation:

$$\frac{\text{Total Tangible Assets} - \text{Liabilities}}{\text{No. Shares}}$$

$$\frac{7,800+7,750-4,280-500}{2,000} = \frac{10,770}{2,000}$$

$$= \$5.38$$

14. After-Tax Return on TSE after Revaluation

$$\frac{320}{11,270} = 2.9\%$$

*Comments:*

1. *Profitability:*

    i.   Low rates of return on sales and shareholders' funds (given risk involved).

    ii.  Low dividend yield c/f Commonwealth bond rate for a zero share price growth stock, and for a company with moderately high leverage.

    iii. Retained earnings not causing share price to rise; ∴ not in shareholders' interests; likewise increase in NTA per share.

    iv.  After allowing for revaluation of premises, profit performance dreadful.

2. *Financial Position:*

    Superficially liquid — WC ratio looks O.K. in providing cover for CL but:

    i.   Debtors' turnover too low, and decreasing. Take more than twice the credit period to pay their bills. Bad credit control. No bad debts written off and perhaps there could be a problem here. Require ageing schedule of debtors.

    ii.  Stock turnover low and declining. Excessive inventories of obsolete stock or prices too high, etc. Poor by industry standards.

    Sources of funds:   Long-term assets are being financed from LT sources, therefore appears O.K.

    Leverage:          Getting high but probably O.K.

    NTA per share appear to approximate share price in 19X7.

    ∴ appears to be no excessive risk of takeover or need to terminate company's operations.

    But in fact NTA per share at CMP substantially exceeds share price; ∴ danger of takeover bid.

    *Financial Policy:*

    Financing growth in WC from CL and retained earnings. In fact it should endeavour to increase sales and at same time reduce WC investment by speeding up inventory and debtors' turnover.

    Reinvestment of profits not justified from shareholders' viewpoint. Company cannot justify use of premises at their current market value — r/r on TSE is 2.9% at CMPs. Unless profit can be increased substantially without further shareholder investment, the business is not viable.

# Index